THE WORLD IN
1969

"We cannot escape history . . . . No personal significance or insignificance can
spare one or another of us. The fiery trial through which we pass
will light us down, in honor or dishonor, to the last generation."

Abraham Lincoln, message to Congress. 1862

THE WORLD IN
1969

History
as we
lived it...

by the

Writers,

Photographers,

and Editors

of The Associated Press

CONTENTS

Foreword

Men have lived magnificently or miserably, fought wars, changed societies and governments, developed myriad cultures, revolutionized science and engaged in ten thousand activities, some of which reflected magnificently upon man and some of which degraded him.

But in 1969 something occurred, nothing like anything that had happened before.

Men walked on the moon.

Three dauntless astronauts in an age of emotion, war and turmoil brought a renaissance of the human spirit all over the world. They proved once again that man can rise to the heights.

Of all the events covered by The Associated Press during this year, the flight of Apollo 11 was undoubtedly the most satisfying for reporters and readers alike and this book is dedicated to those who made this magnificent feat possible.

Wes Gallagher

Wes Gallagher

General Manager

New York, January 1, 1970

January

"We Cannot Learn... until We Stop Shouting"

*President Nixon's inaugural address urged Americans
to speak softly in the quest for national unity,
pledged "peace among nations" as primary goal*

THERE WAS NOTHING intrinsically dramatic about a presidential inauguration in the United States. Everyone knew months in advance who the principal character would be. The most important words he would utter, only 35 in number, had been prescribed by the Constitution in 1787. The entire script of ceremony, pageantry and jubilation was familiar, the setting virtually unchanged from one inaugural to the next.

There would be a speech, of course, but hearers and historians would not scan it for startling content; they would seek the golden phrase or two that might be enshrined in some future edition of Bartlett's *Familiar Quotations.* Usually they were disappointed.

For all of that, an air of drama inevitably surrounded the quadrennial induction of the Chief Magistrate of the world's most powerful state. There was drama in the realization that a fellow citizen was about to be entrusted with the terrifying power of global life and death, to be shadowed throughout his term in office by an unobtrusive man with a black satchel full of secret nuclear codes. There was drama in the quiet presence of armored limousines and bullet-proof glass, and of Secret Service agents, well armed, on the platform roof above the new President's head.

And it had become a matter of unspoken national pride that, even in a United States riven by internal discord and embroiled in a nasty war on foreign soil, the scepter of leadership would pass peacefully from one man to another. For a fraction of time, at least, there was domestic tranquility, even though it was confined to a fraction of U.S. territory—the East Front of the Capitol in Washington.

A few minutes before noon on the 20th of January, Lyndon Baines Johnson heard *Ruffles and Flourishes* and *Hail to the Chief* played in his honor for the last time. Less than a half hour later, Richard Milhous Nixon, 37th President of the United States, heard the martial strains in his honor for the first time.

For Nixon, it was sweet music indeed (as it was for Johnson who said later that he felt immensely relieved when his successor took the oath of office). Vanquished in another presidential contest, Nixon had been a spectator eight years earlier when John F. Kennedy called upon fellow Americans to "ask not what your country can do for you; ask what you can do for your country." Then, after a bruising defeat in a California gubernatorial race, Nixon had stormed out of politics, vowing never to return.

But there he was in 1969, a grocer's son from Whittier, Calif., with his right hand high, his left on two family Bibles opened to the passage in which the prophet Isaiah urged that swords be beaten into plowshares and spears into pruning hooks. There, holding the Bibles, was Pat Nixon—remember Pat who had traveled and smiled and traveled and smiled, and wept one morning in 1960? And, facing an old political foe, Chief Justice Earl Warren, Richard Nixon said:

"I, Richard Milhous Nixon, do solemnly swear that I will faithfully execute the office of President of the United States, and will, to the best of my ability, preserve, protect, and defend the Constitution of the United States, so help me, God."

As a Quaker, Nixon could have affirmed instead of sworn and he need not have said, "so help me, God." But he added his personal touch and became President—the 15th to be elected with less than a majority of the nation's vote, with a plurality of less than one-half million over Hubert Humphrey, but President nonetheless, as firmly and as irrevocably as if he had been elected in a landslide.

Inauguration day had dawned under a threat of foul weather. The day remained gray and cold but the freezing rain predicted for the hour of ceremony held off.

The Nixons attended a prayer breakfast at the State Department. Then a presidential limousine carried them to the White House where a beaming Lyndon and Lady Bird Johnson awaited them. Johnson had a kiss for Mrs. Nixon and the outgoing and incoming Chief Executives chatted warmly over coffee and as they rode, side by side, along Pennsylvania Avenue to Capitol Hill. All was cordiality, a far cry from the frostiness of other transitions, such as those from Herbert Hoover to Franklin Roosevelt, from Harry Truman to Dwight Eisenhower.

At noon, Sen. Everett M. Dirksen of Illinois, the Republican leader, administered the oath to Spiro T. Agnew, a Greek immigrant's son who had risen in less than three years from a Baltimore County job to the vice presidency of the United States, via the governorship of Maryland and dedication to Nixon's cause.

At 12:16 p.m., Nixon was sworn. Not given to public displays of affection, he squeezed his wife's hand. Then he turned to

A spontaneous gesture of recognition

the chilled crowd and began to deliver his inaugural address. He spoke rapidly, quietly, eschewing the jerky gestures with hands and arms that had characterized his campaign. His breath was sometimes visible in the frosty air. His tone was exhortative, almost evangelical. His dominant theme was peace: He promised to "consecrate my office, my energies, and all the wisdom I can summon, to the cause of peace among nations."

"The greatest honor history can bestow is the title of peacemaker. This honor now beckons America—the chance to help lead the world at last out of the valley of turmoil and onto that high ground of peace that man has dreamed of since the dawn of civilization. If we succeed, generations to come will say of us now living that we mastered our moment, that we helped make the world safe for mankind. . . .

"We find ourselves rich in goods, but ragged in spirit; reaching with magnificent precision for the moon, but falling into raucous discord on earth. We are caught in war, wanting peace. We are torn by division, wanting unity.

We see around us empty lives, wanting fulfillment. We see tasks that need doing, waiting for hands to do them.

"To a crisis of the spirit, we need an answer of the spirit. And to find that answer, we need only look within ourselves. . . . We cannot learn from one another until we stop shouting at one another—until we speak quietly enough so that our words can be heard as well as our voices.

"For its part, government will listen. We will strive to listen in new ways—to the voices of quiet anguish, the voices that speak without words, the voices of the heart— to the injured voices, the anxious voices, the voices that have despaired of being heard. Those who have been left out, we will try to bring in. Those left behind, we will help to catch up. For all of our people, we will set as our goal the decent order that makes progress possible and our lives secure. . . .

"But we are approaching the limits of what government alone can do. Our greatest need now is to reach beyond government to enlist the legions of the concerned and the

committed. What has to be done has to be done by government and people together or it will not be done at all. The lesson of past agony is that without the people we can do nothing; with the people we can do everyting.

"To match the magnitude of our tasks, we need the energies of our people—enlisted not only in grand enterprises but more importantly in those small, splendid efforts that make headlines in the neighborhood newspaper instead of the national journal.

"With these, we can build a great cathedral of the spirit —each of us raising it one stone at a time as he reaches out to his neighbor, helping, caring, doing.

"I do not offer a life of uninspiring ease. I do not call for a life of grim sacrifice. I ask you to join in a high adventure—one as rich as humanity itself, and as exciting as the times we live in. . . .

"As we learn to go forward together at home, let us also seek to go forward with all mankind. Let us take as our goal: Where peace is unknown, make it welcome; where peace is fragile, make it strong; where peace is temporary, make it permanent.

"After a period of confrontation, we are entering into an era of negotiation. Let all nations know that during

Parade watchers, Washington, D.C.

On inaugural eve, a demonstration

*this administration our lines of communication will be
open. . . . The peace we seek—the peace we seek to win—
is not victory over any other people, but the peace that
comes 'with healing in its wings, with compassion for those
who have suffered, with understanding for those who have
opposed us, with the opportunity for all the peoples of the
earth to choose their own destiny. . . .*

*"Our destiny offers, not the cup of despair, but the
chalice of opportunity. So let us seize it, not in fear, but
in gladness—and, 'riders on the earth together,' let us go
forward, firm in our faith, steadfast in our purpose, cautious
of the dangers, but sustained by our confidence in the will
of God and the promise of man."*

The new President spoke for 17 minutes. He was interrupted
nine times by applause that was perfunctory rather than spontaneous enthusiasm. Generally, though, the speech was well
received.

Newspapers spoke in a chorus of friendly advice and good
wishes, even some journals that had opposed his election ("We
do not profess any glib optimism, but neither do we join
the prophets of doom. It is our earnest hope that Mr. Nixon
will join the company of Presidents who confounded their

The demonstrators made no serious inroads . . .

The President applauds the passing parade

detractors"—New York Post). In Congress, there was lavish praise from Republicans (Nixon "presented beautifully the basic spiritual elements that together make our country great"—Sen. Wallace F. Bennett, R–Utah), as well as good words from Democrats (the speech "expressed the hopes, aspirations and prayers of most of the people of this globe"—Sen. Richard B. Russell, D–Ga.). The Rev. Ralph Abernathy of the Southern Christian Leadership Conference spoke for the disappointed: "The speech reflected no sense of urgency and no sensitivity to the basic problems of hunger, poverty and race in this nation and said very little about plans to heal the wounds and bring the nation together.")

Nixon's first official act as President was to sign his nominations for Cabinet positions—a lineup dominated by friends, men long known and trusted, all distinguished in the Republican mold *(The World in 1968, 254–256).* (Eleven nominations were confirmed readily by the Senate. The 12th nomination, Gov. Walter J. Hickel of Alaska for Secretary of the Interior, was delayed for five days of hearings in which his commitment to the cause of conservation was questioned. In particular, a remark to a news conference that he opposed "conservation for conservation's sake" was a target for criticism. The Interior Committee finally endorsed the appointment by 14–3 and the Senate followed suit by 73–16 on Jan. 23.)

When the traditional parade began, spectators were reminded in a small way of the violent days of the Democratic conven-

tion *(The World in 1968, 161–166).* Jeering, youthful demonstrators tried to stone the presidential limousine as it led the procession of state contingents to the White House. Secret Service men, surrounding the car, batted down some missiles and none found a mark. For the last blocks of the cavalcade, Nixon ordered the car's roof opened so that he and Mrs. Nixon could stand and wave to the crowds. Nearly 100 arrests were made but, apart from a few sidewalk scuffles, the demonstrators made no serious inroads on the festivities.

At the White House Nixon watched the parade from a bulletproof reviewing stand for more than two hours—blaring bands, tootling fife and drum corps, elaborate floats, strutting majorettes, military units, and a calliope shrilling *I Want a Girl.*

The First Family—the President and his wife, their daughters Julie and Tricia and Julie's husband David Eisenhower—dined on steak, then began the last rite of the day—visits to each of a half-dozen jam-packed inaugural balls. The aggregate attendance was more than 30,000, each of whom had paid from $35 for a single ticket to $1,000 for a box.

The presidential party didn't dance. It would have been next to impossible in the crush and, anyway, only two Presidents had really danced at their inaugurals—the first, George Washington, and the latest, Lyndon Johnson.

At last, it was home to the White House. "They gave me the key to the front door," said the President, "and I'm going home to see if it fits."

Farewell to LBJ

*President Johnson left the White House with
a record of social accomplishment
but the Vietnam war was a dark shadow*

B Y LYNDON JOHNSON'S own timing, he began to relax "within four seconds" after he became a former President of the United States. By observations of the Washington press corps, signs of easing tension had begun to appear a week earlier.

Newsmen who followed the President through the final formalities of his five years in the White House found him "relieved and sentimental," "completely at ease," "calm and composed." His voice had "a richness and timbre it has often lacked." Even his posture, "in the past sometimes a wary crouch," became "relaxed and easy."

He was also philosophical. He concluded his farewell address on the State of the Union with a humble judgment of his Ad-

ministration: "I hope it may be said a hundred years from now that by working together we helped to make our country more just for all its people as well as to insure and guarantee the blessings of liberty for all of our posterity. That's what I hope. I believe that at least it will be said that we tried."

The message enumerated accomplishments and triumphs without braggadocio. He belabored neither Republican foes nor opponents within his own Democratic Party. He spoke no words of anger or frustration. He did not offer one last passionate defense of the American presence in Vietnam. The story had been written beyond his power to change it, he seemed to be saying, and now it was time for the appraisal of history to begin.

The 80th—and last—meeting with his cabinet

Greetings from No. 36 to No. 37

Three days later, on Jan. 17, he made peace with reporters at an impromptu news conference when he and Mrs. Johnson visited the National Press Club. In a long session of give-and-take banter, one participant wrote, "Mr. Johnson's mood was his informal best—sarcastic, earthy and humane, a mixture that has confounded friends and critics." He even poked fun at himself, a rare thing for him to do in public. He recalled the fuss over a Johnson portrait by Peter Hurd *(The World in 1967, 16-17),* denied he had said it was ugly; as a matter of fact, he had "thought it was a pretty good likeness except for one little detail: It left off the halo."

Thus did Lyndon Baines Johnson, 36th President of the United States, depart from Washington in an aura of good will, a far cry from the bitterness that had marred most of his White House years.

He had succeeded to the presidency in the shadow of great tragedy, the assassination of John F. Kennedy in 1963. In a time of national trauma, he had kept the government on even keel, had taken charge with such authority and strength that

he won an unparalleled endorsement from the American people in the 1964 elections.

Then came the birth of the Great Society which, in the words of its founder, "demands an end to poverty and racial injustice. . . . It is a place where every child can find knowledge to enrich his mind and enlarge his talents . . . where leisure is a welcomed chance to build and reflect, not a feared cause of boredom and restlessness . . . where the city of man serves not only the needs of the body but the desire for beauty and the hunger for enrichment . . . where men are more concerned with the quality of their goals than the quality of their goods."

The flood of social legislation was unmatched except perhaps by the fabulous "Hundred Days" of Franklin Roosevelt's New Deal. Three Civil Rights Acts gave new stature and dignity to Negroes and other minorities. Medicare came into being. There were programs for massive aid to education, programs to promote job training and to create job opportunities, to provide housing and to protect consumers, to conserve and beautify natural resources, to combat pollution of air and water. One energetic reporter counted 435 domestic social programs where there had been 45 in 1960.

At the same time, the nation moved into new areas of affluence. The gross national product—measurement of the value of all goods and services—increased by 26 per cent to $861 billion. Per capita income rose by 21 per cent. The unemployment rate dwindled to a record low of 3.6 per cent. Inflation was a disquieting influence but by and large the national prosperity was unequalled in magnitude and duration.

The worm in President Johnson's apple was Vietnam. The onetime "nasty little war" had become a nasty big war with all the consequences of increased cost in lives and dollars. Each step of escalation, beginning with expansion of bombing to North Vietnam in 1965, had been greeted with outcries of protest, not only from those who decried the cost but from those who saw the war's purpose as unworthy.

There were other problems of mounting portent. The poor who had been promised so much demanded fulfillment. Big cities, their areas of discontent too long neglected, exploded into riot, along with many smaller communities. College and university campuses, even high schools, became arenas of violence. Crime in the streets became a national political issue.

Of all the problems, Vietnam cast the longest and darkest shadow. It enveloped even the domestic unrest through the argument that the war's vast costs were crippling, even destroying the Johnson programs. (Even so, the figures for domestic betterment were impressive. President Johnson's last budget message reported that 12 million Americans had "moved out of the bonds of poverty," proposed expenditure of $67.8 billion on "investment in human resources," and remarked that U.S. social outlays, including Social Security, had more than doubled since 1964, increasing by $37.4 billion.)

President Johnson had first curtailed and then abandoned bombing of North Vietnam in the interests of peace. His moves had brought the Communists to conference but the only accomplishment in eight months of talking was an agreement on how the negotiators should be seated.

There was no fragment of doubt that Vietnam was the dominant factor in the President's decision not to seek re-election (The World in 1968, 57–61). Neither was there doubt that he felt most keenly the failure to restore peace. He told that last news conference in Washington: "If I could have one thing presented to me today that I would rather have than anything else in the world, it would be that I could bring back from Vietnam all the men I sent out there and that we could have peace in the world so that these men could come home and enjoy being with their families again. . . . The thing I would like to do most is to find some way, somehow soon, to bring peace to the world. It has eluded me."

Some of the President's problems had been of his own making. Reporters had taken due note that he could be courageous, inspiring, persuasive, charming. They had also taken note that "this extraordinarily complex man" could be vain, devious, bullying, vulgar, malicious.

The judgment of history might be kinder to Lyndon Johnson than contemporary public opinion polls. And there again, the decision might stand or fall on events in Vietnam. In an appraisal in the National Observer of Jan. 20, James R. Dickenson wrote that, "If, as Mr. Johnson and his defenders insist, history judges that his Southeast Asia policies were necessary to contain China and the result is peace and stability in the area, a new American folk hero is in the making. 'There is something about a man sticking to his guns,' says James MacGregor Burns, professor of political science at Williams College and not a

Back home in Texas: "It hurts good"

particularly strong admirer of Mr. Johnson. If he's right, the stories about him are going to sound like those about Lincoln.' "

Dickenson also quoted Professor Eric Goldman of Princeton University who for a time had been a White House adviser: "Lyndon Johnson would be more than forgiven; he would emerge a figure of Churchillian stature, a wise, courageous voice crying out in a crowd of myopic and timid men."

As the Johnson family flew home from Washington, they reflected conflicting moods of weary exaltation, relief, liberation and nostalgia. They talked of their last moments in the White House, of the last special little things they did and their thoughts on leaving. They talked more after they were home in Texas, at the ranch where Lyndon Johnson always had been most assured and secure.

He confessed freely that he would miss the power of the presidency. He said, "I am sure that any person who has been as active as I have in public office for 38 years will notice it when they call the roll and his name is not on it." Then he added, "But I want to miss it. It hurts good."

In Russian artist's view, the space rendezvous of Soyuz 4 and Soyuz 5

Another Way to the Moon

*The Russians were planning to stop en route
—in contrast to America's one-jump technique—
and were moving toward orbiting space stations*

NEVER BEFORE had the Russian people been treated to such intimate, prompt glimpses of their space heroes in action. When Soyuz 4 carried Lt. Col. Vladimor Shatalov into orbit on Jan. 14, pictures of the launching appeared on television in 90 minutes. When Soyuz 5 went aloft on Jan. 15 with three men aboard, a videotape from the ship was on the air within the hour. That was only the beginning.

When the ships linked in space on Jan. 16 for an unprecedented transfer of cosmonauts from one Soyuz to the other, cameras were in action both inside and outside the craft. At other times during the 96-hour mission, frequent telecasts, live and taped, showed the men at work and at rest, displayed their equipment, described their activities. Much of what was

not seen in pictures on television was described in words on radio and in newspapers. In the past, people had waited weeks, even months, for revelations that did not match these.

Still, the barriers of secrecy were not lowered completely. Limitations remained, both technical and puritanical.

At one point in a broadcast to the "Dear Soviet people," Shatalov said, "I shall tell you something about the construction of the spacecraft." Quickly, a voice from ground control cut him off with, "Thank you very much."

At another time, during the linkup, Shatalov nosed his ship into contact with Soyuz 5 with these words. "It took me quite a while to find you but now I've got you." Up spoke a voice from Soyuz 5. "We've been raped! We've been raped!" The comment from No. 5 was erased from later playbacks and reports were heard that flight officials had been scandalized by the failure to delete it from the original.

Perhaps, in permitting such unwonted publicity, the Russians took a cue from the successful exposure to public gaze of the Apollo flights by the United States (*The World in 1968, 202-205, 240-245*). Of a certainty, they did not take a cue from anyone in the achievements of the Soyuz crews.

Earlier pioneers in space had ventured into the infinite void outside their ships, beginning March 18, 1965, with Lt. Col. Alexei Leonov of the Soviet Union (*The World in 1965, 60-61, 106-108*). Subsequent missions, notably in the Gemini program of the United States, had demonstrated how to unite two spacecraft as they whirled around the earth (*The World in 1966, 212-216*). But never had a man transferred from one ship to another in mid-space.

All four of the men involved were rookies in space flight, although two of them had been standby pilots on previous missions. Shatalov, at 41 the senior of the group, had been associated with the Soviet space program for six years. The two who "walked" from Soyuz 5 to Soyuz 4 were Lt. Col. Yevgeny Khrunov, 35, a research engineer, and civilian Alexei Yeliseyev, 34, flight engineer. Lt. Col. Boris Volynov, 34, remained in Soyuz 5 to pilot it back to earth.

The testing hours came at 2:37 a.m., Eastern Standard Time, on Jan. 16 when ground control began maneuvering the ships toward each other. They were completing a circuit of the earth each 88.85 minutes at altitudes ranging from 129.9 miles to 155.3 miles; the problem was to get them on one plane.

When the intervening space dwindled to 100 yards, Shatalov took over with manual controls, nosing his craft forward about 12 feet per minute. "Don't be in a hurry," counseled ground control. "Easy, not so rough," cautioned Volynov. By 11:20 a.m., the docking was complete, the connection was rigid, electric and phone links were set up.

Khrunov and Yeliseyev had donned their space suits, a new, self-sufficient type that enabled the wearer to exist in space without a hose connection to his mother ship's oxygen. First Khrunov, then Yeliseyev emerged into the airless, limitless void of the universe through a hatch on the hull of Soyuz 5, maneuvered across the intervening space and entered Soyuz 4 through another hatch. Television viewers saw a camera float from No. 5 into the arms of a cosmonaut and watched as he took pictures.

The historic transfer was completed in an hour, "strictly on schedule," Shatalov reported; the men had "worked efficiently and confidently." The ships flew on, still shackled, for a total linkup time of 4 hours, 35 minutes.

Shatalov returned Soyuz 4 and his new passengers to earth on Jan. 17, landing on the snowy steppes of his native Kazakhstan in central Soviet Asia. Villagers of the neighborhood greeted the three with heavy overcoats to shield them from howling winds and the numbing cold of 31 degrees below zero. One day later, Volynov piloted Soyuz 5 to an uneventful landing in the same general area.

The exploit brought into sharp focus the differing approaches of Russia and the United States to the conquest of space. In consensus, Russia was ahead in solving the problems of putting up orbiting space "stations;" the United States was closer to putting a man on the moon.

In some measure, the strategies may have been dictated by the tools available. In the huge Saturn 5 rocket, with 7.9 million pounds of thrust in the first stage, the United States had an unequalled propulsion system, capable of sending a space-

craft and crew to the moon in one jump—and had proved it with the flight of Apollo 8 in December. According to intelligence reports, the Russians had not shown any rocket approaching such power. Moreover, recent remarks by Soviet officials had indicated that the Soyuz ships—at least in the current version—would not survive the tremendous heat and pressures generated by reentry into earth's atmosphere, at 25,000 miles per hour, on a direct flight from the moon. Thus, the Russians would fly to—and return from—the moon via an intermediate station orbiting in space.

(The United States, in a budget pinch, did not plan its first embryonic space station, a workshop in a spent stage of a Saturn, until 1971. Larger stations were not in prospect before the mid-1970s.)

The value to the Russian program of January's Soyuz mission was readily apparent. Sir Bernard Lovell, director of England's Jodrell Bank Observatory, described it this way: "In a short time, we can expect to witness the buildup of a permanent space station in earth orbit. This would determine the trend of Russian space activities for a long time ahead. It will certainly be used for important astronomical and geophysical investigations and probably with a shuttle service of Russian scientists from earth."

Other benefits also were possible. In military reconnaissance for example. Chapman Pincher, specialist in military affairs for the London Daily Express, carried that idea a step further. "The Russians have an H-bomb rocket which has worldwide range because it almost goes into orbit," he wrote. "They could now put up multiple satellites carrying a large number of 'jump-down' bombs."

Russian statements had made clear that they had goals in mind other than a lunar landing and scientific explorations. With characteristic Russian reticence, they did not identify those goals.

EPILOGUE. The Soyuz spacemen were honored at the Kremlin on Jan. 22 after a triumphant parade from Moscow airport. The three air force officers became colonels. Each of the four received medals denoting the Order of Lenin and the Gold Star Heroes of the Soviet Union. President Nicolai V. Podgorny and Leonid I. Brezhnev, Communist general secretary, embraced them and Brezhnev delivered a 21-minute speech. The crowd chanted "Glory, glory, glory to the Communist Party" and "Glory, glory, glory to our scientists."

Two days later, a story of unscheduled excitement became known. As the motorcade entered the Kremlin compound through the Borovitsky Gate, a youth had fired several shots at the procession. A chauffeur and a motorcyclist escort were wounded and a cosmonaut of an earlier mission was cut by flying glass. Spectators had grabbed the gunman and police had hustled him away so quickly that people 100 yards distant were unaware of the incident.

Even after the story became known, Soviet officials would say nothing to newsmen beyond confirming that "The facts as you have them took place" and describing the attacker as schizophrenic. Spokesmen would neither identify him nor discuss his motive. It was presumed that Podgorny and Brezhnev were the targets; the Soyuz crewmen, standing in an open car, would have been easy marks. Instead, the youth fired at the second car, apparently in the mistaken belief that it was the officials' car. Actually, they were three or four cars further back in line.

It was the first known violence in the Kremlin since June 1967 when a man had been blown up by his own homemade bomb near the Lenin tomb.

A Super Upset
in the Super Bowl

New York Jets flouted odds to beat Baltimore
and give American League its first championship

Joe Namath (12) hands off to Emerson Boozer (32) for a sweep

THE WAY football prophets previewed the Super Bowl, New York's Jets were not in the same league with Baltimore's Colts, figuratively or literally. They reckoned that the National League Colts would beat the American League Jets by two or three touchdowns in the climactic classic of the professional season.

Of course, there was a certain amount of respect for Joe Namath, the uninhibited free soul who quarterbacked the New York team. Any fellow who could throw footballs for total gains of 4,007 yards in one season—a pro record set in 1967—had the capacity to turn any game upside down. It was acknowledged also that Namath's supporting cast was something more than a lineup of faceless humpty-dumpties. After all, they had won 11 of 14 games and that sort of record was not achieved with mirrors.

As a matter of fact, the Jets looked pretty good in statistics. They had scored more points than the Colts; they had yielded fewer first downs, less total yardage and a smaller percentage of pass completions. Either of two Jet receivers, George Sauer or Don Maynard, had gained 400 more yards with passes than Baltimore's best. The leading groundgainer by rushing was New York's Matt Snell. The leading scorer was New York's Jim Turner.

The point of the one-sided odds was not that New York was so bad but that Baltimore was so good. This Colt team was being mentioned with the all-time greats, particularly on defense. The Jets had an edge in the itemized details but the Colts were mules where it counted most—near the goal line. Baltimore's opponents had scored a mere 144 points, little more than half of the 280 given up by New York. Three Baltimore opponents had failed to score—a rarity in pro football; five had been unable to score a touchdown. In a span of four games in the critical stretch of the season, Baltimore foes had aggregated a meager 12 points.

In the inter-division playoffs, the Colts had upset the Minnesota Vikings 24–14 and then destroyed a good Cleveland team—the only one to defeat them in the regular season—by a crushing 34–0. Cleveland never penetrated within Baltimore's 30-yard line; Leroy Kelly, the National League's premier rusher, gained just 28 yards in 13 carries. In the American League, the Jets had had to scramble from behind to conquer Oakland 27–23 and did it on the wings of superlative Namath passing. But, said the believers in Baltimore, Namath never had faced a pass rush like the stampede of the Colts' front four.

If anyone had suggested in September that the Colts would lose only once in 14 scheduled games and two playoffs and do it without the golden arm of Johnny Unitas, he would have been hooted from the hall. If he had suggested that the Colts would do it with Earl Morrall at quarterback, he would have been hooted out of town.

Unitas was a field general of exceptional talent, widely cheered as the No. 1 quarterback in pro football. Morrall was a veteran too but considerably less glamorous. Most of his 12 years in the National League had been spent on the bench as a reserve quarterback, at San Francisco, Pittsburgh, Detroit and New York. The Colts had obtained him in a trade with the New York Giants, when their No. 2 quarterback was injured.

Then Unitas developed elbow trouble and Morrall took over by default because no one else was available. Amid general amazement, he became Most Valuable Player in the National League (as was Namath in the American) and actually excelled Namath in pass completions (57.4 per cent against 49.2) and in touchdowns (29 to 15). He yielded to Namath in yards gained (2,904 to 3,147).

So much for pre-game statistics. There also was an intangible factor in the reasoning and that was the wide belief in the superiority of the National League. In two previous Super Bowls, the Green Bay Packers had methodically dissected the American League champions, 35–10 over the Kansas City Chiefs in 1967 and 33–14 over the Oakland Raiders in 1968. It just didn't seem possible that the American League had closed such a gap in one year.

Nevertheless a few daring souls predicted New York victory. Most prominent among them was Joseph William Namath of Beaver Falls, Pa.

Namath had been a super-star at the University of Alabama. The Jets had signed him to a bonus contract in the plush neighborhood of $400,000 despite a history of knee trouble. In four years at New York, he had built one reputation as a quarterback and another as a swinger. His feats with a football were no better known than the white llama rug in his East Side apartment, his Fu Manchu mustache (sacrificed for $10,000 in a television commercial) and his get-togethers and parties. ("A get-together," he said, "is when the guys come over to eat steak and play cards; a party is when there are girls.")

Namath had a positive idea about the upcoming game: "We're going to win. I guarantee it." He also had an idea about Earl Morrall: He "would be third-string quarterback on the Jets. There are maybe five or six better quarterbacks than Morrall in the AFL." Such brash talk didn't endear him to the Colts.

It was red meat for the fans, though, and 75,377 of them crowded into Miami's Sugar Bowl on Jan. 12, most of them expecting to see Namath eat both his words and the football.

The Colts made the prophets look good the first time they laid hands on the ball. Morrall passed to tight end John Mackey for 19 yards, halfback Tom Matte added 10 yards on a sweep to the right, fullback Jerry Hill gained 7 on a sweep to the left. Tom Mitchell, another tight end, took a pass for first down on the Jet 19. The attack bogged there and Lou Michaels failed in an attempt to kick a field goal. No matter; the Colts would be back.

They were, right soon, when linebacker Ron Porter recovered a Jet fumble 12 yards from the goal line. On third down at the 6, Morrall's pass caromed off Mitchell's shoulder pad into the hands of Randy Beverly, Jet cornerback who had seemed to be maneuvered out of the play.

Tom Matte took the Colts within range for a third time when he sprinted down the sideline for 58 of the 116 yards he would gain this day. On first down at the Jet 16, Morrall threw to Willie Richardson, the fleet flanker, but cornerback Johnny Sample, former Colt who was supposed to be a sitting duck for Richardson's wiles, intercepted just two yards short of touchdown territory.

In the final minute of the first half, Baltimore had another chance. At New York's 45, Morrall handed off to Matte for an apparent right sweep, a play that had been working well. But Matte stopped in mid-sweep and lateraled back to Morrall. Split end Jimmy Orr was jumping up and down in the goal line corner and no Jet was within 20 yards but Morrall didn't see him and threw to Hill in front of the goal posts. Safety Jimmy Hudson swept between Hill and ball and intercepted. By that time, the impression was growing that this was not Baltimore's day.

The impression was strengthened by events between Beverly's end zone interception and Matte's sideline sprint. Namath picked apart the Colts' complex, stunting, zone defenses and in 12 plays took his team 80 yards to a touchdown. He began with four successive handoffs to Snell, 219-pound fullback who

Matt Snell scores for New York from 4-yard line

played the best game of his fifth year in New York. The gain was 26 yards, all of it over the unexpectedly vulnerable right side of the Baltimore line. Then, with the Colts alerted to the ground game, Namath took to the air and began piling up his personal statistics: 17 completions in 28 attempts for a net gain of 206 yards.

He went first to Sauer whose game totals would be eight catches for 133 yards (The Colts concentrated on the speedier Don Maynard and he did not take a pass all day). After an incompletion, the march resumed with a pass to Bill Mathis, in briefly for Snell. Next it was Sauer again for two sizable gains and Snell for a first down on the 9-yard line. (The passes to Mathis and Snell must have confounded the Colts; the figuring was that Namath would have to keep his backs around him for extra protection. Instead, the Jets' offensive line—Winston Hill, Bob Talamini, John Schmitt, Randy Rasmussen and Dave Herman—was more than adequate.)

In the shadow of the goal line, Namath gave the ball twice to Snell and the fullback scored on his second try, from four yards out, behind a tremendous block by Hill. (Said Snell: "I've been telling reporters for a long time that Winston Hill is a great offensive tackle." Said Hill: "Snell is a great runner. He doesn't ask for much room.")

Any idea that the game's pattern might change in the second half was dissipated in the opening sequence of plays. Matte fumbled in the first scrimmage, New York recovered and Jim Turner kicked a field goal. Baltimore's offense was smothered, Namath hit Sauer for a pair of 14-yard gains and Turner kicked another field goal. When the third quarter ended, the Jets were marching toward Turner's third successful kick and the Colts had held the ball for only eight plays in the period.

By that time, Coach Don Shula had played his last card—Johnny Unitas. Obviously unable to throw the long bomb, Unitas' first threat ended as had so many other Colt sorties,

in an intercepted pass, Beverly's second of the afternoon. But on his next try Unitas completed four passes in an 80-yard drive and Hill ploughed across for the touchdown that made the score 16–7.

Then Baltimore recovered an onside kickoff at the Jets' 44-yard line and Unitas connected with Orr and Richardson to move to the 24. With more than three minutes to play, the brief dream was born that Unitas might yet reassert his mastery and carry the Colts to victory. But again the Jet defenders, instead of the Colt attackers, made the big play. The ubiquitous Sample tipped one pass away from the receiver, the Jet rush twice harassed Unitas into throwing off target, linebacker Larry Grantham knocked the fourth attempt out of Orr's reach, and the game was secure.

In nine years of existence, the American League had proved itself, given its fans grounds to contend even that it was better than the older National circuit. "We are a great team and this is the start of a new era," said Coach Weeb Ewbank who, back in 1958–59, had coached the Colts to league championships (his quarterback was Johnny Unitas).

Other upsets in sports were hauled out of memory to be compared with the Jets' victory—the 73–0 mauling of the Washington Redskins by the Chicago Bears in 1940, the triumph of the Boston Braves in baseball's 1914 World Series, the knockout of Sonny Liston by Cassius Clay (Muhammad Ali), an 8–1 underdog, to win the world's heavyweight boxing title in 1964. Mayor John V. Lindsay of New York didn't bother with comparisons. To him, this was without question "the greatest upset in the history of professional football."

The championship meant $15,000 for each Jet, twice the reward for each Colt. The game had a financial meaning for Jet fans, too. Six weeks after the Super Bowl, the Jet management announced that the cost of assembling and maintaining a championship team necessitated an increase in ticket prices.

Flying Saucers–
"as Real as Rainbows"

A two-year study found no evidence
of visitors from other planets—
but the controversy was not dispelled

As the late Arthur Edson told the story for The Associated Press, this fellow walked into the office one day in 1957 with the glad tidings that he had just returned from Mars. A spaceship had plucked him from his Ozark Mountain home, he said, and whisked him 141 million miles across the universe to the red planet and then brought him back. Did he have proof of his adventure? Of course. He displayed a hank of hair and identified it as the hair of a Martian dog.

Another tale that sounded like an excerpt from science fiction was related by Barney and Betty Hill of Portsmouth, N.H. They were driving home from Canada in 1961 on a lonely stretch of New England road when a flying saucer appeared above their car. The next two hours were blank in their memories but under hypnosis they gave similar accounts of experiences aboard the saucer.

The mountaineer and the Hills were among more than 100 persons who claimed to have been aboard strange craft from other worlds in the years between 1947 and 1969. Some claimed to have communicated with the strangers. One of them, the late George Adamski, told in a book *Flying Saucers Have Landed* of a telepathic conversation with a being from Venus who had landed in the California desert in 1952. Then there were rumors, like the one that the U.S. Air Force had in its possession the charred remains of three spacecraft captured in the American Southwest, along with the scorched bodies of three midget crewmen.

Another five million Americans, according to a Gallup Poll, reported they had at least seen something they believed to be a flying saucer. The U.S. Air Force, in the interest of national security, had investigated more than 11,000 reported sightings.

Sure, some were attributed to kooks. Others were found to be the work of pranksters. Many were explained scientifically—meteors, asteroids, stars, clouds, weather balloons, marsh gases, mirages, reflections on aircraft lights. There was no evidence, said the Air Force, to indicate any of the objects came from another planet. Yet, there were incidents to which there seemed to be no answers—or no answers that flying saucer buffs could accept.

Psychologists explained the phenomenon by saying the public expected big answers for big events. Just as the ancient Greeks, unable to explain lightning, had believed it a weapon of Zeus, so had modern man, unable to identify strange objects in the sky, concluded that they must be vehicles from other planets.

For centuries, people had been seeing mysterious lights in the skies. Ancient legends in Peru, China and elsewhere were interpreted as meaning that beings came from space to inhabit the earth. The Bible was a happy hunting ground for believers. For one example, the "pillar of fire" which lit the way for the Israelites on their journey to the Holy Land was regarded as evidence that a spaceship guided the travelers.

In 1893, a British warship reported strange lights in the heavens near Korea. In 1896, reports were heard of strange objects in the sky over California. They were called "airships" —although the Wright Brothers' flight at Kitty Hawk still was a decade in the future—and the reports multiplied.

"That some of the recent tales are mere inventions is probable, of course," commented Harper's weekly in 1897, "but that all of them are hoaxes is as hard to believe as the stories themselves. If they are true, we have invented the ship; if untrue, we have invented the stories. In either case, we are remarkable people."

The modern version of such visions began in 1947 with the story of an aviator named Kenneth Arnold. While flying over Mt. Rainier in Washington, he said he spotted nine objects swerving among peaks and canyons "like geese in a diagonal chain-like line." Arnold described the objects as "saucer-like." The name "flying saucer" was coined and the craze was on.

In the next two decades, flying saucers in many forms were sighted around the globe—England, Spain, Iran, India, China, Japan, Australia, Russia, Alaska, Canada, the United States, Mexico, South America. The Russians dismissed the reports as optical illusions growing out of war psychosis or inventions of capitalists to fan war hysteria. Nevertheless, the U.S. Department of Defense decided it would be prudent to look into the situation.

Project Blue Book, sponsored by the Air Force, was set up in 1948 to investigate reports of what were called unidentified flying objects, i.e., an aerial object the observer was unable to identify. The purpose was two-fold: to determine whether UFOs (1) posed a threat to U.S. security and (2) exhibited any unique scientific information or advanced technology that could contribute to scientific or technical research.

In the next 20 years the project, headed by Maj. Hector Quintanilla at Wright-Patterson Air Force Base, Ohio, and budgeted at $72,000 annually, delved into thousands of reports. With the aid of Dr. J. Allen Hynek, a Northwestern University astronomer, they came up with scientific answers for all but eight per cent: six per cent unidentifiable and two per cent with insufficient information to attempt identification. Still there were "ufologists," self-described believers in UFOs, who were dissatisfied with Air Force conclusions and formed their own investigative groups. One of the most prestigious was the National Investigations Committee on Aerial Phenomena (NICAP), a $50,000-a-year voluntary civilian organization.

Donald Keyhoe, a retired U.S. Marine major who headed the non-profit group, was among the critics of Project Blue Book. He charged the Air Force with "an intolerable degree of secrecy, keeping the public in the dark about the amount and possible significance of UFO evidence."

Keyhoe's assistant, Richard Hall, a Tulane University graduate of philosophy, said "the most reasonable working hypothesis is that they (UFOs) are extra-terrestrial. We try to be open-minded and objective, but we can't rule out the possibility that there have been landings."

Dr. Hynek added that "95 per cent of all sightings are easily explicable as balloons, meteors, fireballs, birds, satellites, mirages or other things." But, "I know of 20 or 30 baffling cases that I would love to have time to pursue further." In his mind, so long as there were some "unidentifieds," the question of whether some were extra-terrestrial must remain open. Otherwise, he said, we might be making the same mistake as the French Academy of Sciences made in dismissing stories of "stones that fell from the sky," when in fact they were proved to be meteorites that were respectable in the eyes of science.

Dr. Hynek was among those who campaigned for a hard, fully scientific, objective study, a plea that contributed to formation of a committee headed by Dr. Edward U. Condon, a University of Colorado physics professor and former director of the National Bureau of Standards. In October 1966, Air Force Secretary Harold Brown announced that the Condon committee had been commissioned for a $500,000 two-year endeavor "to analyze phenomena associated with UFO sightings" and to make recommendations on the Air Force methods of investigation and evaluation.

This UFO was identified as the result of a defect in film development

The committee included Condon; Robert J. Low, project co-ordinator and a key operations man whose background included a degree in electrical engineering; Dr. David Saunders, professor of psychology at the University of Colorado, and Dr. Norman Levine, scientific investigator. In addition, the group received information from Keyhoe, Quintanilla, Hynek and Dr. James E. McDonald, senior physicist at the Institute of Atmospheric Physics and professor in the Department of Meteorology at the University of Arizona.

Condon was not unaware of a couple of inherent problems in such a study. If his group came up with an adverse report, it could be called a whitewash because the Air Force supported it. On the other hand, just the fact that the study was commissioned could become cause for people to believe the government was admitting there really was something to UFOs. Actually, unexpected problems developed and the committee became embroiled in internal discord and external disbelief.

Saunders was among those who gradually became disillusioned with the way the project was progressing. His concern, he said, was heightened when Condon spoke in Elmira, N.Y., in 1967 and said of the UFOs: "My attitude right now is that there's nothing to it . . . but I'm not supposed to reach a conclusion for another year." A memo written by Low to University of Colorado officials before the project contract was signed caused more concern when it turned up in project files. The memo, labeled "Some Thoughts on the UFO Project," read in part:

"Our study would be conducted almost exclusively by non-believers, who, although they couldn't possibly prove a negative result, could and probably would, add an impressive body of evidence that there is no reality to the observations. The trick would be, I think, to describe the project so that, to the public, it would appear a totally objective study, but to the scientific community, would present the image of a group of nonbelievers trying their best to be objective, but having an almost zero expectation of finding a saucer."

The memo further suggested stressing the psychology and sociology of those who reported seeing UFOs. "I'm inclined to feel at this early stage that, if we set up the thing right and take pains to get the proper people involved and have success in presenting the image we want to present to the scientific community, we could carry the job off to our benefit. . . ." After the memo was shown to Dr. McDonald and to news media, Saunders and Levine were dismissed from the project

This UFO was a camera lens cap, suspended on fine thread outside truck window

for what Condon termed incompetence. Saunders maintained the two were fired because Condon thought he and Levine had a part in taking the memo to McDonald.

In May 1968, NICAP, which had worked closely with the committee, announced it had broken its relationship, charging the Condon study lacked impartiality. That same month Rep. J. Edward Roush, D-Ind., called for a congressional investigation of UFOs, saying the Condon study was foundering in dissension. In July the House Space and Astronautics Committee conducted a UFO seminar. Ground rules prohibited specific discussion of the Condon project but Rep. William F. Ryan, D-N.Y., asked Dr. McDonald if more study than the Colorado project was needed. "Emphatically yes," said McDonald. "We need a broader base. The National Aeronautics and Space Administration or the National Science Foundation ought to support some universities to make studies of UFOs."

The Condon committee plodded on in its quest. On Jan. 1, 1969, a carefully worded, well-documented 1,485-page report was distributed to news media in Washington by the Air Force. The report, filled with scientific terminology, graphs, and charts, was dropped on newsroom desks in the Pentagon with no covering letter and no comment from the agency that had commissioned it.

The committee's conclusion: There was no evidence that UFOs were visitors from outer space; there was no evidence that UFOs posed a hazard to U.S. security; there was no reason to continue Project Blue Book or any other such investigation.

"Our general conclusion," said the report, "is that nothing has come from the study of UFOs in the past 21 years that has added to scientific knowledge." In that vein, "further extensive study of UFOs probably cannot be justified." The report was endorsed by the 11-man board of the National Academy of Sciences.

Of the thousands of reported sightings, the Condon committee researched 59, some suggested by NICAP, and scrutinized photographs of 35 others. More than half of the 35 photos, 19 to be exact, were unintelligible or produced inconclusive results. Nine were ruled fakes and seven were deemed mistaken shots of manmade or natural objects.

One of the unidentifiables was captured in two photographs taken by a McMinnville, Ore., farmer in May 1950. The photos showed a disc-like object as it allegedly moved across the sky. Said the committee: "This is one of the few UFO reports in which all factors investigated—geometric, psychological and physical—appear to be consistent with the assertion that an extraordinary flying object, silvery, metallic, disc-shaped, tens of meters in diameter and evidently artificial, flew within sight of two witnesses." But the committee did not rule out the possibility of a hoax. "The fact that the object appears beneath the same part of the overhead wire in both photos can be used as an argument favoring a suspended model."

A couple of other incidents also left the group mystified. Both involved airplanes pursued by objects that were apparent on radar but not to the naked eye. One such incident occurred in 1956 at Lakenheath Air Base, England, used by both the U.S. Air Force and the Royal Air Force. Radar operators on the ground detected one or more targets that seemed to be moving at speeds up to 4,000 miles an hour although no sonic boom was heard. The targets made right angle turns at a few hundred miles an hour. Two RAF fighters were sent up. One said it had obtained radar "gunlock" on the target. However, the UFO circled the fighter's tail and remained there regardless of the plane's evasion tactics. The RAF plane finally ran low on fuel and landed. "Although conventional or natural explanations cannot be ruled out," said the committee, "the probability of such seems low in this case." A similar occurrence at the Colorado

"Stay calm, Dr. Condon—just tell them you don't believe in them!"

Flying saucers? No; just a freakish cloud formation

Photo from Aerial Phenomena Research Organization

Springs, Colo., airport 11 years later "must remain as one of the most puzzling radar cases on record, and no conclusion is possible at this time," said the committee.

The committee debunked other theories or evidence that ufologists clung to in support of extra-terrestrial spacecraft. With scientific calculations, it summarily decided that the planet Clarion, believed hidden by the sun, did not exist and therefore, could not be the source of extra-terrestrial visitors. It also analyzed a fragment of metal that reportedly fell to earth in 1957 when a UFO exploded above Sao Paulo, Brazil. The metal, reported to be magnesium purer than any made by man, proved to contain more impurities than that produced commercially.

Needless to say, the report was not to the liking of all. Mc-Donald charged that the committee "wasted an unprecedented opportunity" to make a scientific study of the UFO problem. Saunders countered the report with a book *UFOs? Yes*, which attacked his former colleagues, their motives and their methods. "Inasmuch as credibility was the primary goal when the UFO project was first conceived and established," Saunders wrote, "the University of Colorado study can only be regarded as a failure."

Believers in scientific circles found it hard to accept the stated fact that, more than 10 years into the Space Age, a group of scientists could find no evidence that UFOs could originate on other planets.

Believers who were more romantic than scientific clung to a statement made some years earlier by a Harvard professor of astrophysics: UFOs were "as real as rainbows."

IN CONGRESS, ANOTHER KENNEDY TO THE FORE

The Congress of the United States was a creature of custom, at least in the conduct of its internal affairs.

Committee chairmanships were assigned according to seniority. Positions of leadership in party councils were reserved for elders in service. Challenges of the system were rare and usually futile.

It was a matter of some astonishment, therefore, when two members of the new 91st Congress defied tradition. In the Senate, Edward M. Kennedy of Massachusetts, still serving his first full six-year term, stepped forward to oppose Russell B. Long of Louisiana, a veteran of 20 years in the upper house, for assistant majority leader or, in popular parlance, party whip. In the House, Morris K. Udall of Arizona entered the lists against John W. McCormack of Massachusetts, speaker for four terms and a congressman while Udall was in grade school.

Both challengers were Democrats. Both actions illustrated the party's unrest and divisions in the wake of the 1968 elections in which the White House had been lost and Republicans had made significant gains in Congress. Both Kennedy and Udall were forthright in describing their conception of their party's role under a Republican administration.

In the opinion of Kennedy, "The Democratic majority of the Senate has an obligation to the country to present the best possible program in keeping with our historic role as the party of progress and change." To Udall, "The House, if properly organized and led, can again become the independent, constructive force it once was."

The testing time came first for Udall, 46, brother of outgoing Secretary Stewart Udall of the Interior. Tradition and age were served. On Jan. 2, House Democrats nominated McCormack, 77, for a fifth term as speaker by 178-58 and he was elected one day later. Believers in the status quo breathed easier; perhaps the old order was not dying after all. But the Kennedy-Long contest was another story entirely.

Edward Kennedy was the survivor of four illustrious brothers in whose careers triumph and tragedy had strangely mingled: A Navy bomber pilot had died in World War II, a President and a Senator had been assassinated. When Edward was elected in 1962 for the unexpired term of the brother who became President, he devoted himself to learning the job, performing so creditably that Majority Leader Mike Mansfield of Montana remarked that he, "of all the Kennedys . . . is the only one who is a real Senate man."

After the assassination of Robert Kennedy, the younger brother retreated into his grief. He gave much time to enlarged family responsibilities. He rejected proposals that he seek the party's nomination for President or Vice President (*The World in 1968, 143-145, 156-160*). Now,

in the dawning of 1969, he was ready to move forward again.

Kennedy moved against odds. Russell Long's mercurial flamboyance had offended colleagues but he had been the Senate's Democratic whip for four years and he had another power base in the chairmanship of the Finance Committee where he was in position to grant or deny many favors. Moreover, he had the opportunity to rally support while Kennedy still was debating whether to enter the ring.

Kennedy announced his candidacy only four days before the party caucus. He held off until another prospective contender, Edmund Muskie of Maine who had been the Democratic vice presidential nominee, decided not to challenge Long. He made his first soundings of potential support from a ski lodge in Idaho. In the pressure of time, Kennedy was his own campaign manager and chief advocate, working almost wholly by phone. The meticulous preparation and groundwork that were hallmarks of a Kennedy campaign may have been missing but it was a safe assumption that Edward, in the manner of all Kennedys, looked well before he leaped.

The secret ballot on Jan. 3 favored Kennedy by 31-26. "The winds of change that were so evident in 1968 have expressed themselves in the Senate," he said. To Long, the result demonstrated the magic of a name: "I don't think I would have been defeated by anyone else in the U.S. Senate."

In one swift strike, the youngest Kennedy had propelled himself into a position of national Democratic leadership. The post of whip, concerned with rounding up votes on crucial issues and monitoring floor proceedings, was known more for drudgery than drama but it had been a stepping stone to greater things (in the cases of Lyndon Johnson and Hubert Humphrey, for two examples). In Edward Kennedy's hands, given Mansfield's chief interest in foreign affairs, it was deemed likely that the whip would be the party's chief Senate spokesman on domestic matters.

Kennedy professed that there were "not really any implications" beyond his desire to broaden his service in the Senate but few political seers did not believe that the real meaning of his move would be more apparent in 1972 than in 1969.

(Republicans had to settle three contests in organizing for the 91st Congress but all were occasioned by vacancies. In the Senate, Hugh Scott of Pennsylvania defeated Roman L. Hruska of Nebraska for whip, an open position when Thomas H. Kuchel of California lost his bid for renomination. In the House, Gordon Allott of Colorado defeated Robert P. Griffin of Michigan for chairman of the policy committee, vacated when Bourke Hickenlooper of Iowa retired. Also in the House, John Bayard Anderson of Illinois was chosen over two rivals for chairman of the Republican conference, succeeding Melvin Laird of Wisconsin who became Secretary of Defense in the new Nixon Administration.

(Other positions were filled without opposition, among them:

(Democrats: Senate leader, Mike Mansfield of Montana; president pro tempore, Richard B. Russell of Georgia; House leader, Carl Albert of Oklahoma; House whip, Hale Boggs of Louisiana.

(Republicans: Senate leader, Everett Dirksen of Illinois; House leader, Gerald R. Ford of Michigan; House whip, Leslie C. Arends of Illinois.)

A strategy huddle: Sens. Kennedy and Gore of Tennessee

The scarred deck of "Big E"

DISASTER ABOARD "BIG E"

The aircraft carrier *Enterprise* limped into Pearl Harbor with her deck punctured, charred and littered with twisted wreckage of her planes. The world's largest warship had been wracked by destruction which an enemy would have been hard put to equal.

"This is the worst condition I've seen a ship in since World War II," said Samuel Spencer, a rigger at the shipyard for more than two decades.

The "Big E," as the nuclear-powered carrier was known to her 5,300 officers and crewmen, was engaged in routine maneuvers en route to her fourth tour of duty in Vietnam waters on Jan. 14. Lt. Cmdr. Ronald Foster, 33, was in the cockpit of his F4 Phantom jet checking out instruments. He heard an explosion and "saw an orange fireball coming across the deck. Bodies were coming out of the fireball." Another explosion knocked the canopy off his aircraft. A third "blew me out of the plane."

Flames rolled along the 4½-acre flight deck where Navy aircraft loaded with 500-pound bombs, rockets and air-to-air missiles were poised for takeoff. The blaze ignited rockets and exploded bombs. Airplane fuel added to the inferno. Crewmen trapped by fire leaped 60 feet to the sea. They and others who were blasted off their feet returned to perform heroics.

"I was walking forward on the flight deck when the first explosion knocked me down," said Petty Officer Billy Hawk, 25, "I picked myself up, ran to a fire station and started getting out gear. A fire unit went by me into the scene. There was another explosion and the man who had the end of the fire hose wasn't there any more."

From the cockpit of his plane, Lt. Cmdr. Perry Gard "saw what I thought was a piece of burning shrapnel. Then I saw it was my plane captain." Gard ripped off the man's flaming clothes and led him to safety. Another crewman was credited with herding 30 shipmates out of the flames' reach.

When the fire was quenched, 27 crewmen had been killed and 85 injured. It was the eighth major fire or explosion aboard a U.S. aircraft carrier since World War II. But it was far from the most disastrous. Firefighting techniques and equipment for the seven-year-old $444-million vessel had been improved since a fire aboard the *Oriskany* when 43 men died (*The World in 1966, 209*) and another one year later on the *Forrestal* that killed 134 crewmen (*The World in 1967, 147–148*).

While repairs, estimated to cost $6.4 million, began, the Navy probed for the cause of the disaster. "All we know," said a spokesman, "is that it took place in or near a Phantom. It could have been a rocket or a bomb, or a break in a hydraulic line that caused a fire and triggered the first explosion."

HOW MINI CAN A BIKINI BE?

How much cloth was needed for decency in a bikini? The ruling in Sydney, Australia, was that there must be two inches on the side of each female hip. Anything less would be considered indecent exposure.

Many girls pouted and some invited pursuit by showing too much girl per suit. Two were chased off a beach for wearing mini bikinis that measured 1¼ inches under the minimum. Another, a 36–24–36 model, appeared in a triangle of white cloth held in place by two strings. "When the inspector comes," she said, "I put on a two-inch belt that I carry with me."

The inspectors generally were delighted with the prospect—until the Council of Civil Liberties announced that charges of indecent assault would face any officer who "measures the costume while the girl is in it."

One puzzled inspector complained: "How can we do our duty?" A few did not think that measuring bathing suits was their responsibility. "My job is to keep people from drowning," said Brian Davidson, a veteran of 29 years service. "I wouldn't think of throwing one of the girls off the beach. They're too nice."

There was some sentiment that the regulations didn't go far enough. "On some women," said a laboratory technician, "two inches wouldn't cover a freckle."

WINTER VISITOR—HONG KONG FLU

Someone breathed in Hong Kong and sneezed in California and 40 million Americans felt the effects. For most victims of the virus A2-Hong Kong-68, better known as the Hong Kong flu, it meant a few miserable days in bed. For those who suffered from heart conditions, respiratory ailments or the infirmities of age, however, there were possibly fatal complications.

First came the fever and the headache. Then the cough and the chills. And the aches in the muscles and the pains in the joints. And the lassitude that made drinking a glass of water more work than it was worth. Schools closed early for the holidays, some industries shut down, visiting in hospitals was curtailed, government offices operated with short staffs and Christmas shopping was interrupted—all because of a submicroscopic speck of protein and nucleic acid less than one-millionth of an inch wide.

The American Red Cross declared a "disaster situation." The call went out to drug makers to whip up lots of vaccine but it was easier said than done. It seemed that most of the farmers already had sent to market the roosters that fertilized the hen's eggs that produced the chick embryo that was used to make vaccine. Besides, less than six months earlier, the U.S. Public Health Service had predicted, on the findings of a worldwide surveillance network, little flu for the winter.

By early January, less than two months after the bug was discovered in Needles, Calif., the National Communicable Disease Center in Atlanta reported that all 50 states, the District of Columbia and Puerto Rico had been hit by the biological brother of the Asian flu. A survey of 122 U.S. cities showed three times the normal number of deaths from pneumonia and influenza. Some 3,500 deaths were reported for December, 213 in Christmas week alone.

The bug bit such luminaries as President Johnson, Vice President Humphrey, Sen. Edmund Muskie, D-Me., Chicago Mayor Richard Daley, Richard Cardinal Cushing of Boston, Natalie Wood, and Angela Lansbury. Actress Tallulah Bankhead was one of those who died.

Hardest hit was the densely-populated Northeast. In New York City alone, some 1.5 million residents were felled by the Oriental culprit and the effects were complicated by a strike of fuel oil truck drivers. The week-long tie-up left some quarter-million New Yorkers, many bedded down with the bug, shivering in heatless dwellings. When the strike ended, deliveries were slowed because 500 drivers had the flu.

The flu was inexplicably light in Europe. Russia vaccinated 70 to 80 per cent of the population in major cities. A million doses of vaccine were stockpiled in Britain.

Asia was hard hit—Malaysia, Singapore, the Philippines, Vietnam, Taiwan. Delegates from the Far East were blamed for carrying the virus which felled many medical scientists attending a congress in Teheran, Iran. Appropriately, the topic of discussion was infectious disease.

In Hong Kong, where the flu first surfaced outside Communist China, one in five persons fell victim and some 130 died. Officials lamented the fact that, although the epidemic had started in Central China, the British colony of four million was blamed. "We have," noted a Hong Kong newspaper, "acted unwillingly in our role as an entry port for a sneeze by person or persons unknown."

DEATH OF A SPYMASTER

Allen Welsh Dulles, mustachioed master of American espionage, made spying an occupation for professionals. As director of the Central Intelligence Agency for eight years, Dulles devoted unrelenting enthusiasm and expertise to developing the government's most sophisticated cloak-and-dagger organization.

Dulles was well prepared for appointment to the post by President Eisenhower in 1953. As head of the Office of Strategic Services in Switzerland during World War II, he had directed a complex operation that, in six months, led to the surrender of nearly one million German troops in northern Italy nearly a week before the collapse of the Third Reich. His network also was responsible for filtering from Berlin to Bern some 2,000 secret Foreign Office documents on microfilm and for tipping him to the assassination plot against Hitler in 1944. He also became aware of the German V-2 rocket experiments at Peenemunde in 1943, knowledge which led to Allied air raids that crippled the program.

During his tenure with the CIA, in the midst of the coldest of cold wars, it was mostly his failures that were brought to public attention. "If something goes wrong, that's too bad," said Dulles. "If it goes right, I just hope we can keep it a secret as long as possible." One success, aimed directly at countering Communist propaganda, wasn't unveiled until 1967, six years after his retirement, when militant National Student Association leaders denounced the CIA for helping to finance the NSA for 15 years. "We obtained what we wanted," said Dulles. "We stopped them (the Communists) in certain areas, and the student area was one of them." (The World in 1967, 41–43).

Among the setbacks were the Soviet capture of Francis Gary Powers and his U2 reconnaissance plane in 1960 and the Cuban Bay of Pigs fiasco in 1961.

The U2, an aircraft capable of taking detailed photographs from a height of 70,000 feet, had provided the United States with vital information about the Soviets, including their missile development program. When the plane, piloted by Powers, was shot down over the USSR, Premier Khrushchev angrily called off a Summit conference that had been scheduled in the hope of easing world tensions.

The biggest blow to the CIA, and to the nation's stature in world affairs, was the ill-fated attempt to invade Cuba early in the Kennedy administration. President Kennedy blamed himself for agreeing to the invasion and publicly shouldered responsibility. Five months later, however, he appointed a successor to Dulles, saying, "Under the British system I would have to go—but under our system, I'm afraid it's got to be you."

Dulles retired to his Washington home, the Highlands, where he lived quietly until his death Jan. 30.

Born April 7, 1893 in Watertown, N.Y., Dulles was the second son of the Rev. and Mrs. Allen Macy Dulles. His father was a Presbyterian minister and nephew of John Welsh, ambassador to Britain during the Rutherford B. Hayes Administration. His mother, the former Edith Foster, was a daughter of John W. Foster, Secretary of State under President Benjamin Harrison, and his brother, John Foster Dulles who died in 1959, was Secretary of State in the Eisenhower Administration.

A CONGRESSMAN AGAIN

Once more the question before the House was the future of Adam Clayton Powell. Would he be reinstated as a U.S. Representative in good standing or would he again be consigned to exile? The issue came up in the early hours of the 91st Congress when the minister from New York's Harlem presented the credentials of his second election since his banishment for misuse of public funds (The World in 1967, 57–59).

Rep. Emanuel Celler, D-N.Y., who had directed the investigation of Powell's affairs as chairman of a special committee, now became his chief defender. "Any additional punishment would be vindictive," Celler said. ". . . He who is without sin, let him cast the first stone. Judge not that ye be not judged—especially in regard to loved ones on the payroll." Even some who opposed Powell tempered their opposition. "Adam Clayton Powell is not my idea of a congressman," said Morris Udall of Arizona. "But . . . don't close the door again on the 500,000 people of the 18th district of New York." They had not been represented in the House for nearly two years.

For five hours, the House debated while Powell, debonair and jaunty as always, joked and fidgeted in the rear of the chamber. A resolution to restore his seat without conditions was defeated. So was a proposal to convene another special committee. A call for stiffer punishment was ruled out of order. Finally came the voting, and a tally of 252–160 to readmit him.

There would be a price, however. Powell would have to pay a fine of $25,000—to be ex-tracted from his salary at the rate of $1,150 per month—and he would lose 22 years of seniority. He accepted the conditions and was duly sworn. "It might be a good idea if everybody had to pay $25,000 to get in here," he said.

The last word had not been spoken. Late in 1968, the Supreme Court had agreed to hear arguments on Powell's suit that his exclusion by the 90th Congress was unconstitutional. On Jan. 7, his lawyers again went before the Court to complain that the $25,000 fine was part and parcel with the "unconstitutional conduct" of 1967.

The Court announced its decision on June 16—a 7-1 vote that Congress indeed had acted unconstitutionally in excluding Powell while he met the requirements of age, residence and citizenship. The effect was something less than complete victory for the congressman: The Court said explicitly that only the right to exclude was involved; Congress retained the authority to expel the wayward. Similarly, nothing was said about the fine or the loss of seniority. The question of back pay was returned to a lower court.

The Court did assert its right to rule on the constitutionality of exclusion: "It is the responsibility of this Court to act as the ultimate interpreter of the Constitution," said Chief Justice Warren in the majority opinion.

On Bimini, Powell rejoiced. "From now on," he told reporters, "220 million Americans will know that the Supreme Court is the place where you can get justice."

The people of Prague: "Sorrow is Silent"

"A PROTEST OF DESPAIR"

Jan Palach saw himself as the second Czecho-slovak in history to die by fire for his convictions. The first was Jan Hus, a 15th century religious reformer, who was burned at the stake for heresy in 1415. Palach, a 21-year-old university student, set himself afire in Prague's St. Wenceslas Square on Jan. 16 in protest of the abolition of government reforms by Soviet invasion *(The World in 1968, 172–179)*.

"I saw this figure running toward me, burning from head to foot," said a witness. "The youngster yelled 'throw your coat over me.' I did." As Palach slumped to the pavement he whispered, "I did it myself. In my briefcase is a letter." The letter contained two demands: an end to government censorship of the press and a ban on distribution of the Soviet occupation newspaper Zpravy. It also threatened more self-immolations if the demands were not met. The note was signed "Torch No. 1."

For three days, Palach lay in a room on the top floor of a gray, five-story clinic about 600 yards from where he had set himself ablaze.

With third degree burns over 85 per cent of his body, Palach slipped in and out of consciousness. In his more lucid periods, he begged for every detail of public reaction to his deed. What he heard was not unlike listening to a eulogy at one's own funeral. Fellow students called the act a "protest of despair" by a "deeply human, thoughtful, political thinking man." They lashed at the Soviets for crushing democratic reforms and at the Czechoslovak Communist Party for bowing to Russian demands. Trade unions vowed general strikes, if necessary, similar to the ones that helped to wage a war of nerves with the Soviet troops after the August invasion.

When Palach died on Jan. 19, thousands of people converged on Wenceslas Square. Students carried Czech flags and black banners of mourning. Candlelight played against wreaths at the base of St. Wenceslas' statue. Four persons set up a tent in the square and began a hunger strike.

"We support Palach," shouted the crowds. "We want new policies, not more dead people."

After five days of mourning, countrymen gave Palach a martyr's funeral. The government, fearing violence, ordered troops into the city but the mourners were restrained and somber. In keeping with the student slogan "Sorrow is Silent," all traffic stopped for five minutes at noon.

Palach had given his people a new symbol, and new enthusiasm in their struggle against Soviet pressure. But the demands put forth in his final note went unheeded. Jaroslav Havelka, chairman of the government committee for press and information, said some press controls were needed so interests of the country would not be "seriously damaged by the activity of the information media." As for the distribution of Zpravy, Havelka said, it "was never permitted by us; therefore, legally no further act is necessary to prohibit it."

Nevertheless, Palach told a friend that "my act has achieved its purpose. But it would be better if no one repeats it. Lives should be used for other purposes."

"MAKE THIS A HOLIDAY"

On the eighth day, Reuven Horesh rose and told the assembled mourners: "Last Monday, my brother, Charles Horesh, with eight other innocent Jews, were publicly hanged in one of the squares of Baghdad while 500,000 rejoiced and danced; singing, clapping their hands and tapping their feet. And the bodies were kept dangling a whole day from the scaffold while the Baghdad radio and TV was calling on the mobs, to come and rejoice . . .

"A sign was pinned to the victims' prison garb with the word, 'Jew.' That was all their crime."

Reuven Horesh had left Iraq many years before. At the memorial service he said he had begged his brother to join him in New York.

Now it was too late. At dawn on Jan. 27, Charles and 13 others were executed by the Iraqi government on charges of being Israeli spies. The trials had not been public.

Gray prison vans carried 11 of the dead to Liberation Square in Baghdad. In front of a waiting crowd, the eight Jews, two Moslems and one Christian were suspended from hastily-built scaffolds. Pinned to their red prison uniforms were papers listing name, age, religion and crime. The other condemned men, two Moslems and a Jew, were exhibited in the port city of Basra.

Baghdad Radio exhorted listeners: "Make this a holiday. . . . Come in your thousands to express your contempt for the Zionist conspirators." The grisly scene was televised for the aged, infirm and distant.

A wave of protest swept the world.

U Thant, secretary general of the United Nations, expressed "regret and concern" about the trials and executions. He said they "are particularly abhorrent and dangerous when they are carried out in such a way as to inflame the emotions of the populace." He said he had expressed his concern to Iraq's U.N. ambassador, and had been told that he was meddling in an "entirely internal affair."

The Vatican newspaper, L'Osservatore Romano, revealed that Pope Paul VI had appealed vainly for clemency through the apostolic delegate in Baghdad. A plea by Great Britain also had failed. William P. Rogers, U.S. Secretary of State, said the hangings were "repugnant to the conscience of the world."

After the Arab countries were defeated in the six-day war of 1967, Iraq's 2,500 to 3,000 Jews found they were thought of as Zionists. Scores were arrested. By the middle of 1968 the Jewish community was living in virtual isolation: Personal property could not be sold; there was no employment; Jews were allowed to draw only about $280 a month; they were discouraged from talking with diplomats and foreigners.

It was ironic that, like Charles Horesh, they thought of themselves as Iraqis first and had chosen not to join the 120,000 Jews who left after the 1948 Israeli war of independence.

Many felt the reason for Iraq's behavior was a weak government. Since the overthrow of the monarchy in 1958, there had been four bloody changes of government. The military junta which took power in July 1968 under the direction of Ahmed Hassan Al-Bakr, was beset by religious, racial, tribal and political differences. To distract attention from its weaknesses and to move against political foes, the government-in-power turned to the basic propaganda ploy of scapegoats: "Zionists, imperialists and counter-revolutionaries."

(On Feb. 20, seven more young men were executed and put on display, propaganda blaring from Baghdad radio. None of them were Jews.)

FOR THE RECORD

MARRIED. Sandy Koufax, 33, television sportscaster and former star baseball pitcher for the Los Angeles Dodgers, and Ann Heath Widmark, daughter of actor Richard Widmark, at West Los Angeles, Calif., Jan. 1.

OBITUARY. The Saturday Evening Post, which began publication in 1821, announced that it would cease publication with the Feb. 8 issue. Prolonged financial losses caused the death of the magazine which had introduced many notable characters of American fiction—Scattergood Baines, Tugboat Annie, Charlie Chan, Alexander Botts—and had numbered many giants of American letters among its contributors: James Fenimore Cooper, Jack London, O. Henry, Theodore Dreiser, Edna Ferber, Thomas Wolfe, F. Scott Fitzgerald, Fannie Hurst, J. P. Marquand.

ELECTED. Sen. Fred R. Harris of Oklahoma to be chairman of the Democratic National Committee, at Washington, Jan. 14. He succeeded Lawrence F. O'Brien who resigned to join an investment firm.

RELEASED. Morton Sobell, from the federal prison at Lewisburg, Pa., after serving 17 years and 9 months of a 30-year sentence for conspiracy to commit espionage. Sobell had been a co-defendant with Julius and Ethel Rosenberg who were executed in 1953 for stealing American atomic secrets.

Two of the dead in Baghdad's Liberation Square

In California, a battle to save the beaches ➝

February

Three Plagues in California—
Water, Mud and Oil

*And when they had passed, there were prophecies
of greater disaster to come—an earthquake;
the people responded with a quip and a party*

Mud, mud, and more mud

CALIFORNIA WAS not the Golden State in the early months of 1969. Floods of mud from the hills and tides of oil from the sea made a multimillion dollar mess in a big expanse of prized scenic and vacation lands.

More than 100 persons died as record rains poured down in January and February. Some smothered in avalanches of mud. Others drowned in torrents of water rushing through streambeds that normally were dry. Many died in traffic accidents amid the storms.

The tides of oil—more than a quarter million gallons—came from an undersea well that blew out as it was being drilled from an ocean platform six miles off the scenic shoreline at Santa Barbara, a showplace community of 73,000 population about 100 miles northwest of Los Angeles. Oil spewed to the surface at the rate of 21,000 gallons per day, spreading a gummy carpet up to six inches thick over 800 square miles and contaminating 35 miles of beaches. Picturesque Santa Barbara Channel became a Sargasso Sea of iridescent slime, reminiscent of the *Torrey Canyon* disaster in 1967. When that supertanker wrecked on the rocks off Cornwall, England, 36 million gallons of oil gushed into the sea to menace fish, birds and beaches along 120 miles of coastline (*The World in 1967*, 50–53).

Technicians said the well erupted, like champagne from an uncorked bottle, when the drill was withdrawn to permit replacement of a worn bit. The drill had tapped a high pressure pool of petroleum and gas 3,486 feet beneath the Pacific Ocean's floor. Bubbles 100 and 200 feet in diameter boiled up around the platform, each one adding to the thickening, spreading scum.

Ordinarily, the weight of a drilling compound in the shaft would have contained the oil. In this case, the upward surge hit a smaller pool at 350 feet and, when pressure built there, was vented to the ocean floor through uncharted faults or fissures created by earthquakes sometime in the past. The shaft was encased in pipe to a depth of 239 feet as required by federal regulations. Below that point, it was an unsheathed hole through layers of sand and shale.

Offshore drilling was not new to California, particularly within the three-mile limit of state jurisdiction. Thousands of derricks dotted the waters from Santa Barbara to Huntington Beach, 125 miles to the south. However, the field had been expanded a year earlier when the Department of Interior leased, for $603 million, drilling rights in nearly 1,000 square miles of ocean floor to a dozen oil companies. The runaway well was among the first of hundreds expected in the Santa Barbara Channel.

On Feb. 5, the white beaches of Santa Barbara turned black. A correspondent for Sports Illustrated wrote that the oil "lay so thick on the water that waves were unformed; they made a squishing sound. . . . The smell of oil followed me up the canyon to our house, a mile from the sea. . . . The tideline was a broad black band that looked from the air like something made on a map with a black crayon."

As the slick spread, so did casualties mount among the birds —loons, gulls, grebes, cormorants, sandpipers. By official count, 1,053 birds were brought to three improvised laundries with their feathers matted, eyes inflamed and intestines burned by crude oil. Nearly 200 died, despite heroic treatment; uncounted hundreds of others lay inert on the beaches and in the sea. Other wild life was affected. Colonies of sea lions abandoned the blackened rocks of their island sanctuaries. Porpoises and whales were seen surfacing for air in the polluted channel, and then disappearing.

In the harbors, the skin of oil befouled the bright hulls of hundreds of pleasure boats, trapped at their moorings by an order forbidding travel through the volatile scum. Sixty persons

The straw absorbed five times its weight in oil ⟶

The houses slid down the hills

who lived on their boats were evacuated because of fire hazard and noxious fumes.

The Union Oil Co. of California, operator of the miscreant well, sent out boatmen to lay miles of booms in an effort to corral the oil and keep it away from the beaches. Winds of the same storms that were spreading misery inland broke the booms and the creeping fingers of oil seeped through to tar seaside rocks and saturate the sands. The slick was sprayed with chemicals to break down the oil into particles small enough for marine organisms to digest. Crews scattered tons of straw which soaked up five times its weight in oil. As the straw absorbed oil, it was sucked up by giant vacuums, or raked up and stuffed into barrels for removal. Beyond the harbor, one ship used a blower to broadcast the straw across a slick as big as two football fields. Miles of beaches were scoured with steam.

At the same time, riggers worked to kill the leaking well. Tons of a cementlike compound were pumped into the shaft, building a plug which eventually was 3,400 feet thick. Two new holes were drilled to ease pressure in the blown shaft.

The dual effort to disperse the slick and stop the flow had a salutary effect. Within 11 days, the leakage dwindled to a comparative and harmless trickle. In early April, the beaches were clean and operations in the Channel were back to normal. The only visible evidences of disaster were tenuous fingers of oil still seeping from beneath Platform A.

There were other reminders, though. A new set of rules, for one thing. Walter J. Hickel, Secretary of the Interior, had flown to California and found the pollution "much more severe" than

he had anticipated. On Feb. 7, he ordered suspension of all operations under federal leases. Ten days later, he issued new regulations, chief among them a provision that wells be encased to greater depth than the 239 feet previously prescribed. In that respect, the new rules conformed with state requirements which had been cited by California officials as the reason why no similar disaster had occurred within state jurisdiction.

Another reminder was the temper of Santa Barbara. Much of the city's early California-Spanish architectural atmosphere had been preserved by municipal specification and the profusion of stucco homes roofed with red tile, palms, pines and beaches made it a popular tourist attraction. Wealthy residents had seen the value of shore properties rise to as much as $2,000 per front foot. The people never had become accustomed to the sight of oil derricks in their seaward view.

Now many residents who had been devoting spare time to washing oily birds turned to circulating petitions which demanded the permanent shutdown of all drilling in their Channel. A new conservationist group, Get Oil Out (GOO), organized protest demonstrations and picketed the municipal pier with signs, "Ban the Blob." More than 12,000 letters and telegrams went to Congress, the Department of Interior and the Department of Housing and Urban Development. Mass meetings were called to hear geologists warn of future disasters in the heavily faulted, quake-prone region.

Experts gave an oil-soaked bird a 50 per cent chance of survival, depending on how soon it was found, but said unless a bird was very sick it could not be captured. An Audubon Soci-

as he slept. In all, more than a dozen deaths were caused by suffocating mud.

In a tragic incident of flood, six young hikers and their leader were trapped with three men who were guiding them to safety when a bulldozer stalled in a raging stream. One by one, they were carried away, succumbing either to cold or the turbulent waters.

The trials by mud, water and oil did not end California's troubles. Another source of public unease was a rash of predictions by assorted seers and oracles that a major earthquake would rock the state in April or May. Some prophets pinpointed the date—April 18, anniversary of the great earthquake and fire which ravaged San Francisco in 1906. The alarm was not stilled by a work of fiction, *The Last Days of the Late, Great State of California,* which climaxed in a description of a quake, in 1969, that would tear the state from the continent and sink it beneath the Pacific.

A number of families were so impressed that they moved away. Newspapers, radio stations and government agencies were deluged with demands to name the date when disaster would strike. The Geological Survey was moved to announce, "There is no scientific basis for the rash of predictions of a major California earthquake in April." Pessimists noted that the Survey didn't say "absolutely."

The great majority of the people were optimists. They expressed their sentiments in bumper stickers—"California Deserves a Fair Shake"—and in jokes—Howard Hughes was buying Nevada property because he wanted beachfront locations.

One of the scoffers was Mayor Joseph Alioto of San Francisco. He organized a predawn party on the anniversary, to be held defiantly astride the San Andreas fault, where the 1906 quake originated. Five thousand people turned out to sing, hear music and cheer lustily as the sun rose over the sleeping—and unquaked—metropolis.

April and May passed without disaster. One tremor described as "sizable" was recorded on April 28 but the center was lonely desert country and damage was slight. Nonetheless, seismologists were aware that the prophecies of doom were not entirely fancy. They agreed that a major earthquake was inevitable sometime in California's future.

The state was earthquake country; more than 80 per cent of the world's biggest ones occurred around the rim of the Pacific Ocean from Chile northward to Alaska. In California, underground stresses were building along the 600 miles of the San Andreas fault which cut across the southwestern corner of San Francisco and ran 20 miles east of Los Angeles. The only thing which could relieve those stresses was an earthquake.

For the same geological reasons which made the region earthquake-prone, a recurrence of the flood and oil disasters was not unlikely. Centuries earlier, the earth's crust was shot through with cracks, big and little. Where the layers of underlying rock were sheared and piled on top of each other, pockets were formed, natural collecting points for oil. Even a minor earth shock could be enough to tear open one or more of those pockets. In the same manner, rain seeped into the cracks between the tilted layers of rock and formed a lubricating mud which caused the upper layers to slide down from their moorings.

Despite the underground threats, California's population continued to surge upward. A geologist who had firsthand experience explained: "I live on a hillside. I lost part of my back yard in the winter rains. I own some beach property that was smeared by the oil slick. I work in a building that was built on an old earthquake fault. But I wouldn't live anywhere else if I could. I like it here."

ety spokesman called the bird-studded beaches "a very sad looking mess." A witness said pelicans dove right into the oil. "It's a sickening sight."

Thus, the costs of the oil invasion were measured largely in non-human terms; in dollars and dead birds. Such losses paled beside the personal tragedies of the inland disaster wrought by the same series of storms that helped to push the oil ashore.

Along the slopes of the San Gabriel Mountains, 52 inches of rain fell in three storms which hit in close succession. In other areas, rainfall totaled 34 inches, with as much as 12 inches in 24 hours. In Los Angeles, downpours adding up to 17.25 inches were 2.5 times normal for the period.

The affected area extended nearly 200 miles northwestward from Los Angeles to San Luis Obispo County. Hundreds of homes were wrecked or seriously damaged by water and mudslides from hills that had been denuded by brush fires in 1968. In the hills behind the seacoast town of Carpenteria, 10 miles south of Santa Barbara, citrus groves were uprooted and the trees were washed to the beaches where broken branches and rotting oranges mingled with other debris blackened by the seaborne oil. In the town, residents counted 291 homes damaged or destroyed, one in every seven in the community of 7,200 people. Bridges were washed out, rail and highway traffic blocked or seriously impeded.

In Orange County's Silverado Canyon, 17 of 60 refugees who had found shelter in a fire station were buried when mud engulfed the building. Twelve were rescued; five died. An investment banker smothered when mud cascaded into his home

Garrison Finish,
New Orleans Style

*The jury concluded that district attorney's theory
of Kennedy assassination was one man's opinion
and acquitted Clay Shaw of conspiracy charge*

Pistol packin' district attorney and aide

AFTER NEARLY two years of tall talking, the showdown hour had arrived for Jim Garrison's investigation into the assassination of President John F. Kennedy.

Now was the time for the flamboyant, crusading district attorney of New Orleans to produce his evidence, all of his evidence, in court. Now was the time for him to prove beyond resonable doubt that the killing in Dallas on Nov. 22, 1963, had been the fruit of a conspiracy and that Clay L. Shaw, retired managing director of the International Trade Mart and a prominent, respected citizen of New Orleans, had been one of the conspirators.

Legally, Shaw was the only defendant in the trial that began on Jan. 21 in crowded, closely guarded Criminal District Court. In a larger sense, there were two co-defendants—the Warren Commission which had found that Lee Harvey Oswald acted alone in plotting and carrying out the assassination, and the federal government itself, accused of complicity in a coverup.

Garrison read the opening statement and then retired, leaving the prosecution to a team of aides headed by James L. Alcock, assistant district attorney. Under the team's direction, the case developed in two phases. One dealt with the charge against Shaw. The other concentrated on the action in Dealey Plaza, Dallas, on that bleak day in 1963.

Both sides agreed that the case against Shaw hinged on the testimony of one witness, Perry Raymond Russo, a swarthy, muscular book salesman and a onetime taxi driver. He had been the state's major witness also in an earlier hearing which determined that Garrison had enough evidence to warrant a trial *(The World in 1967, 212–214).* His tale varied somewhat in the second telling, during eight hours of testimony and cross-examination.

Russo told that he had attended a party in September 1963, two months before Kennedy was shot, at the home of David W. Ferrie, a brilliant, eccentric homosexual who had been named by Garrison as one of Shaw's co-conspirators. Among those present were Oswald, known as Leon Oswald, and Shaw, under the name of Clay Bertrand. Russo testified that he heard Ferrie, Oswald and "Bertrand" talking about killing the President with a "triangulation of fire," and plans for alibis and escape. His memory had been sharpened, he said, in three sessions with a hypnotist provided by the district attorney. (Judge Edward A. Haggerty Jr. prohibited trial testimony by the hypnotist.

He had narrated at the preliminary hearing how he had taken Russo back through "a time tunnel" to "relive" the party.)

The defense maintained that, even with hypnotic help, Russo's story was wonderfully vague. He had not given a specific date. Aside from Shaw, the only guests identified were Ferrie and Oswald, both of them dead. (Ferrie had been found dead in bed soon after Garrison's investigation became public knowledge. The official medical finding was that he had died of a ruptured blood vessel in the brain; Garrison insisted he had committed suicide.)

At the preliminary hearing, Russo had named a girl, Sandra Moffett, as one of several friends who accompanied him to the party. At the trial, with Miss Moffett (now Mrs. Harold McMaines) ready to testify for the state that she never had attended such a party and had not known Ferrie until 1965, Russo insisted to Alcock that, "I don't know if anyone accompanied me."

There were other erosions in the bizarre story which Russo had unfolded at the earlier hearing. Cross examination brought out that he had expressed doubts about his identification of Shaw. Had he once said there were times when he could not distinguish between fact and fantasy? Yes, said the witness, but they were due to the enormous mental pressures deriving from his role in the case, and to the persistent skepticism of newsmen. "I was 100 per cent sure," he said, "but in a case like this you want to be 1,000 per cent sure."

There was other testimony on that point. Lt. Edward O'Donnell of New Orleans police, a defense witness, recalled an official interview in June 1967 at which Russo had admitted doubt but said he was "afraid Garrison would charge him with perjury if he said Shaw was not at that meeting." O'Donnell had reported the conversation to Garrison, he said, and Russo "did a retake" when Garrison confronted him.

Then, with the testimony of Vernon Bundy, a hoarse-voiced narcotics addict, that he had seen Shaw and Oswald together on a Lake Ponchartrain seawall in 1963, the stage was set for an important new witness.

Charles I. Spiesel, 51, was a little accountant with a gentle smile from New York City. His smile was intact when he left the stand but Alcock, the chief prosecutor, was flushed and grim.

Spiesel told the jury that he, too, had attended a party in New Orleans in 1963, and he, too, had heard talk of killing the President. He had gone to the party with Ferrie and Ferrie had introduced the host as Shaw. The importance of Spiesel's story was that it set up Ferrie and Shaw as something more than casual acquaintances. Shaw had said he never so much as laid eyes on Ferrie or Oswald, either dead or alive.

Under cross examination by F. Irving Dymond of defense counsel, Spiesel's background was bared mercilessly. He agreed that he had been hypnotized "from time to time" by New York police, rival accountants and a psychiatrist. Was he not frequently followed by Communists? "Well, not recently." His tormentors, he said, disguised themselves as members of his family and then refused to recognize him on the street. How many people had hypnotized him? "Oh, 50 or 60." Was it against his will? Yes. How could he tell when he was being hypnotized? "They catch my eye," said Spiesel.

The jury heard him wonderingly. Dymond could not repress a grin of triumph when he left the granite courthouse that day.

Next the prosecution turned to the scene in Dallas. Shaw was relegated to the role of spectator at his own trial while the state mounted a direct attack on the Warren Commission's conclusion that Lee Harvey Oswald was a lone, unaided assassin who killed President Kennedy with rifle fire from the sixth floor of the Texas School Book Depository.

Witnesses were summoned to tell that they heard shots from several directions, this to show that more than one gunman was involved. But the core of the case was a motion picture film taken by Abraham Zapruder, a Dallas dress manufacturer. The amateur production ran about 20 seconds and carried tremendous emotional wallop. With the courtroom darkened, the prosecution showed the film repeatedly, over furious defense objections. Jury and spectators saw the President lurch under the impact of the first shot, gasped at the spray of blood and tissue when he was hit in the head. The fact that Kennedy's head jerked backward was proof, the state argued, that he was shot from the front. Oswald was firing from above and behind the presidential limousine.

The Zapruder film was not new evidence. It had been studied intently by investigators, amateur and professional. Still photo-

Clay Shaw

The jury poses for a picture

graphs from it had been published in newspapers and magazines. The Garrison presentation added little to public knowledge.

When the defense turn came, Dean Andrews of New Orleans was called; he was a short, fat, brash lawyer who called himself Mr. Five by Five. He had reported a telephone call in 1963 from one Clay Bertrand who had asked him to go to Dallas to represent Oswald. Pressed by investigators, Andrews became evasive: He knew Bertrand mainly as "a voice on the telephone"; he didn't know where Bertrand lived; he had not actually seen Bertrand for some time.

After questioning by an attorney for the Warren Commission, Andrews faded into the background—until Garrison began his hunt for Bertrand. Under Garrison's pressure, Andrews finally said he had made up the whole story. He was convicted of perjury in 1967.

Now, in 1969, Andrews repeated that the phone call was a figment of imagination. No one had asked him to represent Oswald; so far as he knew, there was no Clay Bertrand. "The only explanation I can give you is my mouth ran ahead of my brain," he told the jury.

What about his testimony to the Warren Commission's interrogator, asked Alcock. "It's page after page of bull," said Andrews. "You mean page after page of lies?" "If you want to call it that."

In final argument for the defense, Dymond spoke of Russo as a liar, and described Spiesel as "the most obvious paranoid case I've ever seen in my life." As for Andrews, "This little fat man with a peculiar manner of speaking took the stand, a ruined lawyer, bared his chest and said do to me what you can, I'm going to tell the truth now."

Dymond argued that Garrison's case simply did not add up;

Shaw had been accused and brought to trial "for no other purpose than to create a forum for an attack on the American government."

Garrison left the state's final legal arguments to his assistants. For himself, he spoke in quiet, conversational tones as he leaned against the prosecutor's table.

Conviction, he said, would be "the best way to communicate to the government that we do not accept fraud." "The government murders truth," he said, "and if it can murder truth, it can murder freedom."

He said "the strange and deceptive conduct of the government began while (Kennedy's) body was still warm and has continued until this day." The Warren Commission was a matter of "men of high position and prestige sitting on a board and telling you what happened but withholding the evidence. . . . There are forces in America today which are not in favor of the truth coming out about President Kennedy's assassination. . . . You can cause justice to happen and, if you do that, nothing you have ever done will have been more important."

The trial had continued for 34 days. The verdict was returned in less than one hour. The clerk took the slip of paper from the jury foreman and read it: "We find the defendant not guilty." It was 1 a.m. on March 1—exactly two years after the day that Garrison had arrested Shaw.

Afterward, as the jurors left the motel where they had been quartered, they said that only the case as it involved Shaw had been considered. The agreement for acquittal had been reached on the first ballot. One of them, David I. Powe, summarized the thinking:

"Garrison had a right to his opinion about the government and the Warren Commission, but I just don't feel his 'opinion' is enough to convict a man."

"It is Necessary to Consult..."

President Nixon banned
"showboat diplomacy" on mission
to "revitalize" U.S. ties with Europe

O N RICHARD NIXON's 17th day as President of the United States, he surprised his countrymen with an announcement that he soon would visit Western Europe. Mrs. Nixon and the rest of the family would stay home, he said, because it would be a working trip, aimed at "strengthening and revitalizing the American-European community."

The most energetic tourist would have been hard put to devise a more rigorous itinerary: 13,500 miles of travel in eight days with stops in Brussels, London, Bonn, West Berlin, Rome, Paris and then back to Rome for a visit to the Vatican before heading home. Each day had its own dawn-to-midnight schedule of conferences, luncheons, formal dinners, speeches, toasts and protocol ceremonies—the daily tests of stamina and intellectual acuity that did not confront the ordinary tourist.

Many a diplomatic observer was surprised by the new President's decision to venture so quickly into the treacherous realm of personal diplomacy. Nixon had not had time to get a firm grasp on the governmental machinery of the United States. Was he not buying trouble needlessly by so soon attempting substantive conferences with such seasoned European leaders as Charles de Gaulle?

Predictably, Western Europe's Communist leaders called for massive protests wherever Nixon traveled. While presidential advisers and bodyguards fretted, Nixon ordered the Secret Service (criticized for its high visibility during European trips by Dwight D. Eisenhower and John F. Kennedy) to be as unobtrusive as possible and to leave his armored limousine at home. Where appropriate, Nixon would ride in the limousines of his hosts and, on other occasions, in a sedan that would offer no outward evidence of its bulletproof plating.

To every objection, Nixon had a response. If the risks, political and personal, were great, the need for trans-Atlantic consultation was urgent after four years in which the United States was criticized for preoccupation with Vietnam and Asia.

Rain fell at Andrews Air Force Base, outside Washington, as Nixon stepped before cameras and microphones on Feb. 23 to voice his farewell. "The problems we face are too complex and too difficult," he said, "to be settled by what I would call the 'showboat diplomacy.' On the other hand, before we can make progress . . . with our opponents, it is necessary to consult with our friends. And we are going to have real consultation, because we seek not only their support but their advice and their counsel on the grave problems that we face. . . ."

The weather in Brussels was more hospitable when Nixon arrived there after dark that Sunday evening. King Baudouin and respectable numbers of his subjects welcomed the American to the home city of the North Atlantic Treaty Organization and the Commission of European Communities. Nixon reminded his greeters that no U.S. President had visited Belgium since Woodrow Wilson in 1919.

Next morning, at the drab, sprawling NATO headquarters, Nixon delivered the principal formal address of the trip to members of the NATO Council. He said:

"I know there have been rumblings of discontent in Europe —a feeling that too often the United States talked at its partners instead of with them, or merely informed them of decisions after they were made instead of consulting with them before deciding. The United States is determined to listen with a new attentiveness to its NATO partners, not only because they have a right to be heard but because we want their ideas. I believe we have a right to expect that consultation shall be a two-way street."

The gathering clearly appreciated Nixon's pledge of two-way partnership. But the warmest applause came later, when the American visitor promised that Western Europe would not be dealt out of any direct dealings between Washington and Moscow that would involve its interests:

"I have said before that we are ending a period of confrontation and entering an era of negotiation. In due course and with proper preparation, the United States will enter into negotiations with the Soviet Union on a wide range of issues, some of which will affect our European allies. We will do so on the basis of full consultation and cooperation with our allies, because we recognize that the chances for successful negotiations depend on our unity.

After an elaborate luncheon at the Royal Palace and handshaking exchanges with shrill crowds of school children in the heart of Brussels, Nixon headed for London where, at foggy Heathrow Airport, he took a cautious look ahead toward an East-West détente for which he hoped he was building a preliminary foundation: "I believe, as I stand here today, that we can bring about a durable peace in our time. But it cannot come to those who seek it frantically with overnight deals or dramatic gestures . . . Peace will come, I believe, step by step, measured and deliberate, continuing to pursue the goal we seek despite setbacks and disappointments."

Nixon and Prime Minister Harold Wilson had planned to fly directly by helicopter to Wilson's official country residence, Chequers, for a working dinner. Fog and drizzle forced them into a British-made automobile. Police officers were deployed hastily along the route and, by their presence, attracted hundreds of cheering villagers at every major crossroads. In the gathering darkness, an occasional American flag could be seen. The two leaders and their advisers spent a productive evening at Chequers.

Tuesday, Feb. 25, was crowded with activity: a conference at 10 Downing Street, lunch at Buckingham Palace with Queen Elizabeth and Prince Philip, a visit to Westminster Abbey, a lengthy meeting with private citizens, an appearance at the American embassy, and a dinner conference with the British cabinet.

Squeezed into the day was an unscheduled visit to the House of Commons during a question period that saw the Prime Minister field often-ascerbic questions from occupants of the opposition benches. Said Nixon to Wilson: "I believe that your question period is much more of an ordeal than our press conference." The President, the first ever to witness a session of the House, sat in a remote corner, chin cupped in his hands and listened intently to the spirited give-and-take. Spectators in the public gallery were unaware of his presence.

In Bonn, capital of West Germany, the homeland of his mother-in-law, Nixon held lengthy meetings with Chancellor Kurt Georg Keisinger and Foreign Minister Willi Brandt, then addressed the Bundestag before flying to West Berlin, which at that moment faced threatened Communist belligerence (page 68). "Berlin is known as a four-power city," said Nixon, "but there is a fifth power in Berlin . . . I stand here today as a symbol of that fifth power—the power which will not be intimidated by any threat, by any pressure from any direction."

Berliners by the tens of thousands lined the city's boulevards as Nixon drove to the ugly, ominous wall dividing the old German capital. Their cheers and waves repeatedly lured the President out of his limousine to shake hands and exchange greetings. The Communists had promised a major anti-Nixon demonstration here but it fizzled. Paint bombs, eggs, ripe fruit and nail-studded snowballs were aimed at his car at one intersection, but few found their mark.

At the Seimens electric appliance plant, 6,000 workers pressed into a factory building to hear the President's second and final major address of the trip. They liked what they heard:

"Let there be no miscalculation: No unilateral move, no illegal act, no form of pressure from any source will shake the resolve of the Western nations to defend their rightful status as protectors of the people of free Berlin. . . . Berlin must be free. I do not say this in any spirit of bravado or belligerence. I am simply stating an irrevocable fact of international life."

Then, stepping down from the platform, Nixon pushed into the crowd, inspiring a lusty rendition of the Berlin equivalent of hip-hip-hooray: "Ha-ho-hay! Nixon okay!" A grinning President returned to the microphone and shouted, "Ha-ho-hay! Berliners are okay!"

Nixon's entry into Rome, later that day, had a storybook quality. His motorcade moved from Campiano Military Airport down the Appian Way under a hot sun that seemed even more than 4,300 miles removed from the winter cold of Washington. Between brick ruins of Roman fortresses and tombs, the presidential car bounced over cobbles put in place when Christianity was in its infancy. Then came the Coliseum and, after a drive through city streets crowded with an impressive number of traditionally blasé latter day Romans, the turreted and massive Quirinale Palace—the White House for a night.

Another Communist demonstration was expected there and it developed on schedule. Nixon did not see it. Down side streets, military trucks formed wall-to-wall barriers as riot police fought a night-long running battle to contain rebellious youth. The toll: one student dead, scores on both sides injured, 200 or more hustled into jails.

Next stop was Paris—and the big test. At Orly Airport, President Charles de Gaulle was at the foot of the ramp when the front door of Air Force One opened and Nixon emerged. The general escorted his guest into a red-carpeted V.I.P. pavilion and there, for Frenchmen to see on their television tubes, declared: "How could we not attribute the greatest interest and the utmost importance to these exchanges! . . . Long live the United States of America!"

Never caring much for set speeches, Nixon cast his text aside and responded off the cuff: "Speaking in a personal sense, I look forward to the opportunity to receive from you your judgment, your counsel, not only on the relations between our two countries but even more on the great problems that divide the world."

President Nixon with President de Gaulle

. . . . with Prime Minister Wilson

. . . . with Chancellor Kiesinger

Riding into Paris in De Gaulle's limousine, the two Presidents found the crowds friendly, sizeable, but not massive. Only at a few points was the motorcade showered with "Get Out of Vietnam" broadsides.

The first talks went well enough. Honoring Nixon at a dinner that evening at the Elysee Palace, De Gaulle began by saying, "Mr. President, you did very well to come." The U.S. President replied with a blend of truth and flattery that he hoped would break the ice for a more extensive conference next morning at the De-Gaulle-restored Petite Trianon Palace at Versailles:

"Mr. President, your life has been an example to millions of European countrymen and to millions throughout the world —an epic of courage, an epic also of leadership seldom equalled in the history of the world, leadership which now has brought this great nation to the rightful place that it should have in the family of nations."

Inasmuch as it had been unusual for the French president to greet Nixon personally at Orly, the American press had wondered at Nixon's omission of explicit praise for his host. That gap now was filled. The next question: how would things go at the Petite Trianon?

The two chief executives looked cheerful enough as they interrupted their lengthy talks inside the structure that once housed the mistress of a French king. Then came Nixon's black tie dinner for De Gaulle, at the official residence of the American ambassador, R. Sargent Shriver.

Nixon called attention to the menu: ". . . we had cheese from Wisconsin, asparagus from California, and beef from Kansas City. But there was one very unusual combination: For the first time I have seen on one plate together plain American baked potato and Russian caviar. There may be some significance in the fact that it took a French chef to bring the two together."

De Gaulle was delighted, perhaps not so much by the flattery as by the fact that a President of the United States had taken the trouble to think ahead about such niceties. He responded: "As I am learning to know you better—and by this visit you have given me that opportunity which I consider historic—I appreciate more the statesman and the man that you are."

At that point, it was difficult to decide who was flattering whom. But from the standpoint of the United States, the payoff would come next day—and it did. Said Nixon on departure from Orly for the Vatican:

"I am very pleased to announce that President De Gaulle has accepted an invitation to visit the United States. He will visit Washington sometime in January or February at a time that is mutually convenient for our two schedules . . ."

Neither he nor De Gaulle could have anticipated that within scant months the French president, who had given so much of his life and thought to the future of his corner of the globe, would be repudiated by his own people. But even De Gaulle's subsequent resignation did not erase the impression made by Nixon in Paris. Georges Pompidou, the newly-elected President, was a Gaullist who got to know Nixon during the visit.

Most important of all, when weighing the merits of the journey, was the matter Nixon stressed at every stop: consultation. He made this evident in responding to the first question put to him at a news conference after his return. Asked by Frank Cormier of The Associated Press if there was a relationship between his journey and a possible future summit conference with the leaders of the Soviet Union, the President replied:

"Mr. Cormier, this tour was a condition precedent to an East-West summit at a later time."

The Winds of Change in Baseball

*The centennial year of the professional game
brought a new commissioner, new rules, new teams
and plans for a "bold and imaginative" future*

IN 1869, the Cincinnati Red Stockings became baseball's first professional team and won 69 consecutive games with a payroll topped by $1,400 for shortstop George Wright, the best player in the game.

In 1969, stars like outfielder Willie Mays and pitcher Bob Gibson collected annual salaries exceeding $100,000. Major league club owners could afford to allot $5.45 million per year (in addition to salaries) to give the athletes financial comfort. A man who spent no more than four years in the big leagues qualified for a pension of $240 per month at the age of 50, more than twice George Wright's pay in his best years. Pension? It was an unknown word in Wright's day.

Professional baseball had come a long way since the Red Stockings adopted the first uniform with short pants and exposed the hosiery that gave them their nickname. But, judging by the drastic changes of the centennial year, it had not come far enough.

For years, there had been increasing outcry about baseball: Major league owners had locked the game in a straitjacket of tradition; petty jealousies were blocking progress; baseball was too much business and not enough sport; it was losing popular favor to livelier sports like football and basketball. The protests reached a peak after the 1968 season in which the cold supremacy of pitching stifled the bats that provided most of the action and refueled arguments that games moved too slowly and lasted too long *(The World in 1968, 207–209)*.

Some changes had been made in the lineup of teams and both National and American leagues had expanded from eight to ten clubs; a pension system had been established; television was a financial bonanza, but the traditional format of the game remained unchanged. The process of electing a commissioner disclosed the extent of stagnation and stalemate in baseball's leadership.

The office of commissioner had been established in the aftermath of a scandal that involved the bribing of Chicago White Sox players to throw games in the 1919 World Series. Judge Kenesaw Mountain Landis, rugged in countenance and in character, was elected and ruled like a czar for 20 years, employing all of the broad powers granted to him and any others that he felt needed "for the good of the game." His uncompromising, forthright administration was a major factor in restoring public confidence in baseball, but the owners' enthusiasm was diluted by distaste for any authority higher than their own.

Through the terms of three succeeding commissioners, the power and influence of the office waned. It became evident that the owners regarded the commissioner as only an administrator. When the players formed an association with a director as their formal representative, the commissioner's function as arbitrator between employes and management disappeared. In such circumstances, the time came to choose a successor to William D. Eckert.

Eckert, a retired lieutenant general of the Air Force, had been elected in 1965 after a long search for "the best man available." He was conscientious, sincere and well meaning but he was so little known in baseball that sports writers dubbed him "the Unknown Soldier." He knew little more about baseball than baseball knew about him and he had not served half of his seven-year term before even the apostles of the status quo decided that something must be done.

The "something" was done at the midwinter meeting of major league magnates in San Francisco. Euphemistically, Eckert retired, acknowledging "the crying need . . . for a man who knows this world of baseball." Realistically, it was a dismissal at a cost of $260,000, the amount he would collect for his non-services through the last four years of his contract.

At the same time, baseball began moving toward changes far more revolutionary than any fresh concept of the commissioner's functions. Three men were assigned to develop nothing less than a program for "the bold and imaginative restructuring of baseball." They were Jerold Hoffberger of the Baltimore Orioles, John Holland of the Chicago Cubs, and Richard Meyer of the St. Louis Cardinals.

"We need an executive with more clout," said Michael Burke of the New York Yankees. "We must get everyone to accept a new philosophy, to divorce our thinking from the present structure of baseball—which is an anachronism we couldn't live with any longer."

Hoffberger, Holland, Meyer and Burke represented a new breed in the management of baseball. The old guard—men like Walter O'Malley of the Los Angeles Dodgers and Tom Yawkey of the Boston Red Sox—had spent a lifetime or at least a generation in the game. The new guard came from the world of business with businesslike viewpoints. Hoffberger and Meyer were brewing company executives; Burke had been a vice president of the Columbia Broadcasting System when the network bought the Yankees. "None of these fine owners would allow the disorganization we have in baseball in their own industries," said one club leader who cheered new ideas. "It's like a breath of fresh air."

It was significant that one of the late-comers became baseball's spokesman in announcing the changes. He was Frank L. Dale, publisher of the Cincinnati Enquirer, who had bought the Cincinnati Reds two years earlier. But, influence for reform though the younger generation was, it could not yet take command. That became evident when the two leagues met in Chicago to select Eckert's successor. Thirteen hours of wrangling and argument accomplished exactly nothing.

There was no shortage of candidates, formal or informal. The basic trouble was that National leaguers would not vote for American leaguers and American leaguers would not vote for National leaguers.

The deadlock persisted when the moguls of baseball met again at Bal Harbour, Fla., in February. Separate caucuses uncovered a crystallization of sentiment: The American League supported Burke and the National rallied around Charles S. (Chub) Feeney, vice president of the San Francisco Giants. Between the two, frustrating stalemate. Informal talks deepened the feeling that league was arrayed against league and never the twain would meet.

In one last bid for unity, a committee of seven was appointed to canvass the field of alternates to Burke and Feeney and come up with a nomination. The committee went to work in an atmosphere of gloom. Then, in the course of the proceedings, the name of Bowie Kuhn was mentioned. The reaction was electrifying: "Of course" . . . "Yes" . . . "Why not?" In quick agreement, Kuhn's name was submitted to a joint meeting of the leagues. The vote was unanimous by the 24 clubs: Kuhn was elected commissioner for one year at a salary of $100,000. Burke and Feeney were added to the committee planning the "bold and imaginative" restructuring.

Bowie Kuhn was as little known to baseball fandom as Gen. Eckert had been. But he was a familiar, respected figure in the high councils of the game and the only wonder was that he hadn't been mentioned much earlier. He was a lawyer, a member of the firm that had handled National League legal affairs since 1936. (Interestingly, the first suggestion of a Kuhn nomination came from an American leaguer). Since 1950, Kuhn had taken over an increasing share of the baseball business and had been connected intimately with franchise shifts, pension plans, player negotiations and congressional hearings.

Moreover, he liked baseball as much as baseball liked him. He traced his interest from the time he worked on the scoreboard at Washington's old Griffith Stadium for $1 per day. He was 42 and married, with four children. Two governors of Maryland, his native state, were among his ancestors and he and a race track had been named for one of them, Robert Bowie.

Kuhn had a definite idea who held the key to baseball's future. "The players are the game. The focus has to be on them," he said. "If the commissioner becomes better known, that's well and good but it's the public interest in our players and our game that really counts." The focus was very much on the players in the first test of his leadership.

Negotiations for a new agreement on financing pensions had been proceeding intermittently since November. The owners had offered to increase their annual allotment from $4.1 million to $5.3 million. That was not enough for the athletes who had their eyes on a new television deal which, including Game of the Week and World Series broadcasts, would pay baseball $16.5 million, up from $12 million. Ninety per cent of the

Players Association's 800 members were on record as refusing to sign contracts or report for spring training until a new agreement was reached.

The owners had refused to submit the dispute to binding arbitration. They believed that the players would not stand firm and united and insisted that Marvin Miller, negotiator for the Association, submit the last $5.3 million proposal to a vote of the membership, a procedure that might take two weeks.

The first roll calls in the training camps were not encouraging to management. Most of the players who appeared were untried rookies. A few of the absent stars showed signs of wavering but a big majority stood pat. So did the owners; persisting in the belief that the holdouts would not hold out very long, they refused even to negotiate until the Association poll was completed.

In the impasse, Kuhn acted. He persuaded the owners to return to the bargaining table and to stay there until agreement was reached.

The pact, announced Feb. 25, put $5.45 million annually into the pension fund. The minimum service for eligibility was lowered from five to four years and the scale of payments was raised—at the age of 50, the player could collect a minimum of

Bowie Kuhn: "The players are the game"

43

$240 per month for four years of service and a maximum of $800 per month for 20 years. Medical benefits were improved, a program of dental insurance was established and a form of severance pay was set up: A man could take part of his accrued pension benefits in a lump sum when he quit playing.

Thus it was assured that the 1969 season would not open with unknowns dominating the batting orders. Nonetheless, the face of baseball would be changed dramatically for its centennial year.

Four new teams would come into the majors: the Kansas City Royals and Seattle Pilots in the American League, the Montreal Expos and San Diego Padres in the National. With the number of teams rising to 24, the two leagues would split into Eastern and Western divisions of six teams each and the division winners would meet in a playoff preliminary to the World Series. It was the first change in the championship format since 1901.

Not all changes were geographical. The height of the pitchers' mounds was lowered from 15 to 10 inches and the strike zone narrowed to the area over home plate between the batter's armpits and knees. Both innovations were designed to make life tougher for the pitcher in the belief that pitching duels bored and batting duels exhilarated spectators.

More startling changes were in prospect but baseball was not rushing blindly into restructuring. There would be experimental periods in training camps and in minor leagues before the new propositions would be adopted for all of baseball.

Thus, spring exhibition games tested a livelier ball and more liberal use of pinch-hitters and pinch-runners. Through the season, the International League would try "designated pinch-hitters," appointed before the game to bat for the pitcher without forcing the pitcher out of the lineup. In the Eastern League, the designated hitter could be sent to bat during the game and still the superseded pitcher would not have to retire. The Texas League would use "free pinch-hitters" who could bat once every inning for any player on the field, although the one supplanted would go to the bench. In the New York-Pennsylvania League, the experimenting would involve a "pinch-hitting specialist" who could appear twice during a game without replacing the regular player.

Whether all or none of the innovations endured, the important thing to many believers in baseball was that the seeds of change had been planted firmly. In the centennial year of the professional game, 125 years after Alexander Joy Cartwright devised the first set of rules on a New York sandlot, baseball was astir with new life.

Handclasp for Peace: (left to right) John Gaherin, representing the owners; Ed Kranepool of the New York Mets (National League) and Steve Hamilton of the New York Yankees (American League), player representatives, and Marvin Miller, executive director, Major League Baseball Players Association

THE CROSSROADS OF THE WORLD—Times Square, New York—was a lonely place in the midst of a February storm which dumped 15 inches of snow on the city.

NEW FACES IN WASHINGTON

The United States government was not the only Washington institution to change management in early 1969. Within a month after Richard Nixon became the 37th President, the Washington Redskins of the National Football League and the Washington Senators of baseball's American League also acquired new leadership.

The new coach of the Redskins was Vince Lombardi, a stern disciplinarian and an astute tactician who had climaxed a 30-year career by piloting the Green Bay Packers to six divisional and five league championships, plus two Super Bowl victories over the champions of the rival American League. He had retired from coaching in 1968 although retaining the general manager's portfolio and was lured to Washington by an offer which also made him executive vice president and a stockholder of the club.

A stock-owning opportunity also was one of the attractions which brought Ted Williams out of eight years in retirement to manage the Senators. Williams was one of baseball's all-time great hitters; with the Boston Red Sox, he had won six league batting titles, capped with a .406 average in 1946, and finished with a career average of .344. As a player, his mercurial temperament had sparked differences with fans and sports writers; how he would fare as a manager was one of baseball's most interesting pre-season speculations.

Capitol Hill was tired of standing up to be counted, risking election defeat, just to get a raise in pay. So in 1967, Congress passed a law setting up a nine-man commission which would review salaries at least every four years.

Well, the commission made a study and concluded that the nation's lawmakers, and a lot of other government officials, were indeed underpaid. "The compensation of the key leaderships in each of the three branches of government is seriously out of step with today's standards," said the commission headed by Frederick R. Kappel, former chairman of American Telephone & Telegraph Co. Pay increases were recommended ranging from $27,500 for the chief justice of the United States to $20,000 for congressmen. The commission estimated the annual package affecting some 2,000 officials would run $34.5 million.

President Johnson, who had approved doubling Presidential pay to $200,000 effective with Richard M. Nixon's inauguration, was hesitant to endorse such hefty salary hikes for other officials. So he scaled them down and sent the package to the Hill. By law the salaries would become effective 30 days after they reached Congress—unless either house said "we don't deserve it."

In the House, a resolution to veto the pay raise never gained enough momentum to reach the floor.

MORE PAY IN WASHINGTON

In the Senate, a similar resolution was defeated 47–34 and on Feb. 14 it was happy Valentine's Day for the upper echelons of the nation's government. It was payday and the checks were bigger. For at least the next four years, Congressmen would receive $42,500 annually, the chief justice $62,500, and associate justices of the Supreme Court and Cabinet members $60,000.

FOR THE RECORD

ABOLISHED. The patronage system for selecting postmasters, by President Richard Nixon, Feb. 5. The President said the practice of handing out the nation's 32,200 postmasterships as political rewards had had "detrimental effect" on morale and efficiency in the postal service. Henceforth, appointees would be chosen on the basis of competitive Civil Service examinations.

RESIGNED. Ray C. Bliss as chairman of the Republican National Committee, Feb. 18; he had served since Jan. 12, 1965 (The World in 1965, 23–24). His successor was Rep. Rogers C. B. Morton of Maryland, who would retain his seat in the House and serve without salary. Morton, 54, was a young brother of former Sen. Thruston B. Morton of Kentucky, Republican chairman in the Eisenhower years.

DEATH OF AN AQUANAUT

Near San Clemente Island, some 60 miles off the California coast at Long Beach, a nine-man team of aquanauts was about to embark on one of the U.S. Navy's most ambitious undersea ventures. It was the first of five teams which for 12 days each would live more than 600 feet beneath the surface of the Pacific Ocean. They would work and live in 47-degree waters under pressures 19 times normal at depths no man ever had lived before—deeper even than World War II submarines could dive in safety.

Sealab III, about the size and shape of an oil tank car, would be their residence. The project was part of the Navy's Man-in-the Sea Program operated under the Deep Submergence Systems Project (DSSP), designed to pioneer equipment that would open the world's submerged continental shelves to exploration and use. Sealab tasks included setting up an underwater trolley line, building a dry and lighted hut on the sea floor, starting a lobster farm and training porpoises and sea lions to fetch and carry.

The program had been scheduled for the spring of 1968 as a follow-up to Sealab II, an experiment in which three teams of 10 men each spent 15-day periods 205 feet under the surface off La Jolla, Calif. *(The World in 1965, 194–195).* But Sealab III had been plagued with problems. On Nov. 30, 1968, the personnel transport capsule (PTC), a special diving bell, was flooded during a repair operation, causing a two-month delay. Later, when the capsule was being lowered into the well of the support ship, a hoist connection broke. Two generators on the ship failed, forcing a power cut off to the habitat and threatening to flood it. The day before the program finally was to get under way, the habitat, already on the ocean floor, sprung a leak.

Four team members—Barry Cannon, Robert Barth, Richard Blackburn and John Reaves—donned diving gear and made a nighttime descent to fix the leak. Cannon returned to the capsule to report that his "umbilical cord," carrying communication and breathing facilities from the capsule, was fouling. Barth also returned, saying the water was too cold. The capsule was pulled to the surface.

Before dawn the next day, Feb. 17, the men again descended into the dark, frigid waters. Barth, team leader and a Navy warrant officer, and Cannon approached the Sealab hatch while Blackburn and Reaves remained in the capsule. Minutes later Barth and officials watching a television monitor on the support ship *Elk River* saw that Cannon was in trouble.

"I saw his body jackknifing, making a rapid motion," said Capt. George Bond, Sealab's chief medical officer. Barth turned around and saw his companion in convulsions: "He looked like a man jumping rope. . . ." When the diving bell reached the surface Cannon was dead.

Cannon, 33, was the first fatality of the Man-in-the-Sea Program. "We don't know what happened," said a Navy spokesman, "but we are certain that it was not equipment failure because the equipment was checked carefully."

An autopsy showed that Cannon died of carbon dioxide poisoning. Some doctors believed cold and fatigue contributed to his death. A Navy board of investigation learned that a breathing apparatus, possibly used by Cannon, lacked chemicals needed to filter out the carbon dioxide.

Capt. William Nicholson, commander of the DSSP, testified that the aquanauts were "in top physical condition—apparently peaked up for the operation." But Blackburn said "the dive should never have been made. We were all pushed to a point where mistakes were inevitable. Our bodies had not adjusted to depth. . . . Our mental and physical dexterity were affected by the cold."

Other testimony disclosed additional problems of the $10 million program. Cmdr. J. M. Tomsky, on-the-scene commander, testified that on three occasions there was evidence that oxygen valves had been tampered with while divers were undergoing decompression. Had it not been for backup valves, the divers would have died.

After two weeks of hearings, investigators said they could not determine how the tragedy occurred or who or what was responsible. Sealab III was still undergoing an extensive overhaul and the program was postponed once again, at least until autumn.

While Sealab III went into drydock, the "beehive," a habitat of similar purpose, rested on the Atlantic Ocean floor off the Virgin Islands. Called Tektite One, a 60-day experiment in living 50 feet underwater began two days before Cannon's fatal dive. Four marine scientists of the U.S. Department of the Interior returned to the surface on April 15 and the $3 million joint endeavor by the Interior Department, the Navy and NASA was described as very successful. The four aquanauts—John Van der Walker, Conrad Mahnken, Richard Waller and Edward Clifton, all in their early 30s—had doubled the previous record set in August 1965 by former astronaut M. Scott Carpenter in Sealab II. "It was a nice place to visit," quipped Van der Walker, "but I wouldn't want to live there."

NO TEARS, JUST MUD. Diane Crump picked up some mud in the face when she rode into sports history as the first female jockey in a regular race at a U.S. track. She rode Bridle n' Bit and finished 10th at Hialeah on Feb. 7

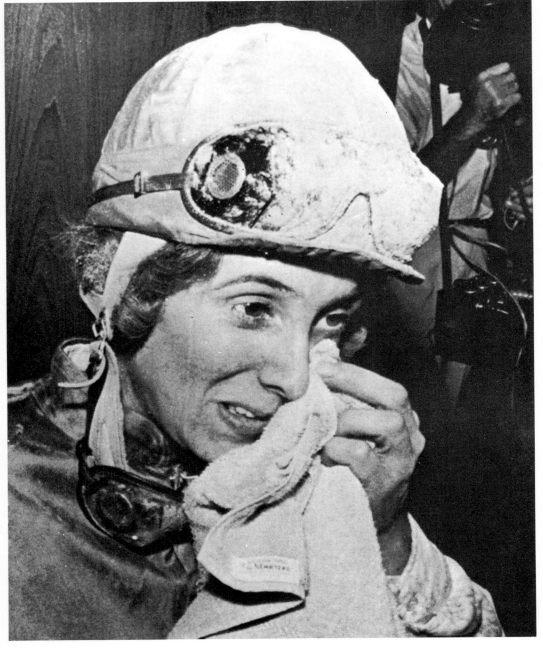

AN ARTIST'S SKETCH of Sealab 3 in operation. Barry Cannon was swimming near the Personnel Transfer Capsule, the diving bell suspended just above Sealab, when he was stricken. On the surface is the mother ship Elk River

LESSON IN BROTHERHOOD

Teachers at Cabin John Junior High School in Potomac, Md., a suburb of Washington, thought they had a way to give practical meaning to Brotherhood Week. Instead of lecturing about the evils of racial discrimination, they would illustrate by segregating blondes from the rest of the student body of 800 boys and girls. The 120 blondes would be required to use separate rest rooms, doors, stairways and drinking fountains, to sit at specific tables in lunchroom and library, to sit apart in classrooms.

The experiment, set up on a voluntary basis, continued for two days of the scheduled week. Then it was canceled because of protests from parents, including threats of lawsuits and picketing.

The youngsters protested the protests, to no avail. "Those parents who complained are narrow minded and intolerant," said a blonde girl. "They were showing off their own prejudices." Said a brunette, "It honestly made me realize for the first time how prejudice hurts."

THE GOLDA ERA IN ISRAEL

The third and the fourth premiers of Israel had much in common: they were born in the Ukraine, immigrated to Palestine as young people and were workers for the underground army Haganah. When Israel gained independence, the two friends served their country as political leaders and as cabinet ministers.

There were differences: one was a folksy man who told jokes to make peace between warring political factions; the other was a pragmatic, political infighter, called "the only man in my cabinet," by premier number two, David Ben-Gurion. He was speaking of the spirit, not the substance, for he lauded Golda Meir, perhaps the most famous Jewish mother in the world.

On March 17, the 70-year-old grandmother was sworn in as 21-year-old Israel's fourth prime minister. She said she was "terrified" but, she told President Zalman Shazar, "it is my fervent wish that it will be my lot to achieve what we all want—peace with the Arabs." She succeeded her friend Levi Eshkol, who had died of a heart attack Feb. 26 in Jerusalem. Eshkol, 73, had adopted a hard-line policy regarding territories won during the 1967 war *(The World in 1967, 110–117).*

Golda Mabovitz had emigrated from Russia to the United States with her carpenter-father when she was eight. She grew up to become a Milwaukee school teacher who, the story went, married commercial artist Morris Myerson on condition they make their life in Palestine.

They moved in 1921 and the new bride quickly became a pioneer in the women's labor movement. She ran guns during the 1948 war of independence, joined Ben-Gurion's cabinet a year later and was named Israel's first minister to Moscow. In 1956 she was appointed foreign minister, a post she held for 10 years. She had retired—or so she thought—in June 1968.

She and Eshkol had traveled the road together. He, along with Ben-Gurion, had gone to Palestine from Russia during the second great "aliyah" or wave of immigration. After years of working to develop Israel, Eshkol became Ben-Gurion's top aide, then premier when Ben-Gurion retired in June 1963.

Golda Meir had been Eshkol's most loyal political friend in the tense days just before the June 1967 war with the Arabs. She supported him in his bid to continue as minister of defense as well as premier. Flamboyant, one-eyed Moshe Dayan, 53, won the defense job, and the stunning victory in the six-day war brought him tremendous popularity.

During the period of mourning after Eshkol's death, Deputy Premier Yigal Allon, 50, became acting premier. He and Dayan had been comrades in arms during the 1948 war of independence, but in the months before Eshkol's death they had become bitter rivals in competition for the premiership. Allon was Golda Meir's choice. He was not glamorous or as popular as Dayan, but he had played his politics well and had few enemies.

A fight between them would be disastrous for the country, most party members felt. To head off the probable divisive effect of a showdown, Golda Meir agreed to form a new government despite her poor health.

She would govern until November and the general elections. Would she use her influence to help Allon? She had answered in January. "Either he is already built for the job, or this won't help him any."

Eulogy for a fallen leader ➡

Dwight David Eisenhower
1890-1969

Shortly after noon on Friday, March 28, 1969, the American flag waving above Walter Reed General Hospital in Washington slowly fell to half-staff. Dwight David Eisenhower, perhaps the most popular President in the history of the United States had died at the age of 78.

His passing was not unexpected. Through the week, the medical bulletins from his doctors had indicated that life was ebbing. Even so, a shadow of sadness spread across the nation and, swiftly spanning the oceans, touched the millions who admired him in many other lands as well.

"Ike is gone," people told each other, and the bells tolled for a much-loved man.

The official announcement of death was issued by Brig.-Gen. Frederic J. Hughes, commander at Walter Reed. It said:

"General of the Army Dwight David Eisenhower, 34th President of the United States, died quietly at 12:25 this noon (Eastern Standard Time) after a long and heroic battle against overwhelming illness. His passing was peaceful and he experienced no distress . . ."

Eisenhower had been flown to Walter Reed from California on May 14, 1968, after suffering the third heart attack of his life. The "overwhelming illness" cited by Gen. Hughes included four more heart attacks, abdominal surgery, and an attack of pneumonia while he was in the hospital. Time after time, it appeared that he could not survive. After each ordeal, to the amazement of the medical profession, he rallied and the famous grin flashed again. After the seventh heart attack, doctors spoke

of his "miraculous recovery." At one time, it appeared that he had recuperated to the point that a return to the farm in Gettysburg, Pa., where he had lived in retirement since 1961, might be possible.

It was not to be. At long last, life gently slipped away.

In the universal mourning, Eisenhower's family and friends found solace in recalling the unusual satisfactions he had known in the last year of his life. During that time, events had combined to bring him a succession of happy, even joyful, hours.

In January 1969, the Gallup Poll had reported that the General led the list of men most admired by the American people. He never lost the immense popularity that was born when he was Allied Supreme Commander in Europe, a quarter century earlier.

His fourth book, *At Ease: Stories I Tell to Friends*, became a best seller soon after it was published. It was a warm, rambling, often nostalgic account of his experiences as a boy in Abilene, Kan., at West Point, in the Army, during the White House years, and beyond. Three previous books had covered the Second World War and his two terms as President; as he often said, they were "reports of matters of interest that came across my desk." Readers found little Eisenhower in them, very little of his personal feelings about the events he discussed. The personalized fourth book was acclaimed as his best. Apart from the reviews, which he read with keen interest while in hospital, hundreds of letters came to him. Often chuckling, he dictated replies to some of them. Eisenhower liked to write, and he worked hard at the task. He was preparing another book of reminiscences in the last months of his life.

His paramount interest in 1968, of course, was the presidential election. He followed closely the maneuverings for nomination in both major parties. During the summer, he called a small press conference in his suite at Walter Reed to announce his support of his Vice President, Richard M. Nixon, for the Republican nomination.

Then, to the dismay of his physicians, Eisenhower insisted on addressing the Republican convention at Miami Beach in August. He worked several days over his statement and it was transmitted to the delegates via closed-circuit television. He watched his own performance that night, something he rarely did when he was in the White House. Then he went to bed, satisfied that he had made his contribution to the nation and to his party.

He suffered another heart attack on the following day, but his doctors said it was not necessarily attributable to delivering the speech. Thereafter, however, he was permitted to read only the sports pages—no political news—in the newspapers. One of his doctors said, "He is so involved in this that anything critical of Nixon, even a cartoon, upsets him. So we try to keep politics away from him." Eisenhower was delighted when the convention nominated Nixon.

During the ensuing months, Nixon regularly visited him to report on the campaign. He sought Eisenhower's advice and made the General feel that he was playing a part in the struggle. Eisenhower enjoyed these sessions enormously.

An event of a wholly different nature also engaged Eisenhower's interest—the approaching marriage of his grandson, David, and Nixon's younger daughter, Julie. David observed during the summer of 1968, "My grandfather is living to see two things, Mr. Nixon's election and our marriage." The marriage took place Dec. 22, 1968.

The crowning satisfaction for the General came when Nixon won the election. He had said often that the greatest disappointment in his own public life had been Nixon's defeat in 1960. Now that setback was reversed.

As President-elect, and after inauguration, Nixon continued to display the greatest consideration for Eisenhower. He often went to the hospital; "His eyes would light up and he grinned as though he hadn't seen you in a year," Nixon recalled. Almost to the end, he found Eisenhower alert and avid to have the new President's thoughts on policy. Nixon did not attempt to restrict the conversations to innocuous subjects so as not to disturb an aged and ailing man. Eisenhower wanted to hear about the vital issues, foreign and domestic, and Nixon obliged him.

When Nixon completed his roster of the men he intended to nominate for his Cabinet, he sent Herbert Brownell, attorney-general in Eisenhower's first term, to notify the General. As was his habit, Eisenhower took a pad of yellow, legal-size paper and jotted down the names. Brownell noticed that he penciled a short observation beneath each of them. Finally, Eisenhower asked. "Does the President want a comment from me about this?"

"I'm sure he would appreciate it," Brownell said.

"Just tell him I am delighted with all those I know," Eisenhower said. Of course, he was acquainted with most of the men Nixon had designated to serve in his Administration.

As Brownell was about to leave, the General said, "I hear he is planning to introduce the whole Cabinet on television at the same time after they are confirmed. Is that true?"

Brownell said he understood this to be Nixon's intention.

"That isn't the way we did it," Eisenhower said. "I announced you and George Humphrey (Secretary of the Treasury) first, and all the others separately."

Brownell murmured something about "every man to his taste." Eisenhower was silent for a moment. His next remark clearly showed that he did not consider himself either aging nor on the threshold of death. "That's true," he said. "It's another time and we all have to change with the times."

Finally, his son, John, brought two more measures of satisfaction in the last month. He published a book about the Battle of the Bulge, *The Bitter Woods*, which was well received by critics. The General was reading the book one afternoon. Suddenly, he put it down and said to his wife, "Hey, this is good. Darned good."

He was delighted, too, when Nixon appointed John Eisenhower to be ambassador to Belgium. Father and son talked at length about the assignment. Having dealt so much with heads of state and their representatives, the General was in a position to give his son a vast amount of useful information.

Summarizing all the satisfactions and happy events in the closing days of Eisenhower's life, one of his most intimate friends said, "Ike died at the right time."

The news of his passing no sooner reached Paris than doughty old Gen. Charles de Gaulle, president of France, announced that he would fly to Washington for the funeral. Other heads of state followed suit, or named high-ranking representatives.

A Pulitzer Prize winner: Eisenhower and President John F. Kennedy at Camp David during Cuban crisis, April 22, 1961

One of the last Eisenhower photos: with President Nixon at Walter Reed Hospital, Feb. 2, 1969

On Saturday, March 29, newspapers filled pages with the Eisenhower story. Television and radio networks canceled scheduled programs and devoted hours to the principal episodes in the General's life. Seldom had there been such an outpouring of affectionate memories about one man.

They recalled the farm boy who came from a poor family in Kansas and peddled home-grown vegetables for money to give to his mother . . . the boy who worked hard for his appointment to the United States Military Academy, not because he wanted to be a professional soldier, but because he was eager to have a college education that he could not otherwise afford.

Photographs were published of Cadet Eisenhower playing football at West Point . . . and others showing Lieut. Eisenhower standing proudly beside his pretty bride, the former Mamie Geneva Doud of Denver, on their wedding day, July 1, 1916.

Eisenhower's swift rise from the rank of a one star brigadier in 1941 to the five stars of the Supreme Commander in 1944 had often been told, but now the story was repeated in full . . . his organizing ability and his previously unsuspected gift for welding into a smooth-working machine strong-willed men of different nationalities . . . his successful campaigns in North Africa, Sicily, on the Italian mainland, the gigantic land, sea and air force that he put together for the assault on Normandy, and the swift sweep across France into Germany until May 7, 1945, when the Naxis surrendered.

Eisenhower stood as an unusual figure in history in that, with a single exception, he sought none of the great offices that he held. Gen. George Catlett Marshall, chief of staff, picked Eisenhower from among hundreds of competent officers and named him chief of the War Plans Division in 1942. When the time came to name the American commander for the European Theater of Operations, Eisenhower recommended another officer, Gen. Joseph T. McNarney; Marshall gave the assignment to Eisenhower, jumping him over the heads of many officers senior to him.

Eisenhower expected that Marshall would be named Supreme Commander for the climactic struggle in Western Europe; President Roosevelt and Prime Minister Churchill agreed that Eisenhower was the man to direct the armies. Recalling the great days, the French magazine, Paris Match, said, "He earned his title of immortal glory: Ike the Liberator."

When the North Atlantic Treaty Organization was formed, President Truman told Eisenhower that the European member nations unanimously had asked that Eisenhower be its first chief. The President said he would be pleased if Eisenhower would undertake the task. Eisenhower would have preferred to continue his work as President of Columbia University, where he was enjoying himself very much, but with reluctance he agreed.

The single exception to the pattern came in 1952 when he fought hard to become the first Republican President in 20

Mrs. Eisenhower and John Eisenhower at Capitol service

years. Even then, it could be argued that here was a classic instance of the office seeking the man. In 1948, Eisenhower had adamantly refused the importunings of many men to run for that office. Four years later, in his judgment, conditions both abroad and at home had changed to such a point that he considered it his duty to offer himself for the presidency. The decision having been taken, he worked with might and main to win.

In Eisenhower's lexicon, "duty" was the all-compelling word. If he became convinced that it was his duty to undertake some task, he did so, selflessly. Mrs. Eisenhower often related how, as a bride of a few weeks, she came to feel the force of this concept to her husband. "I was 19," she said, "and to me being a good wife and making a good home for Ike was the most important thing in life. I thought I was quite something. One day, he said to me, 'Mamie, I have to make something very clear: My duty to my country will always come first, you will always be second.' It took me down a peg, but that's the way it has always been between us."

The last rites for the General took three forms, official, religious and military. They began Saturday, March 29.

In an ordinary GI casket, his body was taken to the Bethlehem Chapel in the Washington National Cathedral. The brief service was private, for members of his family and immediate friends. The honor guard, representing the Army, Navy, Air Force, Marine Corps, Coast Guard and Merchant Marine, took

station around the bier. Among those who rode to the Cathedral was General of the Army Omar Bradley, Eisenhower's classmate at West Point and his top American commander during World War Two.

Sunday, March 30, brought the official tributes in the Rotunda in the Capitol. It was a raw, grey day. A chilling wind swept the streets of Washington, driving spatters of rain. Even so, the route from the Cathedral to Capitol Hill was lined with countless thousands. An exceptionally large crowd massed at the intersection of Constitution Avenue and 16th Street where the casket was transferred from the hearse to a horse-drawn caisson.

The tableau that followed had become familiar in Washington during three enactments in five years, for the assassinated John F. Kennedy, former President Herbert Hoover and General Douglas MacArthur . . . the flag covering the casket . . . the riderless horse with cavalry boots pointing backward in the stirrups, a military tradition said to have started with the funeral of the Mongol conqueror, Genghis Khan . . . the military band's ruffles and flourishes, followed by the strains of the Presidential salute, *Hail to the Chief* . . . the muffled drums and the slow funeral step of those walking in the cortege.

In the Capitol Plaza, facing the noble flight of steps leading to the Rotunda, other thousands of spectators had massed. Mrs. Eisenhower, dressed in black with a black veil, ascended the steps on the arm of her son, John. Nixon and his wife and daughters, and former President Johnson and his wife, followed.

In the great circular chamber, the dignitaries waited in their assigned positions, members of the House and Senate, the Supreme Court Justices, the Cabinet, heads of state, and members of the diplomatic corps.

When all where assembled, Nixon stepped forward to pronounce a brief eulogy. He sounded the dominant theme when he spoke of the extent of the affection for Eisenhower—"a giant among men." "Many leaders are known and respected outside their own countries," the President said. "Very few are loved outside their own countries. Dwight Eisenhower was one of these few. He was probably loved by more people in more parts of the world than any President America has ever had. He captured the deepest feelings of free men everywhere."

After the eulogy, De Gaulle, tall and erect, stepped to the foot of the bier. He wore a simple tan uniform and a tan military greatcoat. He raised his hand in a salute, stood motionless for perhaps 10 seconds and saluted a second time. Later, he called on Mrs. Eisenhower. At the news of the General's death, the French President had said, "For me, I see disappear with much sadness, a dear comrade-in-arms and a friend."

Before the bronze doors of the Rotunda were opened for public tributes, people had formed, two abreast, in a line that stretched two blocks. Until late that night people continued to file slowly past the bier.

On Monday, the casket was returned to the National Cathedral where three clergymen officiated in services which combined the traditions of the Episcopal and Presbyterian faiths. They were the Rev. Edward L. R. Elson, minister of the National Presbyterian Church which Eisenhower attended during his eight years in Washington; Dean Francis B. Sayre Jr. of the National Cathedral; and the Right Rev. William F. Creighton, Episcopal Bishop of Washington. The rites lasted 30 minutes.

Ninety two nations were represented in the Cathedral, either by chiefs of state or high-ranking delegates. They included De Gaulle, the Shah of Persia, Australian Prime Minister John Gorton, Canadian Prime Minister Pierre Trudeau, King Constantine of Greece, President Habib Bourguiba of Tunisia, President Shazar Zalman of Israel, President Ferdinand Marcos of the Philippines, King Baudoin of Belgium, Prince Bernhard of the Netherlands, Crown Prince Hussein of Jordan, Premier Chang Il Kim of South Korea, Deputy Premier Nguyen Cao Ky of South Vietnam, former Prime Minister Nobusuke Kish of Japan, Chang Ching Kuo of the Republic of China, Lord Louis Mountbatten and former Prime Minister Sir Alec Douglas-Home of Great Britain, Marshal Vassily I. Chuikov of the Soviet Union, and U Thant, Secretary-General of the United Nations.

The cathedral glittered with dress uniforms, medals, fourrageres, ceremonial sashes and the robes and turbans of Africa and the Middle East.

Then it was time for the last journey home, to Abilene. Because of Mrs. Eisenhower's aversion to flying, the casket was taken from Washington by train over a route arranged long before the General's death.

As the funeral train sped westward, the most impressive tribute of all took shape. Thousands of persons stood beside the tracks, waiting to see the train pass. For example, more than 5,000 gathered near the depot in O'Fallon, Ill. Men removed their hats and placed them over their hearts. There were so many such scenes that, when the train stopped in St. Louis, Mrs. Eisenhower stepped out on the rear platform to say, "I am most grateful for all the expressions of love."

It was after midnight when the train reached Abilene. More than 5,000 people were waiting near the depot. Abilene was a community of 6,000; on the day of the funeral, state highway officers said 100,000 people streamed into the town.

The rites in Abilene were predominantly military. On the stroke of 10 A.M., a military band played *Hail to the Chief* and soldiers removed the casket from the train to a hearse. Again, both Nixon and Johnson were present.

The Joint Chiefs of Staff and other dignitaries had taken their places on or in front of the portico of the Eisenhower Library where the rites were held. The library, part of the Eisenhower center in Abilene, was across the street from the museum which housed the thousands of trophies, flags, medals and be-jeweled ceremonial swords given to him. Not far away, on the same side of the street was the white frame house where he grew

In the Capitol Rotunda: Farewell to "a giant among men"

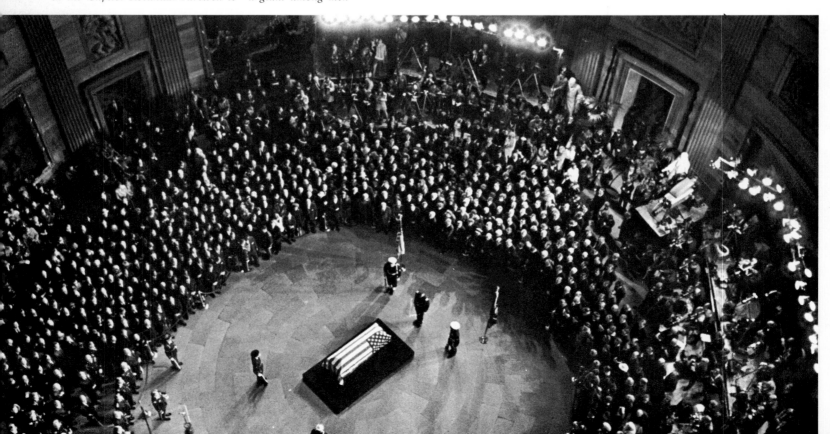

Rain and dark of night cannot stay the mourners

to manhood. Diagonally opposite the family home was the chapel in which a crypt had been prepared to receive the casket.

The route from the railway station to the Eisenhower Library passed a number of buildings that had been meaningful to the General in his lifetime. There was the home of his friend, Charles Case, in which a group of Kansas Republicans, the first to line up beneath his banner, pledged to support him for the nomination for President. Across the street was an apartment house which was the Sunflower Hotel when he announced his candidacy in 1952; standing on a balcony, he reviewed a colorful parade in his honor that day, laughing and waving to friends he hadn't seen in many years. Turning into another street, the cortege passed the Belle Springs creamery where Eisenhower worked nights after he graduated from high school, and where he studied for the examinations for the U.S. Military Academy. Nearby was Abilene High School. Finally, the procession passed the family home, beside it the olive-colored staff car which he used during the war years when his headquarters were in England. As it passed that point, the band played *A Mighty Fortress Is Our God*.

Everyone stood while the casket was carried from the hearse and up the steps of the Library portico where it was placed on a bier. The Joint Chiefs and other officers saluted and the troops stationed on both sides of the Library were ordered to "Present Arms."

The sunshine was steely bright. A chill wind blew from the north. A hush fell over the scene and the watching thousands, a silence broken only by the snapping of flags and pennants whipped by the wind.

Mrs. Eisenhower and John sat in the front row of chairs to the left of the bier. Nixon, Johnson and their wives were directly behind them. As in the services in Washington, John Eisenhower from time to time turned and glanced at his mother in a gesture of tender solicitude. She appeared quite composed.

Two Presbyterian ministers, the Rev. Robert MacAskill of Gettysburg, Pa., and the Rev. Dean Miller of Palm Desert, Calif., officiated. MacAskill said that, although Eisenhower became a citizen of the world, he always thought of Abilene as home. "And he loved this town," the clergyman said. "It is fitting that Dwight David Eisenhower be laid to rest near his family home."

When the rites ended, the casket was carried by the pall bearers down the walk from the Library to the small, spired chapel, some 200 yards away. Mrs. Eisenhower and her son rode; the other mourners walked.

The traditional military salutes followed, three volleys of rifle fire and the notes of a bugle, sounding "Taps." Inside the chapel, the flag was removed from the casket, folded into a tight square and handed to Mrs. Eisenhower.

A retired Army chaplain, Major-Gen. Luther Miller, intoned the words, "Unto God's gracious mercy, we commend you, old friend."

Several hours later, Mrs. Eisenhower returned to the chapel with her son and his wife, Barbara, their daughters, David and Julie Eisenhower, and Sgt. John A. Moaney, Jr., the General's valet since World War II days. Mrs. Eisenhower placed a spray of yellow gladiolus on the buff colored slab of marble covering her husband's crypt. The slab lay well to the left in a sunken area surrounded by a metal railing beyond which visitors might not pass. A three-sided wall separated the burial area from the tiny main chapel with its six pews. The chamber was dimly lighted through the narrow, stained glass windows.

At 3 P.M., Mrs. Eisenhower and the members of her family and the official party went back to the train. It pulled out of the station two minutes later, starting the return journey to Washington.

As it rolled out of the little depot, Mrs. Eisenhower appeared on the back platform of the rear car and waved goodbye.

Toward eternal rest at Abilene

Glory in Space for an "Ugly Duckling"

*The LM wasn't pretty but it worked flawlessly
in test of its capability as a ferry
between an orbiting mother ship and the moon*

LM in flight

Aᴛ ꜰɪʀꜱᴛ ɢʟᴀɴᴄᴇ, the ungainly craft did not impress the beholder. Col. James A. McDivitt, one of the two astronauts who would test it in the endless void of the universe, took one look and asked himself, "Holy Moses, we're really going to fly that thing?" It was, he said, "like a tissue paper spacecraft. If we're not careful, we could easily put a foot through it."

This was the lunar module of the U.S. space program, LM for short, to which would be entrusted the daring and delicate task of ferrying men from an orbiting space ship to the surface of the moon and back. It was a 16-ton package of 18 engines, 8 radio systems, fuel tanks, life support systems and instruments, the product of six years of design and construction. It was also the only major piece of hardware involved in the Apollo 9 mission that had not been tested in space by men and the mission would not succeed without it.

The LM was unique; it was the first vehicle designed to operate only in the airless, limitless reaches of space and as such was the first true space ship. It was not intended to withstand the terrific heat of re-entry into earth's atmosphere and so lacked the sleek, aerodynamic lines of craft like Apollo 9. Instead, with bristling antennae and four spindly legs, it looked like a weird, awkward, giant bug.

The space train that flew into space from Cape Kennedy on March 3—Saturn 5 rocket, lunar module and Apollo command ship—weighed 150 tons, the heaviest satellite ever blasted into orbit. It represented a direct investment of $340 million—$185 million for the Saturn, most powerful rocket ever built with 7.7 million pounds of thrust in the first stage; $55 million for Apollo; $41 million for LM; $59 million for manpower in the launch team and the recovery force. The total was increased by $500,000 (for overtime pay) when the three men of the crew fell ill with colds and a three-day postponement became necessary.

The three men aboard were McDivitt and Col. David R. Scott, both of the Air Force, and Russell L. (Rusty) Schweickart, a civilian and the rookie of the team. . . . McDivitt, 39, had commanded Gemini 4 in 1965, the mission that featured the nation's first space walk. He was a veteran of Korea where he flew 145 combat missions and won nine decorations; holder of a degree in aeronautical engineering from the University of Michigan in his home state; possessor of a low-key wit; known for coolness under pressure. . . . Scott, 36, was a veteran of Gemini 8 in 1966, a flight that ended in an emergency splashdown when an electrical malfunction set the ship to spinning out of control. He grew up at Air Corps bases around the world where his father, a pilot who retired as a brigadier general, was stationed. He held a master's degree from Massachusetts Institute of Technology, was a specialist in guidance and navigation, and a physical fitness enthusiast. . . . Schweickart, 33, also held a master's degree from MIT, in aeronautics and astronautics. He was called to an astronaut's role from a research scientist's post at MIT and had been interested in aviation since his boyhood in New Jersey. He was systems engineer on Apollo 9 and had been in training five years for his first space flight.

The LM rode into space from a beautifully precise launch in a nest atop Saturn's third stage, protected by metal shrouds like shielding hands. Once established in orbit, Scott separated the cone-shaped Apollo from the rocket, turned and nosed his craft into a docking collar on the lunar module. When Apollo and module were linked securely, powerful springs ejected module from rocket, and Apollo and LM floated free, a 90,000-pound package of something like four million parts. "We have made a successful ejection," McDivitt reported calmly. "Beautiful," said Mission Control. (The engines of the abandoned third stage sent it flashing at 1,000 miles per minute toward an orbit around the sun.)

The next two days were devoted to maneuvers with the joined craft, testing reactions to the stresses and strains of space flight, gaining knowledge for the time when the moon would be the target. The next critical experience put men inside the LM for the first time in space flight.

The test began at 6:30 a.m., March 5, when McDivitt and Schweickart opened internal hatches and moved to the LM through 47 inches of connecting tunnel. It was the first transfer between spaceships in flight for U.S. astronauts; two Russians had performed the feat in January *(pages 16–17)*.

Before returning to the command module for the night, the two pioneers thoroughly checked LM's multiplicity of systems, extended its four landing legs and successfully fired the large engine designed to brake the craft to a landing on the moon. They also beamed a live telecast to earth, showing earthlings how they worked in their cramped cabin.

During the day, Schweickart twice became nauseated and vomited. As a result, doctors on the ground cancelled a two-hour space walk scheduled for Thursday, March 6, in which he was to move from the LM to the command ship and back to the LM to demonstrate an emergency transfer.

A good rest overnight apparently helped Schweickart. On Thursday morning, commander McDivitt reported: "He's feeling a lot better and he looks a lot better," and suggested an abbreviated walk in which Schweickart would stand on a platform outside the LM hatch.

Mission Control concurred: "Okay, that's your judgment there and we say go ahead if you feel that way."

Schweickart donned a suitcase-sized 125-pound backpack that provided him with life-giving oxygen and communications and made him a true human satellite once he stepped outside. The equipment and suit were the same that later astronauts would wear on the moon.

Before opening the hatches, Scott depressurized the command module and McDivitt did likewise in the LM, bleeding out oxygen and pressure until atmosphere in the cabins matched the harsh vacuum outside. Both were protected by their suits, connected to their respective ship's life support system.

Schweickart opened his hatch and floated carefully out into a weird, weightless world where danger was always a companion, a world where only eight other men had ventured—five Americans and three Russians. On the platform, he inserted his moon boots into a pair of "golden slippers," which resembled wooden Dutch shoes and held him fast, freeing his hands for photography and other tasks. In case he floated away, he was attached to the LM by a 25-foot cord.

"Boy, what a view," he shouted as he gazed at the grand vista of sky, sun, stars, earth and moon. "That's a pretty sight."

While Schweickart was on the platform, Scott poked the upper half of his body out the command module hatch—the first time two U.S. astronauts were simultaneously outside or partially outside an orbiting ship.

Schweickart was relaxed, oblivious to the 17,500-mile-an-hour speed, as he slipped out of the foot restraints and moved hand over hand a few feet along the LM handrail. He tried some space gymnastics, angling his body away from the ship. He braved the eerie, empty void for 46 minutes, then climbed back into the LM cabin and shut the hatch.

"Good show," commented Mission Control. "You've just heard a live broadcast from Red Rover and his friends, Gumdrop and Spider."

These were the radio code names used by the three astronauts—red for Schweickart's red hair and the other two for the appearance of the spaceships.

The fifth day of the mission, March 7, was the most critical; it would determine whether the LM was capable of free flight, whether it could be maneuvered between moon and mother ship. McDivitt and Schweickart began by moving again through the tunnel to the lunar module, activating its systems and advising Scott that they were ready to fly alone.

Scott began to slip Apollo's arrow-like docking probe from the LM's nose. There was fleeting tension as something stuck. "We seem to be hanging up," he reported. "I'm going to back up a bit." In a few seconds, the probe jiggled from the docking latches and the two ships were separate entities.

Initially, the vehicles maneuvered around each other in a sort of orbital ballet to make certain all was right with the LM. For the first time, men were orbiting a ship that could not return to earth. To get home, they had to get back to the command ship.

With everything functioning well, McDivitt and Schweickart took off, firing a series of jet thrusts that placed them in an orbit 155 miles above earth, 10 miles above Scott. At the higher altitude, the LM needed longer time to make a circuit of the globe and gradually fell behind, reaching a maximum separation distance of 113 miles.

Then, firing the ascent engine designed to boost men off the moon, McDivitt and Schweickart started a tricky rendezvous, pursuing the command module by executing maneuvers nearly identical to those that would be made when two men left the moon to catch up with the orbiting mother ship.

The LM shifted to an orbit 10 miles below that of Scott, and the gap between hunter and hunted narrowed as the astronauts consulted their computers and swapped radio and radar signals.

When the LM was 23 miles behind and 10 miles be-

Schweickart on "porch" of lunar module

low, McDivitt pointed his ship's nose up and triggered an engine blast that drilled it toward the command module on a collision course.

Half an hour and two midcourse corrections later, he applied the brakes, trimming his speed to match Scott's. The ships then were 100 feet apart, and Scott moved in for a linkup with this comment: "You're the biggest, friendliest, funniest-looking spider I've ever seen."

"I've got capture," Scott radioed as the two docked firmly after a separation of more than six hours.

"Wow! I haven't heard a sound that good for a long time," McDivitt exclaimed after a signal tone indicated the two ships were locked together.

At Mission Control, space agency officials were elated. The LM, that ugly duckling of a flying machine, had worked flawlessly.

The two LM pilots moved back to the command module and then kicked the Spider loose in space, watching it dart into a 4,000-mile-high orbit as ground controllers fired its ascent engine by remote control.

"It's going like mad, Houston," Scott called as he watched the flaming farewell. "I hope I didn't forget anything aboard it," Schweickart joked.

With the LM gone, Apollo 9 had completed 97 per cent of its major objectives and the astronauts settled down to the restful holiday half of their mission. For the last five days they had a light schedule as they stayed aloft mainly to test the durability of the command ship. They slept 8-to-10 hours a night, but made good use of their awake time.

They gained experience in space navigation and tracking, plotting their positions by the stars and earth landmarks. Using four special filter cameras, they conducted photographic experiments designed for study of earth's resources. Conclusions drawn from the infrared pictures might help to design satellites to make a global resources inventory.

On March 13, with a storm churning up the prime Atlantic recovery area southwest of Bermuda, Mission Control decided to keep Apollo 9 up an extra orbit, 97 minutes. That shifted the landing point nearly 500 miles southward, to gentle waters off Grand Turk Island in the Bahamas.

McDivitt, Scott and Schweickart fired their retro-rocket high over the Pacific and started the 30-minute downhill trip back to earth. A pair of sonic booms above the recovery area heralded their approach as Apollo 9 plunged back through the thickening atmosphere. At 10,000 feet, three 83-foot parachutes blossomed and slowed the speed of the spaceship to a snail's pace of 22 miles an hour.

As the craft broke through a high thin layer of clouds, it was spotted quickly by hundreds of sailors lining the decks of the main recovery ship, the helicopter carrier *USS Guadalcanal.*

Television pictures, relayed from the carrier through a communications satellite, enabled millions of Americans to share the triumph of their newest space heroes as they splashed into the sea. Forty-eight minutes later, a helicopter deposited the bearded spacemen on the deck of the *Guadalcanal.*

"It's good to be back," McDivitt told the cheering sailors.

The bull'seye landing was a fitting climax to a perfect mission that had taken the three astronauts 151 times around the earth for a flight distance of 4.2 million miles. Official judgment came from Dr. George E. Mueller, director of the manned space program for NASA: It was "as successful a flight as any of us could ever wish for—as successful as any of us has ever seen." The United States had taken a giant step toward the moon.

Command module noses toward hookup with LM

Red carpet of welcome: (left to right) Schweickart, Scott and McDivitt ➞

Blood and Bombast
on a Distant Border

*The dispute between Russia and Red China was old but there were
ominous new tones in fight for an uninhabited island*

*". . . at 04.10 hours Moscow time . . . a Chinese detach-
ment crossed the Soviet state frontier and made towards
Damansky Island. Soviet frontier troops guarding this area
were suddenly fired upon from the Chinese side. . . . Over
200 Chinese troops took part in this provocative attack on
Soviet frontier troops. As a result of this bandit-like raid,
Soviet troops were killed and wounded."*

(From an official note of protest by Moscow)

*"On the morning of March 2 (at 09.17 hours), Soviet
frontier guards intruded into the area of Chenpao Island,
Heilungkiang Province, China . . . and killed and wounded
many Chinese frontier guards by opening fire on them, thus
creating an extremely grave border armed conflict. . . . This
grave incident of bloodshed was entirely and solely created
by the Soviet authorities."*

(From an official note of protest by Peking)

THE SCRIPT, no matter who wrote it, was a cliche. With other
names, the two accounts might have applied to Arab-Israeli
conflict in the Middle East or to any of many other frontier
disputes. There was gunfire. There were casualties. The other
fellow was the aggressor. The area of argument was insignifi-
cant—an uninhabited island in the Ussuri River, known as
Damansky to Russians and Chenpao to Chinese, a miniscule
part of the 4,150 miles of border between the Communist
Goliaths.

Nevertheless, there were new twists to the old tale. Both
casts were Communist, leaving the audience of nations to decide who was villain and who was victim. It was a rare acknowl-
edgment of bloodshed in a vast theater where there had been
perhaps 2,000 incidents since 1960. In another departure from
practice, both sides chose to tell their stories promptly and
volubly.

What made Damansky—or Chenpao—important was the
steadily increasing hostility between the Soviet Union and
Communist China. Even the possibility of war between the
two could not be ruled out entirely, although each side had
innumerable reasons to avoid it.

The dispute over the world's longest political border, cutting
through the heart of the world's largest land mass, had endured
for centuries, going back to the imperialistic days of the Ro-
manovs and the Manchus. The frontier from the Pamir Mountains eastward to the Sea of Japan separated the Chinese provinces of Sinkiang and Heilungkiang from Outer Mongolia, a

Soviet satellite. Chinese cartographers pushed the boundary
northward from Russian mappings to embrace as much as
900,000 square miles of Soviet-claimed territory.

No treaty fixed the border along the northern rim of Sinkiang,
important to China because it was the site of nuclear testing
grounds and missile range and was rich in uranium and other
strategic minerals. To the east, the Peking Treaty of 1860 had
decided the Amur and Ussuri rivers would be the border line.
Below the rivers was China's Manchurian province of Heilungkiang. Above was Khabarovsk and the Maritime Territory of the
USSR. The 1860 agreement failed to take into account the
waters' changing course and the islands in their midst.

In the Ussuri, the Soviets contended that the border was the
Chinese bank, making the river islands Russian territory. Peking
claimed that the treaty gave the land west of the river to China
and territory to the east to Russia, leaving the islands in a
legal limbo. One of those islands was the center of controversy
that first Sunday in March 1969.

It was an area of contrasts. In summer, dense forests were
in full foliage, mosquitoes haunted myriad swamps and temperatures rose to a humid 95 degrees. Winter brought desolation. The river was stilled by ice, the ground blanketed by
snow and the thermometer plunged to 40 degrees below zero.

On many a frosty day, Chinese troops were known to pass
the time by staging provocations. One antic was to line up on
the river ice and in unison stick out their tongues at Russian
troops on the far shore, then turn and drop their trousers in an
ancient gesture of contempt. The Russians responded by taking
refuge behind big portraits of Mao Tse-Tung, thereby aiming
to make the Chinese leader the target of the gesture.

It was Chairman Mao's cultural revolution *(The World in
1967, 156–162)* that had widened the ideological split between
Moscow and Peking and heightened tensions between them.
It was the change in the Ussuri River's course with each spring
thaw that provided an outlet for those tensions.

There had been frequent reports of flare-ups along the border
but neither side bothered to confirm or deny them—until
March 2. That battle was barely ended before Moscow reported
it to the world. Then, in moves as unprecedented as acknowledging the conflict, the two capitals exchanged formal protests,
staged massive demonstrations and let loose with barrages of
propaganda.

The Soviet Foreign Ministry said 330 Red Chinese soldiers,
camouflaged in white, had crossed the ice and fired point-
blank at surprised Soviet border forces. Peking said Russia was
the intruder. Russia counted 31 dead, including the post com-

mander, and 14 wounded in the "brazen gangster raid." China didn't tally fatalities beyond saying there were "many."

Moscow said reinforcements, "displaying courage, bravery and gallantry, by resolute action expelled the intruders." China claimed her forces turned back the Soviet soldiers. Russia accused China of "extreme cruelty and brutality" by firing at wounded Soviet soldiers and bayoneting them until "they became unrecognizable."

Likewise, in a second clash, reported on March 15, Peking charged that Soviet border troops had attacked Chinese forces: "The intruding troops were the first to open fire. . . . The Soviet side has kept on sending out more armored vehicles, tanks and armed troops and has opened artillery fire on areas deep within Chinese territory." The Soviet Union simultaneously accused China of attacking Soviet border guards with "a big armed detachment of Chinese soldiers, supported by artillery and mortar fire from the bank. . . ." Three Soviet border guards, one a colonel, were reported killed.

To express displeasure with Mao, with whom Russia once had pledged "undying friendship," an estimated 50,000 Russians stormed past the Chinese Embassy compound in Moscow, hurling rocks and ink pots that left multi-colored blotches on the stone walls and shattered more than 100 windows.

Probably more vehement and certainly more voluminous were the demonstrations in front of the Soviet Embassy in Peking. During the weeks following the March 2 incident, there were estimates that at least 150 million Chinese protested. Tass, the Soviet news agency, said Red Chinese demonstrators were shouting themselves hoarse in two-hour shifts outside the embassy, and also reported that kindergarten and grade school children were drafted to help fill the ranks. Some four dozen loud speakers kept up a torrent of anti-Soviet slogans.

Charges and countercharges bounced between the two nations. The Chinese editorially attacked Soviet leaders as "imperalialists and prototype czars," and accused Moscow of always having been hostile to the Chinese people, particularly since the cultural revolution. In Moscow, Tass said Peking was creating "nationalistic hysteria in the country . . . to rally its supporters on a platform of adventurism and extreme chauvinism."

Diplomatic observers believed the Russian outrage was intended to provide "the right background music" for an impending meeting of world Communist parties, a meeting at which they were expected to try to mobilize other Communist governments against Red China in a continuing struggle for political domination. The Chinese aim, they believed, was similarly to arouse domestic public opinion in preparation for the Ninth Chinese Communist Party Congress and to "deal a blow to Moscow's move to retain a central role in the world's communism movements."

Nevertheless, the troop buildup along the border in the wake of battle over an island that was economically and strategically worthless could not be ignored. Nor could the fact be ignored that China—who saw her inexorable destiny as war with a great power, either Russia or the United States,—had cut off all Soviet shipments across its territory to North Vietnam. Another sign of deepening hostility was the steady deterioration of trade beween the two nations—from $2 billion annually in 1959 to $90 million annually a decade later.

By April 1, the inflated border incident had been squeezed fairly flat. Both sides exercised military restraint along the Ussuri. Moscow had sent a note to Peking calling for talks on the issue, a move viewed as less an effort to promote discussions than to convince the public both at home and abroad of the soundness of the Soviet position.

"6-Minute War"

There were red faces in London when Britain invaded tiny Anguilla to protect islanders from greedy Americans

Doesn't this sun ever go down?" a British paratrooper asked as he squinted toward the cloudless Caribbean sky. No complaint came from a London bobby, equally sunbaked: He was glad to 'ave a 'oliday on the coral sands. Back home in England, the sun was not so hot but there were red faces nonetheless—red with embarrassment at the Crown's military invasion of the island of Anguilla.

"I say, chaps, the natives are friendly," proclaimed a headline in the London Evening News. "British troops have landed," blurted a BBC announcer. "It's a phrase we thought we would never hear again." In the House of Commons, a Tory challenged Foreign Secretary Michael Stewart to "congratulate the Prime Minister for at last taking on someone his own size."

Anguilla—the French word for eel—was a skinny slip of coral in the Caribbean—among the least of the Lesser Antilles. It was discovered by Columbus in 1493, colonized by Britain in 1650 and became a federation with St. Kitts and Nevis islands in 1873. While the partners in the federation grew, few things changed on the flat ugly duckling. The only electricity was sparked by a few jumpy generators. The battery-operated telephone system had been knocked out by Hurricane Donna in 1960 and the poles stood unwired. The water system was one brackish well, an old pump and a few dribbling public spigots. The dirt roads were broken by few patches of pavement. The tiny airstrip was primitive.

There was little prosperity but there was no hunger. The 6,000 dark-skinned dwellers and 5,000 dusty goats subsisted on what was reaped from plantings in pockets of soil, the profits from a salt pond, and money—estimated at $1,000 a day —sent home by Anguillans gone abroad. Most able-bodied young men left the island soon after high school for settlements in Sough, England; the U.S. Virgin Islands and Perth Amboy, N.J. There were more Anguillans in Greater New York than on their native island.

In 1967, Britain, dismantling her dwindling empire, had granted nominal independence to "The Associated State of St. Kitts, Nevis and Anguilla." Premier Robert Bradshaw, 51, a former sugar cane worker and labor leader with a penchant for fancy uniforms and a yellow Rolls Royce, ruled the trio of islands from St. Kitts. Once, after losing an election on Anguilla, Bradshaw had told the islanders he would "put bones

in your rice, pepper in your soup. I will make Anguilla a desert." He didn't succeed in increasing the island's aridity but Anguillans thought he left them high and dry so far as federal financing was concerned. So on May 31, 1967, they booted out the Kittian police force, declared independence and demanded direct links with Britain.

While Britain hemmed and hawed, the islanders held a referendum and reaffirmed their independence, 1,813 to 5. A second referendum approved a new constitution and set up an independent republic with Ronald Webster, a millionaire merchant, as acting president. Britain, meanwhile, got a little edgy and sent career diplomat Anthony Lee to ease the situation. He stayed for 15 months before the usually placid people, irked by his frequent trips to St. Kitts on administrative matters, gave him his walking papers.

Then William Whitlock, a British government official, was dispatched. He was prepared to offer Webster what his people had requested two years earlier. Before Whitlock could open his mouth, he was ushered off the island. He reported back to the home office with wild tales of American gangster types taking over the island, looking for a kill in real estate and gambling. So the Minigon—as the British War Office in London was dubbed—sent a mini force to the mini republic. The motherland, neglectful for centuries, was ready to return the wayward child to her bosom.

In the predawn hours of March 19, Prime Minister Harold Wilson sent Lee, some 300 marines and paratroopers and 40 bobbies to conquer the sleeping islanders. They paddled ashore in rafts lowered from the frigates *Bothesay* and *Minerva* and parachuted from helicopters. There was no resistance except for a herd of goats that balked at clearing the runway for a cargo aircraft. As the sun rose, bobbies, mighty uncomfortable in

Parachutes and paratrooper

Insults for a British soldier

their British blues, took turns cooling off in the surf. One red-faced soldier was asked if his rifle was loaded. "No, but don't tell anybody," he replied.

Though not a shot was fired, the British carried out the invasion by the book. They searched every house for weapons, uncovering a few rusty rifles in slightly better shape than the Napoleonic cannon aimed at the waterfront from the edge of a hilltop cemetery. A dozen American residents were questioned and one, Jack N. Holcomb, was deported. Rumor had it that Holcomb, a Florida businessman with an extensive law library and a little police experience, was exerting undue influence on the shaping of Webster's government and Anguilla's constitution. His request for permission to build a cement plant and be granted a monopoly and a 15 to 25-year tax exemption was denied.

Prospects of exploitation bothered the islanders less than the British troops who ostensibly had landed to protect Anguilla from greedy Americans. And the idea of returning Anthony Lee as commissioner ruling in the name of Queen Elizabeth II really raised their hackles. The only violence of the British occupation occurred when an angry mob of Anguillans barred Lee from entering his offices. He beat a hasty retreat.

"Lee must go," "Lee must go," the demonstrators chanted. "He just has to go," a young woman said vehemently, but, "We won't eat him or shoot him. We have nothing to shoot him with."

Eventually Lee did go. So did the troops, who were replaced by Royal Engineers imported to begin a $10 million development program. Lee, who had pledged residency "for a number of years" while talks continued to determine Anguilla's future, was quietly withdrawn to Antigua for what was called an extended vacation.

An agreement between Lord Caradon, Britain's ambassador to the United Nations, and Webster, that would have allowed Lee to rule with the elected local council, had failed. Yet to be resolved were three long-range demands by Anguilla: (1) to remain outside the Associated State; (2) to establish direct association with Britain (3) to attain self government.

Britain, meanwhile, had to live with the memories of what critics called "The Six-Minute War," "War in a Teacup," and the "Bay of Piglets." In particular, the critics wanted to know why Anguilla was invaded and breakaway Rhodesians were left to their own devices. They said the reason was that white Rhodesia had a competent army, a small air force, a viable economy and many relatives in Britain. Anguilla had none. The government contended that the two cases were as disparate as the countries themselves and that the Crown had a clear call to act in Anguilla under the West Indies Act which made her responsible for the defense of the Associated State.

Said the Times of London: "All that we have shown is that we can treat 6,000 black people in the Caribbean in a way we would not dare to treat 200,000 white people in Rhodesia."

AN ABDICATION IN PAKISTAN

It was a hot day in Karachi and the thousands of shuffling marchers were veiled in lingering dust. At the head of the procession, a dog—an unclean animal in Moslem eyes—rode in a cart, a representation of President Mohammed Ayub Khan. "Ayub hai" (death to Ayub), the marchers shouted.

One thousand miles away, in steamy East Pakistan, villagers rampaged against Ayub's supporters, crucifying some, throwing others into the flames of their homes, feeding mutilated bodies to wild animals. In ancient Lahore, capital of West Pakistan, students battled bullets, tear gas and club-wielding charges by soldiers and police.

After 10 years of autocratic rule, Ayub's authority was crumbling. The moustached six-footer, whose bearing and behavior still bespoke his training at Britain's Sandhurst, had seized power in a bloodless coup in 1958 at a time of political and economic chaos in Pakistan. He had revived the economy, pushed through political reforms, built Pakistan as a model for other underdeveloped countries. It had been taken for granted that he would be elected to another five-year term in January 1970.

What had gone wrong? In truth, the unrest that exploded into riots in November 1968 had been building for six years.

Ayub's economic gains had seemed to benefit only a small upper crust of the nation's 120 million population. There was much talk of the "Twenty Families," a handful of businessmen and their relatives who were said to control 60 per cent of the national wealth. Ayub himself appeared to lead a comparatively simple life but his family and relatives had built mansions and accumulated personal riches. The second of his four sons, Capt. Gohar Ayub, was reputed to have a fortune of $3 million. Two of his three daughters were married to sons of the Wali of Swat, a wealthy prince whose kingdom in the Himalayan foothills was known for its fabulous emerald mines.

The president was shielded from much of the discontent. Advisers showed him newspapers which had been ordered to print his picture nearly every day. They drummed up crowds to cheer whenever he appeared in public. They assured him all was well. His 10 years in office were celebrated as "a decade of progress and reform." Two weeks after the anniversary, he was battling for survival.

Ayub's downfall began with a relatively simple incident in the dusty Khyber Pass township of Jamrud on Nov. 5, 1968. A group of student travelers was challenged by customs officials about goods bought in the duty-free border

market. The students claimed they had been insulted and hit by the customs men. They took their grievances to a prominent visiting politicia[n], former Foreign Minister Zulfikar Ali Bhutto wh[o] had fallen out with Ayub after eight years in h[is] government.

Police barred the students from Bhutto's hot[el] in Rawalpindi. One who forced his way in w[as] dragged out and beaten. The angry youths r[e-] grouped and in a fresh clash one of them w[as] killed by police gunfire. The news of the dea[th] spread swiftly and demonstrations against th[e] president and his regime flared in many tow[ns] and cities. Their scope quickly broadened fro[m] protests of the death to embrace demands f[or] smaller classes, better facilities, lower fees, p[o-] litical freedom. Workers joined them, seekin[g] higher wages and the right to strike. Politician[s] hopped on the bandwagon with calls for fr[ee] elections and a return to democracy.

When a student fired two shots at Ayub durin[g] a visit to Peshawar, dozens of politicians an[d] student leaders were hauled to jail. Instead [of] quelling the violence, as the government hope[d,] the arrests resulted only in bigger demonstr[a-] tions.

Riots continued through December and Janu[-] ary. Mobs attacked police stations, seized fac[-] tories, burned textile mills, besieged employe[rs]

Zulfikar Ali Bhutto and friends

Flame of riot in Karachi

n their offices until they agreed to pay higher wages. In Dacca, capital of East Pakistan, gangs roamed the streets, ransacking movie theaters and burning the offices of government newspapers. In the west, Karachi's big industrial area was closed by striking workers. The national economy took a beating; Yusuf Shirazi, president of the Chamber of Commerce, said Karachi alone lost a billion rupees—$230 million—in trade during five months of industrial strife. The official count of deaths totaled about 200; unofficial estimates put the number at three times 200.

Ayub began making concessions in an effort to get the opposition leaders to peace talks. He ended a three-year-old state of emergency. He released Bhutto. But Bhutto and the 86-year-old leader of East Pakistan, Maulana Bhashani, refused to attend a roundtable conference held by Ayub at Rawalpindi, his capital. This unspoken alliance between Ayub opponents in east and west made it apparent that there would be no compromise with the old regime.

On Feb. 21, a tired and seemingly ill Ayub (he had suffered an embolism early in 1968), bowed to the pressure and announced that he would not be a candidate for re-election. He agreed to free elections and the establishment of a parliamentary government. Bhutto was not appeased. "Concessions are not enough. Ayub must go now," he said. Violence continued.

The situation climaxed on March 25 in a strike by employes of the Pakistan International Airline (PIA) in Dacca. Hundreds of demonstrators swarmed over the airport, threatening damage to aircraft. An army officer lined up his troops and warned the demonstrators that, unless they dispersed before his count of 10, he would order the soldiers to fire. The officer began counting. The demonstrators broke ranks and departed.

Gunfire at that point could have brought on civil war between the people of East Pakistan and the West Pakistani-dominated army and government elite. The government had sent a division of troops by ship and plane from the western province and they were ready for trouble when an announcement came from Rawalpindi: President Ayub would address the nation.

"This is the last time I shall speak to you as president," he began. He handed power to Gen. Yahya Khan, tough 52-year-old commander-in-chief of the army, who immediately clamped martial law on the country. Demonstrators vanished from the streets, workers returned to their jobs, students went back to their classes.

Yahya pledged his regime to work toward free elections, to be held when "conditions are right." He assumed the title of president "for legal reasons" and dismissed the top civil servants who had been associated with Ayub. He opened a campaign against corruption, tidied the cities, made people pay taxes, ousted currency manipulators, ordered employers to pay the wage increases which had been obtained under duress, promised concessions to students.

It all had a familiar ring to observers of Pakistan politics. Ayub Khan had done exactly the same things 10 years earlier.

A CRISIS THREATENED AND AVERTED

The risks in West Germany's presidential election seemed high. Communist troops along the autobahns leading to West Berlin threatened "grave measures" of reprisal if Federal Republic electors came to the divided city.

The Bonn government met the Communist bluster squarely. By March 5, more than 1,000 delegates had converged on the one-time capital of a once-united Germany. It was the fourth time since 1954 they went to West Berlin to elect a president. It was the first time the Communists had objected, on the reasoning that Berlin was a separate and independent German entity and should not be associated with West German politics.

In the days before the election, West Germany had offered to pull out the elections from Berlin in exchange for more free movement between East and West, but Walter Ulbricht, East German leader, offered only free passes for the Easter holiday.

On election morn, East German border guards blockaded the main West German-West Berlin autobahn for the fourth time in five days. In the afternoon, they closed all roads leading to West

Berlin, releasing the traffic just half an hour before the electors voted. The Communists said the blockade was necessary because Warsaw Pact troops were maneuvering along the routes, but few believed it was such innocent coincidence. A threat, to interfere with air corridors leading to the vulnerable city, never materialized. It was the noisiest infringement on Berlin's access roads in years.

The electors had been threatened on two fronts. In addition to East Germany's threats, militant leftists exercised their "extra-parliamentary opposition" to the established government by pelting delegates' cars with eggs and other missiles, and vowed to disrupt the proceedings in a cavernous building reminiscent of past glories, East Prussia Hall. In response, a total of 8,000 riot police ringed the huge concrete hall. All they had to do was keep warm and fight boredom.

Inside, the 1,021 delegates devoured nearly 10,000 hot dogs, thousands of beers and sodas and, on the third ballot, elected 69-year-old Gustav Heinemann president of the German Federal Republic. The office was West Germany's

highest, but it was largely honorary; the chancellor was the power behind the republic.

The new president had spent 20 years working for the reunification of Germany. A tough minded pacifist and liberal, Heinemann had been Justice Minister for two years in the coalition government of his own Social Democratic Party and the Christian Democratic Union. In that position the silver-haired lawyer was responsible for West Germany's first major penal code reform, liberalizing treatment of sex offenders and Communists.

He had been a member of Konrad Adenauer's first cabinet in 1949, but when the chancellor approached the West about rearming Germany a year later, Heinemann resigned and formed his own pacifist party dedicated to reunification. Finding it impossible to get enough votes for parliamentary representation, Heinemann joined the Social Democrats and in 1969 became their first president.

And one with a sense of humor. When asked about his love for his homeland, Heinemann replied: "I love no states. I love my wife and that's enough."

No. 7 swats one

"I CAN'T HIT ANY MORE"

The news was not unexpected and still it was a shock. Never again would No. 7 step to the plate and sock one for the New York Yankees.

Looking back, it seemed that baseball fans around the American League had sensed in 1968 that they were seeing Mickey Mantle in action for the last time. In every park, when the Yankees made their farewell appearance of the season, there were demonstrations to show that Mantle, 37 and limping on gimpy legs, still was something special. He appeared as a pinch-hitter in the All-Star game in Houston's Astrodome, struck out, and received a standing ovation.

The blond Oklahoman had been Most Valu-

able Player three times in his 18-year career. He had led the American League in home runs four times and ended with 536, enough for third place in the all-time list behind Babe Ruth's 714 and Willie Mays' still climbing 587. On March 1 at Fort Lauderdale, Fla., where the Yankees were setting up training camp, Mantle made his retirement official. "I can't hit any more," he told newsmen. His batting average, which had hit a peak .365 in 1957, was .237 in 1968 and his lifetime mark had faded to .298. That represented the one disappointment: "I feel bad that I didn't hit .300, but there's no way I could go back and get it over .300 again."

HAT TRICK IN THE UNDERGROUND

For four months, this "man in green pants" roamed New York City's subways, snatching mink hats from the heads of surprised women. By police figures, he grabbed 100 hats averaging $100 each in value.

His tactic was to wait until the subway door began to close, snatch the hat and run. The women couldn't complain until the next stop.

Detective Eugene Healey was on vacation when he spotted the bright green pants. He trailed the wearer in and out of trains until the quarry actually snatched a hat. Then he pounced and arrested Joseph Lee Jr., 25, of the Bronx, on a charge of grand larceny.

Holocaust in Maracaibo

THE WORST IN HISTORY

The Venezuelan airliner soared briefly into the air, then smashed to earth in the crowded suburbs of Maracaibo. Disintegrating into hundreds of projectiles, pieces of fuselage and wing and equipment sliced through the little houses. All of the 84 persons aboard the plane were killed; 71 more died on the ground; another 100 suffered burns, broken bones, shock.

It was the worst disaster in aviation history, eclipsing the collision above New York on Dec. 16, 1960, which had taken 134 lives.

Daniel de la Hoz had watched the plane strug-gle to gain altitude. It seemed to be crippled, he said; it clipped an electric utility pole and broke up.

The twin-engine jet had taken off from Grano de Oro airport at 11:45 a.m. on March 16. Just two minutes later, it cut a tragic swath through a five-block area—splintered poles and trees, at least 12 shattered homes, crushed cars, buses and trucks that spread liquid fire. In houses only slightly damaged, pieces of luggage and clothing from the plane were strewed among wrecked furniture. And there were bodies, many bodies.

Forty-six Americans had been on board, on the second and final leg of a flight that had left Caracas, flown 325 miles to Maracaibo, and was on its way to Miami. Ten of the Americans had attended a convention of Clark Equipment, Inc., in Caracas where the company had a plant. Another 15, mostly retired couples, were on a tour organized in California.

No one knew what had gone wrong. The plane had been in service only ten days, and its captain was a veteran pilot. The skies were clear and the sun was shining.

"Buck" Jones: "God had His arms around me"

EIGHT DAYS ENTOMBED

One rescue crew labored to dig through solid rock. Another tackled a heap of rubble. Nearly four days had passed since the cave-in and hope dwindled that William Jones would be found alive. Then startled workers heard a muffled, impatient, plea: "When are you going to get me out of here?"

The 61-year-old Jones was known as "Buck" in the Lark, Utah, mining area where he toiled to support his wife and 11 children. The cave-in caught him and another miner 4½ miles inside a mountain where miles of tunnels stretched toward rich veins of lead, zinc and silver. The buddy jumped free; Jones ducked into a small adjoining tunnel. In that cubicle, too small for a man to stretch his limbs, Jones crouched for four days without food, water or light. Then his shouts were heard and supplies were pushed to him through a narrow pipe.

Jones passed the hours by directing rescuers and bantering with them: "Why don't you send me up a pickax and I'll smash my way out?" The rescue effort was threatened by new cave-ins. One route through 15 feet of debris had to be abandoned. Finally, on the eighth day, Jones was pulled through a passageway less than two feet in diameter, dug through solid rock. Then he scrambled down a ladder to a waiting mine train that chugged him to 300 well-wishers waiting at the entrance.

At a hospital in Salt Lake City, 20 miles distant, Jones had a bath, shaved, dined on ham and eggs, then watched a television replay of his rescue. Examination showed his only injuries were, in the words of a nurse, "awfully red knees, probably from having to kneel a lot." "All I have to say," said Jones, "is that God had His arms around me."

UCLA ALL THE WAY

For a while in March, some optimistic people believed there was a chance that the basketball team of the University of California, Los Angeles, might be thwarted in its quest for a third consecutive national championship. The belief was born when UCLA's Bruins, seemingly headed for an undefeated season, were twice forced into overtime to win.

Then, in the final game of the schedule, after 41 successive victories, UCLA was beaten 46-44 by the Trojans of Southern California. USC played possession basketball, took only 20 shots at the basket and made 12 of them good, sinking the winner with six seconds to play. Lew Al-

cindor, 7 feet, 1½ inches, kingpin in UCLA's remarkable record of 88 wins and two losses over three years, scored a meager 10 points (The World in 1968, 26, 68). All at once, the word was going around that this UCLA team was not invincible.

The Bruins silenced the talk temporarily by romping through the western regionals of the National Collegiate Athletic Association's tournament, particularly by a 90-52 destruction of highly rated Santa Clara. But the doubts revived in the semifinals at Louisville when UCLA met Drake, compiler of a 24-4 record, champion of the rugged Missouri Valley, winner of the mid-

west regionals. Drake's harassing defense harnessed Alcindor and his mates and only a streak of spectacular shooting by guard John Vallely squeaked the Bruins to an 85-82 decision. The doubters found more ammunition in the fact that Purdue, UCLA's opponent in the final on March 22, was much the same sort of team as Drake and was sparked by the best marksman in the tournament, Rick Mount. He had scored 36 points in Purdue's smashing 92-65 win over powerful North Carolina in the semifinals, and had averaged 33.8 points over the season.

The towering Alcindor, who had tasted defeat only three times in his New York high school and California college career, controlled the opening tap and pretty well controlled the game. He scored UCLA's first three baskets on soft shots from close range and continued to score virtually every time his mates gave him the ball. He wound up with 37 points, 24 in the first half, and grabbed 20 rebounds. Close guarding by Kenny Heitz kept Mount in check; the Purdue star connected on only 3 of 18 shots in the first half and most of his 28 points were counted when the game was out of reach. The final score was 92-72 and no spectator, in person or on television, doubted that the margin could have been wider.

For the pupils of coach John Wooden, it was an unprecedented third championship in succession and the fifth in six years. Alcindor was the tournament's Most Valuable Player for the third time, also an unprecedented feat. Two weeks later, he signed a contract to play professionally with the Milwaukee Bucks of the National Basketball Association. The best information was that he would be paid between $1 million and $1.4 million over the five-year term of the pact.

President Nixon at the piano, with former President and Mrs. Truman and Mrs. Nixon

HARMONY IN INDEPENDENCE

A couple of presidential piano players got together in Missouri on March 21 and, if the result was not exactly *Love in Bloom*, it was at least sweeter than the tunes which had characterized their relations in the past.

Former President Harry Truman and President Richard Nixon had often been at each other's political throats. In the 1952 election campaign, for example, Nixon had attacked Truman and some of his associates as "traitors to the high principles in which many of the nation's Democrats believe." In reply, Truman had been quoted as calling Nixon an SOB. He later denied the remark: "I would never call him that. After all, he claims to be a self-made man."

When Nixon visited Truman in Independence

to present him with the grand piano that had graced the White House during Truman's residence, all was harmony. The two chatted privately for 30 minutes, then rode together to the Truman Library for the presentation.

The 84-year-old former Executive accepted the gift with, "Mighty nice of you. I appreciate it." He applauded when President Nixon sat down and banged out a vigorous rendition of the *Missouri Waltz*. In a brief speech, Nixon spoke of his predecessor as the White House's "most distinguished pianist" and a leader in the cause of world peace. He said that, where national defense and security were concerned, "We are not Republicans or Democrats; we are Americans." Truman murmured, "That is right."

FOR THE RECORD

APPOINTED. Dr. Thomas O. Paine, 47, to direct the National Aeronautics and Space Administration, by President Nixon, March 5. He had been acting administrator since the resignation of James E. Webb (The World in 1968, 213). Paine was a submarine officer in the Pacific during World War II and was a veteran of research at General Electric's Center for Advanced Studies in California.

RECOMMENDED. By an examiner for the Interstate Commerce Commission, the merger of two railway systems, the Norfolk & Western and the Chesapeake & Ohio, March 20. The consolidation would create the nation's longest rail network with 27,000 miles of track in 21 states and $6.1 billion in assets. It would exceed the recently created Penn Central by 4,000 miles and $1.1 billion (The World in 1968, 25). Approval by the 11-man commission and prolonged legal maneuvers remained before the merger could be effective.

WEDDINGS. Paul McCartney, 26, of the singing Beatles, and Linda Eastman, 27, an American divorcee, at London, March 12. McCartney was the last of the quartet to desert bachelorhood. . . . Another Beatle, John Lennon, 28, married Yoko Ono, a Japanese sculptress, at Gibraltar, March 20. It was the second marriage for both.

Sirhan Sirhan with his attorneys, Russell E. Parsons (left) and Grant Cooper ➡

April

"I Felt He had Betrayed Me"

Sirhan Sirhan contended he "was not aware" that he had killed Sen. Robert Kennedy, but jury decided he was guilty and should die

THE PROSECUTION WITNESS, a public school official with thinning gray hair, was droning along about high school grades and achievement test scores. Eventually he got around to mentioning an intelligence quotient of 89, which he described as subnormal. At that, the wiry defendant sought to catapult himself from his chair; force was necessary to restrain him.

The man in motion was 25-year-old Sirhan Bishara Sirhan, on trial for his life in Los Angeles superior court for the assassination of Sen. Robert F. Kennedy *(The World in 1968, 114– 121)*. It was not the only courtroom explosion by the volatile, moody defendant in the 15 weeks of his trial on a charge of first degree murder. But there was a difference: "At this time," Sirhan told Judge Herbert V. Walker, "I wish to withdraw my original plea of innocent and plead guilty to all counts—I will ask to be executed."

Judge Walker refused to accept the plea. He warned Sirhan that he would be masked and strapped into his chair if he persisted in emotional outbursts. And the trial continued, in a courtroom flooded with security officers and its four windows armor-plated for the prisoner's protection.

Sirhan could listen calmly, even smilingly, to the grim recounting of his deed—how he had stepped from a crowd in a kitchen area of the Ambassador hotel in Los Angeles at 12:20 a.m., June 5, 1968, shouting, "Kennedy, you son of a bitch," and put a bullet into the brain of the 42-year-old senator from New York. Kennedy was shot at the peak of a celebration of his victory in the California Democratic presidential primary. He was campaigning for the office which his elder brother, President John F. Kennedy, had held when he, too, was assassinated —in Dallas on Nov. 22, 1963.

These details left Sirhan undisturbed. But not so the suggestion that his IQ was subnormal. And not so the questioning of his honor on another occasion, when he protested testimony that he had lied to police officers who were investigating the assassination.

The prosecution dismissed the outbursts as "dramatic improvisations." The defense depicted them as evidence that the young Palestinian Arab, Christian rather than Moslem, was at the time he shot Kennedy "an immature, emotionally disturbed and mentally ill youth." His lawyers argued that Sirhan's mind had deteriorated to the extent that he could not meaningfully and maturely premeditate the assassination—a defense of diminished responsibility which was recognized in California law.

Defense psychologists and psychiatrists called Sirhan a paranoid and a schizophrenic—a split personality whose darker side was at war with a world in which he was hopelessly out of step. Chief Defense Attorney Grant B. Cooper would say in his summation: "There is a good Sirhan and a bad Sirhan and that bad Sirhan is a nasty Sirhan. But I have learned to love the little good Sirhan."

Sirhan had been a lifelong loser, the defense told the jury. He was exposed to the horrors of 1948 warfare between Zionists and Arabs in his native Jerusalem, and the seeds of a virulent anti-Semitism were planted. A fall from a horse erased his hopes of becoming a jockey. He was forced to drop out of college to tend a dying sister, whom he loved deeply. Sirhan's father was said to have beaten him, before returning to Jordan and deserting the family shortly after arrival in the United States in 1957. To compensate for these traumatic experiences, the defense said, Sirhan took refuge in studies and experiments involving the mystic and the occult.

"Then came another heavy shock," the defense argued. "In late May and early June of 1968, Sen. Kennedy, whom he admired and loved, said during the campaign both in Oregon and California, in essence, that if he were President he would send 50 Phantom jets to Israel.

"That did it! Back to mysticism. According to methods he read in a book he acquired, he concentrated in front of a mirror in his room and thought and thought about Sen. Kennedy until at last he saw his own face no longer, but that of Sen. Kennedy himself in the mirror. . . . The killing was unplanned and undeliberate, impulsive and without premeditation or malice, totally a product of a sick, obsessed mind and personality. At the actual moment of the shooting, he was out of contact with reality, in a trance in which he had no voluntary control over his will, his judgment or his actions."

The state took a different view. Conceding that Sirhan was not normal mentally, the prosecution insisted that he wasn't too abnormal to plan meaningfully and maturely the Kennedy assassination.

There was state testimony to tell how Sirhan acquired the murder weapon, a snub nosed .22 caliber pistol, and to record that he practiced rapid fire with it on at least two occasions within a week of the assassination. There was testimony that he told at least one person in advance that he intended to shoot Kennedy. There was testimony that he stalked his victim two

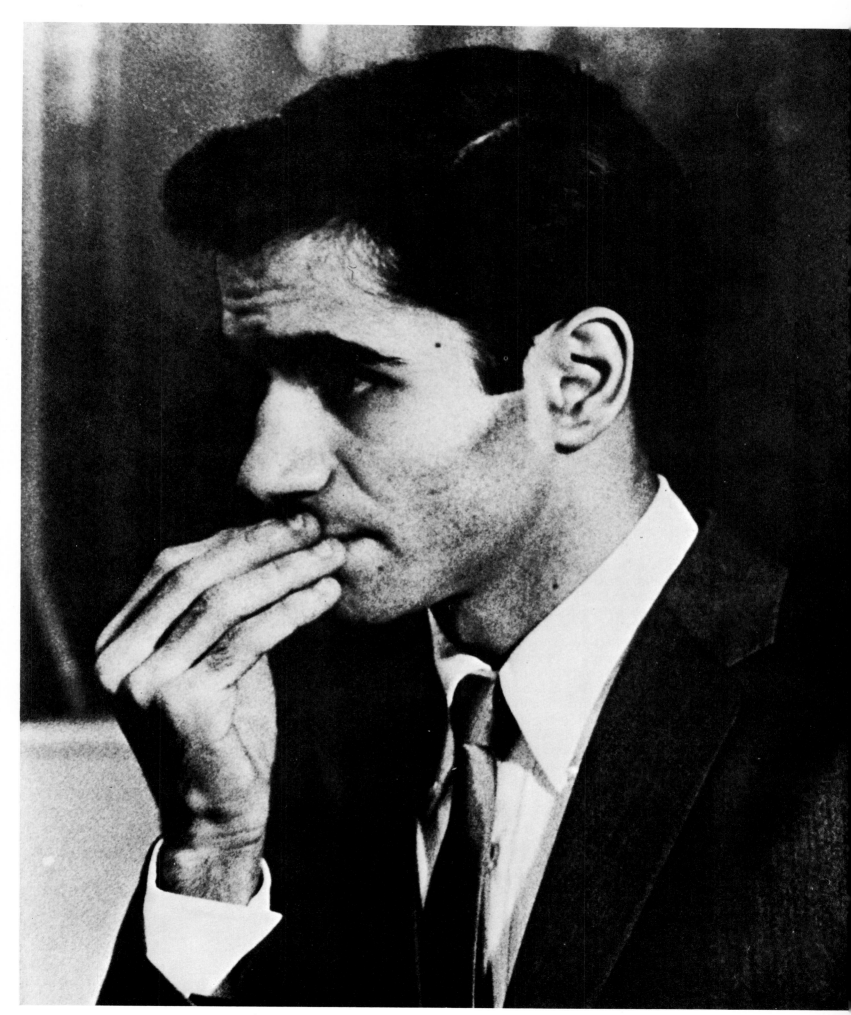

Sirhan Bishara Sirhan: "I felt he had betrayed me"

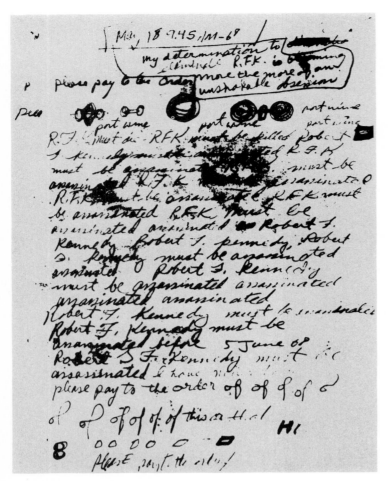

A page from "the incredible Sirhan notebooks"

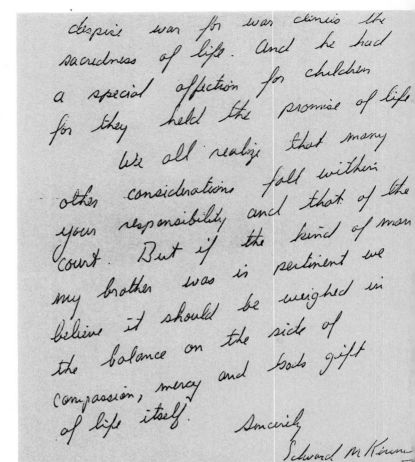

A letter from Sen. Kennedy

nights before the actual shooting, during a campaign rally in the same Ambassador hotel where the murder took place.

Then there were the notebooks, the incredible Sirhan notebooks. They were introduced in evidence over the vigorous objection of the defendant and his attorneys. Sirhan exploded again in court when they were read. In the notebooks, over and over, amid incoherent jottings, was written "RFK must die," "RFK must be killed," "My determination to eliminate RFK is becoming more the more (sic) of an unshakeable obsession."

One entry read: "Robert F. Kennedy must be assassinated before 5 June 1968"—the first anniversary of Israel's victory in the brief 1967 war with the Arabs (The World in 1967, 110–117), a victory that had shaken Sirhan to the core of his being.

For the defense, Sirhan's mother, Mary, a drab little woman with her graying hair in an unfashionable bun, testified to the hardships her son had experienced as a boy in war-ravaged Jerusalem. "I tell you," she cried to the jury, "we are blessed to be in this country after what we went through. I want you to know this!"

On the late afternoon of March 3, the dark-eyed, dark-haired defendant, the five o'clock shadow of his beard clearly visible, took the witness stand. For three days, during his testimony and under cross examination, he grimaced, waved his hands in emphasis and pounded on the rail to emphasize his points.

"I was not aware of anything," Sirhan testified of the moment in which he shot Kennedy, and wounded five bystanders.

Sirhan told of his devotion to the occult, of experiments with candles and mirrors, of mind control efforts he directed against others—all of which he called "white magic." He testified that he steeped himself in anti-Jewish propaganda, in furtherance of his support of the Arab cause in the Middle East. Time and again, he returned to the subject of Israel and its Zionist supporters in America who, in Sirhan's words, "burned the hell out of me."

He had loved President Kennedy, Sirhan testified, "because he was working to bring about a solution to the Palestinian refugee problem." And, he said, he had loved Robert Kennedy too, and wanted him to become President—until the senator's pro-Israeli campaign statements.

Then, Sirhan said, he realized that Kennedy was "doing a lot of things behind my back that I didn't know about." "I felt he had betrayed me," declared the defendant, his eyes flashing. He said he subscribed to an old Arab proverb that "a friend of my enemy is my enemy."

Sirhan could not recall writing his "RFK must die" exhortations in his notebooks. But he did not deny that the writing was his, explaining that apparently "that's what I felt at the time."

He was asked if he had entered in his notebooks the slogan "Long live the Arab dream." Sirhan admitted he had and, half rising from the witness chair, cried: "I say it again—long live the Arab dream!"

He was willing to fight for the Arab cause, Sirhan vowed, and "I'm willing to die for it."

It was purest chance, Sirhan maintained, that placed Kennedy under the murder gun in the Ambassador. Sirhan said he left the hotel at one point but returned because he was intoxicated and felt he needed some coffee before trying to drive to his home in Pasadena. His next memory, he claimed, was of being overpowered after the shooting. Not until he appeared in court the next day did he know he had shot Sen. Kennedy, Sirhan added.

"Are you glad he's dead?" he was asked.

"No sir."

"Are you sorry he is dead?"

"No sir, not sorry," Sirhan responded, "but I'm not proud of it, because I have no exact knowledge of having killed him."

With Sirhan's testimony ended, the defense opened what was to become a sort of a seminar among psychologists and psychiatrists. They varied in their assessment of Sirhan's mental condition. They disagreed on what motivated the assassination.

Psychologist Martin Schorr, later admitting that he borrowed his phraseology from a psychiatrist-author's book, offered this theory:

"By killing Kennedy, Sirhan kills his father, takes his father's place as heir to his mother . . . He hated his father and feared him. He would never consciously entertain the idea of doing away with him, but somewhere along the line the protecting mother fails her son. The mother finally lets down the son. She whom he loved never kept her pledge and now his pain had to be repaid with pain.

"Since the unconscious always demands maximum penalties, the pain has to be death. Sirhan's prime problem becomes a conflict between instinctual demand for his father's death and the realization through his conscious that killing his father is not socially acceptable.

"The only real solution is to look for a compromise. He does. He finds a symbolic replica of his father in the form of Kennedy, kills him, and also removes the relationship that stands between him and his most precious possession—his mother's love."

Dr. Bernard Diamond, testifying for the defense, offered an explanation geared to the space age. He recalled Sirhan's fanatical hatred of Jews, his notebooks, his occult studies, his flirtation with self-hypnosis, his interest in Rosicrucian theories of mind control and his use in experiments of candles and mirrors. Then he continued:

"With absolutely no knowledge or awareness of what was actually happening in his Rosicrucian and occult experiments, he was gradually programing himself, exactly like a computer is programed by its magnetic tape, programing himself for the coming assassination. In his unconscious mind there existed a plan for the total fulfillment of his sick paranoid hatred of Kennedy and all who might want to help the Jews. In his conscious mind, there was no awareness of such a plan or that he, Sirhan, was to be the instrument of assassination.

"It is my opinion that through chance, circumstances, and a succession of unrelated events, Sirhan found himself in the physical situation in which the assassination occurred. I am satisfied that he had not consciously planned to be in that situation. I am satisfied that if he had been fully conscious and in his usual mental state he would have been quite harmless despite his paranoid hatreds and despite his loaded gun.

"But he was confused, bewildered and partially intoxicated. The mirrors in the hotel lobby, the flashing lights, the general confusion—this was like pressing the button which starts the computer. He was back in his trances, his violent convulsive rages, the automatic writing, the pouring out of incoherent hatred, violence and assassination. Only this time it was for real and this time there was no pencil in his hand, this time there was only the loaded gun. . . .

"These are the psychiatric findings in this case. They are

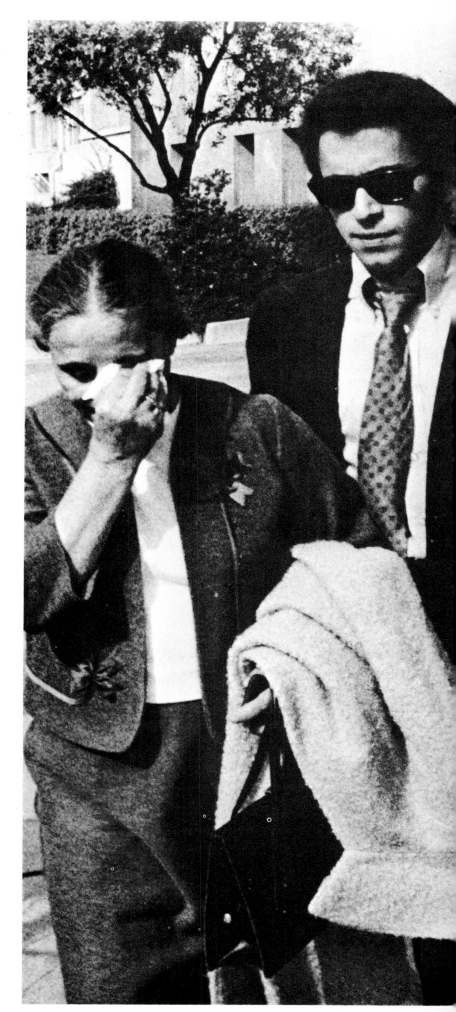

The mother, Mrs. Mary Sirhan, and a brother Munir Sirhan

absurd, preposterous, unlikely and incredible because the crime itself was a tragically absurd and preposterous event, unlikely and incredible. But I am satisfied that this is how Sirhan Bishara Sirhan came to kill Sen. Robert F. Kennedy on June 5, 1968."

The state's star psychiatric witness was Dr. Seymour Pollack, a short, stocky man of ruddy complexion. He described Sirhan as mentally ill, but not to an extent that would absolve him of his crime. "Sirhan at no time expected to be a martyr," Pollack testified. "I don't think Sirhan expected to be caught, or at no time wanted to be caught . . . .

"In my opinion, Sirhan's denial of recall of having written his notes I interpret as his attempt to avoid the serious consequences of these notebooks which would be interpreted as premeditation . . . I do believe Sirhan went to the Ambassador hotel with the conscious intention of killing Sen. Kennedy . . . I believe the possibility of a hypnotic trance is extremely remote . . . .

"Sirhan killed Kennedy because he hated him for what he stood for and Sirhan saw himself as the champion of the Arab world. . . . .

"Sirhan did not believe he should be punished. He believed that if he was caught he should serve only a couple of years in prison. He understood the significance of his act. He understood the full meaning of killing Kennedy."

The long trial had begun on Jan. 7; not until three months later did summations open with Deputy Dist. Atty. David Fitts urging the jurors "to return a verdict of murder in the first degree." "We concede that he's sick," Fitts declared. "How sick? That's a question for you to decide."

Defense Attorney Russell Parsons followed Fitts, to plead in impassioned terms for a measure of leniency for "this poor sick wretch who did not know what he did."

The last word in the argument came from Lynn Compton, chief deputy district attorney who headed the three-man prosecution team. Referring to the psychologists and psychiatrists, he demanded of the jury: "I say throw them all out in one big bag . . . I don't believe anyone can go back to June 5 and look inside his brain."

Judge Walker gave the case to the jury at 2:55 p.m., Monday, April 14. The initial chore was merely to decide the degree of murder attributable to Sirhan. The defense asked for a second degree conviction, punishable by five years to life imprisonment.

At one point in the deliberations in a 20 by 30 foot room just above the eighth-floor courtroom, the jury returned to ask instructions on second degree murder. It was explained that, if the evidence was insufficient to establish that Sirhan had deliberated and premeditated the assassination maturely and meaningfully, he would be guilty only of second degree murder.

Defense hopes rose. It appeared that one or more jurors was holding out for second degree. As it turned out, three were. But at 11:12 a.m., Thursday, April 17, the jury announced a unanimous verdict of first degree murder.

Now, under California law, the panel was required to deliberate anew to assess the penalty—imprisonment for life with parole possible after seven years, or death in the gas chamber.

This time, the suave, gray-haired Cooper had the final word with the jury. He concluded:

"And now, Sirhan Sirhan, I've done all I could do to the very best of my ability for you and for the American system of justice. To you, Mary Sirhan, his mother, I say I can do no more. I now entrust the life of your son to the hands of the jury. Mary Sirhan, may your prayers be answered."

The seven men and five women of the jury received the second or penalty phase of the case at 11:50 a.m., Monday, April 21. At 11:35 in the morning of Wednesday, April 23, they returned with the final verdict—death in the gas chamber should be Sirhan Sirhan's punishment for the assassination of Robert Francis Kennedy.

Asked about the reasoning for the death verdict, one juror said it involved "the gravity of the crime. The cold-blooded murder of an individual. A planned murder."

"Regardless of who the individual was?" he was asked.

"That's right," came the reply.

Sirhan took the decision stoically, ashen-faced but composed. Later he told his lawyers, "Even Jesus Christ couldn't have saved me."

However, there was one mortal man who still could. He was Judge Walker, whose flaring brows and lidded eyes imparted to him a wise-old-owl demeanor.

Back in mid-February, Walker had turned down a deal worked out between prosecution and defense, whereby Sirhan would plead guilty to first degree murder and be let off with a life sentence. To be legally carried out, the agreement required Walker's approval. Walker took the position that the case was of such worldwide interest and importance that not he but the jury should decide Sirhan's penalty.

Now Walker had a second chance to act in Sirhan's behalf. The law gave him the right to reduce the sentence from death to life imprisonment. In 16 years on the bench, Walker had been confronted on 19 prior occasions with such a clemency decision. Only once had he reduced the death sentence.

At a sentencing hearing on May 21, Dist. Atty. Evelle Younger sprang a surprise—a letter from Sen. Edward M. Kennedy.

"My brother was a man of love and sentiment and compassion," the last of the Kennedy brothers had written. "He would not have wanted his death to be a cause for the taking of another life . . .

"If the kind of man my brother was is pertinent, we believe it should be weighed in the balance on the side of compassion, mercy and God's gift of life itself."

After hearing brief arguments, the 69-year-old Walker, hearing his last big case before retirement, announced: "Let the record show I've read and considered the letter. . . . It is the feeling of this court that the jury was right. I find no reason to change my mind now. The motion for a new trial is denied. The motion for reduction of sentence is likewise denied."

Sirhan reacted with a smile and a shrug and told his attorneys: "The real battle has just begun."

Appeal of the death sentence in the California courts was automatic. The defense said it was prepared to go to the U. S. Supreme Court, if necessary. There was always the right of the governor to commute the death sentence.

Even if all legal avenues eventually closed, there remained a growing distaste in many states, among them California, for the death penalty. The apple-green gas chamber at San Quentin prison had been idle since the spring of 1967.

For the time being, Sirhan Sirhan, who had arrived in America from Jerusalem at the age of 12, ended his odyssey of hope and frustration, of hatred and violence, in Cell 33 on San Quentin's death row. It was 4½ feet wide, 11 feet long, lighted by one large bare overhead bulb. The cells on either side were vacated and the area sealed off from other inmates by a steel mesh partition, to protect the assassin of Sen. Kennedy.

"I'm sure someone would like to kill him," said prison Capt. Don Weber. But another death row inmate told a newsmen: "I don't see he'll be any different than anybody else up here. I don't see anything famous about him."

The Shackles of Power

*When a reconnaissance plane was shot down by
North Korea, the United States learned anew
that the strong do not always prevail*

Walkout at Panmunjom, by Maj. Gen. James B. Knapp, U.S.A.

"The weak can be rash; the powerful must be more restrained. . . . Great power does not mean great freedom of action. On the contrary, it often means very narrow choices of action and what we can do to influence events in any given case may well be marginal."

WHEN SECRETARY of State William P. Rogers addressed the words to the American Society of Newspaper Editors, the day's headlines and broadcasts were giving grim meaning to his statement.

North Korea, certainly not one of the world's greater powers, had shot down an unarmed plane of the United States Navy over the Sea of Japan. And, as was the case when that same North Korea captured the *USS Pueblo (The World in 1968, 20-23)*, Washington was discovering that, short of risking world war, little could be done about it.

The plane was known as EC121, a converted Lockheed Super Constellation, four-engined with a top speed of 300 miles per hour, slow for the jet age of aviation. The hull was dark gray on the bottom and white on top, and the only ornamentation was a bar of red and white at the tip of each propeller. The long, lean look of the Constellation had been distorted by bulging domes atop and beneath the fuselage, domes that reminded one reporter of camel's humps and looked like goiters to another.

President Nixon meets the press: "I have today ordered that these flights be continued"

The domes contained the equipment of the ship's function—six tons of electronic gear with which to listen to alien communications, spot military bases and buildups, keep a sensitive finger on the pulse of any potential enemy. In short, the EC121 was an international snoop, as the *Pueblo* had been.

When the plane soared away from Atsugi, Japan, on April 15, the mission was routine reconnaissance, no different from 190 other flights since the turn of the year. Thirty-one men were aboard, all Navy personnel except for one Marine. Orders included an admonishment not to venture within 50 miles of the North Korean coast (the Pyongyang government claimed 12 miles as territorial waters).

The plane was engaged in a methodical sweep over the seas when the screens of U.S. military radar detected two other planes approaching. Abruptly, the blip that represented EC121 vanished.

The first word on what had happened came from a boastful North Korean radio: "a large-size, modernly-equipped plane . . . of the insolent U.S. imperialist aggressor" had committed "the grave provocation of infiltrating deep" into North Korean air and had been shot down in "a brilliant battle success . . . by showering fire of revenge upon it."

In Washington, the Pentagon replied: "All evidence available to us, including North Korea claims and debris sightings, leads us to believe that the aircraft was shot down by North Korean aircraft. . . . From a variety of sources, some of them sensitive, we are able to confirm that, at all times during its mission, the aircraft was far outside any claimed territorial air space of North Korea." Eventually, the plane's position was fixed between 100 and 120 miles off the coast, southeast of the port of Chongjin and roughly 200 miles north of the spot where the *Pueblo* was seized.

A fleet of rescue ships and planes fanned out from South Korea and Japan. Wreckage was found — pieces of fuselage torn by gunfire, lifejackets, a flare, a parachute, a piece of

rudder. Two bodies were recovered, one officer and one enlisted man. Nothing more.

Two strangers appeared in the armada of search—destroyers 429 and 580 of Soviet Russia's navy, based 150 miles distant at Vladivostok. They picked up debris and spread it on their deck for photographing by low-swooping U.S. planes. They sent "condolences in connection with the loss of your aircraft" from the Red Banner Pacific Fleet. (Perhaps mindful that this participation gave the Russians firsthand information on where EC121 was felled, a Communist newspaper in Hong Kong assailed the action for "brazenly and shamelessly selling out North Korea.")

Reaction in Washington developed slowly. President Richard Nixon was awakened to hear the news. He consulted for hours with the National Security Council and military chiefs and advisers. But for three days no word either to denounce or to deplore came from the White House.

There was a confrontation, however, on the dusty plain of Panmunjon where the Korea truce was administered. North Korea summoned a meeting of the Military Armistice Commission on May 17 and opened it by accusing the United States of 39 violations of the truce line in the preceding week. No mention of EC121. Maj. Gen. James B. Knapp broached that subject with a statement accusing North Korea of a "calculated act of aggression." The North Korean reply, by Maj. Gen. Lee Choonsun, was a countercharge of piracy and a request for the name of the unit to which the lost plane was attached.

Knapp ignored the request, saying only, "I have nothing further to discuss. Do you have anything to say?" Lee repeated his query and Knapp again refused to answer. When Lee persisted for a third time, Knapp and his aides arose and walked out of the room. The North Koreans, obviously flustered, sat in silence for two minutes. Then they too departed.

Later that same Thursday, in Washington, President Nixon broke his silence. He told reporters that the attack on EC121 was "deliberate" and "a completely surprise attack in every sense of the word."

"I have today ordered that these flights be continued," he went on. "They will be protected. This is not a threat. It is simply a statement of fact."

He did not specify the nature of protection but other sources spoke of relays of jet fighters from carriers or from bases in South Korea and Japan. As another gesture of strength, Task Force 71 was organized under command of Rear Adm. Malcolm W. Cagle — three cruisers, 16 destroyers, four aircraft carriers, 260 planes. It was what the Navy called a "surge operation," one that could be maintained for a limited time and was "inordinately expensive."

The presence of such an assembly of warships within striking distance of Vladivostok was disquieting to Russia and informal oral complaints were made in Moscow and in Washington. Perhaps as a placating action, the force sailed around Korea, through the Tsushima Strait into the Yellow Sea. Within a week, the task force began to disperse. In early May, only eight ships including one carrier remained on patrol.

Thus the Nixon Administration committed itself to nonviolent response to North Korea's belligerence. It was not a decision of the moment. William Beecher reported in the New York Times on May 5 that the first inclination was for stern military retaliation. He quoted "sources in several agencies of government" that planning went as far as the selection of two bombing targets and, "according to one source," the preparation of a speech of explanation to the people.

The trigger was not pressed at the insistence of close presidential associates, particularly Secretary of State Rogers. Another factor, Beecher wrote, was the President's own belief that, "as time passed, the American people might consider bombing raids against North Korea as hauntingly similar" to the Gulf of Tonkin air strikes in August 1964 which led to deep U.S. involvement in Vietnam.

The White House dilemma was not eased by the recollection of Nixon statements during the 1968 election campaign about the loss of the *Pueblo.* "Unless the United States reacts to these slights," he had said on one occasion, "you are bound to encourage bigger slights and you are going to have more *Pueblos.* In a new Administration, I say we've got to stop that kind of action . . . before it gets started."

In Congress, too, few cried for blood. One of those who did was Mendel L. Rivers, D-S.C., chairman of the Armed Services Committee in the House: "It's time to give them what they ask for. We could dispose of them without full scale war." A majority of opinion either (1) questioned whether the spy flights were worth the risk, particularly with unarmed planes, or (2) took the practical viewpoint of Sen. Jacob K. Javits, R-N.Y.: "Intelligence gathering is a very risky business and you don't go to war over every incident."

The Administration's conclusion was that no great pressure existed for strident talk or action. Accordingly, the goal became a diplomatic procedure that would curb effectively North Korean belligerence and, at the same time, would not advertise the essential impotence of the strong in dealing with the weak. President Nixon made a gesture in that direction when he told his May 17 news conference: "I do not want to leave the implication that the announcement . . . of the continuation of the reconnaissance flights is the final action that can or will be made here. Our action in this matter will be determined by what happens in the future."

North Korea was not impressed. The Central News Agency described the continuation as "new provocation, threat and

A stranger in the search: A Soviet destroyer sends a motor launch in quest of wreckage

blackmail," and dismissed the presidential statement as "preposterous, abusive." The government's response was an 11 per cent increase in the military budget to $561 million, one-third of the national expenditure.

The dimensions of Washington's problem were not reduced by maverick actions in Pyongyang. Premier Kim Il Sung, a hardline Stalinist whose rule had been absolute since a series of ruthless maneuvers eliminated opposition in the mid-1950's, was an adept practitioner of what might be called Small Power Power. He knew that he could act recklessly against bigger nations because they did not dare retaliate lest they spark a general holocaust. By the same token, he was expert in playing Peking against Moscow, never definitely allying himself with either.

Many students of Far Eastern affairs insisted that Sung's real target was South Korea, not the United States. To them, incidents like the *Pueblo* seizure and EC121 attack were items in a long-range plan to demonstrate to Seoul that the United States could not or would not be a fighting ally in case of showdown. At the same time, infiltration activity was being stepped up to sow the seeds of internal discord and discontent that must precede any Communist takeover.

Whatever the intent of the pugnacious actions against the United States, military people were convinced that the reconnaissance flights should be continued. The intelligence missions were "an insurance policy for us," said one Pentagon spokesman. A Navy officer commented: "It would be nice if all countries would observe the mutual and tacit agreement that we and the Russians have of allowing recon missions to go unmolested. It is that practice that lowered our guard. It is well that we've now changed the ground rules to afford protection to our planes."

There was one weak spot in the reasoning. Protection meant the ability to strike back on the spot of attack and that meant fighting and, when fighting started, who could tell where it would stop?

The "January Spring"— a Memory in Prague

Ouster of Alexander Dubcek as leader of Czechoslovakia's Communist party was final blow to democratic hopes

THE COMMUNIQUE from the Communist party's central committee said Alexander Dubcek was "a self-sacrificing and honest Communist . . . whose main aim in life was to serve the Communist party and his people." Then, having praised him, the committee fired him.

With Dubcek's fall from leadership of Czechoslovakia's communism, the Soviet fist finally closed upon the country's cherished reform program and crushed it. The Moscow doctrine of "limited sovereignty," enunciated six months earlier, had claimed its first victim. The action warned other Communist-ruled states of Europe to tread carefully. Big Brother was watching.

It was Thursday, April 17, a bleak and cloudy day in stately old Prague, when the central committee met to take note of what a communique called "shortcomings in the work of Comrade Dubcek in the implementation of approved decisions." The action to replace him was inevitable; it had been demanded by an angry Kremlin.

"God help us without him," cried one distracted woman as she read the news. Her words expressed the thought that lay heavily on many Czechoslovak minds. What now? What of their hopes for political reforms, for a new economic program which might shake the country out of its long lethargy? What would happen now to the new and heady wine they had tasted

Welcome to Budapest: Alexander Dubcek, right, and Janos Kadar, leader of Hungary's Communist party.

—the wine of free expression, of uncensored writing, of free dialogue with foreigners?

Hopes had risen swiftly in what the Czechoslovaks still called their "January Spring." That had been January 1968 when, to the joy of all except entrenched party bureaucrats, the reform-minded members of the Communist central committee dumped their Stalinist boss, Antonin Novotny, despite intense efforts of the Kremlin high command to save him.

The Czechoslovaks had known Stalin-like rule, under a regime which never said "no" to Moscow, ever since the Communists took over the country in the swift coup of February 1948. Now Novotny, symbol of years of oppressive party rule, was gone, to be replaced by the symbol of change, a fresh breeze in the stale political air of Prague.

Few would have expected that Dubcek would turn out to be such a symbol. He had been educated in Moscow's party school. His father and older brother were fanatical Communists. The brother had been killed fighting as a Communist partisan in World War II. Dubcek had risen swiftly under Novotny until he was first secretary—boss—of the party in Slovakia.

At 47, the slender Slovak with the long nose and shy smile emerged as the hope of anti-Stalinists. This was not an anti-Communist manifestation, nor was it anti-Moscow at the time. It was simply a reform movement, an attempt to break the clammy grip of a bureaucracy conditioned to respond to every Soviet whim. The Russians had gone through a de-Stalinization period long before. Czechoslovakia had lagged far behind. The old dictator's ghost still hovered over Prague's medieval grandeur and cast a shadow on the capital's proud European traditions.

A wave of enthusiasm gripped the nation. Things would begin to move, people told themselves. And move they did. Restraints began to fall away. The press was suddenly without censorship. Writers and students, long in the vanguard of the drive for change, found themselves able to speak their minds. Economists plunged happily into the task of drawing up a new program for the country. Frontier barriers fell and Westerners were welcomed. Citizens bubbled with ideas for political change which, although still within the framework of communism, were rank heresy in the eyes of Moscow.

The Russian bear growled in discontent and kept on growling as the Czechoslovaks charged ahead with their reforms. In mid-August of 1968, the growling gave way to action (*The World in 1968 172–179*). Troops of the Warsaw Pact—Russians, Hungarians, Poles, Bulgarians, Romanians and East Germans—swept into Czechoslovakia. Dubcek and other leaders were hauled to Moscow but the Russians could not force them to endorse a Czechoslovak leadership which would be more subservient. Finally the Czechoslovak leaders were released.

Dubcek's aim then was to salvage what he could from the wreckage of Czechoslovak hopes. The outlook was gloomy. In September, the Russians promulgated what became known as the Brezhnev Doctrine, named for Leonid I. Brezhnev, the Soviet party chief. The doctrine contended that, whenever the rule of a Communist Party was threatened or there was any threat to the "socialist community" of nations, the Russians had the right to intervene. The Russians also had the right to decide when such things were threatened. They proclaimed the right to use force to protect what the Kremlin called "proletarian internationalism," and what was in reality a claim to be the center for all Communist affairs.

Henceforth, therefore, sovereignty of a Communist nation, at least in Europe, would be limited. Yugoslavia and Romania, each maverick in its own way, eyed Moscow nervously. Would their turns come soon?

Gustav Husak, the new leader

By early 1969, it was abundantly clear that the Russians were intent on ousting Dubcek in favor of a more pliant leadership. Moscow industriously supported a pro-Moscow, conservative wing of the Czechoslovak party. Russian guns gave encouragement to the conservatives.

The passive resistance, particularly in Prague itself, was getting under Moscow's skin. So unpopular were the Soviet occupation troops that commanders did their best to keep the men out of sight. People turned their backs. Storekeepers served them in stubborn, resentful silence. The protest climaxed in January in the suicide by fire of student Jan Palach *(page 29)*.

Then in March, a Czechoslovak hockey team defeated the Russians in championship play in Sweden. The Czechoslovak public staged joyous anti-Russian demonstrations to celebrate, and Moscow was extremely irked. The "hockey revolt" was hard to take. Moscow growled again, and finally the pressure became too great to resist.

In April, Gustav Husak, a 56-year-old Slovak who recently had proclaimed that the time had come for Czechoslovaks to stop worshipping idols, was moved into the top position in the party. Dubcek was out but the party, in view of his wide popularity, let him down easily. He was relegated to the powerless, ceremonial post of chairman of the federal parliament.

It may have been the "hockey revolt" that finally finished Dubcek. On April 11, a week before the central committee meeting, Husak had made a speech. There had been entirely too much leniency toward anti-Soviet factions, he said, and the party had been too half-hearted and ineffective in measures to impose discipline.

So Husak came in and Dubcek went out, and Dubcek, a few days later, joined the new leaders at a Lenin birthday anniversary rally in chanting "long live the Soviet Union!"

The new party boss, Husak, might not seek to turn the clock all the way back to the time before the "January Spring." But it seemed likely he was prepared to deal harshly with the voice of dissent. The January Spring had become just a memory. Winter had set in again.

"A Widening Circle"

Pope Paul wanted Sacred College of Cardinals to represent both "ancient Christian tradition" and "the flourishing youth" of new nations

THE SUNNY spring week that bridged April and May was a joyous occasion for the Roman Catholic Church with the elevation of 33 bishops to the Sacred College of Cardinals. It also was a time for the birth of controversy in the church.

As pilgrims from five continents streamed into Rome in chartered flights, buses, cars and even on motorcycles, many anticipated the usual round of masses, parties and merry-making which had marked previous consistories. But, true to his intention of updating the church, Pope Paul turned the week into one of the most significant periods of his six-year reign.

He promoted a brand new book of mass giving greater rights to women. He designated a commission to study the roots of much of the unrest facing the Vatican—matters of faith, doctrine and morals. He chose the week to symbolize his compelling concern to bring peace to a war-torn world by meeting U Thant, Secretary General of the United Nations. And, to top his seven days of labor, he named an energetic French cardinal as his "Prime Minister" or Secretary of State.

For exactly one month, the Vatican and the rest of Rome had been a-bustle, preparing for the ceremonies of the largest Consistory in history. Priests thumbed through dictionaries to translate the flood of papal speeches into five languages. Rome tailors snipped away at the regal cloth which would dress the 33 new cardinals. Vatican diplomats mailed in recommendations for members of the theological commission.

On March 28, Pope Paul had announced his choices for the Sacred College of Cardinals, boosting the membership to a record high of 134. Four new cardinals came from the United States—the highest number after Italy's eight. They were Archbishops Terence J. Cooke of New York, John J. Carberry of St. Louis, John F. Dearden of Detroit and Bishop John J. Wright of Pittsburgh.

Another series of firsts: the first cardinals ever were chosen from Korea, Madagascar, Guatemala, the Congo, and New Zealand, and the first Scottish resident cardinal since 1526. One of the new princes vaulted from priest to cardinal. The Rev. Jean Danielou, a noted French theologian, was made a bishop just in time for the ceremonies.

In addition, Pope Paul chose two cardinals *in pectore* (in his heart), who would become princes of the church when and if the Pope revealed their names. Only eight such "secret cardinals" had been chosen since 1900. The identities of six went with the Popes to their graves.

"If its worldwide representation is unfortunately not perfect, full and complete as we would have liked," Pope Paul explained in one of his consistory speeches, "this comes from the fact that, for certain regions, particular circumstances do not make it possible or advisable to freely express our desire." Vatican-watchers took the pope's round-about words to mean he had *in pectore* prelates from Communist Czechoslovakia and Hungary, where the Vatican was conducting secret talks to improve the position of the church.

On April 28, the centuries-old Vatican pageantry unfolded. Gone, however, were the days of the broad-brimmed galero hat, the red shoes and the silver buckles, and the ermine-lined *cappa magna* or great cape. Even the sword bearers and the gentlemen in waiting fell victims of a drastic curtailing of the pomp and regal trappings. Both John XXIII and Pope Paul VI endeavored to eliminate the ostentatious remnants of a long-gone era.

But the gist of the ceremony remained as Pope Paul, wearing his white mitre of office, met in a "secret consistory" with 53 members of the Sacred College to confirm the 33 new cardinals from 19 nations. The whole procedure lasted 15 minutes. Pope Paul read the names in the ornate consistorial hall and asked in Latin *quid vobis videtur?* (how does it seem to you?). A chorus of voices replied *placet* (it pleases).

In a speech asking approval of the cardinals-designate, Pope Paul dwelt on his desire to make the college more representative of the newer, emerging nations. "For this reason," he said, "we have increased still more the number of its members so that it now truly includes in a widening circle the nations of the world, both those from ancient Christian tradition and those which come to the forefront of the world with flourishing youth, with the power of their energies, with the richness of their native cultures, with their will to collaborate for a common peace."

With that, the prelates were officially elevated to cardinals and three messengers set out to notify them as they waited in separate buildings near the Vatican.

For Pope Paul, the day had only started. He marched into another meeting to approve canonization as a saint of the Roman Catholic Church for Sister Marie Rose Julie Billiart, a crippled French-born 18th century nun who had founded an order which spread to five continents.

◀— New Cardinals and Pope Paul concelebrate a mass in St. Peter's Basilica

Then, in a series of announcements, he laid the groundwork for a new policy on sainthood, announced the issue of a new altar book with the latest changes suggested by the Vatican ecumenical council and established his long-awaited theological commission.

Few suspected that the church's new policy on sainthood would have such repercussions. The Consistory measures consisted merely of setting a new calendar for holy days and saints days. But it made room for the veneration of local saints by the removal of some traditional saints. Not until May, when such saints as Christopher and George were demoted, did Roman Catholics realize what had been in the making.

The theological commission was another matter. Controversy broke out immediately over the 30 theologians from 19 nations selected to sit on the commission. The Pope struck a careful balance between liberals and conservatives, but he avoided naming many of the dynamic thinkers who had dared to challenge Roman Catholic doctrine and he brought in some near-unknowns for the sake of geographical representation. The author of a widely-read Dutch catechism, Edward Schillebeeck, was not among the 30. Nor were other innovators—and no member of the commission was a layman. The influence of the commission also remained to be seen. Ultimately, the Pope could accept or reject its suggestions, just as he finally had rejected the recommendation of his birth control commission to end the ban on contraception (*The World in 1968, 186–189*).

At the end of the grueling day, while hundreds of pilgrims were celebrating the nominations at their countries' embassies or pontifical colleges, Pope Paul chose to stress his attachment to the temporal world. "People are growing tired of words and more and more are looking for actions," the pontiff told a solemn reception for Secretary General U Thant and the heads of United Nations special agencies. "At this point in world history," he added "we hope first that the government of the developed peoples, or of those in a condition of relative prosperity, will continue to contribute, or will generously decide to contribute to the cause of developing countries."

The next day, Consistory ceremonies were at a minimum. Pope Paul slipped circular bands of white wool around the necks of the 33 cardinals to symbolize the fullness of episcopal powers. The band or pallium was a purely honorary adornment. But it was significant that Pope Paul had now placed 87 of the white bands around the necks of new cardinals—the equivalent of more than half of the sacred college.

On Wednesday, 33 scarlet birettas were ready for the Pope to place them on the cardinals' heads in a semipublic consistory. Before receiving their hats of office, the new cardinals pronounced a new pledge added by Pope Paul. Until then, the cardinals had promised loyalty to God, Pope Paul and his "legitimately and canonically elected successors." Now they were asked to uphold the secrecy of all ecclesiastical instructions from the Vatican by saying "I will not divulge to their damage or disorder, instructions entrusted to me, directly or indirectly, without the consent of the Holy See." The new provision was overshadowed by yet another surprising announcement by the Pope.

In the midst of his speech in the Hall of the Benedictions in the Apostolic Palace, the pope named as his new Secretary of State Jean Cardinal Villot. Cardinal Villot, who rose through the ranks of the Vatican administration to a cardinal in three short years, succeeded 86-year-old Amleto Cardinal Cicognani, who retired because of age. The resignation of Cicognani—a one-time Papal delegate in Washington—marked the end of an era.

"His age, no other reason, dictates it, even if his strength is thriving and still devoted to the faithful service of the church and of our person," the Pope said. Of Cardinal Villot, a bespectacled gray-haired prelate of 63, the Pope said he was a "true and excellent man of the church." It was the first time in 55 years that the Vatican had a non-Italian Secretary of State—a combination of prime minister and foreign minister, a post second only to the Pope.

The appointment drew grumbles from the Italian members of the Vatican Curia, unhappy about their waning grip on the reigns of power. Some prelates mentioned the resurgence of a "French party," within the Vatican trying to influence the trend of theology and the Papal nominations. Others more bluntly called it "the French Mafia."

As his final message in the Consistory—a public ceremony on the cobblestones of St. Peter's square, Pope Paul spoke against the economic exploitation of man and pleaded for more efforts on behalf of the world's poor. "Development is the new name for peace," the Pope said. "The working class has become less fortunate and even in certain situations is oppressed and humiliated. Hence arise those struggles which have made their mark of deep disturbance on our times . . . (which) often divide men's minds to the real detriment of the common good."

To stress the universality of his message and his concerns for the world beyond Rome, the Pope delivered part of his speech to the 20,000 pilgrims in different languages—Latin, German, French, Spanish and Italian. "Man is sometimes used as a mere tool, according to the cold calculations of the laws of economy; it is therefore necessary that we provide action untiringly, without fear and without remorse." Immediately after the speech, the Pope handed to each of the new cardinals a plain gold ring of the office and together they concelebrated a mass. The last public consistory also marked the largest gathering of U.S. cardinals in history: Besides the four new princes of the church, five others had flown to Rome for the occasion.

Pope Paul pleased the Americans by appointing the jovial Cardinal Wright of Pittsburgh as prefect (head) of the Vatican Congregation of the clergy. Wright became the only American in the Curia and inherited a crucial post in a period of ferment agitating the Catholic clergy. One of his first tasks was to help out a fellow-American, Cardinal Dearden, who received a message from 38 rebellious priests. The priests told him they considered themselves free to marry and continue their work in the Catholic priesthood.

Finally, a Papal order ended experimentation with the Roman Catholic mass. The first new missal in 400 years rounded up all the changes in the liturgy since the Vatican ecumenical council. It confirmed the switch from Latin to modern languages, the use of rock and jazz, and the turning of the altar to face the congregations.

The new missal also gave a greater voice to women in church services, allowing them to go to the altar to read one of the three excerpts from the Bible which come before the Gospel. It allowed women as well as men to convey the wafers and wine of the Eucharist to the altar at the offertory. At first, some Vatican prelates said the missal wiped out a rule that women must cover their heads in church with scarves or hats, since the issue was not mentioned in the book. Two months later, with the cardinals back home and the missal in general circulation, the Vatican denied that women could drop their hats.

"The rule still holds," said one of the Vatican's top liturgy experts." "It has never been abolished."

Hijackers were warned in English and in Spanish

"Pirate Plane to Cuba"

A plague of hijackings posed a problem for airlines, travelers and governments

THE INGREDIENTS of the plot could have been lifted from a late, late movie—danger and adventure on a tropic isle with a cast of thousands including political refugees, ex-convicts, airplane pilots, innocent travelers, secret police, beautiful girls and the FBI. In truth, it was a real life serial which could have been titled "Pirate Plane to Cuba."

The story line did not change much from one episode to the next. One or more of the innocent travelers would turn out to be not so innocent. There would be a brandishing of weapons, an uttering of threats, and the airliner pilot would be forced to digress in midflight and aim his plane toward Cuba. In 1969's first five months, 26 planes were hijacked thus and more than 2,000 passengers and crew taken on unscheduled excursions to the land of Fidel Castro. An additional 20 planes had been abducted in 1968 (*The World in 1968, 146*).

Considering the hazards, it was remarkable that no more than one life was lost. Ricardo Davila, a 21-year-old student, jumped the hijacker of a Colombian plane during a refueling stop at Cartagena and wrested from him what looked like a stick of dynamite. In ensuing gunfire, an airline mechanic was killed and three other men, including the hijacker, were wounded. Later, the "dynamite" was found to be a tube stuffed with talcum powder.

In other skyjackings, tragedy was narrowly averted. A passenger on a Delta Airlines flight in March was big, graying John Reed, an FBI agent en route to a new assignment in

Oklahoma City. When the plane put down at New Orleans for fuel, the pistol-packing hijacker permitted the 89 passengers to leave the plane while he detained the crew as hostages. Reed lingered until all others had left, then quietly told the gunman, Douglas Alton Dickey of Arizona, that he was under arrest. Dickey replied: "I do not intend to kill you but I am going to Havana and I am going to shoot you in the leg." Reed grappled with him, Dickey fired one harmless shot, then he was subdued and arrested.

Another close call occurred when President Carlos Lleras Restrepo of Colombia ordered that fuel should be denied to an Ecuadorian plane which had landed at Barranquilla in the hands of 15 hijackers, three of them women. When the pilot radioed that he would be killed if fuel was withheld, Colombian officials relented "in order to avoid a tragic incident."

It was scary business, particularly when the pirates were nervous or unstable, as many of them were. Capt. James G. Brown of National Airlines told a House committee in February: "There is a good 10-minute period at the initial outset of these hijackings when things are very much in the balance. The slightest move from anyone, or the slightest offending word by anyone, could really bring on an absolute holocaust."

Brown had flown for one hour, 15 minutes with a loaded gun "stuck in the back of my head behind my right ear." The hijacker "had one of his coat pockets full of bullets (and) another full box of bullets that he sat on the console beside my left elbow. So this man was in position to have himself a real shoot-out." He also had a colleague "who was carrying a hand satchel and in this hand satchel he had a cigarette carton. In this carton, he had four sticks of dynamite with fuses wired to each stick."

Despite the underlying terror, some incidents had a lighter side. One concerned a Newark-Miami flight that numbered as a passenger Allen Funt, creator of television's "Candid Camera," which won popularity by recording human reactions to unexpected and unusual situations. Funt reported: "When the captain announced that we were going to Havana instead of Miami, at least four people who recognized me pounced on me, certain it was a 'Candid Camera' stunt."

There was also the case of a long-haired youth who tried to commandeer a Goodyear blimp at Carson, Calif. He carried a guitar and a black box of ominous appearance, and he told the caretaker-crewman that he wanted a ride to a jazz festival at Aspen, Colo. If he didn't get it, he would "blow the thing up." A deputy sheriff came running, the youth pressed a button on the black box and blasted his audience—with rock music. En route to a hospital, he confided how he had eluded a guard: "I'm invisible."

The hijackers were a motley breed. The obvious presumption was that they were Cubans trying to go home. Not so. Fenton Wheeler of The Associated Press explored the backgrounds of 90 sky pirates who had reached Havana and found that, although 61 were Latin Americans, only 15 were Cubans. The

Two-time victim: Lynn Barlow, 19, a New York student, was on a plane hijacked to Cuba twice within two months.

others included 23 North Americans, one Frenchman, one Jordanian and four of undetermined nationality.

By their own explanations, most of them were either mentally disturbed or on the run from the law. Some babbled about family troubles, others complained of mistreatment in the United States. One broke into tears, said he was dying of cancer and didn't care what happened to him. Another offered no more illuminating explanation than that he was "tired of TV dinners." A black nationalist renamed the plane he had captured—*Republic of New Africa.*

Psychiatrists took a turn at explaining the banditry. Dr. Peter Siegel of the Federal Aeronautics Administration developed the "skyjacker's syndrome," a theory that the air pirate was proving to himself that he was a decisive, effective human being by taking control of the plane and its passengers and crew, and steering all of them to Cuba.

In the same vein, another professional said, "With the temporarily omnipotent feeling the skyjacker gets, he actually is in control of his own destiny and the destinies of others. He is next to God, literally, flying to Cuba. With this one grand gesture of power, the skyjacker shows his contempt for the Establishment."

No theory of motivation, however logical, helped to solve the problem of what to do about the continuing piracy. One point upon which everyone agreed was that resistance would be foolhardy. Eastern Airlines told its people in a circular: "It is much more prudent to submit to a gunman's demands than to attempt actions which may well jeopardize the lives of all on board." Ironically, this policy of acquiescence served to assure prospective pirates that they could operate with impunity.

Volunteered ideas ran into the hundreds. One letter to the FAA recommended that everyone be stripped of clothing "so that everybody could see everything and nobody can hide a weapon." Another proposed "sexy" stewardesses who could seduce the hijacker. There were suggestions for trap doors in airliner cockpits through which the attacker could be dumped, depressurizing the cabin until all on board were unconscious, playing the Cuban national anthem on the intercom and arresting anyone who stood up.

The airlines considered armed guards, metal detectors and baggage searches, and dismissed them as prohibitively costly, or impractical. A reward of $25,000 was offered for information leading to arrest and conviction of a hijacker (to avoid disastrous heroics, the reward would not be paid for a midflight capture). Posters in terminals and ticket offices advised travelers: "Aircraft hijacking is a crime punishable by death. Carrying concealed weapons aboard aircraft is punishable by prison sentences and fines. Passengers and baggage are subject to search."

Otherwise, airline actions were calculated to safeguard passengers and crew. Pilots were provided with maps of Havana's Jose Marti Airport and instructed in approach and landing procedures there. They received cards printed in Spanish and English: "I must open my flight bag for maps". . . . "Not enough fuel to reach Cuba"—eight such phrases to facilitate critical communication with a jittery hijacker.

There was little evidence to indicate that the seizures scared travelers. An exception was the woman who announced in a newspaper advertisement that she would sue the airline and the U.S. government if her plane was shanghaied (it wasn't). On the other hand, it was a standing joke at Eastern airports to ask the stewardess: "Is this the plane to Havana?" Tales were told about sports fans en route to football's Super Bowl in Miami: They left New York three days early to allow time for the side trip to Havana and back. Johnny Carson joked on his "Tonight" show: "There are so many hijackings that one airline changed its slogan to 'up, up and olé'."

As time passed, a certain routine developed for dealing with an abducted plane and its people. The nearest air traffic control provided flight path and altitudes for the trip to Havana. Miami alerted Havana to the incoming plane via a direct phone line to Marti airport. The Swiss Embassy in Washington (acting for the United States which severed diplomatic relations with Cuba in 1960) sent a *pro forma* message to its representative in Havana, asking safe return of plane and passengers.

The Swiss reimbursed Cuba for all costs—$2,500–$3,000 in landing fees, fuel, weather reports, food and lodging—and then collected from Washington which in turn billed the airline. "The bill is roughly comparable to what it would cost to land a plane unexpectedly at a U.S. airport," said a State Department spokesman, "although the hotel and meals probably aren't as good." The total cost to the airline could reach $10,000 because of schedule changes, transfer of passengers to other aircraft and diversion of planes from regular routes.

In Havana, whatever the hijackers' expectations, they were not greeted as heroes. Again quoting the State Department: "As soon as a plane lands, the hijackers are grabbed by the Cuban military and carted off to jail for at least two or three weeks. Then they're put under house arrest indefinitely with Big Brother watching all the time." Incarceration and interrogation were intended, it was said, to screen out infiltrators from the United States' Central Intelligence Agency. When the hijackers were released from detention, they were put to work in factories or the sugar cane fields.

The passengers were carried by bus over 85 bumpy, uncomfortable miles to Veradero Beach, once a resort for the wealthy. Invariably, they were well fed, treated courteously and housed in the decaying Veradero Beach hotel ("We had a ball," said one enthusiastic lady) until planes came to return them to the United States. The hijacked planes and crews were held in Havana until clearance was granted for the homeward flight.

The feeling in Washington was that Castro was doing nothing to encourage sky pirates. Neither was he doing anything to discourage them. If hijackers knew they would be extradited to the United States—where death was a possible penalty under legislation approved by Congress in 1961—the passion for piracy would pass. Perhaps the return of even one hijacker would be an effective deterrent. Frank E. Loy, deputy assistant secretary of state, told a House hearing: "We have concluded that the hijacker of a commercial airline carrying passengers should be returned regardless of any claim that he was fleeing political persecution." Castro's reply was to repeat what he had said in the past: Cuba would not turn away anyone who sought political asylum.

Some easing in the treatment of abducted planes and people was achieved in negotiations conducted by the Swiss in Havana. Beginning in February, planes, crews and passengers were detained only a few hours. The foreign ministry did not commit itself to the practice but said each case would be judged on its circumstances.

Simultaneously, the number of piracies began to dwindle and hope arose that time might be the best solution. There were 11 hijackings in January, five in February, five in March, three in April, only two in May. "It's possible the fad has died out," said J. M. Frazier, head of the FAA's office in Miami. "We know there's been a decline in the hijacking but we don't really know why." Like a headache that had passed, who cared so long as the pain had stopped.

A "JOLLY GOOD HOLIDAY"

Two tillers, a jib, a spinnaker, the water tank, self-steering gear and half the cooking stove were useless. The cabin leaked and its canvas cover was cracked. The hull was covered with rust, barnacles and seaweed. "I wouldn't feel safe on her on a one-day trip," said a retired trawler captain. "She could take anyone around the world," beamed Robin Knox-Johnston, a 30-year-old sailor.

The battered 32-foot ketch had done just that. She and Knox-Johnston completed on April 22 a 29,500-mile journey around the globe. They were not the first to do so. Capt. Joshua Slocum did it in 1895. Francis Chichester did it in 1966 and Alex Rose in 1968. But the *Suhaili* and her skipper were the first to do it without once touching shore.

For 10½ months, they were alone against the sea. Shortly after shoving off from Falmouth, England, the fresh food put aboard was rotted. Of the 100 gallons of fresh water, 80 were contaminated with salt water. "I kept a line out stern a lot of the time with a lure on it," said Robin, "but in fact only caught two fish, and one was nabbed by a shark." Although there were "plenty of flying fish on deck for a small fry-up," he was "constantly haunted by visions of big, juicy steaks."

The *Suhaili* was nearly capsized in the Bass Strait between Tasmania and Australia. Soon after surviving what Knox-Johnston called "the stickiest part of the voyage," passing through the Foveaux Strait between New Zealand and Stewart Island in a heavy fog and a gale, the *Suhaili* ran aground on a sandbank off Dunedin, New Zealand. Then the radio went dead.

A mid-Atlantic search by British, Portuguese and American ships and 30 vessels from the North Atlantic Alliance failed to find the pioneer navigator. On April 5, more than 130 days after he was last heard from, a British tanker spotted the *Suhaili* and radioed that all was well.

"The most trying and frustrating days of the voyage," said the skipper, were the last four. With victory in sight, he spent them off the southwest coast of Britain riding out gales, fighting tides and headwinds. Finally, in mid-afternoon of his 312th day at sea, Knox-Johnston came into port to an enthusiastic welcome. With his hands heavily scarred, his beard bushy and his clothes tattered, he had little more to say than to describe his venture—the longest that any man had spent alone at sea—as just "a jolly good holiday."

EXIT MUHAMMAD ALI

The Black Muslims gave and the Black Muslims took away. And the man who had lost the title of heavyweight boxing champion now lost also his name and became again Cassius Clay, as he had been christened.

As Muhammad Ali, minister of the Muslims, he had claimed exemption from the military draft and refused to be inducted into the Army. A jury in federal court convicted him of draft evasion; the World Boxing Association declared his title vacant (*The World in 1967, 133*).

When the Supreme Court ordered a review of his conviction, Ali said hopefully that he would like to resume his boxing career, primarily to pay off indebtedness. The statement aroused Elijah Muhammad, founder and leader of the Muslims, and he announced in April 4 edition of the newspaper Muhammad Speaks: "I want the world to know that Muhammad Ali has stepped down off the spiritual platform of Islam to go and see if he can make money in the sports world. This statement is to tell the world that we, the Muslims, are not with Mr. Muhammad Ali in his desire."

On April 11, Elijah elaborated: "Muhammad Ali is out of the circle of the brotherhood of the followers of Islam for one year. We shall call him Cassius Clay. We take away the name of Allah from him until he proves himself worthy of that name."

Clay said he agreed with the Muslim leader who "has the right to spank us all." Apparently, he also repented his statement; on the night of Elijah's first pronouncement, Clay told an audience in Georgia, "I'll never climb into the ring or go into an arena again."

A FIGURE FROM THE PAST. Rudolf Hess, once deputy fuehrer to Adolf Hitler in Nazi Germany, was photographed on one of his exercise walks in the yard at Berlin's Spandau Prison. Serving a life term for war crimes, he was the only inmate in a prison built to house 660 men and the Big Four of World War II's allies—the United States, Great Britain, France and Russia—were spending $200,000 per year to keep him captive. Hess was 75 years old on April 26.

A lone farm rises above flood waters of Big Sioux River in Iowa

IN SPRINGTIME, FLOODS CAME

The mighty Mississippi's usually placid tributaries, bloated by a heavy snowmelt and spring rains, surged from their channels and swept over lowlands to create a vast inland sea in the Upper Midwest. Floods from Canada to Missouri caused an estimated $100 million damage, killed eight persons and chased 25,000 others from their homes.

The floods were bad although less devastating than those of 1965 which caused $150 million damage, killed 14 persons and drove 38,000 people from their homes (The World in 1965 70–75). Federal, state and local officials said alert planning and accurate forecasting had prevented some $250 million in losses.

George Lincoln, head of the Office of Emergency Preparedness, talked with President Nixon about the impending crisis in early February. At that early date, many local governments foresaw the crisis but had spent all available money on massive snow removal programs necessitated by a severe winter.

"Operation Foresight," a cooperative program of seven federal agencies and the American Red Cross to aid local governments, went into effect March 1. The U.S. Weather Bureau provided ample warning of a record snowmelt in the Dakotas and Minnesota. A weekly "Flood Outlook" bulletin was issued and flood crest figures were predicted accurately, beginning in mid-March. When the high waters came, five states—Minnesota, North and South Dakota, Iowa and Wisconsin—were designated disaster areas.

North Dakota, where the Red River of the

North flowed along the Minnesota border and the Souris curled around Minot, was the first to feel the effects. The normally placid prairie rivers, swollen to as much as 50 times their normal width, drove thousands of persons from their homes in the state's three largest cities. The Red River at Grand Forks was a fraction of an inch below its highest level of the century and created a lake 12 miles wide along a 120-mile route.

Downstream at Fargo, conditions were complicated by an invasion of rats forced from their lowland lairs as waters rose to 21 feet above flood level. At Minot, the Souris, locally called the Mouse, reached its highest level in 65 years. Though there was no loss of life and dikes hastily created by volunteers averted disaster, Gov. William L. Guy said "destruction in many communities is greater than any in history."

All of the flood's fatalities occurred in Minnesota, attacked from the west by the Red River of the North and from the east by the St. Croix River on the Wisconsin border. At Perley, 10 inches of water covered the highest elevation and the St. Croix at St. Paul surged past the city at 1.25 million gallons a second, 15 times normal volume.

Wisconsin was partially spared because of a relatively slow snowmelt, but 30-mile-an-hour winds churned flood waters and threatened dikes and levees barricading land from water. LaCrosse spent $185,000 on levees. At Cassville, hard hit in 1965, new levees held back waters from all but three homes. Streets in Prairie du Chien's low-lying areas were inundated by as much as eight feet of water.

Flood tides moved south. The entire population of North Sioux City, S.D., was chased from homes by the rising Big Sioux. Eighteen square blocks of Sioux Falls were surrendered to the river after a nightlong battle to plug a 100-foot break in a dike. "We dumped in more than 100 tons of rock, we threw in car bodies and anything else we could lay our hands on," said Joe Vanderloo, Minnehaha County Civil Defense director, "but it was undermining faster than we could fill it up."

Iowa was threatened from the east by the Mississippi and from the west by the Big Sioux. The Mississippi's swollen waters were kept on course by sandbags and earthen levees but the Big Sioux ravaged 26 counties in central and northwestern Iowa before flowing into the Missouri River where the runoff spread only across lowlands.

As the Mississippi flowed past Illinois, flood preparations held off the rising waters. The widening of the main stream at the junction of the Mississippi and Missouri accommodated the crests of the two rivers above St. Louis and nearly a month of spring flooding became history.

While the crisis was ended, said Maj. Gen. Frederick J. Clarke, chief of the Army Corps of Engineers, the hurriedly built dikes and other protective measures were for the present, not for the future. He told congressional hearings that the nation's annual flood losses could triple over the next 50 years if the federal government failed to act.

"AN ACT OF DESPERATION"

Transplants of human hearts, averaging two per week since the pioneer operation in December 1967, had become nearly as commonplace as kidney transplants. But, while machines could substitute for useless kidneys until donors were found, the lives of heart patients hinged solely on whether substitute human hearts were available. And then, on April 4, 1969, Haskell Karp lived for 65 hours with a man-made organ.

Karp, a 47-year-old printing estimator from Skokie, Ill., underwent surgery at Houston's St.

Luke's Hospital for repair of a damaged heart chamber. When Dr. Denton A. Cooley, head of the operating team, found that Karp's heart was irreparable, he inserted a mechanical organ.

"It was an act of desperation," said Dr. Cooley who had performed 19 heart transplants, more than any other surgeon in the world. "I was concerned, of course, because this had never been done before. But we had to put up one Sputnik to start the space program, and we had to start here some place."

Karp lived more than two and one-half day with his substitute heart until a human hea was obtained and inserted. Thirty-eight hour later, Karp succumbed to the complications of pneumonia and kidney failure. "I'm more tha satisfied," said Karp's widow. "I know every thing was done for him."

Medical critics said the fact that Karp had bee kept alive by the half-pound, four-chambere mechanism was not enough. Even though he wa conscious while the device was in his chest, the argued, it didn't mean he was getting adequat circulation from it, and a lack of circulatio could have affected his vital organs.

There were questions also of ethics. D Michael E. DeBakey of neighboring Meth dist Hospital said the $25,000 heart and th electrically powered console that kept it fun tioning followed a design developed in h laboratories. If that were true, federal funds ha been used and Dr. Cooley would have been boun by federal guidelines on human experimentatio

Cooley contended the mechanical heart ha been developed in his own labs by Dr. Doming Liotta with a $50,000 grant from the Texa Heart Institute which Cooley headed. Dr. Liott an Argentine, had come to the Cooley tea after five years with DeBakey's artificial hea program, supported by the National Heart Ir stitute through $30 million in federal money Therefore, said Liotta, federal funds finance only the experience and knowledge, not th heart itself.

"I believe I am qualified to judge what is righ and proper for my patient," said Dr. Cooley countering criticism that he had not sought pric approval from a federal review panel nor had h considered it appropriate to do so. "His onl chance to live another hour was to have this de vice attached. If this is cause for censure . . . then I lay myself at the mercy of the court."

Drs. Denton Cooley, left, and Domingo Liotta with a mechanical heart

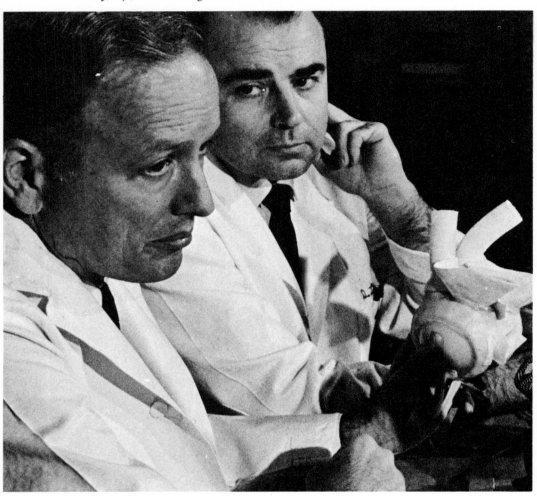

FOR THE RECORD

CONVICTED. Seven men and six women, fc disorderly conduct during the 1968 Democrati convention in Chicago *(The World in 1968, 161 166).* Magistrate Arthur L. Dunne imposed fine of $200–$400 each plus costs on April 14 afte five weeks of testimony. The defendants wer among 79 persons arrested during a protest marc which, the magistrate said, constituted "a clea imminent, and present threat of violence to oι community." Most of the others had pleade guilty and paid fines.

EXONERATED. William N. Oatis of The A sociated Press was convicted of espionage i 1951 while he was chief of the AP bureau i Prague, Czechoslovakia, and served two years a 10-year sentence in prison. A special senate the Prague Municipal Court announced on Apr 25 that the charges against Oatis and two assis tants "were found not to have been based o facts." Since his release in 1953, Oatis had bee reporting for AP from the United Nations.

ELECTED. Barry Goldwater Jr., 30, son of Se Barry Goldwater who was the Republican pres dential nominee in 1964, to Congress in his fir bid for public office, April 30. Goldwater w elected to the House from the 27th district California to fill a seat vacated when Ed Reineck also a Republican, became lieutenant governor

A FLOOR FOR WELFARE PAYMENTS?

The broad variations in state payments to welfare clients became a matter of national concern on April 21 when the Supreme Court struck down as unconstitutional state laws that required one year's residence to qualify for aid. The decision invalidated legislation in more than 40 states.

The ruling made approximately 200,000 needy eligible for assistance and increased welfare costs by something like $175 million annually. Robert H. Finch, secretary of Health, Education and Welfare, said the decision made national minimum standards for welfare payments "inevitable." (As an example of differences, the average payments for a dependent child ranged from $8.50 per month in Mississippi to $71.75 in New York.)

Speaking for the majority in the 6–3 vote, Justice William J. Brennan Jr. said poor people not only had the right to move to another state without loss of welfare benefits but they had the right to move precisely because higher payments were available. He wrote: "We do not perceive why a mother who is seeking to make a new life for herself and her children should be regarded as less deserving because she considers, among other factors, the levels of a state's public assistance."

Chief Justice Earl Warren, speaking for the three dissenters, saw far-reaching implications in the action. He said it could cast doubt on the constitutionality of state residency requirements for the right to vote, to practice a profession and to attend a state-supported university.

Supplies arrive for Firebase Bunker Hill in Vietnam —

May

Hot War in Vietnam; Cold War in Paris

Peace seemed far away on both fronts but United States
took a first step on the road to disengagement

Amphibious landing: Marines charge ashore on island near Da Nang

The day was like many other days in Vietnam. A Communist battalion attacked an American fire base east of the A Shau Valley and was repulsed. United States Marines joined South Vietnamese in an operation designed to trap 200 foemen south of Da Nang. Infantrymen of the 25th Division found an entrenched force of North Vietnamese southwest of Saigon and drove it into retreat in four hours of fighting. Paratroopers of the 101st Airborne were locked in a struggle described as "eyeball to eyeball" on the slopes of a mountain called Ap Bia.

The day was like many other days in Paris. Peace talks were in stalemate. Henry Cabot Lodge, who had succeeded Averell Harriman as chief of the U.S. delegation, had been called home for consultation. Diplomats were appraising a 10-point program put forward by the Viet Cong's National Liberation Front in which the most encouraging point was the absence of invective.

The day was May 13, 1969. One full year had passed since the United States and North Vietnam first met to talk of peace (*The World in 1968, 246–250*). In that year of cold war in Paris, 12,000 Americans and perhaps 170,000 Vietnamese had died

in the hot war in Southeast Asia. The relentless climb of American casualties to 33,614 dead had passed the totals of Korea, and the Vietnam conflict had become the fourth bloodiest in American history, exceeded by the Civil War and two World Wars.

Aside from the decision by the United States to halt bombing of North Vietnam, the one mutual accomplishment in 12 months of wrangling was an agreement on seating arrangements. In the sparring which followed the bombing halt, Hanoi had agreed to accept the presence of the Saigon government—hitherto regarded as an American puppet—but had insisted on recognition of the National Liberation Front, political representative of the Viet Cong, as an equal with all other parties. Saigon had been just as insistent against any setup that even implied recognition of the NLF. Washington had adhered to what became known as the "your side, our side" concept, proposing simply that North Vietnam and the Front sit on one side with South Vietnam and the United States on the other.

A multitude of suggestions had been made—square tables and round tables, elliptical tables and doughnut tables, separate tables and all-together tables, divided tables and undivided tables. Each had been vetoed by one side or the other for one reason or another.

The device which finally won approval on Jan. 15 was a plain round table with rectangular tables for secretaries on either side, an arrangement which preserved the illusions of two parties, or four parties, or three parties, depending on the viewpoint. The surface of the bigger table, 35 feet in diameter, was green imitation leather, uncluttered by name plates, flags or any other identifying insignia. The secretaries' tables, 5½ by three feet, were placed precisely 18 inches from the central one.

Optimism flared briefly when the first expanded session on Jan. 18 produced complete agreement on procedures. But, said spokesman William Jordan for the Americans, "it is always a mistake to take rapid progress at one meeting as an indication of rapid progress over-all. We have many difficult and delicate matters to be dealt with." The words were understatement; one round of oratory was enough to develop obstacles which, one reporter wrote, "seem insurmountable."

The delegates could not agree even on what to talk about. Hanoi sought priority for political discussion. Washington-Saigon wanted first to de-escalate the war. Toward that end, the United States proposed mutual withdrawal of all "external forces," meaning North Vietnamese and Americans. Hanoi insisted that the first requirement for progress of any sort was unilateral, unconditional withdrawal by the United States. With equal vehemence, the Communists argued for "a completely new regime in Saigon"; there was "absolutely no hope" in dealing with the current government. Ambassador Lodge said restoration of a genuinely neutral Demilitarized Zone would be a practical step toward peace. Hanoi agreed; it would be done whenever the United States stopped violating the Geneva agreement which had established the Zone. In the United States view, Hanoi was the violator.

Two formal propositions had been placed on the table. The NLF went to bat first with a 10-point program on May 8. President Nixon countered with an 8-point plan on May 14.

There was some common ground in the proposals—expressions of respect for the fundamental national rights of Vietnam, and declarations that the Vietnamese people should decide their own future in free elections (although argument was certain to develop over definitions of the rights and of "free" elections).

The points of sharp departure included action to de-escalate and end the war. The Front would not acknowledge that North

Vietnam troops were fighting in South Vietnam; it called for withdrawal "without imposing any conditions whatsoever" of only the United States and "other foreign countries in the U.S. camp." The Americans advocated withdrawal of all non-South Vietnamese forces in mutually agreeable stages over 12 months time. At the end of the year, remaining units would retire to designated base areas and cease combat operations; then the United States and its allies would complete withdrawal "as the remaining North Vietnamese forces were withdrawn and returned to North Vietnam." (In arguing for mutual withdrawal, Nixon departed from the so-called Manila formula of his predecessor, Lyndon B. Johnson, which had promised American withdrawal six months after the North Vietnamese departed.)

The American program held special interest because it was the first pronouncement of Vietnam policy by the new Nixon Administration. Commentators generally were impressed, admiring the flexibility in particular. As one exponent of that school of opinion wrote, only two rigid principles were enunciated and these were diplomatically balanced—one assured Hanoi ("We have ruled out attempting to impose a purely military solution") and the other reassured Saigon ("We have also ruled out either a one-sided withdrawal from Vietnam or the acceptance in Paris of terms that would amount to a disguised American defeat."

Neither proposition evoked cheers across the table. To Washington-Saigon, some NLF ideas were "clearly unacceptable." To the Communists, the suggestion of mutual withdrawal was "perfidious" and "a most absurd position."

As the atmosphere of deadlock deepened with each sterile weekly meeting in Paris, the search for crumbs of hope intensified. Diplomats and newsmen weighed carefully every nuance of tone, every hint of emphasis for hidden meaning. In one instance, the fact that a spokesman grinned as he denied a rumor was taken as "unspoken confirmation of the report."

As early as January, talk was heard that nothing would be accomplished until the two sides got together for informal, private discussion and negotiation. Secretary of State William P. Rogers said the United States was ready for such exploration and President Nguyen Van Thieu of South Vietnam seconded the motion for his government. "There are many things we cannot decide at the conference table which we can discuss quite

frankly in private," Thieu said. "We could talk with Hanoi as well as the Front. We could talk with two people or three people."

Despite Viet Cong scoffing that the reports were machinations of Washington to silence anti-war sentiment at home, the word went around that some sort of secret talks were indeed under way. But nothing of substance resulted and John Hightower, specialist in diplomatic affairs for The Associated Press, reported on April 8 that the contacts had "produced little or no progress." He wrote that some Administration authorities "still believe that the North Vietnamese and Viet Cong are convinced they will win the war if they fight on long enough. They conclude, therefore, that the enemy leaders are not yet seriously interested in a compromise settlement."

The tenor of events in Vietnam justified the belief that the Communists were far from abandoning thought of victory. A relative lull in the war was shattered on Feb. 20 by Communist bombardment of 150 cities, towns and military posts. Ground attacks followed a score of the barrages. The burst of action introduced an offensive campaign that endured more than two months.

Despite the sporadic character of battle, the tide of casualties rose inexorably. U.S. deaths mounted to 453 in one March week, the highest total in nine months. In the same time, South Vietnam counted 521 killed and Communist losses were reckoned about 6,000.

In early stages, the offensive was viewed by American commanders as an attempt to repeat the successes of the Tet (lunar new year) offensive 12 months earlier (*The World in 1968, 28–35*). Actually, the 1969 push never attained such dimensions. Most of the targets were rural rather than metropolitan; no massive assaults were mounted such as Saigon, Hue, Ben Tre, Kontum, Ben Me Thuot and other cities had seen in 1968. Moreover, the defenders were alert and prepared. "It was a lot less than we really planned for," a U.S. officer said.

Although the operations did not match the earlier offensive in magnitude of battle, some of the fighting was as vicious as any the war had produced. Suicide squads—sappers with TNT taped to their bodies to blast barbed wire defenses—led an assault force into hand-to-hand combat at Fire Base Russell, a U.S. Marine post south of the DMZ. Three battalions stormed

Ammunition dump explodes at Da Nang

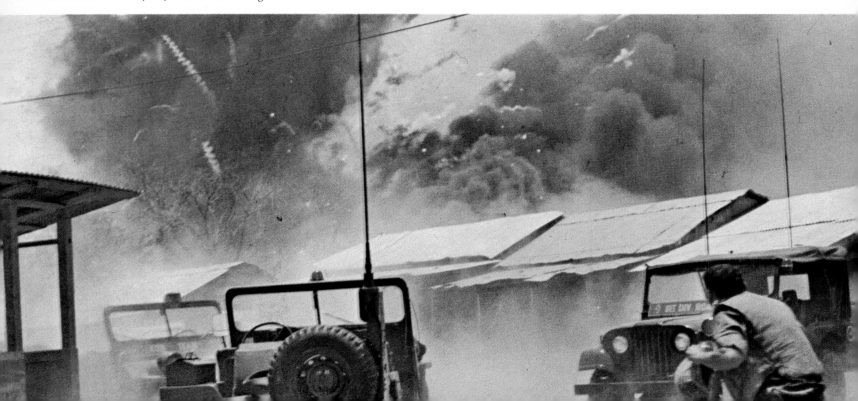

the big base at Bien Hoa, 15 miles north of Saigon, and re-pulsed five counterattacks before they were driven away. Troops of the 25th Division, camped astride an infiltration route north-west of Saigon, frustrated an onslaught by 1,000 Communists, charging from woodland in three directions behind an artillery barrage. In a surprise raid, Viet Cong shot up a training center for South Vietnamese, inflicting heavy casualties and damage at a cost of only two dead.

Also, there was the battle for Ap Bia mountain.

It was not a planned encounter. Helicopters had deposited nine battalions of troops for a sweep of the A Shau Valley, in-filtration route from Laos to the coastal cities of the 1st Corps area. One unit, the 3rd Battalion, 187th Regiment, 101st Air-borne Division, was moving along a ridge line when it hit op-position in unexpected strength and was forced to pull back.

A spokesman for Maj. Gen. Melvin Zais, commander of the 101st, explained what happened: "We ran into a hornet's nest and naturally we cleaned it out. They were North Vietnam sol-diers. They were in our area of operation. People were shooting at us and we went up and got them."

In truth, the fight was not as simple as the spokesman made out. The first attack, in company strength, was repulsed on May 12 by defenders ultimately estimated as the better part of two regiments. Two companies went up the slopes on May 13 and also were beaten back. The whole 3rd Battalion tried on May 14 with no more success. Two other battalions of the 101st and one battalion of South Vietnam's 1st Division were called to action as reinforcements.

The assaults continued, day after day. The mountain known as Ap Bia to Vietnamese and as Hill 937 (denoting its height in meters) to military command became "Hamburger Hill" to GIs. Three times, the crest seemed within grasp. Three times, the attacks faltered in storms of grenades and small arms fire. In all, 10 assaults failed. All the while, U.S. guns and warplanes battered the peak; 20,000 artillery rounds and 155 air strikes literally stripped the covering jungle from the mountain, left it looking like an oversized, pockmarked sand dune.

On May 20, a force of 1,000 Americans and 400 South Viet-namese clawed toward the summit. They routed a stubborn rearguard and Hill 937 was securely in friendly hands. "A great victory by a gutty bunch of guys," said Gen. Zais. One week later, the victors abandoned the ground they had won; "we feel we've gotten everything out of this mountain that we're going to get," said a spokesman.

The guns on Ap Bia fell silent; the voices in Congress did not.

Something like a self-imposed moratorium on criticism had been prevailing in Washington since the Nixon Administration took office. Perhaps the mood reflected that of the nation, evidenced in the decrease in mail decrying the war. One senator reported late in April that he had not received a letter of pro-test in two months; a representative said his Vietnam mail, once mountainous, had dwindled to three letters per week.

The first sparks of revived debate flew in May. Most of them were generated by Republicans. On May 1, Sen. George D. Aiken of Vermont, senior Republican on the Foreign Relations Committee, urged the Administration to begin "immediately . . . an orderly withdrawal" that would be the first step toward returning the war to "its rightful owners" in Saigon. Two days later, Sen. Hugh Scott of Pennsylvania, Republican whip and a, supporter of Vietnam policy, spoke also for withdrawal of "a substantial number" of U.S. troops.

The news of Ap Bia fanned the sparks into flame. Casualties had been heavy—46 Americans killed and 308 wounded; Com-

A Marine artillery base carved from the jungle in one day

95

munist dead were figured at 517. Reports had been heard that GIs, appalled by the bloodshed, had questioned the wisdom of their commanders. Such battles, said Sen. Edward M. Kennedy of Massachusetts, the Democratic whip, were "senseless and irresponsible." He wanted to know: "How can we justify sending our boys against a hill a dozen times or more, until soldiers themselves question the madness of the action?" He and other critics were not appeased when the hard-won ground was abandoned.

Military people had an explanation." "We are not fighting for terrain as such. We are going after the enemy," said a spokesman for Gen. Creighton Abrams, the U.S. commander. The tactic was part of broad strategy to maintain maximum pressure on the Communist foe, harass him wherever he was found, keep him from obtaining any advantage as a result of the halt in bombing of the North. It was a strategy enunciated by Lyndon Johnson and continued by Richard Nixon, at least to the extent that he did not issue any modifying orders beyond telling Abrams to conduct the war "with a minimum of American casualties."

It also was in keeping with tactics initiated by Gen. Abrams when he succeeded Gen. William C. Westmoreland (The World in 1968, 92, 248). Instead of the massive search-and-destroy sweeps favored by Westmoreland, there were numerous small operations, designed in the aggregate to keep the foe off balance and frustrate his offensive plans. In May, military sources described an average day's activity as perhaps 1,000 patrols by units of 100–200 men, all with the common objective of finding and destroying Communist troops, bases and supplies.

Congressional critics were neither impressed nor silenced. "What we ought to do," said Mike Mansfield of Montana, Democratic leader in the Senate, "is not so much apply pressure in Vietnam as to instead apply pressure in Paris. That is where peace is going to be made, not on the battlefield."

The advocates of withdrawal received some encouragement when Presidents Nixon and Thieu, meeting in Midway Island for the sixth council of Washington-Saigon leaders in three years, announced on June 8 that 25,000 Americans would be pulled out of the war. Not all of them would return directly to the United States; about two-thirds would be redeployed to Japan, Okinawa and Hawaii to stand by for emergencies. The bulk of the departures would come from the 9th Division and the 9th Marine Regimental Landing Team and the movement would be completed by August.

The significance of the withdrawal was not the number involved (less than five per cent of American strength, 542,000 men at peak in February), but the fact that it reversed the flow of troops after years of buildup.

In deciding to begin withdrawal, President Nixon faced two problems. He had to avoid any implication of abandoning the Saigon government with consequent damage to morale in the South, and he had to be careful not to undermine the Washington-Saigon bargaining position at Paris. His solution was to seek Saigon's approval for each move and to confront Hanoi with the prospect that, while he was meeting the demand of war critics at home, he was leaving Saigon in position to wage prolonged war. Thus, he hoped, Hanoi would be persuaded to turn from the battlefield to diplomatic and political maneuver.

The key to withdrawal was the readiness of South Vietnam's army to take on more of the world's responsibilities. It had been recognized for months that a reduction of U.S. strength was in the offing. Thieu had said on Jan. 18 that some American combat troops would leave during the year, and he added that Saigon's soldiers were ready to "alleviate the burden for United

States troops." In June, military chiefs who had been opposing any withdrawal were reported as resigned to the inevitable.

It was acknowledged generally that South Vietnam's army was improving. Brig. Gen. James V. Galloway, director of military aid, said in May: "The improvement is steady. In some units, it is significant. Across the board . . . they've shown steady progress in capabilities and effectiveness. There has been great improvement in the regional (militia) forces, due primarily to confidence in improved weaponry."

The reference to weaponry was important. An argument in defense of the Saigon soldier always had been that his equipment was sadly inferior to that of his American brother-in-arms. Now the lack was being remedied. A report in May said that South Vietnam's air force of 18,000 men would nearly double in the next 12 months. U.S. artillery and shells were going to the infantry. The militia was getting M16 rifles. Rivercraft were being assigned to the navy as fast as crews could be trained.

Still, doubts persisted. A survey in June by the New York Times found that the performance in combat of South Vietnam units was "still spotty, ranging from good to abysmal." There were "grievous shortages" of capable officers and "crippling deficiencies" in materiel. "Intensive efforts to correct the shortcomings" were under way, "financed almost entirely by the United States."

Some people, in and out of Congress, wanted Washington to set its own pace in withdrawals to force the issue of a Saigon takeover. On June 18, Clark Clifford, Secretary of Defense in the last year of the Johnson Administration, enlisted in that camp. Writing in Foreign Affairs, quarterly publication of the Council on Foreign Relations, he said orders should be issued "to reduce the level of combat" and to begin a program that would pull out 100,000 Americans by the end of 1969 and "all ground combat forces" by the end of 1970. The United States should continue "to provide the armed forces of the Saigon government with logistic support and with our air resources."

Clifford once had been regarded as a hawk. He had opposed a bombing recess in 1965 and he had argued for pressure on Saigon to support American peace initiatives. Now, he recalled that a trip to Vietnam in July 1968 had left him depressed by "the pervasive Americanization of the war," plus the conclusion that "the South Vietnamese leaders seemed content to have it that way."

"Nothing we might do," he went on, "could be so beneficial or could so add to the political maturity of South Vietnam as to begin to withdraw our combat troops. Moreover, in my opinion, we cannot realistically expect to achieve anything more through our military force, and the time has come to begin to disengage."

President Nixon was moved to rebuttal. "I would hope that we could beat Mr. Clifford's timetable," he told a news conference and a national television audience on June 19, "just as I think we've done a little better than he did when he was in charge of our national defense." He said "another decision" on withdrawals would be made in August.

Some reporters and commentators took the Nixon remarks as a commitment and said he had at least implied that he expected to bring 200,000 men home in the current year. White House aides and other Administration officials hastened to correct such an impression, privately but urgently. The comment, they said, was not a commitment, a schedule or a timetable; only a hope.

Hope. It was a word associated with Vietnam many times in the past and one which most times had gone unrealized.

"A Tragic and Unfortunate Episode"

A storm over a fee for Justice Abe Fortas swept him from Supreme Court and stirred a cry for a code of judicial ethics

NOBODY KNEW it at the moment, but when Justice Abe Fortas took his regular seat at the May 5 session of the U.S. Supreme Court he was wearing his judicial robe for the last time. Ahead were 11 days of turmoil, at the peak of which he resigned—the first member of the court ever to quit under criticism.

People in the courtroom disagreed about Fortas' demeanor on that May day. Some thought he showed no signs of strain. Others said he seemed distracted, "putting his glasses on and taking them off all the time." To those who felt he displayed uneasiness, his manner could have been significant of things to come.

On Saturday night, two days before Fortas made his final appearance on the bench, newsmen had learned the contents of an article to be published May 5 in Life magazine. It reported that in 1966 Fortas had accepted a $20,000 check from the family foundation of financier Louis Wolfson.

On Sunday, Fortas acknowledged in a statement that a fee had indeed been "tendered" by the foundation "in the hope that I would find time and could undertake, consistently with my court obligations, studies and writings connected with the work of the foundation . . . in the field of harmonious racial and religious relations."

Fortas said he later had returned the fee, after deciding that he could not take the assignment. He did not mention the amount of the fee, nor did he confirm Life's assertion that the check was retained for 11 months, until after Wolfson had been indicted on a charge of stock manipulation. Wolfson was convicted of violating the securities laws and, when the Supreme Court refused on April 1 to consider an appeal, he went to prison.

The justice did deny any impropriety, saying he never had used his influence as a judge in Wolfson's behalf and taking note that, as Wolfson's former counsel, he had disqualified himself whenever matters affecting the financier were before the court.

Even before the $20,000 fee was disclosed, the 58-year-old justice had been assailed by rumors and innuendo concerning his extra-judicial activities. Many more conjectures and questions would fill the air, along with outright attacks by members of Congress, during the period between his last day in court and May 14, when he resigned his seat.

The legal career of Abe Fortas had been spectacular. From a brilliant and promising young lawyer, he soon became a prominent—and prosperous—Washington counselor. His wife,

A letter from Justice Fortas: ". . . I've sent a letter of resignation . . ."

Carolyn Agger, also an attorney, was well established as a tax expert.

Following his appointment to the Supreme Court, most of his associates had felt that Fortas had weathered his greatest storm when the Senate refused to confirm his nomination as chief justice (The World in 1968, 210–213). They believed he was settling down to long service as a scholarly, liberal associate justice with an exceptional knowledge of the law.

From the outset, President Nixon appeared determined to disassociate himself from the furor. Various spokesmen hinted that the President feared that the image of the nation's highest court might suffer severely unless the matter was concluded. Another opinion held that Nixon did not wish to create the impression that he was trying to change the liberal atmosphere in the court.

Sen. Robert Griffin, R-Mich., told newsmen on May 7 that "only the tip of the iceberg" had emerged. In 1968, Griffin had led the movement to block Fortas' nomination by President Lyndon B. Johnson to succeed Chief Justice Earl Warren, then 77 and anxious to retire. But the Senate refused to consider the nomination and Fortas' name ultimately was withdrawn at his request.

By May 9, more congressmen were insisting upon a full disclosure by the beleaguered jurist. Accompanying the demands were unconfirmed reports that fellow justices had asked Fortas to spell out his relationship with Wolfson. Then, on May 12, Atty. Gen. John N. Mitchell confirmed a report that he had given secret government information on Fortas' affairs to Chief Justice Warren. Mitchell said his meeting with Warren took place at his own request because "as a courtesy to the Chief Justice, I felt it incumbent upon me to inform him

of certain information known to me which might be of aid to him." The Justice Department then announced it would have nothing further to say about the meeting, although it was known that the department's criminal division had begun investigating reports about Fortas even before Life reported the Wolfson Foundation transaction.

Mitchell's disclosure served to compound the rash of rumors about the wealthy justice's plans and the general clamor for a full explanation of his financial situation. Fortas nonetheless held to the policy of silence he had adopted soon after his reply to Life.

When he went to Northeastern University in Boston to deliver a lecture, he refused to answer questions. Instead, he offered a quip to the cluster of about 50 reporters and photographers: "I can't imagine why all this interest!"

The scene was virtually repeated when Fortas went to Memphis, his home town, to make another speech. Again he refused to answer questions. And, upon his return to Washington, he was equally noncommittal with two reporters who met him at the airport. "I don't see why you fellows came out," he said, smiling.

In a Senate speech on May 11, Sen. James B. Allen, D-Ala., flatly urged Fortas to resign. Allen was echoed the next day by Sen. Joseph D. Tydings, D-Md., who told a news conference: "Mr. Justice Fortas must resign. . . . I have concluded that no explanation at this point can remedy the damage which has been done to our entire judicial system." Less than a year earlier, Tydings had supported Fortas' nomination as chief justice.

As the tempest intensified, Rep. Clark MacGregor, R-Minn., became perturbed about the hints of secrets still untold in the mass of piecemeal revelations. The congressman, a Scottish Presbyterian, told Rep. Gerald Ford of Michigan, Republican leader in the House, that he was convinced some way should be found to bring all the facts about Fortas into the open. When MacGregor told Ford he planned to call for an investigation by the House Judiciary Committee, Ford advised him to go ahead, but to inform the attorney general about his plan. Mitchell offered no objection.

Meanwhile, Iowa's Rep. Gross was holding back introduction of articles of impeachment. Fortas made such proceedings unnecessary when he telephoned the Supreme Court press officer on May 15 and said:

"I'd like you to call the wire services and the news people and tell them that I've sent a letter of resignation to the White House. It was delivered last night."

Fortas' letter of resignation was immediately—and briefly—accepted by President Nixon, who replied: "I have received your letter of resignation and I accept it, effective as of its date."

Although many questions about the affair remained unanswered, the President's press secretary then announced that the case was closed.

In contrast to the White House exchange, a detailed memorandum to Warren said Fortas was resigning so that "the court may not continue to be subjected to extraneous stress which may adversely affect the performance of its important functions." Fortas added:

"Since becoming a member of the court I have not, at any time, directly or indirectly, received any compensation from Mr. Wolfson or members of his family or any of his associates for advice, assistance or any reason whatever, except the foundation fee that was returned. . . ."

Fortas also said that the Wolfson Foundation's board, meeting in 1965 before he became a justice, had formulated a program to improve community relations and promote racial and religious understanding. This was a field in which Fortas said he was interested because there would be "no conflict between it and my judicial duties."

"In January 1966," Fortas continued, "I received a check for $20,000 under the agreement, and began my association with the foundation. . . . Later, in June 1966, I reached the decision that the continuing role in the foundation's work which our agreement contemplated should be terminated."

And so was ended also the career of Mr. Justice Fortas on the nation's highest tribunal, an office to which he had been appointed by his old friend President Johnson (*The World in 1965, 134*).

About the same time, another incident involving the outside activities of a Supreme Court justice came to public attention. He was William O. Douglas. Fortas had been a student of Douglas at Yale law school, and the two had known each other for more than 30 years.

Douglas had written a letter to the Albert Parvin Foundation in Los Angeles, of which Douglas had been president for an annual salary of $12,000. The letter turned up in a packet of documents which multimillionaire Parvin had delivered to The New York Times, ostensibly to show that, despite a three-year Internal Revenue Service investigation, the foundation was innocent of any irregularities.

The Douglas letter told Parvin that the IRS inquiry was "a manufactured case. . . . The strategy is to get me off the Court. I do not propose to bend to any such pressure."

Not long before, Douglas had told the Parvin foundation he planned to resign as its president and he did so on May 22. But when the Times said his letter to Parvin suggested several ways the foundation could avert further difficulties with IRS, suggestions arose that Douglas might have come into conflict with a law barring judges from practicing law.

Sen. Strom Thurmond, R-S.C., in a newsletter to his home state, made this pronouncement: "Justice Douglas is the next one who must go." The reaction of Rep. Emanuel Celler, D-N.Y., was, "If I was in Justice Douglas' shoes, I would never have written that letter."

At one time Parvin had been named as a co-conspirator with Wolfson in a securities law violation case but never was tried. Investigators claimed that the Parvin foundation derived its income from Las Vegas gambling sources, an allegation also raised in the Wolfson case.

Most observers agreed that, while Douglas was president of the Parvin foundation, he had done no more than carry out the foundation's functions: making grants for meetings of jurists and politicians, and issuing scholarships for foreign students at Princeton University and the University of California at Los Angeles.

One immediate effect of the Fortas-Douglas controversy was a surge of concern about the off-bench activities of justices and judges generally. As early as May 5, the last day Justice Fortas wore his robe in court, Sen. John J. Williams, R-Del., called the Fortas fee a shocking allegation and introduced a bill to confiscate 100 per cent of tax fees paid to public officials by tax-exempt foundations and to punish such foundations by canceling their exemptions.

Citing eight canons, an American Bar Association committee announced on May 20 that Fortas' relationship with Wolfson was "clearly contrary" to the ethical code.

Most significant, perhaps, was a plan which Chief Justice Warren set in motion to devise a code of ethics and regulations for financial disclosures, to affect all federal judges. Warren acted after an 11-member committee of the Judicial Conference met secretly May 25 at the Supreme Court. Both the code and the regulations would comprise the first formal standards of conduct to be established by the federal bench.

The conference laid down its new rules June 10. They forbade all federal judges except members of the Supreme Court to accept outside fees.

Warren thereupon asked his associates on the high court to abide by the restrictions placed upon other federal judges. But a majority of the Supreme Court justices chose instead to defer action until October.

Thus the stage was set for possible conflict with Congress over who should police the nation's federal courts. In this respect, the situation left no assurance that any of the three governmental branches had heard the last of Abe Fortas, Justice Douglas or the tax-exempt foundations.

On the whole, Congress reacted favorably to the Fortas resignation. Chairman Celler of the House Judiciary Committee termed it "best for the country and the Supreme Court," and added that further investigation "would be like feeding on a carcass." Congressman MacGregor, however, insisted upon further investigation. "Notwithstanding Mr. Justice Fortas' resignation," said MacGregor, "the American people are entitled to know all of the relevant facts leading to his decision to resign."

Senator Griffin, Fortas' foe when the justice was nominated to replace Warren, had this to say:

"Although this has been a tragic and unfortunate episode in our history, I am confident the Supreme Court and the judiciary will emerge with the respect, strength and vitality that are so essential in these times."

Next Stop, the Moon!

*"We see no obstacles in the path,"
said U.S. space chief after Apollo 10
had scouted landing site
from 9 miles up and LM had
simulated takeoff for return to earth*

Lᴉᴋᴇ ᴀ roller coaster car on a downhill plunge, the spindly, spidery lunar module swooped toward the moon at 3,700 miles per hour. It leveled less than nine miles above the surface—man's closest approach to earth's heavenly neighbor—and flew parallel to the rugged landscape for a few minutes before swinging into a climb.

Aboard the spacecraft, two astronauts of Apollo 10—Col. Thomas P. Stafford, 38, of the Air Force, and Cmdr. Eugene A. Cernan, 35, of the Navy—were tense and excited as they savored the historic moment in man's invasion of space. After 237,000 miles of flight, they were little higher above the moon than commercial jet planes flew above earth.

"We're right there! We're right over it!" cried Cernan. "I'm telling you we are low, we're close, babe!" "All you have to do," added Stafford, "is put your tail wheel down and we're there."

Cernan and Stafford were near the spot where, if all went well, two other astronauts would make an epochal landing later in the year. Their assignment was to scout the landing site, a relatively flat plain in the lunar area known as the Sea of Tranquillity, photograph it from closer range than ever before, and make visual and radar observations that would smooth the way to a touchdown. Apollo 10 was the final rehearsal, the flight intended to tie together all the threads of preparation for Apollo 11. It was the most ambitious, most dangerous space mission yet undertaken.

Both Cernan and Stafford were veterans in space; so was their colleague, Navy Cmdr. John W. Young, 35, who held the fort in the command ship while his mates went down in the lunar module (LM) for a close look at the moon. This was Stafford's third mission; he had taken part in Gemini 6 which executed the first space rendezvous in December 1965, and he had teamed with Cernan in Gemini 9 less than six months later. Cernan, 32 at that time, was the youngest astronaut ever to fly a mission. Young had flown on Gemini 10 in July 1966, a flight notable for a double rendezvous, first with its own Agena rocket and then with another Agena, a "dead bird" from Gemini 8.

The LM en route from closeup look at moon to rendezvous with command module

100

The bleak and hostile dark side of the moon, photographed from Apollo 10

The astronauts of Apollo 10: from left, Eugene Cernan, Thomas Stafford, John Young

Apollo 10 began flawlessly at 12:49 p.m., May 18, when a giant Saturn 5 blasted the capsule and the rocket's third stage into orbit. After nearly two complete circlings of the globe, the third stage fired to increase Apollo's speed from 17,400 to 24,200 miles per hour and send it hurtling on the road to the moon. Minutes later, the astronauts separated the command ship from the stage, pivoted 180 degrees and crept back to link nose-to-nose with the LM, cradled in a nest atop the exhausted stage which then fell away for its own course through space.

The linkup was pictured live to earth by the first color television camera ever carried on a manned space flight. It was the first of a series of dramatic telecasts which enabled earthlings to share the thrills (and, at times, the terror) experienced by the pilots.

The next transmission showed a shrinking earth behind Apollo 10, brilliant as a blue, brown and white-streaked sphere against a cold, black background. "Just for the record," Cernan commented, "it looks to me like a nice place to live."

The first leg of the flight was uneventful. So accurate was it that only one midcourse correction was needed instead of the anticipated four. From peak speed, Apollo gradually slowed to 2,027 miles per hour at the "equigravisphere," a point 18,339 miles from the moon where the ship came within the clutch of lunar gravity and began accelerating again.

The crew was in high humor. Indeed, the three of them behaved with the exuberance of rookies in space. They exclaimed in wonder at every new sight and experience. They bubbled with excitement, talked incessantly, joked with ground controllers in Houston and serenaded them with appropriate pre-taped tunes like *Up, Up and Away* and *Fly Me to the Moon*. The lighthearted mood was evident even in the naming of their craft for blithe-spirited comic strip characters: The command ship was *Charlie Brown* and the LM was *Snoopy*.

They had reason to be cheerful. Unlike previous Apollo crews, they were not bothered by colds or nausea, a relief attributed to a relaxed training schedule in the days immediately preceding launch. Hydrogen bubbles in drinking water caused some discomfort but medication ended it.

At 4:38 p.m., May 21, Apollo 10 slipped behind the moon, out of radio contact with earth. Seven minutes later, the astronauts triggered the engine which braked their speed from 5,700 to 3,660 miles per hour and sent them into lunar orbit. Mission Control and the world waited in suspense for another 24 minutes before they knew whether the maneuver had succeeded. As the ship again came into view, Stafford radioed the good news: "You can tell the world we have arrived." They settled into an orbit 69 miles above the surface.

Before they went to sleep, the three transmitted another fascinating TV program to the earth they had left behind. For 29

A first in space: Astronaut Young's shave

Three Astronauts on a raft await recovery 'copter

Jubilation at Mission Control

minutes, their camera showed a bleak, barren lunarscape of crater-pocked plains, boulder-strewn plateaus, rugged mountains; they marveled at boulders 20 to 50 stories high, canyons a mile deep.

They accompanied the pictures with commentary. "The color looks a brownish gray to us," Young said. "Boy, this moon is lit up like a Christmas tree. . . . I don't mean lit with lights, but it sure is brilliantly illuminated from the earth."

Stafford commented. "Looking at some of the mountains we see, it's going to be a real trick to go down there."

All were struck by the startling, sudden earthrise. "It comes up fast—boom—not like a sunrise or a moonrise," said Stafford.

They were awake early on May 22 to prepare for the most important and most perilous task of the mission—the survey of the landing site for Apollo 11. Stafford and Cernan wiggled through four feet of 32-inch tunnel which connected command ship and LM. In the tunnel, they found their first trouble. During the pressurization of the module, thermal insulation on the sides of the tunnel had loosened, allowing snowy particles of fiberglass to float free in the weightless atmosphere.

The drifting debris was not only a nuisance in causing the astronauts to itch; it clogged a tiny tunnel vent used in depressurization. If the astronauts did not get rid of the extra pressure of oxygen, they would not be able to separate the two craft in safety.

Experts on the ground, working furiously, produced a solution. The crew was told to open the sealed LM hatch, allowing the oxygen in the tunnel to flow into the module where the pressure was lower. The excess oxygen then was dumped into space through LM's vent system.

With one problem solved, another popped up. The docking ring that connected *Snoopy* and *Charlie Brown* had slipped three degrees, with consequent strain on the docking mechanism. Just before Apollo 10 disappeared behind the moon where the undocking was to take place, Mission Control advised not to try it if the twist reached 6.5 degrees.

It was hold-your-breath for 40 minutes of flight behind the moon. Then: "We're about 30 or 40 feet away from *Charlie Brown* and keeping station," Cernan radioed. "Very good, *Snoopy*," said Mission Control, with relief. Seconds later, a vivid color picture of the four-legged *Snoopy* as seen from the command ship was flashed to earth, more than a quarter million miles away.

With Young alone in the command ship, the two craft flew in formation for several minutes. The astronauts did not want to get too far apart until they were sure all systems were working. The LM was built to operate only in airless space and could not return the two pilots to earth. Stafford and Cernan had to get back to the command capsule.

There was a sudden chill as Young reported trouble with a radar transponder, essential to rendezvous.

"How about trying to recycle the power switch?" queried Mission Control. The transponder began to work. "I could kiss you," Cernan radioed.

LM's men were ready as the two ships drifted apart. Once again the critical engine firing that would initiate the daring descent occurred behind the moon. Because of the different orbits, Young emerged 83 seconds sooner and reported: "They are down there among the rocks, rambling among the boulders."

An excited Stafford chimed in: "There are enough boulders around here to fill up Galveston Bay. It's a fascinating sight. Okay, we're coming up over the site. There are plenty of holes there. The surface is actually very smooth, like a very wet clay—with the exception of the bigger craters."

They were 47,000 feet above the Sea of Tranquillity, four miles south of the actual landing site, instead of directly over it, as had been planned. Irregularities in the moon's gravitational field had tugged their orbit southward, and Stafford reported later he would have had a difficult time landing if that had been Apollo 10's goal.

A major goal for Apollo 10 was knowledge of the gravitational problem that would enable future crews to cope with it. As a result of the experience, Stafford reported later, "We see no reason why we can't put Apollo 11 right on the landing spot."

As they left Tranquillity, Stafford and Cernan ignited their engine to send the craft into a looping orbit from 219 miles altitude to another low pass at a height of 13 miles. During that sweep, they would fire the ascent engine, the powerplant designed to lift explorers from the moon and leave the four-legged descent section on the lunar surface.

The astronauts were preparing to blow the explosive bolts that would release the descent section when an explosive "son of a bitch" came from Cernan for all the world to hear. *Snoopy* had begun to pitch and yaw, violently, terrifyingly. Stafford wrestled with the manual hand control, managed to stabilize the bucking vehicle in eight seconds. Cernan's heart beat jumped from his normal 80 beats per minute to 129. "I don't know what the hell that was, babe," Cernan told ground control, "but that was something. We were wobbling all over the skies."

Analysis disclosed a short circuit in the guidance system. Instead of stabilizing the LM at the attitude for separation, it had turned the radar in search of Young and the command ship, still in its 69-mile orbit.

(Cernan's exclamation and other earthy language attracted

much comment and some criticism. At a postflight news conference, Cernan told "those who were offended" that, "I can only say sincerely, from all of us, 'We're sorry'.")

After the brief scare, the astronauts separated the two sections of LM, fired the ascent engine and flew perfectly to a rendezvous with Young four hours later. When the two ships again were locked in company, Stafford reported, "*Snoopy* and *Charlie Brown* is hugging each other. We is back home—almost."

Then the astronauts spent a third, comparatively leisurely day circling the moon, photographing potential landing sites, studying lunar landmarks and perfecting techniques for navigating in the lunar environment.

At 6:20 a.m., May 24, they ended the 61½-hour flirtation, firing their rocket engine to start the 246,000-mile homeward journey.

As they streaked toward planet earth, they pointed the television camera at the rapidly receding moon and shared their thoughts with all mankind.

Earth rises above dark side of moon, seen from Apollo 10's command module

Stafford showed two adjacent dry plain areas, describing one as "chocolate brown in color and the other tannish brown . . . The moon is set against the blackest black you ever saw. It's jet black." Awed by the sight, he added: "It makes you realize how far we've come in a few years and makes you wonder how much farther we'll go in the next few years."

"You've often heard the nursery rhyme about the man in the moon," Young said. "We didn't see one here but pretty soon there will be two men on the moon."

"I've always believed that nothing is impossible and now I'm convinced of it," Cernan said. "I hope that what we're doing here and what's going to go on in the future is going to be something that's going to be a betterment to all mankind."

The 54-hour homeward flight was as perfect as the outward segment. Once again only one small midcourse engine correction was needed.

That put them "right down the slot" for re-entry and, on May 26, eight days, three minutes and 25 seconds after blast-

off from Cape Kennedy, they splashed down in the Pacific Ocean within three miles of the main recovery ship, the carrier *Princeton.* The flight had endured a mere 35 seconds less than the time calculated by mission planners months earlier.

Television cameras on the deck relayed the stirring scene to viewers in the United States and Europe as Apollo 10 floated back to earth, dangling under three large orange and white parachutes. Just 39 minutes after splashdown, the spacemen were on the carrier and were pronounced in better physical shape than any of the three earlier Apollo crews.

President Nixon talked with the new space heroes by radio-telephone and told them: "This is a proud moment for the country."

Back in Houston, Dr. Thomas O. Paine, administrator of the National Aeronautics and Space Administration, said: "The Apollo 10 crew are the pioneers who have brought man to the threshold of a new era. Today we see no obstacles on the path to the moon."

Questions, Questions....

James Earl Ray pleaded guilty in assassination of Dr. Martin Luther King but suspicion persisted that the whole truth had not been told

James Earl Ray (center) and escort

James earl ray did not look like a hardened criminal. Spectacled, dark haired, husky, he could have passed for a respectable middle class businessman.

James Earl Ray also was suspicious and secretive, and he knew the answers to some puzzling questions. He could, if he would, have told the full truth of his role in the assassination of the Rev. Martin Luther King Jr. at Memphis, Tenn., on Thursday, April 4, 1968.

Had Ray acted on his own motion, alone? Had powerful forces worked behind the scenes? Were there men on the streets with blood on their hands, unknown and unpunished? Why did this man arise from nowhere to slay the apostle of nonviolence in the cause of civil rights?

The worst and the best that could be said of James Earl Ray was that he was a workaday criminal. He had been a burglar. He had been an armed robber. He was hardly a sensation as either.

When he escaped from the Missouri State Penitentiary at Jefferson City, Mo., on Sunday, April 23, 1967, no hounds bayed on his trail. Said Warden Harold E. Swenson: "He was an innocuous man. He drew attention only because of previous attempts to escape." The reward for his capture: $50.

One year later, when he was identified as the sniper who killed Dr. King, he was, without a doubt, the most wanted man in the Western world. It was a massive manhunt. Ray's photo and description were broadcast. He was hunted in places he was known to have visited, Mexico and Canada, as well as many states of the United States. The trail led to Portugal and finally to London where, on June 8, 1968, James Earl Ray fell into the hands of Scotland Yard. *(The World in 1968, 75–83).*

How could a man such as Ray have arranged to get false identities, get a passport, pay for his travel? Could he really have done it all alone? And if he was alone, in the planning of the crime as well as in the execution, why did he do it?

To a world hungry for answers, there always remained a promise that some might come in the give-and-take of an open trial. One trial, set for November 1968, was postponed. Ray had dismissed his lawyer, Arthur Hanes, onetime mayor of Birmingham, and the new defense chief, Percy Foreman of Houston, a noted lawyer, needed time to conduct his own investigation and prepare the defense.

Judge W. Preston Battle of the Criminal Court of Shelby County, Tennessee, set a style for decorum. He wanted the case to come to trial—but he also was determined that it should not be conducted in a circus atmosphere. The judge told the prosecution and defense to be ready for trial on Monday, March 10, 1969.

And to those mystified Americans troubled by dark conviction that much was being concealed, there came again the hope that a court trial—with the drama of examination and cross-examination, with lawyers gesturing with spectacles or leaping from chairs to make thunderous objections, with experts explaining graphs and montages and mockups—might finally produce the answers.

It was not to be.

Foreman told Ray, in effect, that he had little chance. The state's evidence was overwhelming; there was the risk, should all defense skills fail, of getting the electric chair. So, plead guilty, escape the chair. Foreman said he'd try for a life sentence. If not that, 99 years at the worst.

Behind-the-scenes maneuvers included seeking the reaction of the Justice Department and of Mrs. Coretta King, widow of Dr. King, among others. Mrs. King, along with others from the Southern Christian Leadership Conference, restated personal dedication to abolition of the death penalty. They did not want to see Ray die in any event.

And so it was settled.

In the *voir dire* of the defendant—the proceeding in which the judge examined the defendant as to his understanding of what was occurring with the change of plea—Judge Battle repeatedly told Ray of his rights. He said that if Ray pleaded innocent to the charge of murder in the first degree, "the burden of proof is on the State of Tennessee to prove you guilty beyond a reasonable doubt and to a moral certainty and the decision of the jury must be unanimous both as to guilt and punishment."

Judge Battle told Ray that if a jury found him guilty, he could seek a new trial. Failing that, he could appeal to the Tennessee Court of Criminal Appeals and the Supreme Court of Tennessee and ultimately seek a review by the Supreme Court of the United States. By pleading guilty, said the judge, Ray would abandon such rights.

"Has anything besides this sentence of 99 years in the penitentiary been promised you to get you to plead guilty? Has anything else been promised you by anyone?" asked the judge.

"No," said Ray.

"Are you pleading guilty to murder in the first degree in this case because you killed Dr. Martin Luther King under such circumstances that would make you legally guilty of murder in the first degree under the law as explained to you by your lawyers?"

"Yes," said Ray.

All was proceeding as had been planned and agreed the day before, Sunday, March 9. Two letters to James Earl Ray, bearing that date, spelled out a private agreement between Ray and attorney Percy Foreman, relating to Foreman's fee. In one letter, signed by both Ray and Foreman, Foreman referred to the guilty plea and the time saved in preparation of a trial, and wrote: "In consideration of the time it will save me, I am willing to make the following adjustment of my fee arrangement with you:

"If the plea is entered and the sentence accepted and *no embarrassing circumstances take place in the court room*, I am willing to assign to any bank, trust company or individual selected by you all my receipts under the above assignment in excess of $165,000." (Italics added).

The second letter, also signed by both, again referred to Ray's courtroom behavior. There was a reference to an advance of $500 to Ray's brother, Jerry, and then the comment: "And this advance, also, is contingent upon the plea of guilty and sentence going through on March 10, 1969, without any unseemly conduct on your part in court."

Now, it was March 10, and Judge Battle had conducted the *voir dire* and James Earl Ray had done nothing "unseemly."

Even with the guilty plea, there still was a procedure to be followed. It was necessary to attest to the fact that the decedent had been alive at a specific time, and then dead. It was necessary to attest to the cause of death. It was necessary to offer proof of the body of the crime and then stipulate what amounted to the state's evidence—evidence which it was prepared to produce for a trial.

Atty. Gen. Phil M. Canale Jr., district attorney of Shelby County, explained the necessity for this procedure and then told the court:

"There have been rumors going all around, perhaps some of you have heard them, that Mr. James Earl Ray was a dupe in this thing or a fall guy or a member of a conspiracy to kill Dr. Martin Luther King Jr. I want to state to you as your attorney general that we have no proof other than that Dr. Martin Luther King Jr. was killed by James Earl Ray and James Earl Ray alone, not in concert with anyone else."

Canale recited the intensive investigation and the massive collection of physical evidence supporting this conclusion.

Percy Foreman then addressed the court: "It took me a month to convince myself of that fact which the attorney general of these United States (Ramsey Clark, at the time), J. Edgar Hoover of the Federal Bureau of Investigation announced last July, that is, what Mr. Canale has told you, that there was not a conspiracy.

"I talked with my client more than 50 hours, I would estimate, and cross examination most of that time, checking each hour and minute, each expenditure of money down to 75 cents for a shave and a haircut pursuing it."

The jury was polled as to its understanding an acceptance of the change of plea and the punishment of 99 years in prison. Then, as the court transcript unfolded:

> "*JAMES EARL RAY—Your Honor, I would like to say something. I don't want to change anything that I have said, but I just want to enter one other thing. The only thing that I have to say is that I can't agree with Mr. Clark.*
>
> "*MR. FOREMAN—Ramsey Clark.*
>
> "*THE COURT—Mr. Who?*
>
> "*JAMES EARL RAY—Mr. J. Edgar Hoover, I agree with all these stipulations, and I am not trying to change anything.*
>
> "*THE COURT—You don't agree with those theories?*
>
> "*JAMES EARL RAY—Mr. Canale's, Mr. Clark's and Mr. J. Edgar Hoover's about the conspiracy. I don't want to add something on that I haven't agreed to in the past.*
>
> "*MR. FOREMAN—I think that what he said is that he doesn't agree that Ramsey Clark is right, or that J. Edgar Hoover is right. I didn't argue that as evidence in this case, I simply stated that under riding the statement of General Canale that they had made the same statement. You are not required to agree with it all.*
>
> "*THE COURT—You still, your answers to these questions that I asked you would still be the same? Is that correct?*
>
> "*JAMES EARL RAY—Yes, sir.*
>
> "*THE COURT—There is nothing in these questions that I have asked you and your answers to them, you change none of them at all. In other words, you are pleading guilty to, and taking 99 years, I think the main question that I want to ask you is this: are you pleading guilty to murder in the first degree in this case because you killed Dr. Martin Luther King under such circumstances that it would make you legally guilty of murder in the first degree under the law as explained to you by your lawyer. Your answer is still yes? All right, sir, that is all.*"

Was this interlude the "unseemly conduct" or "embarrassing circumstances" against which Foreman had warned Ray? If so, it passed without notice. The judicial process continued.

Judge Battle had the curtain speech: "The fact was recognized soon after this tragic murder took place that there was no possible conclusion to the case which would satisfy everybody. It was decided at that time that the only thing the judge could do was try the case as nearly as possible like other cases, and to scrupulously follow the law and his own conscience. This I have done. Memphis has been blamed for the death of Dr. King, to me wrongfully and irrationally. Neither the decedent nor his killer live here, their orbits merely intersected here."

But James Earl Ray had introduced an element of disquietude. What did he mean by his demurrer? What did he mean about not agreeing with the theories of Ramsey Clark and J. Edgar Hoover? Was he saying that a conspiracy did exist?

Ray was on his way to the Tennessee State Penitentiary at Nashville when he bridled at the deal, said it was no good. He said Foreman was fired. He wanted out of the deal.

Elsewhere, discontent and doubt. "Minitrial," was one label put on the March 10 proceeding. Mrs. Coretta King, restating her opposition to the death penalty, said now that other hands were involved in the dirty business.

Again, men wondered aloud whether the plea of guilty was not engineered either to cover up a conspiracy or to put the blame on a man who really was only a dupe.

There were indeed questions that begged for answers. But this did not mean necessarily that, unless the questions were answered, they could be seized upon as evidence of conspiracy. No one had demonstrated with so much as a single piece of evidence that help was involved directly, and with guilty knowledge, in the slaying of Dr. King.

Prison officials were certain Ray had help in escaping from the Missouri penitentiary. But no one had found any evidence that that event—nearly a year before the slaying—had anything to do with it.

The financing of Ray's movements most often intrigued those who wondered how he managed to pay his way. By the best estimates, he spent between $12,000 and $15,000 in the period between his escape, April 23, 1967, and his capture, June 8, 1968. Given the total, the tendency was to assume that he had received money in some large lump sum, or that someone had financed him all along, from the minute he broke out of prison.

But where was the evidence?

To William Bradford Huie, the Alabama author who had exclusive access to Ray under a contract to write Ray's story, the biggest unanswered question related to motive. Huie confessed he began his project with the conviction that a conspiracy existed. But after retracing Ray's trail from escape to capture, he said he found nothing to substantiate the belief.

Huie theorized that Ray—a supporter of George Wallace, the former Alabama governor who sought election as President in the 1968 campaign—felt that the assassination of a key Negro leader such as King would produce cataclysmic rioting which in turn would frighten whites into backing a hardline candidate. Wallace had long been preaching the value and benefit of strict law and order policies to stop crime in the streets.

Huie also contended that Ray felt that Wallace as President would grant him a pardon. When Richard Nixon was elected, according to Huie, Ray wanted his trial postponed from November until after the inauguration in January. The premise was that, with a new administration in office, there might be a different attitude in the courts.

Judge Battle himself wondered in the week after the March 10 hearing whether Americans ever would get the answers to some of the curious things involving Ray. "It seems a miracle to me that he was able to get away from Memphis and reach Atlanta in a white Mustang. I don't know how he could get through an all-points bulletin," said the judge, in one of the last interviews he granted before his death at the end of the month.

An Associated Press inquiry produced the answer: The white Mustang got through because no all-points bulletin had been issued. No roadblocks were established, nor were any particular search-and-seize routines initiated in neighboring states.

On the evening of the slaying, another occurrence lacked full explanation. This was the radio hoax in which at least three

Police on alert at courthouse

police units were preoccupied with the flight of a phantom Mustang. The police were misled by an urgent alarm from a man who began to give a vivid description of a white Mustang moving at high speed. It had already been broadcast on radio news shows that a suspect in the King shooting might be escaping in a white Mustang. The mystery man giving details regarding the high speed Mustang was doing so on a citizen's band channel. The report was picked up by a motorist who flagged a police squad. The police in turn relayed details to the police dispatcher, who put them on the police radio network.

The Associated Press determined that Memphis police as well as the Federal Bureau of Investigation had questioned a high school senior regarding the incident. He was an amateur radio operator with substantial equipment. No charges were placed against him. Authorities said: "We are satisfied to a large degree that he was responsible and that he had no connection with James Earl Ray." But when the youth was questioned a year later at a college far from Memphis, he insisted that he had no role in the matter. He confirmed the keen interest in him by authorities, "But I promise you I had nothing to do with it," he said.

For Ray, there was no halt in his search for a way to reverse the agreement to plead guilty. He had a new team of lawyers and a date to return to court—May 26.

Meanwhile, more facts surfaced about James Earl Ray and his time. He spent hundreds of dollars for camera equipment, including a motion picture camera with a remote control cable—the sort of setup that one might purchase to photograph something from a hidden position. Or, of course, the cable could be used to make photographs of one's self.

Ray also took a correspondence course in locksmithing, a very pragmatic undertaking for a burglar. His progress at first was hardly commendable but then, in February 1968, he began

to show a real interest. "He was a good student," said the director of the school.

The last lesson he completed was the ninth in the course. After Ray was identified as the killer of Dr. King and the FBI began to track down every bit of evidence relating to him, the school director noticed the postmark on the envelope containing the ninth lesson: Atlanta, April 5, 1968—one day after the slaying.

"One can assume that he had either completed the lesson before the killing, or right after it, and then taken the time to mail it from Atlanta, which seems very strange behavior for such a man," said the school director.

There was also an ironic discovery that authorities had a clue to Ray's identity in their hands minutes after he shot Dr. King. Among effects abandoned near the scene was a cheap transistor radio. Laboratory tests found a number etched on the back: 00416. No one knew the significance of the number, and the fact of its existence was not publicized. Only after Ray was identified did the number make sense: It was Ray's prison number in the Missouri State Penitentiary and had been etched onto the case to determine ownership if it was stolen by another inmate.

But whatever the doubts about whether Ray acted alone or in concert with others, whether he was a dupe or decoy, whether he was paid or paid his own way, it remained that no person had come forth, no man had been uncovered, aside from Ray, who had any demonstrable role in the assassination. No single piece of relevant evidence to contradict Ray's guilt or to involve any other person had been produced.

And so, on May 26, James Earl Ray entered the court of Judge Arthur C. Facquin Jr. and asked for a new trial.

The judge said no. Ray was returned to the Tennessee State Penitentiary at Nashville.

"They Have Suffered Enough"

The Secretary of the Navy rejected recommendation
for courts martial and closed the book on the
capture of the USS Pueblo and the captivity of her crew

Cmdr. Bucher and wife

THEY MET, for the first time, as 1966 ended. She was a tired, rusting tramp freighter salvaged from the military's attic; he was a trim, athletic officer fresh from the glamor of the Navy's submarine service.

There was no ceremony. No one piped him aboard at Pier 5 among the cranes and shipways of Puget Sound Naval Shipyard at Bremerton, Wash. Yet, for all the ship's scabby paint and streaks of rust, the man felt pride. This, for the aggressive lieutenant commander, was his first command.

He would have preferred a submarine, but he was all Navy and knew well enough not to question orders. He would make the best of what the Navy gave him. It was the only way. And so did the names Pueblo and Lloyd Mark Bucher become inseparable for history.

On his way to Puget Sound, Bucher had been briefed in Washington, D.C., about his general mission. So he wasn't surprised when a shipyard crane deposited an oblong prefabricated shack on the Pueblo's deck. The workmen who installed it didn't know exactly what it was; they called it the Sod Hut.

Bucher started visiting the Sod Hut almost daily to get acquainted with its electronic equipment and classified publication showing what all the gear could do. A new worry interrupted his concern for getting all of that expensive equipment installed: how to destroy it.

"An explosive destruction means should be provided to the ship which will enable the commanding officer to thoroughly destroy all sensitive classified material quickly should the need arise," he wrote to the Naval Ship Systems Command.

Instead of explosives, Bucher received sledge hammers and fire axes.

Bucher had been orphaned twice—by the death of his mother and the death of his foster mother. He went from an orphanage of Mormon children in Boise, Idaho, to a Catholic children's home at Culdesac, to Boys Town, a Catholic orphanage for boys in Nebraska.

Bucher left Boys Town as a high school senior to enlist in the Navy. He was discharged in 1947 as quartermaster second class, finished high school, then enrolled in the University of Nebraska on a football scholarship.

He liked beer, bawdy jokes, Shakespeare, martinis and a farm girl named Rose Rohling from Jefferson, Mo., whom he met on a blind date and later married.

In July 1953, Bucher was graduated with an ensign's commission in the Naval Reserve. Six months later he was ordered to active service, where he trained for, and fell in love with, submarines.

Across Puget Sound to the shipyard and onto the Pueblo he carried his childhood and his submarine breeding, blended now into a sort of paternalism. He would know his men, teach them, protect them; eventually choose them over his ship; and then suffer with them and suffer because they were suffering. He would feel a responsibility for them that few others ever had felt for him. . . .

The accompanying story of North Korea's capture of the USS Pueblo and the captivity of her crew is a condensation of a narrative by Jules Loh, Sid Moody and Richard E. Myer of The Associated Press. It reconstructs the story from testimony before the Navy's court of inquiry and congressional hearings, numerous interviews and personal research.

In charge of communications was a shy lieutenant named Stephen Harris. He was 32, born and bred in New England in a family of sailing captains whose motto was Amor Patriae Exitat—Love of Country Motivates Me. He was educated at Harvard and was fluent in four foreign languages, including Russian. He liked Rachmaninoff and the esoteric history of street cars. His voice was soft, and he wore black horn-rimmed glasses. Harris was in charge of the Sod Hut, its mysteries and who could come and go through its triple-locked doors.

A dark-haired lieutenant from Principia College, Edward R. Murphy, became Bucher's executive officer. He began handling personnel assignments, manpower authorizations, calibrating navigational equipment and training the crew—particularly in navigation. As executive officer, Murphy would be navigator on the Pueblo.

He came to the Pueblo from the USS Robinson, a destroyer. His entire experience had been with surface ships. And this produced an occasional conflict with his submarine-oriented commanding officer. Murphy was straighter-laced than his captain, too, and perhaps more polished.

Bucher had cause, nonetheless, to respect him. Not many months before, Murphy had been awarded the Navy-Marine Corps medal for saving the lives of three fishermen. He swam through surf and undertow to their capsized boat, carried a line to two of them and helped the third, suffering from shock, back to shore.

It was Saturday, May 13, 1967. "Aye, aye, sir," Bucher replied as a representative of the Navy Department read his orders before an assemblage of brass, friends and kin gathered to wish the Pueblo Godspeed. Then Lt. Cmdr. Lloyd Mark Bucher accepted service into the United States Navy on behalf of his ship, the USS Pueblo. Its ensign was hoisted and Bucher set first watch.

In a simpler time, a sea voyage in a Navy ship was clear cut. In peace: be vigilant. In war: meet the enemy and engage. But 1967 was not a simple time. War had become cold but with an awesomely low boiling point. Armageddon seemingly could spark from the misreading of a crossed wire sending a false signal. And it could come, too, from failure to intercept a true signal.

That was why the Sod Hut was a myriad of electronics, the compact refinement of hundreds of millions of dollars worth of research. For she was a spy ship. Some of her crew—a few —knew it. Some—most—could only swap scuttlebutt.

Yet the Pueblo would go to sea alone, really. Tradition was a safeguard: In 150 years, no American vessel had been seized on the high seas; not since the Civil War had an American vessel struck her colors in the presence of an enemy. The presumption at all levels of authority behind the mission was simply that it wasn't done.

Not until Bucher arrived in Hawaii was he told he would be operating off the coast of Korea, after a stopover in Japan where he was made a full commander. The mission was to be labelled Ichthyic One, more in keeping with the cover as an oceanographic research ship than the original designation—Pinkroot One.

Bucher was ordered to leave Sasebo on Jan. 11, 1968, and sail north about 40 miles offshore of North Korea to avoid radar detection and then move in to listen and watch for shipping activity at Chongjin, Songjin, Mayang Do and Wonsan, the last an active Russian submarine base. Then he was to make for the Tsushima Straits to monitor Russian naval units which had been plotted daily by aircraft. No one was certain why they were there. He was to maintain at least a 500-yard range from them, closing to 200 yards only for photographs. At no time was he to move in closer to land than 13 nautical miles.

* * * *

The *Pueblo's* senior quartermaster, a husky sailor named Charles Law from Chehalis, Wash., saw it first.

About seven miles away, a ship—either a subchaser or a torpedo boat—was standing out from Wonsan and headed their way. Fast. Law called Bucher. The captain told him to call back if the ship got within five miles and to recheck their position (39° 25'N, 127° 35'E) by radar. A quick sweep of the set showed the fix was exact. The stranger kept coming. Bucher went topside and put the ship's "big eyes"—22-inch binoculars—on the vessel and decided she was an SO1, a 147-foot subchaser with 57-mm guns.

At 1,000 yards, the SO1 began circling the *Pueblo.* Her men were at battle stations, her guns trained on the Americans. The SO1 was flying signal flags: "Heave to or I'll fire," then changed to: "Follow in my wake, I have a pilot aboard." Bucher ordered a responding signal: "I am in international waters." Time: 1:05 p.m., Jan 23.

Steve Harris went to the Sod Hut. The operator at the teletype, about to send a situation report to Japan, was ordered to keep the circuit open. Say anything, Communications Technician Don Bailey was told, but don't let anyone else take the circuit.

Three torpedo boats headed toward the *Pueblo*—P4s, 82-footers of Russian design. The SO1 hoisted a new signal: "What nationality?" Bucher responded by breaking out the biggest American flag aboard, the holiday ensign.

The PT boats came up to the SO1 which was circling some 500 yards away. Men in helmets and full battle dress transferred to the smaller ships which had rubber tires and rope mats over their sides for boarding. A fourth P4 showed up. Overhead, two fighter planes—the men believed they were MIG21s—began circling the *Pueblo.*

The SO1, now 3,000 yards astern, began to move. She came at the *Pueblo* at high speed, a 15-foot bone in her teeth. New flags whipped from her signal staff: "Heave to or I will fire." Bucher steamed on.

Bailey to Japan at 1:26—"They plan to open fire on us now. They plan to open fire on us now. They plan to open fire on us now."

The *Pueblo's* guns remained frozen in silence even as the first salvo of eight to 14 shots exploded right over her. Shrapnel hit Bucher six or seven times in the leg and rectum. He fell to the deck. Picking himself up, Bucher, in pain, told the pilot house to order emergency destruction. Then he issued the order for modified general quarters: all hands stay below decks.

The SO1 opened up again. Two MIGs screeched past and fired rockets into the sea ahead of the *Pueblo.* Bucher sailed on.

Bailey: "We are holding emergency destruction. We need help. . . . SOS. SOS. SOS. Please send assistance. . . ."

The SO1 had closed to 800 yards and was firing point blank. The P4s also were shooting from about 30 yards away. Bucher sailed on.

Bucher's primary concern now was to destroy the classified materials. "I really felt strongly about my orders about not provoking an international incident," he said later. "I think this more than anything else guided my actions on this day."

What would happen if the *Pueblo* stopped? Just stopped? Bucher decided to try it. He rang up full stop and the engine room responded instantaneously. So did the North Koreans.

The SO1 wheeled in a spray of foam, sped toward the *Pueblo* and opened up with cannon. The P4s raked the vessel with machine guns.

"Corpsman! Corpsman!"

Duane Hodges' leg was gone and half his abdomen. Hot shrapnel ripped open Steven Woelk's pelvis and cut into his thigh and chest. Blood pulsed from Bob Chicca's thigh and Harry Crandell's legs. Bits of flesh splattered the bulkheads and the passageway, and blood doused burning papers at the door of the Sod Hut.

Bucher ordered the ship under way at one-third speed. As it moved the firing stopped, except for occasional machinegun bursts. At 2:05 p.m., Bucher went to the radio compartment and drafted a hurried message to Japan:

"Have been requested to follow into Wonsan . . . Have three wounded and one man with leg blown off. Have not used any weapons nor uncovered 50-caliber machineguns. Destroying all key lists and as much electronic equipment as possible. How about some help? . . . Do not intend to offer any resistance. . . ."

Japan: "Roger. Roger. We doing all we can. . . . Everyone really turning to and figure by now Air Force got some birds winging your way."

In the pilothouse, Bucher watched the PT boat hoist a familiar semaphore: "Heave to."

He had made his decision. He stopped the *Pueblo.*

"Prepare to receive the North Koreans aboard," he said into the ship's amplifier.

The time was -2:32 p.m. (*The World in 1968,* 20–23.)

The boarders stepped across a little bit of sea between one of the P4s and the *Pueblo.* There were about a dozen of them, dressed in dark green winter uniforms of the North Korean People's Army. The enlisted men had automatic rifles, the officers pistols. As they walked across the deck, Bucher presented himself as the commanding officer. One of the North Koreans put a pistol to his head and ordered him to the pilot house.

He had not resisted the boarding party—despite Navy Regulation 0730 forbidding search. If planes were actually winging his way, he wanted his crew intact to overwhelm the boarders when the planes arrived. And he did not want continuing gunfire to leave his ship helpless should he be able to flee the scene. And there were his orders: no war.

No help came.

Slowly the *Pueblo* headed into Wonsan.

Another torpedo boat backed down, and a second boarding party stepped onto the deck. It included a North Korean colonel with a scar from the top of his head to the nape of his neck—Col. Scar, the men later dubbed him. With him was an interpreter. "Now they're in our country," said the interpreter. "They'll be tried by our laws."

Hodges died at 3 p.m.

At 8:30 p.m., her captors tied up the *Pueblo* in Wonsan Harbor. A North Korean hauled down her colors.

* * * *

The soldiers shoved and kicked their captives in a long stumbling line down the gangway. The last American to leave the ship, bound and blindfolded like all the others, was the captain. The guards herded the crew toward four waiting buses. A thousand or more North Koreans had gathered to view the captives. Lloyd Bucher got a look at them when his blindfold slipped. He was appalled. Men shouted and shook their fists. Women shrieked and spat at the sailors. Children mocked.

In the buses, the Americans were safe from the mob but not from their own fears—and not from the rage of the guards who continued to slap and kick them as they sat in the darkness of their blindfolds and helplessness of their bonds.

A bus ride. A train ride. Another bus ride. At dawn, the trip ended at Pyongyang and a place which would come to be known among the men of the *Pueblo,* and etched in their memories, as "The Barn."

The guards assigned the men four to a room, except for two large rooms where as many as 12 men were confined. After each room was filled, the guards removed the blindfolds and shut the door. No one knew who was in the room next door. Each room thus became its own isolated cell of anxiety. Officers, except for two who wore nothing to identify them, were assigned to separate rooms.

When at last all was quiet in The Barn, a guard opened Bucher's door and led him down the hall to an interrogation room where an interpreter waited with several North Korean officers. The interpreter would earn the nickname Wheezy; he continually tried to cover up his inability to translate rapidly by coughing.

Bucher demanded care for his wounded, demanded to see them, demanded that the crew be kept together. The Communists acted as though they did not hear. For 45 minutes, between coughing fits, Wheezy shouted the accusations: The *Pueblo* had intruded into North Korean waters; it was a spy ship; Bucher was a CIA agent. Bucher uttered denials.

* * * *

That same day, scarcely 100 miles away, at Panmunjom, another American, Vice Adm. John Victor Smith, heard similar accusations from another North Korean, Maj. Gen. Pak Chung-Kook.

"Around 12:15 hours on Jan. 23, your side committed the crude aggressive act of illegally infiltrating the armed spy ship of the U.S. imperialist aggressor Navy equipped with various weapons and all kinds of equipment for espionage into our coastal waters. Our naval vessels returned the fire of the piratical group." Then he got to the heart of the matter: a demand that the United States admit invading North Korean waters, apologize and assure that it would not happen again. That was it—admit, apologize, assure: the Three A's—the policy the North Koreans were not to change for 11 months until the United States did what they asked.

* * * *

Four times Bucher was dragged from his quarters in The Barn and into an interrogation room. There sat a fastidiously groomed North Korean colonel in his early 40s, about five feet one, wearing green tinted glasses. Bucher would come to know the man well during his confinement. He was the colonel in charge of the prison—"Super Colonel" to the men, or for short, Super-C.

Four times Bucher was asked to sign a confession. Three times he refused. Three times he was beaten. The fourth time was different.

"We will now begin to shoot your crew one at a time in your presence, beginning with the youngest, until you sign the confession," said Super-C. He sent a guard to fetch the youngest *Pueblo* crewman. Bucher was stunned.

"No," he whispered, "I'll sign."

Thus in less than 36 hours after the North Koreans accosted

Picket line for the Pueblo

Recreation at recess: pinochle

the *Pueblo* on the high seas Super-C got what he needed: a formal statement signed by the ship's captain admitting espionage and intrusion.

What he wanted was considerably more, and he set out deliberately, methodically, to get that too: an elaboration of the lie.

In the blur of the hours and days that followed, Lloyd Bucher would be forced to copy the typed confession in his own handwriting again and again, to be photographed while copying it, to record it on tape in his own accents. Super-C turned his attention to the other *Pueblo* officers.

As the days passed, torture became more frequent, more cruel. At times the guards placed a stick, a table leg with square corners, behind the prisoners' knees when they squatted so that soon their legs lost all feeling. At other times, the prisoners' upraised hands were bound with wire, or they were forced to hold a chair above their heads while squatting with the stick behind their knees; whenever the chair fell they were kicked savagely. Often the guards stamped on the backs of the captives' legs and ankles, and made them scramble on their knees across the rough floor until their legs were raw and bloody. One marathon session lasted for 39 hours.

Finally all the questionnaires were completed and signed but the North Koreans did not extract from the men any informa-

tion they did not already have in their service records taken from the *Pueblo*.

Later interrogations were far less violent though occasionally the guards would beat someone savagely—to serve, the crew figured, as an example that terror was ever near.

* * * *

Despite numerous acts of defiance against the North Koreans, many *Pueblo* men had courted dishonor. They had broken the military's Code of Conduct for prisoners. Article V of the six-point code said in part: "When questioned, should I become a prisoner of war, I am bound to give only name, rank, service number and date of birth."

But, for all the fear, the beatings, the for-keeps struggle against the tormentors, no one violated Article VI: "If I become a prisoner of war, I will keep faith with my fellow prisoners. I will give no information or take part in any action which might be harmful to my comrades. If I am senior, I will take command. If not, I will obey the lawful orders of those appointed over me, and will back them up in every way."

They remained, to each other, loyal.

That was their strength: They were a crew captured with

morale and command structure intact. And that was their weakness: When the captain broke, they were likely to follow.

* * * *

On the evening of March 5, the 82 men of the *Pueblo* were loaded aboard buses and taken about seven miles to a new place of confinement on the outskirts of Pyongyang. It was a relatively new building, nicer by far than The Barn. The men were quartered eight to a room except for one with four men; the officers had separate rooms. Not only were the accommodations much improved; so was the treatment.

The crew ate in a mess hall instead of their rooms. They received toothbrushes, were allowed to bathe every week or so, get a haircut every two weeks. There were regular periods for recreation and exercise. They were issued a volleyball which the men used as a football until the captors found out they were discussing other matters than plays in the huddle. Then they played soccer.

Life was certainly more tolerable, but they were still prisoners and never were allowed to forget it. Despite the relatively good treatment as contrasted to life in The Barn, there was always present an aura of terror. There would always be someone badly bruised, visible to the rest of the crew.

Bucher also noticed a cyclic repetition of good and bad treatment. For 55–60 days the men would be treated well, for the next 55–60 days, badly.

By late spring, the men began to show the effects of their prison diet, estimated at 500 calories a day. The food was whatever was in season. Some sort of plant resembling spinach. Turnips. Something like cabbage. Something else, the men decided, like grass. They ate three slices of bread a day and an occasional fish.

The ancient diseases of sailors appeared. Scurvy. Diphtheria. Dysentery. Diarrhea. One man developed infectious hepatitis. Another viral meningitis. Another a rash over 90 per cent of his body with running sores. The eyesight of one man failed. Bucher asked, demanded, pleaded that doctors treat his men. Occasionally they did.

In the cycle of good treatment and bad, April and May were bad months except for May Day, when the men were allowed to visit one another's rooms, and June and July were good months. An added reason for the midsummer improvement in prison atmosphere was that Super-C was most happy and self-satisfied. He had been promoted. Now he became GG—Glorious General.

* * * *

On July 16, in the flush of new rank and glory, GG announced to Bucher that the men would be allowed to receive mail. They would be allowed to write home, though of course GG and his men would read each letter and add a few lines of their own. Bucher put out the word: try to discredit every false statement.

The men went to their rooms and set to work. Wheezy, Max, an interpreter called Silver Lips and another known as the Imperialist because when he entered a room he shouted "you imperialist sonabitchee," translated the letters into Korean, and added how kindly the men were being treated. Then the men recopied the letters—three times, as GG was certain the CIA would intercept at least two.

What GG didn't discover was that, in the propaganda portion of one letter, some of the dots over the "i's" were act-

ually dashes, and they spelled in Morse code "This is a lie." Another crewman preceded the propaganda in his letter with the request that his father say hello to an old friend, Garba Gefollows—garbage follows.

At home, the families got the messages.

* * * *

During the era of good feeling, in July, GG enjoyed having long conversations with Bucher. No interrogation, just talk. Bucher expected a reversal of the good treatment to commence in August. To forestall it, during a long session with GG, he said, "General, why don't we have a press conference?"

GG thought it a great idea, and scheduled it for August. The crewmen, watching it on television, were delighted, hardly able to contain themselves as Bucher and the other participants butchered the English language. GG was delighted too. He decided there should be another conference the next month in connection with the 20th anniversary of the founding of his government, and he would invite foreign reporters.

Meanwhile, GG had another chore for the men. He wanted them to write to political figures and news organizations back in America asking them to pressure the government to apologize for what the *Pueblo* had done.

The press conference was held Sept. 12 and while all the crewmen watching it on closed-circuit TV again were able to keep a straight face, many of the foreign correspondents were not. It was so obvious a fraud. But GG was ecstatic. He told everyone that surely the United States would now apologize.

* * * *

GG said he needed one final document from the crew. Well, two. He needed another joint confession of crimes and another joint apology to the Korean government to be used in case the men lied when they got home. Bucher wrote both documents. He read them to the crew.

"The rosy finger of dawn is now replacing the fickle finger of fate upon which we have been rotating for such a long time. . . ." Bucher kept a straight face and read on. He had trusted that the interpreter would run to his English dictionary and look up a certain obscure noun which Bucher would use as a verb, discover that it meant a song of praise, and leave the word in the document. Which the interpreter did. "We not only want to paean the North Korean government," read Bucher, "but paean all the North Korean people."

* * * *

August 29, for Nicholas deB. Katzenbach, Undersecretary of State, was another day to grapple with the problem he had faced for months; how to win freedom for the men of the *Pueblo*. But this day was different. A thought flashed in his mind: what if Maj. Gen. Gilbert H. Woodward, now the U.S. negotiator at Panmunjom, were to ask Gen. Pak: "If we acknowledge receipt of the crew on a document acceptable to you, will you then be prepared to release the crew?"

The genius of the sentence was that it did not commit the United States to sign the North Korean document of May 8 containing the Three A's. But it put the ball squarely in Pak's court. He would have to answer what the U.S. had been seeking to learn for months: What would he do if the Americans signed a document?

On Sept. 17, Pak gave Woodward his answer: "if you sign

our document, we'll give back the crew." There were still barriers. At the end of October there was a stalemate. In November there were no negotiations.

* * * *

In November at Pyongyang, the food suddenly reverted to turnips. Weekly political lectures stopped. GG quit calling on Bucher for friendly conversation. Silence chilled the camp.

"It's going to be a long, cold winter," Bucher mused.

Then GG told Bucher that he and all his men would have to write sincere statements confessing all the "crimes" they had committed while in detention and all those that they knew others had committed and to turn in the statements the following morning. It was a week before the North Koreans translated all the confessions, then told the crewmen these were not sincere, that they would have to write others. And others. The Koreans, to emphasize that they meant business, methodically beat the crewmen.

"It was," said Bucher, "the most concentrated form of terror I've ever seen or dreamed possible." The brutality was unspeakable, the terror constant. Then, as suddenly as it had begun, the 10 days of terror which the men of the *Pueblo* would forever refer to as "Hell Week," just as suddenly ended.

Back in Washington, just before Hell Week, Katzenbach's team was going through some frustration of its own. The planners had pretty much decided the North Koreans were not going to accept any proposal: They would wait out the change in administration, or at least wait until the last days of Johnson's presidency to see if he'd soften at the eleventh hour.

One night in November, Jim Leonard, the State Department officer for Korea, took the problem home with him. He talked it over with his wife. What, she said, if you just formally state that what you are about to sign is false, then you don't jeopardize the record?

On Dec. 17, Pak agreed to the pre-repudiative statement. Why?

"I think the North Koreans knew what they had to deal with in President Johnson," said Leonard. "They knew he hadn't taken any military action against the seizure. Nixon was an unknown quantity. Also, they had gone about as far as they could in extracting propaganda value from the men and in disrupting U.S.-R.O.K. relations."

* * * *

At 9 a.m. on Dec. 22, Gen. Woodward began to read a statement born of a Washington housewife's question:

"The position of the United States Government with regard to the *Pueblo* as consistently expressed in the negotiations at Panmunjom and in public, has been that the ship was not engaged in illegal activity, that there is no convincing evidence that the ship at any time intruded into the territorial waters claimed by North Korea, and that we could not apologize for actions which we did not believe took place. The document which I am going to sign was prepared by the North Koreans and is at variance with the above position, but my signature will not and cannot alter the facts. I will sign the document to free the crew and only to free the crew."

Then he signed.

For two and one-half hours, the men of the *Pueblo* had waited in buses. They were told how to cross over the line; no talking, no running, no looking back, no gestures. If any one violated the rules, he would be taken back to North Korea.

Finally, shortly after noon on Dec. 23, eleven months to the day and almost to the hour after it had all begun, the men of the *Pueblo* began to walk across the Bridge of No Return, into South Korea. Hodges' body was carried across first; then Bucher marched, at the head of his men. Whatever else he had done, Cmdr. Lloyd Bucher had brought his men back. *(The World in 1968, 257–259)*

A Navy court of inquiry met at Coronado, Calif., in January. The hearings went on for eight weeks with the admirals showing they could be stern with their own by questioning Rear Adm. Frank L. Johnson, commander in chief of the Pacific Fleet, as to why no help was sent to the *Pueblo*.

Bucher tried to appear firm, in command. But his lips sometimes trembled. His voice broke and faded. He wept. His face was the only witness needed to tell the torment of the voyage and of the *Pueblo* and of her commander.

His civilian attorney, E. Miles Harvey, called the court " . . . a cruel business . . . It cannot bring back Duane Hodges, cause the return of the *USS Pueblo*, completely heal the scars that many of the crew will carry for the rest of their lives. Probing into disasters at sea may seem merciless because, almost everywhere else, we, as a nation, have abandoned the requirement of accountability. However, on the sea there is a tradition older even than the traditions of our nation and wiser in its trust than our new morality. It is the tradition that, with authority goes responsibility and with responsibility goes accountability."

When the court closed in mid-March, the verdict was expected in two weeks. It came in nearly two months. The court ultimately recommended a general court martial for Bucher and Steve Harris: the skipper for permitting search of his vessel, for following the SO1 into Wonsan, for failing to complete destruction and not properly drilling the crew to do so. Harris was to be tried for dereliction of duty in not taking effective destruct action, failing to inform Bucher of unspecified deficiencies in the intelligence section and for not drilling his men in destruction. Murphy was to get a letter of admonition for failing "to organize and lead the crew on the day of the seizure."

Adm. Johnson was to receive a letter of reprimand for failing to plan effective emergency support, as was Capt. Everett B. Gladding, former director of the Naval Security Group in the Pacific, for failure to coordinate back-up intelligence support to the *Pueblo* and insure the readiness of the men of the Sod Hut for their mission.

Then on May 6, John H. Chafee, Secretary of the Navy, announced the court's conclusions—and his. There would be no court martial for any one, no letter of reprimand for any one.

As for Adm. Johnson and Capt. Gladding, Chafee said: "The consequences must be in fairness borne by all, rather than one or two individuals whom circumstances had placed closer to the crucial event." The secretary said he was not passing judgment on the guilt or innocence of Bucher, Harris or Murphy. He said, simply, "they have suffered enough."

He did note that the admirals of the court had found that during detention Bucher "upheld morale in a superior manner . . . he contributed to the ability of the crew to hold together."

One day after Chafee's announcement, Bucher was reassigned to the Navy's post-graduate school to work on a master's degree in business administration. Steve Harris was assigned to intelligence in Washington. Murphy decided to quit the Navy, as 39 shipmates had already done. Only one of the 82 crewmen, Wendell Leach, a signalman, was ordered back to sea.

THE OLD CELTICS ARE THE CELTICS OF OLD

This was the year, the experts said, when the domination of the National Basketball Association by the Boston Celtics finally would be ended. They had finished no better than fourth in the Eastern Division over the season. They had lost more games than they won through the second half of the schedule. Their regular players averaged 31 years: they were old and tired. So went the arguments.

Murmurs of mild astonishment were heard when Boston eliminated the Philadelphia 76ers, four games to one, in the first playoff round. No matter. The New York Knickerbockers certainly would take care of the Celtics. The Knicks were fresh from four straight victories over the Baltimore Bullets who had come from last place in 1967-'68 to top the Eastern standing in 1968-'69. Moreover, New York had beaten Boston in six of seven seasonal meetings.

The Knicks found out that the old Celtics were once again the Celtics of old. They erased New York four games to two, and suddenly the Los Angeles Lakers stood alone between Boston and an 11th league championship in 13 years. By something more than coincidence, those 13 years represented the career of defensive demon Bill Russell with the Celtics, first as a player and then, for three years, as a player-coach.

The Lakers had reached the finals by conquering the San Francisco Warriors, four games to two, and the Atlanta Falcons, four to one. They had faced the Celtics in five previous years and had lost five times. But in 1969, the Lakers had a third ace—Wilt Chamberlain—to play alongside their high-powered duo of Jerry West and Elgin Baylor.

When Los Angeles obtained Chamberlain in a trade with Philadelphia, the popular impression was that the 7-foot center made the Lakers unbeatable. The going wasn't as easy as predicted. Chamberlain's ideas of his duties did not always coincide with the ideas of Coach Bill van Breda Kolff, and reports were heard of other internal troubles. Nevertheless, the team shook off early lethargy and won the Western title handily.

The first two games of the final series went according to script. Celtic defenses could not effectively harness the high-powered Lakers. They collected 15 points per game above the average for Boston opponents in 11 previous playoff tussles. In particular, the Celtics could not harness Jerry West. He scored 53 points in the first game, 41 in the second, and went on to set a record with 556 points in 18 playoff games. The scores were 120-118 on April 23 (a game in which the lead changed hands 21 times and was tied 15 times). and 118-112 on April 25.

The pattern changed when the scene shifted to Boston. In both the third and fourth games, Boston jumped into command, faded in the heat of a furious Los Angeles spurt, then rallied to win, 111-105 on April 26 and 89-88 on April 29. Larry Siegfried, a guard who had lost his starting job to Emmette Bryant, came off the bench to pump accurate jump shots at critical times and· joined John Havlicek, a tower of Boston strength, in pacing the home team. The second Boston victory in particular was a thriller; the lead changed nine times in the fourth quarter before Sam Jones, playing his last games before retirement, sank a long

jump shot with two seconds to play. Actually, the game was won at the foul line: The Celtics cashed 27 of 31 opportunities while the Lakers, with the same number of chances, made good on only 18.

Back in Los Angeles on May 1, the Lakers rolled up the biggest margin of the series, 117-104, but the victory was costly: West pulled a hamstring muscle late in the fourth period. The effect was apparent in the sixth game at Boston on May 3. West scored 26 points— tied with Baylor for the game's high—but he limped and his mobility was impaired noticeably. Boston rushed into an early lead and kept control all the way to a 99-90 decision. Another Boston substitute, Don Nelson, led his team with 25 points and Siegfried heroics again were in evidence.

In the decisive seventh game at Los Angeles on May 5, a remarkable performance by West was not enough to overcome Boston's smart, opportunistic team play. Despite his limp, West scored 42 points and won an automobile offered by Sport magazine to the outstanding player in the series.

Hot shooting by Bryant, Jones and Havlicek carried the Celtics to an early lead; the Lakers closed the gap to three points at half time. Late in the third quarter, with the Celtics seemingly again in command at 91-74, both Russell and Havlicek were tagged with their fifth fouls and the Celtics lost momentum.

Then Chamberlain also collected a fifth foul and, in addition, injured a knee when he came down with a rebound. Van Breda Kolff kept him on the bench through the final five minutes in a controversial piece of strategy but the Lakers began moving again.

With three minutes to play, Boston's lead was a thin one point, West had a hot hand, and the Celtics were all but exhausted. With 1:17 to go, a Boston pass from out of bounds was deflected from Havlicek's grasp right into the hands of Nelson at the foul line. His shot hit the basket's rim, bounced and fell through for 105-102. With 24 seconds left, two free throws by the omnipresent Siegfried sewed it up and the Lakers' final four points were useless except to make the final score close, 108-106. It was the seventh time that Boston played a seventh game and won.

EPILOGUE. On May 19, Van Breda Kolff resigned as coach of the Lakers "in the best interests of all concerned." Two days later, he signed to coach the Detroit Pistons; Joe Mullaney, coach at Providence College in Rhode Island for 14 years, succeeded him at Los Angeles. . . . On July 30, Bill Russell announced his retirement, with one year still to go on a two-year contract as player-coach. "I've lost my competitive urges," he wrote in a copyrighted article in Sports Illustrated. "I just don't feel like playing any more."

A scramble for a rebound

YORTY WINS AGAIN

Why would Sam Yorty have wanted a third term as mayor of Los Angeles? As a lawyer, he said, he could make much more money than the mayor's $35,000 a year. The view from his hilltop home could only remind him of civic problems badgering him at City Hall:

—A busting-out-all-over population of nearly three million, growing by an estimated 980 per week, in the nation's third largest city.

—Skies filled with gray-brown smog, 13,500 tons of it pouring into the atmosphere daily, 90 per cent from automobiles.

—Nearly 4.5 million motor vehicles throughout the county, many of them congealing in exasperating, bumper-to-bumper jams at rush hours along the city's 136 miles of freeways.

Though lacking authority over smog and transportation, in a welter of city, county and state jurisdictions, Yorty should exert stronger leadership in those areas, critics said. But Yorty claimed, "We've done pretty well with the problem-solving here." He took pride in top-rated fire and police departments . . . racially integrated city commissions . . . city hiring of minorities

. . . a human relations bureau "quietly and effectively doing an outstanding job". . . . a financially self-sustaining harbor and airport . . . a $38.5 million convention center rising downtown . . . and the fact that there had been no teacher or garbage-collector strikes like New York's.

Yorty said "a tremendous number of people" asked him to run again, but the main fact was that he loved political battle. In junior high school in his native Lincoln, Neb., he was elected student-body president and wrote in an essay that his life's goal was to be a politician. Along the way he had been a congressman and state legislator, meanwhile losing seven elections including bids for governor, and U. S. senator. A seasoned campaigner at 59, he was tough, peppery, raspy-voiced, pink-faced. "He's best in a fight," said a Yorty aide, "when the odds are against him."

This time the odds definitely were against him. The 14-candidate primary on April 1 included a television newscaster, a congressman—Republican Alphonzo Bell—and a Negro, City

Councilman Thomas Bradley. In an electorate only about 17 per cent Negro, Bradley emerged on top with 42 per cent of the vote. Yorty was second with 26 per cent and qualified to face Bradley in a May 27 runoff.

Bradley, 51, a calm 6 feet 3 and 195 pounds, with the trim build and athlete's easy stride of his school days, was born on a Calvert, Tex., cotton plantation. As a boy in Los Angeles, he delivered newspapers and in high school became all-city football tackle and quarter-mile runner. He entered the University of California at Los Angeles on an athletic scholarship but quit in 1940 to become a policeman at $170 a month. In 21 years he rose to lieutenant and meanwhile got a law degree in night classes. He was elected city councilman in 1963 from a racially mixed but majority white district in west central Los Angeles and was re-elected, unopposed, in 1967.

The mayor's race was Los Angeles' hottest political slugfest in decades. Yorty told audiences that Bradley, despite his police service, was "antipolice" and that many officers would retire if Bradley were elected. Bradley said he wouldn't destroy an agency for which he had worked so long. He accused Yorty of making "blatant appeals to racism."

Yorty claimed eastern "outsiders" were trying "to take over our city." Bradley called that "laughable" and "ridiculous." The mayor said Bradley had Communist support and the councilman replied: "character assassination . . . gutter type tactics."

The Los Angeles Times, a Yorty foe, said he was waging his re-election campaign along the "ugliest lines possible," and that his "stewardship during the past four years had been characterized by planless drift, record absenteeism, angry discord, and outright corruption among his appointed commissioners." (Three city commissioners had been convicted on charges of bribery and conflict of interest.)

Bradley pledged "the cleanest administration in the city's history." He organized a "coalition of conscience," as he called it, including Negroes, Mexican-Americans, white liberal Democrats and independents. The Herald-Examiner backed Yorty, saying that in eight years he had compiled "one of the best records in metropolitan American history." Billboards proclaimed: "We need Yorty now—more than ever." In a Yorty newspaper ad, the caption under a picture of Bradley asked, "Will your family be safe?"

Polls consistently favored Bradley but, in the words of one pollster, the racial issue was "traditionally a difficult area to survey effectively." The election brought 75.95 per cent of the registered voters to the polls—an all-time record in a Los Angeles municipal contest—and gave Yorty another victory: 449,572 votes for the mayor to 394,364 for Bradley. Political observers said the city's white majority apparently was becoming more conservative. Yorty, like Bradley a Democrat in the race for the nonpartisan office, was called a maverick who had taken conservative stands on issues.

Yorty told an interviewer that goals for his third term included continued civic construction and improved community relations. "The militants get all the attention," he said. "I want to give the good people recognition so Caucasians will get a more balanced viewpoint of what Negroes are doing."

Sam Yorty: "We've done pretty well with the problem-solving"

A NEGRO MAYOR IN MISSISSIPPI

The City Auditorium in Natchez, Miss., was the scene each spring of a pageant, highlight of the annual Garden Pilgrimage, when hoop skirts and Confederate uniforms revived for a brief time the romance of the Old South. In midsummer 1969, the Auditorium was the scene of a ball which celebrated a milestone in the Negro's struggle for civil rights and symbolized the realities of the New South.

The milestone was the inauguration of Charles Evers, 48, field director of the National Association for the Advancement of Colored People, as mayor of nearby Fayette. He was the first Negro to become mayor of a biracial community in Mississippi since Reconstruction days. The ball was transplanted to Natchez because no place in Fayette was big enough to accommodate the 900 guests.

Fayette, the county seat of Jefferson County, had 2,000 population, two-thirds of it black. Once it had been a prosperous center of cotton trade and memories of the earlier era were kept alive by antebellum homes with wrought-iron fretwork, deep shaded lawns, immense pecan and magnolia trees and a profusion of crepe myrtle.

The crucial test for Evers was the May 13 primary in which he won the Democratic nomination from R. J. Allen who had been mayor for 20 years. The vote was 386–285 and five black candidates for the Board of Aldermen were elected with him. The Democratic nomination was tantamount to victory in the June 3 election.

Among dignitaries attending the inauguration were Ramsey Clark, former U.S. attorney general, and John Doar and Burke Marshall, former assistant attorneys general. Each had played a role in passage and enforcement of the 1965 Voting Rights Act under which enough Negro names had been added to registration lists to warrant a determined effort to elect blacks to municipal office. It was estimated that 60 per cent of potential Negro voters and 92 per cent of qualified whites were enrolled in the state.

Along with other towns in southwestern Mississippi which had achieved or were moving toward a black majority in the elec-

torate, Fayette faced problems under a Negro mayor. Evers promised "a clean and righteous town" and expressed the hope that "white people and black people, particularly in Mississippi, understand we are only doing what

God wants us to do—to take part in government and make it work for everybody."

Before the election, City Hall's positions had been filled by 16 whites; all except the fire chief resigned before inauguration day.

Charles Evers: He promised "a clean and righteous town"

THE "ZAP-IN" THAT UNZIPPED ZAP

At first, the idea sounded like a good one. "The Student," newspaper at North Dakota State University, suggested breezily that college youths around the country might like to zip to Zap for a weekend of merriment. It was suggested that the cozy town of 300 population might become the Fort Lauderdale of the North as a scene of student revels.

Mayor Norman Fuchs (he was also Postmaster Fuchs) was among those who cheered. He donned a sweatshirt emblazoned "Zap, N.D., or Bust," and wrote letters to colleges. He promised treats like "Zap-Burgers with special seasoning" and plenty of "good, clean, beer-busting, food-munching, tear-jerking, rib-tickling fun." The word spread to many campuses.

The "Zap-In" was scheduled for Saturday, May 10. At mid-evening on Friday, Zap's population was nearly three times normal as youngsters, 90 per cent of them male,

streamed in from at least five states. They packed Zap's two taverns and one cafe, as they used to pack telephone booths, then spilled onto the one block of dirt road that was Main Street.

When the temperature dipped below freezing, the visitors started to build a bonfire in the street. They used lumber from an abandoned building for fuel. They also used tables and booths ripped from the taverns and the cafe. They broke windows and scattered merchandise in other business houses. Fist fights broke out. Someone called the fire department and, when the volunteers arrived, a score of youths mounted the bright red truck and began to dismantle it.

About that time, Mayor Fuchs decided that maybe the idea wasn't as good as he had thought. He called for help. Gov. William Guy sent 500 National Guardsmen from nearby

Beulah where they were on weekend alert. In less than an hour, the uniformed troopers cleared Zap of its guests.

Some of the ousted ones went to Hazen, others to Beulah. Most of them descended upon Bismarck where they set up a makeshift overnight camp in a riverside park under the watchful eyes of Guardsmen and police.

"It was just like any other beer party except that it was 20 times as big," said one youthful veteran of the "Zap-In." "It was spontaneous combustion," said another. Mayor Fuchs insisted, "It was only 100 to 150 who spoiled it for all the rest."

In Fargo, editor "Chuck" Saga of the student newspaper, began collecting a relief fund to compensate Zap for damages, estimated at $10,000.

"A very considerate gesture," said Mayor Fuchs.

"I WON'T FORGET THE FACE"

Gary Steven Krist: He predicted a death sentence

Slowly the black-shrouded box was wheeled on a casket carriage into the courtroom amid gasps from women spectators. Four deputies trundled the grim burden down the center aisle and stopped in front of the jury in DeKalb County Superior Court at Decatur, Ga.

This was the first public glimpse of the macabre "capsule" in which pretty co-ed Barbara Jane Mackle, 20, had been buried alive for four days after her abduction from a Decatur motel in December 1968 (*The World in 1968, 251–253*).

Beneath its melodramatic black covering, the box was a chilling sight, similar to a pauper's coffin. Built of plywood, it had been coated with fiberglass, then painted gray. A trapdoor, two feet square, was scarred by 15 closely spaced holes for the two-inch screws which had sealed the victim inside.

From the beginning of the seven-day trial, the prosecution had been confident that the box would seal the conviction of bearded Gary Steven Krist, 24, charged with kidnaping for ransom in the scheme that had extracted $500,000 from the girl's father, Robert F. Mackle, a wealthy real estate developer of Coral Gables, Fla.

Krist, too, had predicted conviction and a death sentence as his penalty at the hands of "these barbarian humans." "A farce," he had contemptuously described the courtroom proceedings. "Why should you bring a superior being into court for assaulting a human?"

The jury was more gracious in its verdict: "Guilty with a recommendation for mercy." Krist received a life sentence. His girl friend, Ruth Eisemann Schier, 26, a blonde Honduran biology student at the University of Miami, indicted with him, ultimately pleaded guilty to the lesser charge of simple kidnaping—without the ransom clause. She drew seven years imprisonment.

The victim was the state's 75th and final witness. Poised and smiling, her black hair reaching well below her shoulders, she quietly described her 83-hour ordeal in the box after she had been taken from her mother's motel room. She had been placed inside the six-foot compartment of her prison in the cold, predawn darkness just a week before Christmas.

"I began pleading," she said. She told her abductors: "I'll be good; I will. My daddy will pay the money. Please don't put me in here." Her appeals were in vain. The trapdoor was closed, screwed tight.

"Then," said Miss Mackle, "they put the dirt on top of the box."

The "capsule"—as Krist described it in a ransom note—contained food, a pump, drinking water loaded with a tranquilizer, a battery-powered fan and a light. Within a few hours the light failed, and she remained in pitch darkness until she was freed by FBI agents who followed the kidnappers' telephone directions after the ransom had been delivered. In the climax of her testimony, she arose and pointed to Krist. "That's the man," she said. "I won't forget the face." Later, she identified Miss Eisemann Schier as the other kidnaper.

Earlier in the trial, a parade of FBI agents had built the case against Krist. He maintained an attitude of indifference, putting in much time in reading a book about the origins of life. Witnesses identified him as a "scientist" who had represented himself to be in search of a remote site for sensitive underground experiments with a mysterious coffin-like box just a few days before Miss Mackle was kidnaped and buried alive in a lonely pine forest 20 miles northeast of Atlanta.

Other testimony established that in 1966 Krist had escaped from a California penal institution in a hail of bullets aimed at a car he had stolen. Thereafter, using an alias, Krist had worked at Massachusetts Institute of Technology as a technician before moving to Florida for a job at the University of Miami's Institute of Marine Sciences.

In a surprise move when their turn came, Krist's two court-appointed attorneys decided to offer no defense testimony but to rely wholly on their arguments to the jury.

On May 26, when the case was given to the jurors, Krist suspended his reading and became talkative. He still predicted a death sentence for himself. He expressed his disapproval of capital punishment. What, then, would he consider proper punishment for the crime? "Bury the guy in a box for about three months and see how he likes it," he replied to newsmen.

After three hours and 46 minutes, the jury brought in its verdict. Foreman H. I. Rainwater said the jury decided that Krist's life should be spared because of "the effort and precaution he took to see that she (Miss Mackle) wasn't killed."

AUTOBITUARY

General Motors introduced the Corvair in 1959 as America's answer to the agile, compact imports that were winning an increasing share of the domestic automobile market. The lines were sporty, the design unconventional—an engine mounted in the rear, an engine block of aluminum rather than heavier iron, air cooling instead of the customary water cooling.

The Corvair was a quick success. The car won awards from automotive magazines: "Car of the Year," "best compact sedan." Sales soared to 235,000 in 1960 and to 317,000 in 1961. Then Ralph Nader, a critic of American industry, wrote a book, *Unsafe at Any Speed*, and made the Corvair the target of his attack on auto safety. He said faulty design—particularly in weight distribution and axle suspension—made the car unsafe (*The World in 1966, 172–175*).

Damage suits were filed by owners, perhaps 150 of them. General Motors, defending the car, pointed out that it did not lose one suit that went to trial. Corvair-boosters organized clubs, pasted "I Love My Corvair" stickers on their bumpers.

Still Corvair sales slid downward, to 86,000 in 1966, to 12,977 in 1968. Through the first four months of 1969, only 2,183 were sold.

General Motors bowed to what seemed to be the inevitable. On May 12, the company announced that no more Corvairs would be manufactured. The Corvair plant at Willow Run, Mich., would be converted to the Chevy Nova and to preparing to manufacture components for a new small car to be introduced in 1970.

And Corvair joined the company of defunct automobiles, 3,000 names like Edsel, Maxwell, Packard, Hupmobile, Essex, Durant, Cord, Studebaker, Deusenberg. . . .

FOR THE RECORD

ELECTED. Howard Lee, 34, director of employer relations at Duke University, to be the first Negro mayor of Chapel Hill, N.C., a town of 80 per cent white population, May 5. Lee defeated Roland Giduz, 43, veteran of 12 years' service on the Board of Aldermen, 2,567–2,167.

MARRIED. Film actress Lana Turner, 49, and Dr. Ronald Dante, 49, a night club hypnotist, at Las Vegas, Nev., May 8. Actor Micky Rooney, 48, and Caroline Hockett, 25, of Beverly Hills, Calif., at Las Vegas, Nev., May 27.

CONVICTED. Fred (Ahmed) Evans, a black nationalist, on four counts of first degree murder in the deaths of three policemen and one civilian in racial conflict at Cleveland (*The World in 1968, 181–185*). Evans was sentenced to death in the electric chair.

Students vs. police at Harvard ➞

June

Crisis on the Campus

Many students sought many things,
but was the uproar so great
that the message was unheard?

—"You brought us up to care about our brothers," said Pat Stimer, president of the student body at the University of Colorado. "You brought us up not to run away from injustice, but to recognize it and fight it and destroy it. And now you castigate us. You castigate us because we think and we care. You demean our consciences, the consciences for which you are largely responsible."

—"When I was 10, I was totally fascinated by cars, read all the catalogues," said Henry Norr, a leader of the Students for a Democratic Society at Harvard. "Later it dawned on me that maybe a system which put that much into tail fins and left a lot of people hungry was all screwed up."

—"My father thinks the better world will come through the ballot box and people like Adlai Stevenson," said Jim Nabors, a black student at the University of California. "I think it can come only through revolution and people like Malcolm X."

—So spoke America's students to their elders in the stormy year of 1969.

IT was a year of seething discontent, a year in which campus revolt, once regarded as youthful exuberance, became a matter of national concern. There were protests against the old order and demands for a new order across the land, from Massachusetts to California and Louisiana to Minnesota, from Wilberforce and Stony Brook to Harvard and Wisconsin.

More often than not, the protests bred violence. Great universities as well as small schools were paralyzed or crippled by sit-ins, seizure of buildings, picket lines in which faculty marched with students. When police were called to restore or to maintain order, physical conflict resulted.

Who were the rebels? Saul Pett of The Associated Press toured U.S. campuses and found three broad categories of activists: "Idealists seeking reforms within the system," "radicals vaguely seeking a revolution to replace the system with a vaguely conceived Marxism," and "outrageous nihilists who come to the barricades loaded with their own psychological baggage." He also found "a large group, a majority on some campuses, of moderates who are deeply concerned and highly critical of the American society, its government and its values. They may disagree with the activists on tactics but are usually sympathetic with their goals." Moreover, "you may find it reassuring that most collegians still are typically collegiate and unpolitical."

No one contended that the rebels constituted more than a fraction of the 6.7 million students in U.S. colleges and universities. A Gallup poll found that, while 81 per cent of those interviewed wanted a stronger voice in administration, 72 per cent never had taken part in a demonstration. An Associated Press survey reported that campus protests in which arrests were made involved 60 institutions in 23 states. The total did not include those only under campus discipline in others of the nation's 2,400 institutions of higher learning. Fortune magazine conducted a poll which concluded that 12.8 per cent of America's college students had views that classified them as "revolutionary" or "radically dissident."

What did the discontented seek? A variety of things, from a new name for their school to expanded privileges in relations with the opposite sex. More serious demands concerned reforms in school administration, discipline and curriculum, more students and teachers from minority groups and improved facilities for them, departments for ethnic studies. Some resentment was aimed at the "multiversity," the complex, impersonal education factories which had come into being as college attendance was leaping from one-third to one-half of the nation's high school graduates. "The important thing to remember," said the president of a Georgia college, "is that no student wants to have to rumple his IBM card to get recognition."

As in the nation at large, much of the unrest was rooted in Vietnam, not only in protests of the war itself but in campaigns against the Reserve Officers Training Corps, the military draft, and manufacturers of weapons such as napalm.

A great many words and much time and talent went into explaining what was going on.

The National Commission on the Causes and Prevention of Violence, appointed by President Johnson *(The World in 1968, 119)*, reported: "Today's intelligent, idealistic students see a nation which has achieved the physical ability to provide food, shelter and education for all, but has not yet devised social institutions that do so. They see a society, built on the principle that all men are created equal, that has not yet assured equal opportunity in life. They see a world of nations —states with the technical brilliance to harness the ultimate energy but without the common sense to agree on methods of preventing mutual destruction."

Pett reported after his survey: "This generation is the first in our history, experts agree, which is not going to college just to earn a living. Freed of money problems, it is free to explore its mind and conscience, to delay the traditional burdens of adulthood, to learn more about more things, to concern itself with the quality of life and the needs of others. . . . One generation takes affluence for granted. The other can't and never will. . . . One generation takes comfort in what has

Walkout with weapons at Cornell

been done. The other is outraged by what remains to be done."

The task of explaining was complicated by the fact that, in the words of Austin Scott, specialist in inter-racial affairs for The Associated Press, "what looks on the surface like one big student revolution is really two, a black one and a white one, separate for the most part and not necessarily equal. Tactics are often the same . . . but the goals are different." He illustrated by quoting Walter Adams, acting president of Michigan State University: "The white radicals say to me they're against the (Vietnam) war. I say fine . . . but what can I do about it? The blacks say they want somebody black on the Athletic Committee. That you can do."

Scott also reported: "A careful reading of the demands issued by black student groups at various universities shows that they are shaped very much to deal with those special problems that confront black students. It also shows that today's generation of black college activists is developing a fundamentally different view of what education is all about. . . . The emphasis is on dealing with real problems now, without waiting, linking the world of blacks in college and outside. . . . They really believe that real revolution has to occur for them to get where they are going."

Sometimes the two revolutions mingled. A classic example occurred at the University of Wisconsin.

Blacks on the campus (500 of them in a student body of 34,000) had been campaigning since May 1968 for reforms. In February, the Black People's Alliance called a strike. Demonstrations took place amid rising bitterness and disorder, climaxing when members of the right-wing Young Americans for Freedom clashed with demonstrators massed at building entrances to prevent access to classes.

Gov. Warren F. Knowles called 1,900 National Guardsmen to restore order. The presence on campus of soldiers with fixed bayonets, as well as policemen with tear gas, brought many white students to the black cause. Between 5,000 and 10,000 marched two miles in 10-degree cold to protest at the state capitol. Twenty-four campus organizations sponsored a symposium on "The Black Revolution." Faculty groups joined students in urging action to meet the black demands.

A strong reaction came from the state legislature. The university's budget for 1969–71 was slashed by $38.1 million, a cut which the school's president described as "disastrous." The quota for enrollment from other states was reduced from 28 per cent to 15 per cent by 1975; the reasoning was that increased restriction would keep out trouble makers. In a

companion move, tuition for students from other states was boosted by up to 35 per cent (the fee for Wisconsin students was raised by 5 per cent).

Wisconsin was not alone in attempting to quiet campus storms with legislation. Scores of bills were introduced in state assemblies across the country and at least eight passed laws intended to stifle or discourage campus revolt. "Americans are fed up to their eardrums and eyeballs," said Gov. Tom McCall of Oregon.

California won the championship with more than 80 "crackdown" bills introduced by mid-April. California also led in another department—the number of arrests. An Associated Press survey in June found that more than one-third of 3,747 arrests in campus demonstrations were made in that state. The total did not include nearly 1,000 young people jailed during the "People's Park" riots in Berkeley (page 136).

California was the scene of another *cause celebre* in the tumultuous story, at San Francisco State College. Black and other "third world" (non-white) students had made 15 demands; among those listed as "non-negotiable" were ones for a department of black studies with black instructors and the waiving of entrance requirements for non-white applicants. A student strike was called in September 1968. One-fourth of the faculty joined in, ignoring a court injunction against strikes by public employes. S. I. Hayakawa, acting president of the college, described the striking instructors as "bored, middle-aged adolescents."

Hayakawa, known as an authority in semantics and a professor in English at San Francisco State for 15 years, had no experience in college administration when he became the college's third head in one year. He matched strong words with strong actions, becoming, one reporter said, "a diminutive Don Quixote, wielding a sword of academic freedom, steeled in the belief that a teacher's duty is to teach, a student's duty is to learn, and the school at all costs must remain open" (The World in 1968, 260).

One of Hayakawa's actions was to summon police to keep order and to prevent disruption of classes. Another was an attempt to dismiss striking teachers. He imposed new restrictions on campus demonstrations. There was violence—smashed windows, fires, invasions of college buildings, clashes with police. One student, a 19-year-old Negro, was blinded when a bomb planted in the Creative Arts Building exploded prematurely. In January, a faculty committee reported that attendance for 18,000 students was 50 per cent of normal and, although the college was open technically, it was "rapidly closing intellectually and spiritually."

In February, Hayakawa appointed a committee to meet secretly with leaders of the Black Student Union and the Third World Liberation Front. They achieved an agreement on March 31, embracing essentially what had been offered before: A black studies department with authority to grant degrees; planning for a broader school of ethnic studies; a decision that 10 per cent of each freshman class (up from 4 per cent) would be low-qualification students from the "third world."

Gov. Ronald Reagan said the agreement was "a victory for the people of California." Non-white students issued a statement: "The struggle to end institutionalized racism and the fight of all people to seize power for determining their political, economic and educational destinies is not over but will intensify. We view the settlement as a foundation for revolutionary change."

One place where "revolutionary change" was not anticipated

was the City College of New York, sometimes called "the poor man's Harvard," a tuition-free school which had been the road to middle class stature for many children of the poor. CCNY's location on the fringe of Harlem had made it sensitive of an obligation to the non-whites who were a 40 per cent minority in New York. A program of recruiting freshmen from minority groups had begun. It was not enough.

In April, 200 black and Puerto Rican students locked themselves inside the South Campus and demanded that the school's racial balance reflect that of the city; they wanted also a school of black studies and control of its faculty. White students worried that, if large numbers of "disadvantaged" were admitted, the school's standards would be lowered and their diplomas devalued.

President Buell Gallagher closed the college to permit negotiations. A mayoral candidate obtained a court order to open the school. The governing Board of Higher Education obtained its own injunction requiring demonstrators to leave the campus or face arrest. There was fighting between blacks and whites; an auditorium was burned. Gallagher again closed the school and called for police. Later, he resigned.

In June, the Faculty Senate voted to reject a proposal by blacks and Puerto Ricans under which half of the student body would not need to meet academic requirements. Instead, the Senate proposed that 400 members of the incoming freshman class represent the low-qualified minorities, a number which would bring the total to close to 40 per cent.

The plague of unrest did not leave the aristocratic universities of the East's Ivy League untouched. At Harvard, on April 9, students entered University Hall, ejected the deans, and set up shop by demanding that Harvard drop the Reserve Officer Training Corps (ROTC) and that it stop university expansion into black neighborhoods. Seventeen hours later, at 4 a.m., 400 state and local police clubbed their way into the building, then dragged the occupying students to patrol wagons. In less than 20 minutes, 197 were arrested and 41 injured.

Moderates called a convocation at Memorial Church and 1,500 in a student body of 15,000 voted a three-day class boycott, condemning the "unnecessary use of police." Harvard president Nathan Pusey said he was compelled to call officers because students were rifling confidential files.

After the three-day strike ended, 6,000 young men gathered in Harvard Stadium to vote a three-day extension and to request a statement of the administration's position. The mass meeting was unprecedented in the school's 333-year history.

On the same day, the faculty issued a resolution deploring the students' forcible occupation and "entry of police into any university." They further resolved that all criminal charges be dropped. The administration agreed, but Judge M. Edward Viola refused to honor Pusey's plea, fining 169 youths the maximum $20 each for criminal trespass. A 25-year-old graduate student, Carl D. Offner, was sentenced to one year in jail for an assault on Dean Robert B. Watson.

At the end of the second three-day period, 5,000 students voted to suspend the strike, though the students for a Democratic Society and the blacks said they would continue. The Harvard Corporation—seven Harvard administrators and alumni—which was in charge of all policy decisions, endorsed a faculty request to terminate ROTC contracts as soon as possible and to look into the other demands. Within days, the administration announced plans to alleviate housing problems and the faculty voted to give Negro students a strong voice in professorial appointments for the black studies program.

Harvard protests the protesters

Whites and blacks clash on campus of City College of New York

A few days after Harvard's trial began, Cornell erupted in one of the year's most controversial episodes. To dramatize charges of racism on campus and a request for an autonomous Afro-American College, 250 black students seized the student union building, Willard Straight Hall.

Over the course of months, black demonstrators had received scores of threatening telephone calls. On April 18, one day before they took over Straight Hall, a cross was burned before the black women's dormitory. Now, inside Straight, after an attempted counter attack to "de-liberate" the building, and rumors that other whites were planning to renew the effort with guns, the blacks armed themselves, as some of the Negroes later said. President James A. Perkins said the guns "made it a whole new thing."

After 36 hours, officials agreed to every demand and the dean of faculty pledged to recommend to his teachers that they accept the agreement. The faculty voted no.

Nine thousand of 13,500 students rallied in Barton Hall, the ROTC center. Within hours, the faculty reversed its vote because, as an English professor said, "Basically, we couldn't conceive of watching troops and students battling in conflict. We felt we have to draw back from the abyss of chaos."

Four faculty members resigned in protest and hundreds of letters charging "capitulation" inundated the school. A fraternity man rebutted: "Those people who say 'capitulation' are separating two issues. Blacks for months have been trying to get something done. The seizure was not the first resort; it was a last resort. . . ." The trustees began an investigation. On May 31, James Perkins asked them to find a new president.

Washington concern in the campus crisis became evident when Robert H. Finch, secretary of Health, Education and Welfare, sent a letter to every college and university president in

Sweet girl graduate at Berkeley

the United States, reminding them of 1968 laws which specified that federal assistance to students might be withdrawn under certain conditions. More than a million students were receiving federal aid but college administrators were reluctant to withdraw it, believing the legal proceedings to be awkward and that only a small percentage of the disruptive students received federal loans or grants. "The loan issue is extraneous," said one eastern university official. "If a student tears up a campus, he should be expelled."

The Rev. Theodore H. Hesburgh, president of the University of Notre Dame, told his students on Feb. 17: "Anyone or any group that substitutes force for rational persuasion, be it violent or non-violent, will be given 15 minutes to meditate." If, at the end of that time, the meditation hadn't produced a change of action, the student would be asked for his identi-

Faculty members flee through window at Columbia

fication card and promptly suspended; five minutes more and he would be expelled. Those without cards would be charged with trespassing.

President Richard M. Nixon wrote a "Dear Ted" letter: "I want to applaud the forthright stand you have taken" and asked that Hesburgh give his views on campus revolt to Vice President Spiro T. Agnew who would soon be meeting with all 50 governors.

Hesburgh replied: "The best salvation for the university in the face of any crisis is for the university community to save itself, by declaring its own ground rules and basic values and then enforcing them. . . ." He continued, "Even the most far-out students are trying to tell society something that may also be worth searching for today if they would only lower the volume so we could hear the message."

The governors apparently got the message. They turned down California Gov. Reagan's request for a federal investigation into the campus disorders.

In June, the National Commission on the Causes and Prevention of Violence warned against punitive legislation, saying, "Such efforts are likely to spread, not reduce, the difficulty." Any legislation, the commission said, should "assist the universities themselves to deal more effectively with the tactics of obstruction." Ten days later, the President told Congress he opposed pending legislation that would cut off funds to universities where there had been campus disorders. He reiterated that he did not want the federal government "interfering in and responsible for discipline in every college and university in this country." On July 1, the House Education and Labor Committee quietly shelved the bill.

Not all the unrest was in institutions of higher learning. As one student said, "If you think I'm radical, you should meet my little brother." A survey released by the National Association of Secondary School Principals in May disclosed: "Three out of five principals report some form of active protest in their schools. Many who note no protest as yet add that they expect it in the near future. One of the surprises of the survey was the fact that protest is almost as likely to occur in junior high schools as in senior high schools."

Louis Harris' pollsters conducted 2,500 interviews for Life magazine among parents, students, teachers and principals in 100 geographically balanced schools. They found that students, like their older counterparts, wanted to participate in policy making, curriculum and discipline. They also found that 62 per cent of the parents felt that maintaining discipline was a more important function of the school than encouraging intellectual inquiry.

"Reduced to its simplest terms," Life found, "the generations disagree on the most fundamental question of all: What is education for?" The traditional function—"to absorb all and sundry into a comfortable middle-class democratic pattern— is being challenged" by those who "want to see education used as an instrument for bringing about radical social change."

Another advocate of change was Dr. Calvin H. Plimpton, president of Amherst College. He sent a letter to President Nixon "in behalf of an overwhelming majority of Amherst students, faculty and administration." For two days, the college had discussed student revolt and, "we believe that we must speak out to make clear that much of the turmoil will continue. It will continue until you and the other political leaders of our country address more effectively, massively, and persistently the major social and foreign problems of our society. Part of this turmoil in universities derives from the distance separating the American dream from the American reality. . . ."

Debate in the shadow of campaign posters

"My Mandate... Or My Departure"

*De Gaulle, aging hero president of France, accepted retirement
when loss of his popularity doomed his reform program*

"AT THE START, De Gaulle performed his political flying trapeze act above a safety net," a worried French official confided in January, "then, for a couple of years, he went on without a net. Today he's indulging in dangerous acrobatics with neither a net nor a trapeze."

For all his dexterity, not even Charles de Gaulle could defy the force of gravity for very long. On April 27 he fell.

True to his own very personal notion of leadership, he transformed a national referendum on regional administrative reform into a question of confidence in him and, when the proposal was rejected at the polls, he abdicated the presidency.

So devout were some of De Gaulle's disciples that they preached the doctrine of his infallibility. If De Gaulle committed his office to a clumsily drafted, doubtful reform bill

for which there was no urgent necessity and no assurance of broad public support, they said it was because he knew he would be defeated and therefore had willed his own departure. In brief, they claimed it was a conscious act of political suicide. A less charitable but more plausible hypothesis was that De Gaulle simply had lost touch with the mood of the nation.

This was first evident in May and June of 1968 when the foundations of the Gaullist structure were severely shaken. A revolt by a group of university students determined to overthrow the system spread to most of the country's work force. Strong police repression galvanized university support behind the rebels. Official hesitation followed as sympathy strikes by the trade unions hardened into a generalized work stoppage

129

which practically stilled the national economy. De Gaulle would admit months later that he had been unable to grasp the situation. *(The World in 1968, 94–98).*

Only one man conveyed confidence, a grasp of the stakes and an outline of a solution. That was Premier Georges Pompidou, De Gaulle's faithful No. 2 for six years. Pompidou appeased the students with promises of reform (later fulfilled). He opened wage negotiations with the strikers and, at the cost of a 14 per cent across-the-board salary increase, he induced them to return to work.

Pompidou persuaded De Gaulle to dissolve the national assembly and went to the country in the subsequent election campaign as the leader of Gaullist candidates pledged to order and economic progress. The Gaullists came out of the 1968 elections as the undisputed masters of the National Assembly; for the first time in French history, a single party held an absolute majority in Parliament. As a result, Pompidou emerged as an independent center of power, with most of the newly elected deputies owing allegiance to him. However, he had sinned by succeeding too well.

De Gaulle dismissed his premier in July, saying he was relegated to the "reserve of the republic." The President did add that Pompidou's ministry had been "exceptionally efficacious . . . entirely conforming to what I had expected of you." The President's praise could not disguise the fact that the man whom many credited with having saved the regime had been cashiered like any Elysee Palace servant.

The public never transferred its affection to Maurice Couve de Murville, Pompidou's successor. During 10 years as De Gaulle's foreign minister, Couve de Murville had established a reputation among his colleagues as "a cold fish." He quickly communicated this impression to the public, nearly half of whom in an October opinion poll would list "coldness" as the new premier's chief defect. France needed its confidence re-stored, reassurance which events and Couve de Murville's vaunted intelligence would fail to provide.

The government had proclaimed that the economy could absorb the effects of the strike. The money market decided otherwise. By November the flight of capital from France attained flood proportions, the franc was being discounted in foreign exchanges and rumors of imminent devaluation were commonplace. Recalling that De Gaulle had confronted the French for years with the choice, "me or chaos," one prominent banker lamented, "now we have both."

DeGaulle decided France would not devalue. The parity of the franc, he insisted, would remain unchanged. It did—for nine months. Then, on Aug. 8, 1969, the franc was devalued 12.5 per cent in the dollar exchange rate, or 11.1 per cent in terms of gold, in an effort to bolster the ailing economy.

The decision to devalue was reached three weeks earlier at a secret meeting of top government leaders, but the announcement was delayed until the market fell into its usual summer doldrums while financiers and money dealers vacationed. It followed on the heels of massive losses of French gold and dollar reserves and was described by French labor leaders and left-wing politicians as an example of the failure of financial and economic policies pursued since 1958 by De Gaulle. A vast credibility gap has opened.

Into this gap moved Georges Pompidou on Jan. 17. He had gone to Rome, apparently with De Gaulle's benediction, to see President Giuseppe Saragat and Pope Paul VI. Meeting newsmen afterward, he was asked a question which had become hackneyed with repetition, a question he had always avoided answering directly. Did he consider himself a potential presidential candidate?

"I think it is a mystery for no one: I will be a candidate in a presidential election when there is one," he replied.

The effect in France was electric. Pompidou had crossed the

Meanwhile in Ireleand, De Gaulle attends mass

President Pompidou reviews his honor guard

political Rubicon. Given the neo-monarchistic style of the Gaullist regime, it was easy to see that Pompidou had challenged the sovereign. He had declared De Gaulle was vulnerable and that he, the banished heir-apparent, was available to succeed him.

De Gaulle reacted vigorously with a reminder that his term did not expire until 1972, and that, "I have the duty and the intention to fulfill my mandate." The disavowal came too late. In a poll three months after Pompidou's dismissal, the French were asked: Who would make the best president after De Gaulle? Forty-one per cent replied with Pompidou's name. Couve de Murville was a distant second. Then a New Year's eve poll sought to discover whom the French considered the man of the year in 1968. Pompidou was selected. De Gaulle ranked fifth.

Pompidou, then, had acted in Rome to capitalize on this public support rather than risk oblivion by languishing in the "reserve of the republic." He had announced his availability when his stock with the public and the party apparatus was high. De Gaulle had only to make the mistake that would open the way to the presidency. He wasted no time.

The uprising in 1968, De Gaulle said, had confirmed his belief that there was "a malaise in the human relationships of modern mechanical society" which "gnaws at the regimes sprung from old Marxism as it shakes those abiding still by the dictates of ancient capitalism. . . . Consequently nothing is more important for the moral and social equilibrium of France than a new organization of the contacts and cooperation between those who lead and those who are led, for example, between teachers and students, employers and their employes, the administration and those it administers."

So pressing was this necessity, De Gaulle said, that he would go directly to the people in a referendum April 27, bypassing the National Assembly which had been installed just months before. What his counselors finally produced to implement the reform mocked the simplicity of De Gaulle's grand design. The bill was 8,000 words long, had 68 articles and was expressed in a language that Le Monde's political editor said was barely intelligible to a practicing lawyer. Its substance would have little effect in exorcising the "malaise in human relationships" that De Gaulle had diagnosed.

It provided for the creation of 21 new administrative regions, each with a regional council. These councils, largely appointive, could decide on the priority of some expenditures doled out by Paris. They would have neither taxing authority nor legislative power. "At best," said one critic of the bill, "it is irrelevant."

The other principal aim of the reform was what government spokesmen euphemistically called the "renovation" of the Senate—the bill would end the Senate's role as a legislative body.

Chosen by an essentially conservative electoral college of small-town "notables," the Senate for 10 years had escaped De Gaulle's control. Where it could, it delayed or amended legislation which a compliant national assembly sped to adoption. For years, Senate President Gaston Monnerville was denied De Gaulle's presence. Alain Poher, Monnerville's successor in the fall of 1968, was treated with the same disdain. Clearly the Senate was in presidential disfavor.

It was not surprising that De Gaulle's "renovation" scheme looked to many Frenchmen like a grudge fight. If most people were willing to go along with regionalization in early April, a majority told an opinion poll they opposed the Senate's demise. But the questions couldn't be split. De Gaulle demanded that both issues be resolved with a single yes or no.

Not only was the government's campaign failing to catch fire, the Council of State, which advised on constitutional questions, ruled that the referendum was illegal: The lawyers said the Legislature should be consulted first.

De Gaulle ignored the Council of State—as he had ignored the advice of his most trusted ministers—and on April 10 he threw his full weight into the balance. The reform, he said, was a question of national destiny; therefore "the reply the country makes" will determine "the continuation of my mandate or my immediate departure." Should voters reject the bill, he continued, "what sort of a man would I be if I did not immediately draw the conclusions of such a deep rupture and remained ridiculously in my present functions?" Henceforth, the issue was one of confidence in De Gaulle's management.

A striking indication of how bad things looked for the President was provided a week before the vote when the police trade union said in its weekly bulletin: "Many members have expressed their uncertainty about what should be the attitude of the police and what legitimate authority they should obey if the President resigns . . . the Constitution is quite clear . . . according to the text . . . the President of the Senate takes provisional charge of the public powers. By law it is his instructions which we must obey. There can be no equivocation on this point."

In four previous referendums, De Gaulle had committed his presidency, each time repeating that his departure would bring chaos in its train. In 1958, in 1961 and twice in 1962, the threat was credible. In 1969 it had lost its power to frighten, for De Gaulle's withdrawal would not create a void. Pompidou, the tested lieutenant, assured orderly succession. What politicians came to call "the fact of Pompidou"—his availability and popularity—permitted, if not encouraged, many disenchanted Gaullists to abandon in relative safety a man who had ceased to inspire the blind confidence of former days. As long as De Gaulle was in control of events he could count on them. But the great man had stumbled, and large middle-class defections appeared imminent.

At 8:03 P.M. April 27, three minutes after the polls had closed, two radio stations, which had arranged for computer analysis of the returns, announced that the referendum had been rejected. Official results confirmed this promptly.

Couve de Murville, looking more acerbic than was customary, told television viewers the government considered the game lost. "The French people in its majority has pronounced itself against the proposed reforms, with all the consequences that brings," he said. "Beginning tomorrow, a new page in our history will be turned . . . General De Gaulle has been at the center of our political and national life . . . we remain faithful to him."

Then, shortly after midnight, from the sanctuary of his rural retreat in Colombey-les-Deux-Eglises, De Gaulle made his decision known. An aide distributed a message in which economy of language reflected De Gaulle's military background:

"I am ceasing the exercise of my functions as President of the Republic. This decision takes effect at noon today."

For most of a decade he had appeared larger than life, dominating his country and his countrymen so thoroughly that his name and that of France were not easily separated. Now he was withdrawing to private life, repudiated by the people whom he had regarded with the ambivalent sentiments of love, pride and contempt. Wasn't it he who once remarked, "old age is a shipwreck"?

Hardly was the ink dry on the final returns of the balloting (52.87 per cent "non", 47.13 per cent "oui") before Pompidou was foreclosing on his claim to the inheritance. On April 29 he sought and got Gaullist party endorsement as its presidential candidate in the upcoming elections.

He struck the keynote of his campaign when he promised both "continuity" of Gaullist policies and an "opening" of the Gaullist temple to dissidents De Gaulle had excluded as heretics. Pompidou was moving toward the center, in the selection of new allies.

Senate President Poher, on whom the provisional national presidency had fallen, appeared to be toying with the idea of challenging Pompidou. After some hesitation he joined the race. An unknown, Poher was something of a novelty in French political life. Although he claimed no monopoly on wisdom or virtue, *bonhomie* was a strong quality. At one point public opinion polls showed him a serious contender, but his fortunes declined in almost direct relation to his public exposure.

The rest of the opposition to Pompidou was hopelessly divided. The Communists, unable to come to terms with the Socialists on a single candidate of the left, fielded Jacques Duclos, a septuagenarian party wheelhorse. The Socialists accepted Gaston Defferre, the mayor of Marseilles, whose third-force plan under the Fourth Republic sought the parliamentary isolation of the Communists. Michel Rocard, secretary general of the splinter Socialist party, made his run as the "only true Socialist" in the lot. Louis Ducatel, a self-made millionaire contractor, and Alain Krivine, a self-styled revolutionary given special army leave to run for the Elysee, rounded out the list of candidates. Voting was to be in two rounds; the two front runners in the June 1 balloting would survive for the June 15 runoff.

The first round revealed Pompidou's formidable strength—44.47 per cent, roughly what De Gaulle polled in the opening round of the 1965 elections. Second, nearly 5 million votes behind, was Poher with 23.31 per cent of the vote. Duclos, who nearly caught Poher, weighed in with 21.27 per cent. Defferre's 5.01 per cent unmasked the weakness of the once powerful Socialists. Next, in order, followed Rocard (3.61 per cent), Ducatel (1.27 per cent) and Krivine (1.06 per cent).

If Poher had any illusions about beating Pompidou they were dashed when the Communist Party ordered its disciplined legions to boycott the second round. The choice between the "reactionaries"—Pompidou and Poher—was that of "cancer or cholera," the party said, and Poher was deprived of a possible 4.8 million anti-Pompidou votes.

A confident Pompidou had only to wait two weeks for what looked like certain victory. He won in a landslide, as handily as his advisors had said he would. He led Poher by more than 3 million votes (11,064,371 to 7,943,118).

The old general, meantime, had returned to Colombey-les-Deux-Eglises after a visit to Ireland during the presidential campaign. Colombey had been his asylum during what Gaullists called "the passage through the desert"—the time De Gaulle was out of power between 1946 and 1958. Calm, far from the capital, its most insistent noises were the crowing of cocks and the passage of farm wagons—an ideal laboratory for reflection. In his second floor office, overlooking the walled garden abundant with flowers, De Gaulle once wrote of his passion for France and his isolation:

"Old France, weighed down with history, prostrated by wars and revolutions, endlessly vacillating from greatness to decline, but revived, century after century, by the genius of renewal!

"Old man, exhausted by ordeal, detached from human deeds, feeling the approach of the eternal cold, but always watching in the shadows for the gleam of hope."

Police vs. student demonstrators in Honduras

"THERE IS URGENT NEED FOR CHANGES . . ."

"Do you know what Rockefeller brought?" one Nicaraguan asked another.

"No, what?" his companion replied.

"Greetings!"

Probably apocryphal, the anecdote nonetheless typified the reactions of many foreign aid-hungry Latin Americans while Gov. Nelson A. Rockefeller of New York visited 20 nations on a fact-finding mission for President Richard Nixon.

More often than not, bombings, riots, gunfights, fires and other terrorism heralded his arrival for conferences with heads of state. Eight persons were killed in incidents directly or indirectly connected with the trip. Banners bearing critical references to the multimillionaire visitor were flaunted even in the more peaceful demonstrations.

Venezuela, Chile and Peru declined to receive him at all. The rebuffs were called "postponements," but the meetings never did take place. In Bolivia, the visit was cut to three hours after numerous threats of violence. In Argentina, he stayed 36 hours instead of three days.

What inspired the hostility? Almost from the start Rockefeller's reception indicated that, among younger Latin Americans at least, he was considered not only an exponent of traditional capitalism but a spokesman for what they saw as imperialism.

Rockefeller's instructions were to find out if his country needed a new Latin American policy. He found ample evidence that a great many citizens south of the border were indeed unhappy about their relations with the United States. Specifically, they were interested in U.S. concessions: minimum prices for raw materials, preferential tariffs, unconditional monetary assistance. In general, the Latin nations complained that they were required to spend most of the aid funds in the United States. In some countries, U.S. foreign aid had been suspended.

The United States viewpoint, in contrast, appeared to be that the country had its hands full conducting its own subsidy program, that tariffs were vital needs, and that a balance of payments problem required that Washington aid money be spent principally in the United States. As Rockefeller said in Colombia, assistance to Latin America had to be reduced "because the (U.S.) budget has a large deficit and there is an inflationist trend which is very dangerous."

When he set out in May with 23 aides, Rockefeller took along no promises. "New United States policies may grow out of this mission," he told Colombia's President Carlos Lleras Restrepo, "but do not arrive with it."

However frustrating his receptions were, the governor did not falter. Repeatedly, after massive disorders—most of them involving students and police—he declared his journey would continue. At one point he said that to call the demonstrations humiliating, as some critics had done, would be "farthest from the truth. These are my friends; I know them, I love them, I understand them."

He found ways to discount or excuse the violence that followed and sometimes preceded him. When nearly 50 persons were injured as police and students battled with clubs and tear gas in Bogota, Rockefeller's comment was, "This is something that has been happening everywhere in the world, including the United States." In Quito, after an even more disruptive outbreak, he said he didn't blame Ecuadorian students for using his visit as "an outlet for a demonstration." The next day, however, he told a news conference that "we do not need more violence; we are not here to fight but to listen," and he invited student leaders to sit down with him to discuss their grievances. Almost immediately the students rejected his offer, as they had earlier in Bolivia.

The mission, divided into four trips, began May 11, taking the Rockefeller party to Mexico, Honduras, Guatemala, Nicaragua, Costa Rica, El Salvador and Panama on the first leg. Bolivia, Colombia, Ecuador and Trinidad-Tobago comprised the second leg, started May 27. The third segment, beginning June 16, included Brazil, Paraguay and Uruguay. On June 27 the delegation left for Argentina, Haiti, the Dominican Republic, Jamaica, Guyana and Barbados.

Back in New York July 6, Rockefeller said the mission had been worth while despite the disorders. The number of demonstrators did not surprise him, he said, but "the violence was more than I expected." Even so, he maintained that his trip had provided "a new insight into one of our country's most delicate and complex international situations."

"The problems that developed during the course of the trip," he said, "are clear evidence of the fact that all is not well and that there is urgent need for changes in our policies."

The major problems, he suggested, were unfavorable trade balances between the United States and Latin American countries, shrinking exchange reserves due to heavy dollar outflows to pay for debt service, and an increasing U.S. protectionist policy.

President Nixon expressed satisfaction with the mission and, by that time, there were some signs of ameliorative measures. In mid-June, the administration had announced that it would terminate a restriction on foreign aid known as "additionality." This rule had required recipient countries to spend most of their aid funds in the United States. Then, early in July, the United States lifted its ban on credit arms sales to Peru and Ecuador, penalties that had been imposed in retaliation for the seizures of tuna fishing boats by those countries. The end result was an open door to conferences on fishing rights in offshore waters. Peru, furthermore, announced its reconsideration of the expulsion of U.S. military missions, and Chile disclosed a plan for the "negotiative and progressive" nationalization of Anaconda Co. copper mines in that country.

A MEDAL FOR INTRANSIGENCE

Coal mines throughout the United States and Canada fell silent on June 12 as workers walked off their jobs in a manner reminiscent of the days of bitter, sometimes bloody strikes led by John L. Lewis. "Our men didn't threaten to strike, they just struck," Lewis once said. "We would turn our water buckets upside down . . . and that meant 'we ain't working today'."

This time a labor dispute wasn't at issue. The men were honoring the memory of their loquacious leader of four decades who had died quietly and alone in a Washington hospital. Lewis, president of the United Mine Workers from 1920 to 1960 and the last of the big time labor bosses, was 89. The work stoppage which began hours before Lewis's successor, W. A. "Tony" Boyle, authorized it, continued until after the funeral.

In the 1930s and 1940s, few men made more frequent headlines and few, with the exception of President Franklin D. Roosevelt, exerted more influence in shaping the political and economic face of the nation. Probably nobody more than Lewis was responsible for the rapid growth of labor unions in the decades of his power. His thick mane of hair and bushy eyebrows that bounced with every facial expression became the trademark for himself and his union.

Born into an Iowa mining family on Feb. 12, 1880, Lewis inherited his ardent unionism from his father, Thomas, an active member of one of the old Knights of Labor unions. The young Lewis quit school at the age of 12 and went into the coal pits. He also dug copper in Colorado, silver and coal in Montana and gold in Arizona, but returned to Lucas, Iowa, where in 1906 he was named a delegate to the United Mine Workers convention. In 1919, as a field worker for the AFL, he ended his first mine strike, meekly for him, by telling his union "we cannot fight the government." A year later he became president of the UMW and soon changed his attitude, waging notable battles with the White House and the coal industry during three decades of frequently bloody organizational battles and strikes.

Lewis was a prime mover in founding the Congress of Industrial Organizations, later merged into the AFL-CIO, but he pulled the UMW out of the Congress after he clashed with other labor movement leaders. He led the revolt of unions against the AFL in 1935, sitdown strikes against the auto industry and organization drives on mass production industries in the 1930s.

His strikes in the coal mines forced related industries to halt production, caused trains to be cancelled, curtailed electrical power over wide areas and threw thousands of workers out of jobs. Lewis-led strikes during World War II were the only major defections from a labor no-strike pledge. For his workers he won fringe benefits and higher wages and set the pattern for other unions in collective bargaining.

Lewis often was hauled into court for ignoring injunctions. He paid several million dollars in fines for defying judges. His jousts with the government were a major factor behind passage —over a presidential veto—of the Taft-Hartley Act to provide more stringent controls on labor unions.

After World War II Lewis agreed to automation in the mines despite the resulting loss of jobs. "It is better to have a half-million men working at good wages and high standards of living than to have a million working in poverty and degradation."

Possessor of quick wit, sharp tongue and a powerful personality, Lewis denounced Presidents, Vice Presidents and other labor leaders. He called Vice President John N. Garner in 1939 a "labor-baiting, poker-playing, whiskey-drinking evil old man." For Walter Reuther, head of the United Auto Workers, he reserved this description: "a pseudo-intellectual nitwit."

When FDR dismissed a conflict between labor and management with a comment, "a plague on both your houses," Lewis retorted in stentorian rhetoric, "It ill behooves anyone who has supped at labor's table and who has been sheltered in labor's house to curse with equal fervor and fine impartiality both labor and its adversaries when they become locked in deadly embrace. . . ."

Lewis had been an early supporter of FDR but broke with him in 1940 to support Republican Wendell Willkie.

In 1960 Lewis retired from the UMW presidency. He was given the title of president emeritus and spent his last years as trustee for the union's health and welfare fund. He shunned interviews, public appearances and fabulous financial offers from publishers to write his biography. He stuck to his word— with one exception. Shortly before his 85th birthday, Lewis granted an interview to Associated Press labor writer Neil Gilbride—on the condition that it not be published during his lifetime. In the interview, published at Lewis's death, he advised what he had since the dawn of the century: "Organize."

As a recent recipient of the Freedom Medal, presented by President Johnson, Lewis commented to Gilbride: "So they gave me a medal for doing all those things they fought me for doing all those years."

ORDEAL FOR SURVIVAL

Flight 942, Iberia Airlines from Cuba on June 4, carried a stowaway in one of the metal pods that housed the landing wheels. He tumbled unconscious from his hideout when the jetliner landed at Madrid.

He had endured more than seven hours in cold as bitter as 40 degrees below zero and in the thin atmosphere of 29,000 feet altitude. Doctors were amazed that he had survived. Usually, they said, a human could not live more than a few minutes in such temperatures and such height. It was another wonder that he hadn't been bounced from his precarious perch in the wheel housing or crushed when the wheel was retracted.

The refugee, Armando Socarras Ramires, 22, told Spanish officials that he had fled Havana "because in my country youths have to be home at midnight."

Also, there was a call to military service; "I and my companions decided that we didn't want to join." "It was risky, of course," he said, "but . . . it's necessary to risk one's self, at least in my conditions."

One companion had joined him in the adventure, he said, but he was missing when the plane reached Madrid. Another had backed out at the last minute.

"THE FLOWER GIVES JOY . . . THEN WILTS AWAY"

The gold brick path in The Wizard of Oz seemed to pave for Judy Garland a highway of triumph with crossroads of turmoil.

Judy Garland was born Frances Gumm on June 10, 1922, to vaudeville parents in Grand Rapids, Minn. It was in her hometown 30 months later that she made her first stage appearance singing Jingle Bells. There were no chants of "More, more," as she so often heard later in life, but she sang the song seven times before her father pulled her from the footlights.

At 17, as the plaintive Dorothy in The Wizard of Oz, she captured the hearts of millions while musing about blue birds flying Over the Rainbow.

Miss Garland made more than 35 films and scores of personal appearances. She once set a vaudeville record in New York with an engagement of 19 weeks and 184 performances. Her films, which reportedly made $100 million, included Every Sunday, Babes in Arms, Little Nellie Kelly, For Me and My Gal, The Harvey Girls, Meet Me in St. Louis, The Pirate, Easter Parade, A Star is Born, Judgment at Nuremberg and A Child is Waiting. But trouble seemed to accompany each triumph.

When she was good, she was great. When she was bad. . . . She was nominated for Oscars and fired by studios for failing to show up. She enthralled audiences by singing and infuriated them by arriving late. She was overcome by fans crowding on stage and shouting "More, more," and "We love you, Judy." She was driven from the stage with jeers and missiles. Her voice in its prime was pristine but later it faltered and often left her in midperformance.

The pressures of adolescent stardom sent her to a psychiatrist's couch at age 18. The peaks and valleys of her career were cause for a dependence on drugs to pep her up, calm her down, keep her awake, make her sleep. It was an "incautious self-overdose" of sleeping pills, according to an inquest, that caused her death on June 22 at age 47 in the London home she shared with her fifth husband, Mickey Deans. But her elder daughter, Liza Minnelli, said, "I think she was just tired, like a flower that blooms and gives joy and beauty to the world, and then wilts away."

Liza and Miss Garland's two other children, Lorna and Joseph Luft, brought Judy back to the states for a farewell with her fans. Some 20,000 persons crowded into a New York funeral chapel to bid good-by before a private funeral service and burial.

"HE WOULD NOT BE ABLE TO FUNCTION...."

From the moment Robert H. Finch was appointed secretary of Health, Education and Welfare, he let it be known that John H. Knowles was his personal choice to become assistant secretary for health and scientific affairs. The choice won a nod from President-elect Nixon and on Jan. 15 Finch asked Dr. Knowles, director of Massachusetts General Hospital, to accept the post. The 43-year-old Knowles readily agreed.

Formal nomination and routine Congressional approval appeared to be all that stood between Dr. Knowles and the job of presiding over the Medicare and Medicaid programs, most federal support of biological and medical research and a broad range of other efforts to improve the nation's medical care. But, as the tale was told, the American Medical Association, Congressional conservatives and some pending presidential programs intervened, and it was nearly six months before there was a doctor in the house. Then it wasn't Dr. Knowles at all, but Dr. Roger O. Egeberg, dean of the University of Southern California's Medical School.

Dr. Knowles, a graduate of Harvard College and Washington University's Medical School (cum laude), had an excellent reputation in the field of public health. He criticized doctors' fees as excessive and preached preventive medicine. His concern for the poor led him to advocate the need for all-inclusive health insurance and to back causes—such as Medicare—that long had been unpopular with organized medicine.

In the coming months, there was a lot of political jockeying. President Nixon agreed to nominate anyone Finch could get the Senate to approve. Finch was optimistic. Senate opposition to Knowles appeared minimal, although Everett M. Dirksen of Illinois, Senate minority leader, was leading the battle to block the nomination. Dirksen said he opposed Knowles because the AMA objected and he believed the professional organization of doctors should have a say because of its broad influence in the field of health. Also the AMA's political arm, the American Medical Political Action Committee (AMPAC), was traditionally a heavy campaign contributor. The White House asked the AMA to submit its own list of potential nominees.

"I never shop for trouble, Bob," Dirksen told Finch, "but if you send it (the Knowles nomination) up, I'll put a hold on it."

"I'm going to hang in there," Finch told Knowles. "I've got nobody else. I want you. I'm not going to back down."

Nixon reiterated his earlier promise, this time on a nationally televised news conference: he would nominate whoever Finch recommended—so long as Finch could persuade Congress to approve his choice. Finch again put out the word that Knowles was the man. Dirksen was all but admitting defeat; when queried by newsmen on what he would do when the nomination reached the Senate, Dirksen answered: "When Napoleon sent Marshal Ney to Russia, he told him he would have plenty of time to discuss with him how he conquered that country and no time to discuss how he lost the battle. I have no time to discuss Mr. Knowles."

The AMA redoubled its lobbying efforts. There were reports of political trading: You support my bill and I'll support yours. "It's a whole new ball game now," said Rep. Bob Wilson of California, chairman of the Republican Campaign Committee in the House.

On June 27, President Nixon and Finch conferred for several hours at the White House. Then Finch issued a statement; "I have reluctantly and regretfully decided and today advised Dr. John Knowles that the protracted and distorted discussion . . . has resulted in a situation in which he would not be able to function effectively. . . ."

Five and one-half months after Finch's first efforts to nominate Knowles, President Nixon named Dr. Egeberg, 65-year-old friend of Knowles. Dr. Egeberg, a registered Democrat but an admirer of President Nixon, was a graduate of Cornell and Northwestern universities. Like Knowles, he was described as a medical liberal and as being hospital-oriented. He formerly was chief of medical services at the Veteran Administration Hospital in Los Angeles.

Dr. Knowles was the only person directly involved in the issue who professed no anger. He blamed the outcome on the AMA, called for an investigation of AMPAC, praised Finch and said of Nixon: "If he has had to meet certain promises or debts made during his campaign, I think that he should."

Finch, a personal friend, political ally and confidant of Nixon, said Republican congressmen had threatened not to support key administration programs if President Nixon nominated Dr. Knowles. "If Nixon had nominated him, the administration would have had to seek broad Democratic support to pass its programs, and this would have divided the Republican Party." Knowles, said Finch, "had become a symbol. It could have been very difficult for him to solve the great problems we face carrying the extra weight of this particular symbolism on his back. The man I chose instead—equally brilliant, equally dedicated—does not have that handicap. He will be able to do more, which is the ultimate criterion."

WATERLESS NIAGARA. The American Falls, normally flowing at the rate of 4½ million gallons per minute, went dry on June 12. A cofferdam upstream diverted the entire torrent of the Niagara River to the larger Horseshoe Falls. The American Falls were shut down to permit geologists to inspect and determine ways of clearing away the hundreds of tons of rock eroded from the brink and thus preserve the beauty of the scene.

THE WAR OF "PEOPLE'S PARK"

Berkeley slept. A large marijuana plant in a Dana Street apartment stood out against white curtains. The sun still hid below the lovely green hills backing the city. In Berkeley, the University of California community, which the world knows as the capital of U.S. campus unrest, it is axiomatic: If there is no trouble, wait a few minutes.

The waiting was over at 6 a.m. on a university-owned 270-by-450-foot vacant lot between Dwight Way and Haste Street, three blocks off the campus. The war of "People's Park" was about to start.

Before the day of bricks, clubs, tear gas and shotguns was over, one man would lie mortally wounded, among more than 100 injured, including 60 officers.

For a month, hundreds of Telegraph Avenue "street people"—a mishmash of students, nonstudents, revolutionaries, barefoot hippies, free livers and lovers, intellectuals, acid-heads and pot-puffers—had been using and "improving" the property as a park. They put in brick walks, grass, shrubs and slides and defied authorities to recover the lot. Such was the gauntlet thrown down when, in predawn quiet, some 275 policemen, sheriff's deputies and California Highway patrolmen marched to the lot.

Helmeted faces scanned some 75 figures huddled in the gloom in blankets and sleeping bags. The signal was given. The squatters were ordered to move or be arrested. Sullen, muttering curses, most of the crowd scattered. Three refused to budge and were hustled off, charged with trespassing.

Under police protection, workmen hastily erected an 8-foot-high chain-link fence around the lot. No-trespassing signs were posted.

"We caught them unprepared," said a police captain in a boast shortly to turn to ashes.

At noon, as officials congratulated themselves, hell broke loose.

"Let's go down and take the park," cried a youth to a mob rallying on the campus.

About 1,000 of them marched within a half-block of "People's Park," to be faced by a small contingent of California Highway patrolmen on guard while other officers had lunch. An angry rumble pervaded the crowd. A rock flew out of the mass. The roar grew louder. More

missiles flew. Clubs were raised. The battle was joined in the most violent day in Berkeley's long history of activist rebellion. The patrolmen were reinforced by Berkeley police and Alameda County deputies on a dead-run. Officers met assaults with tear gas, clubs and shotguns.

Relatively nonlethal birdshot began to fly, hitting, among others, San Francisco Chronicle newsman Don Wegars and Los Angeles Times newsman Daryl Lembke. The demonstrators hurled bricks, chunks of cement, steel reinforcing rods, assorted bits of plumbing, broken bottles, tools—anything throwable.

Rioters overturned and burned a car. A highway patrolman was knifed in the chest. Enraged youths climbed to rooftops to bombard police with anything they could get their hands on. Shopkeepers hastily closed for the day.

The melee surged in a cloud of curses down Telegraph toward Dwight—toward the street fronting the Granma Bookstore, where the words of the revolutionary Che Guevara are more likely to be found than those of George Washington, an earlier revolutionary. On the roof of the Granma Bookstore stood a mustachioed man who had driven 60 miles from San Jose that morning to watch the action. He was James Rector, 25, and he had a front seat at the uproar.

Whether he was throwing anything at police is still a question. Down on the street, a uniformed figure took aim, squeezed the trigger of his shotgun, and Rector fell to the roof, his body perforated by buckshot. Most of the shotguns used were loaded with tiny birdshot, but Rector was hit with double-o buckshot. He died four days later.

Rector was a convicted burglar, registered narcotics user and wanted as a parole violator. A rifle was found in his car.

Gov. Ronald Reagan told an Anaheim audience:

"He (Rector) was killed by the first college administrator who said some time ago it was all right to break the laws in the name of dissent."

Despite his record, the Berkeley street people hailed Rector as a martyr. He was memorialized in a long, silent march, and eulogized in at least two church services.

During the tense night of May 15, Reagan alerted the National Guard, which clamped a ring of steel around a wide perimeter of People's Park. Gatherings were banned. A curfew was ordered.

The day after Rector's death, tear gas from a hovering National Guard helicopter scattered a crowd near the campus and seeped into classrooms. On May 22, about 300 guardsmen, bayonets fixed, outflanked some 500 people prowling the streets for a new people's park. Warned they were in violation of an emergency ban on assemblies and parades, they were trapped in an alley, booked on the spot and hustled to jail in vans.

Arrests totalled 482, the biggest mass haul of the crisis.

Indications that things were cooling down came May 30 when 30,000 marchers staged a Memorial Day promenade in altogether peaceful fashion.

The score: More than 900 arrests, one death, some 200 injured, $1.2 million expended for officer regular and overtime pay, equipment and supplies for all agencies.

What was behind the People's Park confrontations?

Berkeley Mayor Wallace Johnson said the radicals and revolutionaries had found themselves a "territorial imperative" with which to clobber one of the dearest elements of the capitalist system—private property. Not so, said self-styled "non-ideological socialist" Steve Delacour, 32, an activist who accepted responsibility for the original idea for the park.

He said he and others started talking last spring about a do-it-yourself park. Interest waxed, and a committee was formed to collect donations and materials.

Too late, university officials awoke to the fact the land they had bought for $450,000 to build dormitories had indeed been appropriated.

When the dust settled from the People's Park crisis, the university made its move. The entire lot was cleared. Not a stick or leaf contributed by the street people was left. Grass carpeting was laid by workmen, and hardtop installed for soccer courts. That's the way it will stay, according to UC officials, until those dormitories are finally built.

LEFTIST ELEMENTS SPLIT SDS

In its prime years, the Chicago Coliseum had echoed to the bombast of national political conventions that hailed Presidents-to-be of the United States. Then its fame faded while roller derbies and thrill shows took over. But in 1969, discord again reverberated within the soot-stained walls of the decaying old structure.

The occasion was the convention of Students For a Democratic Society, a meeting that had been turned down by more than 60 colleges across the nation. Its 1,500 delegates and observers provided five chaotic days of conflicting views, fiery speeches, spontaneous demonstrations, a few scuffles and finally a 26-hour caucus that ended in the divorce of the organization's two major factions.

These were the Progressive Labor party group and the SDS regulars. Ultimately each was to characterize the other as spurious.

SDS began as an organization of liberal students. Leftward leanings appeared, however, and

when the convention opened in June many delegates unfurled their new colors—they wore Red Guard arm bands, waved copies of The Quotations of Chairman Mao and denounced the American Communist party as right wing.

The Progressive Labor party (PL) contingent, a doctrinaire Leninist minority in the estimated 100,000 SDS membership, made a bid for control of the convention. For four days, these and allied groups wrangled and demonstrated and vilified one another. Among them were representatives of the paramilitary Black Panther party and a splinter group known as the Revolutionary Youth Movement (RYM), both of them inimical to the PL.

The Black Panthers made two appearances before the convention, on both occasions denouncing PL members as racist and counterrevolutionary. Calling thereafter for expulsion of the PL group, a Panther leader said, "SDS will be judged by the company it keeps." Supporters

of PL leaped to their feet, shook clenched fists and shouted: "Smash red baiting! Smash red baiting!"

Members of RYM, appalled by the PL attack on their Panther allies, stalked out of the convention.

By this time SDS regulars had concluded that the well disciplined PL might manage to seize the power of national officers. The officers thereupon called a closed caucus, in a church across town. With the subsequent support of the RYM and the urgings of the Panthers, the caucus voted to expel the Progressive Laborites. Each of the two major factions then elected its own slate of officers.

Such was the state of confusion and disagreement that the election appeared to be the convention's biggest accomplishment. Most observers agreed that PL and RYM, both revolutionary but diametrically opposed in ideology, were incapable of coexistence within SDS.

"COLLISION COURSE . . . REPEAT, COLLISION COURSE"

Moonlight played brightly on a calm South China Sea. A half-dozen ships, part of the SEATO naval exercise "Sea Spirit," plied the waters some 650 miles southwest of Manila. The five destroyers, one the *USS Frank E. Evans,* and a carrier, the *HMAS Melbourne,* made up an antisubmarine task group to detect and destroy "enemy" submarines. They were zigzagging at 18 knots in a defensive posture, the destroyers providing an antisubmarine screen for the Australian carrier two miles astern.

Lt. (jg) Ronald Ramsey, 24, officer of the deck of the *Evans* while his superiors slept, received a message from the *Melbourne* ordering him to move to a "plane guard" position. The *Evans'* truck lights would serve as a beacon for incoming planes and the ship itself would serve as a rescue craft should any planes ditch.

As outlined in Navy manuals, standard procedure for the maneuver would have required the *Evans,* moving about two miles ahead of and 10 degrees to the left of the *Melbourne's* bow, to put its rudder left, taking it out of the path in a wide semi-ellipse to a position astern of the *Melbourne.* The *Evans,* however, turned right, and from the *Melbourne's* bridge came an urgent warning from the skipper, John P. Stevenson:

"You are on a collision course. . . . Repeat, collision course. . . ."

The day was June 3. The time 4:15 a.m. The 16,000-ton carrier ripped into and bisected the 2,200-ton destroyer. Within minutes the bow of the *Evans* sank in 5,400 feet of water, carrying 74 of her 273-man crew with her. "I was sitting in radio central talking to one of the other radiomen when she hit," said Radioman Wayne Rickard of Port Arthur, Texas. "I crawled out through a hole in the bulkhead and started swimming. That's when you could hear them cry for help. They were underneath the surface. You could hear them hollering. We couldn't do anything for them."

Only one body was recovered. Among the victims were three brothers from Niobrara, Neb.—Gary, Gregory and Kelly Sage. Their deaths created the worst Navy family tragedy since 1942 when five Sullivan brothers perished aboard the *USS Juneau.*

Within minutes after the collision, early dispatches reaching Australia from the *Melbourne* said "searchlights from the *Melbourne* and her helicopter lit up a scene of tragedy and heroism. All *Melbourne's* sea boats were lowered and picked up survivors. Some of *Melbourne's* crew dived into the water to aid struggling U.S. sailors.

Officers and sailors from *Melbourne* jumped from her flight deck and quarter deck onto the shattered *Evans* and secured ladders and scrambling nets."

Meanwhile, in the stern of the *Evans,* crewmen tossed from their bunks by the impact ran from compartment to compartment securing hatches and doors and performing other emergency measures "just as we had done during drill."

Among the last of the swimmers to be rescued was Cmdr. Albert S. McLemore, the *Evans'* skipper since February 1968 when he was given his first command in his 20-year career. "I was asleep in the sea cabin," recalled McLemore. "My first recollection was a tremendous noise and fire. I thought we had been torpedoed or mined. I bent back the jagged metal with my hands to force my way out. I found myself in the water with the wreckage. I don't know how I survived."

At Subic Bay, the Philippines, where the *Evans* and her survivors were taken, a joint investigation got under way—not to inflict punishment but to determine the cause of the disaster. Seventy-eight witnesses appeared in the unprecedented inquiry conducted by a panel of three American and three Australian naval officers headed by U.S. Rear Adm. Jerome H. King. Witnesses included Adm. G. J. B. Crabb, commander of the Australian fleet, who was aboard the carrier commanding the task force; Stevenson, McLemore and Lt. (jg) James A. Hopson, who with Ramsey directed the final movements of the *Evans.*

Both Hopson and Ramsey were warned that they were "suspected of having committed the offense of neglect hazarding a vessel of the armed forces." Hopson testified that Ramsey gave the order turning the *Evans* directly in front of the carrier. Ramsey declined to testify on constitutional grounds, saying he and his counsel were denied a request to cross-examine witnesses, review previous testimony and to recall earlier witnesses.

The board released its findings some 10 weeks after the fatal collision. It placed primary blame on the *Evans* and said a number of errors contributed to the tragedy, including "the incorrect decoding of the task unit commander's signal . . . which announced that the *Melbourne's* course was 260 degrees." *Evans,* the panel reported, "decoded this signal to mean that the carrier was turning left to 160 degrees."

In a one-man court-martial McLemore was found guilty of negligence and was sentenced to a reprimand Sept. 15. Earlier, Ramsey pleaded guilty to dereliction of duty and negligence and was given a reprimand along with a reduction of 1,000 points in his standing on the list for promotion. On Aug. 25 an Australian military court acquitted Capt. Stevenson, the *Melbourne's* commander, of negligence.

The *Evans* was named for a late Marine Corps brigadier general and hero of the Spanish-American War and World War I. Launched in October 1944, she once was rated the best ship in her squadron. On July 1, at Subic Bay, she was decommissioned, destined to become a target for destruction, to provide training for other fleet units.

"I think it is a fitting end," said Commander McLemore. "It's a hell of a lot better than ending up as razor blades."

One-half a destroyer (right) reaches port

"WE SERVE ONLY THE PUBLIC INTEREST"

The scene, somewhat undramatic, was at least unprecedented: Never before had a President of the United States addressed the Supreme Court. Chief Justice Earl Warren stepped down, into retirement, with Richard Nixon's praise ringing in his ears. Warren E. Burger stepped up, from a relatively obscure career as a federal judge to the highest position in the nation's judicial system.

Thus one era ended and another began.

The last session of the so-called Warren court began on June 23 with announcement of its three final decisions, all cast in the Warren mold. One put fresh restriction on the investigative power of police in the arrest of suspects. The others unified in all states the Fifth Amendment's protection against double jeopardy, and blocked heavier second sentences for those who had won reversal of a first conviction and then had been found guilty again.

In a half hour, the court had formally concluded its term. Chief Justice Warren then arose and said:

"I recognize the President of the United States."

President Nixon, attired in a cutaway coat and striped trousers, extolled Warren as "a symbol of fairness, integrity and dignity" during the years of greatest change in American history and as a judge with "a humanity that is all-encompassing." He added: "The nation is grateful for that humanity."

There was a tremor in Warren's voice as he replied by comparing the mutual obligations of President and chief justice in speaking "the last word" for 200 million citizens and those to follow in the future. "It is," he said, "a responsibility that is made more difficult in this court because we serve no constituency. We serve no majority. We serve no minority. We serve only the public interest . . . guided only by

the Constitution and our own consciences. . . ."

The white-haired Burger, 61, wearing his black robe, then took the oath of office.

The new chief justice had learned his law in night school, developed a practice in St. Paul, Minn., and achieved judgeship by way of the Justice Department in Washington. There, for three years, he was an able but not well known prosecutor. When he decided in 1956 to return to private practice, he was offered a seat on the U.S. Court of Appeals for the District of Columbia. Almost immediately he found himself—like Warren—a controversial jurist but for an opposite reason: His views collided with those of the court's two most liberal judges, and his dissents increased in number and sharpness. He argued frequently that trials were never perfect, that crime was never pat and that courts should not be so quick to free criminals because of technical errors by courts and police.

More than once, President Nixon had indicated that he considered Burger a law-and-order man. Burger himself, in speeches and in dissenting opinions, was on record as disputing some of the Supreme Court's decisions broadening the rights of suspects in criminal cases. Addressing Ripon College students during his appeals court years, Burger had said: "Governments exist chiefly . . . to protect (citizens') homes and property, their persons and their lives. If a government fails in this basic duty, it is not redeemed by providing even the most perfect system for the protection of defendants in the criminal courts."

Yet, just a few days after he assumed office, Chief Justice Burger told a Wyoming judicial conference that anyone who had the idea he favored more stringent criminal prosecutions "couldn't be more wrong." "What I believe is the defense must be strengthened," he said. "We

need better trained lawyers on the defense side."

Most of the comment on Burger's appointment agreed that he was eminently competent through somewhat colorless. One referred to him as "gray." According to another, "he looks like a chief and sounds like a chief. He positively exudes rectitude."

Warren, at 78, was anxious to retire after a half-century of public life. He had, in fact, announced his intention nearly a year earlier, but he remained in office after the Senate refused to confirm Abe Fortas as his successor (*The World in 1968, 210–212*).

Warren's career as a lawyer led to his election as California's attorney general and, in 1942, as governor. In the latter office he served three terms, during which his liberal views brought him into contention with many of his fellow Republicans.

The late President Eisenhower had appointed him chief justice in 1953, and Warren moved even more aggressively into the most controversial of legal and political areas.

Perhaps the greatest storm of protest grew from rulings that expanded the rights of persons accused in criminal cases. But, in an interview published after his retirement, Warren maintained that such rulings "have in no way adversely affected the prosecution of crime."

In one of his last speeches before retiring, Warren summarized his position this way:

"I have heard a great many people say to me, 'Well, I agree with your opinions on these civil rights, all right, but don't you think you are going too fast?' Of course, the answer to this is, 'We haven't anything to say about how fast we go.' We go with the cases that come to us. . . . We either hear them and decide them or we let them go and sweep them under the rug . . . for future generations."

HAIL and FAREWELL! Chief Justice Burger (right) and Chief Justice Warren

FOR THE RECORD

ACQUITTED. Ronald August, 30, Detroit policeman accused of murder in the death of a Negro youth at the Algiers Motel during the 1967 race riots (*The World in 1967, 136–144*). August admitted shooting Auburey Pollard, 19, but claimed it was done in self defense during a struggle for possession of a shotgun. Earlier he had denied that he fired the gun.

ELECTED. Charles S. Stenvig, 41, to be mayor of Minneapolis, June 10. Stenvig, a police detective and a political unknown, campaigned on a "law and order" platform, pledging his support for officers who made unpopular arrests in Negro neighborhoods. He received 62 per cent of the vote in a contest with Dan Cohen, president of the City Council.

APPROVED. By the voters of Rhodesia, a new constitution which would perpetuate the rule of the white minority, June 20. The vote was 54,724 for and 20,776 against. In another referendum, expressing the electorate's view on establishment of a Rhodesian republic that would sever the last remaining ties with Great Britain, the majority also voted in favor, 61,130 to 14,327.

Man, his footprints and flag on the moon ⟶

July

Men on the Moon:
One Small Step....
One Giant Leap....

*Earth's silvery satellite trod upon for first time in history
by heroic Americans who delivered an entire world's
hopes for peace while millions watched in wonder*

Men on the moon: Armstrong, left, and Aldrin secure flag

THEY CAME by the hundreds of thousands to witness history. For days they streamed into Brevard County, Fla., home of Cape Kennedy and the nation's moonport. They jammed the roads and hotels and camping grounds. There were congressmen, diplomats, bankers, industrialists, movie stars, newsmen, tourists and the curious. A physical fitness buff ran all the way from Houston. The Rev. Ralph David Abernathy of the Southern Christian Leadership Conference showed up with the poor people's mule train as a reminder that poverty existed in the United States while billions of dollars were spent on space.

Now man was ready to fly to the moon.

Wednesday, July 16

The success of the nation's space program in preparation for this epic flight had made the proceedings on launch complex 39A seem almost routine: the 36-story-tall Saturn 5 rocket loaded with 3,242 tons of propellant, the Apollo spacecraft that crowned it, even the astronauts that climbed aboard—all were veterans; the countdown for lift-off, the dazzling sheet of flame, the thunderous sound that assaulted ears and pressed against bodies of bystanders—all had occurred before.

But at 9:32 o'clock on this morning all was different.

The assembled thousands cheered, prayed, cried or looked on disbelievingly as Apollo 11 punished the launch pad, lifted off, soared southeast and sped out over the Atlantic. Millions around the world watched the blazing departure on television, among them President Richard Nixon in Washington, who later issued this proclamation:

"In past ages, exploration was a lonely enterprise. But today the miracles of space travel are matched by miracles of space communication; even across the vast lunar distance, television brings the moment of discovery into our homes and makes us all participants."

The huge rocket was visible for nearly three minutes and the spectators viewed the flash that signaled ignition of the five engines on the second stage. Twelve minutes after the trio—civilian commander Neil A. Armstrong, Air Force Col. Edwin E. Aldrin Jr. and Air Force Lt. Col. Michael Collins—left their home planet, and the third stage drilled them into a 118-mile-high earth orbit, where they remained for 2½ hours checking all systems before committing themselves to the moon, 250,801 miles distant.

With everything working flawlessly, the still attached third stage of the Saturn 5 was re-ignited high over the western Pacific. The firing increased Apollo 11's speed from 17,427 to 24,245 miles per hour, enough to break the grip of earth's gravity, and propelled them along the lunar trail blazed twice in the previous seven months—by the astronauts of Apollo 8 (*The World in 1968, 240–245*) and Apollo 10 (*100–105*) who came tantalizingly close as they orbited the earth's only natural satellite to pave the way for the momentous landing attempt.

As Apollo 11 streaked across the vastness of space on its three-day outward journey, Collins separated the command ship and pivoted around 180 degrees to face the lunar module, or LM, cradled atop the spent third stage. Collins gingerly approached and poked a harpoon-like docking mechanism into a connecting device in the LM. Once the linkup was completed, the third stage was jettisoned and the two ships flew nose-to-nose toward the moon. By this time the astronauts were already 50,000 miles from home.

Before retiring for their first night in space, the spacemen pointed a color television camera out the window and gave earthlings a view of their planet, rapidly shrinking in the eyes of the Apollo 11 crew.

Thursday, July 17

While the astronauts ate breakfast, Mission Control read them the news, including a Russian announcement that its Luna 15 spacecraft, launched July 13, had orbited the moon. The Soviets were mum on the mission of the unmanned vehicle. But there was considerable speculation it might try to land, scoop up lunar soil and return it to earth before the Apollo 11 astronauts could collect moon samples.

In Washington, President Nixon announced the astronauts planned to place on the moon medals honoring five men—three Americans and two Russians—who died for the conquest of space (*The World in 1967, 8–13; 79; The World in 1968, 67*).

At 11:33 a.m., Apollo 11 soared past the halfway point of the journey to the moon when the spaceship was exactly 120,003 miles from both earth and moon.

Less than an hour later, the astronauts fired their spaceship engine for three seconds to adjust their path so Apollo 11 would pass within 69 miles of the moon's backside on Saturday—precisely where they wanted to be for injection into lunar orbit.

The successful firing of the 20,500-pound thrust engine was a reassuring sound to Armstrong, Aldrin and Collins. For this engine also must insert them into moon orbit and later start them on the way back to earth.

In the evening, the astronauts beamed another TV show to earth, once again showing a greenish-blue globe streaked with clouds. They took viewers on a tour of their cabin, showing the sextant and other navigation equipment.

"We have a happy home," Collins reported. "Plenty of room for the three of us. We're all finding our favorite little corners."

Such a home in space was not foreign to the trio. All were veterans of previous flights—Armstrong Gemini 8, Collins Gemini 10 and Aldrin Gemini 12 (*The World in 1966, 56–58, 212–216*). Armstrong, a native of Wapakoneta, Ohio, and graduate of Purdue University, lived for one thing—flying—and earned his pilot's license before he was licensed to drive a car. The former Navy combat pilot and one of the world's most accomplished test pilots was the first civilian to be admitted to the elite corps of astronauts.

Aldrin, born in Montclair, N.J., was, like his father, an Air Force colonel. He finished third in his class at West Point, earned a Doctor of Science degree from Massachusetts Institute of Technology, flew 66 combat missions in Korea and joined the astronaut team in 1963. Collins, like Aldrin, was from a military family—this one Army—and was born in Rome where his father was stationed. Collins, also like Aldrin, was a graduate of West Point and an Air Force lieutenant colonel.

All three astronauts were born in 1930 and all created a fortunate balance of personality and interests. Armstrong, commander of the flight, took pride in the skills of man mastering machine. Aldrin, who studied geology to better judge lunar rocks, was the computer expert. Collins, the command module pilot, was fascinated by the variety of tasks required in running the mother ship alone while the other two astronauts descended to the moon in the LM.

Friday, July 18

As Apollo 11 raced unerringly toward the moon, Christopher C. Kraft Jr., director of flight operations, asked astronaut Frank Borman to telephone the Russians for information on Luna's orbit. Borman, who commanded the Apollo 8 moon orbit in 1968, had recently received a warm welcome in Russia. In reply, the president of the Soviet Academy of Sciences, Dr. M. V. Keldysh, cabled Borman that Luna 15 would not intersect the "published trajectory" of Apollo 11. He reported that Luna was on

Aldrin: His First Step . . . he begins his walk

an entirely different path and that Borman would be notified of any changes. It was the first time the Soviets had communicated directly with the U.S. about a Russian mission in progress, and some observers saw it as a step toward space cooperation between the two powers.

Friday afternoon the astronauts turned on the television camera and let earthlings come along as Armstrong and Aldrin crawled through a connecting tunnel into the lunar module to check its systems. Clear pictures showed them inside the fragile spidery craft, inspecting switches and dials and the back packs that would provide them life support on the moon. While in the LM, Armstrong and Aldrin used the radio code name they had selected for the moon lander—Eagle. Collins used the call sign Columbia for the command vessel.

Just before midnight, Apollo 11 sped across an invisible line called the equigravisphere, and the moon's gravity exerted a greater force than that of earth. The spaceship's speed, now slowed to 2,300 m.p.h., began accelerating. The moon was 43,495 miles away.

Saturday, July 19

Armstrong, Aldrin and Collins raced into the shadow of the moon at 8:50 a.m. and reported a spectacular first sighting of their target. Armstrong reported a brilliant solar corona as the moon eclipsed all but the halo of gases surrounding the sun.

"It looks like an eerie sight," he commented. "I can pick out features on the moon in earthshine. I see the crater Tycho fairly clearly. I can see the sky all around the moon, even on the rim of it, where there's no earthshine or sunshine." Collins said that despite the sudden darkness, the light reflected from the earth was bright enough in the cabin to read by.

As Apollo 11 bore down on the moon, Russia's Luna 15 shifted into a slightly higher path than it had been following, but still far from the course intended for the astronauts.

At 1:13 p.m., Apollo 11 slipped behind the darkside of the moon, where the astronauts were to trigger the engine that was to fire them into moon orbit—reducing their speed from 5,645 to 3,736 m.p.h. After 34 suspenseful minutes the spaceship reappeared around the edge of the moon and flashed the good word it was in orbit. "It was like perfect. Everything looks good up here," Armstrong reported on the six-minute engine burn.

They were in an orbit ranging from 70 to 195 miles high, precisely what they sought. After circling the moon twice, the spacemen again fired the engine to achieve a more nearly circular orbit with a low point of 62 miles and high point of 75 miles. As Apollo 11 zipped over the cratered plain in the Sea of Tranquillity, where Armstrong and Aldrin planned to land the next day, Armstrong said: "We're getting our first view of the landing site approach. The pictures and snapshots brought back by Apollos 8 and 10 have given us a pretty good preview of what to look at here. It looks very much like the pictures, but it's like the difference between watching a real football game and one on TV. There's no substitute for actually being there."

The astronauts shared their view with the earth, transmitting vivid color pictures of the lunar landscape with its boulder-strewn plains, deep craters and rugged highlands. Then Aldrin wiggled through the tunnel into the lunar module to again check systems to make certain they were functioning for Sunday's landing attempt.

Sunday, July 20

None of the astronauts slept very long before awakening for the historic day. Collins logged six hours and Armstrong and Aldrin five each. Mission Control awakened them at 7:02 a.m.

Aldrin, LM and wind experiment on moon

They ate breakfast and Armstrong and Aldrin donned their moon-walking suits.

As the world waited for the incredible moment, prayers were offered in many lands for a safe journey.

In mid-morning Armstrong and Aldrin transferred through the tunnel into the LM and began preparing for the dangerous descent to the surface. Russia, meanwhile, announced another course change for Luna 15, sweeping the mystery probe as close as 10 miles to the moon, but still far from the Apollo path.

Armstrong stood at the commander's post at the left of Eagle's cabin, Aldrin at the right. Both were restrained by loose harnesses. They extended the four landing legs and reported they were ready to go. Two minutes before the spaceship disappeared behind the moon on its 13th orbit, Mission Control relayed the word: "You're 'go' for undocking." Tense minutes followed until the two ships—now separated—emerged from the far side and Armstrong reported: "The Eagle has wings!"

The two ships remained a few feet apart for half an hour while Armstrong and Aldrin evaluated Eagle's condition. Collins fired Columbia's maneuvering rockets to move about two miles away and into a slightly different orbit and both ships sailed behind the backside, where Eagle was to ignite the engine that would start it down. Firing was set for 3:08 p.m.

Suspense built in Mission Control until contact was reestablished with Columbia and Collins reported: "Listen, baby, things are just going swimmingly, just beautiful." Two minutes later the ground acquired Eagle and Armstrong reported: "The burn was on time." They were headed for the Sea of Tranquillity.

They had fired themselves into an orbit that took them within 9.8 miles of the surface. Eagle swooped closer, with the thrust of an engine started by Armstrong, and skimmed dangerously low over the moon's hostile craters and mountains. Then computer alarm lights began to flash in the cabin. The computer was overtaxed and they were rapidly approaching an abort situation.

Cool thinking by both the astronauts and the ground saved the day. A young guidance officer, 27-year-old Stephen Bales, quickly reached a solution. He told them to stop asking the computer to display landing information. Instead, Bales, through capsule communicator Charles Duke, passed up the data in a series of dramatic "go's."

Lt. Gen. Samuel Phillips, Apollo program manager, described it later as "a team landing, with Neil at the controls and Aldrin calling out the readings of velocities and altitudes, with the guidance officer on the ground calling out 'go's' in spite of the alarms and with the capsule communicator calling all this up to the crew. . . . I had a strong feeling that, without the ground team part, it might well have been necessary to abort it."

Then Armstrong and Aldrin received a shock as they approached the landing area. As the commander reported later:

"The automatic targeting was taking us right into a football field, a football-field sized crater with a large number of big boulders and rocks for about one or two crater diameters around us. It required flying manually over the rock field to find a reasonably good area." Armstrong needed 90 seconds to find a smooth touchdown spot. That consumed valuable fuel. He had only 15 seconds search time left after he found what he wanted, zeroed in, and the five-foot-long probes dangled like curb feelers from three of the legs. Then they touched the surface.

"Houston, Tranquillity Base here. The Eagle has landed," came the momentous words from Armstrong.

Man landed on the moon at 4:17.42 EDT Sunday, July 20, 1969.

There were cheers and tears in Houston—at Mission Control Center and at the homes of the astronauts.

"Good, good, good," shouted Mrs. Armstrong.

"I just can't believe it," exclaimed Mrs. Aldrin.

"I thought it was fantastically marvelous," said a happy Mrs. Collins.

From Mission Control: "Be advised there are lots of smiling faces in this room and all over the world."

"There are two of them up here," Armstrong advised.

"And don't forget one in the command module," chimed in Collins, who was to become an almost forgotten man for the next day as he orbited 65 miles overhead.

For the next three hours, Armstrong and Aldrin busily checked Eagle's systems, making ready for a quick takeoff in case of an emergency. With no problems and excitement running high, the astronauts asked permission to step outside early, skipping a planned four-hour rest period.

"We will support it," Mission Control replied.

While waiting to go out, Aldrin, a deeply religious man, privately celebrated communion with bread and wine.

Armstrong and Aldrin then struggled into their boots, gloves, helmets and back packs. They depressurized the cabin, and Armstrong opened the hatch. He climbed out backwards, cautiously stepping onto a platform at the top of a nine-rung ladder. On the second step he pulled a lanyard which opened a compartment, exposing the black and white television camera that permitted the world to share a great moment in history.

An estimated 528 million people, the largest TV audience ever, watched breathlessly as the Apollo 11 commander negotiated the remaining steps, resembling a ghostly-white figure as he descended toward an eerie, alien surface. He placed both feet in a 37-inch diameter footpad at the bottom of the ladder. Then he extended his left foot, encased in a thick size 9½ B boot, and stepped onto the dusty surface.

Man first touched the moon at 10:56.20 p.m. EDT Sunday, July 20, 1969.

"That's one small step for a man, one giant leap for mankind," said Armstrong.

With an almost shuffling gait, Armstrong began to move about in the harsh light of the lunar morning. His first steps were tentative tests of the moon soil's firmness and his ability to move about in the one-sixth gravity field. "The surface is fine and powdery," he reported. "It adheres in fine layers, like powdered charcoal, to the soles and sides of my boots. I only go in a fraction of an inch, maybe an eighth of an inch, but I can see the footprints of my boots and the treads in the fine, sandy particles."

He moved stiffly away from the ladder and, using a tong-like device, collected about two pounds of lunar soil which he put in a plastic bag and stuffed in a pocket in the left leg of his suit. This was called a contingency sample, a small prize for scientists in case the astronauts had to leave the moon before gathering a larger supply of rocks and soil.

"It's a very soft surface," Armstrong said. "But here and there where I bored with the contingency sample collector, I ran into a very hard surface. It appears to be very cohesive material of some sort."

Then he permitted himself a long look at the level, rock-strewn moonscape around him. "It has a stark beauty all its own," he described. "It's like much of the high desert areas of the United States. It's different, but it's very pretty out here."

Aldrin stepped onto the surface 19 minutes after Armstrong's first step. "Beautiful, beautiful," he exclaimed. "Magnificent desolation."

While Aldrin acquired his "moon legs," Armstrong carried the television camera about 60 feet away and mounted it on a post he had driven into the soil. This gave earthlings a dramatic, panoramic view of the entire moon walk. The centerpiece of the picture was the strange-looking LM, silhouetted against the deep blackness of space.

The astronauts continually tested their ability to function in the one-sixth gravity field, loping like antelopes and bouncing like kangaroos. "It's not difficult at all moving about in one-sixth G," Armstrong reported as he flashed before the camera like a graceful gazelle. "The rocks are rather slippery," Aldrin said. "When I'm about to lose my balance in one direction, I find recovery is quite natural and very easy."

Together, the astronauts planted a 3-by-5-foot American flag and Aldrin stepped back and saluted it. Wire stiffeners enabled it to stand out in the airless vacuum. But they made it plain they came as ambassadors for all mankind. They unveiled a stainless steel plaque on the ladder leg which bore these words: "Here men from planet earth first set foot upon the moon, July, 1969, A.D. We came in peace for all mankind." It was signed by Armstrong, Aldrin, Collins and President Nixon.

They also left on the moon a disc on which messages from the leaders of 76 nations had been inscribed.

Three experiments then were set up. The first, which they brought home, was a four-foot strip of aluminum foil that was unrolled for an hour to capture particles streaming from the sun. The others, intended to provide data for months after the astronauts left, were a seismometer to record moonquakes, meteor hits and other disturbances, and a mirror-like reflector to beam back to earth laser beams fired from a California observatory. The latter was an experiment to measure the precise distance between earth and moon.

They described vividly their wild and wondrous world and collected about 50 pounds of rocks which they packed in airtight containers for the trip back to earth.

As the astronauts moved about they were protected by their bulky, multi-layered space suits which cost $300,000 each. They reported no discomfort from the 243 degrees (Fahrenheit) above zero heat in sunlight and the 279 degrees below zero cold in the shadow of the LM.

Monday, July 21

It was after midnight, and time to return to the cabin. The astronauts hauled the two rock boxes up on a conveyor device that resembled a clothesline. Aldrin re-entered the cabin at 12:58 a.m., followed minutes later by Armstrong. Aldrin had been outside one hour 44 minutes and Armstrong two hours 14 minutes.

They sealed the hatch and repressurized the cabin. They connected their suits to Eagle's life support system and removed their back packs, hoses and boots, which they placed in a bag with other unneeded equipment. Then they depressurized, opened the hatch and tossed the bag onto the surface. The lunar littering was recorded by the TV camera and was registered as a thump by the seismometer.

At 5 a.m., still on the moon, the explorers settled down to rest. Neither slept well. There were no couches in the LM, so Aldrin stretched out on the floor, and Armstrong leaned back against a cabinet. The ground aroused them after a few hours to prepare for the critical takeoff from the moon and the start of the long journey home.

Two hours before they left, Luna 15 plummeted to a crash-landing at 300 m.p.h. in the moon's Sea of Crises. It died without any announcement from the Russians on the nature of its mission. The incident pointed up the great lead the United States had built up in space exploration after trailing so badly in the early years of the space age.

The world waited anxiously as the time for blastoff approached. For if the 3,500-pound thrust engine in the LM's ascent stage failed to fire, the astronauts would be stranded on the moon with only 18 hours of oxygen remaining and no hope of rescue.

"You're cleared for takeoff," Mission Control radioed.

"Roger. We're No. 1 on the runway," Aldrin answered.

Eagle worked in close radio harmony with Collins in the command ship as the firing neared. Precisely 69 seconds after Columbia passed over the landing site, Armstrong and Aldrin blasted off.

It was 1:55 p.m. Eagle had been on the moon 21 hours 37 minutes.

Engine and guidance systems worked flawlessly and after 7 minutes 12 seconds, Armstrong and Aldrin were in a low orbit ranging from 10 to 54 miles above the surface.

"The Eagle is back in orbit," Armstrong announced happily, "having left Tranquillity Base and leaving behind a replica from our Apollo 11 patch with an olive branch."

Columbia was 300 miles ahead of them, and the chase was on. Eagle raced to its high point of 54 miles on the far side of the moon and executed the first of four maneuvers that caught the fleeting Collins after a tricky pursuit lasting more than 3½ hours. While Armstrong held Eagle steady, Collins moved in and inserted the docking harpoon into the LM's nose. There was a slight misalignment and for a few seconds the combined vehicles vibrated.

"All hell broke loose," Collins said. But the coupling held, and Columbia and Eagle were back together after a separation of 27 hours 47 minutes. Armstrong and Aldrin wasted little time returning through the tunnel to rejoin Collins.

Mission Control asked the Columbia pilot how it felt to have company. "Damned good, I'll tell you," Collins replied.

The astronauts had no more need for the LM, so the faithful Eagle was kicked loose, to orbit the moon for several weeks before lunar gravity tugged it down for a crash landing.

The spacemen settled down for several hours sleep before shooting themselves out of moon orbit.

Tuesday, July 22

At 1:56 a.m., behind the moon, the astronauts triggered Columbia's big engine to break out of the clutch of lunar gravity and start the 60-hour quarter-million-mile voyage home.

"Open up the LRL doors, Charlie," said Collins. "We're coming home." He referred to the lunar receiving laboratory where the moonmen were to be quarantined for 16 days to make certain they brought back no germs that would be harmful to life on earth. "Roger," said capsule communicator Charles Duke. "We got you coming home."

Mission Control told the astronauts everything was working fine and suggested they take a nap. All promptly fell asleep for nearly 10 hours. They were awakened in time to conduct a small 10-second firing of Columbia's maneuvering thrusters to take dead aim at Thursday's planned landing area in the Pacific Ocean.

In the evening Apollo 11 transmitted a 20-minute telecast that included a picture of earth as a half sphere 175,000 miles away.

"It's nice to sit here and watch the earth getting larger and larger and the moon smaller and smaller," Aldrin commented.

"No matter where you travel, it's nice to get home," Armstrong added.

During the homeward trip, the astronauts doffed their dust-covered moon suits and packed them in plastic containers. They sucked up loose moon particles with a vacuum and placed the material in chemically treated bags. The air within the capsule was circulated more than 100 times through special filters. Although scientists were fairly certain the moon supported no life, the precautions were necessary on the remote chance lunar bacteria did exist.

Wednesday, July 23

Streaking like a tiny speck in the limitless, unyielding vastness of space, Apollo 11 sped past the halfway point of the homeward journey with the astronauts resting and yearning for the good earth.

"It's getting appreciably larger now," said Collins of the globe. "It's looking more like a world."

As their eight-day voyage of discovery neared an end, the astronauts beamed a final 12-minute telecast in which they thanked God and all the people on earth who made the trip possible.

Late Wednesday the ground informed the astronauts that the weatherman forecast thunderstorms for their planned landing area about 1,200 miles southwest of Hawaii. The main recovery ship, the carrier *Hornet*, was directed to a new landing zone 250 miles to the east. The astronauts were told to target for that spot by changing the angle of the spaceship slightly as it dipped into the atmosphere.

Thursday, July 24

Apollo 11 hurtled back toward earth like a speeding bullet, slamming into the atmosphere 400,000 feet above the Pacific at 24,602 miles an hour.

The velocity was slowed dramatically by the thickening atmosphere, and forces six times that of gravity pressed the three astronauts to their couches.

During the hottest part of re-entry, with temperatures of more than 4,000 degrees searing the heat shield, ionized gases enveloped the plunging craft and blocked radio communications for more than three minutes.

Once Apollo 11 came out of the blackout, recovery ships and planes quickly established radio and radar contact.

On the deck of the carrier *Hornet*, President Nixon, Secretary of State William P. Rogers, NASA Administrator Thomas O. Paine, astronaut Borman and hundreds of sailors strained for a glimpse of Apollo 11 dangling under its three 83-foot orange and white parachutes.

The spaceship landed just 13.8 miles from the carrier, but a combination of hazy skies and pre-dawn darkness prevented those on the *Hornet* from seeing the splashdown. The carrier steamed quickly to the landing scene, and Nixon and the others and a worldwide television audience had a ringside seat for the most bizarre welcome ever accorded returning space heroes.

Columbia landed in six-foot waves and was tipped upside down. The astronauts swiftly righted it by inflating flotation bags attached to the side. Within minutes helicopters were overhead and three Navy swimmers had jumped into the warm Poly-

Apollo 11: Splashdown

nesian waters to attach additional flotation collars and to inflate a life raft.

"All three of us are excellent. Take your time," the astronauts told the swimmers when they plugged a telephone into the side of the capsule.

Navy Lt. Chancey Hatleberg jumped into the sea with another raft, three biological isolation garments called BIGs, and several cans of disinfectant. Hatleberg wore a BIG. After the other three frogmen moved upwind, Hatleberg knocked on the window and told the astronauts to open the hatch. They did, and he quickly threw in the three BIGs and reclosed the opening.

Several minutes later the spacemen climbed into the raft in their strange garb, which had gas mask-like filters on the face to trap any moon germs exhaled by the astronauts. Hatleberg shut the hatch and sprayed the area around it with Betadine, a decontaminant. He decontaminated the astronauts, using sodium hypochloride and a glove to scrub down their suits. Aldrin, in turn, scrubbed down the Navy lieutenant.

Armstrong, Aldrin and Collins were hoisted one by one into a helicopter which deposited them on the desk of the carrier at 1:57 p.m., one hour and seven minutes after splashdown.

Nixon clapped and waved as the helicopter touched down and the ship's band played *"Columbia, the Gem of the Ocean."*

The chopper was lowered by elevator to the hangar deck. The astronauts quickly moved 12 steps from the helicopter to a 35-foot quarantine trailer—their home for the trip back to Houston. Welcoming them were Dr. William Carpentier, a NASA physician, and John Hirasaki, NASA engineer, both of whom volunteered to be isolated with the astronauts.

Far away in Houston, the men of Mission Control laughed, cried, patted one another on the back and waved American flags. Flashed on the huge displayed board were the 1961 words of another President, John F. Kennedy: "I believe that this nation should commit itself to achieving the goal, before this decade is out, of landing a man on the moon and returning him safely to earth."

Beside the words was a large replica of the Apollo 11 patch,

an Eagle descending to the moon with an olive branch, and above it this cryptic message:

"Task accomplished. . . . July, 1969."

Post-flight

For two days the *Hornet* steamed toward Hawaii, while the astronauts underwent medical checks, read, played cards and watched films of the moon walk in their isolation van.

In Pearl Harbor, the van was transferred by truck to Hickam Air Force Base and flown by C141 transport to Houston, where it was trundled by truck to the Lunar Receiving Laboratory early on the morning of July 27. Here they remained for 16 days, completing a 21-day quarantine period that started the day they closed Eagle's hatch on the moon. Housed with them were 14 other persons, doctors, technicians, a cook, photographer and public information officer. Six others, accidentally exposed to moon dust in another part of the laboratory, joined them before the quarantine ended.

In other sections of the lab, engineers examined the Apollo 11 command ship and scientists and geologists eagerly analyzed the 50 pounds of lunar rock and soil—the first material ever brought to earth from an alien world. Experts said it would be months before any definite conclusions could be drawn from the moon rocks. The material was handled carefully in vacuum chambers, with technicians inspecting and cutting them through glove ports. Solutions made from the dust were injected into sterile mice, cockroaches, fish and various plants to determine if any germs or illness developed.

No ill effects were recorded. And the astronauts, in excellent shape, were released from quarantine Aug. 10. They rushed home to their families.

Aldrin stated their purpose well when he noted the plaque they left on the moon with the inscription: "We came in peace for all mankind."

"I hope," he said, "that some wayward stranger in the third millennia may read it and say, 'this is where it all began.' It can be the beginning of a new era when man begins to understand his universe and man begins to truly understand himself."

Men on the Moon: The Acclaim

"THIS OPERATION is somewhat like a periscope of a submarine," said Mike Collins as he soared through space aboard Apollo 11. "All you see is the three of us, but beneath the surface are thousands and thousands of others."

Those thousands were multiplied into millions: the leaders in Washington who for a decade goaded the feat to reality . . . the brains and brawn that assembled the magnificent machines and primed the astronauts . . . the brave who had gone before . . . the taxpayers who footed the bills . . . those whose age or nationality prevented them from giving anything but enthusiasm. None of these facts phased America, nor the world, as humble homage was paid the men of Apollo 11—civilian Commander Neil A. Armstrong and Air Force Col. Edwin E. Aldrin Jr., the first from planet earth to touch another celestial body, and Air

Force Lt. Col. Collins, the man in the mother ship that hovered above the men on the moon.

An estimated half-billion persons around the globe watched, via television, man's first step on the moon and shared in the exhilaration expressed by leaders of more than 100 foreign governments, both friendly and frigid. That same exhilaration abounded on July 24, when the astronauts splashed down safely in the Pacific. Church bells pealed, automobile horns and whistles sounded. Prayers were offered, cheers erupted.

For a few moments at least the world seemed to bask in unity and America glowed in a glory it had bestowed upon itself and the universe. But in the eyes of a grateful nation it was the three astronauts who deserved a lions' share of the credit. And that which was due was paid two days after the trio, de-

President Nixon welcomes astronauts Neil Armstrong, Michael Collins and Edwin Aldrin Jr. in their quarantine quarters

clared free of any ill effects of their mighty mission, emerged from three weeks of clinical isolation.

The one-day orbit of acclaim was launched well before dawn from Houston, where the three astronauts and their families boarded Air Force One, the Presidential jet, for a three-hour flight to New York, the first leg of a cross-continent hop that touched down in Chicago and ended, 19 hours and 3,875 miles later, in Los Angeles.

New York City greeted the astronauts in a manner some said was equalled only twice in the century—first in 1927 for Charles A. Lindbergh, the first man to fly non-stop alone from New York to Paris, and then in 1962 for John H. Glenn Jr., the first American to orbit the earth.

A fireboat hurled six jets of water 60 feet into the air and pleasure craft and tugboats in the East River sounded their whistles as Marine helicopters, transporting the guests of honor from Kennedy International Airport, set down on the tip of Manhattan. As the astronauts in open limousines rode up Lower Broadway—Apollo Way for the day—the crowd, squeezed five deep along the route, unleashed its emotions. A deafening roar of approval assaulted the astronauts' ears as a deluge of ticker tape and confetti rained down on the parade.

The astronauts alighted at City Hall for a brief respite from the well-wishers, then a short public ceremony. But back on Lower Broadway, where 300 tons of ticker tape awaited clean-up crews, crowds continued to gather, only to be dismayed by the word that the parade had passed more than 30 minutes ahead of schedule.

"This is one of New York's great moments," Mayor John V. Lindsay told the astronauts and 10,000 onlookers at City Hall. "We have honored many voyagers before—men who sailed around the world, men who flew alone across the ocean. But today we honor three men who forged the first link between earth and the stars. Today we honor three men who have affirmed the best we have within us. All that New York has given today —its cheers, its praise, its medals, its glory—is dwarfed by what you three men have done."

Replied Aldrin: " . . . it is rather for us to be congratulating you for your support—the support that made our mission possible."

The space heroes then motored through the midtown area en route to the United Nations. At 42nd Street the confetti, made up more of paper towels and pages from telephone directories than ticker tape, was so dense that the astronauts could hardly see or be seen as the motorcade turned east. At the UN Secretary General U Thant said the flight "brought us a renewed realization of what we, as members of the human race, can accomplish on this planet with our resources and our technology if we are prepared to combine our efforts and work together for the benefit of all mankind."

"I can tell you share with us the hope that we citizens of earth who can solve the problem of leaving earth can also solve the problem of staying on it," said Armstrong, addressing some 1,000 persons, many of them UN delegates.

Next stop: Chicago, where the Windy City's welcome for the astronauts was exceeded only by that for General Douglas MacArthur in 1951, upon his return from the Far East.

An estimated two million persons lined the five-mile parade route though the loop. State dignitaries and a throng of 1,500 onlookers greeted the moon voyagers as their aircraft touched down at O'Hare International Airport, where helicopters whisked them off to the bunting-bedecked business district.

As the astronauts passed along State Street and Michigan Avenue in an open limousine once custom built for Pope Paul,

18 bales of confetti fluttered in the afternoon breeze. Some 500 homing pigeons and 5,000 balloons were released, and a mother lode of fireworks blasted into the sky.

The 2½-hour stopover also included an official welcome at Civic Center, where the astronauts became honorary citizens of Chicago, and a meeting with 10,000 young people gathered in Grant Park along the lakefront.

In Los Angeles it was not the city but the nation, headed by its President, that honored the men who gave mankind a new planet to walk on. The event was billed as a state dinner. As such it would have been the biggest—10 times as many persons as the 140 normally accommodated in the White House state dining room—the costliest—about $50,000—and the farthest afield from Washington. But technically it was just a formal fete since, according to strict protocol, the President may throw a state dinner only for another head of state. Nonetheless, it was a fitting climax for one of America's proudest days.

The ballroom of the Century Plaza Hotel, a crescent on the Avenue of Stars, was decorated in orange and gold—the colors of the earth as it appears from the moon—with candlelight and silver creating a quiet regal glow.

The fanfare was begun by the white-uniformed Army Herald Trumpets. Then to ruffles and flourishes from the Marine Corps Band, President Nixon, Vice President Agnew and the astronauts, all in black tie, and their wives, in flowing gowns, strode in and seated themselves amid thunderous applause from those who had accepted invitations that were considered the most sought after in decades.

The guest list included a liberal sprinkling of the Hollywood set and Republican leaders. Democrats were decidedly thin. Former Presidents Truman and Johnson had been invited but sent regrets. Former Vice President Hubert H. Humphrey and Gov. Lester Maddox of Georgia were there, but Sen. Edward M. Kennedy, D-Mass., whose brother, the late President, launched the space program, and California's junior senator, Alan Cranston, weren't invited. Diplomats from 86 nations, the Supreme Court, the Cabinet and about 50 congressmen showed up. Representatives of labor, the news media, the military and religious and business sectors were there, as were aviation heroes, former space heroes and those yet to soar into space. So was the President's brother.

The Strolling Strings wound through the ballroom providing entertainment by singing and strumming such tunes as "Around the World," "Stairway to the Stars" and "Fly Me to the Moon." While the 1,440 guests dined on a seven-course repast 3,000 pickets patrolled the front of the Plaza protesting war, poverty and the space program.

Before the evening was over, President Nixon presented each of the three astronauts with the Medal of Freedom, the nation's highest civilian award. Honors also were bestowed posthumously upon the three astronauts killed in a launch pad fire (The World in 1967, 8–13) while the trail to the moon was still being blazed.

And, of course, there were speeches.

"We thank you for your courage," said President Nixon, "we thank you for raising our sights, the sights of men and women throughout the world, to a new dimension. The sky is no longer the limit."

Collins declared himself "proud to be an inhabitant of this magnificent planet" and Aldrin said "this is an honor to all Americans who believed, who persevered with us."

"I was struck this morning in New York by a proudly waved but carefully scribbled sign," said Armstrong. "It said: 'through you, we touched the moon.' It was our privilege today to touch America."

Men on the Moon: The Future

NEIL ARMSTRONG's small first step from the bottom rung of Eagle's ladder to the moon's powdery surface was indeed "one giant leap for mankind." By landing on the moon, Armstrong and Edwin Aldrin carried man's eternal questing for the unknown to another celestial body. They opened the gateway to the limitless frontier of space.

After centuries of dreams and prophecies, man had broken his terrestrial bonds and set foot on another world and afforded himself a magnificent opportunity to look deeply into the origins of the moon, the earth and perhaps the universe. It was an exciting preview of the future. Beyond lay the planets and stars. Man would go there too, for he now had demonstrated what his ingenuity and courage could achieve when harnessed to a grand design.

But most of all, Armstrong and Aldrin and Michael Collins had placed man's problems, as well as his world, in new focus.

For, as the world reflected on the incredible events taking place 250,000 miles away, it also reflected on what was happening on earth. It seemed that the world sensed the threshold of a new era, the Age of the Moon, in which the earth and the universe were shrinking.

If much of the world could pull together as one for three astronauts headed for the moon, people asked, why could not nations work in harmony? They seemed to look to the United States for the answer. America had demonstrated its overwhelming technological capability. And its policy of an open space program for all to see paid rich dividends. Never had the U.S. image shone brighter.

America showed that it was willing to share its triumphs, tragedies and knowledge with all who cared to participate. Certainly it was time to recall President John F. Kennedy's May 25, 1961, decision that set this nation's course to the moon.

Moon rock: Aldrin, Collins and Armstrong study two-pound specimen

The lunar landing goal transformed the U.S. space program from a sluggish, reluctant reaction to Soviet triumphs into a vibrant challenge that required the meshing of science, industry and technology. Kennedy made it clear he was calling for a long-term commitment that would be difficult and expensive to accomplish.

Congress and the American people backed the young President, who tragically did not live to see his goal achieved. His successor, Lyndon B. Johnson, supported the effort to the hilt.

The largest, most imaginative government-industry-university team ever assembled for a single peacetime project went to work and the miracles began. In eight years the team, reaching a peak of 420,000 persons, built a remarkable and powerful set of machines that carried the first men to the moon. It was done with things that didn't exist a dozen years before—sophisticated computers and guidance systems, micro-miniature electronics and new metal alloys.

Development of these devices vaulted the United States into the world's technological leadership, and tangible technical benefits began falling from space research—pointing the way to better education, better communications and weather forecasting, less pollution and better food production. Man, unfortunately, was slow to utilize this spinoff to create an aura of better world understanding. But he gradually began to get the message.

Apollo was a U.S. program. Its rockets and spaceships bore the Stars and Stripes. But history will record that the voyage to the moon belonged to all men. It was truly a triumph of man's indomitable spirit to push to new horizons. Visionary men like Galileo, Kepler, Newton, Archimedes, Copernicus, Tsiolkovsky, Oberth, Goddard and others from many lands provided the basic knowledge years and centuries ago. And man dreamed of landing on the moon long before he created nations. So Armstrong, Aldrin and Collins went as representatives of everyone on earth.

Thus, man's urge to seek the unknown of space, which began in a spirit of competition, could reach maturity in a cooperative effort to explore the universe. The U.S. and Russia for several months had been moving closer together in the field of space cooperation. Apollo 11 seemed to narrow the gap. Soviet leaders sent unprecedented messages of praise. The Russian people were permitted to see delayed television pictures of the moon walk and to watch the landing and recovery operation as it happened. There was accelerated talk of these two space-faring nations joining with scientists of other nations to develop a base on the moon.

The three American Apollo crews who had flown to the vicinity of the moon gave man a new perspective of his home planet, whirling a lonely vigil through the solar system, protected from the deadly radiation from the searing sun and the cold of night only by a thin layer of gases trapped in a gravitational field. These adventurers expressed surprise at what a small planet earth really was when viewed in the unyielding and limitless blackness of space and how friendly it seemed in contrast to the bleakness of the moon. Beyond the earth's protective veil of gases, they found a world that many nations might want to conquer together. That was one of the hopes engendered by Apollo 11. Armstrong, Aldrin and Collins took the first tentative step. They proved man could safely go to the moon and function there. Gone were the science-fiction horror stories of man's difficulties in operating on the moon. Vanished were the theories that man and spaceship would be engulfed by deep layers of dust or battered by streams of radiation and meteorites.

And Apollo 11 was a conclusive demonstration of the need for man to carry out a meaningful exploration. Without the astronauts to steer Eagle to a safe landing, the craft almost certainly would have crashed in a rock-filled crater to which it was being guided by automatic systems. No unmanned vehicle could have completed the evaluation and selective rock collecting that Armstrong and Aldrin did in their short stay. Unmanned precursors certainly were necessary to pave the way. But it is man who must conduct the detailed exploration.

The rocks returned by the astronauts would provide more answers about the origin and composition of the moon than centuries of peering through telescopes on earth. Scientists, who would study the samples for years, were elated. Examiners initially identified many materials similar to those on earth and discovered unusual and fascinating features. They found no evidence of life and made no major conclusions. Most held to their pet theories about the makeup and origin of the moon.

But some would change their ideas. Within a few days after the arrival of the rocks, advocates of a cold moon began to falter—faced with considerable evidence of molten material, indicating a hot interior.

The scientists hoped detailed analyses eventually would reveal the age of the moon. From this and other information they believed it might be possible to determine how the moon was formed and thus explain many baffling mysteries about lunar-planetary relationships. On the moon there were no oceans or atmosphere to destroy surface features. Thus, it could retain a record dating back more than four billion years to the infancy of the solar system. Was the moon once a part of the earth? Is it a wanderer from space trapped in earth's gravitational field? Were earth and moon formed essentially at the same time by the same giant gas cloud?

The rocks also could help settle the ages-old scientific debate whether the moon's craters were formed by volcanic action or meteor impacts, or both. Because Apollo 11's rocks came from only one small area of the moon, they only whetted the appetites of those seekers of the unknown. So other astronauts would go to other parts of the moon and bring back other precious bits of lunar soil.

These early flights could determine the feasibility of building an Antarctica-type lunar base, and the possibility of international cooperation in such an endeavor. At such a camp man would look back on his earth and he would contemplate the remarkable series of events that brought him to the moon. He would gaze, too, at the planets and the stars, he would wonder, and he would go there too. That was the nature of his questing.

Tranquillity Base was only the gateway.

Dr. George E. Mueller, the space agency's director for manned space flight, put it this way, as Apollo 11 streaked for home:

"Apollo 11 conclusively proved that man is no longer bound to the limits of the planet on which for so long he has lived. The organization that brought men to the moon stands ready for the next step. The knowledge possessed by man is sufficient, the resources are adequate for the task of carrying out this next step. The will of the people of this nation and the world will determine whether mankind will make the great leap to the planets.

"This nation," Mueller said, "should join with all men in the pursuit of this destiny."

Aldrin, after his safe return, said:

"The footprints on the moon are a true symbol of the human spirit. They show we can do what we want to do, what we must do and what we will do."

Goodbye, Eagle

Men on the Moon: Farewell

Ave atque vale, Eagle. See you around the old cosmos.

You surely were the most exciting bird in history, Eagle, and for a few singing hours you made a family of man. Now we go our separate ways again, but we'll remember, we'll remember. *Dosvidanya* and so long, Eagle.

From a quarter of a million miles, through the blackness of space, you gave us a sense of our bigness and our smallness, Eagle. A vision of living creatures, more alike than unalike, hanging by their thumbs to the one warm, blue sphere we yet see on the lifeless void. *Salaam* and *shalom,* Eagle.

Try to forgive and understand us, Eagle, but you had to be left behind; you were expendable. You weren't designed to get back through the earth's atmosphere but only to fly around the moon. Sorry, Eagle. *Au revoir* and *auf wiedersehen.*

Take comfort, Eagle, if it is you who needs comfort more than we. Columbus' *Santa Maria* didn't make it back either; it was wrecked far from home. They brought Lindbergh's plane back to the Smithsonian and the tourists gawk at it every day.

His was called *The Spirit of St. Louis,* but you, we like to think, were the spirit of all of us. *Sayonara* and *ciao,* Eagle.

You were strictly a moon bird, Eagle, and to the moon you will return. Remember, Robert Falcon Scott lies buried in the Antarctic and John Keats died in Rome, Lord Byron in Greece, all three far from that "sceptered isle" called England.

And you, Eagle, will circle the circle of your glory for months and slowly the circle will grow smaller and you'll fly lower and, finally, back to the moon. The Sea of Tranquillity would be a nice touch, don't you think, Eagle? You looked like no bird that ever flew, Eagle, but you had a soaring grace and a thrilling style all your own and we'll remember.

We'll remember when you took life of your own and, singing down the stars, came the message: "The Eagle has wings." And we'll remember, we'll remember that mountain top of our lives, that crescendo of the ages: "The Eagle has landed."

Happy landings, Eagle. *Adios* and goodbye, Eagle. We'll never be the same.

A PAPYRUS EXPERIMENT

For many years the mystery of early human migrations had haunted Thor Heyerdahl. Captivated by the theory that ancient peoples were capable of crossing oceans in vessels of their own construction, the Norwegian ethnologist decided that the best way to test his conclusions was to duplicate the voyages he believed these intrepid pioneer explorers had survived.

His first venture in this direction was made two decades ago, when he set out in search of evidence that the original population of Polynesia had come from South America. Accordingly, in 1947, Heyerdahl and five other Scandinavians successfully navigated a 4,300-mile crossing of the Pacific from Peru to Polynesia in the primitive balsa-log raft Kon-Tiki, named for a pre-Incan sun god.

This adventure captured the world's imagination and sold 20 million copies of the book he subsequently wrote. It also bolstered his idea that Polynesia's first inhabitants had come from South America and not from Southeast Asia, as most authorities had supposed.

More recently Heyerdahl became equally fascinated by the possibility that the highly sophisticated pre-Colombian civilizations of Mexico, Central America and Peru did not simply create their calendars, pyramids and hieroglyphs by themselves but might well have developed them through contact, during some indefinite time in history, with the cultures of ancient Egypt and North Africa.

Such contact, he speculated, could have been the result of mischance, in which hapless Egyptian sailors 5,000 years ago may have been hugging the North African coastline when strong winds drove them out of the sight of land to drift across the Atlantic to the New World.

Heyerdahl thereupon resolved in 1969 to cross the Atlantic from Safi, Morocco to Central America. For this venture he chose a papyrus boat similar to those designed by early Egyptians. Such a reed boat, he felt, could not sink and thus would withstand the perilous voyage if he and the crew of six could learn to navigate it.

Heyerdahl found papyrus boat builders in the Lake Chad district of Equatorial Africa, where reed boats were still in use. Although papyrus no longer was plentiful in Egypt, Heyerdahl got it in Ethiopia. Two workmen spent 48 days binding the 200,000 reeds into sheaves and lashing them together.

The result was a strange looking craft 15 feet wide and 45 feet long, weighing just above 13 tons. It carried a brown cotton sail, 10 oars for rowing and two more for steering. An Egyptologist designed it, using as guides drawings and models from ancient tombs. Heyerdahl christened the vessel Ra, after the Egyptian sun god, and said, "I am putting my faith in the ancient peoples just as I did with Kon-Tiki."

Heyerdahl provisioned Ra as the Egyptian sailors would have done 50 centuries earlier—with bread, honey, dates, olives, nuts, live hens and ducks. Ra's only modern equipment was a radiotelephone and scuba-diving gear. He selected his crew on the premise that the best possible cooperation was expectable from men of widely different backgrounds, provided they had a common purpose. Recruited were an American business man, a Russian doctor, an Egyptian scuba diver, an Italian mountain climber, a Mexican archeologist and one of the boat builders from Lake Chad.

Heyerdahl, a rugged 54, and his companions

departed May 25, oarsmen in conventional boats towing Ra 20 miles to sea. The sail was then hoisted and Ra began its bizarre journey, Heyerdahl depending on the currents to bear it safely through the narrow passage between West Africa and the Canary Islands.

All went well at first. Then, in July, the Ra lost its yardarm in a two-day Atlantic storm, and its speed dropped from 60 miles daily to 20 miles.

The storm also had caused underwater damage, and the crew's diver was chased by more than 25 sharks as he attempted futilely to repair it. Heyerdahl changed his destination from Central America to Barbados. But a few days later the adventurers abandoned the unmanageable ship, on July 19, 600 miles from Barbados, and boarded an escorting fishing boat for Bridgetown. Nonetheless, Heyerdahl told his wife by radio that he

was very happy and that "my theories have been fully confirmed, even if the voyage was not finished."

The Ra had traveled 2,720 miles in 50 days.

Heyerdahl told newsmen in Bridgetown that continuing the voyage would have endangered the lives of the crew. He added that the trip justified his choice of crewmen because, "being pressed together under extreme conditions and forced not only to coexist but also to cooperate for common survival, we have seen with our own eyes and felt in our bones that whatever separates mankind is artificial, and can be tolerated or ignored."

"None of us had had previous experience sailing in a papyrus reed craft," he said, "but for ancient Egyptians with thousands of years experience in this type of sailing it would have been a walkover."

The abondoned Ra: *200,000 reeds that floated 2,720 miles*

FRANCO'S CHOICE: JUAN CARLOS

The Spanish had been playing a guessing game for years: who would succeed the 76-year-old dictator, General Francisco Franco? Franco finally answered the question July 22 by announcing a law of succession giving Juan Carlos of Bourbon the titles Prince of Spain and Royal Highness. The edict also fulfilled Franco's pledge to restore a constitutional monarchy under Juan Carlos.

Juan Carlos, the grandson of Alfonso XIII, Spain's last king, vowed loyalty to the principles of the Franco regime at his investiture. But speaking of the future he added:

"The cult of the past must not be a brake on the evolution of a society that is changing with dizzying rapidity."

There was little public reaction to the news. A strange exception was Juan Carlos' father, Don Juan of Bourbon, whose dissatisfaction arose from his own claims to the throne. Both father and son had wanted to restore the monarchy, but Don Juan contended it should be an alternative to Franco's rule, while Juan Carlos felt that Franco had the right to appoint whomever he wished to restore the monarchy.

Juan Carlos was well educated for his prospective position. He received degrees from three military academies and studied government at the ministries in Madrid. He often appeared with Franco at official functions and lived in a palace near the general's own residence.

"I CHARLES, PRINCE OF WALES, do become your liege man of life and limb. . . ." Charles Philip Arthur George repeated the ancient vows, donned a golden coronet and ermine and velvet mantle, accepted a ring, a sword and a rod of office from his mother, Queen Elizabeth II, and became the 21st Prince of Wales. The lavish ceremony in Caernarvon Castle, rich in pageantry and tradition dating to the 13th century, was heavily guarded to ward off violence threatened by Welsh nationalists seeking separation from Britain. But the incidents failed to dispel the gaiety of the 20-year-old heir to the British throne who celebrated his investiture July 1 with a party aboard the royal yacht Britannia, then set sail for a four-day tour of Wales.

"HE BELONGED TO US ALL"

Tom Mboya had voiced fears of assassination for several months. As Kenya's Minister of Economic Affairs he had been worried about growing factions within the government and had written to friends that his enemies were getting desperate. Mboya himself was frightened enough by Robert Kennedy's assassination to hire a bodyguard.

On July 5 he made a few purchases at a downtown drugstore in Nairobi. As he reappeared in the doorway a car reported to be carrying three men pulled up. One jumped out, fired three shots and fled. Two of the shots hit Mboya. His bodyguard crouched weeping beside the fallen leader. Mboya was pronounced dead at Nairobi Hospital, where riot police had to use force to hold back grieving crowds. Achisng Oneko, publicity secretary of the opposition party, expressed the feelings of many by saying, "There is no question of party here. He belonged to us all."

Even so the assassination sparked tribal riots. Mboya was a member of the Luo tribe, the second largest in Kenya. He had been mentioned as a possible successor to President Jomo Kenyatta, but was felt to have little chance for success because of Kenyatta's affiliation with the Kikuyus, the dominant tribe.

Mboya had refused to appeal to tribal chauvinism, preferring instead to stake his faith in the ruling multi-tribal Kenyan African National Union and in the labor unions. He felt that Kenya's tribal differences were best minimized. Mboya had wide support among the Luo, however, and riots were especially dangerous in Nairobi and in Luo towns in western Kenya, where mobs of Luos assaulted Kikuyus, believing them to be responsible for Mboya's death.

Mboya was born on August 15, 1930. His parents were illiterate but of the Roman Catholic faith, so young Tom received an education in Roman Catholic schools. In the coalition government that preceded independence he was the minister of labor and he led the campaign for independence, and when freedom finally approached he was the youngest of the 50-man delegation which arrived in London in 1960 to discuss independence.

At his death he was regarded as the third most powerful man in the country. A proponent of non-violence, he said he was a socialist by inclination but still a professed democrat.

After a week of ritual tarnished by tribal and political unrest which prompted President Kenyatta to call an emergency cabinet meeting to discuss the security situation, Mboya was buried. On Sept. 10, Nahashon Issac Njenga Njorge, a Kikuyu tribesman, was convicted of Mboya's murder and sentenced to death by hanging.

FOR THE RECORD

ACQUITTED. Dr. Benjamin Spock, convicted in 1968 of conspiring to counsel evasion of the draft. The First U. S. Court of Appeals in Boston, in a majority decision, held on July 11 that Spock's earlier conviction (*The World in 1968, 130-131*) had violated the First Amendment guaranteeing free speech. "I feel pleased personally, but I'm going to redouble my efforts to bring about an end to the war in Vietnam," said the 66-year-old pediatrician when he heard the news.

RE-SENTENCED. Cassius Clay, by a federal judge in Houston to five years in prison and $10,000 fine. Clay had been convicted in 1967 on a charge of refusing induction into the armed forces (*The World in 1967, 133*). He had sought exemption from the draft as a Black Muslim minister and a conscientious objector, but the judge overruled claims by the defense that illegally obtained wire-tapped conversations had tainted the conviction.

DIVORCED: Dr. Christiaan Barnard, 46, South African surgeon who performed the first successful human heart transplant in 1967, by his wife of 21 years, Gertruida, a former nurse, who said: "I've got a home to run whether we are famous or not." In Capetown, July 30.

Hurricane Camille: Wind and water flung boats onto the levee at Boothville, La. ➡

August

Gulf Coast Wrecked, Virginias Flooded by Hurricane Camille

More than 200 died, 75,000 families suffered property losses in century's most vicious storm, spawned off African coast

Lumber and debris almost buried bridge at Bay St. Louis, Miss.

"No coastline will ever be prepared for a storm like Camille. It was a once-in-a-century hurricane."

Dr. Robert Simpson of the National Hurricane Center in Miami so appraised the shattering tempest that slashed across the southern United States, leaving in its wake nothing but desolation. Another expert called it the worst disaster ever to strike the nation. Spawned off the coast of Africa, Camille made her way across the Atlantic Ocean, blended with the damp air of the Caribbean, then began her deadly trek through the Gulf of Mexico and inland, bearing winds that, in places, reached 200 m.p.h. or more. Before her destructive path faded more than 200 persons were known dead, damage in Louisiana, Mississippi, West Virginia and Virginia was reckoned at nearly $1.5 billion and tens of thousands of families were left homeless.

Mississippi, whose coastline was described as looking "like Hiroshima after the atomb bomb," counted at least 132 dead. Searchers still found bodies five weeks after the storm passed. Louisiana lost at least seven. Virginia and West Virginia, hard hit by floods created by Camille's dying gasp over Appalachia,

listed about 111 dead. But the actual death count would probably never be known. Reconnaissance pilots who flew over the Gulf Coast after the Aug. 17 disaster reported sighting clusters of bodies which had been swept out to sea by incredible tides.

At 9:40 a.m. that Sunday, Camille was 200 miles south of New Orleans. Weather forecasters were all but sure she would smash into the Florida panhandle. But, whipping the Gulf of Mexico into an angry white froth, Camille invaded the marshy coast of Louisiana that afternoon, sliced across the state's oil-rich underbelly, then raged through Venice, Empire and other hamlets as she moved north, barely 60 miles east of New Orleans. All during that grim morning, as radio stations continuously announced weather bulletins, a stream of traffic had choked the highways leading out of the city.

Water rose late in the day in fringe areas of New Orleans, and some families were evacuated. Had Camille held her course toward the city she could have sucked up the waters of Lake Pontchartrain and the death toll "easily would have reached 50,000," Simpson estimated.

While skirting the mouth of the Mississippi, the storm stirred up violent tides that surged up the big river. In Buras, La., virtually deserted, a wall of water smashed over the 15-foot-high levee and the town was temporarily submerged to a depth of 12 to 15 feet. A few Civil Defense workers and others who had remained in the stricken town found an uneasy refuge on the second floor of a school building.

In Louisiana's Plaquemines Parish—a low delta area laid down over the centuries by the Mississippi's silt—martial law was imposed and deputies with cocked shotguns turned back residents seeking to check on their homes. Of one hard hit area, an official said "there are no homes there. There are no grocery stores. Nothing, period. A few telephone poles, tugs in the marsh, houses in the marsh—or parts of them." Operations in the tidelands, where oil worth millions had been pumped annually, were destroyed. One Plaquemines official lashed himself to a building and rode out the storm. He said he felt throughout that long black night that he wouldn't survive.

Although Camille screamed across the Mississippi Gulf Coast just before midnight Aug. 17, it was not until sunrise that her full devastation became known. Little remained wherever the hurricane had struck. Such resort towns as Pass Christian, Miss., and nearby Waveland all but vanished. The bustling vacation centers of Biloxi and Gulfport were blasted. "The wind is blowing rocks," said a deputy at Gulfport. "There's a boat out in the parking lot here, and we're three blocks from the harbor."

Camille's fury seemed indomitable. The six-story Hancock Bank Building, a possible shield for Pass Christian's tiny business district, disappeared. Only its vault remained. Winds estimated well beyond 200 m.p.h. lifted the railroad tracks of the Louisville and Nashville trestle across the Bay of St. Louis. At Biloxi the bottom floor of the venerable Buena Vista Hotel held 12 feet of water which destroyed the facilities of Station WLOX. Steadily rising water levels put out of commission the local plant of the Gulfport Daily Herald for three days, but the paper's plant in Columbia, S.C., set up emergency lines and sent papers by plane to the coast the same day.

Many other communications systems were obliterated. In most cases the only phone lines were those quickly strung for search and rescue operations. Newsmen waited hours for those rare moments in which they could get a call out of the area. When the first photographs reached the wires they revealed damage that was almost unbelievable. Highways too suffered critically. U.S. 90, the four-lane artery across the Gulf Coast—known as the "Old Spanish Trail"—was ripped up; sections of it littered front yards and 26 miles of sand beach.

At first searchers found only a few bodies. Then the toll rose rapidly. At Pass Christian, only 60 miles east of New Orleans and a weekend haven for city dwellers, the dead were draped across tree limbs, pinned beneath the eaves of crushed houses, sprawled under bushes. A monstrous tidal wave, its height estimated at 20 feet, washed over the resort. Graves in the town's little cemetery were opened by the swamping waters and newly buried caskets were found open.

Pass Christian, population about 4,000, was the prime target. The huge storm rampaged through it, leveling almost everything in its way. Only the pilings of a pier and heaps of twisted boards remained. In Pass Christian Isles, Mary and Bill Gatipon had put 20 years' savings into their home. When they visited it a few days after the storm Mrs. Gatipon found her new stove on the front lawn. The new refrigerator leaned uncertainly against the battered and open kitchen window frames. The roof over their 30-foot veranda was found 100 feet away, its concrete pillars still attached. Pieces of the living room rug dangled from the branches of trees more than a block away.

Such scenes were duplicated a hundredfold. Dr. Walter Peat and his family had sent Mrs. Peat to Miami to visit a daughter a few days before the storm, but Peat and his son Buzz decided to remain in Pass Christian. The house crumbled when wind and water slammed into it during Camille's first onslaught. Father and son grabbed a section of masonry still standing and clung to it almost all night. They were found alive, 40 feet above ground, jammed between a tree branch and the remaining wall of another building. Tornadoes

that spun within the eye of Camille had peeled the bark from trees as an Indian might mark a trail.

The storm's concentrated fury stretched from the Louisiana line to Pascagoula, just west of Mobile, Ala. It swept fashionable motel cabins from the beach near Biloxi, and restaurants that had lined the oceanfront disappeared. At Pascagoula snakes invaded the town from the marshes. Merle Palmer, a state senator, reported that "we had to organize to fight them." Mrs. Anne Mansfield, another resident, said, "There were hundreds, and I mean hundreds, of black water moccasins and cottonmouths in the water in my mother's backyard."

Caring for the dead and injured became a herculean task. Bodies had to be tagged and sent to temporary morgues, one of them at Hattiesburg 70 miles north. More than 75,000 families along the storm's lengthy route suffered heavy losses. Food and shelter, of some kind, had to be found for them. The Red Cross and the Salvation Army established temporary kitchens and housing areas.

Why did so many die? Weather bureau advisories all day Sunday had warned that the storm was a killer and had urged all persons in its path to evacuate. But "the people just wouldn't get out," said Gulfport Mayor Philip Shaw. "It's human nature to think that the safest place is their home. If the people had believed us, there wouldn't have been anybody in town."

Nap Cassibry, Gulf Coast Civil Defense coordinator and a member of Mississippi's legislature, said he had lived all his life on the coast. "I just couldn't conceive of 190-mile-an-hour winds," he said. "Hell, we've had hurricanes, and bad ones—or so we thought." There had been hurricanes, many of them, to test the strength of the Gulf Coast. There had been the big one in 1947, whose scars were still there. There had

Louisiana: Homes were smashed like toys at Buras

Mississippi: Pass Christian looked as if it had been bombed

been Betsy in 1965 (*The World in 1965, 175*), Inez in Florida in 1966 (*The World in 1966, 207*), Beulah in Texas in 1967 (*The World in 1967, 188-190*). But none matched Camille.

Among those who faced up to Camille some were lucky—enough to survive—but they paid a price. A few were even luckier. "I lived alone and didn't have any place to go," said Beulah Mae Battiest. "I sat alone all night on the side of the bed and just waited for the house to go over. But it didn't. The water blew right through it."

The job of rebuilding awaited. Some scoffed and said the Gulf Coast would never be the same. Others, like Biloxi Mayor Dan Guice, said things would be "normal" within two years. But "some of us are too old to rebuild," another victim commented. "This home was to have been our retirement home. . . . We can't rebuild now. Why rebuild anyway? We did after Betsy in '65, and now it's all gone. Why ask for the same thing again?"

Camille had made a shambles of the Gulf Coast, but her career of destruction had not ended. She knifed deeper into the nation, her winds tempered to thunderstorm strength by the drag of the land, but her still heavy rains set off a series of life-taking flash floods in West Virginia and Virginia. Most of this downpour was water the hurricane had picked up at sea. The clouds were cooled as they passed over the mountains, and the resulting deluge stripped slopes clean of trees, earth and even whole settlements.

Roaring streams in southern West Virginia drowned many, wrecked houses, washed out roads, smashed bridges. An Army engineer said the concentration of rain—as much as 10 inches in a few hours—brought on the flooding "just as if you'd try to pour a bucket of water into a thimble." In the hamlet of Anjean, about 30 of the community's 35 homes were demol-

Mississippi: Confession after Camille, at Long Beach

West Virginia: Residents fled flood-swept Anjean

Ships blown ashore at Gulfport, Miss.

ished and many families said they planned to move. "There is nothing left to rebuild," said one villager.

In Virginia, rivers flowing down the sides of the Blue Ridge Mountains swept through towns and villages. Giant earthslides thundered down, tearing up or blocking highways. Many towns were cut off, their residents without electricity, telephone service or water safe to drink. An earthen dam at a lake in Louisa County dissolved, releasing a 20-foot wall of water that raced across the surrounding farmland and drowned approximately 400 head of cattle. Massies Mill, a quiet place of 125, was ruined by the Tye River and, for two days, reachable only by helicopter. As the flood waters rose, Miss B. W. Ponton, 70, moved to the second story of her home. The water covered the living room and began to climb the stairs. It stopped at the eighth step. Mrs. R. W. Stratton, standing in her mud-filled living room, said: "Why should people here come back at all? They have nothing to come back to."

As the floods from the battered hill country rolled toward Richmond, workers in the city piled up sandbag dikes and residents braced for the crisis. All of the rivers that flooded converged at the James River, which flowed into Chesapeake Bay, and the normally placid James was swollen to giant proportions. Usually 100 feet to a few hundred yards across, the James above Richmond grew in width to a mile in some places.

Twenty bridges were carried away on major highways and 60 on secondary routes. The James ultimately formed a muddy lake in Richmond's farm and factory flatlands on both sides of the city. Its high water mark was 28.6 feet—19.5 feet above flood stage but well below the expected 34-foot crest.

Debris from wrecked homes and farm buildings floated through the city, and National Guardsmen were summoned to prevent looting. Below Richmond, Coast Guard cutters searched the James for dangerous flotsam, securing tanks of propane and lethal sodium cyanide. The flood, however, had done its worst before reaching the capital, and Richmond escaped heavier damage because it had time to erect dikes and evacuate families in low-lying areas. But merchants along the waterfront counted their losses in the hundreds of thousands of dollars. Among the hazards residents in an industrial area had faced was a lake eight feet deep, topped by an inch of gasoline. The high octane fuel had seeped from a 300,000-gallon storage tank. After the leak was plugged the gasoline was siphoned into the city's sewers.

By the time some semblance of normalcy began to return to the Gulf Coast and the Virginias, the cause of the disaster was gone. Far out over the ocean, after living eight days, Camille merged with a frontal weather system off Newfoundland, and lost all her characteristics of a lethal tropical storm.

"Crisis in the Cities"

Nixon asked Congress for sweeping welfare reforms to fight poverty
after Supreme Court declared unconstitutional state laws
that required needy to establish year's residence

LUMPED UNDER the federal label "crisis in the cities" were most of the nation's social ills and injustices. Though it appeared to be the cities that were being financially squeezed by the migrating poor who sought to escape rural poverty, government leaders were increasingly aware that the cities were not totally responsible for—nor totally capable of—solving these problems. Rather, they believed, the federal government must find ways to overcome urban ills that had been building for decades, partially upon federally-caused rural forces such as the national farm policy. By rewarding farmers for keeping down production, the government had indirectly driven thousands of farm workers into the cities, particularly in the rural north where welfare payments were generally higher.

Urban welfare rolls swelled while shrinking revenues, caused by middle class migration to suburbia, curbed such city services as schools, making it more difficult for the poor to escape poverty through education. Without education, unskilled jobs or welfare were the only alternatives. Unskilled jobs paid minimal wages. A man unable to support his family on these wages often deserted—knowing full well that a household headed by a man, no matter how poor, was ineligible for welfare.

Thus poverty was not an urban problem but a national problem, and the nation's government set about helping to overcome it. Meanwhile, the Supreme Court struck down as unconstitutional state laws that required one year's residence to qualify for welfare aid. Members of a Senate committee toured poverty pockets in the rural south, then set about expanding the food stamp program, and President Nixon sent to Congress a proposal that included the first sweeping reform of the federal welfare system since it was established during the depression years.

In its 6–3 ruling on April 21 the Supreme Court declared unconstitutional the laws and regulations in some 40 states that required new residents to wait at least one year before qualifying for public assistance. Justice William J. Brennan Jr., writing the majority opinion, said poor people not only had the right to move to another state without loss of welfare, but the right to move into it precisely because higher welfare payments were available: "We do not perceive why a mother who is seeking to make a new life for herself and her children should be regarded as less deserving because she considers, among other factors, the levels of a state's public assistance."

The ruling, while it primarily affected the burgeoning Aid to Families with Dependent Children (AFDC), also involved

South Carolina family waited for free food stamps

old age assistance and aid to the blind and totally disabled. It made an additional 200,000 poor people eligible immediately for assistance, thus increasing the nation's welfare rolls by at least $175 million annually. Secretary Robert H. Finch of the Department of Health, Education and Welfare said the decision would "have a substantial impact on federal and state budgets" and make national standards for welfare "inevitable."

Yet, there were those who still were hungry. Worse than the gnawing hunger, though, were the resulting malnutrition and related diseases. Estimates of the number of seriously malnourished Americans ranged from 5 million to 15 million, mostly in the rural south, among migrant workers, Indians and Eskimos, and increasingly among the big-city poor. Some were victims of rickets and endemic goiter, believed wiped out 30 years earlier. Other diseases, commonly associated with underveloped nations of the world also preyed on America's impoverished in an age of unequalled prosperity.

Sen. George S. McGovern, D-S.D., and his Select Committee on Nutrition and Human Needs toured some of the nation's poverty pockets and were appalled by what they saw. Sen. Allen Ellender, D.-La., described it as "dirt and living conditions . . . that one might expect to see in Asia, not America. Most of the cattle and hogs in America are better fed and sheltered than the families we have visited."

Ernest F. Hollings, D-S.C., toured the poorest areas of his home state, then returned to Washington and humbled himself before his fellow senators. Hollings acknowledged both the existence of hunger among his constituents and his own share of responsibility for it. He even said that when he was governor he had supported the "public policy of covering up the problem of hunger" in the hope of attracting industry.

That same month Agriculture Secretary Clifford M. Hardin announced free food stamps would be distributed in two South Carolina counties as a pilot project. They were the first free food stamps available since the federal program was begun in 1964 to enable the poor to buy food with the stamps purchased at a fraction of their face value. Everyone, even those with no income, had had to pay something for the stamps, preventing some of the neediest from taking part.

In rapid succession came a flurry of other proposals for federal assistance, some stop-gap, others long-range. President Nixon, in a special message to Congress in May, advocated a $1 billion annual increase in the $1.5 billion food relief program "to put an end to hunger in America itself for all time." When fully effective in mid-1970, the proposed program would extend government·food assistance to every county in the nation. To get it started, he said $270 million of the fiscal budget would be shifted to food-aid funds effective July 1.

Pilot programs were to be instituted under which needy pregnant women and mothers of infants would receive free food packets and vouchers redeemable at food and drug stores for infant formulas and other highly nutritious special foods. There were plans, too, to expand some of the school lunch programs to summer recreation camps. And there was talk of a White House Conference on Food & Nutrition as well as establishment of a new government agency, a Food & Nutrition Service, to administer separate federal food programs.

By mid-year, the Senate had passed and sent to the House a bill that would more than double the federal funds for food stamps—to $750 million from $340 million—for the first fiscal year. Though McGovern called the measure "acceptable," it was a far cry from the bill he had introduced calling for a food stamp program at an annual level of $1.8 billion.

Then, in August, President Nixon proposed the first major overhaul of the nation's welfare system since it was formed during the depression years. It would more than double the welfare rolls from 10 million to 22.4 million persons and add, in the first year, $2.5 billion to the $4.7 billion already spent by the federal government to aid the nation's poor.

The four-point plan, which President Nixon said was directed toward a "new federalism," included (1) complete replacement of the welfare system; (2) a comprehensive new job training and placement program; (3) a major overhaul in the Office of Economic Opportunity; (4) a start on the sharing of federal tax revenues with state and local governments.

"I have discussed these four matters together because together they make both a package and a pattern," said the President. "They should be studied together, debated together and seen in perspective." The package reflected strongly the imprint of White House urban adviser Daniel Patrick Moynihan, a Democrat, who long had advocated adoption of a national urban policy that would recognize how such vexing social problems as poverty and racial unrest, although centered in the cities, were originated by forces outside the cities— forces that often were immune to remedies applied at the state and local level.

The heart of the President's plan would give a federal income guarantee of $1,600 a year to a family of four, provided that the heads of households—excepting mothers of pre-school children—were willing to work. Recipients would be required to accept suitable employment or register in a job training program. Those enrolled in training programs would receive a $30 a month bonus. Those who accepted jobs would be allowed to keep the first $60 a month of outside earnings with no reduction in aid, plus 50 cents of every dollar beyond that until income for a family of four reached $3,920.

For the three adult welfare programs—aid to the blind, the disabled and the aged—Nixon advocated federal payments of $90 a month to each recipient, replacing the sliding scale of matching payments for the programs. As for the expanded food stamp program, the President proposed earlier it would not be available to participants of the new program but rather to single persons and couples without children—those who could not qualify for welfare payments.

Coupled with these reforms was a plan to share federal funds with state and local governments, in which $1 billion of federal income tax money would be directly turned back to the states in the first year the plan was in effect. This would accompany a proposal to ease the financial plight of state governments by assuming $735 million of the relief burden already paid by the states. During the five-year period from its inception, the shared money would reach a level of one per cent of the federal income tax base, or about $4 billion.

The new program would guarantee that no state would spend more than 90 per cent of what it previously had committed to welfare relief, in effect assuring the state of a 10 per cent savings. Thus, with the direct revenue sharing funds, welfare savings could represent a sizeable easement to state governments. A White House chart, for example, showed that California would receive $112.5 million through revenue sharing and save at least $179.5 million on welfare, thus receiving a total of $292 million.

No action was expected in Congress at least until 1970. What turn it would take was yet to be seen, but initial response among both Democrat and Republican leaders was generally favorable. The real stumbling block appeared to be the revenue sharing program, which would send tax money back to the states with few strings attached.

Protestant vs. Catholic:
Terror in Northern Ireland

Hundreds of homes burned, shops looted and smashed
by barricaded rioters in Londonderry and Belfast

For a week in August, Belfast burned. The capital of Northern Ireland, proud producer of great ships and world-beating aircraft, was back to its old vicious habit of sectarian strife, the unending battle of the Orange and the Green. Street after street of small homes blazed in nights of mounting terror. A 9-year-old boy was shot dead in his bedroom while grown men shot each other on the streets. Hundreds fled to refuge in the neighboring Irish Republic. Neighbor fought with neighbor, and sometimes families fought each other, and Belfast took its biggest beating since the blitz of World War II.

The six counties of Northern Ireland and their 1.5 million people had long been building up to one of the outbreaks of sectarian violence which have seared Belfast's history every generation or so. The Roman Catholic third of the population smarted under a deep sense of injustice. Their charges of discrimination in housing, jobs and voting had been well documented and well publicized by a year-long civil rights campaign but long ignored by the Protestant-dominated provincial government. Protestants, whipped up by the fierce anti-Popery of the Rev. Ian Paisley and his Free Presbyterian followers, countered that Catholics grabbed the welfare state's benefits while refusing to acknowledge the state and its institutions, and were intent on out-breeding Protestants into submission and eventual subjugation by the Catholic-dominated republic to the south.

The year's pattern was set from its very first day. On Jan. 1, about 80 Belfast students ignored appeals from more moderate civil rights leaders and set out to march the 72 miles to Londonderry, protesting against bad housing, unemployment and gerrymander. The organizers were the People's Democracy, a leftist group later castigated by a judicial inquiry as a means of inviting and inciting civil disorder. Marchers included Eamon McCann, an admitted revolutionary, and 21-year-old Bernadette Devlin, soon to become Britain's youngest member of Parliament. A campaign to "harry and hinder" the marchers was announced by the Loyal Citizens of Ulster, a militant offshoot of the Paisleyite movement, and it reached its climax in a brutal ambush at Burntollet Bridge as the march neared Londonderry. The Loyalists first scattered the marchers with a rain of rocks and gasoline bombs from behind hedgerows, then chased and beat them with clubs and iron bars.

That night, Jan. 4, a major riot broke out in Londonderry's Bogside, a Catholic district of ancient streets and new apartment blocks dominated by the city's 17th century walls. Student leaders helped the Bogsiders build anti-police barricades. When the police broke through, some officers went on a rampage of their own, smashing windows and shouting insults until finally they marched off singing the protest movements' own anthem: "We shall overcome." The result was to blacken the police in the eyes of most Catholics and add to the growing pile of political strife. For the week that followed Bogside stayed inside its barricades and the police kept out. A slogan went up on the wall of a house: "You are now entering Free Derry." Catholics never called the city Londonderry, a title granted by the British Crown more than three centuries ago. Radio Free Derry went on the air with a mixture of Republican songs and politics, heralding the battle of the airwaves, that accompanied Belfast's August war.

More rioting followed in Newry a week later. This time the police stood by until the rioters occupied the post office and other public buildings. Three weeks later Prime Minister Terence O'Neill called a general election, determined to smash the hardline rightwingers of his own Unionist party who had been holding back his own limited proposals for reform. Like many another Irish gamble, it failed. O'Neill found himself back as leader of a numerically stronger but still more divided party. More rioting in Londonderry, followed by a series of unexplained explosions which wrecked Belfast's water supplies, preceded O'Neill's resignation, and the premiership passed to his distant cousin, James Chichester-Clark, a 46-year-old ex-soldier whose main qualification was his absence of enemies.

Chichester-Clark's first act as prime minister was an amnesty for all offenses connected with the civil rights campaign. More than 300 persons benefitted from dropped charges, among them prominent politicians. Paisley was released from jail, where he was serving six months after an unlawful demonstration which produced a riot in Armagh, the ecclesiastical capital. Chichester-Clark pledged voting reform in local council elections, which previously had been heavily loaded on the Protestant side, and other measures including a crash housing program and a patently fair method of sharing the resulting houses. But the passions aroused by the civil rights campaign and attendant disorders already had passed from the political to the old Irish issue of Protestant versus Catholic, otherwise known as Unionist (pro-

"Frontier" in Belfast: British troops watch for violence involving rival religious factions ➝

Protestant flag behind barricade in Belfast

British monarchy) versus Nationalist (Republican), or Loyalist versus Rebel. The province generally was quiet until July 12, when Protestants annually celebrated the victory of William of Orange over the Catholic James II at the Battle of the Boyne in 1690. The Orange marches, and their Catholic counterparts on Aug. 15, had traditionally been the starting point for Northern excesses. Through much of the 19th century they were banned under the Party Processions Act. In modern times they had operated under an unwritten convention that each side kept to its "own" territory. Rival conceptions of territorial rights were basic to Northern feuding, and especially so in the Belfast backstreets.

The Orange marches produced riots in Londonderry and Dungiven. Worse followed on the first weekend in August, when Protestants of Belfast's Shankill Road claimed they were attacked with bottles from a Catholic apartment block and turned their fury on the police who stepped in to prevent retaliation. Suddenly Belfast was back to its old habit of drawing the battle lines: Catholics living in mainly Protestant streets around the Shankill were given the traditional Belfast warning "Get out or be burned out"—a warning made the more fearsome in the auto age by the ready availability of gasoline. In this atmosphere Northern Ireland approached another big day in the Protestant calendar, the annual march of the Apprentice Boys of Derry on Aug. 12. The "boys," for the most part middleaged men, were an order celebrating the apprentices who slammed the city gates against James II's Catholic forces in 1689. The apprentices and their families traditionally paraded the walls with fife bands playing Protestant battle songs.

Civil rights leaders and politicians on both sides of the Irish Sea urged the parade be banned. Chichester-Clark, on police advice, decided to let it go ahead. The parade route came close to the Bogside only at one point, and the police

were confident they could keep the two factions apart. Had they succeeded, the province might have seemed settling for peace. But they failed. Catholic and Protestant first jeered then stoned each other. Police waded in with batons, and within an hour the riot was on. The Bogsiders threw up a huge barricade across Rossville Street, a broad thoroughfare which made a natural battlefield and was well supplied with bricks and rubble from building sites. From a 10-story apartment block just beside the barricade they hurled rocks and gasoline bombs against the police. When the police fell back into the narrower and thus more easily cordoned streets nearer the city center the Bogsiders advanced, burning stores and factories. Police used teargas for the first time against the civilian population, and Chichester-Clark mobilized the paramilitary "B Special" reserves. The Bogsiders sent out calls for help.

In Dublin, capital of the Irish Republic, Prime Minister Jack Lynch called up firstline Army reserves, moved troops to the border and prepared to take the North's troubles to the United Nations. Politically his apparent aim was to ensure British intervention to end the rioting and ease the province's festering ills. This was eventually achieved. A side effect undoubtedly was further to inflame the North's 1 million Protestants and heighten their fears of eventual takeover by the Republic's 2.5 million Catholics. Wednesday and Thursday, Aug. 13 and 14, were days of riot in Londonderry which even that troubled old city had seldom seen. Bernadette Devlin marched to the barricades under the plough and stars flag of Irish socialism. The Republic's tricolor, green, white and orange, flew from the rooftops. Women and children manned the munitions factories producing crate after crate of gasoline bombs with sophisticated recipes including soap, paint and sugar. By day the battle was carried on by youngsters, some of them no more than 10, hurling gasoline bombs from the rooftops and pelting police with slingshots. At night the men took over. The police, holding their line between the Bogside and the city center, replied with wave after wave of teargas shells.

The Bogside was a citadel of tears. The black CS 190 gas, never before used against the civilian population in the United Kingdom, drifted remorselessly into the narrow streets on the steady breeze. "If the wind changes we've had it," a police officer said. The immediate effect of the gas was blinding tears, a choking throat and, in severe doses, diarrhea. The longterm effects were put under expert investigation only after the gas had been used. But for all the discomfort, the gas was useless against the youngsters on the rooftops, where the stiffer breeze dispersed it quickly. And though effective in breaking crowds when they charged through to the narrow streets near the city center, it had little more than nuisance value against the frontline rioters in the wide open spaces of Rossville Street. Many were equipped with World War II gas masks, brought out of attics. More would have had them but for a Bogside bonfire of 1939, when the newly issued masks were burned as a protest against British rule. By Thursday afternoon the police had been forced back out of Rossville Street to within 100 yards of their own barracks. Whole streets had blazed through the night. The police admitted defeat and called in the troops. Men of the Prince of Wales Regiment left their barracks across the Foyle River at 5 p.m., and 10 minutes later had the situation under control without firing a shot.

That night, the Bogside's call for support brought renewed rioting in Newry, Armagh, Enniskillen, Strabane, Lurgan, Dungiven—and along the Falls Road in Belfast. Trouble in Belfast, as everyone knew, would make Londonderry's troubles seem a matter of small importance. The Falls Road, running west from the city center, was Belfast's Catholic heartland, just as the Shankill Road, running parallel 400 yards away, was the Protestant heartland. Shankill storekeepers and pubs flew the Union Jack. Without it they would have lost customers and probably their windows. Most storekeepers along the Falls would have flown the flag of the Irish Republic, except that it was banned. The Falls answered Derry's call with a protest parade to Hastings Street police barracks, two blocks from the city center. The protest developed into an attack with bricks and firebombs, more determined but in the pattern that the area had known for more than 100 years, as the Belfast newspaper files showed. The old police answer was to call out the cavalry with sabres drawn. The modern answer had usually been to bring out armored water cannon which, compared to those used in French and Belgian riots, were little more than mobile garden sprinklers.

Once word reached the Shankill that the Falls was up, the long foretold Protestant backlash erupted in blind fury. Mobs advanced down the red brick streets of terraced houses in no-man's-land, throwing rocks, bottles and firebombs. The Catholic ends of Dover Street, Percy Street and Cupar Street were quickly blazing. Scores of families fled in terror. Catholics insisted that the B Specials, a part-time, half-trained all-Protestant force originally formed to fight the outlawed Irish Republican Army, led the attack on Catholic homes, and that behind them came armed men of the Ulster Volunteer Force, underground counterpart to the IRA. Who fired the first shot could not be determined. Police insisted that three of their officers were the first wounded. One of the first to die was Trooper Hugh McCabe, a British soldier on leave from his unit in Germany. Protestants said he was shot through

Bernadette Devlin: Northern Ireland's fiery Catholic spokesman, sought aid in New York

Helmeted police, with tear gas and shields, in front of blazing shop

the head by a police marksman who spotted him sniping into Protestant streets from a Davis Street apartment block. His family said that he had done no more than throw rocks and gasoline bombs from the apartment balcony and that he took seven machinegun bullets in the back while bending over another boy who had been shot through the knee. Another to die was 9-year-old Patrick Rooney, shot through the head by a bullet which pierced the wall of his bedroom in a neighboring apartment block.

As the battle hardened, the cry went up from the Catholic side: "Where is the IRA?" The answer was that the IRA, in its old guise as a trained military force, had largely evaporated. "A few come in when they're needed," an old man said, "and then they vanish. We don't know who they are. It's not like the old days." The police manning the gun turrets of the armored cars along the Falls Road in the small hours of Friday, however, were certain that the IRA was operating, and armed with modern machine guns. "That's sophisticated weapons they're using, and they know how to use them," one officer said. Chichester-Clark was of the same opinion. His government, he said, faced an armed uprising. The precise part played by the IRA was hard to establish. One reason was that there were at least two versions of the organization, a situation resulting from a split in 1962, when IRA leaders in Dublin called off their campaign against police and customs installations along the border. Younger members, drawn from Republican Clubs in universities in Dublin and Belfast, saw little point in nightly forays and wild shooting which brought only the deaths of six Northern policemen and a hardening of Protestant attitudes against a united Ireland.

The younger element began instead to plan a political campaign for the socialist republic which was the stated aim of leaders of the 1916 uprising against British rule. "The aim is revolution in Belfast," one of this younger element told a reporter in 1962. It seemed a remote chance then, less remote amid the blazing streets of Belfast 1969. Shooting continued throughout the Friday, and the city prepared for civil war. More than 50 doubledecker buses and scores of trucks and cars were hijacked at gunpoint to form barricades. Protestants with long memories built their barricades with dozens of delivery vans lifted from Hughes Bakery. The firm's founder, Bernard Hughes, was born in 1826 and was the first Roman Catholic member of Belfast Town Council. In 19th century riots his house and bakeries frequently had been the target of Protestant attack. The armed IRA men in the Falls Road area, no more than 30 by most accounts, were on the streets directing the building of Catholic barricades. Many were thoroughly professional constructions of scaffolding and steel shuttering hijacked from a builders' yard. Youngsters were on factory rooftops spreading gasoline. Soon the factories were ablaze and of no more use for snipers. Troops moved into the Falls Road in early evening and scattered the mobs with teargas. The effect was to shift the battle scene further north, where the Crumlin Road divides an area of mixed population.

Clonard Monastery had been built amid a maze of tiny streets named for onetime outposts of British Imperialism. Bombay Street and Kashmir Street were gutted in an attack on the monastery, which Protestants believed was sheltering a sniper. Catholic-owned pubs along the Crumlin Road took a terrible battering. By dawn on Saturday more than 50 had been looted and burned out. More houses blazed along Hooker Street, where Paisleyites claimed a 78-year-old man had been put out of his lifelong home by Roman Catholics.

When the Army finally completed its cordon around the whole feuding area Saturday evening, the death roll was eight—six Catholic and two Protestant. Hundreds had been wounded and more than 400 houses burned out, most of them beyond repair. Many people insisted the true death roll was higher. Both sides had, in fact, a long tradition of concealing their dead. As the smoke cleared from a weekend of mourning, the extent of the damage began to emerge. Conservative estimates started at 15 million pounds ($36 million), equal to a tax of 10 pounds ($24) a head of the population. The British army commander, Lt. Gen, Sir Ian Freeland, touring the devastation soon after taking control of internal security, said he had seen nothing like it outside total war.

Soon the political pattern emerged too. One third of Londonderry and one eighth of Belfast were behind barricades flying the Irish Republican flag. Their residents called the areas "Free Belfast" and "Free Derry." Their rulers were Citizens' Defense Committees, an alliance of old-style Republicans, many of them veterans of years in jail for IRA activities, and the new-style leftist insurrectionists of the People's Democracy. From behind the barricades came a series of political demands, not always coordinated: Disband the B Specials, disarm the police, abolish Stormont (the provincial Parliament), repeal the Special Powers Act. Sometimes one demand headed the list, sometimes another. But always prominent was the attack on the Special Powers Act, dating from the IRA campaign of 1956–62, by which suspected IRA men or other subversives could be jailed indefinitely without trial. Jim Sullivan, the sandy-haired carpenter who fronted the committee running barricaded "Free Belfast," had himself spent four years in the Crumlin Road jail as a suspected IRA leader. Inside the barricades a whole new way of life sprang up which, for a time at least, most people seemed to like. Rival pirate stations poured out round the clock their mixture of pop and politics, plus songs normally banned from the airwaves—"*The Soldier's Song,*" anthem of the Republic, from "Radio Free Belfast," and Protestant battle songs like "*Dolly's Brae*" (*. . . And we kicked*

five hundred Papishes over Dolly's Brae) from the rival "Radio Free Shankill."

"Radio Free Derry," first on the air the previous January, claimed it was building an audience in Dublin 120 miles away. Posters proclaimed: "Barricades are beautiful." In the Falls, lampoons featured Chichester-Clark as "The Mad Major." On the Shankill, caricatures of Bernadette Devlin carried the legend "Nine out of 10 members of Parliament use soap." "Free Belfast" set up its own hospital, manned by qualified volunteers. Vigilantes closed the bars each night 90 minutes ahead of the regular 10 p.m. shuttering to aid sobriety and avoid any drunken brawls that might have given the army or police necessity to move in. Within three days of the rioting, milk and bread trucks and the mailman came into "Free Belfast" each day at "Checkpoint Charlie," the only access point for vehicles.

The barricades enclosed 75,000 Catholics in Belfast, 27,000 in Londonderry. The repeated justification for them was: "Now we feel safe." Women felt safe from nights of repeated riot. IRA men felt safe from arrest. Student activists and anarchists felt safe to run their newssheets and radios and to promote and study the growth of what they called "spontaneous democracy." To remove this "safety" line and to emphasize its own role as protector, the Army threw a "peace fence" of steel and barbed wire across Belfast, dividing the Catholic Falls Road area from the Protestant Shankill District and reducing the chance of more mob clashes. But scattered shooting and arson continued. And the intimidators with their "Get out" messages, mainly directed at Catholics, ensured that Belfast remained a city of fear. Bernadette Devlin flew off to the United States, intending to raise a million dollars for relief for the hundreds of homeless. She returned ahead of schedule and far short of her target. Paisley made a similar mission to further the Protestant cause. And the British Government, anxious for half a century to avoid entanglement in Irish affairs, despatched a Welshman with an Irish name, Home Secretary James Callaghan, to seek the peace in Belfast and Londonderry.

Embattled Northern Ireland's Londonderry

Innocent victim: Spectators mourn at grave of Patrick Rooney, 9, killed by stray bullet

Callaghan knew from the outset his mission would not be easy. At Belfast Airport he said: "I can't hope to solve in three days the problems of three centuries." In the Bogside he addressed a crowd from a bedroom window. "You have engaged my sympathies and my energies," he told them. "I will try to ensure that in Northern Ireland there is justice and equality, a lack of fear and an absence of discrimination." To Protestants he gave an equally welcome message: the border, and Northern Ireland's link with Britain, would stay so long as a majority of Northerners wanted it. Callaghan went back to London generally acclaimed as having produced a political triumph by winning time. His parting communique, issued jointly with Chichester-Clark, provided for senior British experts to work with the Northern Ireland government on a crash reform program to ensure equal opportunities for Catholics in public employment, protection against incitement to religious hatred, and guaranteed fairness in housing and local government voting.

But Callaghan's main triumph, it seemed, was achieved in a 30-minute meeting with William Cardinal Conway, Archbishop of Armagh and Roman Catholic Primate of All Ireland. What Callaghan told the Cardinal was not disclosed, but from that moment the Church began to swing itself 100 per cent behind the government's reform package and the Army's protection plans. When the Army finally announced that the barricades must go, Catholic leaders like Dr. William Philbin, Bishop of Down and Connor, and Father Padraig Murphy, Admistrator of St. Peter's pro-Cathedral inside Free Belfast, were instrumental in talking them down and averting violence. With the long nights coming, the Army settled in for the winter and the soldiers began to talk of a two-year stay. Their task: to keep apart

a small, educated, highly intelligent people whose only real difference lay in their differing interpretations of the same Christian religion and their widely different views on Ireland's place in a troubled world. From the smoldering wreckage came the first tentative feelers for a new deal between London, Dublin, and Belfast, perhaps leading to the sort of Federation originally envisaged when Ireland was partitioned nearly 50 years ago. Dublin leaders, with Cardinal Conway's approval, began to think of amending their own constitution to remove the "special place" specifically afforded the Roman Catholic Church in the Republic's affairs—a place which Northern Protestants had always seen as a major obstacle to reunification.

Could a new deal on Federal terms write an end to the long years of faction? Few believed it could. For their reason they turned to this: "On Saturday morning the streets around Millfield, the Pound, Shankill Road and Falls Road were in a state of utter desolation. There was scarcely a house without broken windows. Everywhere the pavements were torn up. In some streets barricades were erected and shops boarded up against attack. In every street which bordered on the Catholic and Protestant districts pickets of armed police and soldiers stood guard."

It read like an exact description of Saturday, Aug. 16, 1969. It came, in fact, from a description of Saturday, Aug. 17, 1872, and could be matched in accounts of Belfast riots in 1857, 1864, 1886, 1898, 1935 and 1964. Already the rising generation was schooled in violence and the language of hate to an extent that shocked even the hardened soldiers manning the Peace Line. "Little girls of five and six," said one of them, shaking his head, "using the sort of talk that would get a man run out of our barrack room."

". . . THE END OF THE ROAD"

Dr. Philip Blaiberg was not the first person to receive a heart transplant but he was the first to hold his own heart in his hands. The surgery, performed in January 1968 by Dr. Christiaan Barnard, a pioneer in the technique, was followed by a long and valiant battle against tissue rejection.

During this critical period Blaiberg, a retired dentist in Cape Town, South Africa, lost and regained his hope for survival while Barnard and his aides tried desperately to effect a lasting physiological acceptance of the new heart.

Their efforts, and Blaiberg's courageous co-operation, were destined to fail. Blaiberg died 19 months and 15 days after the operation. He was 60 years old.

Blaiberg's first post-surgery crisis occurred in June 1968. He had been admitted to Groote Schuur hospital for routine tests, but hepatitis developed, along with lung complications, while he was there.

Barnard revealed then that he was considering a second transplant. But Blaiberg told his wife, "You know as well as I do that this is the end of the road."

Instead Barnard resorted to anti-lymphocyte serum. In July he reported that his patient "has the will to live again," since the heart symptoms had disappeared. Blaiberg was discharged from the hospital Sept. 26.

On the first anniversary of the operation Blaiberg's condition remained good, and he celebrated with a dinner party. He was able to travel, answer his large volume of fan mail, receive visiting celebrities and drive his car. He even wrote a best-selling autobiography, "Looking at my Heart." After the surgery Barnard had allowed Blaiberg to hold a glass jar containing his original heart.

Blaiberg remained healthy until May 13, 1969, when he was admitted to the hospital again, complaining of back pains and breathlessness. Doctors were suspicious of rejection, but they later blamed over-exertion. Blaiberg was released May 23.

The last crisis began Aug. 11. Doctors noticed that Blaiberg's blood pressure reading was only one-third its normal level. He had been in poor health for some weeks, and hospitalization was ordered once more. Doctors found that rejection had caused constriction of blood vessels leading to the heart. Blaiberg was barely able to move

his arms and legs. The cortisone drugs which were used to fight rejection had further weakened his body tissues.

The end came peacefully, on Aug. 17.

Barnard said that Blaiberg had been subject to chronic rejection of his transplanted heart. He said so much of the heart tissue was destroyed that Blaiberg was "back to where he started before we did the transplant." When reporters asked why he did not perform another transplant Barnard replied, "He was a man who had not only a disease of the heart muscle but extensive disease of other arteries. We felt that

in this case the rest of his body was so ill it would not be worth it."

Blaiberg was the third man to receive a new heart *(The World in 1968, 17–19)*. His death could have served as a reminder of the extra months of life the operation could bestow. But Dr. Denton Cooley of Houston, Tex., said that the stream of heart donors had dwindled because of transplant criticism from the public and the medical profession *(page 90)*.

Barnard defended the transplant despite the mortality rate, saying, "It is worthwhile, this operation."

Third heart transplant: Dr. Philip Blaiberg and portrait of his surgeon, Dr. Christiaan Barnard

GREATEST ALL-TIME TEAM

As part of the centennial celebration of professional baseball, fans and sports writers collaborated to select the game's greatest heroes, living and dead. Fans in each major league city voted for their choices from the all-time lineups of their local teams. From the resulting lists of eligibles, members of the Baseball Writers Association of America then chose the greatest all-time team. A committee of writers selected the greatest living team. The choices were announced at a black tie, $35-per-plate dinner in Washington on July 21.

Babe Ruth, the fabulous hitter of home runs, was elected the greatest player of all time. Joe DiMaggio, retired from his sleek outfield patrols for the New York Yankees, became the greatest

living player and the greatest center fielder, both all-time and living.

The selections for the all-time team: First base, Lou Gehrig; second base, Rogers Hornsby; third base, Pie Traynor; shortstop, Honus Wagner; outfield, Ty Cobb, Ruth and DiMaggio; catcher, Mickey Cochrane; righthanded pitcher, Walter Johnson; lefthanded pitcher, Lefty Grove; manager, John McGraw.

The living team: First base, George Sisler and Stan Musial (tie); second base, Charley Gehringer; third base, Pie Traynor; shortstop, Joe Cronin; outfield, Ted Williams, Willie Mays and DiMaggio; catcher, Bill Dickey; righthanded pitcher, Bob Feller; lefthanded pitcher, Grove; manager, Casey Stengel.

Two day later, after a postponement because of rain, the stars of the National League defeated their rivals from the American League for the seventh consecutive year, 9-3. In contrast to the domination by pitchers in recent years, this was a hitters' picnic. Five home runs were hit: two by Willie McCovey of the San Francisco Giants and one by Johnny Bench of Cincinnati for the National League; one each by Frank Howard of Washington and Bill Freehan of Detroit for the American. Steve Carlton of the St. Louis Cardinals was the winning pitcher and Mel Stottlemyre of the New York Yankees was the loser in the game which elevated the National League's All Star record to 22 victories, 17 defeats and one tie.

MYTHS OF MARS DISPELLED

Mars lost much of its mystery when two U.S. spacecraft whizzed past in August 1969. Two hundred pictures televised across 60 million miles showed the small red planet, once believed the most likely in our solar system to harbor extraterrestrial life, was barren, cold, dry, nearly airless and heavily cratered like earth's moon. Mariners 6 and 7, with cameras sharp enough to pick out details 900 feet across, dispelled many myths fabricated over the centuries by astronomers wielding telescopes.

The long dark lines called canals—on the assumption they carried water from melting polar caps to vast areas which turn blue-green in spring—all but vanished in photographs taken when the spacecraft were little more than 2,000 miles away. Scientists speculated they actually might be the dark and ragged rims of giant craters created by meteorite impacts. Mariner 7 flew over the great white south polar cap and electronic sensors determined it was made of frozen carbon dioxide, not ice, and when it melted it turned to gas, not water.

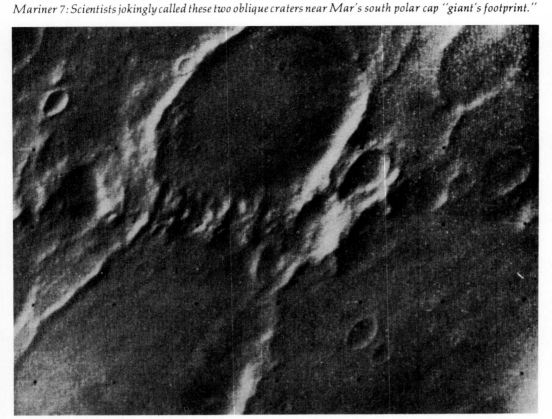

Mariner 7: Scientists jokingly called these two oblique craters near Mar's south polar cap "giant's footprint."

Whatever the vast green areas were they weren't vegetation. Mariner 6 flew across them and found Mars was too cold, with temperatures down to 200 degrees below zero during the night.

Instruments which detect chemicals by analyzing radiations failed to find nitrogen, essential to known life forms. Preliminary reports that there were traces of ammonia and methane, two other vital substances, turned out to be wrong.

Scientists controlling the flights from Jet Propulsion Laboratory in Pasadena, Calif., said they had found nothing to encourage a belief that life could exist on Mars—but did not rule out the possibility that some microbial forms might have adapted to the hostile environment. Final determination could not be expected, they said, until Viking spacecraft had landed and scratched Mars' surface in 1973—or possibly until men eventually set foot there.

When, if ever, that would be remained a controversy likely to be argued for years by space planners who pondered where next to look in their ever-widening search for life beyond earth.

VICTORY FOR MRS. GANDHI?

Bookmakers in Bombay had given even odds on both candidates in India's fourth presidential election. Mrs. Indira Gandhi, as Prime Minister and a leading member of the ruling Congress party, had defied her colleagues by refusing to endorse their nominee, Sanjiva Reddy, and lent her unspoken support to Verahagiri Venkata Giri, who campaigned as an independent.

Reddy was a long-time political foe of Mrs. Gandhi, and it was no real surprise when she declined to accept the Congress party's appeal for its electors to support him. Reddy had been associated with the Syndicate, a group of right wing Congress party members she had vigorously opposed.

Siddavanahalli Nijalingappa, the Congress party president, accused Mrs. Gandhi of siding with communists. History, he said, had recorded no instance of a Prime Minister in India who worked for the candidate of the opposition. But Mrs. Gandhi was well aware that the election would have a strong influence on her political future.

She was an early voter in the contest, which proved to be close. In the second count of the ballots cast by the electoral college of state and federal legislators. Giri, former vice president, defeated Reddy by 14,650 votes.

Mrs. Gandhi said afterward that she did not regard the election as a personal victory. However, political analysts commented in reviewing the campaign that, had Reddy won, the Syndicate probably would have had sufficient political power to oust her from office.

Giri, a 75-year-old trade union patriarch, began his political career in 1912 as a student in Ireland, where he associated himself with the independence movement. The British deported him four years later, charging that he participated in the Sinn Fein rebellion.

On his return to India he joined the trade union wing of Mohandas K. Gandhi's government and was twice elected president of the All-India Trade Union Congress. Later he served as labor minister under Prime Minister Jawaharlal Nehru and as governor in three states during a ten-year period.

He was elected vice-president in 1967 but resigned the post to seek the presidency.

As India's new president Giri succeeded Dr. Zakir Husaid, who had died in May. The office is largely figurative, active national authority resting in the Cabinet. Mrs. Gandhi's help had been enough to cause an estimated 30 per cent of the electors to desert the cause of the Congress party's favorite.

FOR THE RECORD

DIVORCED. George Randolph Hearst Jr., 41, publisher of the Los Angeles Herald-Examiner, by Mary Thompson Hearst, after 17 years. At Santa Monica, Calif., Aug. 6.

RETIRED again, in a Defense Department economy drive, the battleship *New Jersey*, six months after being reactivated. The 45,000-ton veteran of World War II and Korea underwent a $22.5 million facelifting for her new role in the Gulf of Tonkin but was able to fire her 16-inch guns at North Vietnam shores only one month before the Communist country was declared off limits to U.S. air and naval bombardment. Announced Aug. 23.

MARRIED. James P. Shannon, former auxiliary bishop of the St. Paul-Minneapolis Roman Catholic Archdiocese, who resigned in a disagreement with Pope Paul VI over the birth control encyclical, and Ruth Wilkinson, a Rochester, N.Y., divorcee. The Aug. 2 marriage at the First Christian Church in Endicott, N.Y., automatically excommunicated Shannon . . . Claire Bloom, 38, stage and screen actress and former wife of actor Rod Steiger, to Hillard Elkins, 39, producer of the off-Broadway nudist revue "Oh! Calcutta!" In New York City, Aug. 14.

North Vietnam's president: Ho Chi Minh, who died at 79 ➡

September

After Ho Chi Minh:
A Change for Better or Worse?

Death of North Vietnam's leader stunned Communist world, ended an era

THE SITUATION in Vietnam changed dramatically at 9:47 on the morning of Sept. 3, although at the time no Westerner—least of all the Americans—could say whether the change would be for better or worse. That was the moment when, according to the Central Committee of the North Vietnamese Laodong (Workers Party), President Ho Chi Minh "passed away after a sudden, very serious heart attack at the age of 79." Hanoi did not announce the death until almost a full day after Ho breathed his last. Bulletins telling of his grave condition evidently were intended to prepare the public for the shock.

And shock it was, in Vietnam and the Communist world. The North Vietnamese and their Viet Cong allies in the South had lost the very symbol of their cause. World communism had lost the last but one of its living legends and of the movement's giants. Only China's aging and ailing Mao Tse-tung remained of those who could rank with Lenin, Stalin and others in the pantheon of Communist demigods.

Inevitably an event of such magnitude meant change, but what sort of change? Only time would disclose the full impact upon developments in Asia and upon the sanguinary war which steadily corroded the moral and physical stamina of the United States while it threatened general peace.

Long an agent of Moscow's Comintern (Communist International), for 60 years a revolutionary, for 23 years leader and symbol of North Vietnam, a poet, adventurer and philosopher who imparted an Asian flavor to the European idea of Marxism, Ho Chi Minh in many ways was the man nobody knew. Was he good or evil, saint or devil? It depended upon who made the judgment, and there were many judgments. Ho well could have been the most widely misinterpreted man of modern times.

Whatever he was, whatever verdict history would produce, Ho's death surely meant the end of an era. From events which his passing set in motion, it was soon possible to discern indistinct outlines of things to come. There would be a swift effect on international communism. There would be a shift in the political struggle between the two giants of communism, the Soviet Union and China, for influence in North Vietnam and the rest of Asia.

Ho Chi Minh's adopted name meant "he who sheds light," and it seemed that before he died he intended to shed some light on the path he wanted his heirs to pursue. His last testament, dated May 10—just nine days before his 79th birthday—was worded as if to invite only one interpretation by the members of his often-divided Politburo.

"Unity," Ho told his heirs, "is an extremely precious tradition of our party and people. All comrades, from the central committee down to the cell, must preserve union and unity of mind in the party as the apple of their eye . . . Our young people as a whole are of excellent nature. . . . The party must give much attention to their education in revolutionary morality and train them into continuers of the building of socialism, both 'red' and 'expert.' "

In the same document, Ho described himself as "grieved at the dissensions that are dividing the fraternal parties." To any Asian Communist, there could be little doubt that the reference to "red" and "expert" was a thrust at the Red Chinese. Maoists for years, in their assaults on their internal foes, had loudly insisted that "redness" was all good while "expertness" was suspect. The "experts," professional military and civilian leaders, tended to downgrade ideology in favor of practicality.

Did Ho, in his last days, intend to tip the scales in the Hanoi leadership in favor of Soviet influence in the Moscow-Peking struggle for North Vietnam's allegiance? The impression that he did was strengthened by the curious behavior of Red Chinese Premier Chou En-lai, who paid his last respects to Ho in Hanoi and left before the funeral, to be replaced later by lesser dignitaries. While this might have been motivated by an unwillingness to share the same rostrum as Soviet Premier Alexei N. Kosygin at the rites, in some respects it could be considered an affront to Hanoi. Soviet propaganda was quick to leap on this. Moscow Radio called the Chinese behavior "particularly strange and improper," and said it would be "interpreted as an irreverent act toward the heroic Vietnamese people and their honorable leader."

If, indeed, it was intended as an affront, the assumption would be that Chou was aware of Peking's defeat in the influence contest, and that the North Vietnamese Politburo had opted for the ally who was supplying it with sinews of war and props for its economy.

What happened a few days later tended to confirm this line of speculation. The rivalry over Hanoi had not ended, but Peking was persuaded—in an obvious official afterthought—to agree to a meeting between Kosygin and Chou. Just how this surprising event was brought off probably never will be made entirely clear. It had seemed that the Russians were the ones who wanted the meeting, possibly to bring home forcibly

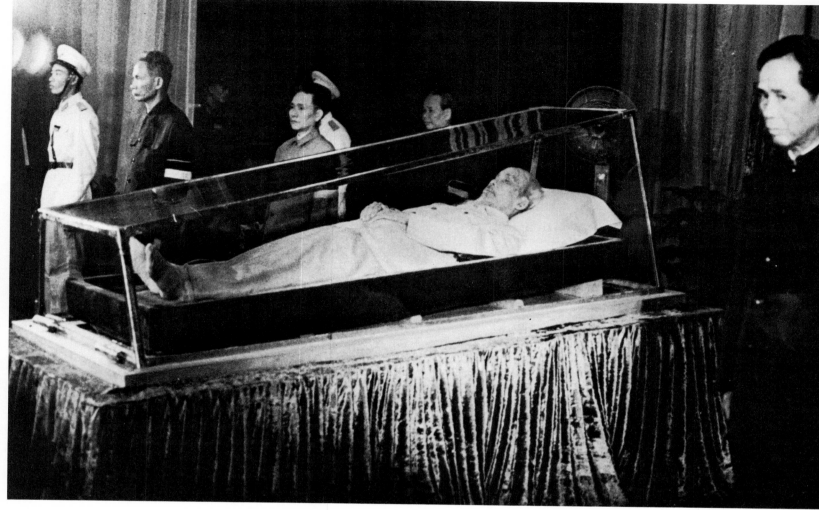

Body of Ho Chi Minh as it lay in state, attended by his North Vietnamese leaders

to Peking that Soviet patience was wearing thin and that China would be wise to avoid future military clashes on the frontier.

It was clear enough, however, that the machinery for that chilly meeting at Peking's airport was set in motion in Hanoi, during the funeral rites. It betokened increased and probably predominant Soviet influence with the ruling Hanoi Politburo. For the Red Chinese, it would mean that, for the time being, "left" Communists in Hanoi standing for long years of protracted war, had lost out to "right" Communists. The "right" Communists also stood for victory, but appeared less enthusiastic than the others about the open-endedness of the conflict. A try for quick military victory in the South seemed worth the gamble.

That gamble failed at the time of the 1968 Tet—Lunar New Year—offensive *(The World in 1968, 28-35)*. Now many questions were raised. If Ho's injunction to his party meant that Soviet influence would prevail, what effect would this have on the war? Would Moscow use that influence to hasten some sort of agreement and thus reduce the overall danger in Asia? Would Hanoi's leaders, now pledged to solidarity in a "collective," interpret Ho's testament as meaning that the Vietnamese people were entitled to peace and pursuit of a better life? Would Hanoi be more attentive to American gestures, such as those which quickly followed Ho's death, seeking to lessen the violence? Had public morale in North Vietnam sustained a devastating blow in the loss of the celebrated leader? Would North Vietnam's people be as willing to suffer and sacrifice endlessly for lesser men?

What did have meaning for average North Vietnamese was that the man who had for a quarter century claimed them as his "children" and his "nephews and nieces" no longer was among them. They knew of Uncle Ho only what they were told and what they could see. People would see him from time to time wandering among his "children," dispensing avuncular advice on "revolutionary virtues."

This was the kindly old man with the silken frizzly beard and liquid brown eyes, his features translucent with oriental saintliness, the composer of poetry, the gentle, people-loving philosopher. This was the sweet old man with the thin, soft voice, the humble patriarch who wore crude peasant clothing and sandals fashioned from rubber tires.

There was another Ho, an implacable hater, a dedicated revolutionary for whom any means justified the end. The other Ho was a veteran and obedient agent of Moscow's Comintern conspiracy to guide world revolution. The other Ho worked diligently at fomenting violence and terror. The other Ho was a top aide of the redoubtable Comintern chieftain, Mikhail Borodin, in China. The other Ho, ten years after assuming power in Hanoi, showed he could be hard as granite.

The occasion called for hardness in 1956, when peasants, frustrated and bedevilled by Communist party restrictions on their livelihood, rose in revolt in Ho's own native Nghe An Province. Under Ho, the party staged a campaign against "landlords and capitalists." All that was required was an anonymous denuciation of any person, whatever his status, and that person was marked for doom. The purge was frightful. Thou-

After paying respects to late Ho Chi Minh in Hanoi: A. Kosygin, left, USSR Council of Ministers chairman, conferred with Chou En-lai at Peking

sands were executed. The party itself, in later years, would concede that it had gone too far in exterminating "enemies of the people."

Ho was born Nguyen That Tan on May 19, 1890, the son of a minor official in an aristocratic Mandarin family which lived in a tiny Annamese village in Nghe An. His father hated the French and considered himself a patriotic nationalist. He conspired constantly against colonial rule.

Ho's family sent him to the Lycee National in the imperial city of Hue. This was the same school which a generation later would educate a young man destined to become Gen. Vo Nguyen Giap, architect of the military defeat of France.

Young Nguyen That Tan spent little time with formal education. He was seized by an urge to see the world of his country's masters and to probe into western revolutionary ideas. He signed on as a cabin boy and went to sea. Eventually he became a ship's cook on a long voyage to the United States, England, Germany and France. In New York he lived briefly in Harlem, and his education prospered. He became proficient in languages. By the end of his adventuring abroad, he could speak French, English, German and Russian in addition to his native tongue and Mandarin Chinese. For six years he lived in London, writing poetry and working at the plush Carlton Hotel as a pastry cook under Escoffier.

The young man moved on to France for a stay which was a decisive turning point in his life. He watched the big powers, after the dreadful carnage of the first World War, struggle to hammer out a peace at Versailles. While he supported himself as a photographer's retoucher, he spent his spare time haunting Versailles, lobbying for Vietnamese nationalism. He composed

and sent to the British, French and American peace delegations an eight-point petition stating the case for Indochinese independence.

But Ho became disillusioned by what he considered the West's broken promises of self-determination for peoples. He began writing articles for the extreme leftist press in France. In 1920 he attended, as an Indochinese delegate, a French Socialist congress at Tours. When it split into factions, he joined the Communist group.

As a Communist Ho followed the conspiratorial custom of adopting "party" pseudonyms. It was as Song Man Cho that Ho went to Russia for the first time in 1923, a presidium member of a Comintern peasants' organization. At Lenin's funeral in 1924 Ho met Stalin and his future as a Comintern agent was assured. The Comintern enlisted him for service in China, and he went there using the name of Ly Thuy. His job: adviser to Borodin on oriental affairs.

It was in Canton, while he was serving with Borodin, that Ho formed the "League of Oppressed People," intended to orient revolutionaries in Asia toward the Soviet brand of communism.

From China Ho went to Thailand, then called Siam, to organize exiled Annamese under the Communist banner and to attract young rebels to the party with his Revolutionary League of Vietnamese Youth—the Thanh Nien—of which Vo Nguyen Giap eventually would be the militant leader while still a boy of 15 in the Vietnamese underground. In this enterprise Ho used the name of Nguyen Ai Quoc—Nguyen the Patriot—to suggest nationalist aims. But Ho never hesitated to plot against and betray other patriotic nationalists whose organizations he viewed as a threat to his own party.

Again, as Song Man Cho, Ho showed up in Hong Kong in 1930 for a conference of expatriate Vietnamese political leaders whom he wanted to unite under the Communist egis. It was then that he formed the Indochinese Communist party. The French in Indochina, meanwhile, had sentenced him to death in absentia. Hong Kong authorities arrested him in 1931 and were about to deport him to Indochina, but he was released on an appeal and he returned to Moscow. He spent five more years in Russia taking a refresher course at the school for Communist leaders, and thereafter began shuttling back and forth between Asian points on revolutionary errands. He was always obedient to Stalin's orders.

When Japan invaded Southeast Asia, Ho was in China's Yunnan Province, where he set to work organizing underground resistance for Indochina, purportedly intended to cross into neighboring Tonkin and fight the Japanese. Events later would

Ho Chi Minh: in 1966

indicate Ho was more interested in what would happen after the war. In any case, in 1941 he slipped back into his native land and, on his 51st birthday, founded the Viet Nam Doc Lap Dong Minh Hoi, or "League of Independence of Vietnam," thereafter to become famous as the Vietminh. He returned to China and again cheerfully collaborated with both the Chinese Nationalists and the Americans. Although he had met and stayed for a time with Mao Tse-tung in the Communist hideout in Yenan, he also collaborated with Chiang Kai-shek and the Americans until Stalin reversed the field after the war.

The Chinese nationalists were not entirely happy with him. They arrested him at one time in 1943, but soon after released him. The Americans in China, meanwhile, saw in him a possibly useful instrument for harassing the Japanese occupation forces in Vietnam. Members of the OSS—the wartime Office of Strategic Services—cooperated with Ho and his chief aide, young Giap, in China. Vietminh guerrillas were trained and armed by Americans. Finally, in 1944, Ho crossed back into his native land, this time using the last of his many names: Ho Chi Minh.

Ho took command of the Vietminh guerrillas, a handful of armed men in the mountains of Tonkin, and by the war's end had them entrenched and ready to move into the vacuum left by the departing occupation forces.

Ho waited for the inevitable, the defeat of Japan by the enormous military might of the United States. While the armies of the Rising Sun reeled from American assaults, Japanese ocupation forces in Indochina, in a desperate move, placed the emperor, Bao Dai, on the throne as a puppet, hoping to use Vietnamese nationalism to alienate the nation from the allies. Ho rejected Bao Dai.

At last, the bloodiest war in history ended with Japanese surrender. At Potsdam in defeated Germany, President Harry Truman, Premier Stalin and Prime Minister Clement Attlee of Britain had already agreed that the Japanese should be disarmed by the British up to the 16th parallel in Indochina and by Chiang in the north.

Ho was ready for the war's end. Troops of France had been interned by the Japanese and Ho had been able to operate free of interference. On Aug. 16, 1945, he proclaimed an independent Republic of Vietnam, borrowing from the American Declaration of Independence in his proclamation. British forces arrived in September to disarm Japanese in the South and found Ho's Vietminh in strong position. It was then that the seeds were sown for agonizing years of guerrilla warfare.

The French began returning to the British-occupied South. They had a more difficult time in the North. Chiang's Chinese were extremely reluctant to get out. The Chinese long had ambitions in the area. They managed to impede the French return to Tonkin, and the climate was even more favorable for Ho's buildup. Not until February 1946 did the Chinese leave.

Ho offered to negotiate with the French, although suspecting that the French intended to set up a puppet government, ostensibly independent, within the French Union. Supposedly, French troops would return peacefully under such an arrangement. In March 1946 the French agreed to recognize Vietnam as independent within the union, with French troops replacing the Chinese in the North. Ho accepted. But Ho's suspicions of the French were confirmed when France declared it would cling to Cochin China in the South as apart from the rest of Vietnam. Violent anti-French rioting broke out and then the beginnings of guerrilla warfare. And, in December 1946, came a Vietminh uprising in Hanoi. By French account, French men, women and children were slaughtered. There remained no more hope for peaceful

solution. The French bombarded Haiphong and the war was on, a phase which would last another seven years.

The hard-pressed French in 1949 announced readiness to unify Tonkin, Annam and Cochin China into a single Vietnam, independent within the union, but Ho wanted no more French agreements. By then he had several hundred thousand guerrillas armed with weapons secured from obliging Nationalist Chinese, who sold arms from American and captured Japanese stocks.

The end of 1949 brought a decisive change. Communists under Mao overran the China mainland. Now Ho had a pipeline to outside help, in the form of arms and coolie labor. The bloodletting rose, at a staggering cost to an already politically confused France. The United States, shocked by Communist invasion of South Korea in 1950, became involved in Indochina with military advice and assistance to the French. Washington feared a red intention to overrun the whole Asian continent.

The American help was to no avail. The end for France came on May 7, 1954, at the remote Dienbienphu fortress deep in the jungled interior of Tonkin. Once it fell to ferocious Vietminh attack, France's position in northern Vietnam was hopeless.

Even before Dienbienphu fell, the big powers were meeting in Geneva on both the Indochina and Korea problems. With French defeat they reached agreement: Vietnam would be divided at the 17th parallel between north and south.

Ho at this time may have felt sold out by the Russians for the sake of Moscow's policy, and robbed of his chance to lead a unified Vietnam.

Now there was a new vacuum, in the South. The Americans stepped into it, pledged to keep out the Communists and make the South viable. Partition brought hundreds of thousands of northerners, mostly Roman Catholics, into the South. Many Vietminh remained in the South to await their chance to move again. They laid low while Ho's Politburo nailed down authority in what now would be the "Democratic Republic of Vietnam."

Elections proposed in a final Geneva declaration on Vietnam—which neither Americans nor South Vietnamese signed—were not permitted to take place in 1956. Many experts believed "Uncle Ho" would have had no trouble winning throughout all of Vietnam. But the South did gradually take on a viable look under the iron-fisted rule of President Ngo Dinh Diem.

Ho's Vietminh, hidden in the South, continued harassing hit-run attacks for years without seeming too much a menace. But in September 1960 Hanoi announced that it would be a good idea for the "patriots" in the South to have a political front. The Popular Socialist party, southern wing of the North Vietnamese Communists, had been active, but strategy called for masking any Communist leadership of insurrection. At the end of 1960, Hanoi Radio announced that there had been formed in the south the Mat Tran Dan-Toc Giaiphong, or National Front for Liberation of South Vietnam. That was the real beginning of the war for the Americans. Until then there had been only a relative handful of U.S. military men in South Vietnam to advise the southern forces. As guerrillas—whom Saigon derisively named "Viet Cong," meaning Vietnamese Communists—stepped up their pressure, President John F. Kennedy reacted, by increasing the number of U.S. military advisers.

Political trouble engulfed the South. By 1963 it exploded. Diem and his brother Nhu were murdered. It was the beginning of a period of political instability which would topple regime after regime in a series of military coups. And by mid-1964, the Viet Cong guerrillas were scenting victory.

Then, in August 1964, came a North Vietnamese gunboat attack on American warships in the Tonkin Gulf (*The World in 1964, 152-156*). The United States, under President Lyndon B.

Ho Chi Minh applauding children he had invited to his Hanoi residence shortly before his death

Johnson, responded with an air attack on North Vietnamese ports. The escalation was beginning in earnest. From then on, the war would grow daily more bloody.

As he neared the end of a picturesque career, Ho Chi Minh became less the active leader and more the symbol. He met often with his ministers in the role of North Vietnam's president, but he abandoned much of the routine to others. Frequently he stayed at a remote village hideaway, leaving routine to a "collective leadership" in Hanoi. Frequently "appeals" were issued in his name for war to the end "against the American aggressors and for national salvation."

Ho often acted like a ceremonial ruler. He seemed to exercise hypnotic power on foreigners, even those visitors from the non-Communist West who came as representatives of his foes. He would go out of his way to be sweetly polite and considerate. He caused even his enemies to wonder whether this old man had not been misunderstood, whether he had not, all along, been basically a nationalist patriot rather than a dogmatic Communist.

There were clear indications before Ho died that his Polit-buro of "Comrade Leaders," as they called themselves, was divided between pro-Soviet and pro-Chinese factions. It had

been Ho who had arbitrated their disputes all along. It had been Ho's father-figure which probably had kept the party from going the way of most other Communist parties in history: the way of power struggle and purge.

Now the spindly old legend had passed into history. In Hanoi a huge, black-bordered portrait of him hung over the grandstand where his successors stood to conduct the solemn last ceremonies.

"After my passing away, great funerals should be avoided in order not to waste the time and money of the people," Ho had directed in the testament read out publicly at the funeral. That injunction was patently disobeyed at a funeral which brought the highest and mightiest from Communist and from many other lands around the world.

Three weeks after Ho's death the National Assembly elected Vice-President Ton Duc Thang to succeed him in the presidency. However, the 81-year-old Ton was not named to Ho's more powerful post as head of the party.

Ho, without question, was for North Vietnam the irreplaceable man. Only time could demonstrate what would be the full meaning of his passage from living legend into history.

179

Peace, Love— and Music

Thousands of youthful vagabonds
shared hunger, hardship
at Music Festivals in
United States and abroad

LIKE LEGIONS of rag-tag vagabonds they trudged their way across the country. From virtually every state they came—by car, by thumb, by foot. They found their way to White Lake, a Cats- kill Mountain hamlet about 70 miles northwest of New York City. With packs on their backs and enthusiasm in their hearts, youth—300,000 to 400,000 strong—packed the Woodstock Music and Arts Fair billed as "three days of peace and music."

They found the music and kept the peace. They were part of a late summer and early fall movement that spread from the State of Washington to the Isle of Wight, symbolizing the life style of what adults called the "hippies" and of what many of the young called the "NOW generation."

The boys and girls—lookalikes in dungarees, bell bottoms and open-necked shirts, beads and headbands—had been drawn to the 600-acre dairy farm in the gently-rolling Catskill country by the lure of perhaps the greatest assemblage of rock music groups ever, and by the prospect of grooving freely with nature and with one another. But they were ill-prepared to live on damp and muddy ground, to go without sufficient food and water or to cope with squalor and the massive traffic tangles created by their very numbers. Many had no shoes, but they shared what little they had—food, cigarettes, blankets, wine, water and drugs.

These youngsters, so often and so severely criticized by their elders for their manner of dress, their tastes and their morals, spent more than three days together under severe hardship. All the while local residents and scores of policemen and security officers waited apprehensively for discomfort to ignite the fuse— for the kids to riot. Stifling heat, throbbing music, sex, nudity and drugs accented the hours. The life cycle went full course, with at least one birth and several deaths. But peace prevailed.

In September, other gatherings took place in the United States and abroad. At Lewisville, Tex., where some 100,000 music lovers milled about during a three-day rock festival, one security officer commented: "This crowd is a lot better than

Isle of Wight: Bob Dylan's audience ——➤

Art at Woodstock: A booth selling colorful posters

Lewisville: A happy hippie singer in Texas

Dallas football crowds. I've worked Southwest Conference games and the professional football games, and generally these kids are better behaved." The only crowd control problem, according to Mayor Sam Houston, was created by motorists, boaters and private pilots who swarmed over the festival area to gawk at nude swimmers in the Garza-Little Elm Reservoir.

Oppressive heat at the New Orleans Pop Festival at Prairieville, La., failed to generate disorder among some 30,000 youngsters attracted by such name performers as Janis Joplin, the Iron Butterfly, Country Joe and the Fish, Canned Heat and The Grateful Dead. These kids merely romped about in various states of undress. As a result, doctors reported treating numerous cases of sunburn and minor cuts. "If we could just get them to wear shoes," complained one physician, "we wouldn't have so many cut feet."

Calm prevailed, too, at the Sky River Rock Festival and Lighter Than Air Fair, which opened on a cattle ranch near Tenino, Wash., only after the state Supreme Court overruled objections of merchants, the John Birch Society, landowners, and the Northern Pacific Railroad. As tens of thousands of young folk flocked to hear the Frumious Bandersnatch, the Cleanliness and Godliness crew, folk singer Gordon Lightfoot and the Flying Barritos Bros. (a country-western ensemble), one resigned Tenino resident commented: "It's a new age, and we are behind the times." But those that were "with it" smoked pot, stripped to the waist in the dry, dusty heat and rocked with the music that pulsated till dawn. When silence finally fell the crowd climbed into sleeping bags and tents or curled up on the ground to sleep.

Sleep, however, was in short supply on the Isle of Wight in the English Channel, invaded by devotees of Bob Dylan for his first major performance in four years. Thousands of fans from the United States, Europe and Australia steamed to the holiday spot under banners echoing the slogan: "Help Bob Dylan sink the Isle of Wight."

181

Woodstock rock enthusiasts shared grass shack

Listening to rock music at Tenino, Wash., Sky River festival

"Oddly dressed people of uncertain sex are arriving in droves by every boat," said a spokesman for the island's 150-man police force. Then there were those who weren't dressed at all. One teen-age girl tore off her clothes, danced naked, and shouted "I just want to be free" before she was escorted from the scene by bobbies. A young couple disrobed and cavorted in a thigh-high sea of man-made foam. "Ain't that the greatest," shouted the applauding crowd.

Thirty-six hours after the festival began, the object of all the adulation appeared. In white suit, yellow shirt and olive green buckle boots, Bob Dylan, the 28-year-old high priest of pop music, took to the stage amid applause so thundering that most agreed it was the greatest ovation ever given a pop singer—including the Beatles—in Britain. For 14 songs and two hours Dylan enchanted the crowds, then disappointed them by cutting the songfest short by 60 minutes. At the festival's end officials estimated the assemblage as 150,000. Promoters put the total at 200,000. No matter the figures; the throng was, according to the organizers, numerous enough to turn a profit, an achievement that the promoters of the Woodstock festival would have envied.

Woodstock, the brainchild of four young men, originally had been planned for the Hudson River village of Woodstock, famed for its artist colonies and known to the young as Bob Dylan's hometown. But property problems plagued the foursome, and the festival—already publicized as Woodstock—was moved to White Lake. Thousands of dollars in improvements at the original site had to be scrapped and started anew at White Lake. Complications continued to take their financial toll, particularly at the gates. There were so many back roads leading to White Lake, and so few ticket-takers, that efforts to check those who had purchased the $18 weekend tickets went awry. Backers took a $1.3 million loss on one of the nation's best-attended entertainment events.

What really went wrong at Woodstock was that no one had anticipated the numbers that came. At best the planners had expected 100,000. By noon the first day the caravan of cars and trucks jammed with youngsters and their camping gear, had choked exits from the superhighway that served the Catskill communities. Many of the vehicles had been decorated with the exotic symbols and bright colors of the "NOW Generation." By mid-day traffic in the area was crawling at about one mile an hour. Automobiles were abandoned on the spot, adding to the already critical congestion, and the kids began hoofing it the rest of the way.

Then the rains came, turning the fields, roads and amphitheater into a sea of mud. Tents of plastic and canvas were pitched and lean-tos of blankets and strips of clothing provided poor shelter from the downpour.

Though the music worshippers were soaked from head to foot and knee-deep in mud, their spirits weren't dampened. Their troubles created a common bond, and the young people camped out as one big family, dividing what they had. One youth said their drugs—mostly marijuana—helped to heighten the "vibrations," to "groove" more deeply with the hard rock music and to experience the pleasurable states of euphoria and gentle inhibition. But the potent, dangerous drugs—LSD, STP and methadrine—were there too. Doctors manning first aid stations reported treating 72 persons felled while trying to get high. A few "freaked out" into a terrifying, crazy state of mind and were flown by helicopter to nearby hospitals. Two died of overdoses.

"This isn't a music festival, it's a drug convention," said a disgruntled state trooper who helped direct the festival forces.

Woodstock: Pop music fans jammed highways serving the site of their music and art fair

Lewisville: Taking a break at Texas festival

But if the policemen didn't like what they saw, they did little to combat it. About 50 youths were arrested the first day on drug charges, but by festival finish only 80 arrests had been recorded. "There aren't enough jails in the county to hold them all," said one official, rationalizing the low toll.

Whether the cause was drugs, easy familiarity or unknown influences, dozens of youngsters, mostly male, shed their clothing to wash or wade in two lakes, or to stroll in the altogether with nature and their fellow man.

It was casual nudity, seemingly devoid of exhibitionism. There was an apparent lack of concern or even open interest on the part of the clothed. One youth, asked why he wore no clothes, replied: "Why, that's where it's at, man. I'm free this way. I've lost my ego. I'm me, I'm you. I'm part of everyone and everything."

Whatever else they had, water and sanitary facilities were in short supply. Rumors were rampant, particularly false ones. These included claims of hepatitis, typhoid or dysentery outbreaks. A true one was that some local officials sought to persuade the state to declare the festival site a disaster area. Yet when things were at their worst help came from about 100 members of a Taos, N.M., commune, the Hog Farm, who had been imported by festival promoters, and about 30 members of a similar group, Ken Kesey's Merry Pranksters, who had driven their wildly-colored bus caravan cross-country from Oregon. They set up free kitchens and dished out high protein gruel of peanuts, oatmeal, raisins and sunflower seeds. They also put up a hospital tent where they ministered mainly to kids on bad drug trips.

Many local residents—and even the security officers—opened their hearts to the youngsters. A shaggy, dirty youth, sloshing along a muddy roadway asked a state trooper if he could spare a cigarette. Smiling, the trooper reached into the glove compartment of his car and handed the youngster two packs. The boy gave a grateful nod and moved along. Some of the local folk invited kids into their homes for food, water and shelter. When hospital facilities ran short on food and dry clothing, groups and individuals in surrounding communities donated supplies.

Others took advantage of the situation. One man barbecued hamburgers on his front lawn and sold them for 65 cents each. Some sold water for 25 cents a glass. A few local merchants jacked up their prices for the commodities the kids needed most. And some had ambivalent feelings about helping those in need. "They're just average, good, polite kids," said a woman attending a gasoline station. "They didn't know what they were getting into. Yesterday a kid with no money came by here. I wanted to feed him, but I didn't for fear they'd all hear about it and I'd be swamped. Now I'm sorry."

There had been other music festivals, beginning in 1954 with the Newport Jazz Festival which became an annual event. In 1967, 45,000 youngsters showed up for the Monterey, Calif., pop festival, and not long before Woodstock some 130,000 youths converged on a pop festival in Atlantic City, N.J. Although nobody knew exactly how many invaded Woodstock, or how many would have made the scene had they not been turned back by police roadblocks and by warnings of scarce food, water and shelter, one thing was fairly certain: Woodstock represented a festival of three worlds.

There was the world that encompassed countless thousands, probably the majority, who came to hear the acid rock music of Joan Baez, Jimi Hendrix, the Jefferson Airplane, Janis Joplin, Sly and the Family Stone and the Creedence Clearwater Revival. The audience jammed together hip to hip, back to back on blankets and in sleeping bags. They covered the sloping alfalfa

Heart of festivities at Woodstock: The stage

field amphitheater like a sea of multi-color dots on a massive impressionist painting. And when the rains came the kids held to their patch of muddy earth lest they lost it to another.

There was the in-between world of the restless wanderers who crossed and recrossed the dirt roads and weed fields looking for friends old and new and for something to keep them busy. And the world of the "Biblical" people, who sought and found a pastoral haven in a gently rolling pasture and adjacent woods where winding trails were named Gentle Way and Groovy Path and where the sweetish scent of marijuana mingled with woodsy smells.

These were fluid worlds, constantly changing with the ebb and flow of humanity; worlds peopled by a strangely silent and seemingly unenthusiastic melange of youngsters, mostly white and apparently high school or college students. In these worlds they endured the discomforts, enjoyed the music and instilled peace. "We're just normal American kids," said one youth. "Just because we dress differently from what our parents would like, and think differently from them, why do they always expect trouble?"

"How can you be against these kids?" asked one man. "You walk by and they smile and say 'hello.' They raise their hands in the sign of peace and shout 'peace' out the windows of their cars.

"Maybe they know something that we don't. Maybe we should begin to listen."

"New Nixon" in First Year Sought Fresh National Course

After slow start events began to overtake him

Nixon: He bowed before addressing United Nations

During the first eight months of his Presidency, Richard Nixon rarely broke his Inaugural pledge to go about his chores with lowered voice. He spoke so softly, in fact, that by September some fellow Republicans wished he had made a dual pledge: to speak softly and carry a big stick. But wielding a Teddy Roosevelt-size stick was not Nixon's style. He brought to the nation a low-key, low-profile chief executive. Gone was the bellicose, ultra-partisan campaigner of the 1950's. Here was a "new Nixon" who, by calculated avoidance of needless bombast, made an immediate and notable contribution toward healing the multiple and dangerous divisions that had sundered the Republic during the cyclone years of Lyndon Johnson's Presidency.

Not even Franklin D. Roosevelt, taking office at the depth of the Great Depression, faced greater challenges than those that confronted Richard Nixon on Inauguration Day. The nation's ills were manifold and seemed almost beyond healing: a costly, unwanted war in Vietnam, revolution among youth, street crime on a scale never known before, an incipient racial civil war, great cities choking on a myriad of social burdens, the economy in disarray. The United States had to be set on a new course, said Nixon, seemingly confident that the many problems would yield to the ministrations of the first Republican President in eight years. Moving cautiously with lowered voice, he was slower off the starting blocks than any chief executive since the 1920s—and the voting public seemed not to mind. Quiet on the Potomac had a soporific effect on the nation as a whole.

True, young people revolted on their campuses, crimes of violence did not abate, living costs rose ever higher, the fighting continued in Vietnam. Still, there was something pleasantly lulling about Summer 1969. No major city burned. And the President of the United States enjoyed a restful August on the beaches and golf courses of Southern California. Not since the Eisenhower administration had such somnolence prevailed. Then came September and, with autumn's first chill, a renewed awarness that not a single national problem had vanished during the pleasant summer. Some Nixon aides began asking outsiders how things seemed to be going for the new President. It was at least a tentative indication that an element of self-questioning, if not self-doubt, had found its way into the Nixon White House.

Historians of the future might mark September as the month when events began to overtake Nixon and his quiet, undemonstrative approach:

—Nixon received a notably enthusiastic welcome during a hurricane inspection stop at Gulfport, Mississippi—and the

Civil Rights Commission assailed the civil rights record of his administration. A particular target: the Nixon decision to ease enforcement of school desegregation in the South. At the Justice Department, several score staff attorneys publicly rebelled against the civil rights policy of Atty. Gen. John P. Mitchell. And Mrs. Martin Luther King Jr., accusing Nixon of failure to evolve from "racist reflexes," predicted unspecified trouble if the administration did not alter its approach to Negro problems.

—Clement F. Haynsworth Jr. of South Carolina, the President's nominee to succeed Abe Fortas on the Supreme Court *(pages 97–99),* wrestled with conflict of interest charges before a Senate Committee. Haynsworth conceded that, in retrospect, he should have avoided a particular stock investment, but he denied that any conflict of interest actually existed. The President thereafter stated, "I still have confidence in Judge Haynsworth's qualifications, in his integrity."

—Having earlier lost the initiative on tax reform legislation to the House Ways and Means Committee, Nixon countered by urging the Senate to reduce House-passed tax cuts for individuals and assign the potential savings to corporations. This roused the ire of organized labor, and presumably some individual taxpayers.

At high noon on Sept. 26, still speaking softly and eschewing the big stick, Nixon tried to take the offensive against his critics. He chose one of his most effective forums: the televised news conference from the ornate East Room of the White House. Early in the year, the chief executive had earned high marks from the public for his deft, no-notes handling of the news conference format. Vietnam was the paramount topic and, on this issue, Nixon came out punching—against some fellow Republicans. Sens. Charles E. Goodell of New York and Hugh Scott of Pennsylvania, the latter just elected to succeed Everett M. Dirksen as Senate GOP leader, had suggested it might be time to pass legislation putting a time limit on involvement of U.S. troops in Vietnam. Goodell, facing a stiff 1970 election

challenge, promised to introduce a resolution fixing Dec. 31, 1970 as the deadline. Scott talked about 1971. Said Nixon:

" . . . If the administration were to impose an arbitrary cutoff time, say the end of 1970, or the middle of 1971, for the complete withdrawal of American forces from Vietnam, that inevitably leads to perpetuating and continuing the war until that time and destroys any chance to reach the objective that I am trying to achieve of ending the war before the end of 1970 or before the middle of 1971."

Terming the proposition "defeatist," he argued it would "inevitably undercut and destroy the negotiating position that we have in Paris."

Nixon at this point continued to enjoy the approbation of most Americans, according to the pollsters. But he had a negative popularity rating on his handling of Vietnam and seemed in danger of becoming a hapless prisoner, caught between public impatience for an end to the war and the public's undoubted wish to find a graceful means of exit. Ironically, Vietnam was to be counted as one area in which Nixon recorded noteworthy achievements during his first eight months in office. After a characteristic delay while pondering the problem, Nixon unveiled a ground-breaking approach to the search for peace in his first major television-radio address, on May 18. Couched in terms both reasonable and flexible, the Nixon policy toward the Paris negotiations seemed to offer new hope. Everything was negotiable, he stated, except the right of the South Vietnamese people to determine their own destiny without interference from Hanoi, Washington or any other quarter. He mentioned such possibilities as mutual troop withdrawals, internationally supervised elections, and a future voice for the Viet Cong in the Saigon government. Further, he expressed willingness to give serious consideration to any proposals put forward by the other side.

While the world waited to find out how the enemy would react, Nixon flew to Midway on June 8 and, after meeting there with President Nguyen Van Thieu, announced that

A wave to the crowds in Bucharest by two Presidents, Nixon and Romania's Ceausescu

In Vietnam: President Nixon with troops

Saigon's military forces now had achieved sufficient strength to permit an initial withdrawal of American fighting men. By Aug. 31, he said, 25,000 U.S. troops would be "replaced." He indicated plans for a further withdrawal would be announced in August. After more than four years of increasing American involvement, the President's move was deemed momentous for its symbolism. At last, deescalation was becoming a reality—and perhaps at a faster pace than the Midway announcement indicated. Back home, Nixon told a news conference he hoped to withdraw more than 100,000 Americans from the war zone by the end of 1969.

With no hopeful word emerging from the Paris talks, Nixon sustained his momentum on the Vietnam issue by heading for Asia and six nations on the periphery of Communist China: the Philippines, Indonesia, Thailand, South Vietnam, India and Pakistan. The trip was planned to coincide with the mid-Pacific splashdown of the triumphant Apollo 11 moon crew, an event Nixon witnessed through zoom binoculars from the bridge of the recovery carrier Hornet. The President had another mission most in mind, however. Stopping overnight on Guam en route to Manila, he called the large traveling contingent of newsmen together and enunciated his own Asian policy, widely interpreted as meaning he would tolerate "no more Vietnams." Signaling a cutback in the American military commitment to Asia, he declared: "Peace in Asia cannot come from the U.S. It must come from Asia. The people of Asia, the governments of Asia—they are the ones who must lead the way."

Nixon's welcoming crowds everywhere were sizeable and friendly, if hardly enormous by Asian standards. Anti-

American demonstrations were rare. And leaders of the host governments were pleased by a Nixon promise to send them bits of moon rock. There was one small difficulty: the "no more Vietnams" stance that had seemed clear enough on Guam became obscured as Nixon's travels progressed and he fell victim to the temptation to tell local audiences what they wanted to hear. In Bangkok, even as he urged Asians to provide the manpower for their own military security, he asserted: "The U.S. will stand proudly with Thailand against those who might threaten it from abroad or from within." The statement presumably fell into the category known back home as "campaign oratory."

Nixon had no intention of visiting Asia without making a side trip, unannounced for security reasons, to South Vietnam. Neither did he want to go to the relatively secure American bastion at Cam Ranh Bay—twice visited by Lyndon B. Johnson. Nixon headed straight for Saigon and the downtown palace of Nguyen Van Thieu. Let there be no mistake, he said, that Saigon would become "Ho Chi Minh City." Standing beside Thieu, Nixon dotted another "i" of his Vietnam policy: "I believe the record is clear as to which side has gone the extra mile in behalf of peace. Now is the time for the other side to respond." The United States, he declared, had gone as far as it should or could go in offering concessions to the enemy.

Next stop was the Di An base camp of units of the 1st Infantry Division, also relatively secure (no attacks in 18 months) although located barely a dozen miles from frequently-rocketed Saigon. There Nixon talked baseball with the troops and, in an off-the-cuff speech, made one of his more puzzling pronouncements of the trip, inasmuch as he was trying to get out of the Vietnam quagmire as quickly as feasible: "I think history will record that this may have been one of America's finest hours, because we took on a difficult task and succeeded." Since everything in Vietnam seemed up for grabs at that point, it was to be presumed that once again Nixon's thoughts were concentrated on his immediate audience of combat troops, forgetting momentarily that his words echoed around the globe.

On the way back to Washington, Nixon stopped for a day in Bucharest, capital of Communist Romania which, for all its insistence on pursuing an independent foreign policy, is a stolid Soviet ally in defending Communism domestically, as witness the fact that it maintains the largest police force in Eastern Europe. There was one curious facet about Nixon's welcome: its warmth and dimensions. Plainclothesmen lining the motorcade route seemed one with the "captive peoples" behind them in cheering the American President, the first to visit a Communist country since Franklin D. Roosevelt journeyed to Yalta in 1945. People raced each other into the streets to retrieve paper Stars and Stripes—distributed in advance—that tore loose from their tiny wood standards. Romanian flags remained on the pavement, perhaps reason enough for Moscow to have viewed the visit with a measure of unease.

Between lengthy talks with Romanian President Nicolae Ceausescu, Nixon, often taking the Communist chief in tow by the arm, ventured into street crowds that seemed willing to wait until any unseemly hour—even without umbrellas or raincoats through a sudden and violent thunderstorm—to catch a glimpse of the visiting American. Nixon obliged them by getting wet, too—and by hauling Ceausescu into a dampened throng. The Romanian, seeming to smile despite concealed disquiet, did his best to ape Nixon in politicking American style.

Back in Washington via a refueling stop visit in England with Prime Minister Harold Wilson, Nixon paused long enough to chalk up another administration milestone, which some thought belated. In the first week of August he addressed the nation once more to disclose major elements of his domestic legislative program—just as Congress settled down for a month-long recess. The President outlined an imaginative "new directions" approach to the ailing public welfare program, urging Congress to, among other things, give welfare recipients strong incentives to find jobs and get off the dole (Pages 162-163). He also called for a government-guaranteed minimum annual income of $1600 for all families of four and proposed sharing, in growing fractions, federal revenues with state and local governments. Although Nixon's long-awaited domestic program was well received, some Congress members complained that it came too late in the session to invite serious consideration in 1969. With all that, it could yet become the cornerstone of a successful Presidency should some other nagging problems get solved along the way.

Nixon seemed unworried. He immediately departed the capital for his own working holiday, a full month at his newly-purchased seacoast home in San Clemente, Calif. There he discovered that a comfortable "Western White House" had been erected, seemingly overnight, next door to his Spanish-style house. Also new was a paved heliport, ready to serve him instantly should he care to fly to beach, golf course or football stadium. Nixon favored all three alternatives—and he would have enjoyed a quick visit to nearby Disneyland save for his obvious lack of anonymity.

Congress returned to Washington a few days before the President, and ready to press forward with its own legislative

program, leaving in limbo many of Nixon's recommendations. If there was anything surprising about the freshman chief executive's first eight months, it was the fact that, time and again, Congress seized from him the policy-making initiative in the domestic arena, on tax reform, repeal of the 7 per cent investment tax credit for industry, expansion of the food stamp program, voting rights and others. Even in the national security realm, Nixon's watered-down plan for limited deployment of an antiballistic missile system—"Safeguard" he called it—survived a crucial Senate test by a single vote. But Vietnam, despite his exertions and good intentions, remained Nixon's No. 1 problem. Because of lack of progress in Paris, a mid-August increase in Communist offensive actions and, it could have been assumed, misgivings in Saigon and at the Pentagon, the President had postponed his promised August review of the second-step U.S. troop withdrawal.

Gathering key advisors around him from at least three corners of the world, Nixon announced in mid-September the dimensions of the second withdrawal: 35,000 more men by Dec. 15—far short of earlier hopes embracing 100,000 or more in total for the year. This time there was no advance indication that December would produce a third withdrawal. To some, Nixon seemed to have become a prisoner of President Thieu and the Pentagon brass—a suspicion that helped prompt abrupt Congressional suggestions for setting a date when the United States, for the first time in its history, would "cut and run," as Lyndon Johnson used to phrase it with curled lip.

Mindful that thousands of rebellious young people—alienated as much, perhaps, by the Vietnam war and the military draft as by other concerns—were returning to restive colleges and universities, Nixon sought to maintain mastery of events.

Ho Chi Minh's death in early September (Pages 173-179) produced new outcries from home front dissidents that the time for peace was now. But Washington and Saigon had difficulty meshing signals on a Communist-promoted temporary truce to mark Ho's passing. Still determined to show who was minding the store, Nixon ordered a 36-hour pause in B52 bombing missions over Vietnam.

Reserving still another string in his bow, the President—just three days after aides had foreclosed any possibility of a temporary suspension of the draft—aimed a new announcement at youth: November and December draft calls, scheduled to total 50,000 men, were cancelled forthwith; he didn't call it a suspension. And if Congress failed to heed him and act sooner, he would reform the draft by executive decree early in 1970—to limit to 19-year-olds the period during which young people needed to worry about enforced induction. As Nixon's eighth month ended, Congressional Republicans urged Vietnam policy critics to hold their fire for just 60 more days, suggesting that might give the President sufficient leeway to find an exit from the maze called Southeast Asia. The critics seemed not to hear.

More than ever, Nixon was preoccupied with the issue. Addressing the United Nations General Assembly, he produced but one new thought on the war: a somewhat plaintive appeal to all U.N. member countries, East and West, to exert their best diplomatic efforts in the cause of a Vietnam peace. That seemed a slender reed indeed.

Yet the relative newcomer to the White House still could insist: "I know the job I have is supposed to be the most difficult job in the world. But it has not yet become for me that great, awesome burden that some have described it."

FOR PIKE, THE "PLACE TO DIE"

Dr. James Pike spent most of his career on a clerical odyssey, questing for what he could accept as true religious doctrine. His itinerary in this behalf was fraught with controversy inspired by his outspoken opinions on church concepts. This course led first to his resignation as Episcopal bishop of California, then to his complete departure from the organized church, with the assertion that it was a sick and "dying institution."

Pike said thereafter that he and his bride, Diane, would found a "Church Alumni Association" for those on the fringes of organized religion, but first he wanted to finish writing a book on the historical Jesus. Research for the book in September took him and Mrs. Pike to the Israeli-controlled territory southeast of Jerusalem where, according to the Gospel of St. Matthew, Jesus had gone to meditate for "40 days and 40 nights." They went to Bethlehem and then into the desert in a rented car, without a guide and equipped with only a map and two bottles of soft drink.

The excursion became a nightmare when the Pikes made a wrong turn and found themselves driving down a dry riverbed. As Mrs. Pike related later, their car soon stuck in a rut. When they were unable to extricate it the two started looking for help. Two hours later they were lost. Pike was too exhausted to go on but urged his wife to do so.

Guided only by moonlight Mrs. Pike wandered through the bleak hills for 10 hours before she stumbled into a work camp on the northwestern shore of the Dead Sea. Workmen there took her to Bethlehem, where she told her story to of-ficials. Israeli police, Bedouin trackers and army volunteers hurriedly set out on a rescue mission, fearing Pike would succumb to 120-degree heat and lack of water. Helicopter and land crews were handicapped by the thousands of caves in which Pike might have found refuge, not realizing he was out of sight from the air or the ground.

After three days the official search was abandoned when authorities decided it would have been impossible for Pike to survive any longer. Mrs. Pike, however, refused to give up. "I don't think my husband is dead," she said. "Had he died I would have felt it." She told volunteers who had agreed to continue the search that she had experienced a vision of her husband in a cave. A message from a Philadelphia medium, Arthur Ford, bolstered her faith: Ford said he too had visions of the former bishop, alive but ill in a cave.

On the sixth day the volunteers came upon a map, a pair of glasses, a contact-lens case and footprints leading from two pools of fresh water. Then they found Pike's body on a narrow ledge in the Judean wilderness, two miles from the Dead Sea, and theorized that he had fallen to the ledge, 70 feet below, while trying to climb out of a canyon. Later a pathologist said Pike probably had died instantly in the fall and had been dead two to five days.

Mrs. Pike was with the party when her husband's body was found. "There was no more appropriate place for Jim to die, if he had to die," she said.

The 56-year-old former bishop was buried in a tiny Israeli cemetery, after his widow had placed on the coffin a medallion symbolizing the life of Christ and the drive for peace.

Pike's stormy and much publicized career was climaxed by his denial of certain clerical precepts. The man who jokingly referred to himself as "God's maverick" began life as a Roman Catholic, so devout that he turned down a Harvard scholarship and chose to study for the priesthood at the Jesuit-run University of Santa Clara in California. While there, however, Pike espoused agnosticism and left for the University of California, only to move on to Yale Law School where he received a doctorate in jurisprudence.

In 1938 he married the former Jane Olvies, but two years later the marriage was annulled and he married Ester Yanovsky. During World War II his religious interest was rekindled at National Cathedral in Washington, D. C., and on Easter Sunday in 1944 Pike said he "suddenly became overwhelmed by the beauty of the liturgy and the music." Deciding that the Episcopal Church had "an intellectual sophistication and breadth," he chose to pursue that faith, and studied for holy orders. Ordained to the priesthood in 1946, he served as rector of Christ Church in Poughkeepsie, N. Y., and as chaplain at Vassar College. Two years later he was appointed chaplain at Columbia University in New York City, and while in New York he earned a bachelor of divinity degree from Union Theological Seminary.

Doctrinally Pike first stayed on orthodox ground. As he later explained, "I was an apologist. My feeling was that you've got to make the church look good." On secular matters, however, he was an independent. He was appointed bishop of California in 1958, and, in his words, "inherited a fast-growing diocese with a half-finished cathedral and no budget." So effective was he at fund raising that Grace Cathedral in San Francisco was finished in two years.

It was as a bishop that Pike first began to voice his opposition to church doctrine. Asking for "fewer beliefs and more belief," he said he wanted to rid the church of "theological baggage." He questioned the Episcopal doctrines of the Virgin Birth, the Trinity and salvation through Jesus Christ alone. Finally, in 1966, a group of bishops circulated heresy charges against him, but the House of Bishops dismissed the call for a heresy trial. They did, however, censure Pike's unorthodox theology as "offensive and irresponsible."

His troubles worsened that year when his 20-year-old son committed suicide in a Manhattan hotel. That tragedy produced Pike's interest in psychic phenomena, and his efforts to contact the spirit of his dead son were recorded in the book, "The Other Side," he wrote in collaboration with Diane Kennedy, who was to become his third wife.

Soon thereafter Pike resigned as bishop and joined the staff of the Center for the Study of Democratic Institutions in Santa Barbara, Calif. His troubles with the church continued, however, when he divorced his second wife and married Miss Kennedy. His successor as bishop claimed that permission to solemnize the marriage had not been granted.

In 1969 Pike left the church altogether. He said then that he was still a Christian, maintaining that he saw in Christ's resurrection a sign that all men could live after death. Death he compared to going to another country to live, "frightening maybe, but exciting too."

Dr. James Pike and his wife, Diane. Dr. Pike, former California Episcopal bishop, was found dead in Judean desert

Actress Sharon Tate, victim in mass murder

Miss Tate's husband, Roman Polanski, in tears

MYSTERY: THE MURDER OF 5

The big house at 10050 Cielo Drive rambled along a ridge overlooking Benedict Canyon, a wooded refuge-in-the-city for the wealthy and talented of Los Angeles and Hollywood. Once owned by Cary Grant, the $200,000 mansion in recent years has been rented out to transients for $1,000 a month. It needed paint. A wooden fence along the driveway had been cracked by a car maneuvering to leave one of the parties frequently held at the secluded home.

Access to the estate was through a wire gate operated by a silver push button on a waist-high pipe at the side of the road. Someone pushed that button one night in August and turned 10050 Cielo Drive into a slaughterhouse.

Police answering a disturbance call found five bodies—two in the house, two on the lawn and one in a car in the driveway. On the door, scrawled in blood, was the word: "Pig." In the huge, two-story living room was the body of actress Sharon Tate, 26, honey blonde, pregnant and clad in bra and panties. She had been stabbed a dozen times.

Around her neck was a nylon rope. The other end of the rope was looped over a ceiling beam and knotted around the neck of Jay Sebring, 26, a hairdresser once engaged to Miss Tate and who later became a friend of her husband, Polish film director Roman Polanski, who was in

Europe. Sebring, fully clothed, had been shot and stabbed and a hood was tied over his head.

Outside on the lawn was the clothed body of Voityck Frokowsky, 37, Polish emigre who had worked in some of Polanski's films. He had been stabbed, shot and beaten. Not far away was the nightgown-clad body of Abigail Folger, 26, daughter of board chairman Peter Folger of the J.A. Folger Coffee, Co. and a longtime friend of Frokowsky. She had been stabbed in the chest. In a car parked in the drive was the body of Steven Parent, 18, who had been visiting William Garretson, 19-year-old caretaker at the estate. Garretson was cleared by police, who theorized Parent got in the way of the killer or killers as he was leaving Garretson's cottage some distance from the main house.

The hood over Sebring's head, the rope that tied him to Miss Tate, the multiple stabbing of the actress' body all led police to describe the slayings as ritualistic, perhaps reflecting the beliefs of some weird cult. Nineteen detectives were assigned to the case. They questioned more than 300 people in the United States and Canada.

The murders were committed Aug. 8, but after weeks of investigation they reported in September, through Police Inspector Harold Yarnell:

"We've got a helluva mystery on our hands."

DEATH IN SKY FOR 83

The skies over Indianapolis were clear and there was no warning of disaster when, for the 19th time since the start of 1969, two airplanes collided and crashed. None of the 83 persons aboard the planes survived in the Indiana accident.

As had been the case in many previous collisions, a private plane was involved. This time it was a single-engine Piper Cherokee, flown by a student pilot on a solo training exercise. Officials said the Cherokee lacked the sophisticated equipment which might have enabled air-traffic controllers to spot it on their radar in time for a warning.

The other plane was an Allegheny Airlines jet, flight 853 out of Boston and headed for a landing at Weir Cook Airport in Indianapolis. Its pilot had just been in communication with ground control when the Cherokee knifed into its tail-section. Two farmers who lived near the scene of the crash reported that the smaller plane chopped off the tail of the jetliner and "people began falling out of the rear of the bigger aircraft."

The jet plunged into a soybean field about 10 miles southeast of Indianapolis, scattering wreckage, personal effects and unidentifiable bodies.

It was the third fatal crash for Allegheny Airlines in nine months. The earlier tragedies took 31 lives.

TV: LESS VIOLENCE?

"Violence on television encourages violent forms of behavior and fosters moral and social values about violence in daily life which are unacceptable in a civilized society."

So observed the National Commission on the Causes and Prevention of Violence in the United States, but its September report also noted signs of improvement in TV programs.

The 13-member commission, a study and advisory body headed by Milton S. Eisenhower, was established by former President Lyndon B. Johnson following the assassination of Sen. Robert F. Kennedy *(The World in 1968, 114–121)*. In its fourth appraisal the panel cited only dramatic portrayals; violence as reflected in TV newscasts was not included.

Commission members found that 95 per cent of American homes each had at least one television set, used 40 hours a week on the average, and that "children begin to absorb the lessons of television before they can read or write. In a fundamental way, television helps to create what children expect of themselves and of others," and what constitutes "the standards of civilized society."

Even so, the report added, "we daily permit our children during their formative years to enter a world of police interrogations, of gangsters beating enemies, of spies performing fatal brain surgery, and of routine demonstrations of all kinds of killing and maiming."

Executives of the three major TV networks said the findings leaned too heavily on past performance, and took insufficient notice of the substantial changes in program content during the ensuing season. In the view of CBS President Frank Stanton, "We have taken substantial steps to alter the basic context in which violence is presented in television drama. We are continuing extensive research into the behavioral effects of violence depicted on television."

President Nixon stood in silent tribute: The Capitol memorial service for Sen. Everett Dirksen

DIRKSEN: "HE CHOSE CALMLY TO RISK HIS LIFE"

"If you have some kind of trademark, like un- ruly hair, people get to recognize you," Everett McKinley Dirksen once remarked. And Dirksen definitely was recognizable. Not only for the ruffled white hair that always looked as if the wind had been toying with it, but for the voice —the rich, resonant voice he used as skillfully as an accomplished musician; so skillfully that it reportedly brought tears at a $100-a-plate dinner in Chicago in 1966, when he said:

"No, you can't eat freedom, or buy anything with it. You can't hock it downtown for the things you need. When a baby curls a chubby arm around your neck, you can't eat that feeling either, or buy anything with it. But what in this life means more to you than that feeling, or your freedom?"

The voice, familiar in Congress for more than three decades, was stilled Sept. 7. Dirksen, 73, leader of the Senate Republican minority, suc- cumbed five days following surgery for lung cancer.

"In the end," said Sen. Howard H. Baker Jr. of Tennessee, Dirksen's son-in-law, "he chose calmly to risk his life, electing uncertain surgery in order to gain the opportunity to live and serve further, and he lost."

Dirksen, who had been elected to his fourth Senate term less than a year before, had suf- fered recurrent illnesses requiring hospital-

ization. He blamed tension for stomach and intestinal disturbances, and he was also troubled by a bleeding ulcer, emphysema, and a pinched nerve in the back. But even in the hospital he got in his thrusts. In 1964, after he had missed a week of debate on a tax cut bill, he sent this message to the Senate:

"Perhaps you can imagine my bedridden amazement, my pajama-ruffled consternation, yes, my pillow-laden astonishment this week, to learn that three Republican-sponsored pro- posals to assist in achieving laudable goals had been defeated by very narrow margins, victims of that new White House telephonic half-nelson known as the 'Texas twist.'"

Washington, where Dirksen had spent much of his adult life since winning his first term to the House of Representatives in 1932 and serv- ing there for 16 years, paused to pay him honor.

"I feel his loss deeply and personally," said Sen. Mike Mansfield, who had worked closely with Dirksen since becoming Senate Democratic leader in 1961. "He was an old pro. His word was good. Everything was on the table. It was a perfect relationship between the leaders."

As Dirksen's body lay in state beneath the vaulted rotunda of the Capitol, beneath the great dome, President Richard Nixon eulogized the dead leader to members of the Senate and the House, the Cabinet, diplomats and judges

who had assembled in funeral salute. Nixon, who had served with Dirksen in both houses of Congress, said, "Our great men are the common property of the country. Everett Dirksen of Illinois was and is the common property of all the 50 states. He was an outspoken partisan, he was an individualist of the first rank. Everett Dirksen added a grace and eloquence and courtliness to the word 'politician'. That is how he became leader of the minority. He culti- vated an appearance that made him seem old fashioned, but his character was as modern as Saturn V."

In the Senate, a lonely marigold marked Dirk- sen's front row desk. In his office, down the hall, a bouquet of marigolds, as always, was on his desk. The marigold was Dirksen's favorite flower—so much so that he made an annual Senate speech to unsuccessfully champion its cause as the national flower. In one of these he said, "It is as sprightly as the daffodil, as deli- cate as the carnation, as aggressive as the petunia, as ubiquitous as the violet and as stately as the snapdragon."

After the eulogies, after the righthand star in a row of six over his office door lit up to indicate the Senate was in session again, Dirk- sen began his last journey—back to his home- town of Pekin, Ill., for burial.

On Sept. 17, Gov. Richard Ogilvie of Illinois

named Republican Ralph T. Smith, speaker of the Illinois House of Representatives, to succeed Dirksen in the Senate. Sen. Hugh Scott of Pennsylvania was elected by Senate Republicans Sept. 24 to take Dirksen's place as Senate minority leader. Scott defeated Sen. Baker by a 24-to-19 vote.

Dirksen made his opening bid for a Congressional seat in 1930, but lost in the Republican primary to the incumbent by 1,100 votes. In 1932, he tried again, and this time he won the seat by more than 23,000 votes. From then until 1946 he was reelected regularly. As a legislator he displayed a massive capacity for hard work, arising at 5:30 a.m. and taking home a bulging briefcase each evening. Even so he completed his legal education in night school.

During his first four terms in the House, Dirksen voted against a number of New Deal measures but did support Social Security and the minimum wage and hour bill. In foreign affairs he was regarded as an isolationist, although later he urged fellow Republicans to show "a unity of purpose" behind the President. Not to do so, he felt, "could only weaken the President's position, impair our prestige and imperil the nation." In 1941 he voted for additional lend-lease funds.

At 51 Dirksen awoke one 1947 morning to find his right eye clouded. The ailment was diagnosed as degeneration of the retina, and specialists recommended that the eye be removed. But Dirksen, after "weeping and praying," said no. He retired from the House at the end of 1948. With rest and treatment, his eye improved, and Illinois voters returned him to Washington in 1951—this time as Senator.

Bucking the forces favoring Dwight D. Eisenhower for the presidential nomination in 1952, Dirksen became a major supporter of Sen. Robert A. Taft of Ohio. During the convention, as the Taft forces battled those favoring Eisenhower, Dirksen waved his finger at New York's Thomas E. Dewey and cried: "We followed you before, and you took us down the path to defeat." But after the Eisenhower camp won, Dirksen became one of the general's closest advisers, during the campaign and after the election. Although once an isolationist, he championed Eisenhower's internationalist foreign policy.

When Adlai Stevenson referred to Eisenhower's administration as "dreary," Dirksen retorted:

"Quite often Adlai has a sense of fitness in selecting his adjectives. Dreary is the word. It is no glamorous or dramatic adventure to cleanse the temple of government of its defilement, indicating grafters and boodlers of the 22 major scandals of the Truman administration . . . it goes forward with vigor even though it be a dreary job."

Dirksen's power was at its pinnacle when Lyndon B. Johnson and the late John F. Kennedy were in the White House. It was to him that Democratic presidents came seeking the votes they needed for key proposals. In 1963 he first opposed the limited nuclear test ban treaty, but later took to the Senate floor to argue the case for Kennedy in the struggle over ratification of the treaty. He had not, he said, lost faith in his President. "Take one little step with some hope and some faith," he urged. And the Senate did.

". . . Sometimes," Dirksen once said, "you have to change your position."

He was a key element in passage of the Civil Rights Act of 1964, and again when Congress dealt with voting rights the next year. Consistency never seemed to hobble Dirksen. He backed

Barry M. Goldwater for the GOP presidential nomination, made the nominating speech for the Arizona conservative, and campaigned for him for the White House even though he was aligned against Goldwater in Senate decisions on foreign policy and civil rights.

At some of the weekly news conferences dubbed "The Ev and Charlie Show" which he held with House GOP Leader Charles A. Halleck, Dirksen gibed at Democratic social programs. Once he said the Johnson administration was pushing such programs with "the pop-eyed ardor of a Harpo Marx chasing blondes." After Nixon took office Dirksen at times stood opposite the Republican president, blocking a widely publicized appointment and agreeing with the Democrats on a six-month extension of the income tax surtax although the White House wanted a year.

One of many anecdotes circulated in Washington purported that, when relaxed, Dirksen liked to amuse party guests with an imitation of an intoxicated goose alighting on Chesapeake Bay. "Sir," he said when asked about this, "I do not know how an intoxicated goose behaves. You must have me confused with Red Skelton."

Before he plunged into politics Dirksen engaged in a varied series of occupations that dated from his childhood.

Everett and his twin brother Tom Dirksen were born at Pekin on Jan. 4, 1896, the sons of German settlers Johann Frederick and Antje Conrady Dirksen. When Everett was 5 his father suffered a stroke and died four years later. He and his brother helped their mother slop hogs, milk cows, and tend the chickens and bees.

Young Dirksen enrolled as a pre-law student at the University of Minnesota in 1914, earning the money to pay his fees by working as a newspaper ad taker, a lawyer's assistant, and in a railroad office. He left school before graduation to join the Army in 1917 and was sent to France. He was commissioned a second lieutenant in the field and, in 1919, discharged. Thereupon he returned to Pekin to make washing machines, share the ownership of a bakery and manage a dredging company. In 1927 he married Louella Carver, with whom he had appeared in a community play. Their daughter, Danice Joy, was born two years later.

Also in 1927, Dirksen was elected to the part-time job of city commissioner of finance and his political career was off to a modest start.

After Dirksen died, Sen. Frank Church, D-Idaho, characterized him as "an authentic product of an earlier period who remained prominent and powerful to the moment of his death. We will not see the likes of him again."

The Senate's Republican leader: Everett Dirksen shortly before his death

AMBASSADOR'S "UNEASY TIME"

It was an uneasy time. First there were rumors that the president of Brazil was dead. Then the 90 million people of Latin America's largest nation were told Arthur da Costa e Silva had been stricken by a "circulatory crisis"—a stroke. With the president disabled, a triumvirate of military leaders announced it was taking over control of the country.

An uneasy time—a suitable time for terrorist opponents of the government to strike. They did.

Their target was C. Burke Elbrick, the United States Ambassador to Brazil. Moving quickly —Costa e Silva's illness was announced Sunday night, Aug. 31—the terrorists ambushed the 61-year-old Elbrick's limousine Thursday, Sept. 4, several blocks from the embassy residence in Rio de Janeiro. Several gunmen forced their way into the car, overwhelmed the ambassador, and forced the chauffeur at gunpoint to drive to a deserted street. Elbrick was put into another car and spirited away. His driver, left unharmed, reported the kidnaping.

It was, a Brazilian official said, "an act of pure and simple terrorism."

The kidnapers left behind a lengthy ransom note. It was signed by two of the several underground guerrilla groups operating in Brazilian cities—the National Liberating Action and the Revolutionary Movement of Oct. 8. It made two demands: Release 15 political prisoners and fly them to political asylum in Chile, Algeria, or Mexico; and publish and broadcast widely their anti-government manifesto, charging the government was a dictatorship exploiting the people. If the demands were not met in 48 hours, they said, Elbrick would be killed as an act of "revolutionary justice."

"With the kidnap of the ambassador," the manifesto said, "we want to demonstrate that it is possible to defeat the dictatorship and the exploitation if we arm and organize ourselves. We show up where the enemy least expects us and we disappear immediately, tearing out

the dictatorship, bringing terror and fear to the exploiters, the hope and certainty of victory to the midst of the exploited. Mr. Elbrick represents in our country the interests of imperialism, which, allied to the great bossers, the big ranchers and the big national bankers, maintain the regime of oppression and exploitation."

Acts of political terrorism in Brazil had increased since the 1964 civil-military revolt (The World in 1964, 66), especially after Costa e Silva closed Congress and assumed virtually dictatorial powers in December 1968, two years following his election (The World in 1966, 210). Assaults and robberies of arsenals and banks had been blamed on leftist terrorists. The terrorists contended they turned to crime to raise funds for an armed struggle against the military-dominated government.

Since becoming dictator, Costa e Silva had stripped nearly 300 prominent citizens of their political rights, fired a number of government workers, and made many arrests. Following his stroke, the military chiefs took power by bypassing the 1967 constitution which decreed the vice president's succession in case of presidential illness or death. Military leaders selected Gen. Emilio Garrastazu Medici, 63, on Oct. 6, as their choice for the country's next president.

The military triumvirate faced its first test with Elbrick's abduction. After a hastily called meeting of the National Security Council and an unsuccessful search for the ambassador, the new administration said it would meet the kidnapers' demands. Two hours after the announcement was broadcast an anonymous telephone call directed police to the suggestion box of a supermarket. There they discovered a list of the prisoners to be released, and a note saying Elbrick would be freed when the 15 prisoners had arrived safely by plane in Mexico. Political sources in Brazil called the list a "Who's Who of political prisoners" ranging from a

long-time Communist party member to a student activist. Police found another note from the kidnapers in an alms box at a church in Rio, saying Elbrick was "perfectly well." Along with it was a hand-written letter from the diplomat to his wife urging her not to worry.

Reluctance of some military officers to release the prisoners caused minor delays at first, but in a matter of hours both the government and the kidnapers kept their promises. Soon after the plane's arrival in Mexico had been confirmed, Elbrick was freed in Tijuca, a residential section of Rio. A taxi driver recognized the ambassador and took him to the American embassy. In Mexico, one of the released prisoners called the three-day kidnaping "a natural act of resistance to imprisonments, tortures and violence by the Brazilian government."

Elbrick told a news conference he had been held in a bare room and had discussed politics with his captors, who "seemed to attribute all troubles and difficulties they saw in Brazil to what they called North American imperialism. I told them that that reflected a colonial mentality on their part."

As for his own discomfort, he said being an ambassador "is not always a bed of roses."

FOR THE RECORD

APPROVED. By the executive committee of the Episcopal Church, $200,000 for the interdenominational National Committee of Black Churchmen. The move followed issuance by James Forman, former executive director of the Student Non-Violent Coordinating Committee, of a "Black Manifesto," which demanded that white churches and synagogues pay Negroes $500 million in "reparations." Episcopal regulations forbade grants of funds to groups advocating violence. So it was decided to channel the promised money to the National Committee, which had never endorsed the Black Manifesto's language but was allied to Forman's group through the overlapping membership of their executive boards.

OVERTHROWN. The civilian government of President Luis Adolfo Siles Salinas of Bolivia by a military junta Sept. 26. Siles, 44, had been elevated from the vice presidency when Gen. Rene Barrientos was killed in a helicopter crash five months earlier. With Gen. Alfredo Ovando Canadia, 52, commander in chief of the armed forces, assuming the presidency, Bolivia became the ninth Latin American nation under military rule. The new government's first act was to invalidate the oil law under which the U.S.-owned Bolivian Gulf Oil Co. operated. Later the firm was seized and nationalized.

COUP. By a military coup Sept. 1, King Idris I of Libya, while the 79-year-old monarch was undergoing medical treatment at a Turkish spa. The junta establishing the new "Libyan Arab Republic" quickly announced it would respect all international obligations, defense treaties and concessions granted to American and other foreign oil companies. The United States formally recognized the new revolutionary regime Sept. 6 and voiced hope for continued "close ties" with the oil-rich Arab land astride North Africa's Mediterranean.

U.S. Ambassador Charles Burke Elbrick, welcomed by his wife Elvira after he had been held captive for three days by Brazilian terrorists

Fans invaded field when Mets won World Series ⟶

October

Destiny's Darlings

The New York Mets were baseball's poor folks for seven years; then, in one giant leap, they vaulted to the world championship

THIRTY-THREE Americans turned impossible dreams into reality in 1969. Three of them rode to the moon with Apollo 11. Thirty rode to the championship of baseball's world on the roster of the New York Mets of the National League. Plenty of people would have said that the Mets' achievement was the more impossible of the two.

Two of Apollo's crew trod the surface of the moon, the first humans to do so in all time. The flight represented a vast investment of talent and treasure; it was the climax in a series of climaxes, each in turn more startling than the last, as man pushed into the void of space *(pages 140–146)*.

No preliminary feats hinted that the Mets were approaching success. Born in a major league expansion in 1962, they had lost more than 100 games and finished a miserable last in five of their seven seasons. In 1968, the pinnacle of their career, they had wound up ninth in a 10-club league. They had explored all known ways of losing a game, then had invented new ones.

So skilled were they in ineptitude that they attracted a large and vocal following, reminiscent of the faithful who inhabited Ebbets Field in the departed days of the Brooklyn Dodgers. The audiences were so raucous, so happy in the throes of defeat that a new Met joke was born: If ever the Mets attained mediocrity, their fans would desert them.

It was appropriate that the Mets (so nicknamed in honor of the Metropolitans, one of New York's first professional teams) should win unprecedented victory in a season without precedent. For the first time, National and American leagues split into East and West divisions, with divisional playoffs preceding the World Series. The change was part of a movement to revitalize professional baseball in its centennial year *(pages 42–44)*.

The new alignment was a great success, at least in terms of public interest. Attendance swelled to more than 28 million, a record, just one year after pessimists were wailing that the game

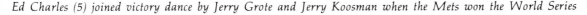

Ed Charles (5) joined victory dance by Jerry Grote and Jerry Koosman when the Mets won the World Series

was dying. The majority of the turnout, by 3½ million, belonged to the National League, testimony to tighter races.

In the American East, the Baltimore Orioles, cool, confident and capable, sprinted to the front in April, quickly built a commanding lead and never were challenged seriously; they coasted home 19 games ahead of the Detroit Tigers, the defending World Champions. In the West, the Minnesota Twins won 13 of 18 games with their strongest rival, the Oakland Athletics, and breezed to the division title when the Athletics faded in the stretch.

The National League's West was a brawl. As late as Sept. 11, five teams were bunched within two games of the lead. Then the Atlanta Braves took charge, winning 19 of their 25 games in the final month. When they clinched victory on Sept. 28, they ran a winning streak to nine games. The National's East was the arena for the Mets' spectacular.

The marvels of September were not foreshadowed in April. The Mets stumbled and fumbled in the manner to which their customers were accustomed while the Chicago Cubs, also a stranger to the altitude of first place, rode serenely in the lead.

The first sign of a new order came in May when the New Yorkers turned from five straight losses to build a winning string of 11. That was "the real turning point," Manager Gil Hodges said later, that was when the players "really got to believing in themselves."

In July, Mets and Cubs collided head-to-head. The Mets won two of three games at their home Shea Stadium and duplicated the feat at Chicago's Wrigley Field. Suddenly they were a mere three games from the top. Unused to high places, they couldn't hold the pace. By Aug. 13, they had slid to third, trailing the St. Louis Cardinals by one game and the Cubs by 9½.

That was the farewell appearance of the old Mets. Over-

night the new Mets were born. In the next six weeks the new darlings of destiny won 34 games while losing only 10. Over the same period the Cubs lost 22 of 39 games and the Cardinals, overwhelming favorites in the springtime to repeat their pennant show of 1968, dropped 24 of 41.

Suddenly the Mets were the young Lochinvars, the Galahads, the underdog that unexpectedly was showing teeth. They were kissed by the gods, favored by fortune, possessors of a magic touch.

Example: They took a doubleheader from the Pittsburgh Pirates, then still a contender for the division title, each game by a 1–0 score. In the first, pitcher Jerry Koosman batted in the only run; in the second, pitcher Don Cardwell did likewise. Rarely did any pitcher bat in a winning run; it was unheard of that two pitchers on one team should do it on the same day.

Example: Pitcher Steve Carlton of the Cardinals set a record by striking out 19 Mets in a game in which he yielded only two hits. Both were home runs by outfielder Ron Swoboda, who hit only seven others all year, and the Mets won, 4–2.

Example: The team came home from a winning road trip to drop a doubleheader to the Pirates, performing so poorly that their admirers began walking out before the second game was half played. One day later, the Pirates' Bob Moose pinned a no-hit shutout on them. The net result of the three humiliating defeats was a tighter hold on first place, occupied on Sept. 10. The explanation was that the Cubs were wallowing in an eight-game losing streak and each loss reduced the combination of Met victories and Cub defeats that would put the title beyond the Cubs' reach. Even the calendar was working against the Cubs.

On Sept. 24, a 6–0 defeat of the Cardinals assured the triumph. The fans responded by surging onto Shea Stadium turf for a

Tommie Agee, Mets centerfielder, hits the dirt in the third game to snag Paul Blair's fly ball

Pete Richert's throw hit J. C. Martin on wrist as he raced for first. Rod Gaspar's score from second won fourth game for mets

Mets' pitching ace Jerry Koosman moments before he burned one across

demonstration of unbridled exuberance. They ripped up chunks of sod for souvenirs, tore the rubber on the pitchers' mound from its moorings, dislodged home plate. They kidnaped the bags from second and third bases but, perhaps in an echo of their heroes' futile days, they forgot to touch first.

In the National League playoffs against the Atlanta Braves, as in the stretch of the regular schedule, the Mets could do no wrong although things did not so appear at first glance. Both Tom Seaver and Koosman, aces of the young pitching staff that was the keystone of Met success, retired under fire. Gary Gentry, a prize rookie, did not last through the third inning. But Gil Hodges' choice of relief pitchers was flawless. Ron Taylor, Tug McGraw and Nolan Ryan—particularly the fireballing Ryan—combined to yield only two runs in an aggregate of 13⅓ innings. The Braves' relievers gave up 9 runs in 11 innings.

At bat, New York produced some unlikely heroes to help their regular stalwarts, outfielders Cleon Jones and Tommie Agee. The important blow in the first game, a pinch single with the bases full, was delivered by J. C. Martin, a second string catcher who had a lowly .209 batting average for the year. The third game was won with a home run by third baseman Wayne Garrett whose only other homer of 1969 was hit 'way back in May. Second baseman Ken Boswell had hit three home runs in 362 times at bat during the season; now he clouted two in 12 trips to the plate. In all, the robust Met attack totaled 37 hits and 27 runs in the three games needed to win the best-of-five series. The scores were 9–5, 11–6 and 7–4.

Over in the American League, Baltimore chewed up Minnesota with equal dispatch in a display of balance, depth and versatility. The Orioles won the first game, 4–3 in 12 innings, when, with shortstop Mark Belanger on third, outfielder Paul Blair laid down a surprise squeeze bunt. In the second game, it was Baltimore pitching: Lefthander Dave McNally yielded only three singles en route to a 1–0 decision in 11 innings. In the third game, it was Baltimore power: 18 hits, including

eight for extra bases, and a rousing 11–2 win. Blair clouted a homer and two singles and batted in five runs.

So the lines were drawn for a World Series of princes versus paupers, the swaggering Orioles, rich in talent, and the poor little Mets whose bubble now must surely burst.

Aside from the pitching staff, an ardent optimist could not give the Mets an advantage at more than two positions—left field where Jones' .340, third best in the National League, overshadowed Don Buford's .291, and at catcher where Jerry Grote was rated a more polished performer than either Andy Etchebarren or Elrod Hendricks. The Mets had no one to match Boog Powell's 121 runs batted in or Frank Robinson's 100 RBI, they had no player to challenge third baseman Brooks Robinson in defensive skills.

Team statistics also were convincing. Baltimore led in batting, .265 to .242; in home runs, 175 to 109; in total bases, 2,300 to 1,904; in runs batted in, 722 to 598.

New York was given an edge in pitching, particularly if Seaver, 25 wins with an earned run average of 2.21 per game, or southpaw Koosman, 17 wins and a 2.28 ERA, was on the hill; this pair had won 17 of 18 starts during the drive to the division title. Even in pitching, however, the Baltimore staff collectively had an ERA of 2.83 against 2.98 for the Met corps.

The first game, at Baltimore on Oct. 11, was strictly according to the book. Lefthanded Mike Cuellar, 23-game winner in the regular season, gave up only six harmless hits. Brooks Robinson's play at third base was spectacular. The first batter, Don Buford, hit a home run and later contributed a run-scoring double. Seaver retired for a pinch hitter in the sixth inning. The Orioles won, 4–1.

Second guessers questioned Hodges' platooning strategy, although it was what he had been doing all year. With a lefthander pitching for Baltimore, he benched his lefthanded hitters and fielded an orthodox righthanded lineup. The questions arose because the replaced players had been so prominent in the playoff route of Atlanta. In particular, the substitution of Al Weis for Ken Boswell at second base was a target. Boswell had batted a lofty .422 during the stretch drive and his five runs-batted-in led the team against the Braves. Weis was a journeyman infielder with a batting average for the season of .215.

Undaunted by initial defeat, Hodges retained the right-handed batting order in the second game against southpaw Dave McNally. Koosman threw a no-hitter for six innings, yielded only two hits in all—although he needed help in the ninth when he walked two men—and the Mets evened the Series with a 2-1 victory. How did the Mets score their runs? Donn Clendenon, platooning with Ed Kranepool at first base, hit a home run. With two out in the ninth, Ed Charles, at third base instead of Garrett, singled. Grote singled. And then Weis smacked the first pitch into left field to send home the run that won. The criticism of Hodges' platooning was silenced.

The third game was Tommie Agee's show. He hit a home run in the first inning and made two catches hailed as among the greatest in Series history. In the fourth inning, with two Orioles on base and two out, he galloped a long way into left center to snare a drive by Elrod Hendricks two steps from the bleacher wall. Three innings later, with the bases full of Orioles and again two out, he sprinted the opposite way for a diving, sliding catch of a ball off Blair's bat. The press box figured that the two plays cut off at least five runs which, by coincidence, was the Met total for the day. Baltimore netted four hits and a zero against Gentry and Ryan.

Aside from Agee's stellar play, the game illustrated again the Met penchant for unlikely heroes. With two out in the second inning, Grote walked and went to second when shortstop Bud Harrelson singled. Up came Gentry with an average of .081 and a lone run batted in for the season. Now he jumped on Jim Palmer's first pitch, lined it into right center for a double, and two runs scored.

The fourth game was critical for the Orioles. If they had won, they would have tied the Series at 2-2 and assured a return to their friendly home park. They didn't win and again the supposedly secondary righthanded platoon was prominent on the New York side.

Clendenon hit his second homer in the second inning. Seaver protected the narrow advantage into the ninth, yielding only three hits and working on five consecutive hitless innings at that point. Then, with one out, Frank Robinson and Powell singled and Brooks Robinson smashed a liner into right center. Ron Swoboda, in the lineup instead of Art Shamsky, made a diving catch that was startling for any fielder, let alone one not noted for fielding ability. A potential triple became a sacrifice fly and Baltimore was retired with one run.

The tie thus created endured into the tenth when gremlins intervened on behalf of the Mets. Grote lifted a high fly into left. Buford lost the ball in the sun just long enough to make sure that he couldn't catch up with it and it was just too far out for shortstop Belanger to reach. After Weis was walked intentionally, pinch hitter J. C. Martin laid down what was intended to be a sacrifice bunt. Pitcher Pete Richert and catcher Hendricks both went after it, Richert reached the ball first and his hurried throw hit Martin on the left wrist and rolled around the infield while the winning run scored. Anguished wails when a news photograph showed Martin running illegally inside the foul line were ineffectual.

By that time, the most ardent Baltimore backers were beginning to believe that 1969 was not their year. When the teams squared off for the fifth time, the feeling around Shea Stadium was that the Mets were on the verge of victory. Three

Man on ledge waited to clean up Wall Street paper blizzard

Hail to the conquering heroes

runs by the Orioles, when pitcher McNally and Frank Robinson tagged Koosman for homers, merely delayed the inevitable.

The inevitable began to happen in the sixth when each team in turn argued about whether a batter was entitled to first base because he had been hit by a pitch. The Orioles lost their argument, the Mets won theirs.

The Oriole contention was that a fast ball hit Frank Robinson on his right thigh. Umpire Lou DiMuro agreed but added that the pitch first had glanced off Robinson's bat and therefore was truly a foul ball and strike two. Then Robinson struck out. The same situation came up in the New York half of the inning when Cleon Jones was hit on the right instep. Hodges retrieved the ball, showed DiMuro a swatch of shoe polish on it, and the umpire waved Jones to first.

The importance of the decision quickly became apparent when Clendenon bounced his third home run off the auxiliary scoreboard in left field and two runs came in. One inning later, the Mets tied the score on the wings of a home run by, of all people, Al Weis. (His output for all of the regular season: two).

Finally, in the eighth, Jones doubled and, with one out, Swoboda doubled to send him home. Buford almost made a brilliant backhand catch but this was a Series in which Met outfielders were making brilliant catches while Oriole outfielders could do no better than "almost." Swoboda scored an insurance run when Powell booted Grote's line drive, and the Orioles were finished. After the third inning, Koosman gave up only one hit, retired 19 of the last 21 batsmen.

Incredibly, unbelievably, magnificently, the New York Mets had won the championship of the world. A mere one season out of baseball's dungeons, they had taken all the marbles that the game could offer.

New York went crazy. Wall Street erupted in a blizzard of confetti, ticker tape and shredded newspapers. Broadway and other avenues of commerce were similarly engulfed. The scene at Shea Stadium made the demonstration when the division title was won look like a Sunday School picnic. There was dancing in the streets. The city had seen nothing like it since the end of World War II.

Statistics showed how thoroughly the Mets had subdued the Orioles. In particular, the figures on the shackling of Baltimore power by Met pitching was revealing. Baltimore's Series batting average, a meager .142, was 124 percentage points under the seasonal level. Baltimore had eight men who batted better than .280 during the regular schedule; in the Series, only three topped .200 and two of them were pitchers. After the first game, the Orioles put their leadoff man on base in only one inning.

On the other side of the field, five Mets batted above .300. Weis led the pack with .454. Swoboda hit .400 and Clendenon .357. The three hit an aggregate 513 points above their gait for the season. And they played with the righthanded platoon.

There was no disposition among the second-guessers to downgrade the Orioles. They were the same splendid team that they had been since April. But, for these five days in October, the Mets were the better club. They simply had outplayed the Orioles, made the big play when it was needed, hit the big hit when it counted most.

Baltimore fans had seen enough of New York to last them through the rest of the year. New York's Jets had trampled Baltimore's Colts in pro football's Super Bowl. New York's Knickerbockers had knocked Baltimore's Bullets out of the National Basketball Association playoffs. And now, most amazing of all, the Mets had conquered the Orioles. It was enough to make a man take up soccer.

200

Willy Brandt, who became West Germany's new Social Democratic chancellor, and his Norwegian-born wife

Willy Brandt, Twice a Loser, West Germany's New Chancellor

"Emigre and Outcast" received Bundestag majority of only two votes
but victory for Social Democrats was their first in 39 years

Konrad Adenauer, the strong-willed patriarch of West German democracy and rebirth, became the Bonn republic's first chancellor by a one-vote majority in 1949. On this meager basis his Christian Democratic Union (CDU) began two decades of dynastic rule. Under Adenauer and his two successors, Ludwig Erhard and Kurt Georg Kiesinger, West Germany rose like a phoenix from the ashes of Hitler's Third Reich. The "economic miracle," for which the Christian Democrats claimed chief credit, brought West Germany into the forefront of the world's industrial and trading nations.

As West Germany began preparing for its sixth postwar federal parliamentary election, there was little on the surface to signal a momentous shift in the balance of political power. The economy was booming. The deutsche mark was one of the world's hardest currencies. West Germany's foreign currency reserves topped $4 billion. Its foreign trade surplus soared to $2.6 billion in the first eight months of 1969. Industrial plants were stretching their capacities to keep up with mounting orders. Unemployment was a scant ½ of one per cent of the total labor force. For each jobless worker, there were eight job openings. A record 1.5 million foreign workers had been imported to fill gaps in production lines. Most of West Germany's 60 million inhabitants were enjoying unprecedented prosperity. Workers' monthly average wage of 1,080 marks ($270) made them among the best paid in Europe.

But the boom could not soothe underlying frustration of a divided nation still burdened by war guilt that inhibited it from playing a political role in the world commensurate with its economic power. "We are an economic giant but a political dwarf," was a catch-phrase summing up this frustration.

Kurt Kiesinger and Ludwig Erhard (background), ex-chancellors, heard their successor, Willy Brandt, as he addressed Bundestag

There was simmering discontent among those who felt themselves bypassed in the general prosperity. About 40 per cent of the factory workers and more than half of the manual laborers were earning only slightly more than the 500 marks ($125) monthly minimum the government considered necessary for the subsistance of a family of four. Pensioners, war widows and disabled veterans complained their benefits were lagging behind the rising cost of living. Small shopkeepers felt themselves increasingly threatened by department stores and supermarkets as American-style shopping centers sprouted from fields on the outskirts of cities. Farmers complained that small family farms were being driven out of business. The number of farms had dropped from 2 million in 1949 to 1.2 million.

Student unrest had decreased in violence since the attempted assassination of Rudi Dutschke (The World in 1968, 89, 103), the firebrand student leader, the previous year. But one of the main causes for the unrest was still there: universities, heavy on tradition but light on the modern accoutrements of learning and research, were overcrowded and sorely in need of reform.

Labor unions, whose members had been among the most disciplined and least demanding in the world, were clamoring for participation in the policy-making decisions of industry. The myth that West German workers were practically immune to strikes was shattered as the 1969 election campaign moved into its final phase. Steel workers, miners and public service employes joined by the tens of thousands in a wave of wildcat strikes to claim a greater share of the boom. The strikes added to a general uneasiness about the economy. Two disastrous world wars, resulting inflations, the boom to bust of the late

20s, the "cigarette barter economy" after World War II had made Germans wary of good times.

The late summer of 1969 also presented the specter of re-emerging ultranationalism under the banner of the National Democratic party (NPD), the strongest rightwing organization since the collapse of the Third Reich. The NPD, labled neo-Nazi and "melting pot of malcontents" by its foes, was already represented in seven of West Germany's 10 state parliaments. Now it was making a concerted drive to win a foothold in the Bundestag, the federal parliament. Many Germans feared even a modest NPD success would cost them much of the goodwill they had won in the west and touch off menacing invective from the Soviet Block. In this atmosphere of uncomfortable prosperity, the Christian Democrats waged their election campaign according to the old formula employed so successfully by the late Konrad Adenauer. "No experiments," was the gist of their message to the voters. This was complemented by a "law and order" theme designed to offset the appeal of the National Democrats among conservative voters.

The official CDU campaign slogan, "It's the chancellor that counts," was proclaimed from countless posters depicting the fatherly image of 65-year-old Chancellor Kurt Georg Kiesinger. The reason for this emphasis on the chancellor was that, for the first time in West Germany's brief history, the Christian Democrats were sharing power with their traditional opponents—the Social Democrats. This odd coupling resulted from the collapse of the Erhard government in November 1966. Erhard was forced aside after his coalition with the small, but pivotal, Free Democratic party (FDP) collapsed in a fiscal dispute. At the time, West Germany was experiencing its first serious recession and Erhard's reputation as economic miracle worker was severely tarnished. The proponents of a coalition of Christian and Social Democrats believed only such a "grand" alliance could tackle the serious economic and social problems facing the country. The advocates, ironically enough, included former Chancellor Adenauer, who once had dismissed the "Sozis" as unfit to rule.

Together the two parties could muster an overwhelming 447 votes—245 CDU and 202 SPD—in the 496-member Bundestag. The Free Democrats, the only opposition, had the remaining 49 seats. Handsome and urbane, the silver-maned Kiesinger was called to the Bonn chancellery from Stuttgart, where he had served as minister-president (governor) of the state of Baden-Wuerttemberg since leaving the Bundestag in 1958. Willy Brandt, SPD chairman and mayor of West Berlin, became vice-chancellor and foreign minister. For Germans still struggling to come to terms with their past, the coalition also had symbolic value. Kiesinger had been a Nazi party member from 1933 to 1945 and deputy head of the radio propaganda section in the Nazi Foreign Ministry. Brandt had fled Nazi Germany in 1933 to escape a witch-hunt against socialists. He returned after the war in a Norwegian uniform.

For Brandt and his chief deputy, Herbert Wehner, the "grand coalition" was a windfall chance to prove that, after 17 years in the opposition, the Socialists were capable of governing. The coalition did not live up fully to the high hopes of its matchmakers, but it did register some notable gains.

The controversial state of emergency laws, held up for years because the necessary two-thirds majority could not be mustered in Parliament, were passed despite hefty opposition from labor unions and leftists. Long overdue amendment of the criminal code was carried out. Among the more progressive features were the legalization of homosexual relations between consulting adults and the abolition of prosecution for adultery.

Under Brandt's prodding the government launched a dip-

Riot police used clubs on demonstrators in Hamburg during West German election campaign

lomatic offensive in Eastern Europe that led to the establishment of relations with Romania and the restoration of ties with Yugoslavia. There even was prospect of intergovernmental talks between Bonn and East Berlin. But these efforts suffered a staggering setback with the Warsaw Pact invasion of Czechoslovakia in August 1968 *(The World in 1968, 172–179).*

The most resounding success of the Kiesinger-Brandt coalition was the revitalization of the sagging economy. However, the absence of a strong parliamentary opposition gave impetus to West Germany's militant New Left, which formed a loose confederation known as the Anti-parliamentary Opposition (APO). It used the streets as a forum for frequently violent dissent.

For more than two years, the coalition leaders succeeded in bridging over the fundamental differences that divided their parties. Cracks in coalition unity widened as the Bundestag election drew near. In March 1969, came the first big hint of a possible future alliance between the Social Democrats and the liberal Free Democrats, who had veered to the left under their new chairman Walter Scheel. The Free Democrats joined with the Social Democrats to elect Justice Minister Gustav Heinemann as federal president. Heinemann, the first Social Democrat to hold the post, succeeded Heinrich Luebke, a Christian Democrat, July 1.

Stung by the defeat of their candidate, Defense Minister Gerhard Schroeder, the Christian Democrats reacted angrily when President-elect Heinemann prophetically observed in a newspaper interview that his election by the Federal Assembly constituted "a partial shift of power."

In May, the Christian Democratic majority in the cabinet overrode the proposal by Economics Minister Karl Schiller, a Social Democrat, to revalue the mark. Kiesinger's veto had been preceded by waves of speculation that had poured billions of dollars into the country in expectation of an upward change in the mark's parity. Schiller, who had collected most of the laurels for pump-priming the economy to new heights, did not accept defeat lightly. He carried his fight for revaluation to the electorate and made this the burning issue of an otherwise lackluster election campaign. The scholarly looking 58-year-old professor of economics argued forcefully that the mark was undervalued and therefore a continuing source of instability on the world money market. At home, he contended, revaluation would dampen the boom before it overheated and stave off the importation of inflation from abroad. Schiller became the Social Democrats' "election locomotive," outshining Brandt and rivaling Kiesinger in public opinion polls.

Brandt, 55, a two-time loser in bids for the chancellorship, maintained a low profile in the campaign, realizing he would be the loser in a popularity contest with Kiesinger. Brandt may have been "our Willy" to the West Berliners he long served, but in West Germany proper there seemed to be more Germans ready to damn him for his wartime emigration and the illegitimacy of his birth than to resent Kiesinger for his Nazi past. In place of the CDU slogan of "It's the chancellor that counts," the socialists boasted: "We have the better men." Brandt shared the spotlight with such SPD cabinet stars as Schiller, All-German Affairs Minister Wehner and energetic Transport Minister George Leber.

By the final week of the campaign, it was becoming increasingly clear the CDU-SPD marriage of convenience was on the rocks. Word was out that Brandt and FDP chairman Scheel already had agreed to confer on election night on the possibilities of forming a new coalition. With some public opinion polls showing the SPD leading the CDU, speculators again poured millions of dollars into the country in the hope that an SPD government would revalue the mark.

Four days before the election, Kiesinger threw a surprise Sunday punch at the Social Democrats and Schiller. He ordered the country's foreign exchange markets closed until after the balloting and blamed what he called the Social Democrats' election "propaganda" for the new wave of speculation. The two coalition partners did go into the election strongly united on one issue: both appealed to the voters to soundly rebuff radicalism, especially that of the right as represented by the National Democrats.

Election Day, Sept. 28, dawned mild and clear, drawing a record 32.9 million voters—86.8 per cent of those eligible—to the polls. First computer projections after the polls closed at 6 p.m. indicated Kiesinger had been given the chance to fulfill his pledge to guide West Germany "securely into the 70s." They gave the CDU nearly 48 per cent of the vote. The Socialists trailed with 41 per cent and the Free Democrats were barely hovering above the 5 per cent necessary to win seats in the Bundestag. Any hopes for a SPD-FDP mini-coalition seemed to be fading. A reconciliation of Christian Democrats and Social Democrats again became a possibility. FDP chairman Scheel, usually witty and ebullient, glumly conceded: "It will be difficult to go into the government." Kiesinger was tasting victory. "I had a feeling it would be like this," he said jubilantly.

CDU parliamentary floor leader Rainer Barzel appeared on nationwide television to state his party had a "clear claim to leadership." But as later returns came in, the CDU share of the vote began dropping by small but decisive fractions away from the 48 per cent level that could have meant a clear majority in the Bundestag. The Socialists and Free Democrats inched upward. Even then, some key members of Brandt's party seemed to have abandoned all hopes of a mini-coalition. Wehner, SPD vice chairman, gave vent to his old distaste for the Free Democrats, calling them an old "commuter party"—a reference to their erratic behavior in past coalitions with the CDU.

The prospect of a SPD-FDP coalition hung like a thin straw in the wind. Some time between 9 p.m. and midnight Brandt made a daring decision to grasp it. He telephoned the downcast Scheel and the two agreed a mini-coalition was worth a try. When the final returns were in, the Christian Democrats had 46.1 per cent of the vote—1.5 per cent less than in the 1965 election. The CDU was still the strongest party, but their 242 of 496 Bundestag seats were not enough for them to rule alone. The Social Democrats burst out of the "30 per cent ghetto" of past elections and polled 42.7 per cent, 3.4 per cent more than four years earlier. They were the only ones to gain rather than lose votes, and laid claim to 224 seats in parliament.

The Free Democrats were the big losers, dropping from 9.5 to 5.8 per cent and from 49 to 30 seats. But, as the 1969 election turned out, "it was the loser that counted"—as one magazine said in a play on Kiesinger's campaign slogan. Added to the SPD bloc, the 30 seats gave the Social Democrats and Free Democrats together a 12-seat edge over the Christian Democrats.

If the election failed to give any party a clear mandate to rule, it was decisive in one respect: German voters over-whelmingly rejected the National Democratic party. The NPD polled only 4.3 per cent of the vote—seven-tenths of a per cent short of the five per cent hurdle. NPD chairman Adolf von Thadden, who had predicted his party would poll 8 to 10 per cent, blamed defeat on anti-NPD "hate-propaganda" and government obstruction of his campaign. He vowed to challenge the election results. The NPD defeat was widely greeted at home and abroad, including the Soviet Union and its allies.

In the days that followed the election, the Christian Democrats stood by as if in a state of shock while Brandt and Scheel sealed their agreement. In final desperation, Kiesinger made a sweeping offer of his own to the Free Democrats, promising a long-term pact beyond the 1973 election. The offer was flatly rejected although several conservative members of the FDP were sympathetic. Despite doubts of the loyalty of the FDP's conservative wing, Brandt predicted he would receive a Bundestag majority "200 or 300 per cent" greater than that afforded Adenauer in 1949. The prediction was correct.

Brandt was voted into office on Oct. 21 by 251 votes—only two more than the required absolute majority. Of the 495 deputies who voted, 235 cast their ballots against Brandt, five abstained and four votes were declared invalid, bearing such scribbled comments as "poor Germany" or just "baloney."

Twenty years of Christian Democratic rule had come to an end.

When asked by Bundestag President Kai-Uwe von Hassel whether he accepted the vote, Brandt appeared to be near tears as he stood up and said in a vibrant voice:

"Yes, Mr. President, I accept."

The tears overflowed when Herbert Wehner, the behind-the-scenes SPD strategist, embraced his boss.

"I am thankful and a little bit proud that I am able to hold this office," Brandt, the ex-emigre and outcast, told newsmen after the vote. He became the first Social Democratic German chancellor in 39 years.

Still feeling cheated of a victory, Kiesinger commented: "The majority Brandt got is very small. He got two more votes than he needed. That is a sign of what is ahead."

Reaction to Brandt's election from foreign capitals, including Moscow, was overwhelmingly favorable. At home there was a sense of fresh wind and a feeling of expectation, much like that in the United States at the outset of the Kennedy Administration. Pledging he would be a chancellor of inner-reform, Brandt also promised to be the leader "not of a defeated Germany, but of a liberated Germany."

Of the 15 cabinet posts—four less than in the previous government,—12 were allotted to the SPD and three to the FDP. Walter Scheel was appointed vice-chancellor and foreign minister. His party also received the key interior and agriculture ministry posts. Most of the SPD ministers were carried over from the "grand coalition," including Schiller. Wehner was shifted to the job of SPD floor leader in the Bundestag, replacing Helmut Schmidt, who became defense minister.

Brandt's policy declaration to the Bundestag on Oct. 28 reflected his stated concern for internal reform in areas ranging from public health and education to the tax structure and armed forces. It also displayed a more flexible approach to East Germany and the rest of the Soviet bloc. While restating West Germany's allegiance to NATO, he declared his readiness for talks with the Soviet Union, Poland, Czechoslovakia and East Germany. West Germany's relations with the United States, he said, "need neither additional assurances nor repeated declarations. They are strong enough to allow for a more independent German policy within a more active partnership."

Supreme Court's Edict: Immediate Integration

Administration had stirred fresh controversy by policy shift favoring delay in withholding federal funds from schools resisting desegregation of students on racial grounds

IN mid-1969 the Nixon Administration made a major policy shift on the sensitive issue of school desegregation—a decision that stirred a new storm of controversy. The President moved to place more emphasis on court enforcement of the 1954 Supreme Court school desegregation ruling and less on direct action by the Department of Health Education and Welfare to back up the 1964 Civil Rights Act. In essence, Nixon thus followed what he called a "middle course," steering between demands for instant integration and views of those who thought in terms of segregation forever.

But the Nixon desegregation slowdown received a setback when the Supreme Court in a unanimous judgment at the end of October flatly ruled out any further delay in integration of the nation's schools. In its first major decision since Nixon named Warren E. Burger chief justice, the court ruled that "the obligation of every school district is to terminate dual school systems at once and to operate now and hereafter only unitary schools."

The ruling dealt specifically with 14 Mississippi school districts, but its implications were obvious for all of the deep South where school districts had managed to stave off desegregation. Nixon's reaction to the court ruling was swift. He said his Administration would do all it could to carry out the Supreme Court's new desegregation decision and he called on the rest of the country to do the same "in full respect for the law."

Nixon had declared in July that the policy of the Johnson Administration—to cut off federal funds to school systems that failed to desegregate—should be used "only when it is absolutely

White and Negro students of integrated public school in Jackson, Miss., where some schools had operated on a desegregated basis for several years under a Freedom of Choice plan

A hand up—

necessary." He summed up his position this way: "I do not consider it is a victory for integration when the federal government cuts off funds for a school and thereby, for both black and white students in that school, denies them the education they should have."

Some liberal groups had argued that too much time already had been taken to achieve the mandate of the Supreme Court in its landmark 1954 decision. To them the Nixon shift appeared to be a deliberate retreat on desegregation. They voiced angry suspicions that the President was paying off a political debt to the South. There also were reports, denied by the White House, that Mississippi's Sen. John C. Stennis managed to win a reprieve for schools lagging on desegregation in his state by threatening to abandon his critical role as a principal defender of the Administration's military procurement bill.

Asked at a news conference how long it would take to achieve the school desegregation ordered 15 years ago by the Supreme Court, Nixon replied: "Only as long as is absolutely necessary to achieve the goal of desegregated schools without at the same time irreparably damaging the goal of education for hundreds of thousands of black and white students . . . ."

A House of Representatives vote in August sharply curbing efforts to further speed school desegregation had discouraged supporters of integration. The effect of the House measure was to legalize the so-called freedom of choice plans under which students, black or white, were permitted to attend schools their parents preferred. Just one year earlier the Supreme Court ruled freedom of choice alone would not show sufficient evidence of efforts to achieve desegregation.

The House measure specifically proposed to bar withholding of federal funds to force the busing of students, to close a school or to require any student to attend a particular school against his parents' will. Administration officials claimed that placing additional emphasis on court enforcement of desegregation would bring about integration faster. Yet past experience had indicated enforcement usually was slower under court

orders than under government use of Title VI in the 1964 Civil Rights Act, which prohibited racial discrimination in any federally assisted program.

Secretary of Health, Education and Welfare Robert Finch reported late in the year that in 11 southern states school districts under court order had 11.5 per cent of their Negro students in formerly all-white schools while districts operating under government enforcement of Title VI had 20.3 per cent of Negro students in schools with whites. During the year the Administration stated the deadline for desegregation compliance would be extended for districts with "bona fide educational and administrative problems." The furor over this public announcement obscured the fact the Johnson Administration had followed the same approach. But the Nixon Administration's announced policy appeared to some to be an invitation for certain districts to find "bona fide problems."

Finch reported the most pressing questions regarding compliance with school desegregation rulings were concentrated in those states which, in the past, had maintained racial segregation as official policy. Involved were 4,477 school districts located primarily in southern and border states. Of these, 2,994 had desegregated voluntarily. Another 33 were in the process of completing desegregation plans as the first semester of the new academic year got under way. Agreements to desegregate came from an additional 234, and 96 said desegregation would be in effect by the opening of the new year. As a result of action by the Justice Department or private lawsuits, 369 districts were under court orders to desegregate as 1969 drew to a close. In many of these cases, courts had instructed school districts to seek assistance of professional educators in the U.S. Office of Education to ease school desegregation problems. A total of 121 school districts had been completely cut off from all federal funds because they had refused to desegregate or even to negotiate, and 263 other districts faced the prospect of a federal fund cutoff for the same reasons toward the close of the year.

Finch said these particular districts represented a steadily shrinking core of resistance to school desegregation.

Looking ahead to 1970, Finch said the Administration would press to insure equalization of expenditures to guarantee equal educational opportunity.

In the wake of what critics regarded as a disappointing beginning by the Nixon Administration in pursuing school desegregation, the National Association for the Advancement of Colored People in July urged the President to strengthen integration policies. An NAACP convention deplored what it termed weak plans and unanimously adopted a resolution declaring: "We cannot too strongly condemn any politically motivated decision that would weaken the school desegregation guidelines." NAACP delegates, representing 450,673 members, charged Nixon was trying to water down school integration guidelines to placate southern Republicans.

At the other end of the spectrum, blacks sought in some areas to gain control of schools in neighborhoods that were totally Negro. Some succeeded as the much-debated concept of community control went into effect in Washington, D.C., Harlem, and Ocean Hill-Brownsville, Brooklyn. Black educators pushing for community control argued, often convincingly, that the improvement of education in existing all-black schools was more important than integration, which they considered patently impossible in cities such as Washington, D.C., with a school population more than 93 per cent Negro.

The National Education Association, in convention, also voted overwhelming approval of a resolution calling on the

Nixon Administration to step up school integration. NEA President George D. Fischer telegraphed the White House to express shock over the shift in policy. "We are convinced any school district which had approached the problem of school desegregation in good faith would have found a solution to the problem of integration before this time," Fischer said.

The widow of Dr. Martin Luther King Jr., Mrs. Coretta King, assailed Nixon's July 3 statement that the desegregation deadline would be extended for school districts with bona fide education and administrative problems as "a tragic mistake that must not be allowed to stand."

"It will vindicate those who contend that the most intense callers for law and order are not interested in law or order if it will benefit black people," she said.

The Presidential shift on desegregation also stirred controversy inside the Cabinet. It left Finch out on a limb and created sharp divisions among some GOP members of Congress. Finch consistently had predicted the September school desegregation deadline would stand. But after the President's announcement, Finch noted in briefing newsmen that the Supreme Court itself had held: "There is no universal answer to the complex problems of desegregation. There is obviously no one plan that will do the job in every case. The matter must be assessed in the light of the circumstances present and the options available in each instance."

Commenting on the shift of enforcement from the government to the courts, Finch said later:

"All the way through there is that ability on my part to cut off funds. Now what we have found is that simply cutting off the funds hurts the people you're trying to help. You know, it's nice to draw blood, but let's draw blood for a purpose and where it will accomplish something.

"Too often, what we've found in the months since I've been in, in the cases where I have cut off funds, is that, yes, we cut it off to the district, but we still forward the funds to the state system and some of these state superintendents have a remarkable ability to shuffle dollars around and still achieve the same result they want."

Finch acknowledged most of the progress achieved to date in school desegregation stemmed from actions taken by the Johnson Administration, but he claimed the Nixon Administration had maintained the momentum. He predicted the new move to force integration through the courts will accomplish more in the next two years than in the past 15. The U.S. Commission on Civil Rights, meanwhile, charged actions by the Nixon Administration during the year marked "a major retreat in the struggle to achieve meaningful school desegregation," and a conference in Washington of 500 elected black officials late in September accused the Administration of doing "little or nothing" about school desegregation.

Governors of 16 southern states who met in Williamsburg, Va., early in the fall, asked the government to clarify its stand on school desegregation. They complained there was too much variance in enforcement of the guidelines, and federal agencies were providing conflicting information. The Civil Rights Commission issued its own report, claiming more than 1,000 of the 3,327 school districts which the federal government said were "completely desegregated" had no black students. Desegregation "is a thing more often proclaimed than practiced," the commission held. It contended Congress had not provided HEW with enough funds to force compliance, and voiced the opinion that the new emphasis on court enforcement would slow integration, primarily because of what it called the outlook of federal judges in the south.

The commission reiterated its conviction that withholding federal funds had proved the most effective method of insuring compliance, but Atty. Gen. John N. Mitchell claimed the new Nixon policy of school suits would have "a hell of a lot more impact" than those of prior administrations. Mitchell denied the desegregation shift was made to attract southern voters and said the Administration was not following a southern strategy to build a political base for 1972.

"I'm not worried about politics in 1972," Mitchell said. "If I were, we wouldn't be filing all these suits in the South."

Integration gains during 1969 were most substantial in Alabama, South Carolina and Louisiana, Mitchell said. He did not provide figures but told a news conference that even Mississippi had made significant progress. The northern part of the state, he said, had moved ahead with meaningful integration. In September HEW issued a 19-page report forecasting civil rights enforcement in education under the new Nixon policy would surpass that of the Johnson Administration.

While the desegregation emphasis continued to be focused on the south, Senator Stennis, a powerful southern Democrat, came up with what he called "shocking" statistics of near-total school segregation in some northern cities. Stennis directly challenged Finch to do something about it. He said his statistics showed 214 Chicago schools were 99 to 100 per cent black and more than 100 of them were all black. In Cleveland, Stennis said, 68 schools were 81.3 to 100 per cent black. He maintained that Newark schools were also 81.3 to 100 per cent black, and that in East St. Louis 24 schools were 92.2 to 100 per cent black.

"I don't see why it's illegal in the south and all right in the north," Stennis said. Addressing himself to Finch, he added: "You haven't tried in the north. Your predecessors haven't tried." The reason he gave was: Such an effort would be "politically hazardous."

A member of the Senate Armed Services Committee and a ranking member of the Senate Appropriations subcommittee, which oversees the HEW budget, Stennis met face to face with Finch in a hearing on the department's $15 billion money bill for 1970. He said if a government policy of rapid school integration were applied in northern cities it would generate enough public reaction to force "a more moderate policy" by the government on school integration in the south.

Finch had never disputed the Stennis figures but he had stated his department lacked the manpower to check into school racial patterns nationwide. The secretary said de facto segregation in the north often posed a more difficult legal problem than dual school systems in the south. The reason he gave was that there were housing patterns in the north which could not be affected merely by court decisions.

As the year neared its end, HEW teams were at work in Chicago, New Jersey, San Francisco, and other areas looking into racial patterns of public schools. Finch also had requested authorizations from Congress to hire additional personnel to intensify anti-bias efforts in all parts of the nation.

The school desegregation issue clearly loomed as a continuing and vexing problem for the nation in 1970, accompanied by more controversy and more experimentation as the government grappled with ways to implement the historic Supreme Court order of 1954. In one 1969 decision the court ruled: "In this field (school desegregation) the way must always be left open for experimentation." This opinion recalled the prophets' prediction often cited by some black educators:

"*. . . The fathers have eaten a sour grape, and the children's teeth are set on edge.*"—Jeremiah XXXI, 29

The Case of the Green Berets

*A curious incident it was: Alleged slaying of Vietnamese national
threatened to reflect upon those in high places, and charges
were dropped when CIA declined to provide witnesses*

*Happy Col. Robert B. Rheault greeted in Boston by his wife, Caroline,
and daughter, Susanne*

*" 'Curiouser and curiouser!' cried Alice. 'Now I'm opening
out like the largest telescope that ever was!' "*

THE CURIOUS CASE of the accused Green Berets—one of them
the former commanding officer of all of the elite unit's
3,000 troops in Vietnam—opened with a sober, routine news release in Saigon. Three months later the case had blossomed
into a convoluted, emotion-laden incident that touched top
Army officers, Congress, the Central Intelligence Agency, the
Secretary of Defense, the Secretary of the Army and even the
President of the United States.

The Aug. 6 Army news release said eight men of the U.S.
Army 5th Special Forces Group (Airborne) "are being held
pending investigation of charges growing out of the fatal
shooting of a Vietnamese national." The eight were identified
as Col. Robert B. Rheault, the group's former commander;
Majors David E. Crew and Thomas C. Middleton Jr.; Captains Leland J. Brumley, Robert F. Marasco and Budge E.
Williams; CWO2 Edward M. Boyle, and Sgt. 1.C. Alvin L.
Smith Jr. The investigation, the release said, was ordered by
Maj. Gen. G. L. Mabry, commanding general of the Support
Troops, U.S. Army, Vietnam, "following charges of premeditated
murder and conspiracy to commit murder of a Vietnamese
national near Nha Trang (a coastal city 200 miles northeast of
Saigon, where the 5th Special Forces were headquartered)
last June 20." Other than to say the victim was a man, the Army
gave no further details.

While the Army remained tight-lipped, a variety of reports
as to what might have happened began to circulate almost
immediately. Some held the dead man, identified as Thai Khac
Chuyen, was a double agent working for both the Green
Berets—as chief of a team assigned to watch enemy movements in nearby Cambodia—and the North Vietnamese. They
said that in early June secretly taken films showed the man
meeting with North Vietnamese agents. The Green Berets,
these reports said, then consulted with the CIA and the order
was to get rid of the agent. The man supposedly was slain and
his body was put into a weighted sack, then dumped into the
South China Sea. Efforts to recover the body were not successful.

Sources sympathetic to the Green Berets contended that
several days before the agent was slain members of the elite
group asked the CIA to fly the agent away. They said the CIA
turned down a request to provide a plane to take the man "to
an island someplace—to get him out of the picture because he

Mother and son: Pham Kim Lien said she was the wife of slain Vietnam agent

was dangerous." However, other sources close to the CIA disclaimed any CIA connection with the incident other than a recommendation that the Green Berets turn over the suspected agent to the South Vietnamese, who could check his activities and knowledge. They said the CIA only learned of the reported death after it occurred, denying claims by at least one of the lawyers for some of the Green Berets that the CIA ordered the assassination. At one point one of the attorneys said, "I know and I have evidence to prove the CIA has ordered the killing and effectuated the killing of over 100 people in South Vietnam in the past year."

While the differing stories circulated, the accused men, arrested July 20, continued in custody. A formal Army probe, similar to a grand jury proceeding, had been in progress since July 30 to determine whether they should stand trial at a general court-martial. George W. Gregory, attorney for Middleton, cabled Secretary of Defense Melvin R. Laird in mid-August that his client—and by implication the other seven prisoners—was being held under "inhumane conditions" at the Army stockade at Long Binh, 12 miles north of Saigon. Gregory contended "the actual confinement of this man is frankly unbelievable. His cell is 5 feet by 7 feet. When I was allowed to visit him in his cell the only light and air were reflected from the vents of the tin roof and a peephole in the door. The cell was unbelievably hot, as circulation was almost non-existent." Shortly afterward, the men were taken out of

solitary confinement and allowed to stay in regular billets. More than a month later, Sept. 25, Defense Secretary Laird, with the first official word that he had become involved directly in the case, said he sought the release of the eight soldiers because he felt they were being "unfairly confined."

The handling of the case also stirred reaction among some Congressmen. Sen. Ernest F. Hollings, D-S.C., remarked that "simply taking these men out of solitary confinement is not enough. These men were soldiers who were doing a job that had to be done." Hollings said the case was "not only giving the Green Berets a black eye, but is undermining confidence in the military." In a letter to Laird, Rep. L. Mendel Rivers, D-S.C., chairman of the House Armed Services Committee, said: "This case is going from bad to worse, and the American people are entitled to know the facts involved." And Sen. Edward W. Brooke, R-Mass., a member of the Senate Armed Services Committee, told newsmen, "I have some understanding that there is much more to this case than what has been reported to the public, and I intend to get to the bottom of it."

With its investigation finished, the Army announced Sept. 18 that Rheault and his five staff officers were to face trial on charges of murder and conspiracy to commit murder. It said the charges against the two other Special Forces soldiers, Boyle and Smith, were being held in abeyance, pending trial of the other cases. Maj. Gen. Mabry specified the accused men would not face the death penalty, which he had the

Five Green Berets in South Vietnam: from left, Col. Robert Rheault, Maj. Thomas Middleton Jr., Maj. David Crew, Capt. Robert Marasco and Capt. Leland Brumley, behind Marasco

authority to invoke. Attorneys for some of the men quickly asked President Nixon to intervene and to shift the trial to the United States. They contended their clients could not get a fair trial in Vietnam because Gen. Creighton Abrams, commander of all U.S. forces in Vietnam, and Maj. Gen. Mabry were "prejudiced because they have prejudged the defendants." One said, "Abrams caused this whole thing simply because of service rivalry" between the regular Army and the elite Green Berets. Other sources contended Abrams was made furious by the slaying and had used his full authority in deciding to prosecute the case.

Breaking its relatively strict silence on the case, the Army in the closing days of September had released charges and specifications against the six Green Beret officers. The charge sheets accused Rheault of premeditated murder, although they said he did not participate in the actual slaying. Although the Army listed Marasco as the man who fired the pistol, the specifications on the premeditated murder charge were the same for all six officers. There were no charge sheets or specifications listed for Boyle and Smith.

Trials for three of the officers were set for Oct. 20, but as September ended so did the planned prosecution; the Army abruptly dropped its entire case against the Green Berets. The reason: Secretary of the Army Stanley R. Resor said the CIA had refused to provide any witnesses. Because of this, Resor, who said he was informed the CIA refusal was made "in the interest of national security," said, "It is my judgment that under these circumstances the defendants cannot receive

a fair trial. Accordingly, I have directed today that all charges be dismissed immediately. The men will be assigned to duties outside of Vietnam."

Resor also went on record as disapproving the kind of act the Green Berets originally were accused of carrying out. "I want to make it clear," he said, "that the acts which were charged, but not proven, represent a fundamental violation of Army regulations, orders, and principles. The Army will not and cannot condone unlawful acts of the kind alleged."

White House Press Secretary Ronald L. Ziegler first contended that President Nixon had nothing to do with dismissal of the charges. But later he acknowledged the President was somewhat involved, although he insisted the Army acted on its own in deciding to drop the charges. According to Ziegler, CIA Director Richard Helms decided the agency's employes would not be allowed, in the interests of national security, to testify at the planned courts-martial. "The President," Ziegler said, "approved the decision."

On Oct. 31 the Pentagon announced that Rheault had retired from the Army as of that date. Earlier in the month Marasco had received, at his own request, an honorable discharge for personal reasons.

And that apparently tied up the controversial case—except for one small strand. The widow of the missing Vietnamese agent threatened to kill herself and her two children unless she was given compensation and an explanation of his death. She received $6,472. A U.S. Command spokesman said the widow had accepted a "missing person gratuity."

"THANKS" FOR THE INVASION

When the conservative Dr. Gustav Husak and his Czech Communist party delegation arrived in Moscow Oct. 20 for an official visit, virtually every Kremlin leader was on hand to extend a warm welcome, and Husak lost no time in thanking the Soviet dignitaries for sending Warsaw Pact troops into his homeland 14 months earlier. He called it "an act of brotherly assistance," and said "anti-socialist and counter-revolutionary forces . . . suffered a heavy defeat in Czechoslovakia."

It was a far cry from the reaction of Husak's predecessor, liberal Alexander Dubcek *(The World in 1968, 172–179)*. When informed in August 1968 that Soviet-led troops had entered Czechoslovakia, Dubcek was said to have cried, "How could they do this to me? I have served the cause of the Soviet Union and communism all my life."

The Soviet Union had a heavy hand in changing the viewpoint of Czechoslovakia's leaders. In April 1969, Dubcek was ousted as First Secretary of the Czech Communist party *(pages 80–81)*. He was allowed to retain his seat on the 11-member ruling Presidium, however, and was given the largely ceremonial position of President of Parliament. Right-winger Husak replaced him as head of the party.

In August thousands of citizens marked the first anniversary of the Soviet invasion by taking to the streets in demonstrations of defiance that lasted for three days and left at least 10 persons dead. Although observers estimated that 70,000

of the occupying Warsaw Pact troops still remained in Czechoslovakia, none was in evidence when the anniversary disturbances took place. Instead the demonstrators were dispersed by Czech riot police and the Czech people's militia. As one observer said, "These are not Russians. These are Czechs fighting Czechs."

There were signs that the Czechoslovakians still rested their hopes of reform in Dubcek. Among their cries were, "We want Dubcek." In reply, conservatives mounted a propaganda campaign in the government-controlled news media against Dubcek and other liberals. Then, on Sept. 19, the Presidium called for a meeting of the 181-member Central Committee to discuss "the present situation and tasks now facing the party." Many Czechs felt that the very announcement of the impending meeting indicated the Presidium had decided the fate of Dubcek and expected the Central Committee to approve.

The Central Committee meeting opened Sept. 25. Three days later it was announced Dubcek had lost his place on the Presidium and had been removed as President of Parliament. He had retained a seat on the Central Committee, but in that group of conservatives his liberal leanings would carry little weight.

In a report to the committee, Husak portrayed Dubcek as weak and wavering, "incapable of stemming right-wing opportunistic forces" inside the party and anti-Communist and counter-revolutionary forces outside it. He charged Dubcek had failed repeatedly to inform the rest of the

leadership of warnings from the Soviet Union about growing strength of anti-Communist forces in Czechoslovakia and about possible military intervention again. Husak also said that, during 1968, if the Dubcek party Presidium "had proceeded from internationalist positions with a political and statesman-like responsibility in the negotiations . . . with the Soviet Union and the other fraternal parties . . . the allied troops would not have entered our territory."

A purge list published after the meeting showed 29 men who had backed Dubcek were removed from the Central Committee. Changes also were announced in Premier Oldrich Cernik's cabinet, in which nine members were unseated or had their jobs abolished. Cernik himself, a former admirer of Dubcek, had switched his allegience to the conservative group and survived the purge. He was asked to form a new cabinet. In a final move the Central Committee repudiated August 1968 party resolutions which had criticized the entrance of Warsaw Pact troops and had praised the historic popular resistance. Soon afterwards Parliament followed suit with a resolution thanking the Soviet Union and its Warsaw Pact allies for invading the country, saying it "appreciates the selfless internationalist assistance of the five fraternal socialist countries granted to our peoples in order to defeat counter-revolution."

On Oct. 9 the government announced a ban on trips made by individual citizens to Western countries in a move to counteract the flow of refugees and to halt the drain of hard currency.

All looked serene when Russian and Czech leaders met at Moscow airport: From left, Alexei Kosygin, Soviet premier; Oldrich Cernik, Czech premier; Leonid Brezhnev, Russian Communist party leader; Gustav Husak, Czech Communist party leader; Ludvik Svoboda, Czech president; Nikolai Podgorny, Russian president

A QUIET REVOLUTION

In Mogadishu, capital of the Texas-sized country of Somalia on the tip of East Africa, many citizens slept while soldiers moved quietly through the streets in pre-dawn hours. Before the sun rose, the Somali troops—in full battle dress with fixed bayonets—seized control of the city, and Somalia's government was overthrown by a military coup.

The takeover by a self-styled revolutionary council on Oct. 21 was the first in Somalia's nine-year history of independence. It came less than 24 hours after the funeral of President Abdirashid Ali Shermarke, shot down Oct. 15 by a member of his police guard who was arrested at once. The new rulers quickly clamped a curfew on the capital city and, as residents sat and waited, sound trucks cruised the streets to announce that a new government was being formed.

The council said the revolution was staged to "save Somalia from the corrupt malpractices of the ruling classes." It promised to "abolish all bad things left behind," and said Shermarke's policies, treaties and agreements with friendly nations would be respected.

Some observers attributed the coup to the government's failure to solve unemployment— a condition worsened by drought in a country heavily dependent on grazing areas for livestock. This frustration, they said, apparently came to a head after Shermarke was assassinated while touring an arid area.

Motives for the slaying were not clearly set forth, but some reports said the president was shot in revenge for the death of a relative, slain during the spring parliamentary election campaign.

Oil rich North Slope of Alaska

SEVEN FRIENDS IN ORBIT

"It was nice to meet with friends in orbit. When you fly among the stars alone it is lonely, but when you are together with friends, your spirits are high and you work well." When Lt. Col. Georgy Shonin was launched on the Soviet Union's 13th manned space shot from the Baikonur Cosmodrome, 1,400 miles southeast of Moscow, on a cool, rainy Oct. 11 he had one companion riding with him in the Soyuz 6 craft. But the spacemen soon got plenty of company as the USSR sent Soyuz (which means union) 7 aloft with three aboard Oct. 12 and Soyuz 8, with two, Oct. 13.

As the seven cosmonauts—four military pilots and three civilian engineers—hurtled around the earth in their three spacecraft they represented the biggest assembly of men in space at one time. As the three manned capsules maneuvered in space, the USSR on Oct. 14 launched an unmanned satellite called Intercosmos-1. It was not connected with the manned mission and was to "study the ultraviolet and roentgen radiations of the sun and their influence on processes taking part in the upper atmosphere," the Russians announced.

Official secrecy shrouded much of the purpose of the high-flying troika, but many observers first thought the Soyuz craft were part of a Soviet effort to construct a permanent orbiting space laboratory—or at least to conduct tests leading to such construction. Such a station would serve as a platform for launching flights to the moon and outer space. A Russian specialist indicated, however, that no attempt was made to put together an orbiting space station, and the three craft returned separately to earth after spending five days each in orbit. Soyuz 6, the first up, also was the first to return, landing Oct. 16. While in orbit, its crew carried out the first welding experiment in space, an operation Tass described as very difficult because weightlessness in space restricts even the simplest movements.

U.S. space experts felt the triple shot carried the Soviet Union a long way toward developing the world's first operational space station. They said they believed that most of the goals of the flight were achieved and that within a few months Soviet cosmonauts might begin putting together an orbiting space station.

SUDDENLY RICH ALASKA

When Secretary of State William H. Seward agreed in 1867 to buy Alaska from Czarist Russia for $7.2 million, the deal promptly was dubbed "Seward's Folly." But time more than justified his purchase. Just 102 years afterward, Alaska put up merely a portion of its state-owned lands for oil lease bids. The rush to get a piece of the action marked the state's most profitable day.

Bids totaled more than $900 million in bonus money on the acreage. Seward, if he had been around, would have had the last laugh.

The tracts were tundra-covered land and off-shore plots in the Prudhoe Bay area, where the biggest oil field on the North American continent was discovered in 1968, about 380 miles north of Fairbanks. At stake were reserves estimated to contain from 5 billion to 10 billion barrels.

Six Eskimos from Barrow picketed the lease sale. They contended all the oil rights on the North Coast should belong to their people, since they were the first inhabitants of the desolate Arctic Ocean area.

Tabulating and reading the bids was an all day job. "A lot of us have headaches," said State Natural Resources Commissioner Tom Kelly, "but it's the best headache we've ever had."

Alaska wasted no time putting the big financial windfall to work. The bid money was loaded on a jet, chartered for $23,000, and flown to banks in New York and other cities to start drawing $45,000 a day interest. Although the total was below the $1 billion originally hoped for, the total due to the bonuses was far higher than the state could have realized under its own laws, which allowed it to lease oil lands at only $1 an acre per year. The law did not prohibit oil companies from sweetening the pot as much as they liked per acre by the September bonus offers. One combine of five companies posted the largest single bid—$72.2 million—for one 2,560 acre lease.

NOVARRO SLAYERS GET LIFE

Two Chicago brothers tried to win freedom in the slaying of silent screen star Ramon Novarro by accusing one another of the crime. But a jury found both guilty of first-degree murder. On Oct. 27 Superior Court Judge Mark Brandler sentenced them to life imprisonment and recommended that they never be freed on parole.

Novarro was found dead in his Hollywood home on Oct. 30, 1968 (*The World in 1968, 275*), presumably the victim of robbery and bludgeoning.

Judge Brandler said that evidence during the two-month trial of Paul R. Ferguson, 23, and Thomas S. Ferguson, 18, "established convincingly and conclusively to the jury and the court the guilt as to each of the defendants in the brutal, vicious torture-killing of Mr. Ramon Novarro."

One of the great "Latin lovers," Novarro thrilled audiences in many films, among them such spectaculars as "Ben Hur" and "The Student Prince."

SOCIETY WAS "RUNNING AMOK"

It was just a moment in a millennium, but for the City of Montreal its fleeting glimpse of anarchy might well have seemed to last a thousand years. For 16 hours lawlessness reigned in Canada's largest city while its 3,700 policemen and 2,400 firemen struck for higher pay.

"It's like the war," said one merchant in the fashionable St. Catherine Street shopping area as he surveyed the damage wrought by looters. In a day and a night of unabated crime, windows of some of the city's most exquisite shops were broken and the stores invaded, 10 banks were robbed, the Queen Elizabeth and Windsor hotels were ransacked, firebombs were exploded and two persons were killed.

There was barely a policeman to quell the demonstrators or a fireman to fight the blazes. Nearly all had gathered for a "study session," rather than to report for work, after an arbitration board had granted policemen a $1,100-a-year raise and firemen $1,000. Neither group was satisfied. Both held that the increase failed to meet a 50-year goal—parity with their counterparts in Toronto.

Not only did Montreal's policemen consider themselves superior to Toronto's protectors. They felt they were subjected to more hazardous duty, what with all the French-English frictions that led to violence by extremist separatists, a recent wave of robberies and an upsurge of organized crime and student unrest. Also, said one young constable, "We have to speak two languages—English and French."

The strike was short-lived. While mobs wrecked the city the Provincial Assembly passed emergency legislation that forced the workers back to their jobs by midnight. Failure to comply with the law meant imprisonment and fines of up to $100 per day per striker.

Two weeks after the men were back on the job their goal, based on the standards of living in Montreal and Toronto, had been met. Policemen received an increase of $1,450 a year and firemen's pay was raised by $1,370.

Mayor Jean Drapeau blamed the trouble on the fact that "Montreal is an international city. When anarchy and disorder exist, they are active in the biggest centers. . . . Unfortunately we have to face this condition. It is the price of our success."

Prime Minister Pierre Elliott Trudeau summed it up by saying that society as a whole was "running amok."

Montreal: Looting mobs burned a bus while police were on strike

Canadian troops moved in to replace striking policemen after a night of rioting in Montreal

Death at 57 took skater-actress Sonja Henie, shown here in a scene for a movie she made in 1943

SONJA HENIE "JUST SLEPT AWAY"

Norse beauty Sonja Henie got her first pair of ice skates on the Christmas after her sixth birthday. She learned how to use them quickly. At the age of eight she won the children's figure skating championship of Oslo, and two years later, in 1923, she won the figure skating championship of Norway. The flashing skates, which became her trademark throughout the world, never failed her. Nor she them.

As a young woman she studied with teachers in Germany, England, Switzerland, and Austria. Often she practiced as much as seven hours a day as she worked to apply the techniques she had learned in her ballet studies to her ice skating routines. She won the first of 10 consecutive world skating titles at Oslo in 1927, and over the next decade Miss Henie won most of the major world skating titles. In 1936 she turned professional and toured the United States in an ice show—a move that took her to Hollywood for motion pictures. Her first skating film *"One in A Million,"* was released at the end of 1936 and was a box office smash as were the other films she made over the next dozen years. She also staged and appeared in ice shows and these too were very successful.

In 1969 she became ill from leukemia. While in Paris her condition worsened and it was decided to fly her home. She died Oct. 12 on an ambulance plane en route to her native Oslo. Neils Onstad, husband of the 57-year-old star, said she "just slept away" halfway through the flight.

FOR THE RECORD

OUTGOING. Lieut. Gen. Lewis B. Hershey, 75, as director of the Selective Service System. The White House announced Oct. 10 that Hershey would step out Feb. 16, 1970, to become adviser to the President on manpower mobilization. Hershey, under fire in recent years by some who claimed he was too old and too rigid to continue to head the draft system, took over as director in 1941 and served through three wars and under six presidents. A symbol of antiwar sentiment to some, Hershey once remarked, "Someone has to play the goat, and I'm it."

RESIGNED. The Most Rev. Fulton J. Sheen, Oct. 15, as head of the Rochester, N.Y., Roman Catholic Diocese. Named to succeed 74-year-old Bishop Sheen was Msgr. Joseph L. Hogan, 63. Bishop Sheen, whose televised image made him nationally known in many American homes in the 1950s, said he planned to return to New York City "not to retire but to spend myself and be spent in any work the Lord sees fit to use me." The silver-haired bishop's televised program, *"Life is Worth Living,"* began in 1951 and lasted six years. It was estimated 30 million persons heard or saw him on radio-TV.

FREED. British news correspondent Anthony Grey, Oct. 4, after being confined to his house in Peking by Communist China for 26 months. Grey, 31, a correspondent for Reuters news agency, was confined in reprisal for the arrest of 13 Communist Chinese newsmen in Hong Kong following anti-British riots in July 1967. The last of the 13 was released Oct. 3. Grey spent much of his confinement in one room.

A HERETIC, IN A SENSE

"They call me a heretic. Well, I am a heretic if conventional oratory is the standard. I should be ashamed to live in this generation and not be a heretic."

Dr. Harry Emerson Fosdick, an advocate of theological liberalism in the Protestant church, once made that statement in a sermon. Frequently involved in controversial issues, he questioned such traditional church doctrines as the Virgin Birth, the inspiration of the Scriptures, the atonement of Jesus and the second coming of Christ "externally on the clouds of heaven to set up His Kingdom here."

Dr. Fosdick was the founder of New York City's Riverside Church in 1927 and served as its pastor until 1946. After retiring he remained active, writing books and espousing social, religious and sometimes political causes. Among his books were *"The Meaning of Prayer"* and *"On Being a Real Person."*

He was 91 when he died Oct. 5 in Bronxville, N. Y., of a heart attack. Mrs. Fosdick, the former Florence Allen Whitney, had died in 1964.

Although the clergyman's first position after graduating from Union Theological Seminary was in a Baptist church, he was soon appointed associate pastor of the First Presbyterian Church of New York City. Huge crowds were attracted by his sermons, and one of these, entitled *"Shall the Fundamentalists Win?"* involved him in a major controversy. Dr. Fosdick had attributed to Fundamentalists the intention "to drive out of the evangelical churches men and women of liberal opinion" by insisting that all church members agree to a literal interpretation of the Bible.

In spite of a flood of criticism from Fundamentalists the New York Presbytery refused to remove him. The issue was complicated by the fact that Dr. Fosdick had never formally embraced the Presbyterian creed. Later the matter was taken up at the General Assembly of the Presbyterian Church of the U. S. A. This group asked the New York Presbytery to require that preaching in the First Presbyterian Church must "conform to the system of doctrines taught in the Confession of Faith." Dr. Fosdick submitted his resignation, but his church refused to accept it. When the matter was brought up a second time, however, Dr. Fosdick was told to become a Presbyterian minister or to resign. He chose the later course.

Two months later he was called to the pastorate of the Park Avenue Baptist Church. He accepted with the provisions that the church would not insist on baptism by immersion, would open its membership to Christians of all creeds and would construct a new building near Columbia University.

Thus on Nov. 20, 1927, the cornerstone for the edifice which was to become Riverside Church was laid. Though nominally Baptist, it embraced followers of many creeds, including some with Roman Catholic and Jewish backgrounds.

At Washington Monument: A massive plea for peace ➞

November

Vietnam: A Year of Change

There were new tactics and new strategies, new moods, new policies and new proposals but peace seemed as elusive as ever

Subtly, slowly, the character of the war in Vietnam had changed. The massive search-and-destroy sweeps by United States troops and their allies had vanished long since. Where divisions and brigades once operated, companies and platoons now bore the burden of fighting. Battles in the dimensions of Leatherneck Square, the Ia Drang Valley, Con Thien, Dak To, Hue and Khe Sanh no longer bloodied the scene.

Casualty lists reflected the slower tempo. For four consecutive weeks in September and October, the rolls of American dead totaled less then 100, the lowest figures in three years. Strange phrases began to appear in news dispatches: "No reports of ground action anywhere" . . . "Only four significant skirmishes over the past 24 hours" . . . "American forces reported no contact with the enemy."

The exceptions helped to prove the rule. In August, and again in November, prolonged lulls of seven weeks to two months were shattered by surges of Communist attacks. Neither series lasted long nor developed serious problems and U.S. officers, who had been predicting fall and winter offensives, refused to give the outbursts such stature.

The biggest action in the last six months of 1969 developed almost by accident. Initially, the antagonists were two companies of Americans from the 196th Light Infantry Brigade, pushing through rolling foothills southwest of Da Nang toward the wreck of a helicopter shot down with eight men aboard, and a force of North Vietnamese, perhaps 1,000, massed to attack Hiep Duc, a district capital and a refugee center. The two enemies collided in an area known as the Rice Bowl, five miles east of the town, where the Communists had dug into a labyrith of bunkers, trenches and gun posts.

Both sides threw in reinforcements. Detachments of U.S. Marines and South Vietnamese expanded the attackers to about 3,000 men. Virtually the whole of North Vietnam's 2nd Army Division was engaged.

The cockpit of battle was a knoll identified as Hill 102 on U.S. military maps. For five days, the Communists stood firm, repelling frontal assaults and flanking attempts alike. On the sixth day, GIs of the 196th went up the rugged slope again, found that the enemy had withdrawn, pushed on to the 'copter wreck and the bodies of its eight occupants. "It's the old story," said an American officer. "Five days of fighting like hell and on the sixth day they give it to you for nothing."

Heavy fighting or light, it made little difference to the slogging foot soldier. It was a fact of the war that actions involving small units (company strength or less) accounted for most of the casualties, even in times of large scale battles. The week ending July 5 was an example: Only 46 minor clashes were reported and yet 155 Americans were killed. "No matter how small the action is, the bullets and rockets still kill," said a senior officer. "If there's no action, the soldier out on the fire base is only thankful that no one's shooting at him today."

*   *   *   *

Sharply, unexpectedly, the thrust of Communist initiative had changed. Summer day succeeded summer day and the time of the monsoon passed with a minimum of meaningful action. In one July week, 25 Communist attacks and ambushes were reported; two months earlier, the number had been 200. The total for all of July was 205; for March it was 461.

The experience of the 3rd Brigade, 82nd Airborne Division, was pertinent. The brigade had been stationed for nearly a year in the Iron Triangle north of Saigon, 60 square miles of abandoned rubber plantations which had been a longtime sanctuary for the Viet Cong. "When we first got here," said Brig. Gen. George Dickerson, "we'd have 30 or 40 contacts a night" be-

Marchers protesting war filled Geary Street in San Francisco during moratorium rally

Buddy hit by shrapnel aided by artillerymen at Bu Prang Camp

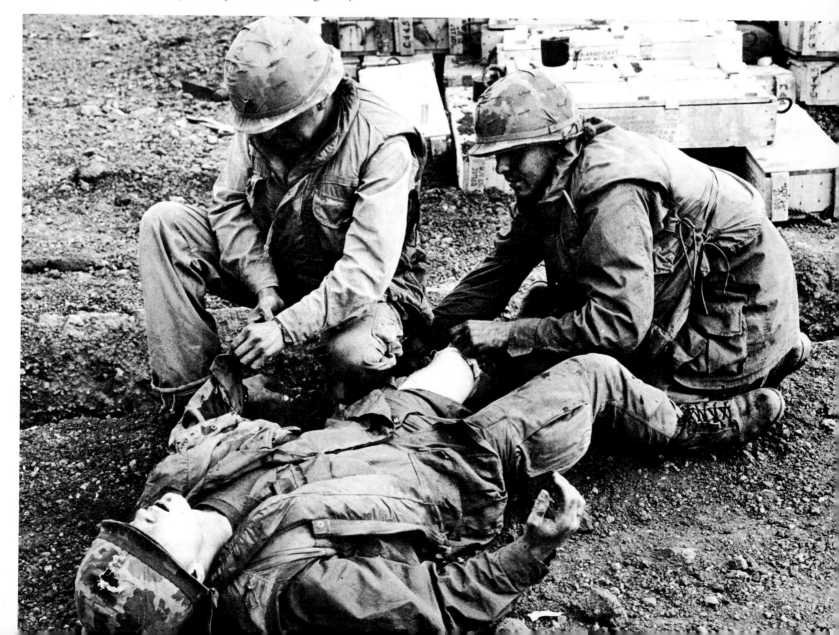

tween American scouts and lurking guerrillas. "Now we're having only about five contacts a week," and as many as 200 patrols were in the field every night.

Infiltration from North Vietnam also dropped from levels estimated at 10,000 in June and 63,000 in the first six months of the year. Some estimates placed the decrease as high as one-third—not enough to replace losses as U.S. intelligence reported them.

In October, Secretary of State William P. Rogers said Communist strength in South Vietnam was down more than 25,000 from the August figures of 100,000 North Vietnamese and 35,000 Viet Cong. The Pentagon, which had disagreed with earlier State Department reports of decreasing Communist manpower, now came around, not only to agree with the statement but to concede that it had "some significance." (In November, Secretary of Defense Melvin Laird told the Senate Foreign Relations Committee that infiltration was on the upswing again. He did not disclose figures).

What was that significance? That's where the experts parted company.

Generally, diplomats thought that Hanoi might be signaling readiness to deescalate the war. The military thought that the Communists were playing 'possum while building muscle for new offensives. A third sector of opinion argued that North Vietnam was having trouble finding manpower—a result of battle losses which, by U.S. figures, were climbing above 500,000 —and was being forced into a cutback in offensive operations. Only Hanoi could have said which school of thought was right and, so far as the public record showed, Hanoi wasn't talking.

* * * *

Quietly, unobtrusively, United States strategy and tactics had changed. The principle of "maximum pressure" enunciated by President Lyndon Johnson had been succeeded by "protective reaction" in the new administration of President Richard Nixon.

In the public mind, the first strategy carried a connotation of offensive action, keeping the enemy off balance, never giving him time to relax. The second meant standing still, waiting for the other fellow to make a move. Military people insisted that the change was one of semantics rather than substance and that as many operations as ever were being undertaken. The difference was that smaller units were conducting them.

Nevertheless, although official orders did not spell it out, there was a tacit effort to avoid heavy casualties. U.S. commanders said holding down losses always had been a concern and that field leaders still had authority to take any offensive action deemed necessary to protect their men. Still, some ranking officers saw a similarity with the last days before armistice in Korea, when anything larger than a company-sized mission had to be cleared all the way to headquarters in Tokyo.

The new name of the game was a new word in the language: Vietnamization. The origin was obscure but the meaning was clear. As President Nixon described it in November: "The primary mission of our troops is to enable the South Vietnamese forces to assume the full responsibility for the security of South Vietnam."

In a subtle way, the American objective had changed. Instead of fighting beside the South Vietnamese, the prime aim now would be to strengthen them to the point where they could stand alone against the Communists.

It would be neither an easy task nor a brief one. The idea of American disengagement had been an active topic of talk and planning among U.S. military and civilian officials in Saigon

◄—— Moratorium: People and placards assembled at Capitol

for more than a year. Their thinking was that a minimum of two years would be required, and then only if U.S. aviation and artillery remained.

A majority of U.S. officers believed that, given time, training and equipment, the material for a competent fighting force was available. But how soon could it be built? Despite general agreement that Saigon's troops had improved, the old problems of high desertion, low pay and lack of dedication persisted. The quality of leadership in the high echelons was uncertain. There was a shortage of trained, experienced officers, particularly in the junior grades.

Vietnamization became a matter of Washington policy in March. In October, Secretary Laird said the new doctrine offered "the best prospect for minimizing American casualties and resolving the war as quickly as possible without abandoning our basic objective, the right of self-determination for the people of Vietnam." He reported that "real momentum" was being achieved.

Evidence of "real momentum" was available. Military training for Saigon's soldiers was stepped up to a pace double that of 1966. Between 425,000 and 475,000 men would come out of 33 training centers and 25 specialty schools before the end of 1969; the goal for 1970 was 560,000.

Casualty lists were revealing. In the first five months of the year, American and South Vietnam battle deaths were not far apart: 4,292 and 4,930. In the next five months, while American deaths decreased to 4,134, South Vietnam's rose to 8,301. It was true that part of the change in ratio traced to an increase in Communist operations against villages guarded by South Vietnam's militia and home guards. But it was also true that government troops were taking more offensive assignments, were moving in to take over fire bases and camps or share them with GIs. In November, President Nixon said that the progress in the training program was "greater than we anticipated."

Another measure of South Vietnamese efficiency was the rate of American withdrawals from the war. The first pullout of 25,000 men (page 96) was completed in August. One month later, the President tagged 35,000 more for departure, including the 3rd Marine Division which had been a mainstay of campaigning along the northern frontier since 1965. Then, on Dec. 15, Nixon said another 50,000 troops would be withdrawn, probably by April 15, 1970.

However, as in the casualty figures, there were diluting factors. President Nixon identified them in a November speech to the nation: "the progress which may be made at the Paris peace talks," and "the level of enemy activity."

"If I conclude that increased enemy action jeopardizes our remaining forces in Vietnam," he said, "I shall not hesitate to take strong and effective measures to deal with that situation. This is not a threat. It is a statement of policy."

*   *   *   *

Sensitively, searchingly, the mood of Congress had changed and changed again.

An impromptu truce which had ushered the new Nixon administration into office faded with the summertime. Almost overnight, it seemed, the voices of renewed criticism became so loud that a group of Republican senators was moved to concerted attack on those who, by calling for more and greater concessions to the Communists, "parrot the voice of Hanoi." "Do more," they were told by Hugh Scott of Pennsylvania, "and you wave the white flag of surrender."

The critics were not silenced. Instead, they gained recruits

American sergeant sets a mine, dashes for safety

Vietnamese mother does her washing in trench

including a number of legislators who had been counseling patience in judging President Nixon's handling of the Vietnam problem.

The congressmen who changed sides in the middle of an argument were not acting without reason. Some of them said they had detected a new and growing restiveness among constituents never associated with peace movements or militant demonstrations. These people were represented as still shunning violence and uproar but becoming exceedingly weary of the war and demanding that the United States have done with it. Consequently, Washington felt there was little political risk and perhaps even some political profit in joining the advocates of immediate peace.

In the beginning, the issue was the pace of U.S. troop withdrawals. When the President announced on Sept. 16 that no more than 35,000 men would be added to the 25,000 previously recalled, the debate gained new vigor. "The prosecution of the war with American troops must be ended, not merely reduced," said Sen. Charles Goodell, R-N.Y. He proposed legislation which would commit the United States to withdrawing all military personnel not later than Dec. 1, 1970.

A group of Republican representatives wanted to terminate the authority "to repel any armed attack . . . and to prevent further aggression" in Southeast Asia which had been granted to the President by the so-called Tonkin resolution (*The World in 1964, 152–154*). A caucus of two dozen senators and representatives voted to make common cause with a massive peace demonstration scheduled in October. Other proposals would have authorized complete withdrawal "with all reasonable haste" unless the Saigon government began internal reforms within 60 days.

"The imperative is that we get out. We have done enough," said Sen. Frank Church, D-Idaho. "We have fought the war for five long years and sacrificed almost 40,000 American lives. It is enough."

In October, the debate broadened with demands that the United States unilaterally declare a cease-fire. Sen. Mike Mansfield of Montana, the Democratic leader, was one of the demanders, arguing that, under the "protective reaction" strategy, the United States had "moved a long distance in the direction of a cease-fire and a stand-fast policy." On the other side of the aisle, Hugh Scott, now Republican leader in place of the deceased Everett Dirksen of Illinois (*pages 192–193*), urged a cease-fire proclamation "as soon as it can be arranged." "It might be a small step for us but a giant step for lasting peace," he said.

In the Pentagon's view, expressed by Secretary Laird, a cease-fire was out of the question unless it was part of an agreement with North Vietnam. So far as withdrawal was concerned, President Nixon said a fixed deadline would destroy "any chance to reach the objective that I am trying to achieve."

He pleaded for a united front against the Communists: "Once the enemy recognizes that it is not going to win its objectives by waiting us out, then the enemy will negotiate and we will end this war before the end of 1970." He embarked on a new review of Vietnam policy and announced that he would discuss the Vietnam situation in a major address to the nation on Nov. 3.

The announcement came from the White House on Oct. 10. It was unusual to schedule a presidential address so far in advance and, in this instance at least, perhaps it was too far. Too much time was available for rumors to rise and to circulate. There was an abundance of them: The President would proclaim a unilateral cease-fire; he would suspend B52 raids;

he would announce (1) complete and immediate withdrawal or (2) a speedup that would have perhaps 100,000 men out of Vietnam by the year's end; he would offer an extended truce at Christmas or at Tet, the lunar new year in the Vietnamese calendar.

The President did none of these things. He announced "a plan . . . for the complete withdrawal of all United States ground combat forces and their replacement by South Vietnamese forces" but he did not disclose the timetable because publication "would completely remove any incentive for the enemy to negotiate." He disclosed some peace initiatives which "we undertook privately and secretly because we thought that we thereby might open a door which publicly would be closed." These initiatives included an exchange of letters with President Ho Chi Minh of North Vietnam, who had died in September (*pages 174–179*).

Nothing was achieved: "The effect of all the public, private and secret negotiations can be summed up in one sentence: No progress whatever has been made except agreement on the shape of the bargaining table."

Nevertheless, "I have chosen a plan for peace. I believe it will succeed." He asked for support by "the great silent majority of my fellow Americans."

A good part of the "great silent majority" spoke immediately in a flood of phone calls and messages to the White House, including a telegram signed by more than 20,000 Colorado supporters. A special Gallup poll found that 77 per cent of listeners applauded the speech and 6 per cent found fault with it (17 per cent of those questioned had not made up their minds). In the House of Representatives, 50 Democrats and 50 Republicans proposed a resolution expressing support of the President "in his efforts to negotiate a just peace."

Senate opponents said they would take their case to the same "silent majority" wooed by Nixon. The vehicle would be a series of "educational" hearings by the Foreign Relations Committee under the chairmanship of J. W. Fulbright of Arkansas, one of the most persistent and outspoken critics of Vietnam policy.

Then, amid the pros and cons of debate, the voice of criticism was muted. One day after he announced the hearings, Fulbright said they had been postponed indefinitely. Instead, administration officials would be invited to explain the presidential peace plan in private. Fulbright said the committee was concerned lest public hearings "contribute to the inflammation of the public mind" at a time of national uproar.

* * * *

Impressively, importantly, the temper of demonstrations had changed.

The seeds of change were planted in April at a meeting in the Boston suburb of Brookline. As the Washington Post reported, leaders of a group organized as Massachusetts Political Action for Peace had gathered to discuss what they saw as a need for a new direction in war protests, something that would rally and reinforce the sentiment for peace.

The idea of a march on Washington was rejected as "tired stuff." The notion of a one-day general strike was vetoed as too drastic to command wide support. But the thought of an interruption of national life hung on to emerge as the plan for a Moratorium on business-as-usual when the demand for peace would come into full and dramatic focus.

Soundings on college campuses won enthusiastic response, headquarters was established in Washington and the movement mushroomed. "The generals," said the Post, were "mostly bright youngsters, not long out of college, given to business suits and medium skirts. They first tasted fire in the civil rights assaults of the early 60s, enjoyed their first victory in the 'dump Johnson' movement and became seasoned veterans, mostly in the McCarthy and a few in the Robert Kennedy campaigns." They were intent on giving impatience with the war "a new and broader dimension," beyond what had been attained by the "hardened and familiar 'peace groups'." Their slogan was "Bring home the troops. All the troops. Now." Their credo was peace, for both Vietnam and their own demonstration. Fourteen senators and 47 representatives endorsed the plan.

Oct. 15 was M-Day. It was impossible to count all those who participated in the wide variety of demonstrations across the land but the figure of one million was not derided as beyond belief. There were solemn vigils and quiet seminars, candlelight processions and religious services, readings of the names of war dead and the tolling of bells. The demonstrators included young and old, militant and moderate, people from cities and from villages and farms.

The roster of protesting organizations included the city council of Miami Beach and the Cleveland Symphony Orchestra. Some universities reported half of their students absent from classes. At Monmouth College in New Jersey, a coffin containing the names of the state's war dead was buried in the athletic field; at Whittier in California, the alma mater of President Nixon, the wife of the acting president lit a "Flame of Life," to burn until the war was ended. Demonstrating students in Wyoming braved snow and zero cold; some in Florida wore bathing suits. Antiwar leaflets were distributed at New York's Shea Stadium, where baseball's World Series was being played, and at bustling O'Hare Airport in Chicago. There were large crowds in some cities—by police estimate, 90,000 on Boston Common, 22,000 in Washington, 20,000 in New York—but the bulk of the turnout was in the host of demonstrations in smaller communities.

There were disappointments for the sponsors. An attempt to hold the House of Representatives in all-night session collapsed after four hours. Some campus protests brought out small minorities of the student body—300 of 19,500 at Texas Tech; 1,000 of 13,000 at Oregon State. And there were counter-demonstrations.

In Philadelphia, the Suburban Transportation Company draped its buses and trolleys with American flags. A full page advertisement in the New York Times, signed by the Citizens Committee for Peace with Security, said, "Everyone who wants peace in Vietnam should tell it to Hanoi." At Spearfish, S.D., demonstrating students were showered with leaflets conveying the advice of a group of Vietnam veterans: "America—Love It or Leave It." In Atlanta, Mayor Ivan Allan Jr. ordered municipal flags to half-staff in memory of the war's dead. Mayor John Lindsay of New York issued a similar order, but as evidence of sympathy with the Moratorium; policemen and firemen ignored the mayor and the color guard at Shea Stadium refused to march until the flag was raised to full staff.

The striking thing about the Moratorium was its peacefulness. There were scattered scuffles, some name-calling, some throwing of missiles, some arrests, but by and large the bitter confrontations of earlier mass demonstrations were missing. The violence, the provocations, the obscenities were muted to a remarkable degree. Said Pennsylvania's Sen. Scott, "These were on the whole gentle people expressing a perfectly proper concern."

Not everybody agreed with him. Sen. John Stennis, D-Miss., chairman of the Armed Services Committee, said the Moratorium

"leaves the enemy with the impression that, if they continue to hold out, we will give in."

As for the administration, President Nixon had made clear previously that he would not "be swayed by public demonstrations." "To allow government policy to be made in the streets would destroy the democratic process," he said. And Vice President Spiro Agnew made the first of a series of speeches that would thrust him to the fore as a creator of controversy; he told a Republican fund-raising dinner in New Orleans that the peace movement embraced "hard core dissidents and professional anarchists" who were encouraged "by an effete corps of impudent snobs who characterize themselves as intellecutals" (page 238).

Joseph Mohbat of The Associated Press appraised the day thus:

"What is clear is that Nixon has not given any indication of doing what the Moratorium demanded. It is equally clear that many who had condemned the Moratorium from the beginning misjudged their people when they prophesied that such a massive, widespread outpouring of feeling could only result in violence. There was no serious violence on Wednesday . . . none, at least, more significant than a brief scuffle in front of the White House during the cool fall afternoon. . . . At the very least, a sizable chunk of America got a sizable chunk of emotion out of its system."

Moratorium leaders believed that another "sizable chunk of emotion" remained to be vented. Sam Brown, 26, of Iowa, who was credited with developing the Moratorium idea and who had headed the student organization for Sen. Eugene McCarthy in the 1968 campaign for the Democratic presidential nomination, offered a prediction: "If there's no change in the Vietnam policy, if the President does not respond, there will be a second Moratorium in November."

There was no change, no response (at least, none of the kind that was wanted) and there was a second Moratorium.

Again thousands of people poured into the streets and onto the campuses of America. Again there were counter-demonstrations, many of them combined with the observance of Veterans Day on Nov. 11. On neither side did the turnouts equal those of October. There were other things to hold attention.

Chief among them was a demonstration in Washington, planned and conducted by the New Mobilization Committee to End the War in Vietnam. The "New Mobe," as it was known, had been organized at Cleveland in the summer. It was an awkward amalgam of people bound together only by their fervent distaste for the war. They included representatives of such disparate organizations as Women Strike for Peace, the Communist Party and the National Council of Churches; and individual pacifists, radicals, moderates and militants.

It was a makeup that aroused unease among government officials and some misgivings in Moratorium leadership although it had endorsed the New Mobe's demonstration. The government predicted trouble and summoned troops to guard buildings or to stand by for emergencies.

The protest began in the dusk of Thursday, Nov. 13, when the vanguard of 40,000 marchers passed the White House in single file, each intoning the name of a man killed in Vietnam or a Vietnam village ruined by war and each carrying a card that bore the name he spoke. The somber "March Against Death" continued through Friday and into the early hours of Saturday. It was wholly peaceful.

Then came the climax, a mass march along Pennsylvania Avenue to the Washington Monument. Police estimated the human sea at 250,000 people; the New Mobe committee said

U.S. Marines on patrol near Danang

Attorney General John N. Mitchell dissented. He acknowledged that "the great majority of participants obeyed the law" but, "unfortunately the planned demonstrations were marred by such extensive physical injury, property damage and street confrontations that I do not believe that—over-all—the gatherings here can be characterized as peaceful." He added that the sponsoring committee "aided this violence through a combination of inaction and affirmative action." Richard G. Kleindienst, deputy attorney general, announced an investigation, aimed specifically at the demonstrations against the South Vietnam Embassy and the Department of Justice.

The New Mobilization denounced the inquiry as an "illegitimate" effort to stifle public opinion against the war and said, "We deny that we have disturbed the peace. . . . We deny that we have conspired to do violence."

* * * *

In the Paris talks—one area where change was essential for progress toward peace—there was no change.

The Communists were obdurate in demanding that complete and unconditional withdrawal by the United States must be the first step. The United States and South Vietnam were equally firm in insisting that withdrawal could be undertaken only as part of a mutual agreement. The future of the Saigon government also was a stumbling block; the Communists denounced it, the United States upheld it.

Publicly, two gestures were made to break the stalemate.

In July, President Thieu of South Vietnam proposed terms which included elections in which the Communists would participate and which would be conducted under international supervision. The proposal was conditioned upon guarantees that the Provisional Revolutionary Government of the Viet Cong renounce violence and join in a pledge to abide by the election results. "Perfidious trickery," said a Communist spokesman.

In October, Xuan Thuy, North Vietnam's chief delegate, called upon the United States to enter into "direct and private talks" with the provisional government, with South Vietnam excluded. The United States retorted that three months had been spent in getting the four delegations to sit down at one table, and, as a nation, "has no desire to shred that (arrangement) by bobtailing it into separate talks."

No gleam of hope was in sight. President Nixon had said, "We have gone as far as we can or should go in opening the door to negotiations that will bring peace." Henry Cabot Lodge, head of the American delegation at Paris, resigned in November, saying that "the other side has flatly refused" to respond to all proposals "in any meaningful way." Vice President Nguyen Cao Ky of South Vietnam said, "Our good will has led us to make many concessions. To make one more concession is nothing but surrender."

On the Communist side, the words of Mrs. Nguyen Thi Binh, chief delegate of the provisional government, were typical: "To restore peace, the United States must put an end to its war of aggression, withdraw from South Vietnam all its own troops and those of other foreign countries in the American camp without posing any conditions whatsoever."

* * * *

And so, 1969 had been a year of change in the Vietnam picture. There had been changes in the character of the war, in Communist initiative, in U.S. strategy, in the mood of Congress and in the temper of antiwar demonstrators.

800,000 took part at one time or another. Without dissent, it was the biggest rally in the history of the movement for Vietnam peace.

There were two incidents of significant violence, neither on the official program. On Friday night, a crowd estimated in the thousands and led by members of the Students for a Democratic Society tried to storm South Vietnam's Embassy and was repulsed with tear gas. On Saturday night, a crowd of equal size and led by the Youth International Party (Yippies) surged around the Department of Justice to protest the Chicago trial of eight men accused of fomenting riot at the 1968 Democratic convention (*The World in 1968, 161–166*). Again, tear gas dispersed the demonstrators.

There were scattered disturbances when the rally broke up and thousands of demonstrators descended upon downtown Washington, some seeking transportation home, some lingering to see what would happen, a few seeking trouble. Dozens of store windows were broken but the consensus of opinion was that march and rally had been planned and conducted with remarkable efficiency. Herbert G. Klein, the President's director of communications; Sen. John Sherman Cooper, R-Ky., and Sen. Scott were among those who praised marchers and their leaders for restrained conduct.

"A Year Later, a Year Closer to Two Separate Societies"

Civil rights efforts since Martin Luther King's death followed new avenues, but blacks and whites remained far apart

Mrs. Coretta King prayed with marchers she led in support of striking Charleston, S.C., hospital workers

"For a year later we are a year closer to being two societies, black and white, increasingly separate."—Report of two urban study groups, Feb. 27, 1969

* * * *

WEARILY THE new year began for the followers of the slain Dr. Martin Luther King Jr. The first week in January they gathered under mossy oaks at a place called Frogmore, S. C., for a retreat, still emotionally benumbed by the assassination nine months earlier and trying to pick up the pieces of the nonviolent movement (*The World in 1968, 180–185*). King's

successor, the Rev. Ralph David Abernathy, dusted off Faith, Hope and Love, and now the staff of the Southern Christian Leadership Conference (SCLC) rallied behind his stocky figure for what he styled "a new thrust."

As he laid out an ambitious SCLC plan for carrying on King's fight against poverty and racism and war, the National Urban League's Whitney M. Young was urging swift White House action on recommendations for a minimum income guaran and a $2 hourly wage floor tied to the cost of living. the continent there was another kind of thrust. Black and members of the also angrily militant and equall fought a gunbattle—at the University of Calif

Angeles. Two Panthers were killed in the Jan. 17 fight in a campus building. Incredibly, the shooting was over selection of a black studies director at the university, authorities said. Three US members got life terms for the killings. Police intelligence sources said the violent rivalry had left six Panthers dead in the Los Angeles and San Diego areas. Several shootings involved police and black gunmen. At Santa Ana, Calif., a policeman was shot to death.

Panthers and police were aprowl elsewhere. San Francisco police raided Black Panther offices April 28 after minor violence was set off outside the place when officers told a speaker to quit using profanity at a "Free Huey Newton" rally. Newton, the Panther "minister of defense," was serving a prison term for the 1967 slaying of a white Oakland policeman (The World in 1968, 191). A few days later nearly 6,000 demonstrators massed at the federal building in San Francisco during a bail hearing for Newton. While the crowd chanted outside, a splinter group looted stores around the corner. Simultaneous Panther demonstrations were staged in New York, Kansas City and Sacramento, Calif.

In the East another Panther was murdered. The victim was Alex Rackley, 24, of New York. His body was found in a swamp near Middlefield, Conn. He had been stabbed with an ice pick, scalded with boiling water and shot in the head and chest. Theorizing Rackley was slain as a suspected informer, police raided Panther headquarters in nearby New Haven May 22, and 15 persons were charged in the killing.

Within a week a Chicago grand jury indicted 16 Panthers in the kidnap-torture of a Negro couple who said they were accused of stealing a gun from the Panthers and then were beaten and burned with a torch. The Chicago Panther lair was raided July 31 and five policemen were wounded. Three men were arrested. On another Chicago raid Dec. 4, Fred Hampton, 21, Illinois Black Panther chairman, and Mark Clark, 22, were killed in a shoot-out with police, who said Clark was the Panther leader in Peoria. Four other Panthers were wounded and two officers were injured. Police said they seized a cache of weapons in the raided apartment.

Even in Cuba, where the Panthers supposedly were moving their base, problems arose. Self-exiled Raymond Johnson, 22, of Alexandria, La., told a Havana news conference that many Panthers who had gone there were not allowed to leave.

In Detroit on the night of March 29 two policemen were shot, one fatally. Officers said that the rifle fire came from men in green army fatigue-type clothing and that the group fled into New Bethel Baptist Church, pastorate of the Rev. C. L. Franklin, father of soul singer Aretha Franklin. Franklin later said he had rented the edifice to the Republic of New Africa (RNA), a black nationalist faction headed by the North Carolina kidnap fugitive Robert Williams. At that time Williams was still in Red China but later he returned to the United States. Police said they were fired upon from the darkened church. They forced their way inside, encountering gunfire from the altar and from a ceiling trapdoor. Officers returned the fire and all 147 within—including women and children—were arrested.

Miraculously, only five in the church were injured. RNA leaders denied any shooting from inside the church. A young Puerto Rican was charged with the policeman's murder and two other men were charged with assault with intent to murder. The rest of those arrested were released subsequently. Judge George C. Crockett of Recorder's Court, a black man who had been summoned to process the arrests, contended that racial ·ertones figured in the case. "Can any of you imagine," he ᵔ reporters later, "the Detroit police invading an all-white

church and rounding up everyone in sight to be bused to a wholesale lockup in a police garage?"

Detroit police action in another case came under jury review in early June. Suspended policeman Ronald August, 30, white, was charged with murder in the shotgun slaying of Aubrey Pollard, 19, black, one of three teen-agers killed in the Algiers Motel incident. August admitted killing Pollard but claimed self defense in a struggle over the shotgun. An all-white jury acquitted him.

* * * *

Gloomy assessment of America's response to the domestic crisis so sharply depicted in 1968 was offered in a report by the Urban Coalition and Urban America Inc., two prestigious organizations. Following up the work of the 1968 presidential commission on civil disorders (The World in 1968, 64–65), these organizations said the trend toward two separate societies continued. "Progress in dealing with the conditions of slum-ghetto life has been nowhere in scale with the problem," and neither had there been "even a serious start" toward altering national priorities.

What would the summer bring? Abernathy had a feeling the summer would be calmer than the past several long, hot seasons of riot. Now Abernathy would summon the nonviolent army again to mark the April 4 anniversary of Dr. King's death by ambush (The World in 1968, 75–83). Abernathy also would launch Chapter 2 of the Poor People's Campaign. "We will not allow America to forget that she killed Dr. King," said Abernathy, "and we will not permit her to forget that 40 million Americans are poor."

Memorial services were held in many cities. In Nashville, about 300 marchers sang "We Shall Overcome" outside the state penitentiary to remind James Earl Ray of his deed (pages 107–109). Ray could not hear from his cell. Violence attended some observances. Upwards of 12,000 marched in Memphis, where Abernathy and Sen. Edward M. Kennedy, D-Mass., stood in the rain to make speeches. Young black troublemakers smashed a dozen store windows. In Chicago, memorial services were followed in two black neighborhoods by shooting, looting and fighting. National Guard Troops were called up. At Selma, Ala., 2,000 thronged down Broad Street and over the Edmund Pettus Bridge to kneel under an 83-degree sun at the spot on U. S. 80 where state troopers routed a 1965 march with clubs and tear gas (The World in 1965, 48–53). Exclaimed the Rev. L. L. Anderson, a Selma black leader: "We want you to know that Dr. King is up in Eternity, clapping his hands!" In Atlanta, the widow laid a simple wreath of red and white flowers in the form of a cross on the tomb of Georgia marble where the eternal flame sputtered in the breeze of a warm spring day.

* * * *

"We ask first that the strong arm of law and order be placed alike over the entire people of this state; that life and property be secured and the laborer free to sell his labor as the merchant his goods."—From a petition to Congress by the Colored People's Convention of South Carolina, Nov. 24, 1865, Charleston.

* * * *

The strong arm of the law was quite visible in Charleston, S. C., after black nonprofessional workers walked off their jobs

The Rev. Ralph Abernathy

at the Medical College of South Carolina and the Charleston County Hospital. National Guard troops, bayonets fixed to their carbines, patrolled the sprawling Medical College complex or scouted from atop its buildings. Charleston, bypassed by the earlier civil rights movement, found itself a rallying ground for labor union-civil rights organizing. When a group of workers sought higher pay and the right to organize at the college's 500-bed teaching hospital, 12 were fired. About 300 employes— most of the nurses' aides, practical nurses, orderlies and food service workers—walked out the next day, March 19. A week later they were joined by 68 black workers from the county hospital, a block away.

Strikers rallied behind Mary Moultrie, tall, stout nurses' aide and president of Local 1199B, Drug and Hospital Workers Union, in demanding higher pay than the $1.30 an hour minimum, union recognition or some form of bargaining rights and rehiring of the 12 discharged workers. Hospital officials rejected any notion of collective bargaining. There was no legal authority, they said, for the state institution to deal with a union. Nor would the 12 be taken back. Instead an injunction was obtained in state court to sharply limit picketing. The union, which in a decade had won contracts with 119 hospitals and nursing homes in the Northeast, eagerly mounted a major campaign and with the arrival of Ralph Abernathy the labor union-civil rights combination made Charleston a new testing ground. It was part of the Poor People's Campaign, Abernathy said, leading a march of about 2,500 April 25—and landing in jail for violation of the court order restricting pickets. Scattered violence brought the

National Guard—800 troops—and more than 150 state police. Ringed by soldiers and troopers, the hospital complex looked like an army camp. While Abernathy was in jail, Coretta King led a march of about 2,000, pledging: "I shall work hard to bring other people here from all walks of life." Gov. Robert E. McNair, backing the hospital's no-union stand, clamped on a 9 p.m. to 5 a.m. curfew May 1 as nightly disorders continued. Strikers and supporters boycotted stores and 12 conventions were canceled in less than a week at one hotel. Tourism and conventions had provided a $30-million yearly income.

Entwined inseparably with the strikers' pay and bargaining demands were complaints of black workers that they were denied basic human dignity at the hospital. Also of long-range concern was the union's hope of organizing the 2.5 million non-professional workers of America. In jail, Abernathy appealed for intervention by President Nixon. In court to answer contempt charges, Abernathy wore his blue denims and evaluated the county jail food: worst of 24 jails he had stayed in, he said. "The macaroni and cheese doesn't have any cheese in it." Gaining release May 3 in $500 bond, Abernathy announced plans for a massive Mother's Day march in Charleston as part of the Poor People's drive. President Nixon, responding to a request by 20 Democratic congressmen that he intervene, ordered Justice Department observers to Charleston and called on the disputing parties to "quiet the situation."

Abernathy took the opportunity to itemize demands of the Poor People's Campaign. They included: free food stamps for families with less than $3,000 yearly income; higher benefits for the poor and jobs "for all Americans able to work;" enforcement of school desegregation; an end to slums; voting rights for 18-year-olds; bargaining rights for public employes, and, finally, "end the war, stop construction of ABM and change the draft."

About 10,000 rallied for the Mother's Day march, rocking to the rhythm of the SCLC Breadbasket Band at County Hall. Natty in pink shirt, pink-and-white tie and white carnation in his light gray suit was Abernathy, who told the hospital workers: "You are today the heroes of poor people all over the world."

In shirtsleeves, with tie and collar loosened, was Walter Reuther, president of United Auto Workers, who delivered a rousing labor speech and then handed Mary Moultrie a check for $10,000 with the promise of more. To Abernathy went a $500 check as the first of weekly instalments in like amount, Reuther said, "until this fight is won."

Abernathy followed through on his antipoverty campaign with a May 13 meeting at the White House with Nixon and some Cabinet members. Afterward he called it his "most disappointing and fruitless" of White House meetings. Next day Abernathy told a Senate committee the Administration's food program "asks the poor and the hungry to wait still another two years before being fed—and even then to be content with a half a loaf."

But there was reason for smiles a few days later in Charleston. The AFL-CIO's George Meany chipped in $25,000 for the strike, moving into its third month as Coretta King returned for another rally. Then back came Abernathy to lead a night march June 20 and go to jail again, this time charged with "common law riot" after some strikers and sympathizers clashed with police. Vowing to stay in jail until the strike was settled, Abernathy fasted a week. Then on June 27 the Medical College dispute was settled under pressure of both state officials and the Nixon Administration.

The hospital agreed to rehire all the strikers, including the

12 who were fired, and pay a $1.60 minimum wage, to set up a grievance procedure and a credit union—through which employes might have union dues deducted. Pay raises ranging from 30 to 70 cents an hour were granted; other state employes also got raises. Union leaders felt the pact would allow the union to continue to function.

Abernathy got his bond reduced from $50,000 to $5,000 and left jail on July 4. The county hospital strike ended July 19 with agreement for a $1.60 minimun wage and rehiring most of the strikers immediately. The union shifted attention to hospitals in Baltimore and other cities.

Abernathy got his "mule train" ready for the Apollo 11 moonshot. He took the Poor People's Campaign to Cape Kennedy (page 141). While he and 45 others in his contingent watched the launch from VIP seats provided by government officials, the Poor People's mules and wagon snarled traffic outside the space center's main gate. Said Abernathy: "We may go on from this day to Mars, Jupiter and even the heavens beyond, but as long as racism, war and poverty prevail on the earth, we as a civilized nation have failed."

* * * *

In Paris two black girls stood in the American Church on May 11 and read an eight-page "ultimatum" demanding reparations to black people. This episode, part of a new racial tack, followed a disruption of services at New York's Riverside Church by black militant James Forman, who demanded 60 per cent of the church's income as reparation for past wrongs to black Americans (page 194). There were disruptions in other cities, sometimes climaxed by arrests, as attempts were made to read the new Black Manifesto. By October the enigmatic Forman had decided the ante would be $24 billion in 1970.

* * * *

On the night of July 20, a Sunday, there was dancing at an enlisted men's club at Camp Lejeune, sprawling Marine Corps base in eastern North Carolina. A white sailor and his black date were dancing when a black Marine tried to cut in. A quarrel ensued, then fighting. Before it ended scores were involved, a Marine was dead and armed patrols walked at Camp Lejeune. Military authorities said gangs of Negro and Puerto Rican Marines roamed the base, hunting white Marines and beating them with chains and other weapons. Five Marines were charged with murder, rioting and 14 counts of assault. Twenty-four others and a sailor were charged with rioting. Some black Marines rejected the official version and charged that a Negro died the year before from a beating by two white Marines behind the service club. This the Corps denied. At Selfridge Air Force Base in Michigan, where two Air Force women had a fight, a demonstration outside the gates protested what was labeled racial bias at the base. But a Defense Department spokesman said the troubles were spillover from civilian racial problems.

* * * *

Sun scorched the dusty, red clay road running past a row of blackened, unpainted shacks and shanties just off the main street of Eutaw, Ala. Ralph Abernathy and his three companions stopped at the porch of a shack where a large black woman pressed snuff between lip and teeth. Abernathy shook hands with her. He wore black jeans, a black pullover and sneakers.

"I want you to vote tomorrow," he said. "Vote under that Eagle."

Black-bearded, black-coveralled Hosea Williams, the SCLC political chief, spoke. "How you plan to vote?"

"Under th' Eagle—if I vote at all," the woman said.

"That Eagle," Williams said, "gonna fly tomorrow."

Abernathy and Williams, together with most of the SCLC staff and a large corps of volunteers, were campaigning for six black candidates in a special election in rural, 81.2-percent-black Greene County on Alabama's southwest border. A U. S. Supreme Court order had put the black slate on the ballot in an old plantation county where the small white minority had run things since soon after the Civil War. All six of the black candidates had run and lost in the 1968 Democratic primary, then filed to run under the Eagle banner of the National Democratic Party of Alabama (NDPA), a splinter group loyal to the national party. But the white probate judge, who also was chairman of the county board of commissioners, left the NDPA off the general election ballot, resulting in the court order and a special election July 29.

At stake were four of the five county commission seats and two of five school board seats. With one Negro already on the school board, the NDPA slate provided a chance for the blacks to gain majority voice on both governing boards. As a result of the 1965 Voting Rights Act (The World in 1965, 150–155), black voters numbered nearly 4,000, contrasted to 1,750 whites. Even with a 2-to-1 edge, black leaders were worried. But when the returns were in a cheer went up from the crowd of waiting Negroes at the courthouse. The Eagle was flying. All six black candidates won. Abernathy exulted. Plans were made by SCLC and NDPA for similar campaigns in other counties in 1970.

For blacks in Greene, it meant a new day. "We never had the opportunity to do anything for our county before," said Levi Morrow, 65, grayed, retired farmer who finished only the sixth grade, reared 12 children and now was a county commissioner. For civil rights leaders, the election gave impetus to the proposed extension of the Voting Rights Act, under which 800,000 Negroes had registered. But as the year waned Rep. William H. Colmer, D-Miss., chairman of the House Rules Committee, bottled up the bill, leaving the 1965 law due to expire in August 1970.

*   *   *   *

Abernathy in mid-August shifted the annual SCLC convention from Charleston to Chicago, to consider deeper involvement in a drive by Negroes for construction jobs. Trade unions, he charged, excluded Negroes and forced them to take the low-paying construction jobs. Seeking 10,000 building trade jobs for blacks, the campaign by the Coalition for United Community Action began picketing construction sites late in July, forcing suspension of work on numerous projects. Police were called frequently. When an assistant U.S. labor secretary held hearings, white construction workers blocked the entrance to the building. Negroes trying to enter said they were roughed up. A settlement was announced Nov. 6 by Mayor Richard J. Daley.

Similar protests developed in other cities. Street marches erupted in Pittsburgh, where a thousand black demonstrators shut down 10 major projects involving about $200 million and caused a massive traffic jam Aug. 26. A clash between marchers and police the next day left 32 injured, including 12 policemen. Mayor Joseph M. Barr halted the city's construction projects two days before the Labor Day weekend, 13,000 white workers were laid off and angry counter-demonstrations erupted. Ne-

gotiations to resolve the dispute were set back in late September when union officials stalked out because the Black Construction Coalition rejected an offer by the unions to train 1,250 black workers. Graphically revealing the problem was a mayor's commission report showing a grand total of 212 black members among 27,000 skilled craft union members in Allegheny County.

*   *   *   *

It was a cooler summer in most cities. A survey indicated contributing factors included new lines of communications as a result of riots, emergence of new black leaders, an apparent switch of tactics by some militants, many new special job and recreation projects and well equipped, specially trained riot police. But violence ranged from standard gang looting and sniper fire at firemen in Winston-Salem, N.C., to a July outbreak that left two dead in Columbus, Ohio. Seattle had three nights of disorders. In Niagara Falls, N.Y., a four-hour state of emergency—probably one of the shortest on record—was declared after racial trouble inspired several beatings. Schools had numerous racial clashes and in Forrest City, Ark., National Guardsmen were called up to keep peace. Father James Groppi, the white Catholic priest who led Milwaukee's siege of open-housing marches in 1967 (The World in 1967, 260), led welfare mothers and university students in an 11-hour occupation of the Wisconsin Assembly chambers to protest a state welfare budget cut. In Hartford, Conn., a week of disturbances in early June resulted in the city's first dusk-to-dawn curfew. More serious trouble followed on Labor Day: Looting and fires in a predominantly black and Puerto Rican section. Four persons were wounded by gunfire and more than 500 were arrested. Damage over a 40-block area was estimated at $600,000; more than 70 stores and other buildings were looted, or damaged by fire.

Similar violence visited Las Vegas, Nev., but the dice kept on rolling. Sunday night, Oct. 5, two black policemen on the west side, where 30,000 Negroes lived, stopped a black cab driver for a routine traffic check. A crowd gathered and a youth waved a shotgun. He was arrested, triggering a looting-burning rampage by 200 young Negroes at a shopping center. After two more nights the toll stood at two dead, nearly 50 injured and heavy property damage. In Fayette, Miss., three white men where arrested Sept. 9 in what Negro Mayor Charles Evers (page 119) said was a plot to kill him. Charged with attempted murder was a former Ku Klux Klan leader, arrested near Evers' office in a car containing two shotguns, a rifle, a carbine and a pistol.

In Philadelphia police said they foiled a plot by a black extremist group to bomb white-owned places with stolen hand grenades after two of the explosives were tossed into a city parking lot, damaging 12 police cars.

Memphis had more demonstrations. Protests by Negroes over school issues and a hospital workers' strike sent thousands into the streets early in November. Nearly 67,000 black children boycotted classes and forced some schools to close. Demands included more black representation in school affairs. The continuing school boycott brought out police to halt a Negro parade Nov. 11 because of disorders during a demonstration the night before, but finally authorities allowed the march to proceed when assured there would be no violence. No serious incidents took place along the route. In the demonstration during the previous night, 53 persons were arrested. By now it was no surprise that one of them was Ralph David Abernathy.

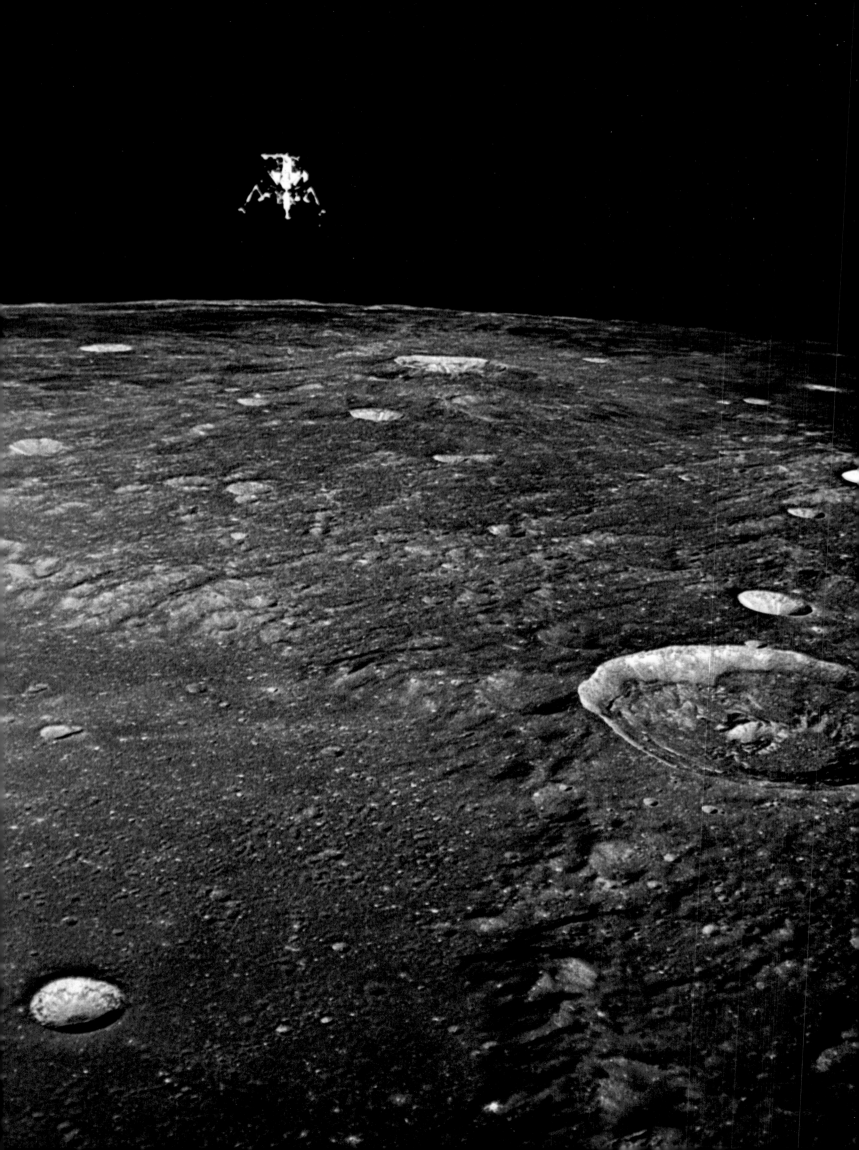

Not Even Lightning
Could Stop Astronauts
on Second Moon Journey

Moment of terror for American spacemen started eerie journey when bolt, probably static electricity, briefly knocked out Apollo 12 power supply, but their reward was a treasure in scientific data

Astronaut stood on moon between lunar module and antenna

THE START of man's second moon-landing voyage was just an hour away when ominous black clouds began moving on Cape Kennedy from the northwest. Astronauts Charles "Pete" Conrad Jr., 39, Richard F. Gordon Jr., 40, and Alan L. Bean, 37, waited in their sealed spaceship atop a Saturn 5 rocket. Launch Control Center had to make a decision. If the approaching storm bore lightning, the astronauts would have to be removed from the capsule and in all probability the launching would be scrubbed until December. This day, Nov. 14, was the only one in the month in which Conrad, Gordon and Bean could start their journey and land on target in the Ocean of Storms.

Launch director Walter Kapryan dispatched weather planes into the clouds. They found no lightning. The countdown continued.

President and Mrs. Richard M. Nixon were among thousands of spectators gathered at the Cape to watch the fiery departure. Twenty minutes before liftoff a light drizzle turned into a heavy rainstorm, lashed by 25-mile-an-hour winds. The launch pad was barely visible. But right on schedule, at 11:22 a.m. EST, the Saturn 5 roared to life. As it powered upward into dense clouds, observers froze as they saw two lightning flashes streak to the ground from the vicinity of the rocket.

"I think we got hit by lightning," radioed Apollo 12 commander Conrad. Then came chilling words: "We just lost the platform, gang. I don't know what happened here. We had everything in the world drop out."

There were so many warning lights flashing, Conrad said, that the astronauts couldn't count them. All three power-producing fuel cells stopped; alternating current circuits went dead, and the gyroscopic platform that measures attitude and velocity tumbled out of control. But the danger lasted only a fraction of a second. Backup batteries delivering direct current automatically took over. Seconds later the spacemen punched circuit breakers to restore all the equipment that failed.

Only systems in the spacecraft were affected. The Saturn 5 with an independent power system fired flawlessly through 11 minutes of powered flight and drilled Apollo 12 into earth orbit 117 miles high. "We had a couple cardiac arrests down here," Mission Control told the astronauts.

"We didn't have time up here," Conrad replied.

Experts later theorized that Apollo had created its own lightning, that static electricity built up by its passage through the rain clouds had suddenly discharged, knocking out the spacecraft power supply. Circling the earth, the astronauts checked all electrical systems and made certain no damage had been done that could pose a hazard once they committed themselves to leave earth orbit and head for the moon. After 1½ circuits of the globe, they triggered the engine of the still-attached third stage and set sail across the vast, unyielding ocean of space. The moon was 227,000 miles away.

"Everything is tickety-boo," Conrad radioed. "We're on our way."

"The earth is starting to get nice and round now," Bean commented as Apollo 12 sped away from its home planet.

The three Navy commanders had selected the nautical names Yankee Clipper and Intrepid for their command ship and lunar lander, respectively. Shortly after they entered the translunar highway, they separated Yankee Clipper, flipped around 180 degrees and docked nose-to-nose with Intrepid, pulling it free of a compartment atop the third stage. The 83-hour outward voyage was uneventful. Intrepid was checked for possible electrical damage. A slight course adjustment was made and the crew rested for four demanding days in the vicinity of the moon.

*   *   *   *

The crewmen of Apollo 12 had much in common. All were Navy men of the same rank. All were nearly the same age. All were dedicated fliers before joining the astronaut corps. All had been test pilots. Two became enamored of flying during childhood. All were family men: Conrad had four children, Gordon six, Bean two.

Conrad took his first flying lessons at 14. He joined the Navy after graduation from Princeton, where he studied aeronautical engineering. He was sent to test pilot school in 1958, and there he met Gordon and Bean. The astronaut program accepted Conrad in 1962, Gordon and Bean a year later. In 1966 Conrad commanded the Gemini 11 flight, with Gordon as pilot (The World in 1966, 213–216).

Gordon, a University of Washington graduate, planned to be a dentist until the Korean War brought him flight training in the Navy. On his first flight he forgot about dentistry. Bean, fascinated by planes as a toddler, started flying with the Navy Reserve at 17. On a Navy scholarship he was graduated from the University of Texas, where he likewise studied aeronautical engineering.

*   *   *   *

Conrad and Bean, who were to walk on the moon, had two major goals: a pinpoint landing in the Ocean of Storms near an unmanned Surveyor spacecraft and an examination of the moon. "Apollo 11 proved that man can land on the moon (*pages 141–146*). Apollo 12 will start the first detailed geological exploration of the lunar surface," Conrad had said before the launching. As they approached the moon Monday, Nov. 17, they televised a look at their strange weightless world. Through one window, they said, they could see the moon. Through another, the earth. Through a third, the sun. "It seems," Conrad said, "we're in suspended animation out here."

At 10:47 p.m. that night, behind the moon and out of radio contact, Yankee Clipper's main engine was fired six minutes to kick Apollo 12 into lunar orbit.

"Yankee Clipper with Intrepid in tow has arrived on time," Conrad said. "I guess that just like everyone else who has just arrived, the three of us are plastered to the windows just looking."

The trio spent most of Tuesday orbiting the moon, gazing down at the bleak, cratered landscape. At 11:16 p.m., with millions on earth watching on live television, Conrad and Bean separated Intrepid from Yankee Clipper and the two spacecraft drifted slowly apart. Against the background of a greyish moon, the lunar vehicle resembled a giant insect from another world, its four landing legs extended and its tracking lights blinking brightly.

"You're on your way, Intrepid," Gordon radioed.

Conrad stood at the commander's post at the left of Intrepid's cabin, Bean at the right. On the far side of the moon they triggered the descent engine and the world waited in suspense for 20 minutes until the fragile craft reappeared around the edge. "We had a great burn," Conrad reported. They had fired themselves into an orbit that would take them within 10 miles of the surface.

As they dropped lower and lower Conrad said: "I sure hope you have us lined up right, Houston, 'cause there's sure some big mountains in front of us right now."

"You're 'go' for powered descent," the ground relayed after checking all systems.

Conrad pressed the proceed button and Intrepid's throttle-operated engine started gently and then built up full thrust of 9,850 pounds. Intrepid swooped closer and closer, skimming dangerously low over the moon's hostile craters and mountains. As they neared the surface, Bean called out the altitude and angles: "1,000 feet, coming down, 33 degrees . . . 600 feet, 35 degrees . . . 330 feet, coming down at 4 per cent fuel, loads of gas . . . contact light on!"

The engine kicked up a lot of lunar dust and Conrad reported: "It's a good thing we leveled off high and came down because I couldn't see with all that dust." Intrepid was on the surface, logging touchdown at 1:54 a.m. Wednesday, Nov. 19.

Conrad and Bean had parked right next to the Surveyor crater in a perfect bull's-eye landing. It proved that flight planners had profited from the lessons of Apollo 11—which overshot its target by four miles—and they could now confidently plan for manned exploration of the more rugged regions of the moon, the mountains, craters and rilles.

"Outstanding!" shouted Conrad, who could not contain his exuberance. "I can't wait to get outside. Those rocks have been waiting 4½ billion years for us to come out and grab them. Holy cow, it's beautiful out here!"

Gordon radioed his congratulations as he orbited 65 miles overhead. "Have a ball," he said.

"Thanks, see you in 32 hours," Conrad answered.

Conrad and Bean went through 4½ hours of essential preparation, donning their life-giving back packs, helmets and gloves. Intrepid's hatch was opened at 6:30 a.m. and Conrad, a ghostly figure in an alien world, backed slowly down a nine-rung ladder attached to a landing leg. At 6:44 a.m. he planted a 13-inch-long boot on the dusty surface, the third human being to leave his imprint on the rugged lunar terrain. "That may have been a small one for Neil, but that's a long one for me." He referred to Neil A. Armstrong's words in July (*page 144*), when he became the first man to walk on the moon: "That's one small step for a man, one giant leap for mankind."

As Conrad climbed down the ladder, he opened the television

Apollo 12 crewman examined Surveyor III which landed on the moon April 19, 1967

camera compartment and gave earthlings a quarter million miles away their first color closeup of the lunar surface.

Conrad walked 20 feet to the edge of a crater and sighted the Surveyor 3 spaceship that landed there 2½ years before *(The World in 1967, 230–231).* "Boy, you'd never believe it," he said. "Guess what I see sitting by the side of the crater: the old Surveyor . . . Good old Surveyor. It can't be more than 600 feet away."

Thirty-one minutes after Conrad stepped down, Bean followed him. But as he tried to move the television camera to a better position something went wrong. After 44 minutes the camera failed and no further pictures were relayed to earth. Engineers at Mission Control speculated that Bean had inadvertently pointed the camera lens at the sun, damaging its sensitive image tube.

The astronauts had difficulty walking at first in the moon's unfamiliar one-sixth gravity field, but they soon became accustomed to the strange environment. "It helps to move if you hop a little," Conrad said. "I'm beginning to feel like Bugs Bunny." They noted the Ocean of Storms appeared to have quite a bit more black dust than Apollo 11's landing site in the Sea of Tranquillity.

They planted an American flag and then unloaded a set of scientific instruments and a nuclear power plant designed to keep the experiments operating and sending data for at least a year.

Scientists on the ground skipped a few heartbeats when Bean reported he couldn't remove the canister containing the nuclear generator's radioactive element, Plutonium-238, from a protective cask. "It seems swollen in there and friction is holding it in," Bean said. "I don't want to pull too hard because it's a very delicate mechanism. Come out of there, you rascal."

"I've got a better idea," Conrad said. "I'll get the hammer." A little pounding did the trick and Bean told the ground: "We got it, babe." Then they carefully moved the five instruments about 1,000 feet from Intrepid and deployed them and the nuclear generator. The instruments were a seismometer to detect tremors in the lunar mantle; a magnetometer to sense magnetic fields; a solar wind spectrometer to sort out the charged particles from the sun, and two detectors to measure the lunar ionosphere and atmosphere. They began transmitting as soon as the nuclear generator was turned on. Mission Control reported the seismometer was recording the astronauts' footfalls on the moon.

Then it was time to end the first excursion, and the two spacemen climbed back into the lunar lander's cabin to sleep and to recharge their back packs with oxygen. Conrad had been outside 3 hours 44 minutes, Bean an even three hours. The astronauts were so excited that they slept only fitfully in hammocks strung up in the cabin. They asked permission to start their second moonwalk about two hours early. Mission Control agreed, and at 10:59 p.m. Nov. 19 the hatch again was opened and Conrad and Bean descended to the surface.

Goals of the second excursion were to gather carefully documented and photographed rock samples on an extended trek to seven craters. Although they walked about a mile, their trail etched an irregular ellipse so that at no time were they more than 1,500 feet from Intrepid in case of trouble with their oxygen systems.

Conrad and Bean kept up a lively commentary for scientists listening in Mission Control as they moved from one crater to another—Head Crater, Bench Crater, Halo Crater, Triple Crater, Sharp Crater, Surveyor Crater and Block Crater. They found varying shades of color in the lunar soil.

"In places the rocks are brown," Bean reported. "In other places they're grey, and in others they're white."

"Man!" Conrad shouted near Head Crater. "Have I got the grapefruit rock of all grapefruit rocks." It was big, he said; adding: "Houston, on my mark, I'm going to roll it. Hit, hit, now! It's just rolling, roll, roll, roll, still rolling. Still rolling, still rolling, slowly, then it stopped." The seismometer needles moved with its bounce and the information was recorded in Mission Control.

Soon they were on the rim of Surveyor crater, with the spacecraft resting 150 feet down the 14-degree slope. Conrad and Bean found the sides of the crater terraced and followed one level around to the dead spacecraft. They reported the vehicle was a light tan and asked what color it was when it left the earth in April, 1967. They were told it was white and blue. "The sun has cooked it," Conrad commented.

They photographed the buildup of dirt around the space-craft to compare it with pictures Surveyor took when it landed. Then they clipped off five pieces of the craft—a television camera, a piece of cable, a strut, a scoop shovel and a section of glass. Examination of the parts by experts could help determine what materials will be needed for building permanent bases or long-term space stations on the moon.

At 2:45 a.m. after nearly four hours outside they returned to Intrepid with their scientific treasure, including about 60 pounds

Returned to earth, astronauts Charles Conrad, Richard Gordon and Alan Bean beamed happily

Astronaut stood beside U.S. flag after it was unfurled on the moon's surface

Sun played tricks with light as astronaut walked on the moon

of rock and soil. Then they spent several hours preparing for the critical engine blast that would lift them off the moon.

"You're 'go' to cast off," Mission Control radioed.

"Liftoff and away we go," shouted Conrad as Intrepid's cabin section blazed upward at 9:26 a.m., using the lower half with the landing legs as a launching pad. They had been on the moon 31 hours 32 minutes. "Man, this is a hot machine," Conrad said as the lunar craft whipped into lunar orbit and began pursuit of Gordon in the Yankee Clipper, some 300 miles ahead. For 3½ hours Conrad and Bean skillfully steered Intrepid in the complex chase. As they executed the final closing maneuvers, a television camera in the command ship relayed the dramatic action to earth. When Intrepid was a few feet away, Gordon took over and guided Yankee Clipper to a stable linkup with the lunar bug. Two and one-half hours later, the moon explorers were safely back in the command ship and they jettisoned Intrepid after setting it up for a death dive to the moon, a maneuver designed to jolt the seismometer left behind.

A signal from the ground ignited the 5,000-pound lunar ship's engine and it plunged downward, striking at 3,600 miles an hour 45 miles from Conrad and Bean's base. The seismometer recorded the shock 5½ minutes later. Then came a big surprise, as the tremors continued for about 55 minutes. On earth a similar impact would reverberate only a few minutes. "We've never seen anything like it on earth," said Dr. Frank Press of the Massachusetts Institute of Technology. "We're not sure what it means, but probably it will be a major discovery." At 3:49 p.m. Friday, Nov. 21, Yankee Clipper's engine fired to increase its speed from 3,700 to 5,700 miles an hour, enough to escape the influence of lunar gravity and start the long journey back to earth.

The three-day homeward journey was uneventful. They held the first news conference from space, answering newsmen's questions from Mission Control.

The astronauts were asked if they would agree to launch again through such a Cape Kennedy storm.

"I'd go again," said Conrad.

"We made it this time. Why not go again?" replied Gordon. "Concur," said Bean.

They were on television again Monday, Nov. 24, as they blazed back through the atmosphere and guided Yankee Clipper into warm Pacific waters just 3.1 miles from the aircraft carrier *Hornet*, about 400 miles southeast of American Samoa.

"We're all okay," Gordon radioed minutes after the ship hit the water. The flight had lasted 10 days, 4 hours, 36 minutes. Helicopters were overhead within minutes, dropping life rafts and swimmers into the white-capped sea.

Because of the remote possibility the astronauts returned harmful germs from the moon, strict quarantine orders were enforced, and one swimmer scrubbed moondust from the spacecraft with a decontaminant after opening it to toss clean flight suits to the spacemen. Conrad, Gordon and Bean emerged wearing face masks to trap any bugs they might exhale. An hour after landing, a helicopter deposited them on the deck of the carrier and a band struck up *"Anchors Aweigh"* for the crew. The astronauts were taken below deck and placed in an airtight quarantine trailer which was their home for nearly five days as the ship steamed for Hawaii, where the trailer was placed aboard a cargo plane for a flight to the Manned Spacecraft Center, Houston, Tex. There they were isolated for another 11 days in special quarters in the Lunar Receiving Laboratory. In another section of the building scientists eagerly began examining the treasure chests of rocks from the moon.

Soon after they were aboard the carrier, the astronauts received a radiophone call from President Nixon. "I am just tremendously proud, personally and representing the American people, of what you've done," he said. Then, in a surprise announcement, he promoted all three to the rank of captain.

Medicare–Medicaid:
The Spiraling Cost
of Health Programs

"A massive crisis" for nation was predicted by Nixon,
with a breakdown of services considered possible in three years

—A doctor in the small Texas town of Jefferson collected $62,000 from Medicare after billing for 4,560 visits to just 54 patients in the nursing home he operated.

—A dentist in the Spanish Harlem section of New York City was suspended from the Medicaid program for alleged fraudulent billings after his clinic received more than $400,000 for dental care for the poor.

—A tiny pharmacy in the Kentucky mountain town of Neon (pop. 700) was paid nearly $330,000 in one year for prescriptions filled under Medicaid. The owner said that without the government program he would have taken in only about $10,000.

—In California, one nursing home continued billing for a patient for several weeks after his death and even doubled the daily rate. In Cleveland, Ohio, authorities sent another nursing home Medicaid checks for a patient for six months after his death.

THESE CASES of mixups, confusion and alleged abuse emerged from investigation files as the Senate Finance Committee took a hard look at the spiraling cost of government medical care programs: Medicare and Medicaid. Federally financed Medicare was established to provide doctor and hospital insurance for persons 65 or older, no matter what their economic need. Medicaid, funded by both federal and state money, aimed to provide health care for the poor and needy, no matter what their age. The financial health of the programs was affected, many felt, because they provided for the first time health care for thousands of persons and thus increased the demand for such care in a time of inflationary pressures as well as a shortage of medical personnel and facilities.

Other groups interested in the steadily rising cost of health care included the President and his advisers; the Department of Health, Education and Welfare; the Internal Revenue Service and the American Medical Association.

Committee Chairman Russell B. Long, D-La., noted in midsummer the programs were running far beyond original estimates, placed the extra cost at $5 billion a year, and said the end was not in sight. He observed that any losses because of

abuses were a much smaller factor than the big cost increases weighing on the program. Some weeks later Dr. Dwight L. Wilbur, then president of the American Medical Association, said of Medicaid that "while there are some abuses being found and the medical profession and government are moving to eradicate them, meaningful economies can come only from better efficiency and management." HEW thereafter issued new regulations intended to check high fees paid to doctors and dentists under Medicaid. The regulations said basically that fees must be based upon the 75th percentile, or what 75 out of every 100 doctors in a given area charged under Medicaid in January 1969. Sen. Jacob Javits, R-N.Y., said at the time that the basic problem was the "unprecedented rise in the cost of medical care. This inflationary trend combined with some abuses and lax administration of federal programs have caused the price of Medicaid to soar far beyond our original expectations."

Social Security Commissioner Robert M. Ball told Long's committee that the biggest increase cited, $4 billion for Medicare, resulted when the need for hospitalization of older persons proved greater than had been anticipated at the outset. Thus, in September, HEW announced that a person covered by Medicare who entered the hospital after Jan. 1, 1970, would have to pay the first $52 of his bill—an increase of $8—for hospitalization up to 60 days. From 60 to 90 days, the patient's share would rise from $11 to $13 of daily costs, and over 90 days, $26 a day instead of $22. Long said the hospital insurance portion of Medicare was costing $3 billion more a year than anticipated when Congress approved the program in 1965 *(The World in 1965, 128–129; The World in 1966, 137; The World in 1967, 153)*, and the portion covering primarily doctor's fees was costing $1 billion more. The senator added that the cost of Medicaid was about $800 million extra.

Dr. Wilbur said of Medicaid that "it is likely that in fiscal 1970 it will cost $4.62 billion and serve 10.2 million people, and estimates of costs, if the present law is in effect in 1975, range from $12 billion to $16 billion."

Dr. John H. Knowles, unsuccessfully proposed by Secretary Robert H. Finch for the post of assistant secretary for health and scientific affairs in HEW *(page 135)*, said in a subsequent

Runaway!

interview that Medicare was "generally a good program, with quality and utilization controls in hospitals, which have worked in the public interest." But Medicaid, he said, was a "poor program with no standards, no quality controls." On the plus side for Medicare, Knowles said, was its funding from "trust funds," largely the Social Security tax, which is "less subject to cutbacks than general tax funds." Also in Medicare's favor, he said, was the requirement that hospitals set up utilization control committees to determine if patients had needed hospitalization, for what length of time, and whether or not they had received proper treatment. There was no such auditing in Medicaid, a lack which he said stimulated the "use of high cost in-patient services."

Dr. Francis L. Land resigned Aug. 31 as chief of Medicaid. Land gave no reason for leaving the post he had taken in November 1966, 10 months after Medicaid's start. When Land took the job, Medicaid was costing the government some $800 million annually. In years following, the costs kept going up, with the government putting some $2.4 billion into the program in fiscal 1969. Under the Medicaid program, some 2,700 doctors collected $25,000 or more each in fees in 1968. In July, Internal Revenue Commissioner Randolph Thrower said his agency planned to audit income tax returns back to 1966 for each doctor who received $25,000 or more a year under the Medicare-Medicaid programs.

The government in August checked the records of Dr. Michael E. DeBakey and Dr. Denton A. Cooley, the two Houston, Tex., surgeons famous for their work in human heart transplants (*The World in 1968, 19, 167, 263*), who received about $200,000 each in 1968. Congressional investigators said that they found no irregularities in the payments, and that the money, which covered more than 1,000 heart and circulatory system operations, went mainly into a college fund. An investigator reported that "DeBakey is an honorable man and so is Dr. Cooley. They are not cheating the government in any way." In Michigan, Dr. Sanford Polansky of Benton Harbor returned $169,000 paid him in 1968 for treatment of Medicaid patients. Polansky also asked Michigan Blue Shield, which administered the program, to audit his work for 1968-69 and

specified that he be paid only on "invoices which are supported to . . . complete satisfaction." A Blue Shield official said nothing significantly incorrect had been found in Polansky's claims. Polansky, whose name was among 13 Michigan doctors listed in a newspaper as collecting $100,000 or more from Medicaid in 1968, said he got an "enormous amount of crank letter harassment" that affected his wife's health and the wellbeing of his family. He said the money "though earned and deserved, is simply not worth the retaining." The physician denied any wrongdoing, saying his mass practice resulted from the refusal of other doctors to treat the poor.

Concerned over health care for not only the poor but for all citizens, President Nixon warned that "we face a massive crisis" and predicted a possible breakdown in medical services in three years if something urgent was not done. The president revealed a health program aimed at holding down costs while providing effective medical care for all. The plan, outlined in an eight page report, called for larger involvement by the private sector as the federal government moved to tighten medical programs and help turn out more medical personnel. The report, prepared by the President's chief health officers, Finch and Dr. Roger Egeberg, said hospital fees per day rose from $44 in 1965 to $70 in 1969, probably would hit $80 in 1970, and could reach $100 in three years.

"This nation," the Finch-Egeberg report said, "is faced with a breakdown in the delivery of health care unless immediate concerted action is taken by government and the private sector. Expansion of private and public financing for health services has created a demand for services far in excess of the capacity of our health system to respond. The result is a crippling inflation in medical costs causing vast increases in government health expenditures for little return, raising private health insurance premiums and reducing the purchasing power of the health dollar of our citizens. Our task now as a nation is to acknowledge the extreme urgency of the situation, to take certain steps to arrest the inflation that is paralyzing us, and to put into motion initiatives that ultimately will reshape the system."

Among the report's main recommendations were the elimination of an allowance to hospitals and nursing homes for unidentified costs, and new regulations curbing Medicaid fees. Finch and Egeberg said the government would require tighter reviews of hospital care and direct the Public Health Service to promote alternative facilities. An Office of New Careers, they said, had been planned in HEW to develop training programs for military medical corpsmen returning from Vietnam, to help relieve the manpower shortage in the health program.

The Administration then called in September for a study to determine if a national health service for all age groups was feasible. Walter Reuther, chairman of the 100-member Committee for National Health Insurance, said his group hoped to propose in 1970 a national health insurance plan which would provide universal coverage of all medical expenses for all Americans.

What would such a national health plan cost the government? Several studies already had indicated it could reach $10 billion a year.

Dr. Russell B. Roth, speaker of the AMA's House of Delegates, appeared before the House Ways and Means Committee in November to present the AMA's proposed "Medicredit" plan which calls for a voluntary national health insurance plan. The plan, geared to tax credits, would allow buyers of private medical insurance to deduct a certain portion of the costs of the premiums from their income taxes.

KENNEDY: FAMILY COUNTED MORE THAN MONEY

Joseph P. Kennedy was a man remembered more as a father than a financier. He believed that "the measure of a man's success in life is not the money he's made. It's the kind of family he's raised."

His father, Patrick, a Boston saloonkeeper and a powerful political figure, was wealthy, but Joseph amassed a fortune—estimated up to $500 million. That, however, was not Joseph's sole goal. Money was chiefly a means toward personal and political prestige, not only for himself but for the fourth generation of an Irish-American family labeled "lace-curtain."

Joseph P. Kennedy's successes had their setbacks, but his ability to survive the extremes of exhaltation and anguish seemed to embody his philosophy: "After you have done the best you can, the hell with it." On Wall Street he was a wizard, although at times the victim of false tips. By the time he was 30 he had made all the money he and his family would ever need.

In politics, he picked a winner—backing Franklin D. Roosevelt in the 1932 Presidential campaign—but turned loser when he was not rewarded, as he had expected, with an appointment as FDR's Secretary of the Treasury. As a family man he fathered nine children, beamed brightly when three sons were elected to the U.S. Senate, one of them to the Presidency, and mourned deeply when four children died violently.

Joseph Patrick Kennedy was born Sept. 6, 1888, destined, according to his father, to rise high in society. He was sent to the best of schools—Boston Latin and Harvard, whose doors seldom had been entered by Irish Catholics—and he was instilled with determination to succeed. First he needed money. Lots of it. For reasons few could understand, he began his career as a bank examiner. The payoff from studying the books of all the eastern Massachusetts banks he visited didn't come from the $1,500-a-year salary but from the opportunity to gain control of Columbia Trust Co., a small bank about to be taken over by a larger institution.

At 25 Kennedy was the bank's president. At 26 he was a member of Boston's first family, taking the hand of Rose Fitzgerald, daughter of Mayor John F. "Honey Fitz" Fitzgerald. Rose, a deeply religious and patient woman often described as the mainstay of the Kennedy family, bore Joe four sons and five daughters. All the while Joe was making his family independently wealthy so his children could follow useful careers without worrying about making a living. Shortly after World War I, he was named manager of the stock division of Hayden Stone & Co. in Boston. He expanded his Wall Street financial empire to include real estate and the motion picture industry. His keen business mind prompted him to sell his movie interests for a $4 million profit in 1928. He not only held onto that cash, he converted his Wall Street holdings into cash too, and by the time the market crash came he was many times a millionaire while others were broke.

His political acumen, however, was not so good. Although he poured money and prestige into Roosevelt's 1932 campaign, the position in FDR's cabinet he had anticipated never came. Instead, he was appointed the first chairman of the Securities and Exchange Commission. He later served on the Maritime Commission and as U.S. Ambassador to Britain. While his charm and lucidity were described as nonpareil in the private company of world political and social leaders, he seemed to have an ability to phrase himself poorly in public, thus making many political enemies.

Of these, Kennedy's third-born son Robert in 1965 said "our opponents became his opponents, our problems his problems" but "he was careful to make sure we understood that his enemies were not to become our enemies."

Thus it was that as the younger Kennedy men —Joe Jr., John F., Robert F., and Edward T.—took their places in society and politics, the patriarch faded into the background. He had done all that he felt he could do for them.

Nonetheless, the triumphs of the carefully cultivated Kennedy clan were destined to be laced with tragedy. Young Joe was killed in the crash of a U.S. Navy plane during World War II. A month later, the husband of daughter Kathleen, the Marquess of Hartington, captain of the Coldstream Guards, died in action in France. In the spring of 1948 Kathleen died in a plane crash. Another daughter, Rosemary, was judged mentally retarded and was destined to spend her life in an institution. John, the oldest surviving son, the first of three to be elected to the Senate and the nation's 35th President, was assassinated in Dallas in 1963 (*The World in 1964, 52–57*). Robert, following his brother's footsteps as a U.S. Senator seeking the presidency, was gunned down in Los Angeles in 1968, moments after winning the Democratic presidential primary in California (*The World in 1968, 114–121*).

With each fatal bullet the burden of telling the elder Kennedy of his sons' fate fell to the youngest, Teddy. But "Old Joe," who had to bear his grief in silence because of an incapacitating stroke suffered in 1961, died without being told of another mishap—an automobile accident near the Kennedy Compound on Cape Cod in the summer of 1969. Teddy Kennedy, driver of a car that plunged off a bridge, escaped injury, but a young woman who had been a member of Robert's office staff was drowned.

Unlike his four children who predeceased him, Papa Kennedy slipped peacefully into death on Nov. 18 at his Hyannis Port, Mass., home that overlooked the sea. He was 81. With him were his wife of 55 years; four children: Teddy, Jean, Pat and Eunice; Jacqueline Kennedy Onassis, widow of the President (*The World in 1968, 200–202*), and Ethel Kennedy, Robert's widow; several of the 27 Kennedy grandchildren and Ann Gargan, a niece and constant companion to Kennedy after his stroke.

Preceding burial at Holyhood Cemetery in Brookline, Mass., was a mass at the little Church of St. Francis Xavier at Hyannis, where the Kennedy family had worshipped for nearly 40 years. It was Teddy who delivered the eulogy, a tribute written by Robert four years earlier, which read, in part:

"He has called on the best that was in us. There was no such thing as half-trying. Whether it was running a race or catching a football, competing in school—we were to try. And we were to try harder than anyone else. We might not be the best, and none of us were, but we were to make the effort to be the best. 'After you have done the best you can,' he used to say, 'the hell with it.'"

The President's father: Joseph P. Kennedy greeted fondly by his late son, President John F. Kennedy

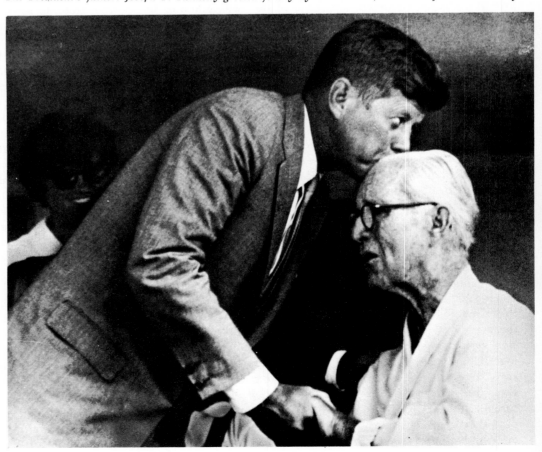

REJECTED: JUDGE HAYNSWORTH

"The chair wishes to caution the gallery that there will be no outbursts at the announcement of the vote. The yeas are 45 . . . The nays are 55. The nomination is rejected." And so, on Nov. 21, Vice President Spiro T. Agnew announced that the Senate had refused to confirm the nomination of Judge Clement F. Haynsworth to the Supreme Court. It was the tenth time in history and the first time in 30 years the Senate had disapproved such an appointee.

When President Nixon announced Haynsworth as his choice on Aug. 18, most political observers predicted easy confirmation. Haynsworth, 56, a native of Greenville, S. C., had been appointed to the U.S. Fourth Circuit Court of Appeals in 1957. His supporters said that although the judge had been essentially conservative, he had liberalized his decisions in response to judicial guidelines handed down by Supreme Court decisions. As a "constructionist" they said he would help restore what Nixon called "the proper balance" to the court.

In retrospect much was made of the fact that since Haynsworth was named to replace Abe Fortas, who had resigned from the Supreme Court in an ethics controversy (pages 97–99), the Nixon administration should have expected its nominee would undergo a thorough scrutiny. Yet Nixon had already named Warren E. Burger as the Supreme Court's chief justice, and the Senate Judiciary Committee had taken only an hour and 45 minutes to approve (page 138).

Sen. Jacob K. Javits, R-N.Y., immediately expressed "grave concern" about Haynsworth's conservative record on the appellate court. Soon after the nomination a Chicago newspaper said Haynsworth had held part ownership in Carolina Vend-A-Matic when in 1963 he ruled in favor of a textile company that did business with the vending-machine firm. Two weeks later the Washington Post quoted South Carolina sources as saying Haynsworth had done "a lot of legal work" after World War II to encourage northern textile firms to settle in the Carolinas.

Testifying before the Senate Judiciary Committee hearings in September, Haynsworth said he thought his action in the textile case was "entirely proper." He added, "The judges in my court thought it was proper and Robert Kennedy (Attorney General at the time) thought so." After the decision the Textile Workers Union

raised conflict of interest questions, but a Justice Department investigation declared Haynsworth free of error. Sen. Birch Bayh, D.-Ind., opposing the nomination, also raised the question. He said examination of Haynsworth's financial record showed the judge held about $16,000 worth of stock in Brunswick Corp., and had ruled in 1967 for Brunswick in a dispute with a bowling alley operator. The nominee had testified he disqualified himself "in all cases . . . in which I had a stock interest," but a Justice Department report showed Haynsworth had acquired the Brunswick stock after he joined in the pro-Brunswick decision but before the ruling was announced. Haynsworth admitted he had made a mistake and said he was "very sorry." Lawrence Walsh, chairman of the American Bar Association Committee on the Federal Judiciary, told the Senate committee he saw no interest conflict.

The committee heard Samuel Tucker of the National Association for the Advancement of Colored People criticize Haynsworth for his "persistent hostility" to the Constitution's promise of racial equality. AFL-CIO leader George Meany called the nominee an "anti-labor" judge whose record was "hostile to workers and Negroes." Edward W. Brooke, the Massachusetts Republican and only Negro member of the Senate, called on Nixon to withdraw the nomination.

Reaffirming his support of Haynsworth in late September, Nixon said: "I believe he will be a great credit to the Supreme Court." Attorney General John Mitchell concurred, adding, "If we had put up one of the 12 Apostles it would have been the same." On Oct. 8, Bayh claimed Haynsworth had held stock in several corporations involved in cases before his court. Deputy Counsel Clark R. Mollenhoff called Bayh's "bill of particulars" an "inaccurate and distorted document."

Despite the White House defense of Haynsworth, further signs of opposition had begun to show among Republican leaders. Hugh Scott, Senate minority leader, said the appointment "justifies some careful thought." Sen. Clifford P. Case, R.-N.J., called upon Nixon to withdraw the nomination in order to restore "public confidence in the integrity of the Supreme Court in its dedication to equal justice under law." Two other leading Republican Senators, Robert P. Griffin and Margaret Chase Smith, announced they would not support the nominee.

Haynsworth's supporters counterattacked. Democrat Ernest Hollings, one of the judge's chief champions in the Senate and a fellow South Carolinean, challenged Bayh to a television debate. Sen. Marlow Cook, R.-Ky., called Bayh's disclosures "sloppy." On Oct. 20 Nixon again affirmed his belief in Haynsworth's ability and told newsmen he would not withdraw the nomination even if Haynsworth asked him to do so. Sixteen past presidents of the American Bar Association signed a telegram to the judiciary committee endorsing Haynsworth, even though the board of governors of the American Trial Lawyers Association stated in a resolution that the judge's confirmation would undermine public confidence in the high court.

Haynsworth, in an interview, declined to reply to the conflict-of-interest allegations. "The Senate," he said, "has the right to decide to what extent I should be scrutinized. I'm not going to find fault with them." The Senate opened debate on Nov. 13, but the outcome was never certain until Nov. 21, the day of the vote. Jean Heller of The Associated Press wrote, "A fistful of senators managed to keep the future of Clement F. Haynsworth as clouded as a Florida sky in hurricane season." At the last minute seven senators had not disclosed their stands.

The roll call itself took only 11 minutes and the only sounds in the hushed senate chambers were the "oohs" and "aahs" from the galleries as the uncommitted senators cast their votes. The biggest response came when Republican Senator Scott said "nay." He called the vote the hardest he ever had to cast. In the end, 17 Republicans and 38 Democrats voted to deny confirmation.

Nixon said he regretted the Senate action and thought the nation regretted it too. From South Carolina a Haynsworth statement read in part: "The resolution is an unhappy one for me, but for our country's sake I hope the debate will prove to have been a cleansing agent . . . I must now consider whether my usefulness has been so impaired that I should leave the court and return to private life. . . ." Then, on Dec. 4, the President announced that Haynsworth would continue to serve as chief judge of the United States Court of Appeals for the Fourth Circuit—and called the attack on Haynsworth "brutal, vicious and . . . unfair."

$7.2 MILLION OIL CLAIMS PAID

The thick crude oil that blighted the beaches of Great Britain and France was cleaned up long ago and the ruptured ship Torrey Canyon from which millions of gallons of oil had escaped was bombed by warplanes after it had been abandoned (The World in 1967, 50–53). Its twisted hulk plunged beneath the Atlantic rollers, to grind to pieces on submerged rocks. But another chapter in the tragedy was to appear more than two years later: In Nov. 11 owners of the giant vessel paid $7.2 million, to be divided equally between England and France, in settling claims.

The 61,263-ton tanker was three times as long as a football field and the largest ship ever to sink in British waters during peacetime. The ship and her oil cargo were valued at $18 million. She ruptured March 18, 1967, when she hit the Seven Stones rocks off the southwest tip of

England and sent 123,000 tons of oil drifting into the English Channel. The escaped oil from the broken tanker slimed some 120 miles of Cornwall's beaches. England alone spent more than $7.2 million to clean up the mess, officials estimated. British Atty. Gen. Sir Elwyn Jones said the payment by the owners and charterers of the Torrey Canyon was "full and final settlement of the claims of the two governments." He added, however, that another $60,000 was set aside to compensate claimants not already reimbursed by their governments. The payment, he said, was made by Barracuda Tanker Corp., a subsidiary of Union Oil Co. of California, which had chartered the ship. Lloyd's insurance brokers said the settlement was believed the largest in maritime history involving oil claims.

Sir Elwyn told Parliament that damages from

the oil had been estimated at $14.4 million—twice the amount paid—by Britain and France, but added, "The owners denied liability and challenged the quantification of damages."

Meanwhile, the tides of oil which blackened the tawny beaches of Santa Barbara, Calif., in January (pages 33–35) resulted in a rash of damage suits seeking a total—conservatively estimated—of over $1 billion. They were filed by the City and County of Santa Barbara, the State of California, and hundreds of individuals.

Major defendants were the four oil companies holding the lease on the oil platform—Union, Gulf, Texaco, and Mobil.

Other defendants included the U.S. Geologic Survey, Interior Secretary Walter H. Hickel, and President Nixon's science advisor, Dr. Lee Dubridge.

"SPIRO WHO?" ZEROED IN

What a difference a year made. "Spiro who?" was a typical tongue-in-cheek critique in November 1968 of the man from Maryland who was elected Vice President of the United States. In November 1969 the name Spiro Agnew was rolling off tongues all across the nation.

The man who vaulted from the governor's office in Annapolis to one step from the Presidency spent most of his first year in Washington without attracting undue attention. Then, suddenly, his phrases made his name a household word and his person highly prized as a dinner speaker. During a New Orleans dinner emerged Agnew's oft-to-be-quoted description of Moratorium Day leaders as "an effete corps of impudent snobs who characterize themselves as intellectuals." While the nation was digesting those words, the Vice President took the electronic and printed news media to task.

In an after-dinner speech in Des Moines Agnew singled out the television networks' treatment of President Nixon's speech on Vietnam two weeks earlier, saying most of the commentators whose "minds were made up in advance" expressed "in one way or another, their hostility to what he (Nixon) had to say." While Agnew said he was not advocating censorship, he urged the public to make known its views on what he called bias by "a tiny and closed fraternity of privileged men, elected by no one, and enjoying a monopoly sanctioned and licensed by government."

The next week, in Montgomery, Ala., Agnew zeroed in on The New York Times and The Washington Post. Noting that the same people who publish the Post also own a radio station, a television station and Newsweek magazine, Agnew said: "I am merely pointing out that the public should be aware that these four powerful voices harken to the same master." Citing the demise of many daily newspapers in New York City, Agnew described the New York Times as being "a better newspaper when they were alive than it is now that they are gone." Agnew also declared that "lacking the vigor of competition, some of those that have survived have, let us face it, grown fat and irresponsible." He added that "just as a politician's words—wise and foolish—are dutifully recorded by the press and television to be thrown up to him at the appropriate time, so their words should likewise be recorded and likewise recalled."

In response, Mrs. Katherine Graham, president of the Washington Post Company, said: "each branch is operated autonomously. . . ." She said the four operations "compete vigorously with one another . . . disagree on many issues." Said Arthur Ochs Sulzberger, president and publisher of The New York Times: "Vice President Agnew is entitled to express his point of view, but he is in error when he implies that The New York Times ever sought or enjoyed immunity from comment and criticism. Indeed, all American institutions from the press to the Presidency should be subjects of free and open debate."

Dr. Frank Stanton, president of the Columbia Broadcasting System, called the Des Moines speech an "unprecedented attempt by the Vice President of the United States to intimidate a news medium which depends for its existence upon government licenses." Julian Goodman, president of the National Broadcasting Co., called Agnew's speech "an appeal to prejudice" and charged that the Vice President wanted "to deny to TV the freedom of the press." Leonard H. Goldenson, president of the American Broadcasting Co., said, "We will continue to report the news accurately and fully, confident in the ultimate judgment of the American public."

A random sampling of 21 radio and television stations a day after the speech indicated that callers had supported Agnew more than 2 to 1. The night the newspapers were attacked the New York Times received 140 telephone calls—58 supporting Agnew, 81 supporting the Times. At the Washington Post 216 calls were received; 129 supported the Vice President, 87 agreed with the Post.

Meanwhile, Washington observers debated whether Agnew was reflecting the Administration's views, acting as President Nixon's sounding board or speaking strictly on his own. Agnew aides held that what he did, he did alone. Others tended to take the view of the man who preceded Agnew:

"Anyone who thinks that the Vice President can take a position independent of the President or his Administration simply has no knowledge of politics or government," said Hubert H. Humphrey in an interview. "You are his choice in a political marriage, and he expects your absolute loyalty."

Vice President Spiro T. Agnew made a prayerful gesture as he discussed news media coverage

UPSETS MARK ELECTIONS

There was a believe-it-or-not quality about some scattered November elections. Republicans scored rags-to-riches victories in Virginia, winning the governorship for the first time in more than 80 years, and they also took the New Jersey statehouse after 16 years of Democratic rule. In New York City, Mayor John V. Lindsay, who looked down-and-out after losing the Republican primary, bounced back to win a second term as a Liberal-Independent candidate.

In the major upset of the off-year elections, Linwood Holton defeated Democrat William C. Battle for the Virginia governorship and became the first Republican to win the office since 1882. President Nixon campaigned for Holton and urged Virginia to set an example for the entire south by breaking with the Democratic tradition.

The President also campaigned for William T. Cahill, who beat Democrat Robert B. Meyner in the race for the New Jersey governorship.

The two victories gave the Republicans 32 governorships and left the Democrats with 18. In hailing the GOP victories, the President suggested they indicated a favorable reaction to his election eve report on Vietnam policy.

Lindsay, who campaigned under the slogan: "It's the second toughest job in America," said of his victory, "I won in New York City as an independent. It obviously means that the tradition of electing a candidate of one of the two major parties—and in New York City usually a Democrat—has been overcome." Lindsay defeated City Comptroller Mario Procaccino, the Democrat who finished second, and State Sen. John Marchi, who placed third with Republican and Conservative party votes.

Lindsay's political fortunes apparently had fallen to a low point after a teachers' strike in the fall of 1968 (The World in 1968, 261) which raised tensions between the non-white com-munities and the predominantly Jewish teachers' union. But he managed to regain much of the Jewish support he had used to win election four years earlier (The World in 1965, 220–221) after a year of relative calm in racial relations. The mayor, all but doomed when he lost the GOP nomination to Marchi, trailed badly early in the mayoralty campaign but thereafter he built a polished and expensive organization that overcame Procaccino's law and order strategy.

A second term also was won by Cleveland Democrat Carl B. Stokes, who had become the first Negro mayor of a major American city in 1967 (The World in 1967, 240). Stokes, the grandson of a slave and a high school dropout who later earned a law degree, got needed support from white voters to beat his Republican challenger, Ralph J. Perk, who sought to become Cleveland's first Republican mayor in 28 years. In Detroit, Wayne County Sheriff Roman Gribbs won the city's nonpartisan election for mayor by beating Richard Austin, a Negro, in a race that was the first in Detroit history matching white and black nominees. Democratic incumbent Frank A. Sedita achieved an unprecedented third term as mayor of Buffalo, New York's second largest city, by defeating a Republican conservative, Mrs. Alfreda Slominski, and Ambrose I. Lane, a Negro independent.

In other November races, Peter F. Flaherty, an independent Democrat, beat Republican John Tabor for mayor of Pittsburgh; Ann Uccello was re-elected mayor of Hartford, Conn., over Democrat Joseph Adinolfi, and in New Orleans, Jim Garrison, who became a center of controversy for his handling of a John F. Kennedy assassination probe (The World in 1967, 212–214, pages 36–38), won the Democratic nomination for district attorney. But Garrison faced another contest, against Republican Phil Trice, in the April 1970 general election.

Re-elected: New York Mayor John V. Lindsay

BOMBS: BLOWS FOR LIBERATION?

The time was a few minutes after one o'clock in the morning. Most New Yorkers were asleep. But Joseph Brando, 26, a maintenance worker, stood in a freight elevator in the new 50-story General Motors Building in the heart of tower-studded Manhattan. There were diners in a restaurant high up in the 70-story RCA Building in midtown Manhattan. Carmella Giannone was among 1,300 persons at work in the 60-story Chase Manhattan Building in the downtown financial district.

At about 1:05 a.m., Nov. 11, a bomb exploded in each of the skyscrapers, all in or near elevator shafts, causing heavy damage but no fire.

Brando's elevator bucked and plunged downward for six floors. It stopped at the 11th floor. Brando escaped. The bomb had gone off on the 19th floor.

Carmella Giannone, an instructor at the Chase Manhattan Bank, was working on the 20th floor when a policeman entered, explained the building was threatened, and began a search. "Seconds later," she said, "we heard the explosion." The bomb had gone off on the 16th floor.

At the RCA Building—the city's fifth highest building and sixth tallest in the country—the blast on the 20th floor "would have killed anybody there," said Deputy Fire Chief Anthony Costa. The explosion sent one elevator tumbling to the ground floor and knocked out four of the building's eight high-rise elevators. Some of the diners and dancers in the 65th floor restaurant walked down to the street.

Each of the explosions occurred minutes after telephoned warnings. About six hours later letters reached some of the news media. They spoke of international problems allegedly caused by large American corporations and added: "From the inside, black people have been fighting a revolution for years. And finally, from the heart of the empire, white Americans, too, are striking blows of liberation."

The next night an explosion shattered walls in a washroom at the Criminal Courts Building. The bomb—on the fifth floor of the 20-story structure—went off while night court was in session, and the building was evacuated. The series of blasts had started four months earlier. Among them were: the bombing of a United Fruit Co. pier July 27, the Marine Midland Grace Trust Co. Aug. 20, the Federal Office Building Sept. 19, and the Armed Forces Induction Center Oct. 7. They caused a score of injuries—19 were hurt in the Marine Midland explosion—but no deaths. Property damage was estimated at $250,000.

Besides the actual bombings, a rash of crank calls and false alarms, as many as 75 in a day, led to the evacuation of such places as the Queens Criminal Court Building, the New York Stock Exchange visitors' gallery, the New York Times Building, and a Penn Central passenger train. Police said "nearly 100 per cent" of the 17,000 people in the 59-story Pan Am Building poured out after one threat. No bomb was found. On the night of Oct. 11 a series of fires started in the giant Macy's Department Store, apparently from small incendiary devices. Similar devices were found in a Bronx department store, Alexander's, Nov. 9 but did not go off.

Two men arrested the night of Nov. 12 were accused of attempting to place dynamite bombs in an Army truck parked outside a Manhattan armory. They were identified as Samuel J. Melville, 34, and George Demmerle, 39. Two others, John D. Hughey III and Jane L. Alpert, both 22, were arrested later. The four were indicted Nov. 18 on Federal charges of conspiring to damage government property with planted explosives. The complaint specified only the bombings of the Federal Office Building, the Armed Forces Induction Center, and the attempt to plant bombs in Army trucks.

Demmerle's bail originally was $500,000. Subsequently he was freed without bail, and later a Federal Court witness testified Demmerle was a volunteer FBI informant.

"A MORE MATURE PARTNERSHIP"

Some four months after Nelson A. Rockefeller returned from his violence-punctuated fact-finding trip to 20 Latin American nations, the text of the New York governor's report was released by President Nixon, who called it the most comprehensive of all Latin American studies commissioned by U.S. presidents over the past 20 years. More than 80 recommendations contained in the report were aimed at dealing with the economic and social situations in the area Rockefeller visited May 11–July 6 (page 133) and at improving its relations with the United States.

The report, delivered to the President Sept. 3 and released by him Nov. 10, contained one major recommendation that had not been disclosed by Nixon in an Oct. 31 speech on hemispheric problems: Creation of a Western Hemisphere Security Council to deal with the "forces of subversion" in Latin America. While noting that "a new type of military man is coming to the fore and often becoming a major force for constructive social change in the American republics," Rockefeller added that to many of them

Marxism seemed a feasible alternative for solving many of the problems of the area. "The essential question," he said, "is which way is this leadership going to go. By cooperation I believe we can strengthen the forces of democracy."

Referring to the recommended security council, Rockefeller suggested it be based outside of the United States, but added: "In view of the growing subversion against hemisphere governments, the mounting terrorism and violence against citizens, and the rapidly expanding population, it is essential the training program which brings military and police personnel from other hemisphere nations to the United States and to training centers in Panama be continued and strengthened." The purpose of the council, he said, "would be to help the hemisphere countries work together in creating and preserving the kind of orderly environment, free from terror and violence, in which each citizen of each country can build a better life for himself and his family."

In releasing the report, Nixon said his administration had liberalized trade and aid policies

toward Latin America under active consideration. One proposal under study, the President said, would liberalize debt repayment on the condition the money saved under such a plan be used for development purposes. A second, if efforts for a global reduction of trade barriers failed, would extend trade preferences to Latin America on a regional basis. The President, in his Oct. 31 speech—broadcast live by satellite to 11 Latin American nations—urged the nations of the Western Hemisphere to join in a partnership. "What I hope we can achieve," he said, "is a more mature partnership in which all voices are heard and none is predominant—a partnership guided by a healthy awareness that give-and-take is better than take-it-or-leave-it."

While expressing a preference for democratic procedures, the President said, "We must deal realistically with governments in the inter-American system as they are"—a remark that was interpreted in some quarters as meaning the United States would deal on an essentially equal basis with both democratic and dictatorial governments.

TRANSATLANTIC "CHARTER"

"There's a man here who wants to go some place, and he's just chartered himself a plane," Capt. Donald Cook of TWA flight 85 called over the craft's intercom. "Drinks are on the house." Facetious as it sounded, Cook's announcement to his passengers nonetheless was made while a boyishly handsome youth held a gun at the flight engineer's head.

"Right away I suspected we would be heading south to pick up a few cigars," pilot Cook said later, "but that wasn't the way it was."

The commercial jetliner, hijacked over California en route from Los Angeles to San Francisco, was one of more than 50 airplanes to be commandeered in the United States in 1969, but unlike most others this one was not going to Cuba.

Rafael Minichiello, 20-year-old U.S. Marine lance corporal, told the pilot to head for New York. However, his ultimate destination wasn't learned until nearly 17 hours and 6,900 miles later, when the longest and one of the most bizarre hijackings in aviation history ended in Rome. James Findlay, a TWA pilot who was among the passengers, said Italian-born Minichiello forced his way into the plane's cockpit by holding stewardess Charlene Delmonico at gunpoint. Cook suggested that the plane could make better time eastward if the 39 passengers disembarked during a refueling stop at Denver. The hijacker acquiesced.

Ground personnel at the Denver airport made no attempt to apprehend Minichiello, but it was a different scene when the plane landed at New York's Kennedy International Airport. Cook had already suspected that Minichiello was determined to leave the continent. He told the youth he was not qualified to pilot transoceanic flights, and Minichiello had agreed to let two replacement pilots come aboard in New York. Neither Cook nor Minichiello had thought that FBI agents might be on hand. "We had arranged that there would be a minimum ground crew when he landed at Kennedy," Cook said later. "When we got there, there was the car with the replacement crew, but there were also many other vehicles and many other men."

Some were dressed as mechanics, but Cook said it was obvious to him they were FBI agents, and when they continued to move toward the plane Minichiello panicked, firing a shot into the ceiling of the cockpit. The bullet bounced off an oxygen bottle and did not puncture the fuselage.

Cook subsequently criticized authorities for "destroying the good faith (in Minichiello) we had built up for almost six hours." The supposed agents did not interfere, however. With the replacement pilots aboard—along with stewardess Tracey Coleman, who had volunteered in Denver to stay with the plane—the craft refueled again at Bangor, Maine, and headed across the Atlantic. Yet another touchdown for fuel took place at Shannon, Ireland, and finally Minichiello's purpose was confirmed: the jet was streaking over Leonardo da Vinci Airport outside Rome.

Minichiello instructed the control tower to direct the plane to a remote parking area and to send an unarmed policeman aboard. Police Chief Pietro Guli, who volunteered to board the plane, became Minichiello's hostage. They finally got off together, and Guli said Minichiello then forced him to drive several miles into the Italian countryside. There the policeman was released.

More than four hours later, the youth was apprehended in a church, just a mile from the Via Appia Antica. "Why did I do it?" the youth wondered aloud after his arrest. "I don't know."

The most often heard explanation was that Minichiello had returned to his homeland to avoid court martial on a charge of breaking into a post exchange. His sister Anna said, "I think the war damaged my brother's mind."

The United States and Italy filed charges against Minichiello on Nov. 1, but Italian officials said Minichiello would stand trial there, charged with hijacking, armed threats and illegal possession of arms. In the United States federal charges of hijacking, kidnaping and interference with a commercial airliner were placed against him. The maximum penalty on conviction in the United States would be death, whereas the worst Minichiello could expect in Italy would be 30 years imprisonment.

FOR THE RECORD

SIGNED. By the United States and the Soviet Union on Nov. 24, a treaty aimed at preventing the spread of nuclear weapons. The treaty was ratified by the U.S. Senate March 13, but President Nixon delayed signing until the two major nuclear powers could do so simultaneously. The treaty commits the U.S., Britain and the Soviet Union to refrain from giving other nations nuclear weapons, control over such weapons, or assistance in their development.

STAGED. The second largest cash robbery in United States history, on Nov. 13, when three men ambushed a Wells Fargo armored car and made off with $1,377,000 in used bills but left behind another $300,000 because the money bags wouldn't fit in the trunk of their getaway car. The armored car, making an eight-mile run from Aqueduct Race Track to a midtown Manhattan bank, was waylaid in Brooklyn when it stopped at a delicatessen. The gunmen disarmed and bound the three guards, drove the armored car a few blocks away, then loaded money bags into their getaway car and escaped. The largest theft was $1,551,277 from a mail truck Aug. 15, 1962, in Plymouth, Mass.

SENTENCED. Army Pvt. Jeffrey Russell, one of the so-called "Ft. Dix (N.J.) 38," a group of GIs charged with various offenses stemming from a June 5 stockade riot, to three years in prison and a dishonorable discharge on Nov. 10 for rioting and arson. Russell, 20, in the stockade at the time of the riot after being convicted of desertion, maintained throughout the court martial he had nothing to do with the uprising. He and others claimed it resulted from mistreatment of prisoners. Another private, Thomas Catlow, 18, was dishonorably discharged Nov. 20 and a third, Terry Klug, was acquitted.

ELECTED. Ferdinand E. Marcos, the first Philippine president to win a second four-year term Marcos, who headed the Nationalist Party ticket, handily defeated Senator Sergio Osmena Jr. who ran on the Liberal ticket, Nov. 11.

Actress Sharon Tate: A victim in mass slaying ⟶

December

Sharon Tate and Friends: They Rivaled Films as Victims of Grotesque Mass Murder

Even Hollywood recoiled in horror when "the Beautiful People" met death, police said, at hands of hippie-style cult dedicated to purge the wealthy of materialism

EVEN WITH help from Roman Polanski, European master of the macabre, Hollywood couldn't have envisioned a film more shocking, found victims more exciting or created murders more grotesque: A young actress with hair the color of honey, in a bikini nightgown and a bra; her former boyfriend, an internationally-known hair stylist; a bright, witty Polish playboy, jet-set lover of luxury; the playboy's brunette friend, socialite heiress to a coffee fortune, and a teen-age boy nobody knew—stabbed, shot and sprawled in and around a rambling, $200,000, tomato-red mansion with "PIG" smeared on the door in blood.

They were among "the beautiful people," luxuriating in the mansion in Benedict Canyon, hidden in the hills where the stars live. And Hollywood, jaded by its make-believe violence, recoiled in horror. Los Angeles, the nation and the world were shaken. Even Hanoi took note, and propagandized the killings as examples of American decadence.

But the biggest shock was yet to come, when police arrested two young men and four young women. They turned out, detectives reported, to be members of a roving, hippie-style "family"—mostly girls—and their leader, a hairy, wild-eyed Svengali, known to his followers as "Jesus," "God" and "Satan," who were bent, one of the "family" said, on purging the rich of their materialism.

For police the carnage recalled the slaughter of a Kansas farm family, chronicled in Truman Capote's *"In Cold Blood,"* and the 1966 killing of eight nurses in Chicago (*The World in 1966, 132–135; 232*). It pushed the unsolved 1922 shooting of film director William Desmond Taylor into second place as The Great Hollywood Murder.

It had a savagery all its own. Some members of the "family" killed a wealthy merchant couple the night after the actress and her friends died, lawyers said, because "Svengali" wasn't completely satisfied with the performance the night before.

It had a touch of mocking macabre beyond Polanski's wildest nightmares. At a London cocktail party, the Polish director, whose film characters are kinky with killing, sex and black magic, remarked about the recent death of a friend.

"Eeny, meeny, miney, mo, who will be the next to go?" he asked.

The telephone rang; he thus learned about the Hollywood slayings, and that the dead actress was his wife.

He collapsed in tears.

It was at the tomato-red home Polanski had rented for his Hollywood visits that a housemaid, Winifred Chapman, reported for work the morning of Aug. 9, saw the butchery and ran downhill to a neighbor screaming: "There's bodies and blood all over the place!"

Sirens pierced the warm quiet. Police arrived, investigated, ticked off the names of the dead:

Sharon Tate, 26, co-star in the movie *"Valley of the Dolls,"* 8½ months pregnant, her baby boy dead inside her; Jay Sebring, 35, whose $50-a-haircut clients included Frank Sinatra, Paul Newman, Henry Fonda and Steve McQueen; Wojieiech "Voityck" Frykowski, 37, Polish friend of Polanski and, police said, a known user of marijuana, and Abigail Folger, 26, of the Folger Coffee family of San Francisco, an honor graduate of Radcliffe College who met Frykowski when she joined the jet set.

It took police a while longer to find out the dead boy was Steven Parent, 18, a sturdy, red-haired high school graduate from suburban El Monte.

He had been visiting the estate's 19-year-old caretaker, who was his friend. "I just don't understand," said the dead boy's father, Wilfred, 44, a construction superintendent. "It don't make any damned sense. Steve wasn't a poshy kid. I didn't even know he knew any of those people." The night after Steven was found, said the elder Parent, "the wife and I finally put the kids in bed with us and the five of us just held onto each other and cried until we went to sleep."

Detectives declared the Polanski estate off-limits, but described what they found inside: a white nylon cord looped loosely around Miss Tate's neck, thrown over a ceiling beam

Indicted in the slayings of actress Sharon Tate and four friends (left to right): Patricia Krenwinkel, 21; Charles D. Watson, 24; Susan Denise Atkins, 21, and Linda Kasabian, 20. They also were charged in the murders a day later of a grocer and his wife.

and hanging limply around Sebring's neck; a hood-like cloth over Sebring's head, and an American flag draped over the back of a sofa.

"It almost looked like a ritual," a police sergeant said.

Whatever it had been, Frykowski and Miss Folger apparently had tried to flee. He was found on the lawn at the end of long, bloody crawl marks; she was in a nightgown under a fir tree where she had fallen 20 yards away.

In his cottage beyond shrubbery and a swimming pool, officers arrested the young caretaker, William Garretson. He said his friend Parent had arrived about 11:45 p.m., to show him a new radio, and had left about half an hour later. Garretson said he had heard no shots and his face wrinkled with horror as police led him past the bodies. He said he wasn't even aware there had been any killings. Questioned and released—"There is no reason to suspect him," an inspector said—Garretson returned to Lancaster, Ohio, his hometown, and said he had decided to go to college.

Then with the gruesome details in Benedict Canyon still vivid, police made another shocking discovery—the bodies of the merchant and his wife, Leno and Rosemary LaBianca, 44 and 38, owners of a grocery chain, stabbed and slashed in their home.

Somebody had carved "WAR" and three big "X"s into LaBianca's chest and smeared "Death to Pigs" on the refrigerator door in blood.

Detectives spent days combing the Polanski estate and the LaBianca home, eight miles away in Los Angeles' Los Feliz district. They traveled thousands of miles questioning more than 400 persons in the United States and Canada.

"The more we think about the whole thing, the more baffling it becomes," one detective said. "We've got a helluva mystery on our hands" *(Page 191).*

It remained a mystery for months. In October police said they had found a pair of eyeglasses with tortoise-shell rims at the Polanski home. Detectives figured one of the slayers had dropped them. But the clue wasn't very helpful. The frames and prescriptions were fairly common.

About the same time, a dozen sheriff's deputies and highway patrolmen raided a hippie-style commune in the hills edging Death Valley, 350 miles away. They found women nude or nearly nude, dune buggies with machine gun mounts, walkie talkies and military-like observation posts. Taken into custody on charges relating to auto theft (the dune buggies, deputies said, were made from stolen Volkswagens) were the leader of the commune, Charles M. Manson, 35, his hair and beard a straggly black halo around his mustachioed face; Susan Denise Atkins, 21, known in the commune as "Sadie Mae Glutz," a choir girl turned amateur go-go dancer; and pretty dark-haired Leslie Louise Van Houten, 19.

Miss Atkins was brought to Los Angeles, where she was charged with murder in the slaying of Malibu musician Gary Hinman. She was put into a cell with Shelly Joyce Nadell, 31, charged with forging prescriptions to obtain narcotics. Then detectives got their biggest break.

Miss Atkins told her cellmate about the Tate and LaBianca slayings. And her cellmate told investigators.

Whereupon stolid, gray Police Chief Edward M. Davis called a news conference. He announced warrants for the arrest of three other members of Manson's "family"—Charles D. "Tex" Watson, 24, Patricia Krenwinkel, 22, and Linda Kasabian, 20. Davis said 40 detectives had spent 8,750 hours on the case.

The telephone rang in "Tex" Watson's home at Copeville, Tex. His parents answered, and young Watson's cousin, the county sheriff, told them about the warrants. Watson, remembered by friends as a high school football, basketball and track star and "a good boy, not the sort to get in trouble," went to the sheriff's office and waited for California officers.

Miss Krenwinkel, daughter of an insurance agent in the Los Angeles suburb of Inglewood, had been arrested in August under the name "Mary Ann Scott" for investigation of auto theft and murder in the Hinman slaying. She had been released without charge, went to Alabama, where she had attended Spring Hill College for a semester in the fall of 1966, and police found her in Mobile. She pulled a ruffled hat over her face when they rearrested her.

Mrs. Kasabian, mother of an 18-month-old daughter and five months pregnant, surrendered at the home of friends in Concord, N.H. The whereabouts of her husband, Robert, wasn't known. Friends at a commune in Taos, N.M., described her as "a nice person, very innocent."

Manson and Miss Van Houten were brought from jail in the tiny town of Independence, Calif., near Death Valley, to Los Angeles. Manson wore handcuffs and buckskin clothing and his reddish-brown hair fell in a tangle over his shoulders.

On Dec. 8 the Los Angeles County grand jury indicted all but Miss Van Houten on five counts of murder in the Tate slayings and one count of conspiracy to commit murder. Miss Van Houten was indicted on one count of conspiracy to commit murder and—along with the others—two counts of murder in the LaBianca slayings.

Prosecutors began preparing their case.

From Miss Atkins, who cooperated hoping for leniency, and from her cellmate, two deputy district attorneys assigned to the case pieced together a story about what had happened.

The cellmate's attorney said she told him she had learned that "family" members "felt the stabbings and the brutal cuttings would help release the souls of the victims." The killers, he reported his client as saying, "were all on acid (LSD) and the more they stabbed the more they enjoyed it."

One of Miss Atkins' attorneys quoted her as saying the killers wore black clothing they called their "creepy-crawlies." The attorney gave this account based on a five-hour interview with her:

"One man had a gun. The girls had knives. They parked the car so they could get away quickly. A man with wire cutters went up a pole and cut utility lines outside the Tate house. They saw Parent starting to leave. He got into his car and was shot. A man went through an open window, then opened the front door. The others went inside. Frykowski was lying on the couch. Sharon Tate and Sebring were talking in her bedroom. The Folger girl was in another bedroom, reading a book. Tate and Sebring were told to stay in the bedroom. Then they were brought out. Miss Tate became very apprehensive.

"She wanted to make sure her baby was not harmed. That was virtually all she pleaded about, 'Let me have my baby.' But she was killed. Sebring said very little. He was killed. Frykowski attempted to escape. As he ran through the front door he was hit on the head with a gun butt. Miss Folger handed them all the money she had, $73, and they took it and killed her and Frykowski anyway."

Another of Miss Atkins' attorneys said he had learned a reason for the slayings was to "liberate" the victims from their materialism.

The attorney said Miss Atkins had been "hypnotized" and "intrigued" into joining Manson's "family" and "had nothing to do with the murders" because she was under Manson's "hypnotic spell" at the time.

Sharon's father, Paul J. Tate, left Army intelligence to hunt killers

Susan Denise Atkins: Acted under "hypnotic spell"?

244

In custody: Charles Manson, 35, cult leader accused in slayings

Some of Manson's friends told about his "hypnotic" attraction. "He was magnetic," said Sandra Good Pugh, 26, a member of the clan. "His motions were like magic."

"We belong to him," Miss Atkins' attorneys quoted her as saying. "Not to outselves."

"He believes that he and all human beings are God and the devil at the same time," said Brooks Poston, 21, who followed Manson for two years. "He belives all human beings are part of each other."

"You see what that means?" said Paul Crockett, 50, a miner who knew Manson in Death Valley. "It means that human life has no value. If you kill a human being, you are just killing a part of yourself. So it's all right."

From prison and parole records, prosecutors pieced together the portrait of a small-time hood. Born to an unwed 16-year-old girl in Cincinnati, Ohio, Manson had lived with his maternal grandmother, then an aunt and uncle. He ran away from a boys' school, landed in a correctional institution and had spent 13 years in reformatories and prisons by the time he was 25. His convictions: auto theft, forgery, transporting women across state lines for prostitution. No killing.

Out of prison on parole, he married and fathered a son—but by the time the boy was born, he was back in jail. His wife divorced him. And he took up the guitar and the occult.

They helped open a new world on his next parole. Manson discovered the hippie life. He went to San Francisco's Haight-Ashbury district and acquired a following, mostly girls.

Then he moved, "family" and all, to a ranch full of old movie sets north of Los Angeles. Deputies raided the place shortly after the Tate and LaBianca killings, but made arrests only for prostitution and drug allegations. Shortly after, Manson moved his "family" to Death Valley.

Among other things, Manson fancied himself a "roving minstrel" and budding song writer. His guitar and a slow, deliberate, moody way of moving gave him hypnotic power over women, said Poston and Crockett.

"This sort of power takes a long time to work to an effect," Crockett said. "Motions are tied to emotions. Certain motions create certain responses if you know how to use them."

"The whole thing was held together by black magic," said Paul Watkins, 19, another who followed Manson for about two years. "You don't belive it? Well, it really exists, and it is powerful."

It matched Roman Polanski's films. In "Rosemary's Baby," a young woman is betrayed by her husband into being raped by the devil, whose diabolical child she bears. In "Repulsion," a psychotic young woman is driven by an abnormal fear and loathing of sex to commit murders of savage ferocity.

It matched Sharon Tate's performances. In "The Dance of the Vampires," she bathed nude. If making love on screen could be done "as a thing of beauty and not embarrassment," she said, "then I would do it with pleasure." In the movie "13" she played a witch in a story of ritualistic murder done by a hooded sect of devil worshippers.

And it matched their romance. Shortly after they met, Polanski and Miss Tate ate dinner late one night in his apartment. Polanski excused himself from the room and put on a Frankenstein mask. Then he crept up behind her, raised his arms and gave a blood-curdling moan.

Miss Tate screamed. Then she wept for an hour.

245

Single Vote Won Victory for ABM

*But bitter four-month battle between party coalitions
ended Congress-Pentagon "honeymoon"*

For more than four months, two great coalitions squared off in the United States Senate. The issue: whether the United States should deploy an antiballistic missile (ABM) defense system.

The coalitions, for the most part, were the familiar ones— Republicans and Southern Democrats on one side, Northern Democrats and moderate Republicans on the other—that have contested most of the nation's major domestic issues of the past three decades.

But, for the first time, the issue was one of national security —and the bitter battle that climaxed Aug. 6 in a one-vote victory for President Nixon and his Safeguard ABM symbolized the end of the decades-long honeymoon between Congress and the Pentagon.

Coming amid widespread national frustration and disillusionment over the continuing war in Vietnam, the ABM fight was more than just the first congressional challenge in memory to a major weapons system sought by the Pentagon. It threw down the gauntlet to what critics called the "military-industrial complex" in a struggle to bring defense matters under the same close scrutiny it had given major domestic social programs.

The effort was complicated by the intricacies, both technical and political, of battling through layers of Pentagon secrecy, and, in large measure, the Senate revolt ended in immediate failure.

The ABM was approved, as were such other controversial proposals as the C5A super transport, the CVAN-69 nuclear attack carrier and the Advanced Manned Strategic Aircraft (AMSA), a new long-range Air Force bomber. Efforts to restrict chemical and biological warfare (CBW) and the billions of dollars of defense contracts were at best only partially successful.

But the groundwork was laid for future battles, a major goal of the effort. As Senate Democratic Leader Mike Mansfield put it, "A lot of us have become more educated, more aware. It's been an educational round, a good one."

There were these further developments:

—The Senate Armed Services Committee, under its new chairman, Mississippi Democrat John C. Stennis, undertook its most extensive examination of the defense budget in years and set up new machinery to keep tighter scrutiny over defense contracts and research, and to watch closely for signs of massive cost overruns on some ships, missiles and planes.

—Opponents, previously outmaneuvered on the Senate floor by Armed Services Committee members who were far better educated on the technical details of military matters, formed discussion groups, brought in outside speakers and started to educate themselves.

—The Pentagon, noting the growing congressional demand

for defense cuts, sought to keep one step ahead of Congress. By the end of November it had cut some $2.4 billion from the $81.1 billion Johnson defense budget—including plans for 300 base closings or reductions, retirement of 11 ships and 86 B58 bombers, and a force reduction of 220,000 men. The last alone would bring an eventual $2.2 billion annual saving. By the end of the fiscal year June 30, 1970, it hoped to have held spending to $77 billion despite the fact that in the first quarter (July to September) it was running at an annual rate of $80.3 billion.

—Individual crusades by Rep. Richard D. McCarthy, D-N.Y., and Sen. Frank E. Moss, D-Utah, blossomed into a full-scale effort to limit the bugs and germs of the nation's CBW program. Congress finally passed a modest restriction, with gaping loopholes, but President Nixon went far beyond it in committing the nation to a halt in testing of offensive CBW weapons and a reduction in CBW stockpiles.

—Despite revelations that the cost of the C5A transport had skyrocketed from about $3 billion to about $5 billion, Congress rejected efforts to cut back the planned 120-plane force. But the Air Force reduced it to 81 as costs threatened to go even higher.

—Amid criticism of duplication between the Pentagon and the National Aeronautics and Space Agency, Secretary of Defense Melvin R. Laird eliminated the program for a Manned Orbiting Laboratory—an immediate half-billion dollar saving.

But Laird, the most politically attuned secretary of defense thanks to 16 years in the House, warned:

"I want the American people to know that there will be an inevitable weakening of our world wide military posture."

And the secretary made it clear that, if anyone was to blame, it was Congress.

There were many reasons why, all of a sudden, a full-scale assault on Pentagon spending developed in 1969. One, Sen. Edmund S. Muskie, D-Maine, said, was the cumulative effect of the government's inability to settle the Vietnam war.

"Today," Muskie continued, "the average citizen wants to know what the choices are and, as he is exposed to them, he begins to become more skeptical about the choices that were made for him by the establishment in the past.

"He begins to discover that those he trusted with the responsibility in the past weren't as wise in their judgments as he thought they were."

Sen. Stuart Symington, D-Mo., a longtime supporter of the Pentagon turned critic, gave another reason: "There has been too much mystery, too much classification, too much secrecy which, at times, is a way of covering up."

Fiscal arguments, including the cost of weapons, became

increasingly prominent, fueled by the continuing disclosure of cost overruns at a time Americans were paying a 10 per cent surcharge on top of their regular income taxes.

Then too, it became known that military planners were drawing blueprints for an entire arsenal of new weapons systems—bombers, missiles and ships—that would quickly use up any funds freed by the possible end of the Vietnam war, money that otherwise could be transferred to domestic programs.

Thus, lawmakers from the industrial states saw the "Great Society" domestic programs they had backed in fields such as education, health and poverty withering for lack of funds despite growing federal revenues from years of economic growth and inflation. They trained their sights on the $80 billion defense budget—some 40 per cent of all federal spending.

Urban-minded Democrats entered the battle with new spirit since the foe was now the GOP administration of Richard M. Nixon.

Hanging over all of this was the arms race, and the widespread fear that decisions to deploy multi-headed MIRV (Multiple Independently-Targeted Re-entry Vehicles) offensive missiles and the ABM, a defensive weapon, would escalate the arms competition between the United States and the Soviet Union to a dangerous and costly new level.

A move to curb U.S. tests of the multiple warheads as an initiative in seeking an arms control agreement with the Soviet Union failed to make much progress. The issue became an important one for the Strategic Arms Limitation Talks (SALT) that began Nov. 17 in Helsinki, Finland, but the likelihood of any agreement was hindered by the fact that U.S. testing had entered its final stages with deployment of MIRVs planned for mid-1970.

Thus, the ABM, authorized originally in 1968 during the administration of former President Lyndon B. Johnson, became the focus of the fight between Congress and the Pentagon as an expensive weapon that might accelerate the arms race but that was so little advanced it could still be stopped.

The first sign of public interest in the ABM came at the start of the year in a series of public hearings, set up for Army officials to explain how they planned to protect major U.S. cities with ABMs in the suburbs of Boston, Chicago and Seattle, Wash.

Each hearing brought an outburst of public opposition. Congressmen from the suburban districts called on the Army to move the ABM bases, and even the late Sen. Everett McKinley Dirksen, R-Ill., a longtime Pentagon supporter, indicated doubts about the ABM.

On Feb. 4, Sen. Edward M. Kennedy, D-Mass., led a broad attack in the Senate on the ABM and, just two days later, the Pentagon let it be known Laird had held up the Johnson ad-ministration's ABM—called Sentinel—pending a review of the project.

"We in the Congress—with the notable exception of a few of our colleagues—have been remiss in bearing our responsibilities," Kennedy said. "National defense programs have somehow been above the battle—it has always been implicit in many of our debates that it is perhaps unpatriotic to question the recommendations of the Department of Defense."

Polls showed more than 40 senators opposed deployment of the Sentinel ABM, half that number in favor and the other 40 undecided.

In the House, where the coalition of rural Republicans and Southern Democrats held sway, opponents mustered only 105 members in their high water anti-ABM effort.

On March 14, President Nixon announced that the ABM was being revised to emphasize defense of U.S. missile and bomber bases, rather than cities, with the first sites to be completed at Grand Forks, N.D., Air Force Base and Malmstrom Air Force Base near Great Falls, Mont., far from the centers of urban-suburban opposition.

This change had little effect on the Senate outlook. Sens. John Sherman Cooper, R-Ky., and Philip A. Hart, D-Mich., said they would continue their efforts against the newly renamed Safeguard ABM. A handful of Republican senators abandoned either opposition or neutrality to back the President, but a solid 40 senators remained opposed. Positions did polarize to the extent that almost all of the Senate's top Republicans supported the ABM while the top Democrats opposed it.

Opponents contended the Safeguard system, budgeted at about $7 billion, would cost more than twice that much; that its components were untested and ill-suited for the type of defense planned; that the system's computers were too complicated to work; that its radars were especially vulnerable, and that its approval would spur the arms race and hamper chances of a U.S.-Soviet agreement.

The administration's director of communications, Herbert Klein, launched a propaganda drive aimed at the country at large, with special emphasis on the media, while Sens. Henry Jackson, D-Wash., and John G. Tower, R-Tex., became the bipartisan captains of the pro-ABM troops, both in the Armed Services Committee and on the floor.

Proponents said the ABM was worth its cost to keep the Soviets from achieving the capability to launch a "first strike" against the United States; that tests of its components—missiles, radars and computers—were going well; that American know-how could make the complex system work; that it gave the President a choice other than massive retaliation in event of an attack, and that it would help arms control talks by putting

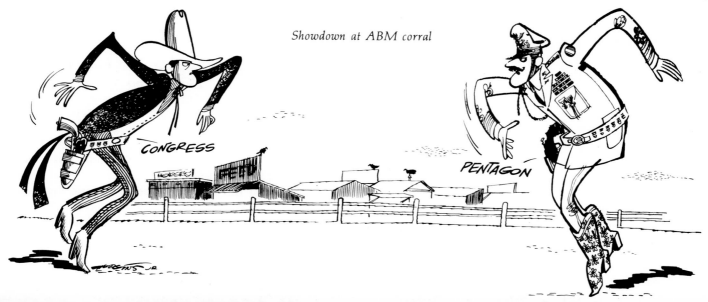

Showdown at ABM corral

CONGRESS

PENTAGON

the United States in a position of strength from which to negotiate.

On June 27, the ABM won approval from the Armed Services Committee by a 10-7 vote—closest ever on a major weapons system. By the time it reached the Senate floor July 7 as part of a $20 billion-plus authorization bill, the 50-50 tie that finally emerged was in sight. On July 10, the balance appeared to tip against the ABM when Sen. George D. Aiken, R-Vt., came out in opposition. But the following Monday, his junior GOP colleague, Winston L. Prouty, announced he would support the President.

Though the breakdown remained close to traditional liberal-conservative lines, four liberal Northern Democrats joined the generally conservative pro-ABM camp: Jackson, Sens. John O. Pastore, D-R.I., a senior member of the Joint Atomic Energy Committee; and Thomas J. Dodd, D-Conn., and Gale McGee, D-Wyo., hawkish members of the Foreign Relations Committee.

ABM proponents waged an intensive but futile battle for the votes of two other Northern Democrats—Alaska freshman Mike Gravel and Washington veteran Warren G. Magnuson. Both ended up in opposition.

Two senators remained undecided—aging and ailing Clinton P. Anderson, a New Mexico Democrat, and John J. Williams, a Delaware Republican. The key vote was scheduled Aug. 6 on an amendment to limit the ABM to research for the next year. Then, on the eve of the showdown, the Senate's only woman, Maine Republican Margaret Chase Smith, introduced without explanation an amendment that would bar research too.

Jackson, recalling afterwards the fight against the Cooper-Hart proposal, said he was elated at the news of Mrs. Smith's move. "The Republicans had been telling me they had 30 votes (against Cooper-Hart)," he said, "and I could only count 29. As soon as she put that amendment in, I knew she was the 30th."

Mrs. Smith had opposed the ABM in committee. After her amendment was rejected 89 to 11—most senators had already gone on record for continuing research on the ABM—frantic maneuvering began to put together an amendment acceptable to both the Cooper-Hart forces and the independent lady from Maine.

Finally the roll was called.

Fourth on the alphabetical list was Anderson. "No," he responded and a murmur went through the hushed chamber. When, 93 names later, the name of Williams was called, he too replied "No."

The vote was 50-50—enough to defeat the compromise amendment which needed a majority to prevail.

Now came the suddenly anti-climactic vote on the Cooper-Hart amendment. It was defeated 51 to 49, with Mrs. Smith joining the ABM proponents in opposition to it. "I've always been against the ABM," she said, explaining she saw no reason to vote any money for it at all.

The next day, a fourth and final ABM vote produced a resounding 73-27 count against the proposal by Sen. Thomas J. McIntyre, D-N.H., to go ahead with the North Dakota and Montana ABM sites while withholding authority to deploy Safeguard's missiles. He called it a compromise but neither side saw it that way.

The ABM fight was now over, but the Senate battled well into September on the rest of the authorization bill. Amendments to block funds for the AMSA, the CVAN-69 carrier and the MBT-70 tank were beaten overwhelmingly or withdrawn. These amendments adopted in the Senate stayed in the final bill: a proposal to bar defense research on nonmilitary items,

conflict of interest provisions, a study of profits by defense contractors and the first limit on a practice whereby defense research contractors get extra funds for so-called "independent" research.

Despite the effort in the Senate, the final military procurement authorization legislation, which totaled $20.7 billion, gave the Pentagon every new weapons system it had sought—though some funds were reduced. In considerable degree, this reflected the fact that the conferees from both houses were the senior members of the Armed Services Committee who had opposed reductions on the floor. But citizens' groups began to grow up with the avowed aim of shifting the budgetary balance from the military to the civilian sector. Within Congress itself, 35 members of the House and Senate called a Congressional Conference on the Military Budget and National Priorities, which produced a 61-page report warning the nation was in danger of becoming a "national security state" and concluding:

"The most urgent challenge confronting Congress today is to reassert control over the military bureaucracy and the policy decisions it has pre-empted." Sen. Ralph Yarborough, D-Tex., hauled out figures showing the Bureau of the Budget had more auditors for the $27 billion in social programs than for the $80 billion defense budget. "The budget bureau tells the civilian departments what to do," he said. "But the Pentagon tells the budget bureau what to do."

Within weeks President Nixon gave an order that henceforth the Pentagon budget would be subject to the same review as those of civilian agencies.

Amid the unprecedented congressional offensive against the Pentagon, its allies in and out of Congress reacted with widely differing responses.

Stennis, a tight man with a dollar, not only strengthened procedures against waste and cost overruns, but indicated his committee planned to make its own determination of what weapons were needed. But his counterpart in the House, Rep. L. Mendel Rivers, D-S.C., made it clear which side he was on. When Rep. George H. Mahon, D-Tex., chairman of the Appropriations Committee and a longtime Pentagon backer, complained in the House that "one of the things that disturbs me is that there have been so many mistakes made by the military," Rivers exploded: "You are playing into the hands of the enemies of the military, and the other body (the Senate) is full of them."

It remained for President Nixon to deliver the year's sharpest attack on congressional foes of the Pentagon.

Addressing the Air Force Academy June 4, Nixon said:

"It is open season on the armed forces. Military programs are ridiculed as needless if not deliberate waste. The military profession is derided in some of the best circles." Attacking those he called "new isolationists," the President said, "We must rule out unilateral disarmament" and keep the peace through military strength and maintenance of U.S. alliances around the world.

The reaction in Congress was immediate, and it symbolized the year-long debate. "Neither I nor this subcommittee is attacking the military forces of the country," Chairman J. W. Fulbright, D-Ark., of the Senate Foreign Relations Committee said. "We are questioning the political judgments that led us into this quagmire." He added that any budget priority that gives 10 times as much to military spending as to education is "cockeyed."

"The greatest threat to peace and domestic tranquillity," he said, "is not in Hanoi, Moscow or Peking but in our colleges and in the ghettos of cities throughout the land."

Officials inspect recovered car in which Mary Jo Kopechne drowned when auto veered off bridge

Tragedy at Chappaquiddick

Mary Jo Kopechne died near Martha's Vineyard when car plunged off bridge; Sen. Ted Kennedy given suspended sentence for failure to report accident promptly and court set January inquest

IT WAS planned as a happy weekend of sailing, swimming and a cookout for a Kennedy group at Edgartown on Martha's Vineyard and on the smaller adjoining island of Chappaquiddick. Instead, the reunion became an occasion of tragedy and crisis for Sen. Edward M. Kennedy—sole survivor among four brothers—and his close associates.

On the night of July 18, as he reported later, the Massachusetts Democrat was driving his automobile on an unfamiliar road to the two-car ferry connecting Chappaquiddick Island and Edgartown. A half-mile down the narrow, bumpy gravel roadway was a small wooden bridge, a hump-backed span 75 feet long and only 10 feet, 8 inches wide. It led off the Dike Road at a 25-degree angle to the left, rising sharply to cross a narrow waterway cut through the dike to allow tidal salt water to flow to and from Poucha Pond.

Kennedy didn't make the turn. The car went off the edge on the right side of the bridge, rolling over as it plunged into the water, and coming to rest upside down on the bottom.

Kennedy managed to escape from the car, but his passenger, Mary Jo Kopechne, 28, who worked for the 1968 presidential campaign staff of Robert F. Kennedy, was trapped inside and perished. Kennedy's delayed report to Edgartown police said the car left the bridge at about 11:15 p.m.

First public word of the accident came nine hours later, at 8:20 a.m. Saturday, when Mrs. Pierre Malm, whose house is only 50 yards from the bridge, called the Edgartown police station to report a car in the water. Two young men, Robert Samuel, 21, of Albany, N.Y., and Joseph Cappevella, 15, of Schenectady, N.Y., crossed the bridge about 7 a.m., to fish in the ocean surf on the other side, she said. They saw nothing then, but on their way back the tide had fallen, and an automobile wheel was visible above the water's surface.

Police Chief Dominick J. Arena went to the bridge, borrowed swimming trunks and dove in. He got the car's license number, sent it by radio to the station for an ownership check, then dove again to look inside the vehicle.

"I couldn't see much because of the current," he said. Arena then sent for John Farrar of the Edgartown Fire Department's scuba team, who soon determined there was a woman's body in the car. He surfaced to report, then dove again with a piece

Tragedy's victim: Mary Jo Kopechne

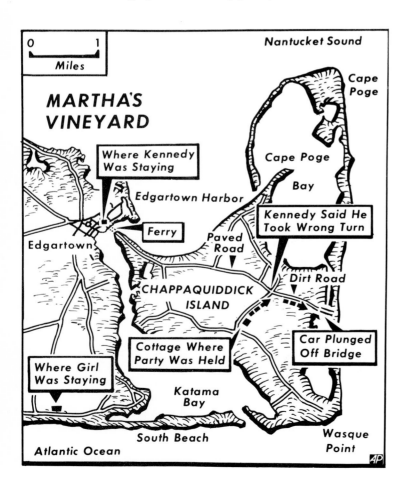

of rope which he tied around the neck to haul the body clear. Arena pulled it to the surface. Farrar brought up a woman's handbag from the rear seat where he had found the body.

Arena was notified by radio the car was registered to Sen. Edward M. Kennedy at his Boston residence. Still in wet trunks, Arena returned to his station. There he found Kennedy and Paul Markham, a Kennedy campaign worker and former U.S. attorney for Massachusetts, waiting to talk to him. He said Kennedy told him: "I was driving. What do you want me to do? It has to be right."

"I told him the first thing was an accident report," Arena said. "He asked me if he could give it to me in a written statement and I agreed. They went into the back room to do it."

Arena returned to the scene of the accident and talked to Dr. Donald R. Mills, associate medical examiner for Dukes County. A week later Mills said in a written statement: "The body was carefully examined . . . and a positive diagnosis of accidental drowning was made." Mills said also that if he had known of Kennedy's involvement he would have ordered an autopsy. But, he added, when he viewed the body he had no idea of the victim's identity except from a bystander's comment that she might be a Kennedy staff secretary. Mills then advised Dist. Atty. Edmund Dinis to send a state pathologist if he planned an autopsy. Later, Mills said, Lt. George Killen, a state police detective assigned to Dinis' staff, sent word that if the medical examiner "was satisfied that there was no foul play, no autopsy would be done."

Subsequently, Dinis said he too would have proposed an autopsy had he been aware Saturday of Kennedy's association in the case. But, when he did find out, it was too late; the body had been released by the medical examiner and flown to Miss Kopechne's birthplace in Pennsylvania Sunday afternoon, Dinis added.

All that was on the record at that time was Kennedy's statement given to Arena on Saturday:

"On July 18, 1969, at approximately 11:15 p.m., in Chappaquiddick, Martha's Vineyard, Mass., I was driving my car on Main Street on my way to get the ferry back to Edgartown. I was unfamiliar with the road and turned right on Dike Road instead of bearing hard left on Main Street. After proceeding for approximately one-half mile on Dike Road, I descended a hill and came upon a narrow bridge. The car went off the side of the bridge. There was one passenger with me, one Miss Mary ---, a former secretary of my brother Robert Kennedy.

"The car turned over and sank into the water and landed with the roof resting on the bottom. I attempted to open the door and window of the car but have no recollection of how I got out of the car. I came to the surface and then repeatedly dove down to the car in an attempt to see if the passenger was still in the car. I was unsuccessful in the attempt. I was exhausted and in a state of shock. I recall walking back to where my friends were eating. There was a car parked in front of the cottage and I climbed into the back seat. I then asked someone to bring me back to Edgartown. I remember walking around for a period of time and then going back to my hotel room. When I fully realized what had happened this morning I immediately went to the police."

Arena explained that, in the initial handwritten report given to him, the surname of the victim was left blank because Kennedy had said he didn't know how to spell it. Neither did Markham.

Arena typed out the statement from the handwritten draft and gave a copy to Kennedy, who, he said, read it through without further comment.

Markham then asked that the statement be withheld from the press until Kennedy had time to consult with Burke Marshall, a former assistant U.S. attorney general on the Robert Kennedy staff. Arena said he agreed, but when he failed to hear from Kennedy for three hours after that, he released the statement to the press.

Arena also announced later that day he intended to bring a criminal complaint against Kennedy, charging him with leaving the scene of an accident without making himself known.

By Kennedy's own story nearly 11 hours elapsed between the time of the accident and Kennedy's appearance at the police station.

Arena received a report in the meantime that Kennedy had taken the ferry from the Edgartown side to Chappaquiddick Island and spent some time in the ferry house there. It had a pay station telephone inside.

A ferryman also reported he saw two men with Kennedy and that he asked if they knew about the accident at the dike where a car went into the water. The ferryman didn't know of Kennedy's involvement. He said that one of the men replied, "we just heard about it," and that Kennedy then took the ferry back to Edgartown. It was near 10 a.m. then, and Kennedy went directly to the police station.

Arena later told newsmen: "If he had time to take the ferry over and back, he had time to see me."

By noon on that Saturday, or soon after, Kennedy and the others who were at the Friday night cookout on Chappaquiddick had left the island and returned to the mainland.

In addition to Kennedy, Markham, and Kennedy's cousin, Joseph F. Gargan, the other men at the outing were Kennedy friends or campaign workers. The oldest among them was John J. "Jack" Crimmins, 63, an investigator for the office of the Suffolk County District attorney in Boston, and a volunteer chauffeur for Kennedy since his first Senate campaign in 1962. Ray LaRosa, 51, of Andover, Mass., crewed for Kennedy on his 24-foot Wianno Senior sloop, which came in ninth in the Friday race in which 31 boats of that class were entered. Kennedy's boat, *"Victura,"* formerly was owned by the late President John F. Kennedy. Charles Tretter, 30, youngest of the men at the weekend gathering, was a Boston lawyer who joined the Kennedy forces as a volunteer campaign worker in 1962.

For the girls it was a reunion of the workers in the "Boiler Room" of the 1968 Robert Kennedy presidential campaign. Mary Jo Kopechne was one of those back-room workers. She was born in Plymouth, Pa., where her father was an insurance salesman. When she died, her parents were living in New Jersey, but her body was taken back to her home town for burial. She had worked on the staff of Sen. Robert F. Kennedy when he came in as a freshman after the 1964 election. Known

Sen. Edward M. Kennedy and Mrs. Kennedy return from Mary Jo Kopechne's funeral

as "M.J.," she was regarded by her associates as a wholesome type, a sort of "nicest girl on the block" who blushed easily at 28, and definitely was not a "swinger." Her friends said the biggest things in her life were the Catholic Church and her jobs in politics, including her work for the Kennedys.

The other girls in the group all were younger than Miss Kopechne. Rosemary Keough, 23, came from Philadelphia, and joined Robert Kennedy's staff in 1967. Esther Newberg, 26, worked for a Senate subcommittee before she joined Robert Kennedy's staff in 1968. Susan Tannenbaum, 24, from Greensboro, N.C., worked for Robert Kennedy in 1967. The other two were sisters, Maryellen and Nance Lyons. Nance, 27, was on the staff of Sen. Ted Kennedy in Washington. Her sister, Maryellen, a year older, worked in the Bobby Kennedy presidential campaign.

Rosemary Keough's pocketbook was found in the sunken Kennedy car because, she said, she forgot it when she returned in the evening after borrowing the car to drive to the ferry for a quick trip to Edgartown to get a radio for the party.

On the Monday after the accident, Arena filed a formal application for a criminal complaint charging Kennedy with leaving the scene of an accident without making himself known. Kennedy's lawyers immediately asked for a "show cause" hearing on issuance of the complaint. District Court Clerk Thomas A. Teller set the hearing for the following Monday, July 28. However, on the intervening Thursday came the announcement that Kennedy would waive the hearing, accept the summons, and appear for arraignment. He did so July 25, accompanied by his wife, Joan, and his brother-in-law, Stephen Smith.

Teller read the complaint, that Kennedy did "knowingly leave the scene of an accident causing injury, without making himself known." The clerk finished with the formal question:

"How say you to this complaint, guilty or not guilty?"
Kennedy stood with head bowed, his hands at his sides.
"Guilty," he said in a low but steady voice.
From a seat at the side of the court, Kennedy's wife stared without expression.

Judge James A. Boyle then asked Prosecutor Walter D. Steele to present the facts in the case. Arena, when called, testified to recovery of the body and told how Kennedy appeared at the police station the next morning to make a report. "The accident happened some time after 11:15 p.m., and it was not reported to me until after 9 a.m. the next day," Arena said.

Kennedy's lawyers, Richard J. McCarron, an island attorney, and Robert G. Clark Jr., a prominent mainland lawyer and former judge, declined to cross-examine.

"Well, I have some questions," Boyle said. "I would be most interested in determining from the defendant or the commonwealth if there was a deliberate effort to conceal the identity of the defendant."

"Identity of the defendant? Not to my knowledge, your honor," Arena replied.

McCarron told the court Kennedy was "adamant" in insisting that a plea of guilty be entered, and that, in effect, his case be left to the mercy of the court. Both he and Prosecutor Steele asked for a suspended sentence. Boyle ordered the minimum sentence of two months in jail, and suspended it for one year.

"It is my understanding he (Kennedy) already has been and will continue to be punished far beyond anything this court can impose," Boyle commented.

As Kennedy left the courtroom, he told newsmen he had asked for time on a Boston television station that night. The networks picked up his appearance nationwide. Kennedy defended the character of Miss Kopechne, saying he never had a "private relationship" with her of any kind. He also denied he was driving under the influence of liquor. He described how his car plunged into the pond and said "water entered my lungs and I actually felt the sensation of drowning, but somehow I struggled to the surface alive."

Kennedy also said he made repeated efforts to reach the girl by diving but failed because of the dark and the strong current. "My conduct and conversations during the next several hours, to the extent that I can remember them, make no sense to me at all," he told the nation. "I regard as indefensible the fact that I did not report the accident to the police immediately." Instead, he said, he walked back to the party cottage a mile away and got his cousin, Joe Gargan, and his lawyer-friend Markham to return to the bridge with him. He said they too tried without avail to dive to the submerged car.

Kennedy said he had "all kinds of scrambled thoughts" during the night which followed the accident, ". . . confused . . . irrational . . . many . . . which I cannot recall, and some of which I would not have seriously entertained." One of these, he said, was "whether some awful curse actually did hang over all the Kennedys. . . ."

Kennedy said that after Gargan and Markham also failed to reach the sunken car ". . . I suddenly jumped into the water and impulsively swam across, nearly drowning once again in the effort, returned to my hotel room about 2 a.m. and collapsed in my room."

In the morning, by Kennedy's own story, he went to the ferry and crossed again to the Chappaquiddick side to use a public telephone to call "a family legal advisor," Burke Marshall.

Kennedy had to pass at least two outdoor public telephones on his way to the ferry which took him across to the smaller island where he made his calls from a phone in a small waiting room. He said in his TV appearance that thereafter he "belatedly reported the accident to the Martha's Vineyard police."

After Kennedy's appearance in court, his plea and his penalty, Dist. Atty. Dinis applied for an inquest to the only court which could grant one, the District Court of Edgartown. The same Judge Boyle set the inquest for Sept. 3 and, at a pre-session courtroom conference with Kennedy lawyers, laid down the ground rules for it.

He said he intended to follow the law as it appeared in the books: witnesses could have lawyers present only during their appearances on the stand; the lawyers could not listen to other witnesses or cross-examine; he would exercise the discretion given him by the law and call it a "public" inquest, but only accredited members of the press would constitute the "public." The courtroom had about 125 seats available. On the eve of the inquest, however, Kennedy lawyers, headed by Edward B. Hanify, went to the State Supreme Judicial Court and filed objections to the procedures.

The petition was brought before a single justice, since the full bench was in summer recess. Justice Paul C. Reardon was the judge on call for the week. It was he who had been chairman of a bar association committee that studied press-bar relations as they might affect defendants' rights, and who decided the press should be shut off from practically all access to information in criminal cases before they came to trial.

Reardon agreed with the pleas of Hanify and other lawyers for the Kennedy group that the accident had indeed generated considerable publicity, and that an inquest conducted under the rules laid down by Boyle might indeed result in additional massive publicity. Then he issued an injunction delaying the inquest, and referred the case to the full bench.

Hyannis Port demonstrators question Kennedy's explanation of accident

In arguments before the Supreme Court, the Kennedy group's lawyers said that, if an inquest were held, Kennedy would be the "focal point" of the proceeding, which possibly could result in further court action. Thus the lawyers asked the Supreme Court to require that the inquest, if held, be secret; that counsel for the witnesses be allowed to remain through the entire inquest, and that they be allowed to cross-examine. The lawyers also told the court that further publicity could affect any future fair trial, if the inquest ruling called for one.

In the end, the court issued a directive for a new set of procedures for inquests, closing them to the press and public, and impounding inquest papers and the judge's report until all prospect of any further court procedure ceased to exist.

In other respects the Supreme Court upheld Boyle's rulings that lawyers could accompany witnesses into the hearing solely to advise them on their rights, but not to question or cross-examine any witnesses.

The district attorney, Dinis, meanwhile had applied to the Luzerne County Court of Common Pleas in Pennsylvania for an order requiring the exhumation of Miss Kopechne's body for an autopsy. Dinis said he needed the autopsy to establish the exact cause of death, and he filed with the court a report which said traces of blood were found on the girl's shirtwaist and in her nose and mouth.

Judge Bernard C. Brominski held up his decision for two months. Not until Dec. 10 did he rule against any exhumation or autopsy. He said he was satisfied with the finding of the associate medical examiner, Dr. Mills, that she died of drowning, and that no evidence indicated any other cause.

The following day Judge Boyle at Edgartown decreed the inquest would be held without autopsy. He set the date for Jan. 5, 1970.

Inflation and Recession Too?

Less spending, more taxing, tighter money formed Administration's economic strategy against threat of trading "Boom" for "Bust"

RICHARD NIXON left Washington in 1961 at the bottom of a recession. He returned as President at the height of an inflation. After one year in the White House he faced the possibility of the only economic headache that could be more painful—an inflation and a recession combined.

The recession threat at the end of 1969 was unplanned and unwanted. The Nixon anti-inflation strategy called "gradualism" —a steadily hardening squeeze of lower spending, higher taxes and tighter money—was expressly designed to avoid collapsing the boom in the classic way—with a bust. Ending the inflation was the foremost aim of Nixon's domestic policy. But he wanted disinflation, not deflation. The cure should be a tapering off, not a shock treatment.

There had been three recessions during his terms as Vice President under Dwight D. Eisenhower. Nixon believed the last one cost him the White House in 1960—there must not be another Republican recession in 1970. Most government economists thought it would be avoided. Many others were less optimistic.

The President's Council of Economic Advisers, headed by Paul W. McCracken, said he could not promise disinflation would be painless. McCracken thought it could be achieved without "substantial" unemployment, but for nine long months of 1969 he was more concerned with watching for the slowdown than with worrying about what to do when it came. And, by October, the effects of gradualism began to show. Not yet in the form of a letup in price increases. But the long-hoped-for deceleration of the boom had begun.

Unwelcome signs included "long holidays" and layoffs in the auto industry, shrinking profits, a depression in housing and the highest interest rates in a century. The unemployment rate baffled the forecasters; it rose in the late summer, dropped sharply in November. The President took to radio Oct. 17 to tell the nation's housewives price stability must be bought at a price, too, and it might be a high one. "We have asked the American people to take bitter medicine," Nixon said. "We are going to experience some slowing pains. Like growing pains, these are a healthy development—but painful, nevertheless."

His chat carried a warning and a promise. The warning was that prices would keep on rising for some time to come, coasting uphill for months to come on the momentum of a five-year inflation. The promise was that the government "is not fooling." The administration would hold firm to its restraints, Nixon vowed, until it had halted the inflation and the inflationary expectations on which inflation feeds.

Whether inflation could be stopped without a recession— whether Nixon's economic command could sense the exact moment to release the anti-inflation brakes before the economy skidded to a halt—remained to be seen. As 1969 ended, economists appeared to be about equally divided as to whether 1970 would bring a real recession or just a pause in history's longest boom.

Nixon's inheritance from the Democrats—besides an inflation and a record of budget deficits—was a business expansion that in eight years had broken all records for velocity and longevity.

In 1960 the nation's output was about $500 billion. By late 1970—barring a truly disastrous recession, which no expert deemed possible—Nixon could expect a production rate exactly twice as great, $1 trillion a year. The expansion of the 1960's was healthy and mannerly in its first five years. The cost of living increase averaged less than 1.5 per cent a year. Then, in 1965, inflation took wings (*The World in 1965, 168–169*). The economy had been stimulated by the massive 1964 tax reduction. President Lyndon B. Johnson had set in motion his large and costly "Great Society" program of welfare, education and antipoverty outlays. In 1965 Johnson learned the ugly truth that the Vietnam war effort was wallowing; he approved a massive escalation. He did not ask higher taxes to pay for it, and he did not shelve his lofty vision of a Great Society. He made in effect a decision that America could afford both guns and butter. Johnson was willing to accept some further red ink financing, but the deficit mushroomed, unbelievably, to $25 billion in the fiscal year that ended in mid-1968. That was nearly twice the size of the biggest previous deficit ever recorded, Eisenhower's $12.9 billion in 1959.

In a retrospective mood, Economist Walter W. Heller commented on what happened after his own resignation as Economic Council chairman:

"The period of the Vietnam War hardly represents the finest hour of U.S. economic policy. Had the President called for— and been able to get—a surtax and suspension of the investment tax incentives early in 1966 (*The World in 1966, 200–203*), we could have eased inflationary pressures without resorting to brutally tight money. And the need for fiscal restraint in 1966–1968 (*The World in 1967, 226–229*), would have been a lot less pressing."

The words, "had the president called for—and been able to get" recalled that many economists had implored Johnson to seek a surtax or some other form of temporary tax increase in 1966 and 1967. But the word in Congress—as it was relayed by the most believable Congressional tax authority, Chairman Wilbur D. Mills of the House Ways and Means Committee— was Congress simply wouldn't swallow a surtax.

When the scale of the fiscal debacle became clear, Johnson asked for a 10 per cent surcharge on individual and corporation

Irate Boston citizens protest prospective tax increase

income taxes. Congress did not oblige until 1968 was half over. Johnson's economists assured Congress in the spring of 1968 *(The World in 1968, 122–123)* the slowing-down effect would be felt by fall. Instead, the spiral of inflation spun faster. When Nixon took office he too was sure the balloon was about to deflate. It didn't.

Nixon disliked the surtax. He had made campaign promises to let it expire on schedule on June 30, 1969, or to reduce it drastically. On election eve, he had dropped the qualification. The surtax, he said, would have to go. But by February price markups were destroying the buying power of Americans at an annual rate of a nickel out of every dollar of take-home pay. Instead of diminishing as expected in the first quarter, the gross national product scored a $16 billion gain in annual rate —exactly as great as in the final quarter of 1968.

McCracken and his colleagues on the Economic Council persuaded Nixon to change his mind. The fiscal strait-jacket would have to be worn another year. Monetary policy could hardly be pulled tighter; money already was so tight the financial markets feared another near-panic like the 1966 "credit crunch."

Nixon made his decision at a meeting of the Quadriad—the four-man high command of economic policymakers—in mid-March, in the Cabinet room of the White House. Ranged along one side of the long oval cabinet table were McCracken, Secretary of the Treasury David M. Kennedy, Budget Director Robert P. Mayo, and Chairman William McChesney Martin of the Federal Reserve Board. The scene was duplicated on most of Nixon's economic decisions thereafter, except there was never again such unanimity among his advisers. After a two-hour general discussion the President pointed a finger and called for a recommendation from each man in turn.

"My recommendation was that we had no choice, we had to go for it (the surtax extension)," McCracken recalled. "We simply could not let it expire."

All agreed. Nixon, assenting, made the decision he had refused to make at the suggestion of Johnson a few months earlier.

Now, having reversed his anti-inflation strategy, Nixon made a series of tactical errors. The first was to assume that if both Johnson and Nixon called for surtax extension, Congress would vote for it with nonpartisan dispatch. Congress did not, but the Nixon team applied little pressure until the June 30 expiration date drew near. When it did begin to push, it met the same kind of delays, haggling, and bargaining for concessions that Johnson had encountered a year earlier.

Congress belatedly gave an extension for six months only. Nixon's hope of demonstrating to the world the government's determination to halt inflation and bulwark the dollar went glimmering. The economic scene was one of conflict, indecision and continuing inflation.

By the end of the year the average city-dwelling family had to pay $1.30 to buy the consumer items $1 had bought a decade earlier. The year 1969 alone whittled 6 cents out of every dollar in the average wage-earner's paycheck. The unions were hitting back with wage demands big enough to catch up with the past year's living cost increases, plus enough more to stay ahead of next year's anticipated rise. About 3.5 million workers automatically would get increases averaging 5.7 per cent in 1970 under long-term union contracts previously bargained. That became the starting point for the 1969 bargaining; wage demands went up from there.

That added to the miseries of the housing industry, already depressed by a drouth of mortgage funds and sky-high interest rates. By October the average new home buyer had to pay an effective rate of 8.12 per cent. In that month new housing starts slumped to an annual rate of 1.33 million, from 1.55 million in 1968.

Two-year and three-year wage settlements, providing for

annual step-ups, assured industry of rising labor costs to come. Output per worker dipped; that, plus a slowing of retail sales, put a squeeze on the profits of many businesses and provided new incentive for price increases to bolster earnings. Secretary of Labor George P. Shultz warned that labor, as well as industry, could price itself out of the market. "Most of the low cost housing is factory-made mobile housing now," he reminded the building trades.

Nixon's message to housewives commiserated with them over more visible evidences: It cost 66 cents to buy a pound of hamburger that cost 53 cents four years earlier. A day in the hospital cost $48, up from $27 in the same four years. The broadcast to housewives signaled a shift of strategy for the Administration. Nixon had insisted, in his campaign and for months thereafter, that the Republican Administration would not resort to voluntary government-set "guideposts" for wage and price settlements. Neither would it use "jawbone price control," the White House promised. That referred to the publicity, pressure and persuasion used in the Kennedy and Johnson administrations to discourage price boosts or to roll back increases deemed excessive.

The absence of jawbone brought criticism on Nixon and his Economic Council from Congress members and others, and one confidential business advisory service reportedly notified its clients: "The President has just said you can raise prices."

By the end of 1969 Nixon was jawboning labor and management in behalf of moderation, but without singling out individual firms or industries. To get its initial extension of the surtax, Nixon had "acquiesced" in a ceiling on budget spending. When Congress began to insist on tax reforms as the next price for a favorable vote, the Administration rushed a tax reform bill to Capitol Hill. To get the support of liberal Democrats, it threw in a sweetener—a virtual exemption from the income tax for almost all Americans with incomes below the officially designated poverty level. When Congress began to talk of extending the surtax at only half the 10 per cent rate, the Treasury became alarmed at the potential revenue loss, and Nixon offered another concession: Let the surtax go to 5 per cent after six months—that is, after Jan. 1, 1970, but repeal the 7 per cent tax credit for business investment. The tax credit was being blamed for helping to stimulate a record volume of plant and equipment outlays, a major inflationary force.

So Congress seized and held the tax initiative. The tax reform bill mushroomed into a major tax reduction measure, with about $9 billion of tax relief provisions outweighing by $2.5 billion or more the revenues gained from closing tax loopholes.

As the first session of the 91st Congress reached its final days the Administration was still battling for a second six-month surtax extension, this time at 5 per cent, and imploring Congress not to go overboard in tax reduction.

Nixon got his extension in the last days of the year, along with a Congress-written tax reform bill which provided $2.5 billion (B) for his new budget.

The tax reductions, Nixon men had argued, would weaken the fiscal curbs on inflation, endanger Nixon's planned budget surpluses, and give away prematurely tax revenues that might be needed later to finance Nixon's own social-welfare programs —or might provide tax cuts needed later to combat a recession.

For, by this time, it was clear that the slowdown had begun. In July the Federal Reserve Board's index of industrial production—a measure of the physical output of mines, factories and refineries—reversed its long climb and began to sink,

month by month. By September the unemployment rate was up to 4 per cent, compared with 3.3 per cent the day Nixon took office.

By October overtime work was vanishing; the factory work week was half a day shorter than in January. Housing starts were one-third slower. The stock market, after recovering from a long slide in the spring, sagged anew in December and finally dropped below the supposed technical rallying-point, 800 on the Dow Jones industrial average. Inflation, for a time, had masked the slowdown. The gross national product had continued its giant strides—another $16 billion in the second quarter, then an astonishing $18 billion in the third quarter.

It appeared the GNP would exceed $930 billion for the year, a gain of roughly $70 billion or 8 per cent over the 1968 record level. But the GNP was a flawed index, distorted by inflation. The GNP is a yardstick of expenditure rather than of actual output. It represents the value of all goods and services produced, as priced in dollars. The 8 per cent increase in the rate of GNP in the summer quarter was three-fourths inflation. After the price increases were squeezed out, the gain in "real GNP" was a mere 2 per cent.

Inflation was surging on, but the eight-year boom was slowing down. The Nixon "package of restraints" was showing results, enough results to hurt.

The financial markets were imploring Washington for relief from the credit squeeze. The "prime rate" had climbed to 8½ per cent; this was the rate at which the major banks made loans to their best and biggest customers. Smaller borrowers paid more, much more. Even the Treasury had to pay 8 per cent, in late 1969, to sell six-month securities backed by the faith and credit of the United States of America. It was the highest rate since the end of the Civil War.

But the Federal Reserve board was backed by the Administration in its refusal to ease the credit reins. And Budget Director Mayo, noting that Congress was considering appropriation bills costing $5 billion more in outlays than Nixon's budget called for, gave notice that the White House would simply "impound" or refuse to spend, the extra money that Congress might provide.

Treasury Secretary David M. Kennedy gave notice to industry: The Administration would not release its grip on the fiscal and monetary reins "until we have restored basic health and stability to the economy." Kennedy predicted that the "real GNP" would decline for "some length of time" in 1970. That might mean a recession; most economists considered that the economy was in recession if the real GNP declined for two or more consecutive quarters.

Economic Adviser McCracken conceded that there was "now some emergent concern" over the risk of a recession; his own expectation, he said, would be "a flat period of business conditions for a time."

The consensus of Washington economists was that there would at least be no gain in "real GNP" in the first half of 1970, with enough pickup in the second half to provide a 1.5 per cent or 2 per cent gain for the year. But inflation would rob the dollar of perhaps another 4 cents in buying power and send the uncorrected, inflated GNP onward to its trillion-dollar rate.

McCracken added a warning:

When the period of hesitation, plateau or recession was over, the government would bend its efforts to see that the growth resumed at a sustainable rate of 5 or 6 per cent a year, "rather than the highly inflationary 8 to 10 per cent rates that have prevailed since 1965."

"A MASSACRE, OR WHAT WAS IT?"

My Lai: (pronounced Mee Lie) the name of a once obscure Vietnamese hamlet. . . . A name unknown to most Americans until late in 1969, when it was thrust before the public eye as the scene of an "alleged" massacre of Vietnamese civilians, reportedly by U.S. troops, on March 16, 1968. . . . A name which became well enough known to draw the attention of the President.

Two soldiers were under charges in connection with the My Lai affair at year's end. On Sept. 5, the day before he was scheduled for discharge after two years in the Army, 1st Lt. William L. Calley Jr., 26, was charged with slaying 109 Vietnamese civilians. S. Sgt. David Mitchell, 29, nine-year Army veteran and squad leader of a platoon of combat infantrymen commanded by Calley, was charged on 30 counts of assault with intent to commit murder. In addition, Army sources said it was probable charges would be filed against a majority of nine soldiers and 15 former soldiers, all members at one time of Company C, 1st Battalion, 11th Infantry Brigade, Americal Division. The Army refused to identify these 24 men or to name any other members of the platoon and company involved. On Dec. 7, it impounded the daily operational records of Company C, dating back to six weeks before the incident.

Two days later, President Nixon was asked at a news conference, "In your opinion, was what happened at My Lai a massacre, an alleged massacre, or what was it?"

The president replied: ". . . What appears was certainly a massacre, under no circumstances was it justified. One of the goals we are fighting for in Vietnam is to keep the people . . . from having imposed upon them a government which has atrocity against civilians as one of its policies. . . .

"Now when you use the word 'alleged' that is only proper in terms of the individuals involved. Under our system a man is not guilty until proved to be so. There are several individuals involved here who will be tried by military courts. Consequently, we should say 'alleged' as far as they are concerned until they are proved guilty."

"The first indication that something extraordinary had taken place at My Lai reached the Department of the Army" in early April 1969, according to Secretary of the Army Stanley R. Resor. Resor said it was a letter by Ronald Ridenhour, 23, to Secretary of Defense Melvin R. Laird and five congressmen which alleged the troops were given the mission of destroying My Lai "and all its inhabitants." Ridenhour, who was not a witness to the alleged slayings but spent a year in Vietnam as a helicopter door gunner, said his 2,000-word letter—written four months after he completed his service time—was based on information he had gathered from soldiers who said they had been in My Lai. The letter, which he said was mailed to 23 Capitol Hill offices, was dated March 29, 1969, and told of "dark and bloody" events which Ridenhour said took place a year earlier. It stated that fellow soldiers told him an American infantry company killed at least 109 and possibly 567 civilians—including babies—at My Lai.

A field level investigation made after the alleged 1968 incident rose no higher than Americal Division headquarters, according to the Army, and concluded there were no grounds for disciplinary action. It came after a helicopter pilot reported the killing of civilians and similar claims were put forth in Viet Cong propaganda leaflets. Pentagon sources said it was CWO Hugh C. Thompson Jr., 27, whose complaint prompted the study. Thompson said he got a military citation for saving the lives of 16 Vietnamese children at My Lai the day of the alleged massacre but declined to comment on details of the incident.

About a year later, a full scale probe was begun on the basis of Ridenhour's letter. The Army began an inquiry April 23, and turned it over Aug. 4 to the provost marshal general. That month the Army received copies of slides taken by Ronald Haeberle, a combat photographer at My Lai. Of the pictures taken by Haeberle, some were turned over to the Army at the time of the alleged massacre but others, taken with his personal camera, were sold to various publications. The Pentagon said the photos he gave the Army did not show a massacre but did establish the presence of certain personnel in Capt. Ernest L. Medina's company in My Lai. Medina, 33, was commander of the company involved in the alleged massacre. Calley was the leader of Medina's first platoon.

Accounts of what happened that day vary widely. Looking back more than a year, Do Chuc, 48, a Vietnamese peasant, recalled that the first two times American soldiers passed through his town they gave candy to the children, but the third time he said the inhabitants were rounded up and then cut down by rifle and machine-gun fire. "My family was eating breakfast when the Americans came," Chuc said. "They ordered us out and gathered us together in three big groups. Then they shot us." Chuc said he was wounded in the leg, his wife in the back, and their daughter, 24, and son, 4, were killed.

In a copyrighted story Dec. 10 the Houston Chronicle quoted Herbert Carter, 23, a former soldier, as saying that he was speaking out about the incident because of "everyone blaming Medina and Calley. Medina (against whom no charge had been placed) didn't have the authority to give an order like that (to kill civilians). He just passed the word along. And as for Calley, he didn't kill the 109 all by himself. There was a company there."

The story said Carter added: ". . . We went through the village. We didn't see any VC (Viet Cong). People began coming out of their hootches (huts) and the guys shot them down and then burned the hootches or burned the hootches and shot the people when they came out. Sometimes they would round up a bunch and shoot them together. It went on like this all day . . . After a while I sat down in the road with a buddy. I heard Bernhardt (Sgt. Michael Bernhardt) tell an officer, 'The hell with this.' "

According to Life magazine, Bernhardt reported in an interview that "the people who ordered it probably didn't think it would look so bad . . . It was point-blank murder. Only a few of us refused. I just told them the hell with this, I'm not doing it. I didn't think this was a lawful order."

Sgt. Mitchell, who said he was "very surprised" when he heard the Army charges read to him "because I was accused of something I had no part of," told a Dec. 12 news conference there was no massacre at My Lai. "In my opinion, what they said happened did not happen," he said when asked about statements by other soldiers that civilians were shot down by American troops. He said he was innocent of the charges.

Capt. Medina's attorney, F. Lee Bailey, said Dec. 1 "the company commander (Medina) received no orders to butcher anyone or to kill any women and children—and he issued none." Bailey said the captain briefed his men the night before the attack "to destroy the village and buildings and to destroy their livestock, an unusual order but it was given by Col. Barker (Lt. Col. Frank A. Barker Jr., commander of Task Force Barker, who was killed about three months after My Lai) and to expect to be outnumbered and to go in shooting like hell." The attorney said Medina thought the village was held by the 48th Battalion of the Viet Cong and did not know there were women and children there.

Medina told a news conference Dec. 5 that "I did not shoot any child in My Lai and . . . I did not order any massacre in My Lai . . . I did not see any massacre in My Lai." Several days later Medina repeated in an interview, according to the New York Times, that he did not order or see any massacre but that "it is possible that it could have taken place." Later he asked his three platoon leaders, including Calley, if any civilians were killed and "I received negative indications from all platoon leaders," he said.

1st Lt. William L. Calley Jr., charged with killing 109 civilians

MIDDLE EAST: PEACE WAS ILLUSIVE

The "Six Day War" entered its third year with no prospect of peace. Hardly a day passed without incident. Secretary General U Thant told the United Nations more than once that "a virtual state of active war" existed in the Middle East and that Security Council cease-fire orders "had become almost totally ineffective."

A Swedish member of the 95-man UN Cease-Fire Observation Team, Maj. B. Roland Plane, was killed by an Israeli artillery shell during an exchange of fire with Egyptian guns. The United Arab Republic said it regarded the cease-fire agreement to be void. "A cease-fire agreement," said Mohammed H. El-Zayyat, chief government spokesman, "must be followed by something—an armistice, a withdrawal, fighting or surrender. There must be something."

There was: Fighting.

Peace plans were projected, and rejected, by various nations and a negotiable solution was sought in formal talks by the Big Four—United States, Russia, France and Britain. All the while dog fights in the air, artillery duels and commando raids on the ground took place along the border that separated Israeli-held territory from her Arab enemy. The concrete issue was land seized by Israel during the June 1967 war—the Golan Heights, the Gaza Strip, the Sinai Peninsula and the West Bank of the Jordan River *(The World in 1967, 110–117)*—but this was complicated by religious and moral convictions dating back thousands of years.

Jewish people had considered the land their own for some 4,000 years. They believed that preservation of their ancient culture—and of themselves as a people—was tightly bound to the re-establishment of a Jewish state in the "land of our fathers." The Arabs, however, held that some sort of statute of limitations should apply; that Hebrews had lived in Palestine for 2,000 years before Christ did not warrant their perpetual title to part of it.

The year 1969 was but a week old when Israeli forces exchanged fire with Lebanese troops and Arab guerrillas in Lebanon in the wake of Israel's commando raid on the Beirut International Airport in the closing hours of 1968. The attack was in retaliation for an assault against an El Al plane in Athens two days beforehand, for which the Popular Front for the Liberation of Palestine (PFLP), a commando group, took the credit.

State-owned airlines, and even those of allied countries, remained a major target. An El Al Boeing 720 commercial airliner with 17 passengers and a crew of 10 was attacked on takeoff from Zurich Feb. 18. Three passengers and three crewmen were injured, an Arab terrorist was killed and three others were captured. The PFLP said the attack was in reprisal for what it called Israeli acts of torture and brutality against "unarmed and innocent civilians in occupied Arab territory."

The PFLP, too, took credit for hijacking a Trans World Airlines jet Aug. 29 while it was en route from Rome to Athens and Tel Aviv. One of the two hijackers who forced the plane and 113 persons aboard to Damascus said "we have kidnaped this American plane because Israel is a colony of America and the Americans are giving the Israelis Phantom planes."

"We would never have made it if we had had to circle the airport one more time," said Capt. Dean Carter, the pilot. What's more, a time bomb set by the hijackers shattered the cockpit moments after the aircraft was emptied. All of the passengers and crewmen eventually were released. The PFLP claimed a victory. But a party of prominent Israelis, expected to be aboard, had cancelled their reservations at the last moment.

Following the hijacking the guerrilla organization let it be known that it planned full-scale war against Israeli and Zionist interests around the world and warned it would not be "responsible for the lives of tourists and foreigners . . . regardless of their nationality" who used Israeli means of transportation. No longer would attempts be made, as in the past, to avert foreign casualties. "We consider ourselves in a state of war and bloody fighting with Israel and those behind Israel until Palestine and the occupied Arab territories are fully liberated."

Commando groups were creating problems not only for the Israelis but for Arab army regulars. Tiny Lebanon, squeezed against the Mediterranean by Syria and Israel, had become a launch pad for the terrorist attacks on Israeli territory. Lebanon, fearing reprisals from its Jewish neighbor, ordered a crackdown on guerrilla activities. The guerrillas answered with gunfire. The 10-day shootout between army regulars and the commandos left nearly 100 warriors dead and several hundred wounded, led to the resignation of Premier Rashid Karami and threatened to plunge Lebanon into civil war.

A 24-hour cease-fire was announced Oct. 29 to give negotiators in Cairo a breather, but more bitter battles preceded the compromise finally reached Nov. 3. The agreement allowed the guerrillas to continue moving through the country. But they were required to remain inconspicuous, avoiding principal cities and tourist centers, and to penetrate deeply into Israel be-

Israeli soldier kicks in door of Arab house in the occupied Gaza Strip

Arab guerrilla troops of the Palestine Action Organization, hooded and heavily camouflaged

fore launching their attacks. To show their co-operation, the guerrillas quickly evacuated areas they had seized in southeastern Lebanon in their effort to control the Bekaa Valley Road from Syria toward Israel.

This "war of liberation" also was touted by

Yasir Arafat, Arab guerrilla leader

President Gamal Abdel Nasser, who stressed that Egypt was considering not only capturing the Israeli-occupied Sinai Peninsula but "all the Arab lands, and Jerusalem first." He acknowledged however, that "the path before us is long and difficult" and would involve "a bitter struggle."

That battle loomed ever more realistically in the wake of a fire that badly damaged portions of the Mosque of Al Aksa in Jerusalem, one of Islam's most sacred shrines. Israel bore the burden of blame for the Aug. 21 blaze, partly because of recurring reports in Arab newspapers that the Israelis wanted to rebuild the Temple of Solomon that once stood atop the mosque compound directly behind the Wailing Wall. Disputes over access to the area by Jewish and Moslem worshippers had been common since 1929. After the 1967 war, however, the Israelis had been in control of all Jerusalem.

A 27-year-old Australian sheep shearer and member of the Church of God, Michael Dennis Rohan, ultimately was arrested by Israelis and charged with the crime at Al Aksa. He was said to have a religious obsession that Jesus would return to earth when Jerusalem became completely Jewish and the Third Temple was built, replacing the second temple destroyed by the Romans in 70 A.D. According to Rohan's premise, the new temple could be built only after all the mosques in Jerusalem had been destroyed.

On Dec. 30 the Israeli court sentenced Rohan to an indefinite period in a mental institution.

Rohan's arrest did not soothe the Arabs. Nasser and other Arab political and religious leaders called for a Holy War against Israel. "In the coming battle," he said, "the Arab soldiers will not be soldiers of the Arab nations alone but soldiers of God and protectors of religion." But before the Arabs could garner their forces following the fire, Israel put them back on the defensive with a devastating 10-hour raid along the Suez Canal. Israeli armored amphibious forces crossed the Gulf of Suez from the Sinai Penin-

sula Sept. 9, attacking Egyptian military positions along a 20-mile coastal strip extending south from El Hafayer. The Israelis reported that 150 Egyptian soldiers were killed and 15 coastal positions, radar sites and missile bases had been wiped out, and that Israeli troops returned home virtually unscathed. Eli Landau of the Israeli newspaper Maariv, wrote: "All hell broke loose. The tanks were firing away at all targets and the road we were following was lined on both sides with burning vehicles of all descriptions, destroyed buildings and shot-up positions. At one stage three Egyptian armored troop carriers confronted the fast-advancing column and put up a fight, but the men inside spilled out and fled as soon as the first Israeli shot came whistling over."

Fighting as well as peace negotiations continued while Premier Golda Meir, the 71-year-old grandmother who succeeded the late Levi Eshkol *(page 47),* traveled to America with a military shopping list. She asked President Nixon particularly for more airplanes to complement the 50 Phantom jets already scheduled for delivery. But Mrs. Meir was concerned about her country's image as well as its arms. Before the war Israel had been regarded by many as a valiant underdog surrounded by hostile giants: some 3 million Israelis versus some 33.5 million Arabs. Israel's victory was widely cheered outside the Arab combine, but as the border conflict continued, the feeling in some quarters was that Israel was too tough in retaliation and in refusal to yield any of the occupied territories without an overall settlement. That hard-line stance seemed unlikely to change soon. Said a Jordanian cabinet member: "Eshkol hated the hawks, but Golda flies in formation with them. She has always been hard as nails."

On Dec. 28 five French gunboats, built for Israel but never delivered because of an arms embargo, departed under mysterious circumstances and reached Haifa on New Year's Eve.

MONEY VALUE: A "CRAWLING PEG"

Some Americans were griping about the new Eisenhower silver dollar not having enough silver in it. In Britain, people were complaining about the awkwardness of a seven-sided coin to replace the old 10 shilling note.

But in West Germany Chancellor Willy Brandt's new government got down to a more basic monetary problem. On Oct. 24 it took the long awaited step of increasing the price of the mark from 25 cents to 27.3 cents. The decision did not change the look of the money; it was designed to have much more important effects.

So was the devaluation of the French franc, arranged in great secrecy during the dead calm of an August in Paris (page 130) by President Georges Pompidou's government, also relatively new in office. Not only was it unexpected just then, but it came at a moment when there were virtually no businessmen in town to expect it.

Both actions were designed to right a lopsided international picture. West Germany was exporting a great deal more than it was importing (page 203). Investors and speculators were falling over one another to send their money into the country, expecting a rise in the price of the mark. The higher rate meant that exported West German goods would be more expensive, imports would come in more cheaply, and there would be fewer exports and more imports.

France had been in exactly the opposite situation, buying more than it was selling. Devaluation was expected to stimulate French sales and dampen purchasing.

In between the French and German actions, on Sept. 23, representatives of 112 countries at a meeting of the International Monetary Fund in Washington took a step that history will probably regard as more important. They created an entirely new money, a kind of "paper gold," designed to help make sudden big changes in currency values unnecessary. More than that, it may some day replace metallic gold altogether in the reserves of nations.

The decision was to issue $9.5 billion in the new money by Jan. 1, 1972.

In 1945, after World War II, a system of deposits and "drawing rights" was worked out to help countries in trouble. But the sum available totaled less than $8 billion. Though it had grown to more than $21 billion in the next 25 years, it had been nothing like enough to finance world trade then worth an annual $240 billion and growing at a rate of $7 billion a year.

A complex system of loans and currency swaps also had grown up for the same purpose, but it too proved inadequate. So were new supplies of gold. In recent years, new gold had tended to disappear more and more into jewelry, industrial uses and the hoards of people with little faith in the system.

France had a series of devaluations up to 1958 because it spent more than it took in. Britain had to drop the price of the pound twice, in 1949 and in 1967 (The World in 1967, 238–239).

But West Germany, after its currency reform in 1949, enjoyed almost uninterrupted prosperity. In 1961 it was doing so well that the mark appeared to be undervalued. Without too much fuss, its price was increased from 23.8 cents to 25 cents. Looking back, it seemed in 1969 that this was not enough.

Although there was an automatic increase in the price of West German goods abroad, the demand for them persisted. They were still cheap, well made, promptly delivered, intelligently marketed and promoted by an effective system of government aid to exports. Besides, West Germany had received a great deal of new plant free, under the Marshall Plan, and for 10 years had no military expenses weighing on its national budget. So West Germany continued to pile up surpluses.

A French crisis came in the spring of 1958. Riots and strikes forced de Gaulle's government to grant big wage increases. Workers bought more foreign goods with their higher earnings. The goods they themselves produced were now necessarily more expensive and didn't sell as well as they had.

Confidence was shaken. Businessmen, scenting a devaluation, got as much of their money out of the country as they could. They paid their foreign debts as quickly as possible and delayed collecting the money owed to them abroad.

Meanwhile, West German surpluses skyrocketed. Investment money arrived in embarrassing quantities. West German businessmen delayed paying their foreign debts and dunned their customers abroad to get their hands on what was owed them as fast as they could.

Experts who were neither French nor West German pretty well agreed the value of the mark should be put up and the franc devalued. But a major monetary conference held in Bonn in November 1968 ended in frustration (The World in 1968, 228).

The West German government made the price of the mark a point of honor. Chancellor Kurt George Kiesinger vowed that he would never raise the value while he was in office. Many West Germans felt foreign pressure was trying to get their government to price its businessmen out of foreign markets in favor of competitors who had not been as efficient or as hard working.

Five months later De Gaulle was defeated; four months after that, the franc was devalued.

Meanwhile, monetary experts had been working for years on the plan for a new kind of money. Why, they asked, should world trade depend for its financing on the amount of gold that happens to be mined in South Africa or the number of dollars the United States has to spend abroad because of a war in Vietnam?

They decided to create "Special Drawing Rights" on the IMF. These "SDR's," sometimes called paper gold, were seen as the beginning of a new system. Under it the members of the IMF, virtually the whole non-Communist world, eventually would be able to create as much money as they considered necessary to finance international trade, even more accurately than the central bank in a single country could determine the amount of money it thought should be circulating within it.

The United States opposed increasing the price of gold. For one thing, that would be equivalent to devaluing the dollar. An American devaluation would have pleased De Gaulle by taking the United States down a peg. But by the same token it was highly unlikely that anything of the sort could get past Congress.

For another thing, although the U.S. government held large gold reserves, American citizens did not. Those who would profit by a higher gold price would be the South African and Soviet governments, neither of them favorites in the United States, and a host of anonymous speculators from other countries.

For a third thing, foreigners had been happily accepting dollars for years. Many countries were holding a large proportion of their reserves in dollars instead of gold. Increasing the price of gold would reduce the value of those dollar holdings, and might well be resented as a breach of faith.

By the time the IMF finally approved the SDR plan, De Gaulle was out of office and the French had lost a large portion of their reserves. France could use SDR's, and any other help it could get.

President Pompidou switched signals and went along with the plan.

Now West German trade surpluses were building up again—$331 million in the month of September alone—and with them the pressure from other countries to revalue the mark. Kiesinger and his Christian Democratic party still refused. But Karl Schiller, his minister of economics, was a Social Democrat and a convert to revaluation. Besides, there was an election coming up (pages 201–204).

One sure bonus West Germans could expect: the millions of them who went on foreign vacations every year would get more francs or lire for their marks. And a bonus for the neighbors: the million and a half foreign workers in West Germany would get more money in their own currencies to send to their families or pile up for future investment at home.

Kiesinger's party lost strength in the election. The day the returns came in, he set the mark free to find its own level on world markets. It immediately started to float upwards. By the time Brandt was elected chancellor, it was being quoted at almost 27 cents.

Kiesinger was out, but Schiller was still in. Four days after Brandt took office, the West Germans let the other shoe drop: the mark was revalued.

An incidental effect of the French and German actions was a severe blow to the European Common Market and one of its most vaunted achievements: a uniform system of farm prices. Under the Common Market system, the currency changes would have meant that prices to French farmers would have had to rise, while West German farmers would get less for their crops.

Neither the French government nor the others in the Common Market wanted French farm prices to go up. That would have increased huge surpluses of food products that already are burdensomely expensive to manage. So France had to be exempted for two years from conforming to the uniform price system.

West German farmers were not ready to accept lower prices. Whatever was done to compensate them was bound to interfere in some way with the uniform price system, or the free flow of goods among the six member countries.

These dramatic effects confirmed economists in the opinion that something must be done to take the pressure out of changes in currency values. They felt that changes should come when economically required, without political fireworks. A favorite suggestion acquired the rather shivery name of the "crawling peg." The idea was to let the value of a currency change by a small amount—say no more than 2 per cent—every year. These changes would be permitted to accumulate. In the course of time, values would adjust themselves with more ease and certainty.

BIAFRA: "BABIES SUFFERED, DIED"

The city of Onitsha grew as Nigeria grew—slowly, as vastly different peoples found themselves under the same roof; quickly, as they learned to get along together. At the edge of the dense network of Ibo clan lands of the hilly green east, it was an Ibo town. But along the Niger River artery, it belonged to the open sandy north. Highways soon connected this marketplace to the west and Lagos.

At secession in May of 1967, Onitsha was the gateway to Biafra and the first obvious objective of a federal drive. It might have fallen quickly, but retreating Biafrans dynamited the $20 million Niger bridge. The explosion neatly lifted a 500-foot section into the air and then dropped it evenly onto the sloping bank.

It took Nigerian forces seven months to capture Onitsha despite gains elsewhere. The victory was heady and the psychological boost immeasurable.

But 18 months later (October), the Nigerian Army was still there and under fire. A scraggly lot of 2,600 refugees and 500 traders remained of the city's hundreds of thousands. The market was burned to the ground.

More than anywhere else in the sapping war that dashed hopes for a vital African model nation, Onitsha showed what could not be done. If Nigeria were to unite itself on the battlefield, it would cost more blood and money than anyone dared consider.

Already the war had killed perhaps two million people. No one really knew how many. Ibo children suffered and died in the dense bush and their mothers buried them if they could. There were no records. Kwashiorkor, a Ghanaian word for protein deficiency, demented minds and withered bodies. Stomachs swelled and arms shriveled. Soldiers disappeared in action, some were killed, others escaped. Either was easy for a soldier with scant weeks of training and maybe not more than 12 years of age.

As the war slogged on into its third year, it became evident that no one was going to give in easily. If Biafra had to cook its own gasoline in backyard distilleries, its homemade armored cars would still roll. Back to back in a tight circle of good roads and concealing jungles, Biafrans seemed ready to stand indefinitely.

With Biafra cut from 30,000 square miles to about 2,000—a little over one per cent of all of Nigeria—advancing Nigerians found every inch fiercely defended. Confined to the roads, federal units had to commit scarce troops to protect their supply lines from infiltrators hidden in the bush on either side.

Even nightly patrols by fighters and bombers could not cut off the stream of supplies and ammunition reaching Biafra's roadbed airstrip well inside the tight circle. Food supplies dwindled when the International Red Cross halted mercy flights, but bullets—and some food—kept coming. Relief workers inside Biafra reported new starvation crises, and once again arose the threat of millions dying, but Biafran leadership showed no sign of relenting.

In fact, Biafra managed a successful offensive in the air behind a fleet of five single-engine Swedish aircraft mounted with rockets. Count Carl von Rosen, a Swedish charter pilot who had flown relief, brought them to Biafra in his summer vacation. With mosquito attacks, the tiny planes sought out strategic oil installations. Hitting only a few times a month, the planes

forced oil companies to reduce production costing the federal government millions of dollars in monthly revenue. By September, Biafra increased its air force, attacking in widely scattered areas of the Midwest State. Until the raids, oil production had already surpassed the prewar level of 580,000 barrels a day making Nigeria the world's 11th oil producer. It dropped so sharply that figures were withheld.

Perhaps worse, the thin fabric that held Nigeria together began to tear. The Yorubas, a tribe of 10 million in the West, began showing general discontent and latent political churning by violently resisting tax collection. Led by agitators, farmers rioted again and again, ambushing police and soldiers with homemade muskets and modern rifles. The Moslem North, removed from the war, felt frustration at draconian control from Lagos.

Just after lunch on Sept. 5, a towering Nigerian stepped from a plane from London to a roar of "Zeeek, Zeeeek." Even soldiers holding back the crowds forgot themselves and joined in the rush. It was 64-year-old Doctor Nnamdi Azikiwe, first president of Nigeria, coming home after years of self-exile. An Ibo, Azikiwe said he decided "enough is enough" and switched from a lukewarm commitment to Biafra to a solid stand for a single Nigeria. He said: "I'm going to do all I can to convince other Ibos to come back . . . that there is no genocide."

Biafran leader Gen. C. Odumegwu Ojukwu immediately disowned him and Biafra's roving diplomats denounced him. The effect inside

Biafra, where millions once had an almost worshipful respect for Zik, was impossible to gauge.

The federal leadership, though, had been working hard for such a windfall. Here was top-level evidence they meant the Ibos no harm.

The Organization of African Unity brought leaders of both sides to the same conference, if not the same table, for the third time. They did not get past the basic issue—whether Biafra must renounce session before talks start.

The sixth OAU Summit in September called for talks but specified a united Nigeria.

At stake, according to Ojukwu, was the Ibos' entire cultural identity. As the war progressed, he broadened his definition of genocide to include the annihilation of a people's culture. Riots in the North that killed thousands of Ibos convinced his tribesmen that they could never live in peace with the rest of Nigeria, Ojukwu said. Federal authorities offered countering arguments, saying that there were identifiable reasons for the 1966 riots, many attributable to the Ibos themselves.

Feeding the civilians inside Biafra became a moving challenge, perhaps the most frustrating in the 105-year history of the International Committee of the Red Cross. Radar-directed Nigerian Mig 17s shot down a Swedish Red Cross DC7 June 5 as it was flying an ICRC mercy mission from the island of Fernando Po. The ICRC suspended operations, which meant hundreds of tons nightly for Biafran civilians, nearly all faced with diet deficiencies. Church and other relief groups maintained limited supply flights.

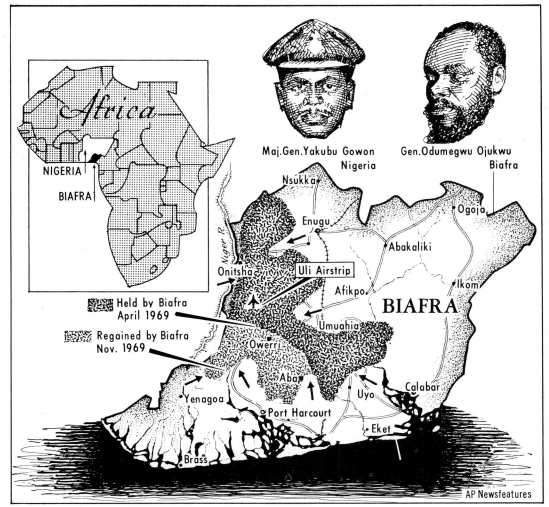

NIGERIA
BIAFRA

Maj.Gen.Yakubu Gowon
Nigeria

Gen.Odumegwu Ojukwu
Biafra

▨ Held by Biafra April 1969

▨ Regained by Biafra Nov. 1969

Nsukka
Enugu
Ogoja
Abakaliki
Onitsha
Uli Airstrip
Afikpo
Ikom
BIAFRA
Umuahia
Owerri
Aba
Uyo
Calabar
Yenagoa
Port Harcourt
Eket
Brass

AP Newsfeatures

MURDER IN MICHIGAN

On the night of July 9, 1967 Mary Fleszar, 19, left her apartment near the Eastern Michigan University campus in Ypsilanti and vanished. Her body was found a month later. She had been stabbed again and again, her fingers and feet had been cut off; they remained unrecoverd. The condition of her body prevented authorities from determining if she had been molested sexually.

The day after she was identified Chester Fleszar, her father, talked to police. "They said he (the slayer) would kill again within the year," Fleszar recalled later. "They hoped they could stop him."

Part, at least, of the official prediction was correct: One year to the day after Miss Fleszar disappeared, James Schell buried his attractive dark-haired daughter, Joan, 20, an Eastern Michigan art student. She had been stabbed and sexually abused. Her blue miniskirt had been twisted around her neck, but the rest of her clothing had been stacked neatly beside the body in a wooded lovers' lane area of Ann Arbor.

Police said Miss Schell had last been seen accepting a ride with three youths who encountered her as she sought to hitchhike from Ypsilanti to nearby Ann Arbor, where she planned to visit a friend. When her body was found July 7, 1968 police recalled the murder of Miss Fleszar, but they hesitated to speculate on similarities of the two cases and they obviously could not foresee that at least five more brutal killings would take place among girls of high school and college age in the Ypsilanti-Ann Arbor vicinity.

Nearly another year passed. By mid-March of 1969 the Fleszar and Schell murders, unsolved, had faded from newspaper front pages. Then, on the first day of spring in 1969 a pretty University of Michigan coed disappeared. The body of Jane Mixer, 23, shot twice in the head, was found the next day. Law officers said she had not been assaulted sexually, but a woman's stocking had been wrapped around her neck—and the stocking wasn't hers.

While details of the three crimes varied, police concluded that they could have one characteristic in common. They could have been conceived by a deranged mind. Miss Mixer's body, they cited as possible evidence, had been carefully laid out in a cemetery grave and all three victims had been coeds.

* * * *

The newspage tag of "coed killer" thus was born, as was widespread apprehension among the 50,000 students of the two cities. Apprehension became outright fear when, the morning after Dr. and Mrs. Dan Mixer buried their daughter at Muskegon, workmen found in an Ann Arbor subdivision the mutilated body of a high school dropout from Romulus, Mich. She was Maralynn Skelton, 16. She too had planned to hitchhike to Ypsilanti, as she had informed friends there by phone the day before. She never arrived. Police said she had been beaten savagely across the back and hips—probably with a leather belt—and on the face. Her breasts had been slashed. An autopsy showed she died of a massive skull fracture.

Caution became the counterpart of terror among most coeds and many other women. After Mary Fleszar was killed Mrs. Sharon Roe, whose husband Ken worked a moonlighting job, worried about going home from an education class at which she spent her

Last rites for Karen Sue Beineman, slain coed

evenings. One night she asked John Norman Collins, a friend and classmate, to walk with her and check her apartment to make certain no assailant lurked within. Collins was accommodating. As Ken Roe reported later, "he walked up the stairs, looked in both bedrooms, the kitchen, closets, under the bed and on the back porch." Sharon had then relaxed. She and Collins sat down in the kitchen, she said, and talked, "a little bit" about murder "but mostly about the class."

No more than the police did she know that four more possibly related violent deaths would follow. Neither did she even imagine that the dark-haired young man with whom she sat chatting in her kitchen would be accused in one of these, almost two years later.

* * * *

Less than a month after Maralynn Skelton's slaying another shock wave jolted the college towns. On April 16 the nearly nude body of 13-year-old Dawn Basom was found alongside a dirt road three miles north of the Ypsilanti apartment house where she lived with her widowed mother, Cleo. Dawn had been strangled and slashed across the breasts, police said. A rag had been stuffed into her mouth. Officers also said they believed the slaying had taken place in the glass-strewn basement of an abandoned farmhouse nearby, inasmuch as bits of glass in her feet matched shards found on the basement floor. They theorized she had tried to escape but her slayer had caught her from behind and had choked her with a length of electric cord.

Nearly two months—weeks of tension but not homicidal—passed before Alice Kalom, 23, of Portage, Mich., a University of Michigan graduate student, was found dead near abandoned farm buildings north of Ann Arbor. She had been shot in the head, stabbed, slashed in the neck and raped. Two nights earlier, at a dance in Ann Arbor June 7, she had last been seen alive.

Karen Sue Beineman, 18, disappeared July 23, a Wednesday. By Friday the feeling that the Eastern Michigan freshman had been slain was growing in police stations, campus buildings and homes throughout the area. On Saturday a couple walking on a gravel road to their mailbox found Miss Beineman's nude body in a ravine. Her face had been beaten beyond recognition. Officers replaced the body with a department store mannequin, then concealed themselves and waited. About midnight someone approached the decoy but fled when the police closed in to seize him. They said he was not found thereafter.

Less than three weeks before Miss Beineman's death yet another coed had been fatally shot, but authorities reported that they were unable to connect this with any of the other killings.

* * * *

John Norman Collins, 22, was arrested a few days after the Karen Beineman tragedy. He was subsequently charged with first-degree murder in the death of Miss Beineman alone; officers said they had not been able to associate him with any of the other cases, but several Eastern Michigan coeds had reported that Collins had offered them rides on his motorcycle on the day Miss Beineman dropped from sight.

Collins denied any connection with Miss Beineman's demise. Sharon and Ken Roe were shaken when they learned Collins was in custody. Said Roe: "My immediate reaction was, 'God, he walked my wife home from school.' He was the kind of guy you trusted. . . . He was welcome any time at our house. . . . John was just as upset and shocked as the rest of us. . . .'"

At year's end Collins had been arraigned on the murder charge but had not entered a formal plea. A preliminary hearing was set tentatively for late in January, and officials said court action was expected to extend well into 1970.

GREETINGS—BY LOTTERY

Birthdays acquired a non-celebrative significance and a new greeting card on Dec. 1. The occasion was the nation's first draft lottery in 27 years. It effected those youths born from Jan. 1, 1944 to Dec. 31, 1950. After it was over some 850,000 young Americans had been assigned places in the order of call, based on the dates they were born.

The primary advantage of the lottery system, sponsors said, was that it limited to one year the period in which a person was liable to be drafted. As long as the lottery continued, a new drawing would be held every year, assigning places to 19-year-olds who would then be exposed to the draft until the next year's lottery. If not drafted within one year they would be virtually free of military obligation. If deferred,

they would be eligible for one year after their deferments lapsed.

The only exception would be a national emergency affecting all young men.

Under the old method of draft selection the period of uncertainty lasted for seven years, from a man's 19th birthday to his 26th, with the oldest men drafted first.

The first date drawn was Sept. 14 and the last was June 8th. If it were only a matter of arithmetic, the first 170 birthdays drawn would just about provide 1970's draftees, but local draft boards warned that varying quotas or needs could blur the dividing line. To differentiate between those with the same birth dates a second drawing was held—this one with the letters of the alphabet.

Some congressmen, cool to the lottery proposal, had said it would hurt officer procurement. Others favored a complete overhaul of draft laws. In 1967 Congress had included in the draft extension bill a sentence that prohibited the President from establishing a random system without prior congressional approval (*The World in 1967, 132*). Pressure for the lottery continued, however, and in September 1969 President Nixon asked Congress to pass a bill removing the prohibition. On Nov. 26 Congress heeded Nixon's request. But in announcing the lottery the President said he would not be satisfied until the draft could be eliminated entirely.

On the day after the drawing draft boards across the country said they were swamped with telephone calls. "We have wives calling to see if their husbands will be drafted, deferred men asking if deferments will continue—you name a question, we've got it," said Helen Bowers, executive secretary of the Albuquerque, N. M., draft board.

FOR PANTHER SEALE, A MISTRIAL

After a tumultuous performance in a Chicago courtroom Bobby G. Seale faced a four-year sentence for contempt and a second trial, in 1970, on a charge of conspiracy. Seale, 32, national leader of the Black Panthers, was one of the so-called Chicago Eight accused of conspiring to incite a riot during the 1968 Democratic National Convention (*The World in 1968, 161–166, 191*).

U.S. Circuit Judge Julius J. Hoffman convicted Seale Nov. 5 on 16 counts of contempt resulting from a series of outbursts during six weeks of proceedings in the conspiracy case. The judge considered Seale so adamant at times that on Oct. 29 he had ordered the Panther leader gagged and shackled. A week later, when removal of the restraints was ordered, Seale re-

sumed a demeanor which Hoffman said "constituted a deliberate and willful attack on the administration of justice and an attempt to sabotage the function of the federal judicial system."

The court also decreed a mistrial for Seale and set the new trial for April 23, 1970.

Seale had contended that he had been deprived of his right to defend himself by the absence of his chosen attorney, Charles R. Garry of San Francisco, who was recovering from surgery at the time.

The conspiracy case had been the first attempt to test a section of the 1968 civil rights act which provided that anyone convicted of crossing state lines to incite a riot may be sentenced to a maximum of 10 years in prison and fined $20,000. Seale was from Oakland, Calif.

FOR THE RECORD

REBOUND. By Brig. Gen. Omar Torrijos. Ousted as commander of the Panama National Guard and the nation's leader by two colonels Dec. 15, while in Mexico City to see a horserace, Torrijos slipped back into Panama the following day and returned to power with the help of those members of the capital guard garrison who remained loyal to him. The coup leaders, Cols. Ramiro Silvera and Amado Sanjur, were arrested.

DIED. Arthur da Costa e Silva, 67, former president of Brazil, on Dec. 17 in Rio de Janeiro at Laranjeiras Presidential Palace where he had been under treatment since suffering a stroke Aug. 29 (*p. 194*). Costa e Silva, who rose to power after a 1964 uprising, ousted the government of Joao Goulart and was succeeded by a military triumvirate when he was stricken.

NAMED. Alexander Dubcek, former Czech party chief (*p. 211*), as Czechoslovak ambassador to Turkey Dec. 15. Dubcek, 48, a liberal whose reform movement was stopped by Soviet tanks in 1968, was named to the post despite strong left-wing opposition. On Dec. 17 Joseph Smrkovsky, 58, who served as Dubcek's main lieutenant during the liberalization period, resigned from Parliament along with 10 other liberals.

BOMBED. The Banca Nazionale Della Agricultura in Milan, Italy, Dec. 12. Fourteen persons were killed. The same night three bombs went off almost simultaneously in Rome. More than 100 persons were injured in the four blasts in the two cities. Milan Police Chief Marcello Guida said, "There could have been no other reason than anarchy in itself." The police Dec. 16 charged nine persons with having engineered the bombings in the two cities.

FINAL CHAPTER. For Project Blue Book, the 21-year-old U.S. Air Force agency that investigated more than 12,000 reported sightings of unidentified flying objects (UFOs). The agency was disbanded Dec. 17 on recommendation of the Condon Committee (*pages 21–24*) which concluded that the project's findings contributed nothing to science or national security.

The Rolling Stones were the chief attraction at the December Rock festival in Tracy, Calif., one of the many musical events that attracted huge crowds of young people across the United States during 1969

Project Supervisor
Keith Fuller
Editors
Howard C. Heyn   Robert D. Price
Photos
Jack Schwadel
Promotion and Distribution
Dan Perkes   Ed Fleming
Staff Writers
Karol Stonger   Phil Thomas   Peace Sterling

Feature Narratives

Elizabeth Bassett, New York
  Student unrest
Howard Benedict, Cape Kennedy
  Apollo space missions
W. Stephens Broening, Paris
  French elections
Frank Cormier, Washington
  Nixon in Europe
  Nixon's first year
W. C. Crider Jr., New Orleans
  Clay Shaw trial
Ralph Dighton, Los Angeles
  California mud,
  oil and water
Otto Doelling, Frankfurt
  German elections
Art Everett, New York
  Sirhan Sirhan trial
Colin Frost, London
  Irish riots
Bernard Gavzer, New York
  James Earl Ray trial
Sterling Green, Washington
  Economic-Tax
Gene Handsaker and
Richard Meyer, Los Angeles
  Sharon Tate slayings
Howard C. Heyn, New York
  Fortas resignation
Garvin Hudgins, Washington
  School integration
Cornelius F. Hurley, Boston
  Kennedy accident
Carl Leubsdorf, Washington
  ABM
Jules Loh and Sid Moody,
  New York, and
Richard Meyer, Los Angeles
  Pueblo inquiry
Don McKee, Atlanta
  Civil rights
Joe Mohbat, Washington
  Nixon inauguration
Relman Morin, New York
  Eisenhower death
Saul Pett, New York
  Farewell to *Eagle*
Robert D. Price, New York
  Farewell to LBJ
  Vietnam
  World Series
Dennis Redmont, Rome
  New Cardinals
Naomi Rock, New York
  Woodstock festival
Bill Ryan, New York
  Dubcek ouster
  Ho Chi Minh death
Karol Stonger
  Flying saucers
  Apollo 11 acclaim
Phil Thomas
  Green Berets
  Medicaid-Medicare
Ed Tunstall, New Orleans
  Hurricane Camille

Contributing Reporters

Myron Belkind, New Delhi
Carl Hartman, Brussels
Lowell McKirgan, Detroit
Timothy Renn, Chicago
Mort Rosenblum, Lagos
Jack Schreibman, San Francisco
Granville Watts, London
Saigon:
  Peter Arnett
  George Esper
  Willis G. Johnson
  David Mason
  Robert Ohman
  Michael Putzel
  Richard H. Pyle
  David Rosenzweig
  Jay R. Sharbutt
  Nguyen Gia Thanh

Photographs
(The illustrations in this volume
were selected for the most part
from the news photo reports of The
Associated Press and, except where
specifically credited, were taken
by staff photographers of The AP
and its member newspapers).

Staff Photographers
Athens
  Aristotle Saricostas
Berlin
  Edwin Reichert
Bonn
  Heinrich Sanden
Buenos Aires
  Max Simon
  Domingo Zenteno Zeggara
Copenhagen
  Mogens Holmberg
  Sigvard Holmer
  Poul Henrik Seifert
  Ejirn Sveegard
Frankfurt
  Dieter Endlicher
  Bernhard Frye
  Peter Hillebrecht
  Kurt Strumpf
Hamburg
  Heinz Ducklau
  Helmuth Lohmann
London
  Leslie C. Priest
  William F. Rider Rider
  Dennis Lee Royle
  Sidney Smart
  Frank A. Tewkesbury
  Edward S. Worth
Madrid
  Leopoldo Gomez Gonzalez
Mexico City
  Jesus Diaz
  Javier Renero
Milan
  Raoul Fornezza
Moscow
  Vasili Semenovich Gritsan

Oslo
  Tom Brauner Jensen
  Paul Oweson
Paris
  Spartaco Bodini
  Pierre Godot
  Jean Herlin
  Ernest Jacquere
  Michel Laurent
  Jean Jacques Levy
  Michel Claude Lipchitz
  Jacques Marqueton
  Georges Raulin Jr.
  Albert Roques
Rome
  Giuseppe Anastasi
  Giulio Broglio
  Giovanni Foggia
  James Pringle
  Mario Torrisi
Saigon
  Yvonne Cornu
  Horst Faas
  Mark Godfrey
  Graham McInerney
  Rick Merron
  Max Nash
  Dang Van Phuoc
  Carl D. Robinson
  Charles J. Ryan
  Hubert Van Es
Seoul
  Ken Chon-Kil
Tel Aviv
  Brian Calvert
Tokyo
  Max Desfor
  Henri Huet
  Uichi Ishizaki
  Mitsunori Chigita
  Keiichi Mori
  Bunji Watanabe
Albany
  Steven D. Starr
Atlanta
  Horace W. Cort
  Lou Garcia
  Joe Holloway
  Charles E. Kelly
Austin
  Ted Powers
Baltimore
  William A. Smith
Boston
  Francis C. Curtin
  J. Walter Green
  A. E. Maloof
Chicago
  Frederick H. Jewell
  Edward S. Kitch
  Charles E. Knoblock
  James Palmer
  Laurence E. Stoddard
Cincinnati
  Harvey E. Smith
Cleveland
  Julian C. Wilson
Columbia
  Louis Krasky
Columbus
  Gene E. Herrick
Dallas
  Ferd Kaufman
  Carl E. Linde
  Dave Taylor
  Harold Waters
Denver
  Robert D. Scott
Detroit
  Mark Foley
  Rich Schweinwald
  Preston Stroup

Harrisburg
  Paul Vathis
Houston
  Edward F. Kolenovsky
Indianapolis
  Douglas L. Roberts
Kansas City
  William P. Straeter Jr.
Los Angeles
  George Brich
  Harold F. Filan
  Wallace H. Fong Jr.
  Harry P. Matosian
  David F. Smith
  Edward C. Widdis
Miami
  James A. Bourdier
  James P. Kerlin
  Howard R. Massey
  Hal Valentine
Milwaukee
  Paul J. Shane
Minneapolis
  Robert J. Walsh
New Orleans
  Jack R. Thornell
New York
  Edward T. Adams
  Murray L. Becker
  Anthony Camerano
  Ron Frehin
  Daniel J. Grossi
  Harry L. Harris
  Jacob Harris
  J. Spencer Jones
  Jack Kanthal
  Robert Kradin
  Martin M. Lederhandler
  John J. Lent
  David Pickoff
  John P. Rooney
  Robert H. Schutz
  Robert A. Wands
Philadelphia
  Wilson G. Ingraham
  Ronald B. Kennedy
  Warren M. Winterbottom
Pittsburgh
  Harry Cabluck
San Francisco
  Ernest K. Bennett
  Robert H. Houston
  Robert K. Klein
  Paul C. Strong
  Sal Veder
Sacramento
  Walter Zeboski
Seattle
  Barry R. Sweet
St. Louis
  Frederick O. Waters
Tallahassee
  William M. Hudson
Washington
  Henry D. Burroughs Jr.
  Robert A. Daugherty
  John A. Duricka
  Harvey W. Georges
  Charles P. Gorry
  Henry Griffin
  Charles W. Harrity
  Byron H. Rollins
  John H. Rous
  William J. Smith
  Charles B. Tasnadi

Research Assistant
  David S. C. Liu
Maps
  George Braunsdorf
Almanac Editor
  John Koehler

AP News Almanac

CHRONOLOGY—1969

JANUARY

1—Marian Elizabeth Habe, 17, daughter of Swiss author Hans Habe and actress Eloise Hardt, was found slain in a ravine, one day after she had been kidnaped from her home in West Hollywood, Calif. She had been beaten and stabbed in the neck and chest.

2—Sen. Edward M. Kennedy, D-Mass., unseated Sen. Russell B. Long D-La., as Democratic whip or assistant majority leader of the upper house.

3—Rep. Adam Clayton Powell, D-N.Y., denied his seat in the 90th Congress on charges of misusing funds, was re-seated by a 252-160 vote, but was fined $25,000 and lost his 22 years seniority.

3—An Eastern Airlines jet carrying 146 persons from New York to Miami was hijacked by a Negro couple and forced to fly to Cuba.

4—More than 110 persons were injured in fighting between Roman Catholic civil rights marchers, Protestant opponents, and police in the worst of a series of riots in Northern Ireland.

5—Henry Cabot Lodge, former U.S. ambassador to Saigon, was appointed by President-elect Nixon to head the American delegation to expanded Vietnam peace talks in Paris.

5—The Soviet Union launched an unmanned spacecraft on a flight to Venus, scheduled to be completed in mid-May.

6—An Allegheny Airlines propjet crashed while attempting a landing at Bradford, Pa. Eleven of 28 persons en route from Washington to Detroit were killed.

6—The French government banned shipment of arms to Israel.

6—The U.S. Treasury Department reported the national debt increased by four per cent in 1968 to $361.2 billion.

7—Jane Britton, 22, daughter of J. Boyd Britton, vice president of Radcliffe College, was bludgeoned to death in her apartment in Cambridge, Mass. She was a graduate student in anthropology at Harvard University.

7—The prime rate for interest on loans by major banks was raised by ¼ per cent to a record 7 per cent in a continuing effort to curb inflation.

8—Two FBI agents were killed in Washington, D.C. while hunting a suspect in a bank robbery. One of the two was the first Negro agent to die in line of duty. The suspect, a fugitive from a federal prison, was captured six hours later and accused of the killings.

9—The Labor Department announced that the nation's unemployment rate in 1968 was 3.6 per cent, the lowest since the Korean War.

9—The Apollo 8 astronauts received Distinguished Service Medals from President Johnson and a standing ovation from Congress.

10—Sweden's government announced its intention to establish diplomatic relations with North Vietnam, the first Western European nation to do so.

10—Directors of the Saturday Evening Post voted to discontinue publication with the Feb. 8 issue, ending a magazine career that began in 1821.

11—Two airliners were hijacked in flight and forced to fly to Cuba. One, a Corvair of Peruvian National Airlines, carried 83 Argentine exchange students among the 110 passengers from Buenos Aires to Miami. The other was a Boeing 727 of United Airlines, en route from Jacksonville to Miami.

14—The nuclear aircraft carrier Enterprise, the world's largest warship, was torn by fire and explosions while on maneuvers in the Pacific 75 miles southwest of Hawaii; 25 men died and 85 were injured.

14—President Johnson delivered to Congress his valedictory message on the State of the Union, urging the nation to press "the quest for peace" and to commit itself to the fulfillment of his social programs.

15—President Johnson sent to Congress a budget proposing expenditure of $195.3 billion in fiscal 1970. A surplus of $3.4 billion was anticipated.

16—A large round table flanked by two rectangular tables was agreed to by parties to the Paris peace talks, ending a 10-week stalemate in negotiations to end the war in Vietnam.

16—Two Soviet astronauts walked through space from Soyuz 5 and boarded Soyuz 4 in a four-hour link-up of the spacecrafts described as the "world's first experimental space station."

16—Scientists at Merck Sharp & Dhome Research Laboratories and Rockefeller University announced simultaneously they had synthesized the enzyme ribonuclease, a complex chemical of life that performed vital functions in almost all cells.

17—Two Negro students were shot fatally during a business meeting of the Afro-American Student Center at the Los Angeles campus of the University of California.

18—Several hundred Czechoslovak students in Prague marched on the Soviet command post and Wenceslas Square where a 21-year-old youth had set himself afire two days earlier and suffered fatal burns as a personal protest against the continued Russian presence in his country.

18—President Johnson signed into law a bill to double the President's salary to $200,000 a year, effective with Richard Nixon's inauguration.

19—A United Air Lines jetliner carrying 38 persons from Los Angeles to Milwaukee crashed into the Pacific shortly after takeoff, killing all aboard.

19—Two airliners en route to Miami—one an Eastern Airlines jet with 171 persons aboard, the other an Ecuadorian airliner carrying 88 persons—were hijacked to Cuba.

19—About 5,000 anti-war, anti-Nixon demonstrators staged a counter-inaugural demonstration along Pennsylvania Avenue in Washington; 18 persons were arrested.

19—A year-long student occupation of Tokyo University ended when police seized the last stronghold, Yasuda Hall; most of the 400 occupiers were arrested after a two-day battle.

20—Richard M. Nixon was inaugurated as the nation's 37th President.

22—Several shots, believed aimed at top Soviet officials, were fired at a motorcade carrying four cosmonauts to a Kremlin rally in Moscow; two persons were injured, and an accused assailant was arrested.

23—The 12th and final member of President Nixon's Cabinet, Interior Secretary Walter Hickel, was approved by the Senate 75-16 after five days of hearings.

23—Tornadoes ripped through 40 miles of Southern Mississippi hill country, killing 31 persons, injuring hundreds.

23—Police at San Francisco State College arrested 380 persons when strikers violated an order against campus rallies.

24—A National Airlines jet carrying 47 persons from Key West to Miami was diverted to Cuba on orders from "a kid with a knife."

24—The Franco regime imposed a state of emergency for all of Spain in the wake of student violence and political protests.

25—Student demonstrators set fire to government buildings, buses and cars in Karachi in the second day of protests against President Mohammed Ayub Khan of Pakistan.

25—A string of railroad tank cars filled with butane exploded in Laurel, Miss., injuring 19 persons and demolishing up to 40 homes.

26—Fourteen Iraqi Nationals, including nine Jews, were hanged in a public execution in Baghdad on charges of espionage for Israel.

27—Nine days of torrential rains in California ended with the worst flooding in more than 30 years, 91 deaths and an estimated $60 million property damage.

27—The Supreme Court agreed unanimously that no court may decide disputes over church property when religious doctrine is involved.

28—Two United States airliners en route to Miami —one owned by National, the other by Eastern— were hijacked to Cuba with 145 persons aboard.

29—The U.S. 1968 balance of trade showed a surplus of $726 million, the lowest since $265 million in the depression year of 1937.

29—The cost of living increased 4.7 per cent in 1968, the biggest hike in 17 years, said the Labor Department.

30—The National Commission on the Cause and Prevention of Violence said in an interim report that the "key to much of the violence in our society seems to lie with the young."

31—A National Airlines plane carrying 55 persons from San Francisco to Miami was forced to fly to Cuba by a lone gunman.

31—Allied troops destroyed a huge Nort Vietnamese base, complete with underground hospital, dining halls, command post and bunkers for 5,000 men some 50 miles northwest of Saigon.

FEBRUARY

1—A piano fantasy believed written by Franz Schubert in 1817 was found in an attic in southern Austria and unveiled on the anniversary of the composer's birth.

3—Four Cubans hijacked to Havana a Newark-Miami Eastern Air Lines jet carrying 93 persons. An attempt to divert a National Airlines plane to Havana was foiled and two suspects were arrested.

3—The president of the Mozambique National Liberation Front, Dr. Eduardo Mondlane, was assassinated with a time bomb in Tanzania.

3—The United Federation of Teachers was fined $220,000 and its local president, Albert Shanker, was sentenced to 15 days in jail on charges of defying court orders to end three New York City strikes early in the 1968-69 school year.

5—A $12,500 annual pay raise for Congress was assured by House action, effective Feb. 14.

5—Sixteen miles of beach at Santa Barbara, Calif., was blackened by a huge oil slick from a leaking well off the coast.

5—The Federal Communications Commission voted 6 to 1 to issue a proposal that would ban cigarette advertising from radio and television.

6—At least 22 persons were killed and 100 injured in the collision of a passenger train and a freight train 100 miles northeast of Melbourne, Australia.

7—A Nigerian jet fighter-bomber strafed a market place and maternity clinic in the Biafrian village of Umuohiagu, killing at least 200 persons.

9—A storm of near-blizzard proportions dumped more than a foot of wind-whipped snow on the Northeastern United States, causing more than 100 deaths.

10—An Eastern Air Lines plane en route from San Juan, P.R., to Miami was hijacked to Cuba.

11—Atty. Gen. John Mitchell authorized federal agents to resume wiretaps in investigations of organized crime.

11—Three days of rioting in Bombay over a long-standing border dispute left 43 persons dead, 200 wounded.

11—A sweeping election victory by the United Front Party in West Bengal gave Communists control of two of India's 17 state governments.

11—I. W. Abel was re-elected president of the 1.2-million-member United Steelworkers of America.

13—At least 27 persons were injured when a homemade bomb exploded in the visitors' gallery of the Canadian and Montreal stock exchanges.

13—National Guard troops at the University of Wisconsin and policemen at Duke University used tear gas to break up demonstrations backing demands of Negro students.

14—New York City longshoremen ratified a three-year contract, the first workers in 20 East and Gulf coast ports to end a strike begun 56 days earlier.

14—United States and Peruvian relations were strained when a Peruvian Navy gunboat fired on American tuna boats fishing off the coast; two boats were damaged.

16—The Year of the Rooster began in Vietnam with a lunar new year truce broken only by minor skirmishes.

16—Three yachts carrying 15 persons—including four Americans—from Hong Kong to Macao were seized by Chinese Communists.

17—Aquanaut Berry Louis Cannon, a veteran of the government's Sealab projects, died 600 feet beneath the Pacific shortly before a 60-day experiment in ocean-bottom living was to begin off the California coast.

17—Peru signed her first trade agreement with the Soviet Union.

18—Six persons were wounded when Arab terrorists ambushed an Israeli airliner as it taxied for takeoff at Zurich airport.

18—Anhydrous ammonia fumes, spewed from an overturned railroad tank car in Crete, Neb., were fatal to eight persons; 12 persons were hospitalized and scores of families evacuated from their homes.

19—Seven persons convicted as spies for Israel were executed in Baghdad.

19—The University of Wisconsin's Afro-American and Race Relations Center was damaged by fire as an 11-day strike to press for a black studies department was temporarily halted.

21—President Ayub Khan of Pakistan, whose government was target for four months of massive demonstrations by opponents, announced he would not seek re-election.

21—An explosion, believed set off by Arab guerrillas, ripped through a Jerusalem supermarket, killing two shoppers and injuring nine others.

22—Hamer H. Budge, former Idaho congressman, was named by President Nixon to be chairman of the Securities and Exchange commission, succeeding Manuel F. Cohen.

23—Saigon, Da Nang and 125 other cities and bases in South Vietnam were shelled by the enemy in the heaviest bombardment in nine months.

23—Former President Eisenhower, hospitalized 10 months with a heart ailment, underwent surgery to remove an acute intestinal obstruction.

24—Mariner 6, an unmanned spacecraft, was launched on a 226-million-mile trek to Mars and a five-year mission to determine if life existed there.

24—The U.S. Supreme Court held that public school pupils might exercise their right of political expression during school hours so long as they did not disrupt classes.

24—The American Federation of Teachers ended a classroom boycott at San Francisco State College, begun Jan. 6 in support of Negro student demands.

25—An Eastern Air Lines jet en route from St. Louis to Puerto Rico with 61 persons aboard was diverted to Havana by a gunman.

25—North Vietnamese suicide squads attacked two U.S. Marine artillery squads near the Demilitarized Zone; 20 Marines and 35 enemy soldiers died in hand-to-hand combat.

26—Torrential rains in Southern California and a two-foot snowfall in New England claimed at least 40 lives.

26—Rep. Rogers C. B. Morton, R-Md., was named to succeed Ray C. Bliss who resigned as Republican National Chairman.

26—General Motors recalled a record 4.9 million cars and trucks for repair of a possibly faulty exhaust system.

MARCH

1—New Orleans businessman Clay Shaw was acquitted by a jury of conspiring to kill President Kennedy; two days later District Attorney Jim Garrison filed perjury charges against Shaw.

2—A race car slammed into the stands at a drag strip near Covington, Ga., killing 11 spectators and injuring 50.

2—The Soviet Union and China fought what was believed the largest single clash on the Ussuri River border in 10 years of tensions; some 70 persons, including the Russian commander, were killed.

2—President Nixon concluded an eight-day, five-nation tour of Europe.

3—Sirhan B. Sirhan testified at his own murder trial and identified himself as the assassin of Sen. Robert F. Kennedy.

3—Columbia University trustees abandoned plans for a gymnasium in Harlem's Morningside Park, focal point of student demonstrations that paralyzed the campus a year earlier.

5—A National Airlines plane carrying 26 persons from New York to Miami was diverted to Cuba by a bearded gunman who robbed a passenger of $1,700; the money was returned by Cuban authorities.

5—Ruth Eisemann-Schier, the first woman on the FBI's "10 most wanted" list, was arrested in Norman, Okla., on charges stemming from the abduction of Barbara Jane Mackle, Miami heiress (The World in 1968, 251-253).

5—Justice Minister Gustav Heinemann, a Social Democrat, was elected president of West Germany by a narrow margin over Defense Minister Gerhard Schroder; the voting in West Berlin was without incident after weeks of harassment by East Germany.

5—A bombardment of Saigon, the fourth since the Communist offensive began Feb. 23, left at least 22 civilians dead, scores wounded.

6—The price of gold soared to a record $47.51 per ounce in Paris on speculation that the franc would topple in the wake of a planned 24-hour general strike.

9—William V. Jones, 60-year-old father of 11, was rescued after being entombed in a Utah silver mine for eight days.

9—Lt. Gen. Abdel Moneim Riad, chief of staff of Egyptian armed forces, was killed during an Israel-Egyptian gun battle across the Suez Canal.

10—The Labor Department reported that employment rose by nearly 380,000 jobs in February, the largest monthly increase on record.

10—The U.S. Supreme Court ruled 5 to 3 that defendants in criminal cases had a right to see transcripts collected through illegal federal bugging.

10—James Earl Ray pleaded guilty in Memphis to the murder of Dr. Martin Luther King Jr. and was sentenced to 99 years imprisonment.

11—Millions of French workers staged a 24-hour general strike in support of demands for a 10 per cent wage hike.

11—A three-week strike by West Virginia's 42,000 coal miners ended as Gov. Arch Moore signed into law a bill increasing compensation benefits for miners disabled by "black lung" disease.

12—Gen. Andrew Goodpaster was named NATO chief and commander of U.S. forces in Europe, succeeding the retiring Gen. Lyman Lemnitzer, effective July 1.

13—The U.S. Senate ratified 83-15 the Nuclear Nonproliferation Treaty.

13—More than 20 crewmen aboard a Soviet fishing vessel were lost when the trawler collided with a Panamanian tanker and sank off the North Carolina coast.

13—The Apollo 9 and its three-man crew successfully ended a 10-day four-million mile earth orbital mission that proved the lunar-landing craft spaceworthy.

14—The Chicago Police Department inquiry into charges of misconduct during the 1968 Democratic National Convention ended with penalties for 41 members of the force.

14—President Nixon called for a modified missile defense system designed to defend missile and bomber bases rather than cities.

16—American Airlines and the Transport Workers Union reached a contract agreement to end an 18-day strike.

16—The worst civilian air disaster in history killed 155 persons, including 47 Americans. A Venezuelan DC-9 airliner crashed into a residential area of Maracaibo on takeoff en route to Miami.

17—The nation's banks increased the prime interest rate for the fourth time in as many months—this time to 7½ per cent—in an effort to curb inflation.

17—Mrs. Golda Meir took office as Israel's fourth premier, pledging to carry on the program of the late Levi Eshkol.

17—A Delta Airlines plane with 64 persons aboard was hijacked to Cuba while flying from Atlanta, Ga., to Charleston, S.C.

17—Some 2.5 million workers staged a general strike in Pakistan to press for better living conditions, wages and working conditions.

18—Some 10,000 troops launched one of the Vietnam War's largest operations—a drive through plantations northwest of Saigon in an attempt to halt an expected enemy thrust toward the capital.

19—Two American tuna boats were seized 23 miles off the Peruvian coast and released after the captains paid fines.

19—A United Arab Airlines crash at Aswan Airport in Egypt killed 87 persons and injured 10.

20—A federal grand jury in Chicago indicted eight policemen and eight demonstrators on charges of conspiracy to start a riot during the 1968 Democratic National Convention.

20—An agreement between the Black Students Union, Third World Liberation Front and their sympathizers and San Francisco State College officials ended a violent strike begun Nov. 6, 1968.

25—The United States, at the Geneva disarmament conference, rejected Russia's proposal for a total demilitarization of the ocean floor, saying it would be "simply unworkable and probably harmful."

25—President Mohammad Ayub Khan resigned and martial law was declared in Pakistan in the wake of mob violence and lawlessness in which at least 200 persons died.

25—A Newark-Los Angeles Delta Airlines jet carrying 114 persons was hijacked to Cuba.

25—Spain's state of emergency, imposed Jan. 24 to cope with student unrest, was lifted on the 30th anniversary of the end of the Civil War.

26—The International Federation of Airline Pilots Association representing 44,000 pilots from 54 countries adopted a resolution threatening boycotts and global strikes if hijackings continued unchecked.

26—Lord Constantine, son of a Trinidad cocoa farmer, was installed as the first black member of the British House of Lords.

27—The United States for the first time had two spacecraft pointed simultaneously toward the same planet when Mariner 7, a television scout ship, was launched to Mars some 5.3 million miles behind Mariner 6.

28—Dwight David Eisenhower, 34th President of the United States and supreme Allied commander in Europe during World War II, died; the 78-year-old five-star Army general was buried in his hometown of Abilene, Kan., after five days' mourning.

30—A Detroit police officer was killed, four black militants were wounded and 135 persons were arrested in a gun battle following a meeting of a group called New Republic of Africa in the area of the 1967 riots.

31—Britain and the Caribbean island of Anguilla signed a truce for a cooperative government, ending two weeks of turmoil, invasion and protest.

31—Some 162 Mexican coal miners were presumed dead in an explosion that trapped the workers some 500 feet beneath the surface of a Coahuila state mine 75 miles southwest of Eagle Pass, Tex.

APRIL

2—Fifty-one persons were killed in the crash of a Soviet-built Polish Airlines plane near the city of Krakow in southern Poland.

3—The American death toll in Vietnam surpassed

the 33,629 fatalities of the Korean War, making the Vietnam conflict the fourth bloodiest in U.S. history.

3—National Guardsmen were ordered into Chicago and a curfew for minors was imposed when racial disturbances broke out following memorial services for the Rev. Dr. Martin Luther King Jr.

3—Two measures aimed at curbing inflation were imposed by the Federal Reserve Board: (1) an increase to 6 per cent in the interest rate charged member banks for loans and (2) an increase in the amount which member banks were required to hold in reserve.

3—Lazaro Kavandame, leader of a four-year guerrilla revolt against Portuguese rule in Mozambique, surrendered, convinced that "no final victory or advantages could be expected."

4—Dr. Denton A. Cooley at St. Luke's Episcopal Hospital in Houston implanted the world's first totally artificial heart in the chest of Haskell Karp, 47, of Skokie, Ill. Karp died four days later.

5—Three motorists were killed and 15 wounded by a sniper on the Pennsylvania Turnpike near Harrisburg; then the gunman, 31-year-old Donald Lambright, killed himself.

5—The U.S. State Department denied re-entry to two Cuban diplomats, alleging the Cuban mission to the United Nations contributed money and support to black militant groups.

6—At least 26 persons were missing after the fiery collision of a Nationalist Chinese freighter and a string of oil barges in the Mississippi River at New Orleans.

9—Three constitutional rights suspended by the Greek regime following the ouster of King Constantine were restored—the rights of assembly and association and the inviolability of the home.

10—Some 200 persons were arrested on the Harvard University campus as policemen broke up a sit-in by students seeking an end to the Reserve Officers Training Corps program.

11—In South Vietnam, the center of the city of Tay Ninh was wrecked and communications were cut by rocket attacks that left 15 persons dead, 100 wounded and 80 missing.

13—Four Spanish-speaking gun wielders forced a Pan American jet enroute from Puerto Rico to Miami to divert to Cuba.

13—Four Arabs were hanged at dawn in Iraq on charges of spying for the U.S. Central Intelligence Agency.

13—Methodist Hospital in Houston announced a 22-hour test of a unique heart preservation chamber that could be used to carry human organs to any point in the world for transplants.

14—A tornado in East Pakistan killed at least 500 persons and injured thousands.

14—Thirteen persons, including five delegates, were found guilty of disorderly conduct during a demonstration at the 1968 Democratic National Convention in Chicago.

14—The ninth congress of the Chinese Communist Party unanimously adopted a new charter stipulating that Defense Minister Lin Piao would eventually succeed Mao Tse-tung as China's leader.

14—Two policemen were killed and four other policemen and a civilian were wounded during a five-hour gun battle on Chicago's south side with Frank Kulak, 40, accused of bombing a Chicago department store.

15—Four aquanauts ended a 60-day experiment in undersea living off St. John, V.I.

15—North Korea shot down a U.S. Navy electronics plane with 31 crewmen aboard in the Sea of Japan.

17—Sirhan Bishara Sirhan was convicted of first degree murder by a Los Angeles County jury in the 1968 assassination of Sen. Robert F. Kennedy. Eight days later, the 25-year-old Jordanian immigrant was sentenced to death in the gas chamber.

17—Alexander Dubcek, leader of Czechoslovakia's reformation, was ousted as head of the Communist Party; Gustav Husak was his successor.

20—Belfast's water and power facilities were crippled and nine post offices were damaged by saboteurs in renewed violence in Northern Ire-

land; more than 260 persons were reported injured.

20—Armed black students who held the Student Union Building at Cornell University for 36 hours ended their sit-in as university officials bowed to demands of the Afro-American Society.

21—A task force of 29 U.S. warships moved into the Sea of Japan to back up President Nixon's pledge to provide cover for reconnaissance flights along the Korean coast.

21—The U.S. Supreme Court, in a 6-3 decision, struck down states' welfare residency requirements, saying they violated the rights of poor people to travel.

22—The first non-stop solo voyage around the world was completed by Robin Knox-Johnston, 30-year-old merchant marine officer, 312 days after he set sail from Falmouth, England, in his 32-foot ketch, the Suhaili.

22—Paul Haney, the voice of Mission Control on the Apollo space flights, was succeeded by Brian Duff as public affairs officer of NASA's Manned Spacecraft Center.

23—The Bureau of Labor Statistics reported that living costs rose .8 per cent in March, the largest monthly increase since the peak of Korean War inflation in early 1951.

23—The Nigerian government said federal forces had captured Umuahia, administrative headquarters of Biafra and the last major center held by the secessionist regime.

24—Premier Rashid Karami resigned after two days of bloody clashes in Lebanon between government troops and Palestinian refugees who were protesting curbs on Arab guerrilla activities.

24—In the heaviest bombing raid of the Vietnam War, U.S. B52s dumped nearly 3,000 tons of explosives along the Cambodian border area northwest of Saigon.

25—The Rev. Ralph David Abernathy, head of the Southern Christian Leadership Conference, was among 50 persons arrested in Charleston, S.C., on charges of violating a state court injunction. The order limited the number of pickets at hospitals where workers had struck for union recognition.

26—Troops of secessionist Biafra recaptured Owerri, fifth largest in the province, from federal Nigerian troops.

27—President Charles de Gaulle resigned after the French people failed to give him a vote of confidence in a referendum; Senate President Alain Poher became temporary successor to the 78-year-old general.

27—René Barrientos, president of Bolivia since a 1964 military coup, died in a helicopter crash during a flying tour of his nation's farm country; Vice President Siles-Salinas became his successor.

28—The U.S. Naval task force deployed a week earlier to the Sea of Japan to protect U.S. reconnaissance flights was reduced from 29 to eight vessels and moved to the Yellow Sea.

28—Nearly 900 students were arrested and 94 policemen injured in Tokyo during leftist demonstrations demanding that the U.S. return Okinawa to Japan.

30—Pope Paul named Jean Cardinal Villot, a Frenchman, to be secretary of state for the Vatican, the first non-Italian appointed to the post in 55 years.

30—The mighty Mississippi River and its tributaries menaced the nation's heartlands during a spring thaw of record snow packs. Thousands of residents fled their rivertown homes and flooding caused tens of millions of dollars damage despite levees and sand bags.

MAY

1—Maj. James D. Chichester-Clark, a moderate in the Protestant-dominated Unionist party, was chosen prime minister of Northern Ireland. He succeeded Capt. Terence O'Neill who resigned in the wake of rioting between Catholics and Protestants.

5—More than 250 Negro and Puerto Rican students, seeking changes in admissions policies and study programs, ended an occupation at the City College of New York that had locked 20,000 students from classes for two weeks.

5—A National Airlines jet carrying 73 persons from New York to Miami was diverted to Cuba by a hijacker.

6—Thirty-four persons were killed and 35 injured in the crash of a U.S. helicopter 75 miles north of Saigon, the worst such disaster of the Vietnam war.

6—The Navy announced that no disciplinary action would be taken against the crew of the USS Pueblo, seized by North Korea 15 months earlier. The decision overruled a Navy court of inquiry recommendation that the ship's two top officers, Cmdr. Lloyd M. Bucher and Lt. Stephen R. Harris, be court martialed.

9—Dr. Buell G. Gallagher, president of City College of New York, resigned after an effort to reopen the campus failed and 11 fires, one of which destroyed a student center auditorium, occurred. Joseph J. Copeland, a biology professor, was named acting president.

9—West Germany ruled out an upward revaluation of the mark as a step to protect the nation's economy against inflation, ending speculation that had sent billions of dollars in foreign currency into German financial centers.

9—More than 200 saints were omitted from a revised Roman Catholic calendar of church feasts; 46 of them, including St. Christopher, were dropped because of doubt that they ever existed.

12—Fred Evans, a black nationalist convicted in the killing of three policemen and a civilian in a shootout in Cleveland's Negro area on July 23, 1968, was sentenced to death.

12—About 75 students at the Union Theological Seminary in New York City occupied the campus administration building to press demands of black militant James Forman that American churches pay Negroes $500 million in reparation for past injustices.

12—Communists staged 159 attacks across South Vietnam, the largest number since the Tet offensive of February 1968.

13—Charles Evers, Negro civil rights activist, defeated a white incumbent to become mayor of Fayette, Miss.

13—Trustees at Columbia University voted to abolish the Naval Reserve Officers Training Corps program, focal point of much student unrest, by June 1971.

13—Violence broke out at Southern University in Baton Rouge, La., between students and deputies guarding firemen who were attempting to extinguish a blaze. Thirty persons were injured, eight by gunfire, and 17 were arrested.

14—President Nixon, in his first full-length report on the Vietnam war, proposed a phased withdrawal of most allied and enemy forces over a 12-month period followed by an internationally-supervised free election.

14—Prime Minister Abdul Rahman suspended the Malaysian Constitution in the wake of the nation's worst rioting following a general election four days earlier.

14—Abe Fortas resigned from the Supreme Court, the first Justice to do so under pressure of public criticism, following disclosure of an extra-judicial relationship with imprisoned financier Louis Wolfson.

15—Five persons were wounded and 21 arrested as policemen and National Guardsmen moved in with tear gas to break up a protest in Berkeley over the seizure by the University of California of a park that had been a hippie haven.

15—The execution of 10 more Iraqis brought to 36 the number put to death since January on charges of spying for Israel, the United States and Iran.

16—A $50 million nuclear submarine, the USS Guittaro, sank to the bottom of San Francisco Bay where it was undergoing final fitting.

16—The third U.S. fishing boat seized by Peru

this year was released after the captain of the tuna clipper *Western King* paid $15,000.

17—One young Negro was killed and two other persons were injured in an exchange of gunfire between snipers and National Guardsmen in Burlington, N.C.

19—Key provisions of the federal anti-marijuana laws were knocked down by the Supreme Court when it reversed the 1966 conviction of Dr. Timothy F. Leary, hallucinogenic drug enthusiast.

19—Mobs roamed the streets and looted shops near the scene of the 1967 riots in Newark, N.J., after a Negro youth was shot by a Negro officer.

20—Some 1,400 allies including 1,000 U.S. paratroops, dislodged the enemy from Apbia Mountain overlooking the Ashau Valley after 10 earlier attempts in as many days.

21—Judge Warren Earl Burger of the U.S. Circuit Court of Appeals in Washington, described as a "law and order" man, was nominated by President Nixon to succeed retiring Chief Justice Earl Warren.

21—Sirhan Bishara Sirhan, convicted assassin of Robert F. Kennedy, was denied a new trial and his death sentence was upheld despite a plea for compassion by the Kennedy family.

22—The military took over Rosario, Argentina's second largest city, after students rampaged to protest the deaths of three youths allegedly shot by policeman.

22—A state of emergency was declared in Greensboro, N.C., and the predominantly Negro A&T University was closed indefinitely following violence in which one student was killed.

23—The military government of Gen. Juan Velasco Alvarado ordered U.S. military aides expelled from Peru following a U.S. decision to suspend military aid in retaliation for the seizure of an American-owned oil company and American fishing boats.

24—Eldridge Cleaver, fugitive Black Panther leader facing a prison sentence for parole violation in California, was found living in Havana.

25—The shaky coalition government in the Sudan was overthrown in a bloodless coup d'etat and former Chief Justice Abubakr Awadallah replaced Mohammed Ahmed Mahgoub as premier.

26—A Northeast Airlines jet en route from Miami to New York was hijacked to Cuba by three armed Latin Americans.

26—The Apollo 10 with three astronauts aboard returned safely to earth after a successful eight-day dress rehearsal for the Apollo 11 moon landing.

26—James Earl Ray, serving a 99-year sentence for the assassination of Dr. Martin Luther King Jr., was denied a new trial. Criminal Court Judge Arthur C. Faquin Jr. ruled in Memphis that Ray gave up his right of appeal when he pleaded guilty.

26—Gary Steven Krist was found guilty by a 12-man jury in Decatur, Ga., and sentenced to life imprisonment in the December 1968 kidnaping of Miami heiress Barbara Jane Mackle. Two days later Ruth Eisemann Schier pleaded guilty to the same charge and was sentenced to seven years in prison.

26—Three Seattle policemen were wounded and 34 persons arrested in a melee at Seattle Community College that broke out during a demonstration urging that a Negro be appointed to the board of trustees.

27—Mayor Samuel W. Yorty of Los Angeles was re-elected to a third term, defeating Thomas Bradley, a city councilman and former police lieutenant who sought to become the city's first Negro mayor.

27—Nine South Carolina state troopers were acquitted of federal charges that they violated the civil rights of three Negro teenagers shot to death and 27 others wounded during a college campus uprising Feb. 8, 1968.

27—Apbia Mountain in South Vietnam, scene of a controversial 10-day battle to dislodge the enemy, was abandoned by U.S. paratroopers.

29—The Atomic Energy Commission disclosed that more than $20 million worth of radioactive plutonium had been destroyed in a fire at a nuclear weapons factory in Golden, Colo., May 11.

29—A 20-year-old Long Island youth, Bruce Mayrock, died of self-immolation on the lawn of the United Nations as a protest of Biafran deaths in Nigeria's civil war.

30—About 5,000 oil refinery workers in Curacao, striking for higher wages, took over the Caribbean resort city of Willemstad, burning and looting shops and gasoline stations and threatening white businessmen. A detachment of Royal Dutch marines restored calm.

30—A 24-hour general strike by commerce, industry and transportation workers in Argentina appeared to culminate three weeks of worker and student demonstrations in which nine persons were killed while protesting alleged police brutality.

JUNE

1—Gov. Nelson Rockefeller of New York cancelled a visit to Venezuela to avoid further student violence that had marred his fact-finding mission in Latin America.

2—Some 74 Americans were killed when the U.S. destroyer *Frank E. Evans* was sliced in two by an Australian aircraft carrier during SEATO maneuvers in the South China Sea.

3—The Curacao government of Premier Ciro de Kroon bowed to labor demands and resigned.

4—A Mexican airliner crashed and burned on a mountain in northeastern Mexico killing 79 persons, including Davis Cup tennis player Rafael Osuna.

4—Chile joined Venezuela and Peru in withdrawing the welcome mat from Nelson Rockefeller, on a fact-finding mission for President Nixon.

4—A 22-year-old Cuban, Armando Socarras Ramirez, survived a shortage of oxygen and temperatures 40 degrees below zero as a stowaway in the wheel pod of a jet airliner bound for Spain. A companion fell to his death during the nine-hour flight.

5—Americans have become "a rather bloody-minded people in both action and reaction," reported a panel of scholars named by a presidential commission to study the history and foreign parallels of violence.

5—President Nixon appointed Donald E. Johnson, a former national commander of the American Legion, to head the Veterans Administration.

6—Twelve of 14 prisoners at the San Francisco Presidio stockade were convicted by a military court of mutiny and received light sentences for a sit-down demonstration to protest the fatal shooting of a prisoner by a Presidio guard.

7—The Rev. John Burgess of Boston was elected the first Negro bishop of America's Episcopal Church.

8—President Nixon announced from his Midway Island meeting with President Nguyen Van Thieu that 25,000 U.S. troops would be withdrawn from South Vietnam by Aug. 1.

9—The minimum interest rates charged for bank loans jumped one percentage point to 8.5 per cent, the highest on record.

9—The Supreme Court, in a 7-1 decision, struck down a law of 17 states permitting creditors to garnishee wages to satisfy debts without a court hearing.

9—Some 135 Harvard students were punished by a special disciplinary board for their part in the seizure of the administration building two months earlier. Sixteen were barred from classes for two years.

10—A teen-aged brother and a sister were charged with murder in Parkersburg, W.Va., in a fire that killed their parents and 10 brothers and sisters.

10—The Judicial Conference of the United States imposed stiff new rules on federal judges' outside activities, excluding Supreme Court justices who were not under conference jurisdiction.

10—Pope Paul VI became the first pontiff to visit Geneva since the 16th century.

10—Ronald W. August, a suspended Detroit policeman charged with murdering a Negro youth during the 1967 riots, was acquitted.

11—A Sino-Soviet border clash, potentially more serious than those along the Ussuri River three months earlier, occurred along the frontier of Sinkiang.

12—The National Liberation Front was replaced at the Paris peace talks with what the NLF called a new "revolutionary provisional government" of South Vietnam.

13—Dan Bullock, a 15-year-old Marine from Brooklyn, N.Y., became the youngest American killed in the Vietnam war.

15—Former Premier Georges Pompidou overwhelmingly defeated Interim President Alain Poher as successor to former President Charles de Gaulle of France.

15—At least 51 diners were killed and more than 175 injured when the roof of a restaurant near the Spanish resort village of San Rafael collapsed on opening day.

16—A $300,000 warehouse was destroyed by flames while firemen were pinned down by snipers in Cairo, Ill., plagued by racial strife since April.

16—Some 300 potential troublemakers were reported in custody in Brazil to prevent anti-American demonstrations during a visit by New York Gov. Nelson Rockefeller.

16—The Supreme Court, in a 7-1 decision, ruled that the House had no right to exclude Rep. Adam Clayton Powell, D-N.Y., from the 90th Congress on charges of misusing public funds.

17—Mayor John V. Lindsay and former Mayor Robert F. Wagner lost their bids for renomination in New York City mayoralty primaries. State Sen. John J. Marchi defeated Lindsay on the Republican ballot, Controller Mario Procaccino won over Wagner on the Democratic ticket.

17—Moscow's International Communist Conference, attended by 75 parties, ended without official condemnation of Red China as had been hoped by Moscow.

17—A TWA airliner en route from Oakland, Calif., to New York with 87 persons aboard was hijacked to Cuba.

18—Israeli warplanes staged the year's heaviest assault on Jordan, pounding Iraqi and Jordanian artillery positions for five hours.

19—The nation's air traffic controllers staged a so-called safety campaign that resulted in major delays at some metropolitan airports.

20—Terrorists in Montevideo, Uruguay, set fire to a General Motors building, causing $1 million damage, to protest a visit to the country by presidential envoy Nelson Rockefeller.

20—Jacques Chaban-Delmas was named premier of France by President Pompidou.

20—Five American tuna boats were seized by Ecuador and later released without penalty.

20—Voters in Rhodesia approved a new segregationist constitution.

22—The Students for a Democratic Society, in the forefront of much campus unrest, split into two rival factions during their national convention in Chicago.

23—Chief Justice Earl Warren ended 16 years in the Supreme Court with three decisions protecting the rights of criminal suspects, then swore in his successor, Warren E. Burger.

23—Israeli commandos sabotaged Jordan's most important irrigation project, the $85 million Ghor Canal.

23—Ten persons were killed, including four crewmen, when a DC-4 cargo plane crashed into a busy Miami street as it attempted an emergency landing at Miami International Airport.

24—Arab saboteurs exploded a pipeline to the Haifa oil refineries, one of Israel's most important facilities, causing fire, the loss of 1,000 tons of fuel and disruption of telephone service.

24—A vast land-reform program, under which all major tracts of property held by Peruvians and foreigners would be seized and divided among the people, was announced by Peru.

24—British Foreign Secretary Michael Stewart

announced the last tenuous ties with rebel Rhodesia would be cut.

24—Millions of dead fish blanketed 200 miles of the Rhine River, victims of an unknown poison that threatened swimming and drinking water.

25—A United Airlines jet, on a Los Angeles-New York flight with 58 persons aboard, was diverted to Cuba by a young gunman.

26—Fourteen supermarkets owned by a Rockefeller-founded corporation were bombed in Buenos Aires by terrorists protesting a three-day visit to Argentina by presidential envoy Nelson Rockefeller.

26—Chile announced an agreement with Anaconda Co. to take over the American company's copper mines and processing plants in the Latin American country by 1972.

28—Dr. Roger Egeberg, dean of the University of Southern California Medical School, was nominated for the top health post in the Department of Health, Education and Welfare, ending a five-month struggle by Secretary Robert H. Finch to get Dr. John Knowles of Boston approved for the job.

28—An Eastern Airlines plane flying from Baltimore to Miami with 104 persons aboard was diverted to Cuba by a lone hijacker.

JULY

1—Charles Philip Arthur George was invested as the 21st Prince of Wales and the Earl of Chester by his mother, Queen Elizabeth II, at ancient Caernarvon Castle.

1—A convoy of South Vietnamese armored personnel carriers rumbled into the Special Forces outpost at Ben Het, surrounded by Communist troops for nearly a month.

2—A jury in Newark, N.J., acquitted Negro author LeRoi Jones and two co-defendants in their retrial on charges of illegal possession of guns during 1967 rioting.

3—Four persons were killed and three wounded by gunfire in Santo Domingo where Presidential envoy Nelson Rockefeller conferred with leaders of the Dominican Republic.

4—A Japanese freighter was heavily damaged and five crewmen were injured by debris from a Soviet spacecraft. The June incident, belatedly reported, was believed to be the first damage caused by man-made space objects.

4—A storm that lashed Lake Erie and northern Ohio left at least 33 persons dead and 300 injured.

5—Italy's six-month-old center-left coalition government headed by Premier Mariana Rumor, a Christian Democrat, collapsed after a split in the Socialist party, a major partner in the coalition.

5—Tom Mboya, Kenya's minister of economics and development, was assassinated in Nairobi.

7—The Nixon Administration announced that desegregation suits were filed against a school district in Illinois and another in South Carolina. Federal funds were cut off from three other districts.

8—Bonny, a ringtail monkey on a 30-day earth orbit, died 12 hours after his flight was aborted on its ninth day.

8—Israel reported downing seven Syrian MIGs and Damascus said four Israeli jets were destroyed in one of the biggest aerial dogfights in the Middle East since the "Six Day War" of 1967.

8—China and Russia accused each other in a new outbreak of hostilities on the Amur River border.

9—President Nixon ordered reductions in U.S. military and civilian personnel abroad by more than 20,000 persons to reduce the international payments deficit.

10—The Nixon Administration continued its campaign against public school segregation with lawsuits against school districts in Mississippi and Arkansas.

11—The draft conspiracy convictions of Dr. Benjamin Spock and three others were overturned by an appeals court in Boston. Spock and Michael Ferber were ordered acquitted and retrial was ordered for

Dr. William Sloane Coffin Jr. and Mitchell Goodman.

14—Armed conflict broke out between Central American neighbors El Salvador and Honduras.

14—Two persons were killed and three injured in an outbreak of violence in a Negro section of San Diego after police tried to arrest a man for throwing rocks in a city park.

15—The Justice Department, charging abuse of trust by a public employe, filed suit to recover part of $1.75 million from Bobby Baker, former secretary to Senate Democrats, convicted in 1967 on charges of stealing political funds and evading taxes (The World in 1967, 14–15).

17—The papyrus vessel Ra, which sailed from Morocco on May 26 in an attempt to prove it was possible that ancient Egyptians crossed the Atlantic in such boats, was abandoned by its seven-man crew 10 days short of Barbados.

18—The first message on population problems ever sent by a President to Congress contained proposals to expand the government's birth control programs and to establish a commission to study implications of continued population growth in the United States.

18—A 113-day strike at Charleston (S.C.) County Hospital ended, two weeks after settlement of a companion strike by Negro nonprofessional workers at South Carolina Medical University Hospital.

19—Sen. Edward M. Kennedy, D-Mass., escaped death when his automobile dived from a bridge into a pond on Chappaquiddick Island near Martha's Vineyard. A passenger, Mary Jo Kopechne, drowned. On July 25, Kennedy pleaded guilty to a charge of leaving the scene of an accident and asked the people of Massachusetts to help him decide whether he should resign from the Senate. On July 30, he announced that he would retain his seat and seek re-election in 1970.

19—John Fairfax of Great Britain became the first person ever to row alone across the Atlantic Ocean; he arrived in Hollywood, Fla., after 180 days at sea.

20—Neil A. Armstrong, command pilot of Apollo 11, became the first man to walk on the moon at 10:56 p.m. EDT, some 6½ hours after he and Edwin E. Aldrin Jr. set their spacecraft down on the Sea of Tranquillity with the words "The Eagle has landed."

21—National Guard troops were deployed to Columbus, Ohio, after one man was killed and about 20 persons were injured in disturbances in a dominantly Negro neighborhood.

21—The nine-day flight of Russia's Luna 15 unmanned spacecraft ended in apparent failure when it landed—and probably crashed—on the moon.

22—The Pentagon, in announcing removal of chemical weapons from Okinawa, acknowledged for the first time that the United States had war gases deployed overseas.

23—Prince Juan Carlos of Bourbon was formally invested as successor to Generalissimo Francisco Franco and future king of Spain.

24—America's Apollo 11 carrying the world's first lunar explorers, splashed down safely in the Pacific, ending an epic-making journey from earth to moon and back.

24—The heaviest and longest battle since the six day war of 1967 raged between Arab and Israeli forces along the Suez Canal.

24—Ten Western nations reached an agreement, after five years of negotiations, to establish "paper gold," an internationally managed reserve unit aimed to increase world liquidity and insure growth of world trade.

24—Sen. Eugene J. McCarthy, D-Minn., announced he would not seek re-election in 1970.

24—Cassius Clay was resentenced by a federal judge in Houston to the same five years imprisonment and $10,000 fine assessed in June 1967 when the former heavyweight boxing champion was convicted of refusing induction into the armed forces.

24—Twenty persons were reported killed in the sinking of the Norwegian tanker Silja after it collided with a French passenger-cargo ship in the Mediterranean off Toulon.

26—A 19-year-old Marine at Camp LeJeune, N.C., died of injuries suffered a week earlier during racial violence at the big Marine base.

28—An Eastern Michigan University coed became the eighth young woman to be slain in the past two years in the area of the universities of Michigan and Eastern Michigan.

29—El Salvador told the Organization of American States that troops which had invaded neighboring Honduras two weeks earlier would be withdrawn.

29—Negroes gained control of the Greene County (Ala.) commission and school board in a special election.

30—President Nixon interrupted a tour of Asian nations to visit Vietnam and told American soliders at a base near Saigon that, "We have gone as far now as we can or should go in opening the door to peace."

30—The space traveler Mariner 6 sent a second set of pictures of Mars, taken as the unmanned craft passed within 2,000 miles of the planet. Mariner had been launched from Cape Kennedy five months earlier.

31—Pope Paul VI began his eighth mission abroad, a trip to Africa to consecrate 12 African bishops and dedicate a shrine to 22 African saints. He was the first Roman pontiff to visit the continent.

AUGUST

1—The Justice Department filed suit against Georgia, charging that the state encouraged continued segregation in its 192 public school systems.

2—Michigan state police arrested John Collins, a 22-year-old college student, and charged him with murder in the slaying of Karen Beineman, the eighth young woman killed in the Ann Arbor-Ypsilanti area in two years.

2—President Nixon became the first President in nearly 25 years to visit a Communist nation. A crowd estimated in the hundreds of thousands gave him a warm welcome in Romania.

3—A panel of 23 space scientists proposed that the United States undertake a program for unmanned exploration of the remote reaches of the solar system, including Jupiter, Saturn, Uranus, Neptune and Pluto. The proposed flights would begin in 1974.

4—The House passed and sent to the White House a bill continuing the 10 per cent surcharge on income taxes until the end of 1969.

4—A group of coal miners and widows of miners filed suit in U.S. district court, accusing officials of the United Mine Workers with mismanagement, conspiracy and exploitation of the union's welfare and retirement fund. A minimum of $75 million in damages was sought.

5—Three Americans arrived in Laos, released from captivity in North Vietnam.

6—Tornados killed 14 persons and injured hundreds in north central Minnesota resort areas, including a church camp, one of the sections hardest hit.

6—A school was firebombed, rocks and bottles were thrown and 18 persons were arrested during racial violence in Passaic, N.J.

6—Charges of premeditated murder and conspiracy in the death of a Vietnamese man were lodged against a former commander of the Green Berets and seven of his men.

7—The government abandoned its case against Dr. Benjamin Spock, yielding without appeal to a circuit court's reversal of his conviction on a charge of conspiring to persuade young men to avoid the draft.

7—California's legislature enacted a law taxing non-church-related income of religious organizations.

8—The franc was devalued by the French government by 12.5 per cent in relation to the U.S. dollar.

8—President Nixon, in a nationwide television

address, called for sweeping welfare reforms, including a minimum standard of federal aid for every needy family with dependent children.

9—At least four persons were killed and 200 injured as a tornado tore through suburban Cincinnati, causing at least $7 million damage.

9—Actress Sharon Tate, wife of film director Roman Polanski, was one of five persons found slain at Polanski's Bel Air, Calif., home.

10—The three Apollo 11 astronauts, pronounced free of lunar contamination, were released from quarantine under which they had been placed since their return from the moon.

10—Nineteen U.S. Marines were killed and 80 wounded during an enemy attack on two bases near the DMZ in which 17 North Vietnamese were killed.

11—Enemy forces attacked more than 100 cities, towns and allied bases across South Vietnam, ending an eight-week lull in the war.

11—Fighting between Negroes and whites at Kaneohe Marine Corps Air Station in Hawaii resulted in the injury of at least 16 U.S. Marines.

12—Heavy fighting broke out in Londonderry, Northern Ireland, between police and Roman Catholic demonstrators who attempted to break up a Protestant festival; scores of persons were injured.

12—Heavy fighting in South Vietnam in a 24-hour period reportedly left 1,450 enemy dead and about 200 allied fatalities.

13—The FBI's annual Uniform Crime Reports showed 4.5 million serious crimes recorded in 1968, a 17 per cent rise over 1967.

14—A Northeast Airlines jet carrying 52 persons from Boston to Miami was forced to fly to Cuba where two passengers deplaned.

15—A two-nation board of inquiry ruled the USS Frank E. Evans was primarily responsible for its fatal collision June 3 with the Australian carrier HMAS Melbourne during SEATO maneuvers in the South China Sea.

16—British soldiers patrolled Londonderry and Belfast, where three days of rioting between Protestants and Catholics left at least eight persons dead and 500 injured.

17—Dr. Philip Blaiberg, the world's longest surviving heart transplant patient, died at the age of 60 in the Capetown, South Africa, hospital where 19½ months earlier he had received the heart of another man.

17—An unarmed U.S. Army helicopter with three persons aboard was shot down over North Korea; the three crewmen later were reported injured.

17—At least 200 persons were feared dead in the wake of hurricane Camille, the second strongest hurricane ever to hit the United States, which unleashed its fury along the Gulf Coast states.

18—Federal Judge Clement F. Haynsworth Jr., a conservative from South Carolina, was nominated by President Nixon to succeed Abe Fortas as an associate justice of the Supreme Court.

19—Red China accused the Soviet Union of as many as 429 incidents along the Chinese-Soviet border during June and July.

20—Anti-Soviet demonstrators clashed with troops in Prague's Wenceslas Square on the first anniversary of the Russian-led invasion of Czechoslovakia.

20—V.V. Giri was elected president of India in what was termed a personal triumph for Prime Minister Indira Gandhi and a bitter defeat for the old-guard rightists.

21—Defense Secretary Melvin R. Laird announced a cut of 100,000 men from the armed forces and $1.5 billion from the Pentagon's budget this year because of Congressional austerity pressures and the "economic needs of our country."

21—The Mosque of Al Aksa in the Old City of Jerusalem, one of the most holy Moslem shrines, was heavily damaged by a fire; the blaze sparked renewed tensions between Arabs and Israelis but an Australian was arrested in the incident.

22—Some 5,000 anti-Soviet demonstrators clashed with police in Brno, Czechoslovakia's second-largest city, and two persons were reported killed.

22—The death toll exceeded 100 in Virginia, inundated by flood waters from the James River, caused by the remnants of Hurricane Camille.

23—President Thieu named Gen. Tran Thien Khiem premier of South Vietnam to succeed Tran Van Huong, who resigned under pressure.

25—Fifteen Iraquis, including two Jews, were executed as convicted spies for Israel or the United States.

26—Some 180 persons were arrested and 45 others, including 12 policemen, were injured in the second day of Negro demonstrations pressing for more jobs on construction projects in Pittsburgh.

28—The Nixon Administration won a delay of court-ordered desegregation of 30 school districts in Mississippi in a ruling handed down by a federal appeals court in New Orleans.

29—A family of five hijacked a National Airlines plane to Cuba.

29—A Trans World Airlines jet carrying 113 persons bound for Athens and Tel Aviv, was hijacked to Damascus by two Arabs. All but two Israeli men aboard the jet were released.

29—The British and Northern Ireland governments announced agreement on a series of civil rights reforms designed to ease causes of religious strife by ending discrimination of the Roman Catholic minority in Northern Ireland.

31—A triumvirate of Brazil's top military commanders, ignoring the constitutional provision on succession, assumed control of the country after President Arthur da Costa e Silva suffered a stroke.

SEPTEMBER

1—King Idris of Lybia was deposed by the military which proclaimed the country a socialist republic and dissolved parliament and other constitutional bodies.

2—Hartford, Conn., was placed under dusk-to-dawn curfew following disorders in a Negro and Puerto Rican area in which 60 businesses were damaged and 300 persons arrested.

3—Ho Chi Minh, president of North Vietnam and the man who gained independence for his country from the French in the battle of Dien Bien Phu in 1954, died at age 79.

3—The Episcopal Church, allocating $200,000 to James Forman's Black Economic Development Conference, became the first major denomination to recognize the group that sought "reparations" from churches for past "racist oppression" of Negroes.

4—The Nixon Administration announced a 75 per cent cutback in new federal construction contracts as an anti-inflation move.

6—Two Ecuadoran air force planes were commandeered, a co-pilot killed and another wounded by 13 hijackers who abandoned one plane during a refueling stop and forced the other to Cuba.

7—The body of former Episcopal bishop James A. Pike of California was found six days after he was reported missing by his wife after their car broke down in the Judean wilderness.

7—C. Burke Elbrick, American ambassador to Brazil who had been kidnaped two days earlier, was released unharmed after the "ransom"—asylum in Mexico for 15 political prisoners—was paid by the Brazilian government.

7—An Eastern Air Lines jet en route from New York to San Juan with 96 persons aboard was diverted to Cuba by an armed hijacker.

9—Eighty-three persons were killed in the collision of a light plane and an Allegheny Airlines jetliner near Indianapolis.

9—Israeli forces crossed the Gulf of Suez for a 10-hour destructive sweep of Egyptian military installations along the coast; more than 100 Egyptian soldiers were reported killed.

10—A 40-kiloton nuclear explosion under the western slope of the Rocky Mountains in Colorado was set off in an effort to free a vast store of natural gas and to demonstrate peaceful use of nuclear energy.

10—Nasashon Isaac Njenga Njoroge was convicted of the murder of Tom Mboya and sentenced by the Kenya High Court to death by hanging.

10—Competitive bidding for oil rights on Alaska's North Slope netted the state treasury more than $900 million as some of the property went for a national record price of $28,233 an acre.

11—Israel reported downing 11 planes during Egyptian air attacks in the Sinai Peninsula in retaliation for Israel's raid along the Gulf of Suez two days earlier.

15—Scientists ruled out the hypothesis that the moon was a fragment ripped from earth, saying a preliminary analysis of Apollo 11 moon rocks indicated their chemical composition was "unlike that of any known terrestrial rock."

15—More than 250 persons were killed, 80 missing and 60,000 homeless in the worst floods to his South Korea in 10 years.

17—President Nixon announced the withdrawal of 35,000 more American troops from Vietnam by the end of the year, raising the total since June to 60,000.

17—Gov. Richard Ogilvie of Illinois named Republican Ralph Smith to succeed the late Everett Dirksen in the U.S. Senate.

19—President Nixon announced a 50,000 cut in the planned draft call for the balance of the year.

22—The SS Manhattan arrived at Port Barrow, Alaska, completing a mission meant to prove that a year-round sea route could be opened through the Northwest Passage but the ice breaker failed in another venture—navigating the never-penetrated ice-choked McClure Strait.

24—Republicans elected Hugh Scott of Pennsylvania as Senate minority leader and Robert P. Griffin of Michigan as whip.

24—Vice president Ton Duc Thang, 81-year-old Vietnamese communist leader, was elected to succeed Ho Chi Minh as president of North Vietnam.

24—Four women—an employee and three customers were shot and killed during a $275 robbery of a suburban Cincinnati savings and loan office; four men later were arrested.

25—Five persons were hurt and nine others arrested when more than 1,000 white construction workers in Chicago barred Negro leaders from appearing at a Labor Department hearing on building trades discrimination.

25—A mob of 200 persons in Ahmedabad, India, attacked two express trains, beating 13 passengers to death, during a tour of the riot-torn city by Prime Minister Indira Ghandi.

26—Bolivia became the ninth Latin American nation to come under military rule as the civilian government of President Luis Adolfo Siles Salinas was overthrown and Gen. Alfredo Ovando Candia, commander of the armed forces, replaced him.

28—The Czech cabinet resigned in response to Communist party orders and Premier Oldrich Cernik was asked to form a new government; the party also ousted its former leader, Alexander Dubcek, from the ruling Presidium and from the chairmanship of the Federal Assembly but allowed him to retain his seat on the Central Committee, a privilege denied 29 other progressives who were purged.

28—The Christian Democratic Union of Chancellor Kurt Georg Kiesinger won by a narrow margin in the West German parliamentary elections, defeating the Social Democratic party headed by Foreign Minister Willy Brandt.

28—Renewed religious violence in Northern Ireland prompted deployment of 600 more British troops to Belfast, where five Catholic homes were set afire and 20 persons were injured in rioting.

29—The West German mark was freed to find its own rate in an effort to halt speculation against an increase in its value.

29—The U.S. Army dropped proceedings against six Green Berets charged in the alleged murder of a Vietnamese agent, saying that Central Intelligence Agency refusal to provide witnesses barred a fair trial.

OCTOBER

1—An earthquake shook Northern California, the worst in eight years, causing injury to 15 persons and thousands of dollars damage.

3—Member nations of the International Monetary Fund voted to create Special Drawing Rights, the first international money other than gold. Commonly called paper gold, it would exist only in writing to settle accounts among nations.

3—Press censorship, arbitrary arrest and trial by military courts, except in cases involving public order and security, were abolished by Greece's military regime.

4—One of the largest Egyptian commando raids since the 1967 war was launched across the Suez Canal but Israeli air attacks drove them back.

5—British troops used tear gas to quell street fighting in Belfast on the first anniversary of the outbreak of savage rioting between Northern Ireland's Protestants and Roman Catholics.

5—A Russian-built MIG17 set down at Homestead AFB, Fla., where its Cuban pilot was granted political asylum.

7—Gen. Emilio Garrastazu Medici was named by Brazil's military government to succeed ailing Arthur da Costa e Silva as president.

7—Criminals in Montreal had a field day, looting some of the most chic shops and robbing 10 banks, as the city's 3,700 man police force walked off their jobs demanding more money. A court order sent them unwillingly back on the beat after one day.

8—A National Airlines jet carrying 69 persons from Miami to Los Angeles was hijacked to Cuba.

8—Some 2,000 National Guardsmen were deployed to Chicago to control student radicals demonstrating during the court trial of the "Chicago Eight."

9—Czechoslovak citizens were barred from private travel to the West in the most dramatic tightening of frontier control since the Soviet invasion in August 1968.

10—President Nixon announced the retirement, effective Feb. 16, 1970, of 76-year-old Lt. Gen. Lewis B. Hershey, ending Hershey's 28-year career as head of the Selective Service System.

10—The United States and Mexico agreed to a modification of Operation Intercept which relaxed almost to the point of eliminating strict border searches for illegal marijuana traffic.

11—Russia launched the first of three spacecraft, beginning what the U.S. described as a "space spectacular" involving seven cosmonauts and welding experiments for a space station.

11—One policeman was killed and three policemen and a British soldier were wounded in renewed religious violence in Belfast one day after sweeping changes were announced for Northern Ireland's police force which had been highly criticized by militant Protestants.

15—President Abdirashid Ali Shermarke of Somalia was assassinated while touring an area of northern Somalia stricken by drought; a policeman was charged with the murder.

15—A Vietnam Moratorium, begun as a student protest against the war, closed the generation gap across the nation as thousands of students, homemakers, businessmen and workers took part despite pleas from President Nixon that it would only aid Hanoi propaganda.

17—A constitutional amendment that would allow President Chung Hee Park to seek a third consecutive term in South Korea was approved in a landslide vote.

17—The Bolivian Gulf Company, a subsidiary of Gulf Oil Corp. in the United States, was seized and nationalized by the Bolivian military government.

17—President Nixon appointed an economic advisor, Dr. Arthur F. Burns, to succeed William

McChesney Martin Jr. as chairman of the Federal Reserve Board, effective Feb. 1, 1970.

18—The federal government, acting on evidence that cyclamate caused cancer in animals, ordered an immediate halt to production of foods and drinks, mostly diet items, containing the artificial sweetener.

18—The last of Russia's seven orbiting cosmonauts returned to earth in the third of the spaceships —Soyuz 6, 7, and 8—sent up a week earlier in what was believed to have been a welding experiment, possibly a forerunner of an attempt to build a space platform.

18—Four American soldiers were killed in an ambush by North Koreans near the southern boundary of the DMZ in Korea.

19—Two young East Germans hijacked a Polish airliner at gunpoint, forcing it to land in West Berlin, where the hijackers were handed over to West German officials for processing as refugees.

21—Willy Brandt was elected chancellor by the West German parliament, succeeding Kurt Kiesinger, after successfully forming a coalition between the Social Democrats and the Free Democrats.

21—A self-styled revolutionary council seized power in Somalia in a bloodless coup less than a day after the funeral of the nation's assassinated president.

21—Tokyo was among 100 Japanese cities rocked by students protesting the Vietnam war, the U.S.-Japanese security treaty and U.S. rule of Okinawa. Arrests totaled more than 1,400—the highest recorded by police in Japanese rioting since World War II.

23—A crackdown by Lebanon on guerrillas operating from within its borders led Palestinian commandos to raid Lebanese frontier posts and to reports that large numbers of armed men were massing along the Syrian border.

24—The West German mark was revalued upward by about 9 per cent to 27.3 American cents, ending nearly a year's speculation that at times threatened to topple the international monetary system.

26—The ruling National Union party in Portugal won National Assembly seats by a landslide in the first significantly contested election in 43 years.

26—A coalition of 13 unions representing 147,000 workers struck General Electric after the nation's fourth largest industrial corporation declined a union bid to submit contract differences to arbitration.

27—At least 21 persons were killed and 400 injured in an earthquake that destroyed the town of Banja Luke, Yugoslavia, leaving 60,000 residents homeless.

27—The Pentagon announced plans to "condolidate, reduce, realign or close" 307 military bases and activities at home and abroad, cutting military spending by about $609 million a year.

27—President Jomo Kenyatta of Kenya put opposition leader Oginga Odinga and seven of his colleagues under house arrest on charges that Odinga's party was responsible for an anti-government demonstration two days earlier in which 11 persons were killed.

28—Premier Golda Meir and her ruling Labor Party were returned to power in an Israeli general election.

29—The Supreme Court, in a unanimous decision, ordered an end to all school segregation "at once," replacing its 14-year-old decision to desegregate with "all deliberate speed." The decision immediately affected 30 school districts in Mississippi and was considered a stinging setback for the Nixon Administration's policy.

29—The South Vietnamese government released 88 Viet Cong prisoners and pardoned a militant monk, Thien Minh, as part of South Vietnam's National Day observance.

31—The longest and most daring skyjacking to date ended in Rome 17 hours and 6,900 miles after it began when a TWA jet was commandeered over California and was forced to leap-frog across two continents and the Atlantic Ocean. A young AWOL Marine was arrested as the accused air pirate.

31—Palestinian guerrillas claimed a major victory in repulsing a Lebanese Army attack on Kfar Kouk, a village under siege by guerrillas for three days.

NOVEMBER

1—The Congress party, which had ruled India since independence in 1947, officially split into two warring groups, one headed by Prime Minister Indira Gandhi and the other by the party's old-guard leaders called the Syndicate. Mrs. Gandhi retained her office.

1—The Judicial Conference of the United States suspended strict limitations on judges' off-the-bench income that were adopted by the group a year earlier.

2—Six Americans charged in separate incidents of hijacking aircraft to Cuba were returned to the United States by Canadian officials upon arrival in Montreal aboard a Cuban freighter.

3—A cease-fire agreement in the two-week conflict over Lebanon's curb of guerrilla activity was reached, calling for the Lebanese government to formally recognize the commando groups in exchange for guerrilla cooperation with the army.

4—In off-year elections New York City Mayor John Lindsay won re-election without major party backing; in mayoral races pitting black against white, Negro Mayor Carl Stokes of Cleveland won re-election but Roman Gribbs was elected Detroit mayor over his Negro opponent. Republicans in New Jersey and Virginia won the nation's only gubernatorial races.

4—Brazilian police shot and killed Carlos Marighella, described as a terrorist and the man who engineered the political kidnaping in September of U.S. Ambassador Charles Burke Elbrick.

5—The 18-year-old son of Richard J. Dolan, an American executive in Brazil, was found murdered after a $12,500 ransom had been paid for his release; a Portuguese father and son were charged with the crime.

5—Three American prisoners of war were released by the Viet Cong.

6—Black Panther leader Bobby Seale was sentenced to four years' imprisonment on charges of contempt of court during the trial of the "Chicago 8" on conspiracy charges stemming from disorders during the 1968 Democratic Convention.

7—A dynamite blast deep within a South African gold mine killed 64 workers and injured 14 in the country's worst mine mishap since 1960.

8—A massive power failure blacked out 90 per cent of Quebec Province, including Montreal and Quebec City, for more than one hour.

10—Nelson Rockefeller's long-awaited report on his Presidential fact-finding mission to Latin America called for a Western Hemisphere Security Council to combat subversion.

10—Policemen armed with riot guns battled 400 young Negroes who wielded rocks and bottles in Memphis after the arrest of 53 persons demonstrating against white resistance to Negro demands for equality.

11—Owners of the tanker Torrey Canyon, whose oil polluted French and British beaches in 1967, agreed to pay $7.2 million in damages.

12—Some $1.3 million in Aqueduct Race Track receipts were taken from an armored truck in a daring daylight robbery in New York, the second-largest haul in the nation's history.

13—Four bombings that damaged three major New York City office buildings and a courthouse in two days led to the arrest of four persons described as left-wing radicals opposed to the Establishment.

13—Robert H. Finch, secretary for Health, Education and Welfare, announced the government planned to ban all but "essential" uses of DDT over a two-year period.

15—Major European cities were clogged with thousands of demonstrators showing solidarity with the Vietnam Moratorium staged in Washington, a generally peaceful anti-war protest by 250,000, and in San Francisco, where 100,000 persons paraded.

17—The United States and Russia began preliminary talks in Helsinki on the limitation of strategic arms.

17—Greece's military government decreed prison terms and fines, effective Jan. 1, 1970, for offenses by the press, which officials described as "responsible for the decadence of Greek democracy" before the military takeover 30 months earlier.

17—Israel bombed and strafed Jordanian artillery positions for two hours in one of the most sustained assaults since the 1967 war.

17—Survivors of Vietnam coastal hamlets of Tu Cung and My Lai claimed that 370 of their villagers were slain and their houses burned by an American infantry unit in March 1968. Two soldiers were charged in the case.

18—Joseph P. Kennedy, one of the nation's wealthiest men and patriarch of an ill-fated political family, died at age 81.

19—Navy Cmdrs. Charles Conrad Jr. and Alan L. Bean made man's second landing on the moon—on the Ocean of Storms—and spent some eight hours walking on the lunar surface.

19—The Senate passed and sent to the White House an administration-backed bill creating a draft lottery.

19—About half of Italy's working population joined in a 24-hour general strike to dramatize demands for better public and private housing programs for low-income workers.

20—Henry Cabot Lodge resigned as chief United States delegate to the Paris peace talks, effective Dec. 8.

21—The Senate, for the first time since 1930, barred confirmation of a Supreme Court nominee —Clement F. Haynsworth Jr. of South Carolina, on a 55 to 45 vote.

21—The United States agreed to return Okinawa to Japan in 1972.

22—The National Commission on the Causes and Prevention of Violence warned that crime was turning America's cities into armed camps—"fortresses for the wealthy and "places of terror" for others.

24—Three American astronauts returned man's second successful mission to the moon, this one aboard Apollo 12, which began the detailed exploration of the moon and a careful documentation of scientific data.

24—The United States and the Soviet Union simultaneously signed the nuclear nonproliferation treaty, becoming the 23rd and 24th countries to ratify the pact.

25—President Nixon renounced any resort to germ warfare and promised to destroy existing stockpiles of such weapons.

26—President Nixon signed into law a bill creating a lottery system for the Selective Service, drafting 19-year-olds first.

27—Fifteen persons were injured, one fatally, by a hand grenade thrown into the passenger terminal of El Al, the Israeli airline, in the center of Athens. Two Jordanians were arrested.

29—A former special assistant to President Nguyen Van Thieu and three other South Vietnamese were convicted of high treason and sentenced to life imprisonment at hard labor. Thirty-seven other persons, including 13 women, were found guilty of lesser charges of espionage.

DECEMBER

1—The first draft lottery since 1942 was staged in Washington, removing much of the uncertainty of military service for the nation's young men aged 19 to 26 years.

2—More than 50 persons were killed in a fire that leveled a home for the aged in Notre-Dame-Du-Lac, Quebec.

2—A TWA jetliner carrying 28 persons from San Francisco to Philadelphia was hijacked to Cuba.

3—An Air France jet en route to Paris from Quito, Ecuador, plunged into the Caribbean, carrying 62 persons to their deaths.

4—The Illinois Black Panther leader, Fred Hampton, was one of two party members killed in a pre-dawn shootout with a police raiding party in Chicago.

4—American war casualties passed the 300,000 mark, the U.S. Command in South Vietnam reported.

5—Chief Justice Warren E. Burger appointed 10 federal judges to oversee financial and out-of-court activities of all federal judges except members of the Supreme Court.

6—Two Americans held captive since Feb. 16 when their yacht was seized between Hong Kong and Macao were released by Communist China. Thirteen other yachtsmen were released April 2.

6—In a two-day prisoner exchange involving three parties to the Mid-East war, Syria exchanged two Israeli civilian passengers of a jetliner hijacked to Damascus on Aug. 29 for 13 Syrian military men, and two Israeli pilots were exchanged for six Egyptian military men and 52 civilians.

6—Col. Nguyen Ba Lien, commander of two South Vietnamese provinces, and nine other persons, including five Americans, were killed in the crash of an American helicopter in the Central Highlands.

8—Three Los Angeles policemen and three Black Panthers were wounded in a pre-dawn raid that turned into a shootout at Panther party headquarters.

8—An Olympic Airways DC6 en route from Crete to Athens crashed into a hillside and burst into flames near Athens during a driving rainstorm, killing all 90 persons aboard.

8—Charles Manson, a 35-year-old nomad said to have possessed hypnotic powers, and five of his followers were indicted by a Los Angeles grand jury on murder charges in the deaths of seven persons, including actress Sharon Tate.

10—A military junta overthrew the government of the African nation of Dahomey.

10—W. A. (Tony) Boyle, president of the United Mine Workers of America, claimed victory in his bid for re-election, defeating Joseph A. Yablonski in one of the most strenuous labor union elections in modern times.

11—A South Korean airliner en route from Kangung to Seoul with 51 persons aboard was hijacked to the North Korean coastal city of Wonsan.

11—Some 75 black students at Harvard University were suspended following a day of occupying the dean's office, faculty club and a major building site to press demands for more black construction workers on campus projects.

12—Greece withdrew from the Council of Europe to avoid being expelled on charges of violating human rights.

12—Two men, one an Arab, the other an African, were shot to death as they attempted to hijack a commercial jet flying over southern Europe en route from Madrid to Addis Ababa, Ethiopia.

13—Carmine G. De Sapio, former Tammany Hall leader, was found guilty in federal court on three counts of conspiracy to bribe former water commissioner James L. Marcus and extort contracts from Consolidated Edison that would have resulted in kickbacks.

13—A 13-week strike by the performers' unions which had postponed the opening of the New York Metropolitan Opera season ended with agreement to a new contract.

14—American troops, supported by helicopter gunships and artillery, killed 53 enemy soldiers in a five-hour battle near My Lai.

15—The 207,000-ton tanker *Marpessa*, the largest ship ever to sink, went down off the coast of West Africa on her maiden voyage after an explosion. Two crewmen were missing.

15—President Nixon announced another 50,000 American troops would be withdrawn from Vietnam by April 15, bringing total reductions since he took office to 110,000.

15—Alexander Dubcek, former secretary of the Czechoslovak Communist Party and leader of the 1968 liberalization campaign who lost power following the Soviet invasion, was named his nation's envoy to Turkey.

15—Israel's coalition government, consisting of 24 ministers and put together by Premier Golda Meir, was approved by Parliament.

16—Gen. Omar Otrrijos, commander of the National Guard and Panama's leader, was back in power after being ousted in a coup a day earlier. Two officers who led the overthrow were arrested.

16—Police in Rome charged nine persons, including a teen-age German girl and an Italian ballet dancer, with engineering bombings in Rome and Milan that killed 14 persons and injured more than 100 four days earlier.

17—The Air Force ended Project Blue Book, a 22-year-old program that investigated 12,618 reported sightings of unidentified flying objects.

17—The last 11 liberals sitting in Czechoslovakia's parliament resigned under fire.

17—Newark Mayor Hugh J. Addonizio was among 15 persons indicted by a federal grand jury on charges of extortion, conspiracy and income tax evasion. Fifty-five persons, including reputed New Jersey Mafia boss Simone De Cavalcante, were indicted on charges involving an alleged $20-million-a-year gambling ring.

18—Britain abolished the death penalty for murder.

18—Arthur F. Burns was confirmed by the Senate as head of the Federal Reserve Board.

19—The United States moved toward improving relations with Communist China by easing a trade embargo of nearly two decades.

22—Bernadette Devlin, independent member of the British Parliament, was sentenced to six months' imprisonment for her part in the religious rioting in Northern Ireland four months earlier. The sentence was appealed.

22—A South Vietnamese airliner with 70 persons aboard slid off a runway at Nhatrang and plowed into a school building and a row of houses, killing at least 35 persons.

22—At least 11 persons were reported killed in the crash of a jet fighter into a hangar at Miramar Naval Air Station in San Diego.

25—Some 27 children were killed and more than 100 persons were injured by a crowd that stampeded a sports arena in Bukavu, The Congo.

25—At least one person was dead and 11 were injured in the aftermath of two tornados that touched down in Southern Louisiana.

25—Ground-to-air missile sites being rebuilt by the Egyptians after earlier attacks came under Israeli air assault for more than eight hours.

26—Twenty of 39 crewmen aboard the *Badger State* were reported missing after abandoning the Vietnam-bound freighter which broke up in the stormy mid-Pacific.

26—A United Air Lines jet carrying 29 persons bound for Chicago was hijacked to Cuba shortly after take-off from LaGuardia Airport in New York.

27—Premier Eisaku Sato's Liberal-Democratic party swept to victory in Japan's election for the House of Representatives.

27—Seventy-nine enemy soldiers were reported killed in a Cambodian border fight, the fiercest battle in Vietnam in six weeks.

28—The temple of Aphrodite of Cnidus was discovered among ruins on a Turkish peninsula that juts into the Aegean Sea.

28—Five French gunboats built for Israel but never delivered because of an arms embargo were headed for the war-torn country after supposedly being bought by a Norwegian company later declared nonexistent.

29—Many European industries and services were virtually paralyzed by a major epidemic of influenza that first swept the continent in mid-December.

30—President Nixon signed into law a mine health and safety bill and the tax reform and relief bill.

30—The trial of Denis Michael Rohan, 28-year-old Australian sheep shearer, charged with setting fire to Al Aksa Mosque in the Holy City on Aug. 21, ended when an Israeli court sentenced him to an indefinite period in a mental institution.

DEATHS—1969

Earl Alexander of Tunis, architect of Allied victories in the Middle East, North Africa and Italy in World War II, fought by the motto "attack and attack, even when on the defensive." It had tragic implications at Dunkirk, where he presided over one of Britain's most heartbreaking retreats. The fourth son of the Earl of Caledon became, at age 46, the youngest Briton to achieve the rank of major general. He was commander in chief of all Allied armies in Italy, supreme commander of British and American troops in the Mediterranean. Gen. Dwight D. Eisenhower, under whom Alexander served, called him the "ace card in the British Empire's hand." After the war Alexander was governor general of Canada and minister of defense in Churchill's first postwar government. At age 77 in London. June 16.

Maj. Gen. Terry Allen, 81, who earned the nickname, "Terrible Terry," never lost a battle. A World War II hero, he led the First Infantry Division in the North Africa and Sicily campaigns and the 104th Infantry Division in the Allied drive into Germany. Although his stanchest military philosophy was that tactics are nine-tenths audacity, he never lost the confidence of his men. For his service with the First Division he was awarded the Distinguished Service Medal and the French Croix de Guerre. He retired from the Army in 1946 at his own request. In El Paso, Texas, Sept. 12.

Gen. Carias Andino, 94, was a power in Honduran affairs for more than six decades and served as president of that country from 1933 to 1948. His tenure in office was marked by labor controversy, legislative conflict and the imprisonment of many opponents. He was credited with stabilizing the country's economy and with increasing stability in Central America. Dec. 23, in Tegucigalpa, Honduras.

Emilio Arenales, 46, aged quickly in his first United Nations job. When the 24-year-old law student found that legal counsels to UNESCO must be 30, he added six years for the record. As Guatemala's representative to the international body from 1955 to 1958, he was elected president of the Trusteeship Council for a year. Then, after a term as his country's foreign minister, the handsome and charming diplomat was chosen president of the United Nations General Assembly in 1968. April 17, in Guatemala City.

Thurman Arnold, 78, was an assistant attorney general in the Franklin D. Roosevelt administration from 1938 to 1943 and was one of the New Deal's chief trust busters. A cigar-smoking, booming voiced westerner, he had been mayor of his home town of Laramie, Wyo., a Wyoming legislator and a lecturer in law at the University of Wyoming before he became dean of the West Virginia University College of Law in 1927. In 1930 he moved to Yale as a professor of law and remained there for seven years. After leaving the Justice Department he was given a lifetime appointment as judge of the U. S. Court of Appeals but resigned after two years and formed a law firm; Nov. 7, in Alexandria, Va.

Adm. Daniel Barbey, 79, known as "Uncle Dan" by officer and enlisted man alike, invented and/or developed both the practical patterns of amphibious warfare and many of the landing craft that made up his fleet. During 1943-1945, he directed the landings of more than one million men in 56 Southwest Pacific assaults. April 11, in Bremerton, Wash.

Herbert W. Barker, 64, supervised the night general news desk of The Associated Press for 26 years. He had been an AP employe for 44 years in all, including stints as general sports editor and night editor in Pittsburgh. He was known for his ability

to make quick decisions under pressure and his steadying and enthusiastic influence. Jan. 15, in Syosset, N. Y.

W. Preston Battle, 60, presided over the trial of James Earl Ray and, when Ray pleaded guilty to killing the Rev. Martin Luther King Jr., sentenced him to 99 years in prison. A criminal court judge in Memphis since 1959, Battle had a reputation for taciturnity, compassion and running a no-nonsense court. March 31, in Memphis, Tenn.

Welton Becket, 66, founder and leader of one of the nation's largest architectural firms. He designed expensive homes for film stars, set a trend in suburban shopping centers by blending stores with residential surroundings and masterminded sleek, functional corporate structures on five continents. His projects included the Los Angeles Music Center; Century City in West Los Angeles; Los Angeles Memorial Sports Arena; Xerox Square in Rochester, N.Y.; Center Plaza, Boston; the Eisenhower Museum in Abilene, Kan., and the American Embassy in Warsaw. Los Angeles, Jan. 18.

Dr. Philip Blaiberg (see page 171)

John Boles, 73, had rugged good looks and a booming baritone that served him well on Broadway and in Hollywood. His movie credits included: *The Desert Song, Imitation of Life,* and two Shirley Temple films. His biggest stage hit was *One Touch of Venus* in 1943. Feb. 27, in San Angelo, Texas.

Charles Brackett, 77, was most successful in his fourth career: movie making. He teamed with Billy Wilder to win Oscars for *Sunset Boulevard* and *The Lost Weekend* and won one of his own for *Titanic* —this out of a total of about 25 films. An urbane, affable and philosophic man, Brackett had been a lawyer, free-lance fiction writer and a drama critic for The New Yorker. March 9, in Hollywood.

Dan Breen, 75, was known for his exploits as an Irish Republican Army commandant leading the "Flying Column" against British troops and the Black-and-Tan auxiliaries from 1918 until the truce of 1921. His book, *"My Fight for Irish Freedom,"* was translated into many languages and made his name well known to guerrilla organizations around the world. In the Irish civil war that followed the peace treaty with Britain in 1922 he again fought on the I. R. A. side against the forces of the new Irish Free State. Dec. 27, in Dublin, Ireland.

Maureen Connolly Brinker, better known as "Little Mo," became, in 1953, the first woman to achieve the grand slam of tennis—the national championships of the United States, Britain, France and Australia. Winner of three United States and Wimbledon crowns, "Little Mo" ruled the woman's tennis world from 1951 until 1954 when a horseback riding accident ended her career. At age 34 of cancer in Dallas, Tex. June 21.

Robert Briscoe, 74, was the son of a Lithuanian immigrant who grew up to be an Irish rebel and Dublin's only Jewish mayor. Briscoe, a founder of the Fianna Fail party, was first chosen Lord Mayor of Ireland's Roman Catholic capital in 1959 when his name was drawn from a hat in city council. So colorful was his life that a movie, *The Fabulous Irishman,* was based on it. May 30, in Dublin.

John Mason Brown, 68, was a drama and literary critic whose gentle wit was bred in Louisville and honed at Harvard. He reviewed plays for New York newspapers before joining the Saturday Review in 1944. A literary gourmand, he stuffed himself with hundreds of books a year and digested them in speeches before scores of luncheon clubs annually.

For years he was a Book-of-the-Month Club judge and wrote some 20 books himself, mostly on the theater. March 16, in New York.

Alisa Mellon Bruce, 65, reported by Fortune Magazine to be the only woman in the United States worth at least $500 million, devoted herself to a number of charitable pursuits, including the donation of $20 million with her brother to the National Gallery of Art in Washington, D. C. She served as her father's social secretary when he was Secretary of the Treasury under President Harding, and was married to Robert Bruce, former Ambassador to London, for 19 years. In New York City, Aug. 19.

Barry Cannon (see page 46)

Gen. Georges Catroux, 92, was one of the highest-ranking figures to join Gen. Charles de Gaulle at the fall of France in 1940. The diplomat general's career spanned much of the establishment and disintegration of French colonialism from the country's campaigns in North Africa, the Middle East and Indochina before World War I to the Algerian revolution. He was ambassador to the Soviet Union from 1944 to 1948. Dec. 21, in Paris, France.

Eduardo Ciannelli, 80, Italian-born character actor, had a 45-year career in motion pictures and on the American stage. His jutting chin and seemingly malevolent eyes were familiar to thousands of fans who could count on him to portray criminal masterminds with great flair. Although he was frequently called upon to play Mafia overlords, he also undertook character roles as priests, restaurant owners and comic grandfathers. His greatest success was his portrayal of the evil Trock Estrella in Maxwell Anderson's *"Winterset."* He was last seen on the stage in 1961 in *"The Devil's Advocate,"* and shortly before his death he finished his last film, *"Boot Hill,"* in Rome, Italy. Oct. 9, in Rome.

Spade Cooley, 59, the country fiddler once known as the "king of western swing," was discovered for motion pictures by western star Roy Rogers. During the peak days of radio he formed a band and subsequently wrote the song *"Shame, Shame on You."* Later he entered the real estate business. In 1961 he was convicted in the slaying of his wife, Ella Mae. Scheduled for parole in 1970, he collapsed during a 72-hour prison furlough; Nov. 23, in Oakland, Calif.

Vicki Cummings, 50, musical comedy actress, was often praised by critics for her portrayals of sophisticated, sharp-tongued women. She made her New York debut in 1931 and continued to appear frequently on Broadway. In 1953 she won the Aegis Club award as best supporting actress of the season. Although she appeared in more than 200 television shows, she only made one movie, *"I Can Get It for You Wholesale,"* in 1951. Her last New York assignment was in the 1966 revival of *"The Butter and Egg Man";* Nov. 30, in New York City.

Dr. William Dameshek, 59, pioneer in the study of blood, was credited with establishing hematology as a separate medical specialty. He often served as a consultant to Federal agencies and was a key figure in national and international meetings on blood problems. At his death he was emeritus professor of medicine at the Mount Sinai School of Medicine in the City University of New York, consultant hematologist to the Mount Sinai Hospital and editor in chief of Blood, the international journal of hematology which he founded in 1946. Oct. 7, in New York City.

Sen. Everett Dirksen (see pages 192-193)

Constance Dowling, 49, began her acting career on the Broadway stage, appearing in *"Panama Hattie," "Hold On to Your Hats"* and *"The Strings, My Lord Are False."* In 1943 she went to Hollywood and appeared in Danny Kaye's first film, *"Up in Arms."* After a few more movie roles, however, she became disillusioned with Hollywood. She returned briefly to the stage and later went to Italy to make such films as *"Duel Without Honor"* and *"Mad about Opera."* Oct. 28 in Los Angeles, Calif.

Dorothy Draper, 79, became one of the best-known interior decorators in the country though she had no formal training. Initiator of the concept of "total coordination" of all elements, from matchbooks to curtains, she worked mostly on commercial jobs using vivid colors—unique in the 30s—and lots of roses. March 10, in Cleveland, Ohio.

James H. Duff, 86, said, "All you need to do to see the governor of Pennsylvania is to have a nickel and a telephone booth; I believe in keeping myself close to the average guy." The Republican leader served as governor from 1947 to 1950 and then was elected to the Senate, where he alienated some of the state's leading industrialists with his program to rid Pennsylvania's streams of pollution. At the Republican National Convention in 1948 he attracted national attention by refusing to support Gov. Thomas E. Dewey of New York. Dec. 20, in Washington, D. C.

Allen Welsh Dulles (see page 28)

Harley J. Earl, 75, innovated longer, lower automobiles, decluttering them by removing the running board, outside luggage compartment and spare tire holder. He brought new ideas of styling to General Motors—such as two-tone paint, hardtop design and fins copied from a P-38 fighter plane—and created "dynamic obsolescence" or annual model changes. April 10, in Palm Beach, Fla.

Max Eastman, 86, was the handsome, egotistical and romantic leader of the Bohemians of Greenwich Village during the teens and '20s. He made a more lasting impact as a center of political and literary controversy: as editor of The Masses, an anti-World War I magazine, he became involved in two sedition trials; as a friend of Leon Trotsky's and foe of Stalin's, he became embroiled in the Communist controversies of the '30s. Age brought him political disillusionment and a job as roving editor for the Reader's Digest. March 25, in Bridgetown, Barbados.

Charles Edison, 78, overshadowed by the fame of his father, inventor Thomas A. Edison, devoted his life to business and civic and political leadership. He was Secretary of the Navy under Franklin D. Roosevelt, governor of New Jersey from 1941-44, president of Thomas A. Edison Inc. until it merged with McGraw Electric Co., when he became board chairman of McGraw-Edison Co. In New York City, July 31.

Dwight D. Eisenhower (see pages 250-256)

Levi Eshkol (see page 47)

Former Queen Victoria Eugenie in Spain, 81, the widow of King Alfonso XIII who abdicated in 1931, was a granddaughter of Great Britain's Queen Victoria. The royal marriage almost ended as it began in 1906 when an anarchist's bomb exploded prematurely, killing and wounding more than 100 persons. When the king and queen left Spain, they lived separately. In 1968, at the age of 80, she returned for the first time, for the baptism of a great-grandson. April 15, in Lausanne, Switzerland.

William A. Fisher, 83, was one of the seven brothers who created the Fisher Body Corp., the company that grew from a blacksmith shop to a multimillion dollar operation. After General Motors bought controlling interest in the firm and established it as a new division he was its first president. He was a donor to cultural and educational projects and an avid yachtsman. Dec. 20, in Detroit, Mich.

Raoul H. Fleischmann, 83, a member of the family that developed the bread yeast, turned from baker to publisher in 1924 when Harold Ross suggested the start of "a new comic paper." In February, 1925 they put out the first issue of The New Yorker. Before the weekly magazine became one of the country's most profitable editorial properties, Fleischmann poured $700,000 of his General Baking Co. fortunes into it and confided, "I didn't think for a moment we'd make a go of it." In New York City, May 11.

Corey Ford, 67, was one of the best literary funnymen of the 1920s and 30s. In his autobiography, *"A Time for Laughter,"* Ford summed up his own approach to comedy: "Much of it was bigger than life" but "there was no malice concealed in a joke. Fun had only one purpose and that was to be funny. Humor was its own excuse." Ford parodied many of his contemporaries and poked fun at American foibles. The author of 30 books, 500 magazine articles and associate editor and columnist for Field and Stream magazine was in on the founding of The New Yorker magazine and provided the name Eustace Tilley for the man-of-all-work. The character, depicted as a top-hatted dude with a monocle, became the magazine's hallmark. In Hanover, N.H., July 27.

Dr. Harry Emerson Fosdick (see page 214)

Lieut. Col. William F. Friedman, 78, was leader of the Army task force that cracked the Japanese "Purple" code shortly before the United States entered World War II. In 1946 President Harry S. Truman awarded him the Medal for Merit, highest U.S. civilian award, for his wartime work. Born in Kishinev, Russia, he emigrated to Pittsburgh, Pa., with his family at the age of two. After college he studied genetics, but his interest soon shifted to cryptology. In 1947 he became chief cryptologist of the Department of Defense. After his retirement he continued to serve as a consultant; Nov. 2, in Washington, D. C.

Romulo Gallegos, 84, was the first president of Venezuela to be elected by popular vote. His four-year term, begun in Feb. 1948, was ended just nine months later by a military coup. For 10 years, he lived in exile, then returned to devote himself to a life of writing and liberal politics. Gallegos was a well-known Spanish-language novelist, essayist and playwright who had spent his first 20 working years teaching. At his death he headed the human rights committee of the Organization of American States. April 4, in Caracas, Venezuela.

Judy Garland (see page 134)

Vito Genovese, 71, reputedly became "boss of all bosses" in the underworld of Cosa Nostra after an assassination attempt on mobster Frank Costello and the execution of Albert Anastasia. His rivals disposed of, the takeover was allegedly completed at the Apalachin, N.Y., meeting in 1957 which police raided. From then on, the short, pallid immigrant ruled a "family" of 450 racketeers and business infiltrators. Even when imprisoned on a narcotics smuggling charge—his only major conviction—he was able to order his "soldiers." One, Joseph Valachi, thought Genovese wanted to execute him and turned state's witness about the American branch of the Mafia. Feb. 14, at the Medical Center for Federal Prisoners, Springfield, Mo.

Kimon Georgiev, 87, mobilized anti-Nazi and anti-royalist feelings of Bulgarians in 1944 to stage a coup d' etat, which led to a communist government. Twice Premier of Bulgaria, he headed the government from 1944 to 1946 and held high-ranking posts in the communist regime following World War II. After his 70th birthday he faded from public view. In Sofia, Bulgaria, Sept. 28.

Adam Gimbel, 75, president of the Saks Fifth Avenue stores from 1926 until his retirement in February 1969, said he strove to create in his stores the warmth of a "home in which the customers are treated as guests." He built the stores into the country's largest specialty chain, with 30 branches stretching from New York to Florida and California. His wife, Sophie, who designed for Saks, was elected a member of the permanent Fashion Hall of Fame. In New York City, Sept. 9.

Leo Gorcey, wearing a tweed peaked cap or a beanie, slouched his way through the 1935 Broadway production *"Dead End"* and a dozen subsequent movies about the Manhattan street gang, first portraying Spit, then Muggs McGinnis. Spit, said a reviewer of the Dead End Kids, was "the littlest, the one most stunted by cigarette smoking, a venomous expectorator for whom the eye of an enemy was like a flying quail to a huntsman." When the Dead End Kids broke up in the 1940s, Gorcey and Huntz Hall, another member of the gang, created the Bowery Boys, based mostly on slapstick comedy rather than the adventures of the endearing gang that backed the underdog. At age 52 in Oakland, Calif. June 2.

Dr. Walter Gropius, founder of the Bauhaus School of Design and Architecture in Germany, was one of the world's leading architects and the father of modern design. Gropius' school was the first to unite art with industry and daily life. He described it as "a new fusion of man and machine," whereby the notion that forms follow function was applied to everything and the young students were trained to "bridge the gap between the rigid mentality of the businessman and technologist and the imagination of the creative artist." Gropius built Harvard's Graduate School of Design into one of the major architectural centers of the world. Among buildings he designed was the Pan Am Building in New York. At age 86 in Boston, July 5.

Frank Gruber, 65, was one of the nation's most prolific writers. In 22 years he produced 37 books, 52 screen plays and 350 short stories. Westerns and mysteries were his specialty. Among the films made from books were *"Broken Lance," "Rawhide,"* and *"Tension at Table Rock."* Born in Elmer, Minn., he grew up in Chicago, found writing success in New York and spent his last years in Hollywood. Dec. 10, in Santa Monica, Calif.

Ricardo de la Guardia, 72, was president of Panama between 1941 and 1945. He was credited with establishing realistic price ceilings on food staples and broadening programs for education and health. In early 1945 he suspended the constitution to prolong his time in office, but on June 15, 1945 he was replaced as president when the Constitutional Congress chose Enrique A. Jimenez as his successor. After he left public life he operated a supply store in Panama City. Dec. 29, in Panama City.

Walter Hagen, 76, a giant in professional golf, entranced galleries in every country in which the game was played. From 1914, when he won his first championship—the United States Open—until 1929, when he retired from competition, he won 17 major golf titles and appeared in more than 2,500 exhibitions. His wizardry included devastating mashie shots, a renowned skill at putting and a knowledge of psychology which frequently unnerved his opponents. After his retirement he headed the Walter Hagen Division of the Wilson Sporting Goods Company, and wrote a book, *"The Walter Hagen Story."* Oct. 5, in Traverse City, Mich.

Fred A. Hartley Jr., 66, was a little-known Republican congressman from New Jersey for nearly two decades. Then in 1947, as chairman of the House Labor Committee, he joined Sen. Robert A. Taft, R–Ohio, in sponsoring the Labor-Management Relations Act, passed by Congress over a veto by President Harry S. Truman. The legislation, known as the Taft-Hartley Act, outlawed the closed shop, protected the right of the worker not to join a union and provided injunctions to compel "cooling-off" strike postponements. In Linwood, N.J., May 11.

Coleman Hawkins, 64, whose musical career spanned nearly half a century, created the first valid jazz style on the tenor saxophone in the mid-1920s. In 1939 he recorded *Body and Soul* as a favor to his producer and made such a hit that he had to play it at nearly every performance for the next 15 years. in New York, May 19.

Cameron Hawley, 63, used his experiences as a successful businessman in four novels. His first were his best known: *Executive Suite* and *Cash McCall,* and both were made into movies. A thorough researcher, the mustachioed executive quit the work-a-day world in 1951 to devote himself to writing. In addition to his novels, he wrote for magazines and television. Feb. 9, in Marathon, Fla.

George "Gabby" Hayes, 83, played the grizzled, cantankerous, trusty sidekick to the likes of William Boyd (Hopalong Cassidy), Roy Rogers, Gene Autry and John Wayne in countless movie and television cowboy epics. In fact, he was a tenderfoot from New York state who headlined a vaudeville act for almost 20 years. With the advent of talking pictures, he left the stage and a few years later struck gold as Windy Halliday, Hopalong's pal. Feb. 9, in Hollywood, Calif.

Walter E. Heller, 78, received $100,000 credit in 1919, and turned it into a $600 million international commercial finance business. Heller broke with tradition by lending on the borrower's customers' credit, or factoring, till then used only in the textile field. He thoroughly researched the borrowers-to-be and boasted he had financed some 13,000 successful businesses in the United States. April 12, in Chicago.

Sonja Henie (see page 214)

Michael Franklin "Pinky" Higgins, 59, played baseball with the Philadelphia Athletics, Boston Red Sox and the Detroit Tigers in the late '30s and early '40s, and set a major league record of 12 consecutive hits. He later became a popular Boston manager. March 21, in Dallas, Tex.

Violet and Daisy Hilton, 60, British Siamese twins, were joined at the base of the spine. Orphaned at the age of four, the sisters were exhibited in circuses and street carnivals in Australia until 1916 when they came to the United States and broke into vaudeville as "our own jazz band." Their last days were spent as checkers in a supermarket. Charlotte, N.C., Jan. 4.

Max Hirsch, 88, was dean of America's thoroughbred horse trainers. After a career as a jockey, he turned to training at the age of 22 and developed three Kentucky Derby winners. One, Assault, added the Preakness and Belmont in 1946, thus becoming racing's seventh Triple Crown winner. The trainer had such confidence in his charges he would on occasion back them with a little wager—like the time he and gambler Arnold Rothstein allegedly won $770,000 on a till then non-winner, Sidereal. April 3, in New Hyde Park, N.Y.

Zakir Husain, 72, an educator who entered politics at the age of 55, was elected India's first Moslem president 15 years later. Husain, India's third president since it became a republic in 1950, was elected May 9, 1967, to succeed Sarvepalli Radhakrishnan. The eloquent, shy and gently humorous scholar was a law student when he became attracted to the

movement initiated by Mohandas K. Gandhi against British rule. With Gandhi's blessings, he worked ceaselessly to reform the educational system. In New Delhi, May 3.

Dr. Karl Jaspers, 86, was described variously as an existentialist or a personalist, but he was a leading philosopher who attempted to explain man to himself, not in scientific or religious terms, but metaphysically: "It can only be learned at the source, non-objectively, beyond all that can ever be known." He imposed on man the awesome responsibility of constantly judging himself in the entirety of his existence. Feb. 26, in Basel, Switzerland.

Boris Karloff, 81, was so horrible he was beautiful to millions of movie monster fans. His acting career had been languishing until 1931 when *Frankenstein* hurled him into a life of terror. The elegant and sensitive Englishman played bodysnatchers, sadists and ax murderers in some 130 films, and a dozen plays of which the longest-running was *Arsenic and Old Lace.* Feb. 2, in London.

Joseph Kasavubu, 50s, the Congo's first president, oversaw, with his arch-rival, leftist Patrice Lumumba, the bloody collapse of their country. When independence was declared in 1960, Belgian colonialists deserted, the army mutinied, diamond-rich Katanga Province seceded and chaos reigned. Finally, army-backed Col. Joseph D. Mobutu took over, forcing Lumumba into exile; a few years later, in 1965, Kasavubu was pushed by Mobutu into retirement. March 24, in Bomba, the Lower Congo.

Jack Kerouac, 47, wrote in one of his novels, "The only people for me are the mad ones, the ones who are mad to live, mad to talk, desirous of everything at the same time." He gave the Beat Generation its name and celebrated its rejection of middle class American conventions. Although his works never gained wide acceptance among literary tastemakers, they served as texts for youth who found their country claustrophobic and oppressive. Among his novels were, *"On the Road,"* based on his travels through the United States, and *"The Subterraneans,"* written in three days. Oct. 21, in St. Petersburg, Fla.

Andy Kerr, 90, was respected as one of the nation's most successful and inventive college football coaches. In his 18 years as Colgate University's head coach, his teams compiled a won-lost-tied record of 95-50-7 and the 1932 squad outscored nine opponents 264-0. He returned to the scene of triumph in 1966 when Colgate dedicated a stadium in his honor. Feb. 16, in Tucson, Ariz.

Frank King, creator of the comic strip "Gasoline Alley," amused millions of newspaper readers for a half-century, mirroring the vicissitudes and triumphs of an average small-town American family. King, who began the comic strip in 1919, became the first American cartoonist to have his family of pen and ink—Skeezix, Uncle Walt, Aunt Phyllis and others—grow and age. Much of the background and setting for "Gasoline Alley" was Tomah, Wis., his boyhood in the Kickapoo Hills. At age 86 in Winter Park, Fla. June 24.

Edwin A. Lahey, 67, former chief of bureau and chief correspondent in Washington for Knight newspapers, was variously described as a crime and labor expert and one of the nation's top reporters although he often said, "I don't know anythink duller than an expert." Lahey, who quit grade school "to bring in five dollars" became a member of the first class of Nieman Fellows at Harvard. Among his best remembered stories were a beat on the resignation of Martin Durkin, President Eisenhower's first labor secretary, and an interview with Sen. Robert A. Taft of Ohio that led to a reconciliation between Taft and General Eisenhower, who defeated him for the Republican Presidential nomination in 1952. In Washington, July 17.

Rod La Rocque, 70, made his Hollywood debut as a villain in Cecil De Mille's production *"The Ten Commandments."* He later appeared in more than 30 pictures, including, *"Gigolo," "Ressurrection"* and *"Captain Swagger."* His marriage to Vilma Banky, the Hungarian-born actress, was a lavish spectacle, planned and supervised by producer Samuel Goldwin. After retiring from the screen La Rocque became a real estate broker. Oct. 15, in Beverly Hills, Calif.

D. B. Wyndham Lewis, 78, for more than 40 years combined scholarship and wit in columns for the Daily Express, the Daily Mail and other London newspapers. He was also the author of lively biographies of Boswell, Moliere, Rabelais and others. Born in Wales, the descendant of an old and distinguished family, he once described himself as "impulsive, lazy, easily imposed upon . . . full of loves and hates and generally unpleasant." His last book, *"The World of Goya,"* appeared in 1968; Nov. 21, in Altea, Spain.

John L. Lewis (see page 134)

Willy Ley lived to within one month of the fulfillment of his prophecy—that liquid fuel rockets would land men on the moon. Ley, a German-born scientist and author who helped usher in the age of rocketry, was one of the earliest protagonists for such a flight. In Germany he helped found the Society for Space Travel and recruited into the organization a young man named Werner Von Braun who ultimately became a leader in German military rocket development. The two later collaborated on several books, including *"The Exploration of Mars."* In 1935 Ley got word that he was in trouble with the Gestapo so he left for Britain and ultimately the United States, where he continued writing and lecturing. At age 62 in New York City, June 24.

Robert Lehman, 77, was an investment banker who could raise millions with little more effort than the lift of an eyebrow. He often said, "The secret of investment banking is to put your money in the right place at the right time." His firm, Lehman Brothers, of which he was senior partner, was one of the giants of Wall Street. He was an art collector with paintings valued at $50 million, a racing horse breeder and a philanthropist. In Sands Point, N. Y., Aug. 19.

Allan H. Lockheed, 80, a barnstorming exhibition pilot in the decade after the Wright Brothers' famous flight, decided while his plane crashed in a small Illinois town that he could build a better one. He and his late brother, Malcolm, founded Lockheed Aircraft and watched it become the nation's 24th largest industrial corporation. Lockheed was born Allan H. Loughead but "people keep calling me Log-head," so the name was changed. In Tucson, Ariz., May 27.

Frank Loesser came from a highbrow musical family—his father a teacher of classical piano, his brother music critic and professor—but Frank was determinedly middlebrow. He never studied music; it just rubbed off on him. "He was one of the greatest songwriters the United States ever produced," said composer William Schuman. ". . . His songs were authentic Americana . . . he sensed the rhythms of American speech and captured them." Loesser brought to Broadway *"Guys and Dolls," "How to Succeed in Business Without Really Trying," "Where's Charley?"* and *"The Most Happy Fella," "Baby, It's Cold Outside,"* written for *"Neptune's Daughter,"* won the 1948 Academy Award. Other songs included *"Once in Love with Amy," "On a Slow Boat to China," "Heart and Soul," "Two Sleepy People."* At age 50 in New York City, July 28.

Barton MacLane, 66. With an adolescent eye on an acting career he built up his biceps so he could "tear a villain limb from limb." But it was he who played the villain in more than 150 motion pictures. Santa Monica, Calif., Jan. 1.

Erica Mann, 63, writer and actress, was the daughter of Nobel prize novelist Thomas Mann. As an anti-Hitler exile from Germany, she came to the United States to lecture and write on the menace of Fascism. She also produced and acted in *"The Pepper Mill,"* a political-literary revue which criticized the Nazis. After the war she returned to Switzerland with her father, who died there in 1955. In Zurich, Switzerland, Aug. 27.

Rocky Marciano, 45, nicknamed Brockton Blockbuster, was former world heavyweight boxing champion with an undefeated record. His greatness in the ring, based on aggressiveness and ability to withstand punishment, was in contrast to his gentle nature in personal life. He began boxing in the Army and turned pro in 1947. In 1956 he retired and tried several business ventures with moderate success. In Newton, Iowa, Aug., 31.

George Preston Marshall, 72, controversial owner and former president of the Washington Redskins, once said: "The cure for the ills of college football is to dismiss 90 per cent of the college presidents, most of whom wanted to play football but couldn't make the team." While he wasn't watching the Redskins from the sidelines in his raccoon coat, spats and derby he tried running the team and calling plays over the phone from his box seat. The title playoff game and Pro Bowl were his ideas and his half-time shows were as spectacular as the games. Once he even hired the National Symphony Orchestra to play at half-time. In Washington, D. C., Aug. 9.

Giovanni Martinelli, 83, was a leading tenor during the Metropolitan Opera's golden age. His 1910 debut was so impressive that six months later composer Giacomo Puccini cast him in *Girl of the Golden West.* By 1913, the sunny-tempered Italian was on the Metropolitan's roster, and he stayed there for 32 years. He estimated that he had sung before 7,000 audiences around the world before his retirement to voice coaching in 1946. Feb. 2, in New York.

Adolfo Lopez Mateos, 59, served as President of Mexico from 1958 to 1964, and was head of the Institutional Revolutionary party which had controlled the Government for more than five decades. As president he cracked down on labor disputes and encouraged private enterprise, especially foreign investments while maintaining what he called "independence" in foreign policy. After retiring from the presidency he was head of the Olympics Organizing Committee, which arranged for the 1968 games in Mexico City. In Mexico, D.F., Sept. 22.

Gavin Maxwell, 55, Scottish naturalist, achieved his greatest popularity with three books he wrote about his experiences with otters. The first, *"A Ring of Bright Water,"* was filmed. His writing career began in 1952 with *"Harpoon Venture,"* a book about basking sharks. He wrote about southern Iraq, the Scottish highlands and Sicily, describing them as places that were not "suburbanized and where there was still something left to see." He was active in many preservation societies, and also campaigned for the abolition of capital punishment in Britain. In Inverness, Scotland, Sept. 6.

Tom Mboya (see page 154)

Paul McCobb, 51, designed elegant natural-wood furniture that won awards from the Museum of Modern Art and the Philadelphia Museum of Art, yet was priced so reasonably that one group was a best-seller for a decade. He believed in modular, cleanly-sculptured design and was credited with innovating room dividers, walls to which desks and cabinets could be attached and the first use of

metal in inside-the-home furniture. March 11, in New York.

Ralph McGill, 70, made his paper, the Atlanta Constitution, a voice for civil rights in the wilderness of entrenched southern separatism. In 1958 he won the Pulitzer Prize for editorial writing. The publisher's columns were not limited to civil rights, but ranged from regional to world problems and were syndicated across the country. Feb. 3, in Atlanta, Ga.

Jimmy McHugh, 74, dashed his father's dream of "my son, the plumber" when he got a job at the Boston Opera House. While working as office boy and rehearsal accompanist, McHugh embarked on a composing career that totaled more than 500 songs, the scores for 55 motion pictures and many Broadway musicals. Among his best known were *Sunny Side of the Street, I'm in the Mood for Love,* and *I Can't Give You Anything But Love, Baby.* In Beverly Hills, Calif., May 23.

Donald McMillan, 82, joined the Salvation Army at 19, and during his 51-year career rose to its highest position in the United States. He was graduated from the Salvation Army Training College in 1906. He held positions in the army's finance, men's social and field departments and on its training staff before becoming a general secretary for three Eastern regions. He was national secretary during World War II, and in 1946 received the Medal for Merit, highest Presidential award to civilians. In 1953 he was appointed national commander and held that position until he retired in 1957. Dec. 3, in New York City.

Gilbert Miller, 84, dean of New York theatrical producers. The son of Henry Miller, actor-manager, and Bijou Heron, actress, made his debut in London in 1916 with *Daddy Long Legs.* He moved onto Broadway in 1919 with *Beaucaire,* the only musical he ever produced. Miller's biggest hit was *Victoria Regina,* starring Helen Hayes. It opened in New York Aug. 31, 1936 and eventually grossed $2.5 million. New York, Jan. 3.

Ho Chi Minh (see pages 174–179)

Maj. Gen. Iskander Mirza, 70, was Pakistan's first President when that country became a republic in 1955. He was considered a shrewd administrator, but ultimately he offended leading politicians and irritated the army. In 1958 he abrogated the constitution and declared martial law. Later that year he was persuaded to turn over the government to Gen. Ayub Khan. After resigning he went to England to live; Nov. 13, in London, England.

Russ Morgan, 65, trombonist and pianist, was one of the leaders of the big band sound. He formed his own orchestra in 1936 and cultivated the sweet jazz style. Born in Scranton, Pa., he started working in the coal mines at 9 to earn money for music lessons. In Las Vegas, Nev., Aug. 7.

Alan Mowbray, 72, had a comic elegance that won him roles in more than 400 movies. As an Englishman-turned-American, he played character roles ranging from butler to nobleman, not only on film but on Broadway and television. He was a founder of the Screen Actors Guild. March 25, in Hollywood.

Clinton Williams Murchison Sr., one of the world's wealthiest men who amassed a $500 million fortune, once said "cash makes a man careless," so he invested in things—oil, gas, railroads, publishing, grocery chains and the like. The Texan, whose forte was the ability to discover and develop deposits of oil and natural gas, put his Midas touch to other people's money to build an empire that extended from Venezuela to Canada and throughout the United States. When he struck natural gas—a waste product in the 1920s—he decided to

exploit it and in 1929 founded the Southern Union Gas Company and a new industry—natural gas piped into the home for heating. At age 74 in Athens, Tex. June 20.

Oliver Noonan, 29 Associated Press photographer, was killed in South Vietnam when the helicopter in which he was traveling was shot down over rugged jungle terrain about 30 miles south of Da Nang. He was the third AP staffer to lose his life while covering the Vietnam war. Noonan had been in the combat areas for five months, working almost wholly in the field. Before joining The Associated Press he was employed by the Boston Globe and Boston Herald Traveler, and had served as president of the Boston Press Photographers Association. Noonan was a native of Norwell, Mass. Aug. 19, in Vietnam.

Frank (Lefty) O'Doul, 72, one of baseball's great hitters, won National League batting titles with the Philadelphia Phillies in 1929 and with Brooklyn in 1932. He finished with a lifetime batting average of .349, one of the highest in the major leagues. After pitching for the Boston Red Sox and New York Yankees during World War I, he switched to outfield and played for the New York Giants, Phillies and Dodgers. In 1935 he left the major leagues and spent 17 years as manager of the San Francisco Seals. O'Doul also managed San Diego, Oakland, Vancouver and Seattle teams. After quitting baseball he devoted his time to golf and the restaurant business. Dec. 7, in San Francisco, Calif.

Bishop John O'Shea, 82, a Roman Catholic prelate, led the first American Vincentians to Kanchow, China. After 31 years there he was arrested on charges of spying for the United States. He was held captive for seven months, and later wrote that he had been confined in a cold, wet cell and kept on a starvation diet. After he had contracted pneumonia and tuberculosis he was expelled from China. On returning to the United States he worked in Vincentian seminaries. Oct. 6, in Washington, D. C.

Franz von Papen, 89, was a midwife in the birth of the Third Reich and a bungler in both politics and war. The former Prussian army officer was expelled from the United States for espionage activities as a military attache in World War I. He became chancellor in 1932 whereupon he opened the door to Hitler and found himself superseded. He served the Fuehrer as vice chancellor and later ambassador to Turkey. At the end of World War II, he was convicted at Nuremberg for his Nazi activities and his sentence later was suspended. In Oberasbach, West Germany, May 2.

Drew Pearson, 71, nationally syndicated columnist, compiled an impressive record of what he termed malfunctions in the government. William L. River, in his *"The Opinion Makers,"* said Pearson's disclosures "sent four members of Congress to jail, defeated countless others and caused the dismissal of scores of government officials." Pearson began as a freelancer, later joined the staff of the Baltimore Sun and became head of its Washington, D. C., bureau. After it was revealed that he had written the book *"Washington Merry-Go-Round"* he lost his job and began his column, which ultimately was carried by more than 650 newspapers. Once he said, "My chief motive is to try to make the Government a little cleaner, a little more efficient, and I would say also, in foreign affairs, to work for peace." In Washington, D. C., Sept. 1.

Westbrook Pegler, 74, was the caustic columnist whose wrath few notables escaped. He dubbed President Roosevelt the "feebleminded fuehrer"; FDR's wife "la boca grande," the big mouth, President Truman a "thin-lipped hater" and FBI Director J. Edgar Hoover "a nightclub fly-cop." In 1949 he wrote that his writer-friend Quentin Reynolds had "a yellow streak for all to see" and that he once had been seen "nuding along a road with a wench in the raw." For that Pegler and his employer, the Hearst Corp., were taken to court. In one of the nation's most famous libel cases Reynolds, represented by Louis Nizer, won $175,000 in damages. The war correspondent, sportswriter, columnist and 1941 Pulitzer Prize winner for exposing labor union corruption, even bit the hand that fed him, attacking not only the Hearst Corp., but William Randolph Hearst Jr. himself. Their relationship ended in 1962. In Tucson, Ariz. June 24.

Leander Perez, 76, was a rich and powerful political boss in southern Louisiana. In his capacity as district attorney and president of a local commission (he later turned these posts over to his sons), he fought integration of the schools; attacked Negroes, Jews, Communists and the U.S. Navy; and almost singlehandedly kept Gov. Huey P. Long from being impeached in 1930. He was excommunicated from the Roman Catholic Church in 1962 for trying to close a parochial school that had admitted Negroes. March 19, in New Orleans.

Dr. James Pike (see page 190)

Henry Francis du Pont, 88, last great-grandson of the founder of the E. I. du Pont de Nemours chemical firm, was an accomplished man in his own right. A top businessman, he was a director of his family firm and of General Motors Corp., in which the du Ponts were major stockholders. He assembled what was considered the largest and finest collection of American decorative art anywhere for his 100-plus-room home, Winterthur, then turned it into a public museum in 1951. The estate's gardens were exceptional and du Pont as "head gardener" was a noted non-professional horticulturalist who won top awards. April 10, in Wilmington, Del.

Eric Portman, 66, leading character actor, appeared in over 100 stage plays in the United States and Britain and in many motion pictures and television programs. He once said, "I don't know if there's a method in acting at all. . . ." His career began at 20, with a walk-on part when a touring Shakespearean company visited his town. He was well-known to Americans for his dual role in the Broadway production of Terence Rattigan's *"Separate Tables."* Nov. 7, in Cornwall, England.

Stephen Potter, 69, was a satirist who wrote *"Gamesmanship, or the Art of Winning Games Without Actually Cheating,"* a book dealing with the view that psychologically well equipped persons could win at the games of life without really being able to play them well. Born to prosperous parents, he was educated at Merton College, Oxford, where he took honors in English. In 1938 he joined the British Broadcasting Corporation as a writer-producer but in 1947 decided to write the book on gamesmanship. It was so popular that he followed it with *"Lifemanship"* and *"One-Up-manship."* Dec. 2, in London, England.

Edwin Posner, 78, began a 61-year Wall Street career as a $5-a-week runner and rose to the chairmanship of the American Stock Exchange. Widely respected as a man of experience and honesty, he was asked to take the helm of the exchange in 1962. His leadership resulted in dramatic reforms, including a new administration with a 32-member policy board. He remained active as senior partner of Andrews, Posner and Rothschild, a brokerage firm, until his death. Oct. 4, in New York City.

Cecil Powell, 65, was a British physicist who won the Nobel Prize in 1950. Internationally known as an authority on cosmic rays and subnuclear particles, he often conducted high-altitude balloon expeditions to gather data. He was a leading promoter of international cooperation in science and was associated with the British peace movement, sometimes serving as Bertrand Russell's deputy. In Milan, Italy, Aug. 9.

Dr. Theodor Reik, 81, was one of the first students of Sigmund Freud. He wrote many books on psychoanalysis, including *"Listening With the Third Ear"* and *"Masochism in Modern Man."* He was born and educated in Vienna and practiced there from 1918–1928. He then moved to Berlin where he practiced and taught until the advent of Hitlerism when he moved to The Hague. In 1938 he traveled to the United States. After he was denied membership in the New York Psychoanalytic Society because of his lack of a medical degree, he helped to found the National Psychological Association for Psychoanalysis. He practiced in New York City and set up a clinic there for those who could not afford the fees of most analysts. Dec. 31, in New York City.

Herman Henry Ridder, 61, member of the nationally-known Ridder newspaper family, was publisher of the Long Beach, Calif., Independent and Press-Telegram. He was also president of Ridder Publications, Inc., with interests in 13 newspapers across the country. Ridder established residence in California in 1952 and played a leading role in state and city affairs. In Long Beach, Calif., Sept. 15.

Thelma Ritter, 64, was mostly a housewife until a friend gave her a small role in the 1946 movie, *Miracle on 34th Street.* A series of movie successes followed which won for the raspy-voiced actress an unprecedented four consecutive Oscar nominations, but no Oscars. Though she gained fame as one of the most skilled character actresses around, she still did her own housework. Feb. 5, in Queens, N.Y.

Charles Ellsworth "Pee Wee" Russell, 62, played a venturesome clarinet with traditional Dixieland bands. One jazz critic wrote, "He does with musical phrases just about what Joyce did with words." The Missouri jazzman did it with the best: Jack Teagarden, Bix Beiderbecke, Red Nichols, Eddie Condon and later with Thelonius Monk and Duke Ellington. Feb. 15, in Alexandria, Va.

Vincent Sardi Sr., 83, was founder of a restaurant described as "the club, messhall, lounge, post office, saloon and marketplace of the people of the theater." Born in Italy, he came to the United States in 1907. In 1921 he and his wife, the former Eugenia Pallera, opened a small restaurant on West 44th Street in New York City which they called The Little Restaurant. It soon became popular with theater people, who called it Sardi's. He respected the accomplishments of his guests and guarded their privacy; Nov. 19, in Saranac Lake, N. Y.

Saud Ibn Abdul Aziz, 67, was one of the world's richest absolute monarchs until overthrown by one of his 39 brothers, Crown Prince Faisal. From 1953 to 1964, King Saud ruled 870,000 acres of desert that covered 10 per cent of the world's known oil reserves. This hidden treasure brought the king of Saudi Arabia $300 million annually which he spent on planes, slaves, concubines, 24 palaces, 25 sons and an unknown number of daughters—a household of 5,000 to 10,000 persons. Although the Western-leaning, anti-Zionist monarch initiated development programs to bring his six million subjects into the present, lack of organization, court corruption and over-zealous personal spending led to his forced abdication. Feb. 23, in Athens.

Nicholas M. Schenck, 87, was known as "The General" to Louis B. Mayer and Irving Thalberg, who ran his film company, Metro-Goldwyn-Mayer, the world's largest. Nick and his brother Joseph, who later headed United Artists Corp. and 20th Century Productions, were running a beer and entertainment concession in New York when they were befriended by Marcus Loew, a theater operator. When Loew died in 1927, Nick took over and by 1932 headed an empire that employed 12,000 people and made millions of dollars during the Depression. After World War II his cavalier attitude

toward television led to stockholder unhappiness and in 1955 he was bounced upstairs by Loew's son, Arthur. March 3, in Miami Beach, Fla.

Harry Scherman, 82, began his career as a reporter for a weekly newspaper but soon moved into the book field and set up the Little Leather Library Corp. In the eight years of its existence the company sold, at 10 cents each, 48 million volumes of classics. Then he became convinced the demand for new books could best be met by sales through the mails. He joined Maxwell Sackheim and Robert K. Haas in setting up the Book-of-the-Month Club in 1926; Nov. 12, in New York City.

The Countess of Seafield, 63, reputed to be Britain's wealthiest woman after the Queen, held vast estates in northeast Scotland which brought her an annual income estimated at $250,000. Her home in Banffshire had 40 bedrooms and about seven miles of corridors. She was the only child of the eleventh Earl of Seafield, succeeding to the title when he died in 1915. In London, England, Sept. 30.

Ben Shahn, 70, said, "How can an artist living in a society ignore it?" And his talent combined with involvement and enthusiasm ranked him as perhaps the foremost social artist of his day. He produced his best work when confronted by social injustice: the Sacco and Vanzetti series of the '30s, posters for the World War II Allies. He wanted to communicate with a large audience, so, with great disdain for skyrocketing art prices, he ran off reams of original posters and prints so everyone could afford them. March 14, in New York.

Ole Singstad, 87, was a designer, builder and consultant on many vehicular tunnels, including the Holland, Lincoln and Brooklyn-Battery tunnels in New York City, the tunnel under Baltimore Harbor and the underwater tube connecting Oakland and Alameda, Calif. He was born in Norway but emigrated to the United States in 1905. From 1910 to 1917 he designed rapid transit subways and tunnels in New York and Brooklyn, and from 1935 to 1945 he served as chief engineer of the New York City Tunnel Authority. He was a visiting lecturer at Harvard University for 20 years and also taught at New York University. Shortly before his death he completed a textbook, *"Tunnels."* Dec. 8, in New York City.

Sir Osbert Sitwell, 76, was a baronet, author and head of a family of distinguished writers and poets. He delighted in scandalizing literary circles with his eccentricity and self-exhibitionism. In writing his own contribution to *"Who's Who"* he described his recreation as "listening to the sound of his own voice." *Miracle at Sinai,* published in 1933, was his most famous novel. In Florence, Italy, May 4.

Joseph Peter Spang Jr., 76, joined the Gillette Co. in 1938 as executive vice president and retired as chairman of the board in 1958. Beforehand he was reported to have tested personally all its products and those of its competitors for six months. Within a few months he became president. He made the company one of the nation's major advertisers of sports broadcasts and was active in the National Association of Manufacturers, serving as national vice president and chairman of its international relations committee. Dec. 19, in Boston, Mass.

Adm. Raymond A. Spruance, 83, was considered the Navy's leading tactician in World War II, having come into prominence as ranking officer in the 1942 battle of Midway Island. For his victory there he received the Distinguished Service Medal. In 1943 he was appointed commander of the Central Pacific force and was in command of the invasion of the Gilbert and Marshall Islands and of the carrier task force strikes against Truk, the Marianas and the Palau Islands. In 1946 he left active duty to become president of the Naval War College. Dec. 13, in Pebble Beach, Calif.

Gen. George Stratemeyer, 78, for years urged that the U. S. keep strong to stay at peace. He was former commander of the Air Defense Command and of the U. S. Air Force in the Far. East. Among those who began the nation's fledgling Air Force, he was a staunch believer in the ultimate efficacy of air power in military effort. He sided with Gen. Douglas MacArthur after the latter was removed from his command in the Far East. In Winter Park, Fla., Aug. 9.

Sharon Tate (see pages 191, 242–245)

Robert Taylor was the modern-day Rudolph Valentino, star of more than 70 motion pictures, idol of millions of matinee matrons. Though Taylor set a Hollywood record with his 27 years at one studio —Metro-Goldwyn-Mayer—it was while he was on loan to Universal in 1935 that he reached stardom in *"Magnificent Obsession,"* co-starring Irene Dunne. His first box-office smash for M-G-M was *"Camille,"* in which he played opposite Greta Garbo. He also was leading man to such stars as Jean Harlow, Ava Gardner, Elizabeth Taylor, Myrna Loy, Joan Crawford, Hedy Lamarr, Lana Turner, Katherine Hepburn and Greer Garson. His movies included *"Broadway Melody," "Johnny Eager," "A Yank at Oxford," "Quo Vadis," "Ivanhoe," "Ride, Vaquero," "Her Cardboard Lover," "Bataan"* and *"Waterloo Bridge,"* his favorite. At age 57 of cancer in Santa Monica, Calif. June 8.

Bruno Traven, 79, lived in mystery and wrote of adventure, his most famous tale being *The Treasure of Sierra Madre.* A recluse who shunned publicity and kept his past secret, he said, "My personal history would not be disappointing to readers, but it is my own affair. . . ." His 15 novels and numerous short stories was peopled with Mexicans and expatriates who lived with danger, horror and cruelty. March 26, in Mexico City.

Rafael Leonidas Trujillo Jr., 40, was the son of the dictator of the Dominican Republic. A flamboyant, colorful figure, he often seemed to prefer the company of movie stars to that of politicians and soldiers. His father commissioned him into the army at the age of 3. At 6 he was a colonel and in his teens a brigadier general. When assassination ended his father's 30-year rule he took command of the armed forces under President Joaquin Balaguer. In 1961 he resigned and left for Europe, never to return. Dec. 27, in Madrid, Spain.

Moise Tshombe was former premier of the Congo, former president of secessionist Katanga Province and political prisoner. Tshombe first gained power by capitalizing on turmoil. He waited 10 days after army mutiny broke out when the Congo was declared independent in 1960 then declared independence for Katanga, the Congo's southernmost and richest province. In 1963 Katanga collapsed under an onslaught of United Nations troops and Tshombe, its president, fled to Spain. He returned to Leopoldville six months later. In two weeks he

was premier of the united Congo. Tshombe fought vigorously to preserve the country but a power struggle with President Kasavubu sent him packing to Spain again in 1965. In 1967 he was kidnaped aboard an airliner over the Mediterranean and was flown to Algiers when it was rumored he was planning another comeback. It was in an Algiers prison that he died at age 49. June 30.

Giovanni Cardinal Urbane, 69, was a strong candidate in the 1963 papal election. He had been president of the Italian Bishop's conference since 1966, after succeeding Pope John XXIII as Patriarch of Venice in 1958. He strongly criticized what he regarded as unorthodox and disobedient church reformers, saying he would oppose any effort to discuss such subjects as birth control and priestly celibacy. In Venice, Italy, Sept. 17.

Mies van der Rohe, 83, with no academic architectural training, designed scores of structures expressing the spirit of the industrial 20th century. He said, "Architecture is the will of an epoch translated into space." Along with Frank Lloyd Wright the German-born master dominated the architectural scene for years. He designed, among others, the Seagram Building in New York, often called the most beautiful building in the U. S. In Chicago, Ill., Aug. 17.

Josef Von Sternberg, 75, was famed as the director of glamorous films starring Marlene Dietrich, notably *"The Blue Angel," "Morocco," "Dishonored"* and *"The Scarlet Empress."* He was born in Vienna and in 1914 came to the United States, where he took a job as a film patcher. His first directorial job was in 1924 with *"The Salvation Hunters."* During the late 1920s he became famous for such melodramas as *"Underworld," "Dragnet"* and *"Docks of New York."* The photography of Miss Dietrich in his films set a new standard in glamor. In 1964 he wrote an autobiography, *"Life in a Chinese Laundry,"* a title from an early movie. Dec. 22, in Hollywood, Calif.

Marshal Kliment Y. Voroshilov, 88, distinguished himself in the Russian Revolution of 1917 and the subsequent civil war. Under the patronage of Josef Stalin, he rose in the ranks of the Red Army and in 1925 was appointed war commissar, a post he held under various titles for 15 years. In the defense of Leningrad during World War II he was said to have blundered in deploying his troops but he was continued on the State Committee of Defense. After Stalin's death he was a member of the group that sought to depose Nikita S. Khrushchev, but was allowed to retain his party honors. Dec. 2, in Moscow.

Maj. Gen. Fred Walker, 82, commanded the 36th Infantry Division in North Africa and Italy during World War II. He and that division were credited with unhinging a German line at Velletri, Italy and thus opening the road to Rome. He was deeply involved in the controversy over Gen. Mark Clark's

ordering the 36th Division to storm the Rapido River line in Italy, and contended that the attack did not make tactical sense. After retiring from the Army in 1946 he reorganized the Texas National Guard. His decorations included the Distinguished Service Cross, the Silver Star and the Purple Heart. Oct. 6, in Washington, D. C.

James P. Warburg, member of an international banking family, financier and board member of various railroads, found public service more satisfying than private enterprise. He expressed his liberal-democratic point of view through more than 30 books and numerous public speeches and severed many of his corporate connections because he felt big business was to blame for much of what he considered misguided U.S. foreign policy. He was a close associate of both Presidents Franklin D. Roosevelt and John F. Kennedy, an early champion of the New Deal and monetary adviser to the American delegation at the London Economic Conference of 1933. In 1935 he broke with FDR over monetary policy and attacked the New Deal in his writings, but he returned to the FDR fold during World War II and served as deputy director of the Office of War Information. At age 72 in Greenwich, Conn. June 3.

Josh White, 61, often sang with a cigarette behind his ear. He became interested in folk and sacred music at the age of 7, when he helped a blind Negro singer home. As a youth he helped other blind minstrels on their tours, learning and later popularizing their spirituals and work songs. He became nationally famous with his "Chain Gang" album and his song, *"One Meatball,"* which recorded his experiences during the Depression. A cabaret favorite, he captivated audiences with his casual style. White had been inactive for three years, following an automobile accident. In Manhasset, N. Y., Sept. 5.

Hugh Williams, 65, appeared in his new comedy, *"His, Hers and Theirs,"* only four days before his death. After years as a character actor he had turned to writing with his wife, Margaret Vyner, as collaborator. They were a successful team, and London theatergoers thronged to their series of drawing room comedies which included *"The Irregular Verb, to Love," "The Happy Man,"* and *"Charlie Girl."* As a film actor he played in *"One of Our Aircraft Is Missing," "Wuthering Heights,"* and other pictures. He made several visits to the United States to appear on Broadway in *"Flowers of the Forest," "The Cocktail Party,"* and other productions. Dec. 7, in London, England.

Charles Winninger, 84, veteran of vaudeville, stage and screen, created the role of Cap'n Andy Hawks in *Showboat.* Both on Broadway in 1927 and in Hollywood in 1929, Winninger charmed audiences and critics with his portrayal of the jovial and rotund master of the *Cotton Blossom* that steamed the Mississippi in the adaptation of Edna Ferber's book. Palm Springs, Calif., Jan. 20.

THE BIG STORIES OF 1969

(Selected by news editors of Associated Press member newspapers and radio and television stations)
1. Man on the moon
2. The Vietnam war
3. Edward M. Kennedy's political fortunes
4. The controversial U.S. Supreme Court
5. Student unrest
6. Hurricane Camille
7. Growing trouble in the Middle East
8. Dwight D. Eisenhower dies
9. The Mets win the World Series
10. Sirhan B. Sirhan and James Earl Ray sentenced for assassinations

TOP NEWSMAKERS OF 1969

(Selected by news editors of Associated Press member newspapers and radio and television stations)
Newsmaker of the Year—Neil A. Armstrong
Foreign Affairs—Charles de Gaulle
Science—Dr. John H. Knowles
Business—William H. Donaldson
Labor—George Meany
Religion—Bishop James A. Pike
Sports—Joe Namath
Entertainment—Tommy and Dick Smothers
Literature—Norman Mailer
Woman—Mrs. Jacqueline Kennedy Onassis

PRIZES—AWARDS

PULITIZER PRIZES 1969

Local Reporting: John Fetterman, Times and Courier-Journal, Louisville, for the story of the return of the body of a Vietnam veteran.

Local Reporting, special: Albert L. Delugach and Denny Walsh, St. Louis Globe-Democrat, for investigative reporting of fraud within the St. Louis Steamfitters Union.

National Reporting: Robert Cann, Christian Science Monitor, for a series on national parks.

Editorial Writing: Paul Greenberg, Pine Bluff, Ark., Commerical, for the general excellence of his editorials.

International Reporting: William Tuohy, Los Angeles Times, for combat coverage in Vietnam.

News Photography: Edward T. Adams, The Associated Press, for his picture of a Viet Cong prisoner being shot in the head by a South Vietnamese general.

Feature Photography: Moneta Sleet Jr., Ebony Magazine, for his picture of Mrs. Martin Luther King at the Atlanta funeral of her assassinated husband.

Cartooning: John Fischetti, Chicago Daily News, for the body of his work as a cartoonist.

Meritorious Public Service: The Los Angeles Times, for an exposure of wrongdoing in city government.

Fiction: N. Scott Monaday for "House Made of Dawn."

General non-fiction: Norman Mailer for "The Armies of Night" and Jules Dubos for "So Human an Animal."

Drama: Howard Sackler for "The Great White Hope."

History: Leonard W. Levy, Brandeis University, for "Origins of the Fifth Amendment."

Biography: B. L. Reid, Mount Holyoke College, for "The Man from New York: John Quinn and his Friends."

Poetry: George Oppen for "Of Being Numerous."

Music: Karel Husa for his "String Quartet No. 3."

OSCARS

Best Acting—Katherine Hepburn of "The Lion in Winter." Barbra Streisand of "Funny Girl."

Best Actor—Cliff Robertson of "Charly."

Best Supporting performers—Ruth Gordon of "Rosemary's Baby." Jack Albertson of "The Subject was Roses."

Best Song—"Windmills of Your Mind" of "The Thomas Crown Affair."

Best foreign—Russia's "War and Peace."

Writing—James Goldman for "The Lion in Winter." Mel Brooks for "The Producers."

Art Direction—"Oliver" John Box and Terence Marsh, set direction.

Vernon Dixon and Ken Muggleston, set decorators.

Documentary feature—"Young Americans."

Documentary short—"Why Man Creates."

Costume Design—"Romeo and Juliet," Danile Donati.

Sound—"Oliver" Shepperton Studio Sound Department.

Cinematography—"Romeo and Juliet," Pasqualine De Santis.

Visual Effects—001, A Space Odyssey, Stanley Kubrick.

Score of musical—"Oliver," John Green.

Short subject—"Robert Kennedy Remembered," Charles Guggenheim, producer.

Editing—"Bullit," Frank P. Keller.

Cartoon—"Winnie the Pooh and the Blustery Day" Walt Disney Studio.

Special Choreography award, Oona White for "Oliver."

Best score not for musical—"The Lion in Winter," John Barry.

NOBEL PRIZE AWARDS

Literature—Samuel Beckett, Ireland, author of "Waiting for Godot," his Nobel eulogy saying that his writing "rises like a miserere from all mankind."

Medicine and Physiology—Max Delbruck, California Institute of Technology; Salvador E. Luria, Massachusetts Institute of Technology, and Alfred D. Hershey, Carnegie Institute, Washington, D.C., for their work between 1940 and 1952 in microbiology and genetics, experimenting with bacteriophages, a group of viruses that infect bacteria.

Physics—Murray Gell-Mann, California Institute of Technology, for his discoveries in classifying elementary particles and exploring their relationships.

Chemistry—Derek H. R. Barton, Imperial College of Science and Technology, London, and Odd Hassel, University of Oslo, for their work to develop and apply "the concept of conformation" in chemistry, their basic research determining the actual, three-dimensional shape of certain organic compounds having been put to practical use by others in making and synthesizing new drugs.

Economic Science—Ragnar Frisch, Norway and Jan Tinbergen, The Netherlands, for their work in developing and applying mathematical models to analyze economic activity.

Peace—International Labor Office.

AMERICAN EDUCATION AWARD

Ralph Emerson McGill (posthumously).

LASKER AWARDS FOR MEDICINE

George C. Cotzias, Brookhaven National Laboratory, for pioneering the use of daily doses of the drug L-DOPA in treating Parkinson's disease.

Bruce Marrifield, Rockefeller University, for developing a simpler way to make proteins and their smaller units, peptides, in the laboratory.

THE COLLIER TROPHY

Awarded to the Apollo 8 Astronauts—Col. Frank Borman, commander; Navy Capt. James A. Lovell Jr., Major William A. Anders.

FREEDOM FOUNDATION AWARDS

George Washington Award—Gen. Harold K. Johson, retired.

American Exemplar Medal—Dr. Leon H. Sullivan of Philadelphia.

Free Enterprise Exemplar Medal—J. Howard Wood, publisher of the Chicago Tribune.

STAUFFER PRIZE

Dr. Jerome W. Conn, University of Michigan.

Dr. Jacques Genest, Clinical Research Institute of Montreal.

Dr. Franz Gross, University of Heidelberg, Germany.

Dr. John H. Laragh, Columbia University College of Physicians and Surgeons.

NATIONAL BOOK AWARDS

Arts and Letters: Norman Mailer for "The Armies of the Night."

History and Biography: Winthrop D. Jordan for "White Over Black—American Attitudes Toward the Negro, 1550–1812."

Fiction: Jerzy Kosinski for "Steps."

Children's Literature: Meindert DeJong for "Journey from Peppermint Street."

Poetry: John Berryman for "His Toy, His Dream, His Rest."

The Sciences: Dr. Robert J. Lifton for "Death In Life—Survivors of Hiroshima."

Translation: William Weaver for his translation from the Italian of "Cosmicomics" by Italo Calvino.

TONY AWARDS

Best Actor: James Earl Jones, "The Great White Hope."

Best Actress: Julie Harris, "Forty Carats."

Best Musical Actor: Jerry Orbach, "Promises, Promises."

Best Musical Actress: Angela Lansbury, "Dear World."

Best Drama: "The Great White Hope."

Best Musical: "1776."

Best Supporting Actor: Al Pacino, "Does a Tiger Wear a Necktie."

Best Supporting Actress: Jane Alexander, "The Great White Hope."

Best Supporting Musical Actor: Ronald Holgate, "1776."

Best Supporting Musical Actress: Marian Mercer, "Promises, Promises."

Best Drama Directing: Peter Dews, "Hadrian VII."

Best Musical Directing: Peter Hunt, "1776."

Choreography: Joe Layton, "George M."

Scenic Designs: Boris Arenson, "Zorba."

Costume Design: Louden Sainthill, "Canterbury Tales."

RECORDINGS

National Academy of Recording Arts and Sciences (Grammies).

Album Of The Year: "By the Time I Get to Phoenix"—Glen Campbell.

Song Of The Year: "Little Green Apples"—Songwriter: Bobby Russell.

Best Contemporary-Pop Vocal Performance, Female: "Do You Know the Way to San Jose"—Dionne Warwick.

Best Contemporary-Pop Vocal Performance, Male: "Light my Fire"—Jose Feliciano.

Best Contemporary-Pop Performance, Vocal Duo or Group: "Mrs. Robinson"—Simon & Garfunkel.

Best Country Song (Songwriters' Award): "Little Green Apples"—Songwriter: Bobby Russell.

Best Classical Performance—Orchestra: (Conductor's Award) "Boulez Conducts Debussy" (La Mer, Apres-midi d'un Faune, Jeux) Pierre Boulez conductor, New Philharmonic Orchestra.

Best Opera Recording: (Awards to the Conductor and A & R Producer) "Mozart: Cosi Fan Tutte"—Erich Leinsdorf conductor, New Philharmonic Orchestra and Ambrosian Opera Chorus/Principal soloists: Leontyne Price, Tatiana Troyanos, Judith Raskin, Sherrill Milnes, George Shirley, Ezio Flagello. A & R Producer: Richard Mohr.

BEAUTY CONTESTS

Miss Teen U.S.A.—Synda Bunton, 17, of Kansas City.

Miss America—Pamela Ann Eldred, 21, Birmingham.

Miss Universe—Gloria Diaz, 18, The Philippines.

No Mrs. America this year.

UNITED STATES GOVERNMENT

EXECUTIVE DEPARTMENT

President: Richard M. Nixon
Vice-President: Spiro T. Agnew

WHITE HOUSE STAFF

Special Assistant to the President: Robert J. Brown

Staff Assistant: Bruce Rabb

Counsellors to the President: Bryce Harlow & Daniel P. Moynihan
  Deputy Assistant to the President for Domestic Affairs (Legislative): Richard T. Burress
  Special Assistant to the President: Dr. Martin Anderson
  Deputy Special Assistant to the President: Jack T. Cole
  Staff Assistant: Wesley G. McCain

Special Assistant to the President (Appointments & Schedule): Dwight L. Chapin
  Staff Assistant: Hugh W. Sloan Jr.

Executive Secretary, President's Foreign Intelligence Advisory Board: J. Patrick Coyne

Special Assistant to the President (White House Visitors): John S. Davies
  Staff Assistant: Michael J. Farrell

Science Advisor to the President: Lee A. DuBridge

Assistant to the President for Domestic Affairs: John D. Ehrlichman
  Deputy Assistant to the President for Domestic Affairs: Henry C. Cashen II
  Deputy Counsel to the President: Harry S. Dent
  Deputy Assistant to the President for Domestic Affairs: Egil Krogh Jr.
  Deputy Assistant to the President for Domestic Affairs: John C. Whitaker
  Deputy Assistant to the President for Domestic Affairs: Edward L. Morgan
  Staff Assistant: John J. Caulfield
  Staff Assistant: Charles Edward Stuart

Assistant to the President: Peter M. Flanigan
  Deputy Assistant to the President: Darrell M. Trent
  Staff Assistant: Daniel W. Hofgren
  Staff Assistant: Clay T. Whitehead
  Staff Assistant: John Rose

Special Assistant to the President: Harry S. Flemming
  Deputy Special Assistant to the President: Lawrence H. Dunn
  Staff Assistant: George T. Bell
  Staff Assistant: William E. Casselman II

Special Consultant to the President: Leonard Garment

Assistant to the President: H. R. Haldeman
  Deputy Assistant to the President: Alexander P. Butterfield
  Deputy Assistant to the President for Administration of The Domestic Affairs Staff: Kenneth R. Cole Jr.
  Staff Assistant to the President (Correspondence): Noble Melencamp
  Staff Assistant: John R. Brown III
  Staff Assistant: Stephen B. Bull
  Staff Assistant: Lawrence Mead Higby
  Staff Assistant: Jay G. Wilkinson

Assistant to the President for Congressional Relations: Open (Nov. 1969)
  Deputy Assistant to the President for Congressional Relations: Kenneth E. BeLieu

Deputy Assistant to the President for Congressional Relations: William E. Timmons
Special Assistant to the President: H. Dale Grubb
Deputy Special Assistant to the President: John Nidecker
Staff Assistant: Lamar Alexander

Special Assistant to the President: James Keogh
  Special Assistant to the President: Patrick J. Buchanan
  Special Assistant to the President: Raymond K. Price Jr.
  Special Assistant to the President: William L. Safire
  Staff Assistant: Lyndon K. Allin ("Mort")
  Staff Assistant: William F. Gavin
  Staff Assistant: Lee W. Huebner
  Staff Assistant: James C. Humes
  Staff Assistant: Tom Charles Huston

Assistant to the President for National Security Affairs: Henry A. Kissinger

Director of Communications for the Executive Branch: Herbert G. Klein
  Executive Assistant to the Director of Communications for the Executive Branch: Paul W. Costello
  Assistant to the Director of Communications for the Executive Branch: Herbert L. Thompson
  Assistant to the Director of Communications for the Executive Branch: Virginia S. Savell
  Administrative Assistant: Margareta E. White
  Staff Assistant: Robert Odle Jr.

Special Assistant to the President for Consumer Affairs: Virginia H. Knauer

Assistant to the President for Urban Affairs: Daniel P. Moynihan
  Deputy Assistant to the President for Urban Affairs: Stephen Hess
  Counsel to the Assistant to the President for Urban Affairs: John R. Price
  Staff Assistant: Richard Blumenthal
  Staff Assistant: Christopher DeMuth
  Staff Assistant: Chester E. Finn Jr.
  Staff Assistant: Michael C. Monroe

Assistant to the President & Director of Office of Economic Opportunity: Donald Rumsfeld

Special Assistant to the President for Liaison with Former Presidents: General Robert L. Schulz

Press Secretary to the First Lady: Gerry Van der Heuvel

Special Consultant to the President: Charles B. Wilkinson
  Special Assistant to the President: James Atwater
  Staff Assistant: John L. Campbell
  Staff Assistant: Jeffrey Donfeld

Social Secretary: Lucy Alexander Winchester

Personal Secretary to the President: Rose Mary Woods

Special Assistant to the President (Press Secretary): Ronald L. Ziegler
  Deputy Press Secretary: Gerald L. Warren

EXECUTIVE AGENCIES

Bureau of the Budget
Robert P. Mayo, *director*

Council of Economic Advisors
Paul W. McCracken, *chairman*
Hendrik S. Houthhaker
Herbert Stein
Charles B. Warden

National Security Council
Richard M. Nixon, *chairman*
Spiro T. Agnew
William P. Rogers
Melvin R. Laird
George A. Lincoln
Henry A. Kissinger

Central Intelligence Agency
Richard M. Helms, *director*

National Aeronautics and Space Council
Spiro T. Agnew, *chairman*
William P. Rogers
Melvin R. Laird
Thomas O. Paine
Glenn T. Seaborg

Office of Economic Opportunity
Donald Rumsfeld, *director*
Robert Perrin, *deputy director*, Actg.

Office of Emergency Planning
George A. Lincoln, *director*
Fred J. Russell, *deputy director*

Office of Science and Technology
Lee A. DuBridge, *director*

Office of Trade Negotiations
Carl J. Gilbert, *special representative*

CABINET

Department of State
William P. Rogers, *secretary*
Elliot L. Richardson, *under secretary*
U. Alexis Johnson, *under secretary for political affairs*
Nathaniel Samuels, *deputy under secretary for economic affairs*
Wm. B. Macomber Jr., *deputy under secretary for administration*
Richard F. Pederson, *counselor*

BUREAU OF INTER-AMERICAN AFFAIRS
Charles A. Meyer, *assistant secretary*

MISSION TO THE UNITED NATIONS
Charles W. Yost, *ambassador*

AGENCY FOR INTERNATIONAL DEVELOPMENT
Dr. John A. Hannah, *administrator*

DEVELOPMENT LOAN COMMITTEE
Dr. John A. Hannah, *chairman*

PEACE CORPS
Jack Vaughn, *director*

POLICY PLANNING COUNCIL
Mariam C. Camps, *chairman*

CONGRESSTIONAL RELATIONS
William B. Macomber Jr., *assistant secretary*

LEGAL ADVISOR
Leonard C. Meeker

BUREAU OF PUBLIC AFFAIRS
Richard I. Phillips, *acting assistant secretary*

BUREAU OF AFRICAN AFFAIRS
Joseph Palmer II, *assistant secretary*

BUREAU OF EUROPEAN AFFAIRS
Martin J. Hillenbrand, *assistant secretary*

BUREAU OF EAST ASIAN AND PACIFIC AFFAIRS
William P. Bundy, *assistant secretary*

BUREAU OF NEAR EASTERN AND SOUTH ASIAN
AFFAIRS
Joseph J. Sisco

BUREAU OF ECONOMIC AFFAIRS
Philip H. Trezise, *assistant secretary*

BUREAU OF EDUCATIONAL AND CULTURAL
AFFAIRS
John Richardson Jr., *assistant secretary*

BUREAU OF INTELLIGENCE & RESEARCH
Thomas L. Hughes, *director*

BUREAU OF INTERNATIONAL ORGANIZATION
AFFAIRS
Samuel DePalma, *asst. secretary*

BUREAU OF INTERNATIONAL SCIENTIFIC AND
TECHNOLOGICAL AFFAIRS
Herman Pollack, *director*

BUREAU OF SECURITY AND CONSULAR AFFAIRS
Barbara M. Watson, *administrator*

AMBASSADORS AT LARGE
Henry Cabot Lodge

Department of Treasury
SECRETARY OF THE TREASURY
David M. Kennedy

UNDER SECRETARY
Charles E. Walker

UNDER SECRETARY FOR MONETARY AFFAIRS
Paul A. Volcker

INTERNAL REVENUE SERVICE
Randolph W. Thrower, *commissioner*

SECRET SERVICE
James J. Rowley

TREASURER OF THE UNITED STATES
Mrs. Dorothy Andrews Elston

Department of Defense
SECRETARY
Melvin R. Laird

DEPUTY SECRETARY
David Packard

JOINT CHIEFS OF STAFF
Gen. Earle G. Wheeler, *chairman*
Gen. William C. Westmoreland, *chief of staff,
U.S. Army*
Adm. Thomas H. Moorer, *chief of naval operations*

Gen John P. McConnell, *chief of staff, U.S.
Air Force*
Gen. Leonard Chapman Jr., *commandant,
Marine Corps*

DEPARTMENT OF THE ARMY
Stanley R. Resor, *secretary*

DEPARTMENT OF THE NAVY
John H. Chafee, *secretary*

DEPARTMENT OF AIR FORCE
Dr. Robert C. Seamans Jr., *secretary*

Department Of Justice
ATTORNEY GENERAL
John N. Mitchell

SOLICITOR GENERAL
Erwin N. Griswold

BUREAU OF NARCOTICS AND DANGEROUS DRUGS
John E. Ingersoll, *director*

FEDERAL BUREAU OF INVESTIGATION
J. Edgar Hoover, *director*

Post Office Department
POSTMASTER GENERAL
Winton M. Blount

DEPUTY POSTMASTER GENERAL
Elmer T. Klassen

Department of the Interior
SECRETARY
Walter J. Hickel

UNDER SECRETARY
Russell E. Train

Department of Agriculture
SECRETARY
Clifford M. Hardin

UNDER SECRETARY
J. Phil Campbell

Department of Comerce
SECRETARY
Maurice H. Stans

UNDER SECRETARY
Rocco C. Siciliano

Department of Labor
SECRETARY
George P. Shultz

UNDER SECRETARY
James D. Hodgson

Department of Health, Education, and Welfare
SECRETARY
Robert H. Finch

UNDER SECRETARY
John G. Veneman

PUBLIC HEALTH SERVICE
vacant, *surgeon general*

SOCIAL SECURITY ADMINISTRATION
Robert M. Ball, *commissioner*

MEDICARE
Thomas M. Tierney, *director*

FOOD AND DRUG ADMINISTRATION
Herbert L. Ley, Jr., *commissioner*

Department of Housing and Urban Development
SECRETARY
George W. Romney

UNDER SECRETARY
Richard C. Van Dusen

Department of Transporation
SECRETARY
John A. Volpe

COAST GUARD
Adm. Willard J. Smith, *commandant*

FEDERAL AVIATION ADMINISTRATION
John H. Shaffer, *administrator*

MAJOR INDEPENDENT AGENCIES
ATOMIC ENERGY COMMISSION
Glenn T. Seaborg, *chairman*

FEDERAL RESERVE SYSTEM
William McC. Martin Jr., *chairman*

CIVIL AERONAUTICS BOARD
John H. Crooker Jr., *chairman*

CIVIL SERVICE COMMISSION
Robert E. Hampton, *chairman*

FEDERAL COMMUNICATIONS COMMISSION
Rosel H. Hyde, *chairman*

FEDERAL POWER COMMISSION
Lee C. White, *chairman*

FEDERAL TRADE COMMISSION
Paul Rand Dixon, *chairman*

GENERAL SERVICE ADMINISTRATION
Robert L. Kunzig, *administrator*

INTERSTATE COMMERCE COMMISSION
Virginia Mae Brown, *chairman*

NATIONAL AERONAUTICS AND SPACE
ADMINISTRATION
Dr. Thomas O. Paine, *administrator*

NATIONAL LABOR RELATIONS BOARD
Frank W. McCulloch, *chairman*

SECURITIES AND EXCHANGE COMMISSION
Hamer H. Budge, *chairman*

SELECTIVE SERVICE SYSTEM
Lt. Gen Lewis B. Hershey (until Feb. 1), *director*

SMALL BUSINESS ADMINISTRATION
Howard J. Samuels, *administrator*

UNITED STATES INFORMATION AGENCY
Frank J. Shakespeare Jr., *director*

VETERANS ADMINISTRATION
William J. Driver, *administrator*

LEGISLATIVE
91st Congress

SENATE

PRESIDENT PRO TEMPORE: Richard B. Russell (D-Ga.)

MAJORITY LEADER: Mike Mansfield (D-Mont.)

MAJORITY WHIP: Edward M. Kennedy (D-Mass.)

MINORITY LEADER: Hugh Scott (R-Pa.)

MINORITY WHIP: Robert P. Griffin (R-Mich.)

CHAPLAIN: Rev. Edward L. R. Elson

Members of the Senate

District	Party	Born	Tenure	Term Expires
ALABAMA				
James B. Allen	D	Dec. 28, 1912	Jan. 3, 1969	Jan. 2, 1975
John J. Sparkman	D	Dec. 20, 1899	Nov. 6, 1946	Jan. 3, 1973
ALASKA				
Mike Gravel	D	May 13, 1930	Jan. 3, 1969	Jan. 2, 1975
Ted Stevens	R	Nov. 18, 1923	Dec. 24, 1968	Jan. 2, 1973
ARIZONA				
Barry Goldwater	R	Jan. 1, 1909	Jan. 3, 1969	Jan. 2, 1975
Paul J. Fannin	R	Jan. 29, 1907	Jan. 3, 1965	Jan. 3, 1971
ARKANSAS				
John L. McClellan	D	Feb. 25, 1896	Jan. 3, 1943	Jan. 3, 1973
J. W. Fulbright	D	April 9, 1905	Jan. 3, 1945	Jan. 3, 1973
CALIFORNIA				
Alan Cranston	D	June 19, 1914	Jan. 3, 1969	Jan. 2, 1975
George L. Murphy	R	July 4, 1902	Dec. 31, 1964	Jan. 3, 1971
COLORADO				
Gordon L. Allott	R	Jan. 2, 1907	Jan. 3, 1955	Jan. 3, 1973
Peter H. Dominick	R	July 7, 1915	Jan. 3, 1963	Jan. 3, 1973
CONNECTICUT				
Thomas J. Dodd	D	May 15, 1907	Jan. 3, 1959	Jan. 3, 1971
Abraham A. Ribicoff	D	April 9, 1910	Jan. 3, 1963	Jan. 3, 1973
DELAWARE				
John J. Williams	R	May 17, 1904	Jan. 3, 1947	Jan. 3, 1971
J. Caleb Boggs	R	May 15, 1909	Jan. 3, 1961	Jan. 3, 1973
FLORIDA				
Spessard L. Holland	D	July 10, 1892	Sept. 25, 1946	Jan. 3, 1971
Edward J. Gurney	R	Jan. 12, 1914	Jan. 3, 1969	Jan. 2, 1975
GEORGIA				
Richard B. Russell	D	Nov. 2, 1897	Jan. 12, 1933	Jan. 3, 1973
Herman E. Talmadge	D	Aug. 9, 1913	Jan. 3, 1957	Jan. 3, 1973
HAWAII				
Hiram L. Fong	R	Oct. 1, 1907	Aug. 21, 1959	Jan. 3, 1971
Daniel K. Inouye	D	Sept. 7, 1924	Jan. 3, 1963	Jan. 3, 1973
IDAHO				
Frank Church	D	July 25, 1924	Jan. 3, 1957	Jan. 3, 1973
Len B. Jordan	R	May 15, 1899	Aug. 6, 1962	Jan. 3, 1973
ILLINOIS				
Charles H. Percy	R	Sept. 27, 1919	Jan. 3, 1967	Jan. 3, 1973
Ralph Smith	R		Sept. 18, 1969	Nov. 4. 1970
INDIANA				
Vance Hartke	D	May 31, 1919	Jan. 3, 1959	Jan. 3, 1971
Birch Bayh	D	Jan. 22, 1928	Jan. 3, 1963	Jan. 3, 1969
IOWA				
Harold E. Hughes	D	Feb. 10, 1922	Jan. 3, 1969	Jan. 3, 1973
Jack R. Miller	R	June 6, 1916	Jan. 3, 1961	Jan. 3, 1973
KANSAS				
Robert Dole	R	July 22, 1923	Jan. 3, 1969	Jan. 2, 1975
James B. Pearson	R	May 7, 1920	Jan. 31, 1962	Jan. 3, 1973
KENTUCKY				
John S. Cooper	R	Aug. 23, 1901	Nov. 7, 1956*	Jan. 3, 1973
Marlow W. Cook	R	July 27, 1926	Dec. 17, 1968	Jan. 2, 1975
LOUISIANA				
Allen J. Ellender	D	Sept. 24, 1890	Jan. 3, 1937	Jan. 3, 1973
Russell B. Long	D	Nov. 3, 1918	Dec. 31, 1948	Jan. 3, 1973

District	Party	Born	Tenure	Term Expires
MAINE				
Margaret Chase Smith	R	Dec. 14, 1897	Jan. 3, 1949	Jan. 3, 1973
Edmund S. Muskie	D	March 28, 1914	Jan. 3, 1959	Jan. 3, 1971
MARYLAND				
Charles Mc C. Mathias, Jr.	R	July 24, 1922	Jan. 3, 1969	Jan. 2, 1975
Joseph D. Tydings	D	May 4, 1928	Jan. 3, 1965	Jan. 3, 1971
MASSACHUSETTS				
Edward W. Brooke	R	Oct. 26, 1919	Jan. 3, 1967	Jan. 3, 1973
Edward M. Kennedy	D	Feb. 22, 1932	Nov. 7, 1962	Jan. 3, 1971
MICHIGAN				
Robert P. Griffin	R	Nov. 6, 1923	May 16, 1966	Jan. 3, 1973
Philip A. Hart	D	Dec. 10, 1912	Jan. 3, 1959	Jan. 3, 1971
MINNESOTA				
Eugene J. McCarthy	D	March 29, 1916	Jan. 3, 1959	Jan. 3, 1971
Walter F. Mondale	D	Jan. 5, 1928	Dec. 30, 1964	Jan. 3, 1973
MISSISSIPPI				
James O. Eastland	D	Nov. 28, 1904	Jan. 3, 1943*	Jan. 3, 1973
John C. Stennis	D	Aug. 3, 1901	Nov. 5, 1947	Jan. 3, 1971
MISSOURI				
Stuart Symington	D	June 26, 1901	Jan. 3, 1953	Jan. 3, 1971
Thomas F. Eagleton	D	Sept. 4, 1929	Dec. 28, 1968	Jan. 2, 1975
MONTANA				
Michael J. Mansfield	D	March 16, 1903	Jan. 3, 1953	Jan. 3, 1971
Lee Metcalf	D	Jan. 28, 1911	Jan. 3, 1961	Jan. 3, 1973
NEBRASKA				
Roman L. Hruska	R	Aug. 16, 1904	Nov. 8, 1954	Jan. 3, 1971
Carl T. Curtis	R	March 15, 1905	Jan. 1, 1955	Jan. 3, 1973
NEVADA				
Alan Bible	D	Nov. 20, 1909	Dec. 2, 1954	Jan. 3, 1973
Howard W. Cannon	D	Jan. 26, 1912	Jan. 3, 1959	Jan. 3, 1971
NEW HAMPSHIRE				
Norris Cotton	R	May 11, 1900	Nov. 8, 1954	Jan. 3, 1973
Thomas J. McIntyre	D	Feb. 20, 1915	Nov. 7, 1962	Jan. 3, 1973
NEW JERSEY				
Clifford P. Case	R	April 16, 1904	Jan. 3, 1955	Jan. 3, 1973
H. A. Williams Jr.	D	Dec. 10, 1919	Jan. 3, 1959	Jan. 3, 1971
NEW MEXICO				
Clinton P. Anderson	D	Oct. 23, 1895	Jan. 3, 1949	Jan. 3, 1973
Joseph M. Montoya	D	Sept. 24, 1915	Nov. 4, 1964	Jan. 3, 1971
NEW YORK				
Jacob K. Javits	R	May 18, 1904	Jan. 9, 1957	Jan. 3, 1973
Charles E. Goodell	R	March 16, 1926	Sept. 10, 1968	Jan. 2, 1971
NORTH CAROLINA				
Sam J. Ervin Jr.	D	Sept. 27, 1896	June 5, 1954	Jan. 3, 1973
B. Everett Jordan	D	Sept. 8, 1896	April 19, 1958	Jan. 3, 1973
NORTH DAKOTA				
Milton R. Young	R	Dec. 6, 1897	March 12, 1945	Jan. 3, 1973
Quentin N. Burdick	D	June 19, 1908	Aug. 8, 1960	Jan. 3, 1971
OHIO				
William B. Saxbe	R	June 24, 1916	Jan. 3, 1969	Jan. 2, 1975
Stephen M. Young	D	May 4, 1889	Jan. 3, 1959	Jan. 3, 1971
OKLAHOMA				
Henry Bellman	R	Sept. 3, 1921	Jan. 3, 1969	Jan. 2, 1975
Fred R. Harris	D	Nov. 13, 1920	Nov. 4, 1964	Jan. 4, 1973
OREGON				
Robert W. Packwood	R	Sept. 11, 1932	Jan. 3, 1969	Jan. 2, 1975
Mark O. Hatfield	R	July 12, 1922	Jan. 3, 1967	Jan. 3, 1973
PENNSYLVANIA				
Richard S. Schweiker	R	June 1, 1926	Jan. 3, 1969	Jan. 2, 1975
Hugh Scott	R	Nov. 11, 1900	Jan. 3, 1959	Jan. 3, 1971
RHODE ISLAND				
John O. Pastore	D	March 17, 1907	Dec. 19, 1950	Jan. 3, 1971
Claiborne Pell	D	Nov. 22, 1918	Jan. 3, 1961	Jan. 3, 1973
SOUTH CAROLINA				
Ernest F. Hollings	D	Jan. 1, 1922	Nov. 9, 1966	Jan. 3, 1969
Strom Thurmond	R	Dec. 5, 1902	Nov. 7, 1956*	Jan. 3, 1973

*Served prior, noncontinuous term in the senate.

District	Party	Born	Tenure	Term Expires
SOUTH DAKOTA				
Karl E. Mundt	R	June 3, 1900	Dec. 31, 1948	Jan. 3, 1973
George McGovern	D	July 19, 1922	Jan. 3, 1963	Jan. 3, 1973
TENNESSEE				
Albert Gore	D	Dec. 26, 1907	Jan. 3, 1953	Jan. 3, 1971
Howard H. Baker	R	Nov. 15, 1925	Jan. 3, 1967	Jan. 3, 1973
TEXAS				
Ralph W. Yarborough	D	June 8, 1903	April 29, 1957	Jan. 3, 1971
John G. Tower	R	Sept. 29, 1925	June 15, 1961	Jan. 3, 1973
UTAH				
Wallace F. Bennett	R	Nov. 13, 1898	Jan. 3, 1951	Jan. 3, 1973
Frank E. Moss	D	Sept. 23, 1911	Jan. 3, 1959	Jan. 3, 1971
VERMONT				
George D. Aiken	R	Aug. 20, 1892	Jan. 10, 1941	Jan. 3, 1973
Winston L. Prouty	R	Sept. 1, 1906	Jan. 3, 1959	Jan. 3, 1971
VIRGINIA				
Harry F. Byrd Jr.	D	Dec. 20, 1914	Nov. 12, 1965	Jan. 3, 1971
William B. Spong	D	Sept. 29, 1920	Jan. 3, 1967	Jan. 3, 1973
WASHINGTON				
Warren G. Magnuson	D	April 12, 1905	Dec. 14, 1944	Jan. 3, 1973
Henry M. Jackson	D	May 31, 1912	Jan. 3, 1953	Jan. 3, 1971
WEST VIRGINIA				
Jennings Randolph	D	March 8, 1902	Nov. 5, 1958	Jan. 3, 1973
Robert C. Byrd	D	Jan. 15, 1918	Jan. 3, 1959	Jan. 3, 1971
WISCONSIN				
William Proxmire	D	Nov. 11, 1915	Aug. 28, 1957	Jan. 3, 1971
Gaylord Nelson	D	Jan. 4, 1916	Jan. 8, 1963	Jan. 3, 1973
WYOMING				
Gale W. McGee	D	March 17, 1915	Jan. 3, 1959	Jan. 3, 1971
Clifford P. Hansen	R	Oct. 16, 1912	Jan. 3, 1967	Jan. 3, 1973

HOUSE OF REPRESENTATIVES

SPEAKER: John W. McCormack (D-Mass.)

MAJORITY LEADER: Carl Albert (D-Okla.)

MAJORITY WHIP: Hale Boggs (D-La.)

MINORITY LEADER: Gerald R. Ford (R-Mich.)

MINORITY WHIP: Leslie C. Arends (R-Ill.)

CHAPLAIN: Rev. Edward G. Latch

Members of the House of Representatives

District	Party	Born	Tenure
ALABAMA (3 Republicans: 5 Democrats)			
1—Jack Edwards	R	Sept. 20, 1928	Jan. 3, 1965
2—William L. Dickinson	R	June 5, 1925	Jan. 3, 1965
3—George W. Andrews	D	Dec. 12, 1906	March 14, 1944
4—Bill Nichols	D	Oct. 16, 1918	Nov. 8, 1966
5—Walter Flowers	D	April 12, 1933	Nov. 5, 1968
6—John H. Buchanan, Jr.	R	March 19, 1928	Jan. 3, 1965
7—Tom Bevill	D	March 27, 1921	Jan. 3, 1973
8—Robert E. Jones	D	June 12, 1912	Jan. 28, 1947
ALASKA (1 Republican)			
AL—Howard W. Pollock	R	April 11, 1920	Jan. 3, 1967
ARIZONA (1 Democrat; 2 Republicans)			
1—John J. Rhodes	R	Sept. 18, 1916	Jan. 3, 1953
2—Morris K. Udall	D	June 15, 1922	May 2, 1961
3—Sam Steiger	R	March 10, 1929	Jan. 3, 1967
ARKANSAS (1 Republican; 3 Democrats)			
1—Bill Alexander	D	Jan. 16, 1934	Nov. 5, 1968
2—Wilbur D. Mills	D	May 24, 1909	Jan. 3, 1939
3—John P. Hammerschmidt	D	May 4, 1923	Jan. 3, 1967
4—David Pryor	D	Aug. 29, 1934	Nov. 14, 1967
CALIFORNIA (21 Democrats; 17 Republicans)			
1—Don H. Clausen	R	April 27, 1923	Jan. 22, 1963
2—Harold T. Johnson	D	Dec. 2, 1907	Jan. 3, 1959

District	Party	Born	Tenure
3—John E. Moss	D	April 13, 1913	Jan. 3, 1953
4—Robert L. Leggett	D	July 26, 1926	Jan. 3, 1963
5—Phillip Burton	D	June 1, 1926	Feb. 18, 1964
6—William S. Mailliard	R	June 10, 1917	Jan. 3, 1953
7—Jeffrey Cohelan	D	June 24, 1914	Jan. 3, 1959
8—George P. Miller	D	Jan. 15, 1891	Jan. 3, 1945
9—Don Edwards	D	Jan. 6, 1915	Jan. 3, 1963
10—Charles S. Gubser	R	Feb. 1, 1916	Jan. 3, 1963
11—Paul N. McCloskey, Jr.	R	Sept. 29, 1927	Dec. 12, 1967
12—Burt L. Talcott	R	Feb. 22, 1920	Jan. 3, 1963
13—Charles M. Teague	R	Sept. 18, 1909	Jan. 3, 1955
14—Jerome R. Waldie	D	Feb. 15, 1925	June 7, 1966
15—John J. McFall	D	Feb. 20, 1918	Jan. 3, 1957
16—B. F. Sisk	D	Dec. 14, 1910	Jan. 3, 1955
17—Glenn M. Anderson	D	Feb. 21, 1913	Nov. 5, 1968
18—Robert M. Mathias	R	Nov. 17, 1930	Jan. 3, 1967
19—Chet Holifield	D	Dec. 3, 1903	Jan. 3, 1943
20—H. Allen Smith	R	Oct. 8, 1909	Jan. 3, 1957
21—Augustus F. Hawkins	D	Aug. 31, 1907	Jan. 3, 1963
22—James C. Corman	D	Oct. 20, 1920	Jan. 3, 1961
23—Del Clawson	R	Jan. 11, 1914	June 11, 1963
24—Glenard P. Lipscomb	R	Aug. 19, 1915	Nov. 10, 1953
25—Charles E. Wiggins	R	Dec. 3, 1927	Jan. 3, 1967
26—Thomas M. Rees	D	Mar. 26, 1925	Dec. 15, 1965
27—Barry M. Goldwater, Jr.	R	Jan. 15, 1938	May 5, 1969
28—Alphonzo Bell	R	Sept. 19, 1914	Jan. 3, 1961
29—George E. Brown, Jr.	D	March 6, 1920	Jan. 3, 1963
30—Edward R. Roybal	D	Feb. 10, 1916	Jan. 3, 1963
31—Charles H. Wilson	D	Feb. 15, 1917	Jan. 3, 1963
32—Craig Hosmer	R	May 6, 1915	Jan. 3, 1953
33—Jerry L. Pettis	R	July 18, 1916	Jan. 3, 1966
34—Richard T. Hanna	D	June 9, 1914	Jan. 3, 1963
35—James B. Utt	R	March 11, 1899	Jan. 3, 1953
36—Bob Wilson	R	April 5, 1916	Jan. 3, 1953
37—Lionel Van Deerlin	D	July 25, 1914	Jan. 3, 1963
38—John V. Tunney	D	June 26, 1934	Jan. 3, 1965
COLORADO (3 Democrats; 1 Republican)			
1—Byron G. Rogers	D	Aug. 1, 1900	Jan. 3, 1951
2—Donald G. Brotzman	R	June 28, 1922	Jan. 3, 1967
3—Frank E. Evans	D	Sept. 6, 1923	Jan. 3, 1965
4—Wayne N. Aspinall	D	April 3, 1896	Jan. 3, 1949
CONNECTICUT (2 Republicans, 4 Democrats)			
1—Emilio Q. Daddario	D	Sept. 24, 1918	Jan. 3, 1959
2—William L. St. Onge	D	Oct. 9, 1914	Jan. 3, 1963
3—Robert N. Giaimo	D	Oct. 15, 1919	Jan. 3, 1959
4—Lowell P. Weicker, Jr.	R	May 16, 1931	Nov. 5, 1968
5—John S. Monagan	D	Dec. 23, 1911	Jan. 3, 1959
6—Thomas J. Meskill	R	Jan. 30, 1928	Jan. 3, 1967
DELAWARE (1 Republican)			
AL—William V. Roth	R	July 22, 1921	Jan. 3, 1967
FLORIDA (3 Republicans; 9 Democrats)			
1—Robert L. F. Sikes	D	June 3, 1906	1940
2—Don Fuqua	D	Aug. 20, 1933	1962
3—Charles Bennett	D	Dec. 2, 1910	1949
4—Bill Chappell, Jr.	D	Feb. 3, 1922	Nov. 5, 1968
5—Louis Frey, Jr.	R	Jan. 11, 1934	Nov. 5, 1968
6—Sam M. Gibbons	D	Jan. 20, 1920	1962
7—James A. Haley	D	Jan. 4, 1899	1952
8—William C. Cramer	R	Aug. 4, 1922	1954
9—Paul G. Rogers	D	June 4, 1921	1955
10—J. Herbert Burke	R	Jan. 14, 1912	1966
11—Claude Pepper	D	Sept. 8, 1900	1962*
12—Dante B. Fascell	D	March 9, 1917	1954
GEORGIA (8 Democrats; 2 Republicans)			
1—G. Elliott Hagan	D	May 24, 1916	Jan. 3, 1961
2—Maston O'Neal	D	July 19, 1907	Jan. 3, 1965
3—Jack Brinkley	D	Dec. 22, 1930	Jan. 3, 1967
4—Ben B. Blackburn	R	Feb. 14, 1927	Jan. 3, 1967
5—S. Fletcher Thompson	R	Feb. 5, 1925	Jan. 3, 1967
6—John J. Flynt Jr.	D	Nov. 8, 1914	Nov. 2, 1954
7—John W. Davis	D	Sept. 12, 1916	Jan 3, 1961
8—William S. Stuckey, Jr.	D	May 25, 1935	Jan. 3, 1967
9—Phil M. Landrum	D	Sept. 10, 1909	Jan. 3, 1953
10—Robert G. Stephens Jr.	D	Aug. 14, 1913	Jan. 3, 1961
HAWAII (2 Democrats			
AL—Spark M. Matsunga	D	Oct. 8, 1916	Jan. 3, 1963
AL—Patsy T. Mink	D	Dec. 6, 1927	Jan. 3, 1965

District	Party	Born	Tenure
IDAHO (2 Republicans)			
1—James A. McClure	R	Dec. 27, 1924	Jan. 3, 1967
2—Orval Hansen	R	Aug. 3, 1926	Nov. 5, 1968
INDIANA (4 Democrats; 7 Republicans)			
1—Ray J. Madden	D	Feb. 25, 1892	Jan. 3, 1943
2—Earl F. Landgrebe	R	Jan. 21, 1916	Nov. 5, 1968
3—John Brademas	D	March 22, 1927	Jan. 3, 1959
4—E. Ross Adair	R	Dec. 14, 1907	Jan. 3, 1951
5—Richard L. Roudebush	R	Jan. 18, 1918	Jan. 3, 1961
6—William G. Bray	R	June 17, 1903	Jan. 3, 1951
7—John T. Myers	R	Feb. 8, 1927	Jan. 3, 1967
8—Roger H. Zion	R	Sept. 17, 1921	Jan. 3, 1967
9—Lee H. Hamilton	D	April 20, 1931	Jan. 3, 1965
10—David W. Dennis	R	June 7, 1912	Nov. 5, 1968
11—Andrew Jacobs, Jr.	D	Feb. 24, 1932	Jan. 3, 1965
ILLINOIS (11 Democrats; 12 Republicans)			
1—William L. Dawson	D	April 26, 1886	Jan. 3, 1943
2—Abner J. Mikva	D	Jan. 21, 1926	Nov. 5, 1968
3—William T. Murphy	D	Aug. 7, 1899	Jan. 3, 1959
4—Edward J. Derwinski	R	Sept. 15, 1926	Jan. 3, 1959
5—John C. Kluczynski	D	Feb. 15, 1896	Jan. 3, 1951
6—Vacancy: Death of Ronan, Sept. 13, 1969			
7—Frank Annunzio	D	Jan. 12, 1915	Jan. 3, 1965
8—Dan Rostenkowski	D	Jan. 2, 1928	Jan. 3, 1959
9—Sidney R. Yates	D	Aug. 27, 1909	Jan. 3, 1965*
10—Harold R. Collier	R	Dec. 12, 1915	Jan. 3, 1957
11—Roman E. Pucinski	D	May 13, 1919	Jan. 3, 1959
12—Robert McClory	R	Jan. 31, 1908	Jan. 3, 1963
13—Philip M. Crane	R	Nov. 3, 1930	Dec. 1, 1969
14—John N. Erlenborn	R	Feb. 8, 1927	Jan. 3, 1965
15—Charlotte T. Reid	R	Sept. 27, 1913	Jan. 3, 1963
16—John B. Anderson	R	Feb. 15, 1922	Jan. 3, 1961
17—Leslie C. Arends	R	Sept. 27, 1895	Jan. 3, 1935
18—Robert H. Michel	R	March 2, 1923	Jan. 3, 1957
19—Tom Railsback	R	Jan. 22, 1932	Jan. 3, 1967
20—Paul Findley	R	June 23, 1921	Jan. 3, 1961
21—Kenneth J. Gray	D	Nov. 14, 1924	Jan. 3, 1955
22—William L. Springer	R	April 12, 1909	Jan. 3, 1951
23—George E. Shipley	D	April 21, 1927	Jan. 3, 1959
24—Melvin Price	D	Jan. 1, 1905	Jan. 3, 1945
IOWA (2 Democrats; 5 Republicans)			
1—Fred Schwengel	R	May 28, 1907	Jan. 3, 1967*
2—John C. Culver	D	Aug. 8, 1932	Jan. 3, 1965
3—H. R. Gross	R	June 30, 1899	Jan. 3, 1949
4—John Kyl	R	May 9, 1919	Jan. 3, 1967*
5—Neal Smith	D	March 23, 1920	Jan. 3, 1959
6—Wiley Mayne	R	Jan. 19, 1917	Jan. 3, 1967
7—William J. Scherle	R	March 14, 1923	Nov. 8, 1966
KANSAS (5 Republicans)			
1—Keith G. Sebelius	R	Sept. 10, 1916	Nov. 5, 1968
2—Chester L. Mize	R	Dec. 25, 1917	Jan. 3, 1965
3—Larry Winn, Jr.	R	Aug. 22, 1919	Jan. 3, 1967
4—Garner E. Shriver	R	July 6, 1912	Jan. 3, 1961
5—Joe Skubitz	R	May 6, 1906	Jan. 3, 1963
KENTUCKY (4 Democrats; 3 Republicans)			
1—Frank A. Stubblefield	D	April 5, 1907	Jan. 3, 1959
2—William N. Natcher	D	Sept. 11, 1909	Aug. 1, 1953
3—William O. Cowger	R	Jan. 1, 1922	Jan. 3, 1967
4—M. G. Snyder	R	Jan. 26, 1928	Jan. 3, 1967
5—Tim Lee Carter	R	Sept. 2, 1910	Jan. 3, 1965
6—John C. Watts	D	July 9, 1902	April 14, 1951
7—Carl D. Perkins	D	Oct. 15, 1912	Jan. 3, 1949
LOUISIANA (8 Democrats)			
1—F. Edward Hebert	D	Oct. 12, 1901	Jan. 3, 1941
2—Hal Boggs	D	Feb. 15, 1914	Jan. 3, 1947
3—Patrick T. Caffery	D	July 6, 1932	Nov. 5, 1968
4—Joe D. Waggonner Jr.	D	Sept. 7, 1918	Dec. 19, 1961
5—Otto E. Passman	D	June 27, 1900	Jan. 3, 1967
6—John R. Rarick	D	Jan. 29, 1924	Jan. 3, 1967
7—Edwin W. Edwards	D	Aug. 7, 1927	Oct. 26, 1965
8—Speedy O. Long	D	June 16, 1928	Jan. 3, 1965
MAINE (2 Democrats)			
1—Peter N. Kyros	D	July 11, 1925	Jan. 3, 1967
2—William D. Hathaway	D	Feb. 21, 1924	Jan. 3, 1965
MARYLAND (4 Democrats; 4 Republicans)			
1—Rogers C. B. Morton	R	Sept. 19, 1914	Jan. 3, 1963
2—Clarence D. Long	D	Dec. 11, 1908	Jan. 3, 1963
3—Edward A. Garmatz	D	Feb. 7, 1903	June 15, 1947
4—George H. Fallon	D	July 24, 1902	Jan. 3, 1945
5—Lawrence J. Hogan	R	Sept. 30, 1928	Nov. 5, 1968
6—J. Glenn Beall, Jr.	R	June 19, 1927	Nov. 5, 1968
7—Samuel N. Friedel	D	April 18, 1898	Jan. 3, 1953
8—Gilbert Gude	R	March 9, 1923	Jan. 3, 1967
MASSACHUSETTS (8 Democrats; 4 Republicans)			
1—Silvio O. Conte	R	Nov. 9, 1921	Jan. 3, 1959
2—Edward P. Boland	D	Oct. 1, 1911	Jan. 3, 1953
3—Philip J. Philbin	D	May 29, 1898	Jan. 3, 1943
4—Harold D. Donohue	D	June 18, 1901	Jan. 3, 1947
5—F. Bradford Morse	R	Aug. 7, 1921	Jan. 3, 1961
6—Michael Harrington	D	Sept. 2, 1936	Oct. 3, 1969
7—Torbert H. Macdonald	D	June 6, 1917	Jan. 3, 1955
8—Thomas P. O'Neill Jr.	D	Dec. 9, 1912	Jan. 3, 1953
9—John W. McCormack	D	Dec. 21, 1891	Nov. 6, 1928
10—Margaret M. Heckler	R	June 21, 1931	Jan. 3, 1967
11—James A. Burke	D	March 30, 1910	Jan. 3, 1959
12—Hastings Keith	R	Nov. 22, 1915	Jan. 3, 1959
MICHIGAN (7 Democrats; 12 Republicans)			
1—John Conyers Jr.	D	May 16, 1929	Jan. 3, 1965
2—Marvin L. Esch	R	Aug. 4, 1927	Jan. 3, 1967
3—Gary Brown	R	Aug. 12, 1923	Jan. 3, 1967
4—Edward Hutchinson	R	Oct. 13, 1914	Jan. 3, 1963
5—Gerald R. Ford	R	July 14, 1913	Jan. 3, 1949
6—Charles E. Chamberlain	R	July 22, 1917	Jan. 3, 1957
7—Donald W. Riegle	R	Feb. 4, 1936	Jan. 3, 1967
8—James Harvey	R	July 4, 1922	Jan. 3, 1961
9—Guy Vander Jagt	R	Aug. 26, 1931	Jan. 3, 1967
10—Elford A. Cederberg	R	March 6, 1918	Jan. 3, 1953
11—Philip E. Ruppe	R	Sept. 29, 1926	Jan. 3, 1967
12—James G. O'Hara	D	Nov. 8, 1925	Jan. 3, 1959
13—Charles C. Diggs Jr.	D	Dec. 2, 1922	Jan. 3, 1955
14—Lucien N. Nedzi	D	May 28, 1925	Nov. 7, 1961
15—William D. Ford	D	Aug. 6, 1927	Jan. 3, 1965
16—John D. Dingell	D	July 8, 1926	Dec. 13, 1955
17—Martha W. Griffiths	D	Jan. 29, 1912	Jan. 3, 1955
18—William S. Broomfield	R	April 28, 1922	Jan. 3, 1957
19—Jack H. McDonald	R	June 28, 1932	Jan. 3, 1967
MINNESOTA (3 Democrats; 5 Republicans)			
1—Albert H. Quie	R	Sept. 18, 1923	Feb. 18, 1958
2—Ancher Nelsen	R	Oct. 11, 1904	Jan. 3, 1959
3—Clark MacGregor	R	July 12, 1922	Jan. 3, 1961
4—Joseph E. Karth	D	Aug. 26, 1922	Jan. 3, 1959
5—Donald M. Fraser	D	Feb. 20, 1924	Jan. 3, 1963
6—John M. Zwach	R	Feb. 8, 1907	Jan. 3, 1967
7—Odin Langen	R	Jan. 5, 1913	Jan. 3, 1959
8—John A. Blatnik	D	Aug. 17, 1911	Jan. 3, 1947
MISSISSIPPI (5 Democrats)			
1—Thomas G. Abernethy	D	May 16, 1903	Jan. 3, 1943
2—Jamie L. Whitten	D	Apr. 18, 1910	Nov. 4, 1941
3—Charles Griffin	D	May 9, 1926	March 18, 1968
4—Gillespie V. Montgomery	D	Aug. 5, 1920	Jan. 3, 1967
5—William M. Colmer	D	Feb. 11, 1890	March 4, 1933
MISSOURI (9 Democrats; 1 Republican)			
1—William Clay	D	April 30, 1931	Nov. 5, 1968
2—James W. Symington	D	Sept. 28, 1927	Nov. 5, 1968
3—Leonor K. Sullivan	D		Jan. 3, 1953
4—William J. Randall	D	July 16, 1909	March 3, 1959
5—Richard Bolling	D	May 17, 1916	Jan. 3, 1949
6—W. R. Hull Jr.	D	April 17, 1906	Jan. 3, 1955
7—Durward G. Hall	R	Sept. 14, 1910	Jan. 3, 1961
8—Richard H. Ichord	D	June 27, 1926	Jan. 3, 1961
9—William L. Hungate	D	Dec. 14, 1922	Nov. 3, 1964
10—Bill D. Burlison	D	March 15, 1931	Nov. 5, 1968
MONTANA (2 Democrats)			
1—Arnold Olsen	D	Dec. 17, 1916	Jan. 3, 1961
2—John Melcher	D	Sept. 6, 1924	June 27, 1969
NEBRASKA (3 Republicans)			
1—Robert V. Denney	R	April 11, 1916	Jan. 3, 1967
2—Glenn Cunningham	R	Sept. 10, 1912	Jan. 3, 1957
3—David T. Martin	R	July 9, 1907	Jan. 3, 1961

District	Party	Born	Tenure
NEVADA (1 Democrat)			
AL—Walter S. Baring	D	Sept. 9, 1911	Jan. 3, 1957*
NEW HAMPSHIRE (2 Republicans)			
1—Louis C. Wyman	R	March 16, 1917	Jan. 3, 1967
2—James C. Cleveland	R	June 13, 1920	Jan. 3, 1963
NEW JERSEY (9 Democrats; 6 Republicans)			
1—John E. Hunt	R	Nov. 25, 1908	Jan. 3, 1967
2—Charles W. Sandman Jr.	R	Oct. 23, 1921	Jan. 3, 1967
3—James J. Howard	D	July 24, 1927	Jan. 3, 1965
4—Frank Thompson Jr.	D	July 26, 1918	Jan. 3, 1955
5—Peter H. B. Frelinghuysen	R	Jan. 17, 1916	Jan. 3, 1953
6—William T. Cahill	R	June 25, 1912	Jan. 3, 1959
7—William B. Widnall	R	March 17, 1906	Feb. 6, 1950
8—Robert A. Roe	D	Feb. 28, 1924	Nov. 4, 1969
9—Henry Helstoski	D	March 21, 1925	Jan. 3, 1965
10—Peter W. Rodino Jr.	D	June 7, 1909	Jan. 3, 1949
11—Joseph G. Minish	D	Sept. 1, 1916	Jan. 3, 1963
12—Florence P. Dwyer	R	July 4, 1902	Jan. 3, 1957
13—Cornelius E. Gallagher	D	March 2, 1921	Jan. 3, 1959
14—Dominick V. Daniels	D	Oct. 18, 1908	Jan. 3, 1959
15—Edward J. Patten	D	Aug. 22, 1905	Jan. 3, 1963
NEW MEXICO (2 Republicans)			
1—Manuel Lujan, Jr.	R	May 12, 1928	Nov. 5, 1968
2—Ed Foreman	R	Dec. 22, 1933	Nov. 5, 1968
NEW YORK (26 Democrats; 15 Republicans)			
1—Otis G. Pike	D	Aug. 31, 1921	Jan. 3, 1961
2—James R. Grover Jr.	R	March 5, 1919	Jan. 3, 1963
3—Lester L. Wolff	D	Jan. 4, 1919	Jan. 3, 1965
4—John W. Wydler	R	June 9, 1924	Jan. 3, 1963
5—Allard K. Lowenstein	D	Jan. 16, 1929	Nov. 5, 1968
6—Seymour Halpern	R	Nov. 19, 1913	Jan. 3, 1959
7—Joseph P. Addabbo	D	March 17, 1925	Jan. 3, 1961
8—Benjamin S. Rosenthal	D	June 8, 1923	Feb. 20, 1962
9—James J. Delaney	D	March 19, 1901	Jan. 3, 1949
10—Emanuel Celler	D	May 6, 1888	March 4, 1923
11—Frank J. Brasco	D	Oct. 15, 1932	Jan. 3, 1967
12—Shirley Chisholm	D	Nov. 30, 1924	Nov. 5, 1968
13—Bertram L. Podell	D	Dec. 27, 1925	Feb. 20, 1968
14—John J. Rooney	D	Nov. 29, 1903	Jan. 3, 1943
15—Hugh L. Carey	D	April 11, 1919	Jan. 3, 1961
16—John M. Murphy	D	Aug. 3, 1926	Jan. 3, 1963
17—Edward I. Koch	D	Dec. 12, 1924	Nov. 5, 1968
18—Adam Clayton Powell	D	Nov. 29, 1908	Jan. 3, 1945
19—Leonard Farbstein	D	Oct. 12, 1902	Jan. 3, 1957
20—William F. Ryan	D	June 28, 1922	Jan. 3, 1961
21—James H. Scheuer	D	Feb. 6, 1920	Jan. 3, 1965
22—Jacob H. Gilbert	D	June 17, 1920	March 8, 1960
23—Jonathan B. Bingham	D	April 24, 1914	Jan. 3, 1965
24—Mario Biaggi	D	Oct. 26, 1917	Nov. 5, 1968
25—Richard L. Ottinger	D	Jan. 27, 1929	Jan. 3, 1965
26—Ogden R. Reid	R	June 24, 1925	Jan. 3, 1963
27—Martin B. McKneally	R	Dec. 31, 1914	Nov. 5, 1968
28—Hamilton Fish, Jr.	R	June 3, 1926	Nov. 5, 1968
29—Daniel E. Button	R	Nov. 1, 1907	Jan. 3, 1967
30—Carleton J. King	R	June 15, 1904	Jan. 3, 1961
31—Robert C. McEwen	R	Jan. 5, 1920	Jan. 3, 1965
32—Alexander Pirnie	R	April 16, 1903	Jan. 3, 1959
33—Howard W. Robison	R	Oct. 30, 1915	Jan. 14, 1958
34—James M. Hanley	D	July 19, 1920	Jan. 3, 1965
35—Samuel S. Stratton	D	Sept. 27, 1916	Jan. 3, 1959
36—Frank J. Horton	R	Dec. 12, 1919	Jan. 3, 1963
37—Barber B. Conable Jr.	R	Nov. 2, 1922	Jan. 3, 1965
38—James F. Hastings	R	April 10, 1926	Nov. 5, 1968
39—Richard D. McCarthy	D	Sept. 24, 1927	Jan. 3, 1965
40—Henry P. Smith III	R	Sept. 29, 1911	Jan. 3, 1965
41—Thaddeau J. Dulski	D	Sept. 27, 1915	Jan. 3, 1959
NORTH CAROLINA (7 Democrats; 4 Republicans)			
1—Walter Jones	D	Aug. 19, 1913	Jan. 3, 1967
2—L. H. Fountain	D	April 23, 1913	Jan. 3, 1953
3—David N. Henderson	D	April 16, 1921	Jan. 3, 1961
4—Wilmer Mizell	R	Aug. 13, 1930	Nov. 5, 1968
5—Nick Galifianakis	D	July 22, 1928	Jan. 3, 1967
6—Richardson Preyer	D	Jan. 11, 1919	Nov. 5, 1968
7—Alton A. Lennon	D	Aug. 17, 1906	Jan. 3, 1957
8—Charles R. Jonas	R	Dec. 9, 1904	Jan. 3, 1953
9—James T. Broyhill	R	Aug. 19, 1927	Jan. 3, 1963
10—Earl B. Ruth	R	Feb. 7, 1916	Nov. 5, 1968
11—Roy A. Taylor	D	Jan. 31, 1910	June 25, 1960
NORTH DAKOTA (2 Republicans)			
1—Mark Andrews	R	May 19, 1926	Oct. 22, 1963
2—Thomas Kleppe	R	July 1, 1919	Jan. 3, 1967
OHIO (18 Republicans; 6 Democrats)			
1—Robert Taft, Jr.	R	Feb. 26, 1917	Jan. 3, 1967
2—Donald D. Clancy	R	July 24, 1921	Jan. 3, 1961
3—Charles W. Whalen, Jr.	R	July 31, 1920	Jan. 3, 1967
4—William M. McCulloch	R	Nov. 24, 1901	Nov. 4, 1947
5—Delbert L. Latta	R	March 5, 1920	Jan. 3, 1959
6—William H. Harsha	R	Jan. 1, 1921	Jan. 3, 1961
7—Clarence J. Brown Jr.	R	June 18, 1927	Nov. 2, 1965
8—Jackson E. Betts	R	May 26, 1904	Jan. 3, 1951
9—Thomas L. Ashley	D	Jan. 11, 1923	Jan. 3, 1955
10—Clarence E. Miller	R	Nov. 1, 1917	Jan. 3, 1967
11—J. William Stanton	R	Feb. 20, 1924	Jan. 3, 1965
12—Samuel L. Devine	R	Dec. 21, 1915	Jan. 3, 1959
13—Charles A. Mosher	R	May 7, 1906	Jan. 3, 1961
14—William H. Ayres	R	Feb. 5, 1916	Jan. 3, 1951
15—Chalmers P. Wylie	R	Nov. 23, 1920	Jan. 3, 1967
16—Frank T. Bow	R	Feb. 20, 1901	Jan. 3, 1951
17—John M. Ashbrook	R	Sept. 21, 1928	Jan. 3, 1961
18—Wayne L. Hays	D	May 13, 1911	Jan. 3, 1949
19—Michael J. Kirwan	D	Dec. 2, 1886	Jan. 3, 1937
20—Michael A. Feighan	D	Feb. 16, 1905	Jan. 3, 1943
21—Charles A. Vanik	D	April 7, 1913	Jan. 3, 1955
22—Louis Stokes	D	Feb. 23, 1925	Nov. 5, 1968
23—William E. Minshall	R	Oct. 24, 1911	Jan. 3, 1955
24—Donald E. Lukens	R	Feb. 11, 1931	Jan. 3, 1967
OKLAHOMA (4 Democrats; 2 Republicans)			
1—Page Belcher	R	April 21, 1899	Jan. 3, 1951
2—Ed Edmondson	D	April 7, 1919	Jan. 3, 1953
3—Carl B. Albert	D	May 10, 1908	Jan. 3, 1947
4—Tom Steed	D	March 2, 1904	Jan. 3, 1949
5—John Jarman	D	July 17, 1915	Jan. 3, 1951
6—John N. (Happy) Camp	R	May 11, 1908	Nov. 5, 1968
OREGON (2 Democrats; 2 Republicans)			
1—Wendell Wyatt	R	June 15, 1917	Nov. 3, 1964
2—Al Ullman	D	March 9, 1914	Jan. 3, 1957
3—Edith Green	D	Jan. 17, 1910	Jan. 3, 1955
4—John Dellenback			
PENNSYLVANIA (14 Democrats: 13 Republicans)			
1—William A. Barrett	D	Aug. 14, 1896	Jan. 3, 1945
2—Robert N. C. Nix	D	Aug. 9, 1905	May 20, 1958
3—James A. Byrne	D	June 22, 1906	Jan. 3, 1953
4—Joshua Eilberg	D	Feb. 12, 1921	Jan. 3, 1967
5—William J. Green	D	June 24, 1938	April 28, 1964
6—Gus Yatron	D	Oct. 16, 1927	Nov. 5, 1968
7—Lawrence G. Williams	R	Sept. 15, 1913	Jan. 3, 1967
8—Edward G. Biester	R	Jan. 5, 1931	Jan. 3, 1967
9—G. Robert Watkins	R	May 21, 1902	Nov. 3, 1964
10—Joseph M. McDade	R	Sept. 29, 1931	Jan. 3, 1963
11—Daniel J. Flood	D	Nov. 26, 1903	Jan. 3, 1955*
12—J. Irving Whalley	R	Sept. 14, 1902	Jan. 3, 1961
13—R. Lawrence Coughlin	R	April 11, 1929	Nov. 5, 1968
14—William S. Moorhead	D	April 8, 1923	Jan. 3, 1959
15—Fred B. Rooney	D	Nov. 6, 1925	July 30, 1963
16—Edwin D. Eshleman	R	Dec. 4, 1920	Jan. 3, 1967
17—Herman T. Schneebeli	R	July 1, 1907	April 26, 1960
18—Robert J. Corbett	R	Aug. 25, 1905	Jan. 3, 1945
19—George A. Goodling	R	Sept. 26, 1896	Nov. 8, 1960
20—Frank Gaydos	D	July 3, 1926	Nov. 5, 1968
21—John H. Dent	D	March 10, 1908	Jan. 21, 1958
22—John P. Saylor	R	July 23, 1908	Sept. 13, 1949
23—Albert W. Johnson	R	April 17, 1906	Nov. 5, 1963
24—Joseph P. Vigorito	D	Nov. 10, 1918	Jan. 3, 1965
25—Frank M. Clark	D	Dec. 24, 1915	Jan. 3, 1955
26—Thomas E. Morgan	D	Oct. 13, 1906	Jan. 3, 1945
27—James G. Fulton	R	March 1, 1903	Jan. 3, 1945
RHODE ISLAND (2 Democrats)			
1—Fernand J. St. Germain	D	Jan. 9, 1928	Jan. 3, 1961
2—Robert O. Tiernan	D	Feb. 24, 1929	Jan. 3, 1967
SOUTH CAROLINA (5 Democrats; 1 Republican)			
1—L. Mendel Rivers	D	Sept. 28, 1905	Jan. 3, 1941
2—Albert W. Watson	R	Aug. 30, 1922	Jan. 3, 1963
3—W. J. Bryan Dorn	D	April 14, 1916	Jan. 3, 1951
4—James R. Mann	D	April 27, 1920	Nov. 5, 1968
5—Tom S. Gettys	D	June 19, 1912	Nov. 3, 1964
6—John L. McMillan	D	April 12, 1898	Jan. 3, 1939

*Served prior, noncontinuous term in the House.

District	Party	Born	Tenure	District	Party	Born	Tenure
SOUTH DAKOTA (2 Republicans)				**VIRGINIA (5 Democrats; 5 Republicans)**			
1—Benjamin Reifel	R	Sept. 19, 1906	Jan. 3, 1961	1—Thomas N. Downing	D	Feb. 1, 1919	Jan. 3, 1959
2—E. Y. Berry	R	Oct. 6, 1902	Jan. 3, 1951	2—G. William Whitehurst	R	March 12, 1925	Nov. 5, 1968
				3—David E. Satterfield III	D	Dec. 2, 1920	Jan. 3, 1965
TENNESSEE (5 Democrats; 4 Republicans)				4—Watkins M. Abbitt	D	May 21, 1908	Feb. 17, 1948
1—James H. Quillen	R	Jan. 11, 1916	Jan. 3, 1963	5—W. C. Daniel	D	May 12, 1914	Nov. 5, 1968
2—John J. Duncan	R	March 24, 1919	Jan. 3, 1965	6—Richard H. Poff	R	Oct. 19, 1923	Jan. 3, 1953
3—William E. Brock III	R	Nov. 23, 1930	Jan. 3, 1963	7—John O. Marsh Jr.	D	Aug. 7, 1926	Jan. 3, 1963
4—Joe L. Evins	D	Oct. 24, 1910	Jan. 3, 1947	8—William L. Scott	R	July 1, 1915	Jan. 3, 1967
5—Richard H. Fulton	D	Jan. 27, 1927	Jan. 3, 1963	9—William C. Wampler	R	April 21, 1926	Jan. 3, 1967
6—William R. Anderson	D	June 17, 1921	Jan. 3, 1965	10—Joel T. Broyhill	R	Nov. 4, 1919	Jan. 3, 1953
7—Ray Blanton	D	April 30, 1930	Jan. 3, 1967				
8—Ed Jones	D	April 20, 1912	April 1, 1969	**WASHINGTON (5 Democrats; 2 Republicans)**			
9—Dan Kuykendall	R	July 9, 1924	Jan. 3, 1967	1—Thomas M. Pelly	R	Aug. 22, 1902	Jan. 3, 1953
				2—Lloyd Meeds	D	Dec. 11, 1927	Jan. 3, 1965
TEXAS (20 Democrats; 3 Republicans)				3—Julia B. Hansen	D	June 14, 1907	Jan. 3, 1961
1—Wright Patman	D	Aug. 6, 1893	March 4, 1929	4—Catherine May	R	May 18, 1914	Jan. 3, 1959
2—Jack Brooks	D	Dec. 18, 1922	Jan. 3, 1953	5—Thomas S. Foley	D	March 6, 1929	Jan. 3, 1965
3—James M. Collins	R	April 29, 1916	Nov. 5, 1968	6—Floyd V. Hicks	D	May 29, 1915	Jan. 3, 1965
4—Ray Roberts	D	March 28, 1913	Jan. 30, 1962	7—Brock Adams	D	Jan. 13, 1927	Jan. 3, 1965
5—Earl Cabell	D	Oct. 27, 1906	Jan. 3, 1965				
6—Olin E. Teague	D	April 6, 1910	Aug. 24, 1946	**WEST VIRGINIA (5 Democrats)**			
7—George H. B. Bush	R	June 12, 1924	Jan. 3, 1967	1—Robert H. Mollohan	D	Sept. 18, 1909	Nov. 5, 1968
8—Robert C. Eckhardt	D	July 16, 1913	Jan. 3, 1967	2—Harley O. Staggers	D	Aug. 3, 1907	Jan. 3, 1949
9—John Dowdy	D	Feb. 11, 1912	Sept. 23, 1952	3—John M. Slack Jr.	D	March 18, 1915	Jan. 3, 1959
10—J. J. (Jake) Pickle	D	Oct. 11, 1913	Dec. 17, 1963	4—Ken Hechler	D	Sept. 20, 1914	Jan. 3, 1959
11—W. R. Poage	D	Dec. 28, 1899	Jan. 3, 1937	5—James Kee	D	April 15, 1917	Jan. 3, 1965
12—James C. Wright Jr.	D	Dec. 22, 1922	Jan. 3, 1955				
13—Graham Purcell	D	May 5, 1919	Jan. 27, 1962	**WISCONSIN (6 Republicans; 4 Democrats)**			
14—John Young	D	Nov. 10, 1916	Jan. 3, 1957	1—Henry C. Schadeberg	R	Oct. 12, 1913	Jan. 3, 1967
15—Eligio de la Garza	D	Sept. 22, 1927	Jan. 3, 1965	2—Robert W. Kastenmeier	D	Jan. 24, 1924	Jan. 3, 1959
16—Richard C. White	D	April 29, 1923	Jan. 3, 1965	3—Vernon W. Thomson	R	Nov. 5, 1905	Jan. 3, 1961
17—Omar Burleson	D	March 19, 1906	Jan. 3, 1947	4—Clement J. Zablocki	D	Nov. 18, 1912	Jan. 3, 1949
18—Robert D. Price	R	Sept. 7, 1927	Jan. 3, 1967	5—Henry S. Reuss	D	Feb. 22, 1912	Jan. 3, 1955
19—George H. Mahon	D	Sept. 22, 1900	Jan. 3, 1935	6—William Steiger	R	May 15, 1938	Jan. 3, 1967
20—Henry B. Gonzalez	D	May 3, 1916	Nov. 4, 1961	7—David R. Obey	D	Oct. 3, 1938	April 3, 1969
21—O. C. Fisher	D	Nov. 22, 1903	Jan. 3, 1943	8—John W. Byrnes	R	June 12, 1913	Jan. 3, 1945
22—Bob Casey	D	July 27, 1915	Jan. 3, 1959	9—Glenn R. Davis	R	Oct. 28, 1914	Jan. 3, 1965
23—Abraham Kazen Jr.	D	Jan. 17, 1919	Jan. 3, 1967	10—Alvin E. O'Konski	R	May 26, 1904	Jan. 3, 1943
UTAH (2 Republicans)				**WYOMING (1 Republican)**			
1—Sherman P. Lloyd	R	Jan. 11, 1914	Jan. 3, 1967*	AL—John Wold	R	Aug. 31, 1916	Nov. 5, 1968
2—Laurence J. Burton	R	Oct. 30, 1926	Jan. 3, 1967				
VERMONT (1 Republican)							
AL—Robert T. Stafford	R	Aug. 8, 1913	Jan. 3, 1961	*Served prior, noncontinuous term in the House.			

JUDICIARY

SUPREME COURT

CHIEF JUSTICE OF THE UNITED STATES

	Home State	Date of Birth	Date took Court seat	Appointed By
Warren E. Burger	Minn.	Sept. 17, 1907	Oct. 6, 1969	Nixon

ASSOCIATE JUSTICES OF THE SUPREME COURT

	Home State	Date of Birth	Date took Court seat	Appointed By		Home State	Date of Birth	Date took Court seat	Appointed By
Hugo L. Black	Ala.	Feb. 27, 1886	Oct. 4, 1937	Roosevelt	Potter Stewart	Ohio	Jan. 23, 1915	Oct. 14, 1958	Eisenhower
William O. Douglas	Wash.	Oct. 16, 1898	April 17, 1939	Roosevelt	Byron R. White	Colo.	June 8, 1917	Apr. 16, 1962	Kennedy
John M. Harlan	N.Y.	May 20, 1899	March 28, 1955	Eisenhower	Thurgood Marshall	Md.	July 2, 1908	Oct. 2, 1967	Johnson
William J. Brennan	N.J.	Apr. 25, 1906	Oct. 16, 1956	Eisenhower					

THE SECRETARIAT

GENERAL ASSEMBLY

SECRETARY GENERAL

U Thant	Burma

UNDER SECRETARIES—GENERAL

Ralph J. Bunche	United States	Special Political Affairs
Philippe de Seynes	France	Economic and Social Affairs
Constantin A. Stavropoulos	Greece	General Assembly Affairs
Jiri Nosek	Czechoslovakia	Conference Services
Jose Rolz-Bennett	Guatemala	Special Political Affairs
Constantin A. Stavropoulos	Greece	Legal Counsel
Leonid N. Kutakov	U.S.S.R.	Political and Security Council Affairs
Chief S.O. Adebo	Nigeria	U.N. Institute for Training and Research
Issoufou Saidou Djermakoye	Niger	Trusteeship, Non-Self Gov. Territories
C. V. Narasimhan	India	Chef de Cabinet
Andrew A. Stark	United Kingdom	Administration and Management

Country	Year of Admission	Permanent Representative
Afghanistan	1946	Abdul Rahman Pazhwak
Albania	1955	Halim Budo
Algeria	1962	Hadj Benabdelkader Azzout
Argentina	1945	Jose Maria Ruda
Australia	1945	Patrick Shaw
Austria	1955	Heinrich Haymerle
Barbados	1966	Oliver H. Jackman
Belgium	1945	Constant Schuurmans
Bolivia	1945	Walter Guevara Arze
Botswana	1966	T. J. Molefhe
Brazil	1945	João Augusto de Araujo Castro
Bulgaria	1955	Miklo Tarabanov
Burma	1948	U Soe Tin
Burundi	1962	Terence Nsanze
Byelorussian S.S.R.	1945	Vitaly Stepanovich Smirnov
Cambodia	1955	Huot Sambath
Cameroon	1960	Michel Njine
Canada	1945	Yvon Beaulne
Central African Republic	1960	Michel Gallin-Douathe
Ceylon	1955	Hamilton Shirley Amerasinghe
Chad	1960	Bruno Bohiadi
Chile	1945	Josef Pinera Carvallo
China	1945	Liu Chieh
Colombia	1945	José Maria Morales-Suarez
Congo (Brazzaville)	1960	Adrien Bakala
Congo (Leopoldville)	1960	Theodore Idzumbuir
Costa Rica	1945	Luis Dobles Sanchez
Cuba	1945	Ricardo Alarcon Quesada
Cyprus	1960	Zenon Rossides
Czechoslovakia	1945	Zdeněk Cerník
Dahomey	1960	Maxime-Leopold Zollner
Denmark	1945	Otto R. Borch
Dominican Republic	1945	Horacio Julio Ornes Coiscou
Ecuador	1945	Leopoldo Benites
El Salvador	1945	Don Reynaldo Galindo Pohl
Equatorial Guinea		Gustavo B. Envela-Makongo
Ethiopia	1945	Kifle Wodajo*
Finland	1955	Max Jakobson
France	1945	Armand Berard
Gabon	1960	Jean Davini
Gambia	1965	(vacant)
Ghana	1957	R. M. Akwei
Greece	1945	Dimitri S. Bitsios

State	Rank in Population	Population (Latest Estimate or Local Census)	Capital	Population of Capital
Alabama	21	3,462,000 (1967E)	Montgomery	164,343 (1967E)
Alaska	50	779,000 (1967E)	Juneau	8,600 (1965E)
Arizona	34	1,660,000 (1967E)	Phoenix	519,000 (1967E)
Arkansas	32	1,936,600 (1966E)	Little Rock	135,500 (1967E)
California	1	19,535,000 (1967E)	Sacramento	266,000 (1966E)
Colorado	31	2,015,650 (1967E)	Denver	477,000 (1967E)
Connecticut	24	2,873,000 (1966E)	Hartford	162,200 (1966E)
Delaware	46	512,000 (1966E)	Dover	14,100 (1966E)
Florida	9	5,996,000 (1967E)	Tallahassee	64,400 (1967E)
Georgia	15	4,511,000 (1967E)	Atlanta	513,000 (1967E)
Hawaii	42	773,609 (1967E)	Honolulu	352,925 (1967E)
Idaho	41	702,300 (1967E)	Boise	72,090 (1966C)
Illinois	5	10,081,158 (1967E)	Springfield	84,649 (1964E)
Indiana	12	4,958,400 (1967E)	Indianapolis	765,000 (1967E)
Iowa	25	2,768,800 (1965E)	Des Moines	206,000 (1966E)
Kansas	29	2,236,750 (1967E)	Topeka	120,467 (1967E)

NATIONS

Country	Year of Admission	Permanent Representative	Country	Year of Admission	Permanent Representative
Guatemala	1945	Maximiliano Kestler	Norway	1945	Edvard Hambro
Guinea	1958	El Hadj Abdoulaye Toure	Pakistan	1947	Agha Shahi
Guyana	1966	P. A. Thompson	Panama	1945	Aquilino Boyd
Haiti	1945	Marcel Antoine	Paraguay	1945	Miguel Solano Lopez
Honduras	1945	Salomón Jimenez Munguia*	Peru	1945	Manuel Felix Maurtua
Hungary	1955	Karoly Csatorday	Philippines	1945	Privado G. Jimenez (Deputy)
Iceland	1946	Hannes Kjartansson	Poland	1945	Eugeniusz Kulaga
India	1945	Samar Sen	Portugal	1955	Duarte Vaz Pinto*
Indonesia	1950	Hadjii Roeslan Abdulgani	Romania	1955	Gheorghe Diaconescu
Iran	1945	Mehdi Vakil	Rwanda	1962	Fidèle Nkundabagenzi
Iraq	1945	Adnan Raouf*	Saudi Arabia	1945	Jamil M. Baroody (Deputy)
Ireland	1955	Cornelius C. Cremin	Senegal	1960	Ibrahima Boye
Israel	1949	Yosef Tekoah	Sierra Leone	1961	Davidson S.H.W. Nicol
Italy	1955	Piero Vinci	Singapore	1965	T. T. B. Koh
Ivory Coast	1960	Simeon Ake	Somalia	1960	Abduerahim Abby Farah
Jamaica	1962	Keith Johnson	South Africa	1945	Matthys I. Botha
Japan	1956	Senjin Tsuruoka	Southern Yemen		Ismail Saeed Noaman
Jordan	1955	Muhammad H. El-Farra	Spain	1955	Don Jaime de Pinies
Kenya	1963	Arthur Elphas Osanya-Nyyneque*	Sudan	1956	Fakher-ed-Dine Mohamed
Kuwait	1963	Muhalhel Mohamad Al-Mudhaf	Swaziland	1968	S. T. Msindazwe Sukati
Laos	1955	Khamking Souvanlasy	Sweden	1946	Sverker C. Astrom
Lebanon	1945	Edouard Ghorra	Syria	1945	George J. Tomeh
Lesotho	1966	M. T. Mashologu	Tanzania	1961	Akili B. C. Danieli
Liberia	1945	Nathan Barnes	Thailand	1946	Anand Panyarachun*
Libya	1955	Wahbi El-Bouri	Togo	1960	Alexandre J. Ohin
Luxembourg	1945	André Philippe	Trinidad & Tobago	1962	P. V. J. Solomon
Malagasy Republic	1960	Blaise Rabetafika (Acting)	Tunisia	1956	S. El Goulli
Malawi	1964	N. W. Mbekeani	Turkey	1945	Umit Haluk Bayulken
Malaysia	1957	Ismail bin Mohamed Yusof	Uganda	1962	E. Otema Allimadi
Maldive Islands	1965	Abdul Sattar	Ukrainian S.S.R.	1945	Mikhail Deonisovich Polyanichko
Mali	1960	Mamadou Moctar Thiam	Union of Soviet Socialist Republic	1945	Yakov A. Malik
Malta	1964	Arvid Pardo	United Arab Republic	1945	Mohamed Awad El-Kony
Mauritania	1961	Abdallahi Ould Daddah	United Kingdom	1945	Lord Caradon
Mauritius	1968	Radha Krishna Ramphul	United States	1945	Charles W. Yost
Mexico	1945	Francisco Cuevas Cancino	Upper Volta	1960	Tensore Paul Rouamba
Mongolia	1961	Mangalyn Dugersuren	Uruguay	1945	Augusto Legnani
Morocco	1956	Ahmed Taibi Benhima	Venezuela	1945	Andrés Aguilar Mawdsley
Nepal	1955	Padma Bahadur Khatri	Yemen	1947	Mohamed Said Al-Attar
Netherlands	1945	Duco G. E. Middelburg	Yugoslavia	1945	Lazar Mojsov
New Zealand	1945	John Vivian Scott	Zambia	1964	Vernon Johnson Mwaanga
Nicaragua	1945	Guillermo Sevilla-Secasa			
Niger	1960	Adamou Mayaki			
Nigeria	1960	Edwin Ogebe Ogbu			

*Charge d'Affaires. Post of Permanent Representative vacant.

THE UNION

Largest City	Population of Largest City	Governor	Party	Term Expires
		Albert Brewer*	D	1971, Jan.
Birmingham	351,653 (1967E)	Walter J. Hickel	R	1970, Dec.
Anchorage	60,000 (1967E)	Jack Williams	R	1972, Dec.
Phoenix	519,000 (1967E)	Winthrop Rockefeller	R	1973, Jan.
Little Rock	135,500 (1967E)	Ronald Reagan	R	1971, Jan.
Los Angeles	2,779,500 (1966E)	John A. Love	R	1971, Jan.
Denver	477,000 (1967E)	John N. Dempsey	D	1971, Jan.
Hartford	162,200 (1966E)	Russel W. Petersen	R	1973, Jan.
Wilmington	95,827 (1967E)	Claude R. Kirk	R	1971, Jan.
Jacksonville	525,000 (1967E)	Lester G. Maddox	D	1971, Jan.
Atlanta	513,000 (1967E)	John A. Burns	D	1970, Dec.
Honolulu	352,925 (1967E)	Don W. Samuelson	R	1971, Jan.
Boise	72,090 (1966C)	Richard B. Ogilvie	R	1973, Jan.
Chicago	3,550,404 (1960C)	Edgar D. Whitcomb	R	1973, Jan.
Indianapolis	765,000 (1967E)	Robert D. Ray	R	1972, Dec.
Des Moines	206,000 (1966E)	Robert Docking	D	1973, Jan.
Wichita	281,110 (1967E)			

*Succeeded Lurleen B. Wallace, Died May 7, 1968.

State	Rank in Population	Population (Latest Estimate or Local Census)	Capital	Population of Capital
Kentucky	22	3,166,000 (1966E)	Frankfort	22,500 (1966E)
Louisiana	18	3,631,000 (1967E)	Baton Rouge	174,000 (1966E)
Maine	38	983,000 (1967E)	Augusta	21,600 (1967E)
Maryland	20	3,100,689 (1960C)	Annapolis	36,340 (1966E)
Massachusetts	10	5,295,281 (1965C)	Boston	616,326 (1965C)
Michigan	7	8,584,000 (1967E)	Lansing	124,400 (1967E)
Minnesota	19	3,576,000 (1967E)	St. Paul	313,000 (1966E)
Mississippi	28	2,327,000 (1966E)	Jackson	168,000 (1966E)
Missouri	14	4,605,000 (1967E)	Jefferson City	32,000 (1967E)
Montana	40	717,000 (1965E)	Helena	23,000 (1966E)
Nebraska	35	1,516,044 (1967E)	Lincoln	142,717 (1967E)
Nevada	47	505,000 (1967E)	Carson City	12,500 (1967E)
New Hampshire	44	674,366 (1967E)	Concord	30,200 (1964E)
New Jersey	8	7,000,000 (1967E)	Trenton	110,640 (1966E)
New Mexico	36	1,041,300 (1967E)	Santa Fe	44,600 (1967E)
New York	2	18,335,000 (1967E)	Albany	134,984 (1967E)
North Carolina	11	4,908,000 (1967E)	Raleigh	105,722 (1967E)
North Dakota	45	652,000 (1965E)	Bismarck	30,584 (1963C)
Ohio	4	10,726,007 (1967E)	Columbus	544,016 (1967E)
Oklahoma	27	2,500,000 (1967E)	Oklahoma City	410,000 (1967E)
Oregon	30	1,999,780 (1966E)	Salem	66,397 (1966E)
Pennsylvania	3	11,582,000 (1967E)	Harrisburg	79,000 (1965E)
Rhode Island	39	892,709 (1965C)	Providence	187,061 (1965C)
South Carolina	26	2,550,000 (1965E)	Columbia	101,300 (1967E)
South Dakota	43	698,800 (1966E)	Pierre	13,000 (1967E)
Tennessee	17	3,925,000 (1967E)	Nashville	250,887 (1966E)
Texas	6	10,652,000 (1966E)	Austin	216,765 (1966E)
Utah	37	1,015,000 (1967E)	Salt Lake City	222,570 (1967E)
Vermont	48	412,000 (1967E)	Montpelier	8,841 (1964E)
Virginia	13	4,538,937 (1966E)	Richmond	217,671 (1966E)
Washington	23	3,183,614 (1967C)	Olympia	20,880 (1967C)
West Virginia	33	1,798,000 (1967C)	Charleston	85,796 (1960C)
Wisconsin	16	4,188,000 (1967E)	Madison	177,000 (1967E)
Wyoming	49	315,000 (1967E)	Cheyenne	43,505 (1967E)
District of Columbia		809,000 (1967E)		

ECONOMICS

EMPLOYMENT

Year	Civilian Labor Force	Un-employed	Percent-age Unem-ployed*
1929	49,180,000	1,550,000	3.2
1933	51,590,000	12,830,000	24.9
1940	55,640,000	8,120,000	14.6
1944	54,630,000	670,000	1.2
1960	70,612,000	3,931,000	5.6
1961	71,603,000	4,806,000	6.7
1962	71,854,000	4,007,000	5.6
1963	72,975,000	4,166,000	5.7
1964	74,233,000	3,876,000	5.2
1965	75,635,000	3,456,000	4.6
1966	75,770,000	2,875,000	3.8
1967	78,402,000	2,942,000	
1968	78,737,000	2,816,000	3.6

1969 by month (seasonally adjusted)

Jan.	79,874,000	2,645,000	3.3
Feb.	80,356,000	2,627,000	3.3
March	80,495,000	2,728,000	3.4
April	80,450,000	2,845,000	3.5
May	80,071,000	2,806,000	3.5
June	80,433,000	2,762,000	3.4
July	80,756,000	2,882,000	3.6
Aug.	81,054,000	2,867,000	3.5
Sept.	81,359,000	3,233,000	4.0
Oct.	81,486,000	3,161,000	3.9
Nov.	81,295,000	2,798,000	3.4

(Source Bureau of Labor Statistics)

GROSS NATIONAL PRODUCT

(The total output of goods and services in the United States measured in terms of expenditures by which they were acquired)

Year	GNP
1929	$103,100,000,000
1933	55,600,000,000
1940	99,700,000,000
1945	211,900,000,000
1950	284,800,000,000
1960	503,700,000,000
1961	520,100,000,000
1962	560,300,000,000
1963	590,500,000,000
1964	632,400,000,000
1965	683,900,000,000
1966	743,300,000,000
1967	789,663,000,000
1968	865,700,000,000
1969 (estim.)	933,000,000,000

(Source: Department of Commerce)

U.S. NATIONAL DEBT

(As of June 30)

Year	Total	Per Capita
1860	$65,000,000	$2
1900	1,263,000,000	17
1920	24,299,000,000	228
1930	16,185,000,000	132
1940	42,968,000,000	325
1945	258,682,000,000	1,849
1960	286,331,000,000	1,585
1961	288,971,000,000	1,573
1962	298,201,000,000	1,598
1963	305,860,000,000	1,615
1964	311,713,000,000	1,622
1965	317,274,000,000	1,631
1966	319,907,000,000	1,625
1967	326,221,000,000	1,638
1968	347,578,000,000	1,727
1969	367,152,000,000	1,743

(Source: Treasury Department)

PER CAPITA PERSONAL INCOME

1950	$1,496	1965	2,765
1960	2,215	1966	2,978
1961	2,264	1967	3,159
1962	2,368	1968	3,421
1963	2,455	1969 (estim.)	3,775
1964	2,586	(Source: Department of Commerce)	

Largest City	Population of Largest City	Governor	Party	Term Expires
Louisville	390,100 (1966E)	Louie B. Nunn	R	1972, Jan.
New Orleans	650,000 (1966E)	John J. McKeithen	D	1968, May
Portland	72,400 (1967E)	Kenneth M. Curtis	D	1971, Jan.
Baltimore	939,024 (1967E)	Marvin Mandel	D	1971, Jan.
Boston	616,326 (1965C)	John A. Volpe	R	1971, Jan.
Detroit	1,612,100 (1967E)	William G. Milliken	R	1970, Dec.
Minneapolis	470,000 (1966E)	Harold LeVander	R	1970, Jan.
Jackson	168,000 (1966E)	John Bell	D	1972, Jan.
St. Louis	831,000 (1967E)	Warren E. Hearnes	D	1973, Jan.
Billings	74,851 (1966E)	Forrest H. Anderson	D	1973, Jan.
Omaha	339,494 (1967E)	Norbert T. Tiemann	R	1971, Jan.
Las Vegas	250,000 (1967E)	Paul Laxalt	R	1970, Jan.
Manchester	87,622 (1967E)	Walter R. Peterson, Jr.	R	1973, Jan.
Newark	397,650 (1966E)	Richard J. Hughes	D	1970, Jan.
Albuquerque	260,000 (1967E)	David F. Cargo	R	1972, Dec.
New York	8,011,000 (1965C)	Nelson A. Rockefeller	R	1970, Dec.
Charlotte	258,000 (1967E)	Robert W. Scott	D	1973, Jan.
Fargo	46,662 (1960C)	William L. Guy	D	1973, Jan.
Cleveland	825,436 (1967E)	James A. Rhodes	R	1970, Jan.
Oklahoma City	410,000 (1967E)	Dewey Bartlett	R	1971, Jan.
Portland	1,999,780 (1967E)	Thomas L. McCall	R	1971, Jan.
Philadelphia	2,080,000 (1965E)	Raymond P. Shafer	R	1971, Jan.
Providence	187,061 (1965C)	Frank Licht	D	1973, Jan.
Columbia	101,300 (1967E)	Robert E. McNair	D	1971, Jan.
Sioux Falls	76,000 (1967E)	Frank Farrar	R	1973, Jan.
Memphis	536,585 (1967E)	Buford Ellington	D	1971, Jan.
Houston	1,122,109 (1965E)	Preston Smith	D	1973, Jan.
Salt Lake City	222,570 (1965E)	Calvin L. Rampton	D	1973, Jan.
Burlington	35,983 (1964E)	Dean C. Davis	R	1973, Jan.
Norfolk	322,030 (1966E)	Mills E. Godwin Jr.	D	1970, Jan.
Seattle	580,000 (1967C)	Daniel J. Evans	R	1973, Jan.
Charleston	85,796 (1960C)	Arch A. Moore, Jr.	R	1973, Jan.
Milwaukee	783,400 (1967E)	Warren P. Knowles	R	1973, Jan.
Cheyenne	43,505 (1967E)	Stanley K. Hathaway	R	1971, Jan.

CONSUMER PRICE INDEX (Living Costs)

(1966 annual average)

	All Items	Food	Apparel	Housing	Rent	Medical Care	Transportation
1913	34.5	33.6	33.8	--	55.7	--	--
1920	69.8	70.8	98.0	--	72.9	--	--
1929	59.7	55.6	56.2	--	85.4	--	--
1933	45.1	35.3	42.8	--	60.8	--	--
1940	48.8	40.5	49.6	--	63.2	--	--
1945	62.7	58.4	71.2	--	66.1	--	--
1950	83.8	85.8	91.5	83.2	79.1	73.4	79.0
1960	103.1	101.4	102.1	103.1	103.1	108.1	103.8
1961	104.2	102.6	102.8	103.9	104.4	111.3	105.0
1962	105.4	103.6	103.2	104.8	105.7	114.2	107.2
1963	106.7	105.1	104.2	106.0	106.8	117.0	107.8
1964	108.1	106.4	105.7	107.2	107.8	119.4	109.3
1965	109.9	108.8	106.8	108.5	109.8	122.3	111.6
1966	113.1	114.2	109.6	111.1	110.4	127.7	112.7
1967	116.3	115.2	114.0	114.3	112.4	136.7	115.9
1968	121.2	119.3	120.1	119.1	115.1	145.0	119.6

1968 by month	All Items	Food	Apparel	Housing	Rent	Medical Care	Transportation
January	124.1	122.0	123.4	122.7	116.9	150.2	120.7
February	124.6	121.9	123.9	123.3	117.2	151.3	122.0
March	125.6	122.4	124.9	124.4	117.5	152.5	124.3
April	126.4	123.2	125.6	125.3	117.8	153.6	124.6
May	126.8	123.7	126.6	125.8	118.1	154.5	124.0
June	127.6	125.5	127.0	126.3	118.5	155.2	124.6
July	128.2	126.7	126.8	127.0	118.8	155.9	124.3
August	128.7	127.4	126.6	127.8	119.3	156.8	124.2
September	129.3	127.5	128.7	128.6	119.7	157.6	123.6
October	129.8	127.2	129.8	129.2	120.1	156.9	125.7

(Source: Bureau of Labor Statistics)

SPORTS

BASEBALL

FINAL STANDINGS

AMERICAN LEAGUE

EASTERN DIVISION

	W.	L.	Pc.	G.B.
Baltimore	109	53	.673	—
Detroit	90	72	.556	19
Boston	87	75	.537	22
Washington	86	76	.531	23
New York	80	81	.497	28½
Cleveland	62	99	.385	46½

WESTERN DIVISION

	W.	L.	Pc.	G.B.
Minnesota	97	65	.599	—
Oakland	88	74	.543	9
California	71	91	.438	26
Kansas City	69	93	.426	28
Chicago	68	94	.420	29
Seattle	64	98	.395	33

NATIONAL LEAGUE

EASTERN DIVISION

	W.	L.	Pc.	G.B.
New York	100	62	.617	—
Chicago	92	70	.568	8
Pittsburgh	88	74	.543	12
St. Louis	87	75	.537	13
Philadelphia	63	99	.389	37
Montreal	52	110	.321	48

WESTERN DIVISION

	W.	L.	Pc.	G.B.
Atlanta	93	69	.574	—
San Francisco	90	72	.556	3
Cincinnati	89	73	.549	4
Los Angeles	85	77	.525	8
Houston	81	81	.500	12
San Diego	52	110	.321	41

Leading Pitchers

AMERICAN LEAGUE			NATIONAL LEAGUE		
(Based on 15 or more decisions.)					
	W.	L.		W.	L.
Palmer, Balt.	16	4	Moose, Pitts.	13	3
Perry, Minn.	20	6	Seaver, N.Y.	25	7
McNally, Balt.	20	7	Maloney, Cin.	11	5
McLain, Det.	24	9	Carroll, Cin.	12	6
Bosman, Wash.	13	5	Regan, Chic.	12	6

NATIONAL LEAGUE

First Game

NEW YORK	ab.	r.	h.	bi.	ATLANTA	ab.	r.	h.	bi.
Agee, cf	4	3	2	2	Millan, 2b	2	1	2	0
Garrett, 3b	5	1	2	1	Gonzalez, cf	4	1	1	0
Jones, lf	5	2	3	3	H. Aaron, rf	5	1	1	3
Shamsky, rf	5	3	3	1	Carty, lf	4	2	1	0
Gaspar, rf	0	0	0	0	Cepeda, 1b	4	1	2	1
Boswell, 2b	5	1	1	2	Boyer, 3b	4	0	1	2
McGraw, p	0	0	0	0	Didier, c	4	0	0	0
Kranepool, 1b	4	0	1	1	Garrido, ss	4	0	1	0
Grote, c	5	1	0	0	Reed, p	0	0	0	0
Harrelson, ss	5	1	1	1	Doyle, p	0	0	0	0
Koosman, p	2	1	0	0	Pappas, p	1	0	0	0
Taylor, p	0	0	0	0	T. Aaron, ph	1	0	0	0
Martin, ph	1	0	0	0	Britton, p	0	0	0	0
Weis, 2b	1	0	0	0	Upshaw, p	1	0	0	0
					Asprom'nte, ph	1	0	0	0
Total	42	11	13	11	Neibauer, p	0	0	0	0
					Total	35	6	9	6

New York   1 3 2   2 1 0   2 0 0—11
Atlanta   0 0 0   1 5 0   0 0 0— 6

E—H. Aaron, Cepeda, Harrelson, Boyer. DP—New York 2, Atlanta 1. LOB—New York 10, Atlanta 7. 2B—Jones, Harrelson, Carty, Garrett, Cepeda. HR—Agee, Boswell, H. Aaron, Jones. SB—Agee 2, Garrett, Jones.

	IP.	H.	R.	Er.	BB.	SO.
Koosman	4⅔	7	6	6	4	5
Taylor (W)	1⅓	1	0	0	0	2
McGraw	3	1	0	0	1	1
Reed (L)	1⅔	5	4	4	3	3
Doyle	1	2	2	0	1	3
Pappas	2⅓	4	3	3	0	4
Britton	⅓	0	0	0	1	0
Upshaw	2⅔	2	2	2	1	1
Neibauer	1	0	0	0	0	1

T—3:10. A—50,270.

Second Game

NEW YORK	ab.	r.	h.	bi.	ATLANTA	ab.	r.	h.	bi.
Agee, cf	5	0	0	0	Millan, 2b	5	1	2	0
Garrett, 3b	4	1	2	0	Gonzalez, cf	5	2	2	2
Jones, lf	5	1	1	1	H. Aaron, rf	5	1	2	2
Shamsky, rf	4	1	3	0	Carty, lf	3	1	1	0
Weis, 2b	0	0	0	0	Lum, lf	1	0	1	0
Boswell, 2b	3	2	0	0	Cepeda, 1b	4	0	1	0
Gaspar, rf	0	0	0	0	Boyer, 3b	1	0	0	1
Kranepool, 1b	4	2	1	0	Didier, c	4	0	0	0
Grote, c	3	1	1	1	Garrido, ss	4	0	1	0
Harrelson, ss	3	1	1	2	Niekro, p	3	0	0	0
Seaver, p	3	0	0	0	Asprom'te, ph	1	0	0	0
Martin, ph	1	0	1	2	Upshaw, p	0	0	0	0
Taylor, p	0	0	0	0	Total	36	5	10	5
Total	35	9	10	6					

New York   0 2 0   2 0 0   0 5 0—9
Atlanta   0 1 2   0 1 0   1 0 0—5

E—Boswell, Cepeda, Gonzalez. DP—Atlanta 2. LOB—New York 3, Atlanta 9. 2B—Carty, Millan, Gonzalez, H. Aaron, Garrett, Lum. 3B—Harrelson. HR—Gonzalez (1), H. Aaron (1). SB—Cepeda, Jones. SF—Boyer.

	IP.	H.	R.	ER.	BB.	SO.
Seaver (W, 1-0)	7	8	5	5	3	2
Taylor	2	2	0	0	0	2
Niekro (L, 0-1)	8	9	9	4	4	4
Upshaw	1	1	0	0	0	1

HBP—By Seaver (Cepeda). PB—Didier, Grote.
T—2.37. A—50,122.

Third Game

ATLANTA	ab.	r.	h.	bi.	NEW YORK	ab.	r.	h.	bi.
Millan, 2b	5	0	0	0	Agee, cf	5	1	3	2
Gonzalez, cf	5	1	2	0	Garrett, 3b	4	1	1	2
H. Aaron, rf	4	1	2	2	Jones, lf	4	1	2	0
Carty, lf	3	1	1	0	Shamsky, rf	4	1	1	0
Cepeda, 1b	3	1	2	2	Gaspar, rf	0	0	0	0
Boyer, 3b	4	0	0	0	Boswell, 2b	4	1	3	3
Didier, c	3	0	0	0	Kranepool, 1b	4	0	1	0
Lum, ph	1	0	1	0	Grote, c	4	1	1	0
Jackson, ss	0	0	0	0	Harrelson, ss	3	0	0	0
Garrido, ss	2	0	0	0	Gentry, p	1	0	0	0
Atou, ph	1	0	0	0	Ryan, p	3	1	2	0
Tillman, c	0	0	0	0	Total	36	7	14	7
Jarvis, p	2	0	0	0					
Stone, p	1	0	0	0					
Upshaw, p	0	0	0	0					
Asp'monte, ph	1	0	0	0					
Total	35	4	8	4					

Atlanta   2 0 0   0 2 0   0 0 0—4
New York   0 0 1   2 3 1   0 0 x—7

E—Millan. DP—Atlanta 1. LOB—Atlanta 7, New York 6. 2B—Cepeda, Agee, H. Aaron, Jones, Grote. HR—H. Aaron, Agee, Boswell, Cepeda, Garrett. S—Harrelson.

	IP.	H.	R.	ER.	BB.	SO.
Jarvis (L)	4⅓	10	6	6	0	6
Stone	1	2	1	1	0	0
Upshaw	2⅔	2	0	0	0	2
Gentry	2	5	2	2	1	1
Ryan (W)	7	3	2	2	2	7

T—2:24. A—53,195.

AMERICAN LEAGUE

First Game

MINNESOTA	ab.	r.	h.	bi.	BALTIMORE	ab.	r.	h.	bi.
Tovar, cf	5	0	1	0	Buford, lf	3	0	0	0
Carew, 2b	4	0	0	0	Blair, cf	4	0	0	0
Killebrew, 3b	3	0	0	0	F. Rob'on, rf	5	0	2	0
Oliva, rf	4	0	1	0	Powell, 1b	3	1	1	0
Allison, lf	5	0	0	0	B. Rob'n, 3b	4	0	2	0
Reese, 1b	4	0	0	0	D. J'son, 2b	4	0	2	0
Mitterwald, c	3	0	1	0	Belanger, ss	5	0	0	0
Cardenas, ss	4	0	0	0	Etchebarren, c	3	0	0	0
Boswell, p	4	0	0	0	Hendricks, c	0	0	0	0
Perranoski, p	0	0	0	0	Motton, ph	1	0	1	1
Total	36	0	3	0	McNally, p	4	0	0	0
					Total	36	1	8	1

Minnesota   0 0 0   0 0 0   0 0 0   0 0—0
Baltimore   0 0 0   0 0 0   0 0 0   0 1—1

E—Cardenas. DP—Minnesota 2. LOB—Minnesota 8, Baltimore 11. 2B—F. Robinson 2. SB—Oliva. S—B. Robinson.

	IP.	H.	R.	ER.	BB.	SO.
Boswell (L, 0-1)	10⅔	7	1	1	7	4
Perranoski	*0	0	0	0	0	0
McNally (W, 1-0)	11	3	0	0	5	11

*Two out when winning run was scored.
Wild pitch—Boswell.
T—3:17. A—41,704

Second Game

MINNESOTA	ab.	r.	h.	bi.	BALTIMORE	ab.	r.	h.	bi.
Tovar, cf	4	0	0	0	Buford, lf	6	0	0	0
Carew, 2b	5	0	1	0	Blair, cf	5	0	1	0
Killebrew, 3b	2	1	0	0	F. Robinson, rf	3	1	1	1
Oliva, rf	5	2	2	2	Powell, 1b	5	1	2	1
Allison, lf	3	0	0	1	B. Robins'n, 3b	5	0	4	0
Uhlaender, lf	1	0	1	0	Hendricks, c	3	0	0	0
Reese, 1b	4	0	0	0	Motton, ph	1	0	0	0
Cardenas, ss	5	0	0	0	Watt, p	0	0	0	0
Mitterwald, c	4	0	0	0	Salmon, ph	1	0	0	0
Roseboro, c	1	0	0	0	Lopez, p	0	0	0	0
Perry, p	3	0	0	0	Hall, p	0	0	0	0
Perranoski, p	1	0	0	0	Johnson, 2b	5	0	0	0
Total	38	3	4	3	Belanger, ss	5	2	2	1
					Cuellar, p	2	0	0	0
					May, ph	1	0	0	0
					Richert, p	0	0	0	0
					Rettenmund, ph	0	0	0	0
					Etchebarren, c	1	0	0	0
					Total	43	4	10	4

292

Minnesota   0 0 0   0 1 0   2 0 0   0 0 0—3
Baltimore   0 0 0   1 1 0   0 0 1   0 0 1—4

E—F. Robinson, Uhlaender, Carew. DP—Baltimore 1. LOB—Minneosta 5, Baltimore 8. 2B—Oliva. HR—F. Robinson (1), Belanger (1), Oliva (1), Powell (1). SB—Tovar. S—Etchebarren. SF—Allison.

	IP.	H.	R.	ER.	BB.	SO.
Perry	8	6	3	3	3	3
Perranoski (L, 0-1)	*3⅔	4	1	1	0	1
Cuellar	8	3	3	2	1	7
Richert	1	0	0	0	2	2
Watt	2	0	0	0	0	2
Lopez	⅓	1	0	0	2	0

*Two out when winning run scored.
Wild Pitch—Lopez.
T—3:29. A—39,324.

Third Game

MINNESOTA   BALTIMORE

MINNESOTA	ab.	r.	h.	bi.	BALTIMORE	ab.	r.	h.	bi.
Uhlaender, lf	5	0	0	0	Buford, lf	5	3	4	1
Carew, 2b	5	0	0	0	Blair, cf	6	1	5	5
Oliva, rf	4	1	2	0	F. Robinson, rf	4	0	1	1
Killebrew, 3b	3	1	1	0	Powell, 1b	5	0	2	0
Reese, 1b	4	0	2	2	B. Robinson, 3b	5	1	1	0
Tovar, cf	4	0	0	0	Johnson, 2b	4	2	1	0
Roseboro, c	4	0	1	0	Hendricks, c	5	2	2	3
Cardenas, ss	4	0	2	0	Belanger, ss	5	2	2	0
Miller, p	0	0	0	0	Palmer, p	5	0	0	0
Woodson, p	1	0	0	0					
T. Hall, p	0	0	0	0	Total	44	11	18	10
Manuel, ph	0	0	0	0					
Worthington, p	0	0	0	0					
Grzenda, p	0	0	0	0					
Renick, ph	1	0	0	0					
Chance, p	0	0	0	0					
Perranoski, p	0	0	0	0					
Nettles, ph	1	0	1	0					
Total	36	2	10	2					

Baltimore   0 3 0   2 0 1   0 2 3—11
Minnesota   1 0 0   0 1 0   0 0 0— 2

E—Oliva 2. DP—Baltimore 1, Minnesota 1. LOB—Baltimore 9, Minnesota 9. 2B—Oliva, B. Robinson, Hendricks 2, Blair 2, Killebrew, Buford. 3B—Belanger, Cardenas. HR—Blair.

	IP.	H.	R.	ER.	BB.	SO.
Palmer (W, 1-0)	9	10	2	2	2	4
Miller (L, 0-1)	1⅔	5	3	1	0	0
Woodson	1⅔	3	2	2	3	2
T. Hall	⅔	0	0	0	0	0
Worthington	1⅓	3	1	1	0	1
Grzenda	⅔	0	0	0	0	0
Chance	2	4	3	3	0	2
Perranoski	1	3	2	2	0	1

Wild pitch—Palmer.
T—2:48. A—32,735.

Series Standing, Figures

	W.	L.	Pc.
Mets	4	1	.800
Orioles	1	4	.200

Five-Game Totals

Paid attendance—272,378.
Total receipts—$2,857,782.78
Commissioner's share—$428,667.41
Players' share (first four games only)
—$1,142,200.93
Clubs' and leagues' share—$321,728.61

World Series
Composite Box Score

BALTIMORE ORIOLES

	G	AB	R	H	2B	3B	HR	RBI	BB	SO	Bat. Avg.	PO	A	E	Fldg. Avg.
Buford, lf	5	20	1	2	1	0	1	2	2	4	.100	8	0	0	1.000
Blair, cf	5	20	1	2	0	0	0	2	5	5	.100	7	0	0	1.000
F. Robinson, rf	5	16	2	3	0	0	1	1	4	3	.187	13	0	0	1.000
dRettenmund, pr	1	0	0	0	0	0	0	0	0	0	.000	0	0	0	.000
Powell, 1b	5	19	0	5	0	0	0	1	4	.263	46	2	1	.939
B. Robinson, 3b	5	19	0	1	0	0	0	2	0	3	.053	1	16	0	1.000
Hendricks, c	3	10	1	1	0	0	0	3	0	1	.100	21	1	0	1.000
Johnson, 2b	5	16	1	1	0	0	0	0	2	1	.063	7	15	0	1.000
Belanger, ss	5	15	2	3	0	0	0	1	2	1	.200	8	14	0	1.000
Cuellar, p	2	5	0	2	0	0	0	1	0	3	.400	0	1	0	1.000
Etchebarren, c	2	6	0	0	0	0	0	0	0	1	.000	16	0	0	1.000
McNally, p	2	5	1	1	0	0	1	2	0	2	.200	1	1	0	1.000
Palmer, p	1	2	0	0	0	0	0	0	0	0	.000	1	0	1	.500
eMay, ph	2	1	0	0	0	0	0	0	1	1	.000	0	0	0	.000
Leonhard, p	1	0	0	0	0	0	0	0	0	0	.000	0	1	0	1.000

fDalrymple, ph   2   2   0   2   0   0   0   0   0   0   1.000   0   0   0   .000

fDalrymple, ph	2	2	0	2	0	0	0	0	0	0	1.000	0	0	0	.000
gSalmon, pr	2	0	0	0	0	0	0	0	0	0	.000	0	0	0	.000
Watt, p	2	0	0	0	0	0	0	0	0	0	.000	0	0	1	.000
Hall, p	1	0	0	0	0	0	0	0	0	0	.000	0	0	0	.000
Richert, p	1	0	0	0	0	0	0	0	0	0	.000	0	0	1	.000
hMotton, ph	1	1	0	0	0	0	0	0	0	0	.000	0	0	0	.000
Total	5	157	9	23	1	0	3	9	15	28	.142	129	51	4	.978

dRan for F. Robinson in 9th inning of second game.
eWalked for Palmer in 7th inning of third game; Struck out for Cuellar in 8th inning of fourth game.
fSingled for Leonhard in 9th inning of third game; Singled for Watt in 10th inning of fourth game.
gRan for Dalrymple in 9th inning of third game; Ran for Powell in ninth inning of fifth game.
hGrounded out for McNally in 8th inning of fifth game.

NEW YORK METS

	G	AB	R	H	2B	3B	HR	RBI	BB	SO	Bat. Avg.	PO	A	E	Fldg. Avg.
Agee, cf	5	18	1	3	0	0	1	1	2	5	.167	19	0	0	1.000
Harrelson, ss	5	17	1	3	0	0	0	0	3	4	.176	12	17	0	1.000
Jones, lf	5	19	2	3	1	0	0	0	0	1	.158	7	0	0	1.000
Clendenon, 1b	4	14	4	5	1	0	3	4	2	6	.357	30	4	0	1.000
Swoboda, rf	4	15	1	6	1	0	0	1	1	3	.400	14	0	0	1.000
Charles, 3b	4	15	1	2	1	0	0	0	0	2	.133	3	9	0	1.000
Grote, c	5	19	1	4	2	0	0	1	1	3	.211	29	2	0	1.000
Weis, 2b	5	11	1	5	0	0	1	3	4	2	.454	8	5	1	.929
Seaver, p	2	4	0	0	0	0	0	0	0	2	.000	2	1	0	1.000
aDyer, ph	1	1	0	0	0	0	0	0	0	0	.000	0	0	0	.000
Cardwell, p	1	0	0	0	0	0	0	0	0	0	.000	0	0	0	.000
bGaspar, rf	3	2	1	0	0	0	0	0	0	0	.000	2	0	0	1.000
Taylor, p	2	0	0	0	0	0	0	0	0	0	.000	0	0	0	.000
cShamsky, rf	3	6	0	0	0	0	0	0	0	0	.000	1	0	0	1.000
Koosman, p	2	7	0	1	1	0	0	0	0	4	.143	0	2	0	1.000
Garrett, 3b	2	1	0	0	0	0	0	0	2	1	.000	1	0	1	.500
Boswell, 2b	3	3	1	1	0	0	0	0	3	0	.333	0	1	0	1.000
Kranepool, 1b	1	4	1	1	0	0	1	1	0	0	.250	7	0	0	1.000
Gentry, p	1	3	0	1	0	0	0	2	0	2	.333	0	0	0	.000
Ryan, p	1	0	0	0	0	0	0	0	0	0	.000	0	0	0	.000
iMartin, ph	1	0	0	0	0	0	0	0	0	0	.000	0	0	0	.000
Total	5	159	15	35	8	0	6	13	15	35	.220	135	42	2	.989

aGrounded out for Seaver in 6th inning of first game.
bGrounded out for Cardwell in 7th inning of first game; Ran for Grote in 10th inning of fourth game.
cGrounded out for Taylor in 9th inning of first game; Grounded out for Charles in 9th inning of fourth game.
iSacrificed for Seaver in 10th inning of fourth game.

COMPOSITE SCORE BY INNINGS

Baltimore   1 0 3   3 0 0   1 0 1   0—9
New York   1 3 0   1 0 3   2 3 1   1—15

PITCHING SUMMARY
Baltimore Orioles

	G	CG	IP	H	R	BB	SO	HB	WP	W	L	Pct.	ER	ERA
Cuellar	2	1	16	13	2	4	13	0	0	1	0	1.000	2	1.13
McNally	2	1	16	11	5	5	13	1	1	0	1	.000	5	2.81
Palmer	1	0	6	5	4	4	5	0	0	0	1	.000	4	6.00
Leonhard	1	0	2	1	1	1	1	0	0	0	0	.000	1	4.50
Watt	2	0	3	4	2	0	3	0	0	0	1	.000	1	3.00
Hall	1	0	0	1	1	1	0	0	0	0	1	.000	0	0.00
Richert	1	0	0	0	0	0	0	0	0	0	0	.000	0	0.00
Total	5	2	43	35	15	15	35	1	1	1	4	.200	13	2.72

New York Mets

	G	CG	IP	H	R	BB	SO	HB	WP	W	L	Pct.	ER	ERA
Seaver	2	1	15	12	5	3	9	0	0	1	1	.500	5	3.00
Cardwell	1	0	1	0	0	0	0	0	0	0	0	.000	0	0.00
Taylor	2	0	2⅓	0	0	1	3	0	0	0	0	.000	0	0.00
Koosman	2	1	17⅔	7	4	4	9	0	0	2	0	1.000	4	2.00
Gentry	1	0	6⅔	3	0	5	4	0	0	1	0	1.000	0	0.00
Ryan	1	0	2⅓	1	0	2	3	0	0	0	0	.000	0	0.00
Total	5	2	45	23	9	15	28	0	0	4	1	.800	9	1.80

Sacrifice—Garrett, Martin, Sacrifice fly—Weis, B. Robinson. Stolen bases—Blair, Agee. Double play—Baltimore 4. Left on base—Baltimore 29, New York 34. Saves—Taylor, Ryan.
Time of games—2:13 (first game), 2:20 (second game), 2:23 (third game), 2:33 (fourth game), 2:14 (fifth game).
Attendance—50,429 (first game), 50,850 (second game), 56,331 (third game), 57,367 (fourth game), 57,397 (fifth game).
Umpires—Soar (A.); Secory (N.); Napp (A.); Crawford (N.); DiMuro (A.); Weyer (N.).

SERIES BOX SCORES

First Game   **At Baltimore**   **Oct. 11**

		R.	H.	E.
Mets	000 000 100 —	1	6	1
Orioles	100 300 00x —	4	6	0

Batteries—Seaver, Cardwell (6), Taylor (7) and Grote; Cuellar and Hendricks.
Winning pitcher—Cuellar. Losing pitcher—Seaver.
Home run—Baltimore: Buford

Second Game   **At Baltimore**   **Oct. 12**

		R.	H.	E.
Mets	000 100 001 —	2	6	0
Orioles	000 000 100 —	1	2	0

Batteries—Koosman, Taylor (9) and Grote. McNally and Etchebarren.
Winning pitcher—Koosman.
Home run—New York, Clendenon.

Third Game   **At New York**   **Oct. 14**

		R.	H.	E.
Orioles	000 000 000 —	0	4	1
Mets	120 001 01x —	5	6	0

Batteries—Palmer, Leonhard (7) and Hendricks; Gentry, Ryan (7), and Grote.
Winning pitcher—Gentry. Losing pitcher—Palmer.
Home runs—New York: Agee, Kranepool.

Fourth Game   **At New York**   **Oct. 15**

		R.	H.	E.
Orioles	000 000 001 0 —	1	6	1
Mets	010 000 000 1 —	2	10	1

Batteries—Cuellar, Watt (8), Hall (10), Richert (10) and Hendricks; Seaver and Grote.
Losing pitcher—Hall.
Home run—New York, Clendenon.

Fifth Game   **At New York**   **Oct. 16**

		R.	H.	E.
Orioles	003 000 000 —	3	5	2
Mets	000 002 12x —	5	7	0

Batteries—McNally, Watts (8) and Etchebarren; Koosman and Grote.
Winning pitcher—Koosman. Losing pitcher—Watts.
Home runs—McNally, F. Robinson, Clendenon, Weis.

PRO FOOTBALL

NATIONAL FOOTBALL LEAGUE

Standings

EASTERN CONFERENCE

Century Division

	W	L	T	Pct.	P.F.	P.A.
Cleveland	10	3	1	.769	351	300
New York	6	8	0	.429	264	298
St. Louis	4	9	1	.308	314	389
Pittsburgh	1	13	0	.071	218	404

Capitol Division

	W	L	T	Pct.	P.F.	P.A.
Dallas	11	2	1	.846	369	223
Washington	7	5	2	.583	307	319
New Orleans	5	9	0	.357	311	393
Philadelphia	4	9	1	.308	279	377

WESTERN CONFERENCE

Central Division

	W	L	T	Pct.	P.F.	P.A.
Minnesota	12	2	0	.857	379	133
Detroit	9	4	1	.692	259	188
Green Bay	8	6	0	.571	269	221
Chicago	1	13	0	.071	210	339

Coastal Division

	W	L	T	Pct.	P.F.	P.A.
Los Angeles	11	3	0	.786	320	243
Baltimore	8	5	1	.615	279	268
Atlanta	6	8	0	.429	276	268
San Francisco	4	8	2	.333	277	319

Playoffs
Minnesota 23, Los Angeles 20
Cleveland 38, Dallas 14

Championship Game   **Jan. 4, 1970**

At Minnesota						
Cleveland	0	0	0	7	—	7
Minnesota	14	10	3	0	—	27

Minnesota: Touchdown—Kapp, 7, run (Cox kick)
Minnesota: Touchdown—Washington, 75, pass from Kapp (Cox kick)
Minnesota: Field Goal—Cox, 30
Minnesota: Touchdown—Osborn, 20, run (Cox kick)
Minnesota: Field Goal—Cox, 32
Cleveland: Touchdown—Collins, 3, pass from Nelsen (Cockroft kick)
Attendance—47,900

AMERICAN FOOTBALL LEAGUE

Playoffs
Kansas City 13, New York 6
Oakland 56, Houston 7

Championship Game

At Oakland						Jan. 4, 1970
Kansas City	0	7	7	3	—	17
Oakland	7	0	0	0	—	7

Oakland: Touchdown—Smith, 3, run (Blanda kick)
Kansas City: Touchdown—Hayes, 1, run (Stenerud kick)
Kansas City: Touchdown—Holmes, 5, run (Stenerud kick)
Kansas City: Field Goal—Stenerud, 22
Attendance—54,544

AMERICAN FOOTBALL LEAGUE

Standings

EASTERN DIVISION

	W	L	T	Pct.	P.F.	P.A.
New York	10	4	0	.714	353	269
Houston	6	6	2	.500	278	279
Boston	4	10	0	.286	266	316
Buffalo	4	10	0	.286	230	359
Miami	3	10	1	.231	234	332

WESTERN DIVISION

	W	L	T	Pct.	P.F.	P.A.
Oakland	12	1	1	.923	377	242
Kansas City	11	3	0	.786	359	177
San Diego	8	6	0	.571	288	276
Denver	5	8	1	.385	297	345
Cincinnati	4	9	1	.308	280	367

COLLEGE FOOTBALL

Ratings*

College	W	L	T
1—Texas	11	0	0
2—Penn State	11	0	0
3—Southern California	10	0	1
4—Ohio State	8	1	0
5—Notre Dame	8	2	1
6—Missouri	9	2	0
7—Arkansas	9	2	0
8—Mississippi	8	3	0
9—Michigan	8	3	0
10—Louisiana State	9	1	0

*Records include post-season bowl games.

Offense

Pos.	Player	College
TE—	Jim Mandich,	Michigan
WR—	Walker Gillette,	Richmond
T—	Bob McKay,	Texas
T—	John Ward,	Oklahoma State
G—	Bill Bridges,	Houston
G—	Chip Kell,	Tennessee
C—	Rodney Brand,	Arkansas
QB—	Mike Phipps,	Purdue
HB—	Bob Anderson,	Colorado
HB—	Steve Owens,	Oklahoma
FB—	Jim Otis,	Ohio State

Defense

Pos.	Player	College
E—	Jimmy Gunn,	Southern California
E—	Phil Olsen,	Utah State
T—	Mike McCoy,	Notre Dame
T—	Mike Reid,	Penn State
MG—	Jim Stillwagon,	Ohio State
LB—	Steve Kiner,	Tennessee
LB—	Dennis Onkotz,	Penn State
LB—	Don Parish,	Stanford
DB—	Tom Curtis,	Michigan
DB—	Buddy McClinton,	Auburn
DB—	Jack Tatum,	Ohio State

Major Conference Champions

Ivy League—Dartmouth, Princeton, Yale
Yankee—Massachusetts
Big Eight—Missouri, Nebraska
Middle Atlantic—Delaware
Southern—Davidson
Southeastern—Tennessee
Big Ten—Michigan, Ohio State
Atlantic Coast—South Carolina
Western Athletic—Arizona State
Southwest—Texas
Ohio Valley—East Tennessee State
Missouri Valley—Memphis State
Pacific Eight—Southern California

Major Undefeated-Untied Teams*

College	W	L
Penn State	10	0
San Diego State	10	0
Texas	10	0
Toledo	10	0

*Excluding bowl games

Bowl Games

Pasadena Bowl—San Diego State 28, Boston University 7
Liberty Bowl—Colorado 47, Alabama 33
Sun Bowl—Nebraska 45, Georgia 6
Tangerine Bowl—Toledo 56, Davidson 33
Gator Bowl—Florida 14, Tennessee 13
Peach Bowl—West Virginia 14, South Carolina 3
Astro-Bluebonnet Bowl—Houston 36, Auburn 7
Cotton Bowl—Texas 21, Notre Dame 17
Orange Bowl—Penn State 10, Missouri 3
Rose Bowl—Southern California 10, Michigan 3
Sugar Bowl—Mississippi 27, Arkansas 22

TENNIS

Davis Cup
Challenge Round at Cleveland, Ohio, Sept. 19–21
Arthur Ashe (United States) defeated Ilie Nastase (Romania), 6-2, 15-13, 7-5.
Stan Smith (United States) defeated Ion Tiriac (Romania), 6-8, 6-3, 5-7, 6-4, 6-4.
Smith and Bob Lutz (United States) defeated Nastase and Tiriac (Romania), 8-6, 6-1, 11-9.
Smith (United States) defeated Nastase (Romania), 4-6, 4-6, 6-4, 6-1, 11-9.
Ashe (United States) defeated Tiriac (Romania), 6-3, 8-6, 3-6, 4-0 (match halted by prior agreement).
(United States won the Davis Cup, 5 matches to 0).

Champions
Wightman Cup (women)—United States
Federation Cup (women)—United States
Wimbledon—men, Rod Laver, Australia; women, Mrs. Ann Haydon Jones, Great Britain; men's doubles, John Newcombe and Tony Roche, Australia; women's doubles, Mrs. Margaret Smith Court and Judy Tegart, Australia; mixed doubles, Fred Stolle, Australia, and Mrs. Jones, Great Britain.
U.S. Open—men, Rod Laver, Australia; women, Mrs. Margaret Smith Court, Australia; men's doubles, Fred Stolle and Ken Rosewall, Australia; women's doubles, Francoise Durr, France, and Darlene Hard, Montebello, Calif.
U.S. Grass Court—men, Stan Smith, Pasadena, Calif.; women, Mrs. Margaret Smith Court, Aus-

tralia; men's doubles, Dick Crealy and Allan Stone, Australia; women's doubles, Mrs. Court and Virginia Wade, Great Britain.

U.S. CLAY COURT—men, Zeljko Franulovic, Yugoslavia; women, Mrs. Gail Chanfreau, France; men's doubles, Bill Bowrey, Australia, and Clark Graebner, New York; women's doubles, Mrs. Chanfreau and Mrs. Leslie Bowrey, Australia.

GOLF

U.S. OPEN—Orville Moody
P.G.A.—Raymond Floyd
MASTERS—George Archer
U.S. AMATEUR—Steve Melnyk
BRITISH OPEN—Tony Jacklin
BRITISH AMATEUR—Michael Bonallack
NCAA (Team)—Houston
NCAA (Individual)—Bob Clark, Los Angeles State
VARDON TROPHY—Dave Hill
WORLD CUP—United States
WOMEN'S OPEN—Donna Caponi
WOMEN'S P.G.A.—Betsy Rawls
WOMEN'S AMATEUR—Catherine Lacoste

HOCKEY

NATIONAL HOCKEY LEAGUE

Final Standings

East Division

	W	L	T	PTS.	GF	GA
MONTREAL	46	19	11	103	271	202
BOSTON	42	18	16	100	303	221
NEW YORK	41	26	9	91	231	196
TORONTO	35	26	15	85	234	217
DETROIT	33	31	12	78	239	221
CHICAGO	34	34	9	77	280	246

West Division

	W	L	T	PTS.	GF	GA
ST. LOUIS	37	25	14	88	204	157
OAKLAND	29	36	11	69	219	251
PHILADELPHIA	20	35	21	61	174	225
LOS ANGELES	24	42	10	58	185	260
PITTSBURGH	20	45	11	51	189	252
MINNESOTA	18	43	15	51	189	270

INDIVIDUAL SCORING

	G	A	PTS.
Esposito, Boston	49	77	126
B. Hull, Chicago	58	49	107
Howe, Detroit	44	59	103
Mikita, Chicago	30	67	97
Hodge, Boston	45	45	90
Cournoyer, Montreal	43	44	87
Delvecchio, Detroit	25	58	83
Berenson, St. Louis	35	47	82
Beliveau, Montreal	33	49	82

ALL-STAR TEAM

Goal—Glenn Hall, St. Louis; Defense—Bobby Orr, Boston, and Tim Horton, Toronto; Center—Phil Esposito, Boston; Right Wing—Gordie Howe, Detroit; Left Wing—Bobby Hull, Chicago.

Second Team

Goal—Ed Giacomin, New York; Defense—Ted Green, Boston, and Ted Harris, Montreal; Center—Jean Beliveau, Montreal; Right Wing—Yvan Cournoyer, Montreal; Left Wing—Frank Mahovlich, Detroit.

TROPHY WINNERS

Hart Memorial Trophy (Most Valuable Player)—Phil Esposito, Boston.

Lady Byng Memorial Trophy (Gentlemanly Conduct)—Alex Delvecchio, Detroit.

James Norris Memorial Trophy (Best Defenseman)—Bobby Orr, Boston.

Calder Memorial Trophy (Outstanding Rookie)—Danny Grant, Minnesota.

STANLEY CUP PLAYOFFS

Series 'A'—Montreal defeated New York, 4 games to 0.

Series 'B'—Boston defeated Toronto, 4 games to 0.

Series 'C'—St. Louis defeated Philadelphia, 4 games to 0.

Series 'D'—Los Angeles defeated Oakland, 4 games to 3.

East Semifinal—Montreal defeated Boston, 4 games to 2.

West Semifinal—St. Louis defeated Los Angeles, 4 games to 0.

Final—Montreal defeated St. Louis, 4 games to 0.

TRACK & FIELD

AAU Champions

100 yards, Ivory Crockett
220 yards, John Carlos
440 yards, Lee Evans
880 yards, Byron Dyce
One mile, Marty Liquori
Three miles, Tracy Smith
Six miles, Jack Bachelor
3,000-meter steeplechase, Mike Manley
120-yard high hurdles, Willie Davenport and Leon Coleman
440-yard hurdles, Ralph Mann
High jump, Otis Burrell
Pole vault, Bob Seagren
Long jump, Bob Beamon
Triple jump, John Craft
Shot put, Neal Steinhauer
Discus, Jon Cole
Hammer throw, Tom Gage
Javelin, Mark Murro
56-pound weight throw, George Frenn
15,000 meters, Garry Bjorklund
50 miles, Jim McDonough
10,000-meter, 15,000-meter, 20,000-meter, 25,000-meter, 35,000-meter and 40,000-meter walks, Ron Laird
50,000-meter walk, Byron Overton

NCAA Champions

100 yards, John Carlos, San Jose State
220 yards, Carlos
440 yards, Curtis Mills, Texas A&M
880 yards, Byron Dyce, N.Y.U.
One mile, Marty Liquori, Villanova
Three miles, Ole Oleson, Southern California
Six miles, Frank Shorter, Yale
120-yard hurdles, Erv Hall, Villanova
440-yard hurdles, Ralph Mann, Brigham Young
3,000-meter steeplechase, Jim Barkley, Oregon State
440-yard relay, San Jose State
One-mile relay, U.C.L.A.
High jump, Dick Fosbury, Oregon State
Pole vault, Bob Seagren, Southern California
Long jump, Jerry Proctor, Redlands
Triple jump, Pertti Pousi, Brigham Young
Shot put, Karl Salb, Kansas
Discus, John Van Reenen, Washington State
Hammer throw, Steve DeAutremont, Oregon State
Javelin, Mark Murro, Arizona State
Team, San Jose State

PRO BASKETBALL

NATIONAL BASKETBALL ASSOCIATION

Final Standings

Eastern Division

	W	L	PCT.	GB
BALTIMORE	57	25	.695	--
PHILADELPHIA	55	27	.671	2
NEW YORK	54	28	.659	3
BOSTON	48	34	.585	9
CINCINNATI	41	41	.500	16
DETROIT	32	50	.390	25
MILWAUKEE	27	55	.329	30

Western Division

	W	L	PCT.	GB
LOS ANGELES	55	27	.671	--
ATLANTA	48	34	.585	7
SAN FRANCISCO	41	41	.500	14
SAN DIEGO	37	45	.451	18
CHICAGO	33	49	.402	22
SEATTLE	30	52	.366	25
PHOENIX	16	66	.195	39

PLAYOFFS

East—New York defeated Baltimore, 4 games to 0; Boston defeated Philadelphia, 4 games to 1; Boston defeated New York, 4 games to 2.

West—Los Angeles defeated San Francisco, 4 games to 2; Atlanta defeated San Diego, 4 games to 2; Los Angeles defeated Atlanta, 4 games to 1.

Final—Boston defeated Los Angeles, 4 games to 3.

INDIVIDUAL SCORING

	FG	FT	PTS.	AVG.
Hayes, San Diego	930	467	2327	28.4
Monroe, Baltimore	809	447	2065	25.8
Cunningham, Philadelphia	739	556	2034	24.8
Rule, Seattle	776	413	1965	24.0
Robertson, Cincinnati	656	643	1955	24.7
Goodrich, Phoenix	718	495	1931	23.8
Greer, Philadelphia	732	432	1896	23.1
Baylor, Los Angeles	730	421	1881	24.8
Wilkens, Seattle	644	547	1835	22.4
Kojis, San Diego	687	446	1820	22.5

ALL-STAR TEAM (FIRST)

Billy Cunningham, Philadelphia
Elgin Baylor, Los Angeles
Wes Unseld, Baltimore
Earl Monroe, Baltimore
Oscar Robertson, Cincinnati

MOST VALUABLE PLAYER

Wes Unseld, Baltimore

ROOKIE OF THE YEAR

Wes Unseld, Baltimore

ALL-STAR GAME

Jan. 14, at Baltimore
East 123, West 112

ALL-STAR TEAM (SECOND)

John Havlicek, Boston
Dave DeBusschere, New York
Willis Reed, New York
Hal Greer, Philadelphia
Jerry West, Los Angeles

AMERICAN BASKETBALL ASSOCIATION

Final Standings

Eastern Division

	W	L	PCT.	GB
INDIANA	44	34	.564	--
MIAMI	43	35	.551	1
KENTUCKY	42	36	.538	2
MINNESOTA	36	42	.462	8
NEW YORK	17	61	.218	27

Western Division

	W	L	PCT.	GB
OAKLAND	60	18	.769	--
NEW ORLEANS	46	32	.590	14
DENVER	44	34	.564	16
DALLAS	41	37	.526	19
LOS ANGELES	33	45	.423	27
HOUSTON	23	55	.295	37

PLAYOFFS

East—Indiana defeated Kentucky, 4 games to 3; Miami defeated Minnesota, 4 games to 3; Indiana defeated Miami, 4 games to 1.

West—Oakland defeated Denver, 4 games to 3; New Orleans defeated Dallas, 4 games to 3; Oakland defeated New Orleans, 4 games to 0.

Final—Oakland defeated Indiana, 4 games to 1.

INDIVIDUAL SCORING

	2-PT. FG	3-PT. FG	FT	PTS.	AVG.
Barry, Oakland	389	3	403	1190	34.0
Hawkins, Minnesota	493	3	425	1420	30.2
L. Jones, Denver	735	24	591	2133	28.4
J. Jones, N. Orleans	763	1	521	2050	26.6
Dampier, Kentucky	514	199	308	1933	24.8
Daniels, Indiana	712	0	400	1824	24.0
Somerset, New York	583	36	484	1758	23.8
Carrier, Kentucky	434	125	447	1690	23.2
Freeman, Miami	649	2	420	1724	22.1
Armstrong, Oakland	562	11	373	1530	21.5

ALL-STAR TEAM (FIRST)
Connie Hawkins, Minnesota
Rick Barry, Oakland
Mel Daniels, Indiana
James Jones, New Orleans
Larry Jones, Denver

MOST VALUABLE PLAYER
Mel Daniels, Indiana

COACH OF THE YEAR
Babe McCarthy, New Orleans

ROOKIE OF THE YEAR
Warren Armstrong, Oakland

ALL-STAR TEAM (SECOND)
John Beasley, Dallas
Doug Moe, Oakland
Austin Robbins, New Orleans
Louie Dampier, Kentucky
Don Freeman, Miami

COLLEGE BASKETBALL

NCAA Tournament

East
Duquesne 74, St. Joseph's 52
Davidson 75, Villanova 61
St. John's 72, Princeton 63
—
North Carolina 79, Duquesne 78
Davidson 79, St. John's 69
—
North Carolina 87, Davidson 85

Mideast
Marquette 82, Murray State 62
Miami, Ohio 63, Notre Dame 60
—
Marquette 81, Kentucky 74
Purdue 91, Miami, Ohio 71
—
Purdue 75, Marquette 73

Midwest
Texas A&M 81, Trinity, Tex. 66
Colorado State U. 52, Dayton 50
—
Drake 81, Texas A&M 63
Colorado State U. 64, Colorado 56
—
Drake 84, Colorado State U. 77

West
New Mexico State 74, Brigham Young 62
Weber State 75, Seattle 73
—
UCLA 53, New Mexico State 38
Santa Clara 63, Weber State 59
—
UCLA 90, Santa Clara 52

Semifinals
Purdue 92, North Carolina 65
UCLA 85, Drake 82

Finals
UCLA 92, Purdue 72

College Division
Kentucky Wesleyan, defeated Transylvania 77–61; Alcorn A&M 83–69; Oglethorpe 82–68; American International 83–82; Southwest Missouri 75–71.

Junior Colleges
Paducah of Paducah, Ky., defeated Robert Morris of Pittsburgh, Pa., 79–76.

Rankings*

COLLEGE	W	L
1—UCLA	29	1
2—La Salle	23	1
3—Santa Clara	27	2
4—North Carolina	27	5
5—Davidson	27	3
6—Purdue	23	5
7—Kentucky	23	5
8—St. John's, N.Y.	23	6
9—Duquesne	21	5
10—Villanova	21	5

*Regular Season

Major Conference Champions
IVY LEAGUE—Princeton
YANKEE—Massachusetts
SOUTHEASTERN—Kentucky
ATLANTIC COAST—North Carolina
SOUTHERN—Davidson
OHIO VALLEY—Murray State
BIG TEN—Purdue
MID-AMERICAN—Miami, Ohio
BIG EIGHT—Colorado
MISSOURI VALLEY—Drake
SOUTHWEST—Texas A&M
WESTERN ATHLETIC—Brigham Young
PACIFIC EIGHT—UCLA
WEST COAST—Santa Clara

Individual Scoring

PLAYER, COLLEGE	G	FG	FT	PTS.	AVG.
Maravich, Louisiana State	26	433	282	1148	44.2
Mount, Purdue	28	366	200	932	33.3
Murphy, Niagara	24	294	190	778	32.4
Haywood, Detroit	22	259	181	699	31.8
B. Tallent, George Washington	25	284	155	723	28.9

All-Americans

PLAYER, COLLEGE	HGT.
Lew Alcindor, UCLA	7:01½
Pete Maravich, Louisiana State	6:05
Spencer Haywood, Detroit	6:08
Rick Mount, Purdue	6:04
Calvin Murphy, Niagara	5:10

BOXING

Heavyweight—Jimmy Ellis, Louisville, Ky., the World Boxing Association champion, failed to defend his title when proposed bouts fell through matching him with Henry Cooper of England, Gregorio Peralta of Argentina and Joe Frazier of Philadelphia, recognized as champion by five states.

Frazier, meanwhile, defended his version of the crown with a one-round knockout of Dave Zyglewicz on April 22 and a seventh-round TKO of Jerry Quarry on June 23.

Light-Heavyweight—Champion Bob Foster defended his title by stopping Frankie DePaula in one round on Jan. 22 and Andy Kendall in four on May 24.

Middleweight—Champion Nino Benvenuti of Italy defended successfully Oct. 6 against Fraser Scott when Scott was disqualified in the seventh round for fighting with his head too low.

Welterweight—Jose Napoles of Mexico won the championship from Curtis Cokes with a 13-round knockout April 18. He defended successfully by stopping Cokes in 10 rounds June 28 and then outpointed Emile Griffith in 15 rounds Oct. 18.

Lightweight—Mando Ramos of Long Beach, Calif., won the crown Feb. 18 with a second-round knockout of Teo Cruz, the champion from the Dominican Republic. Ramos defended successfully Oct. 5 by kayoing Japan's Yoshiaki Numata in the fifth round.

Featherweight—Shozo Saijyo of Japan, the World Boxing Association champion, defended his crown with a second-round knockout of Cuba's Jose Pimentel on Sept. 7.

Australia's Johnny Famechon won the other piece of the title when he outpointed Jose Legra of Spain in 15 rounds Jan. 21. Famechon made a successful defense by outpointing Fighting Harada of Japan, a former champion, July 28.

Bantamweight—Lionel Rose, the Australian aborigine, was the titleholder as 1969 began and made a successful defense March 8 by outpointing England's Alan Rudkin. Rose then lost his title Aug. 23 to Mexico's Ruben Olivares via a fifth-round knockout. Olivares retained the crown Dec. 12 by stopping Rudkin in two rounds.

Flyweight—Mexico's Efren "Alacran" Torres won one version of the title Feb. 23 with an eighth-round technical knockout over Thailand's Charchai Chionoi. He defended it Nov. 28 by outpointing Japan's Susumo Hanagata.

The WBA version was won March 30 by Japan's Hiroyuki Ebihara when he outpointed Jose Severino of Brazil for the vacant crown. But Ebihara was in turn outpointed Oct. 19 by Bernabe Villacampo of the Philippines.

HORSE RACING

Kentucky Derby

May 3, 1969	Churchill Downs, Ky.		$155,700
HORSE	JOCKEY	OWNER	MARGIN
1—Majestic Prince	Hartack	Frank McMahon	Neck
2—Arts and Letters	Baeza	Rokeby Stable	
3—Dike	Velasquez	Claiborne Farm	

Preakness

May 17, 1969	Pimlico, Md.		$182,000
HORSE	JOCKEY	OWNER	MARGIN
1—Majestic Prince	Hartack	Frank McMahon	Head
2—Arts and Letters	Baeza	Rokeby Stable	
3—Jay Ray	Fires	Claiborne Farm	

Belmont Stakes

June 7, 1969	Belmont Park, N.Y.		$147,800
HORSE	JOCKEY	OWNER	MARGIN
1—Arts and Letters	Baeza	Rokeby Stable	5½ lengths
2—Majestic Prince	Hartack	Frank McMahon	
3—Dike	Belmonte	Claiborne Farm	

Awards & Miscellaneous

Horse of the Year—Arts and Letters
Best Older Horse—Nodouble
Best 3-year-old—Arts and Letters
Best 2-year-old—Silent Screen
Best 3-year-old filly—Gallant Bloom
Best 2-year-old filly—Fast Attack, Tudor Queen

THE WORLD IN 1969—Index